RESTRUCTURING ECONOMIES IN DISTRESS

RESTRUCTURING ECONOMIES IN DISTRESS

Policy Reform and the World Bank

edited by
Vinod Thomas
Ajay Chhibber
Mansoor Dailami
Jaime de Melo

PUBLISHED FOR THE WORLD BANK
Oxford University Press

Oxford University Press

OXFORD NEW YORK TORONTO DELHI
BOMBAY CALCUTTA MADRAS KARACHI
PETALING JAYA SINGAPORE HONG KONG
TOKYO NAIROBI DAR ES SALAAM
CAPE TOWN MELBOURNE AUCKLAND
and associated companies in
BERLIN IBADAN

Manufactured in the United States of America
First printing June 1991

Library of Congress Cataloging-in-Publication Data

Restructuring economies in distress : policy reform and the World Bank
/ edited by Vinod Thomas . . . [et al.].
p. cm.
Includes bibliographical references and index.
ISBN 0-19-520870-6
1. World Bank—Developing countries. 2. Balance of payments—
Developing countries. 3. Economic stabilization—Developing
countries. 4. Developing countries—Economic policy. I. Thomas,
Vinod, 1949– .
HG3881.5.W57R47 1991
339.5'09172'4—dc20 90-25999
CIP

Foreword

THE WORLD BANK began lending for structural adjustment in 1980. The balance of payments problems facing developing countries at that time resulted from high oil prices and rising nominal interest rates, as well as inadequate domestic policies. These problems intensified as real interest rates rose, a global recession developed, and the debt crisis was recognized as such.

Initially, adjustment lending for a given country was expected to last three to five years, and its balance of payments was expected to become sustainable in five to seven years. As the 1980s progressed, however, the terms of trade for many developing countries deteriorated further, real interest rates remained high, and the debt crisis persisted. In addition, the sources of domestic inefficiencies proved to be intractable. Instead of disappearing, adjustment lending intensified—both in depth, for a given country, and in breadth, in the range of member countries receiving such loans. Typically, the World Bank started adjustment lending with structural adjustment loans and then moved on to a series of sectoral adjustment loans to effect policy changes in particular sectors.

Almost a decade after the first structural adjustment loans, the World Bank evaluated its experience with adjustment lending in a report that was discussed by the Bank's Executive Directors in September 1988. This volume, a product of the extensive work done for that report, provides a detailed and frank discussion of adjustment lending programs, how they have worked, and how they can be improved.

As external uncertainties and internal problems continue for member countries of the World Bank, it is hoped that the objective of adjustment efforts will shift from the short-term issues of crisis management and stabilization that have dominated the past decade, to the more fundamental issues of long-term growth, sustainable development, and the alleviation of poverty.

Barber B. Conable
President, The World Bank

Contents

Contributors

AFFILIATIONS are those at the time of the conference.

Joe Abbey, *Ghanaian High Commissioner in the United Kingdom*
Sadiq Ahmed, *World Bank*
Elliot Berg, *Elliot Berg Associates, Virginia*
William H. Branson, *Princeton University*
Christophe Chamley, *Boston University*
Ajay Chhibber, *World Bank*
Barber B. Conable, *President, World Bank*
Vittorio Corbo, *World Bank*
Mansoor Dailami, *World Bank*
Jaime de Melo, *World Bank*
Dennis de Tray, *World Bank*
Shantayanan Devarajan, *Harvard University*
Vinod Dubey, *World Bank*
Sebastian Edwards, *University of California, Los Angeles*
Riccardo Faini, *Johns Hopkins University, Bologna Center, Italy*
Mohsen A. Fardi, *World Bank*
Stanley Fischer, *World Bank*
Faezeh Foroutan, *World Bank*
Maxwell J. Fry, *University of California, Irvine*
Alan Gelb, *World Bank*
Manuel Guitián, *International Monetary Fund*
Gerald Helleiner, *University of Toronto*
Peter S. Heller, *International Monetary Fund*
John A. Holsen, *World Bank*
Patrick Honohan, *World Bank*
W. David Hopper, *World Bank*
S. Shahid Husain, *World Bank*
Nurul Islam, *International Food Policy Research Institute*
Edward V. K. Jaycox, *World Bank*
Leroy P. Jones, *Boston University*
Attila Karaosmanoglu, *World Bank*
Javad Khalilzadeh-Shirazi, *World Bank*
Mohsin S. Khan, *International Monetary Fund*
Ben King, *formerly World Bank*
Odin Knudsen, *World Bank*
Hans-Eberhard Köpp, *World Bank*
Chad Leechor, *World Bank*
Pedro S. Malan, *Alternate Executive Director, World Bank*
William A. McCleary, *World Bank*
Peter J. Montiel, *International Monetary Fund*
Cristian Moran, *World Bank*
John Nash, *World Bank*

John R. Nellis, *World Bank*
Mieko Nishimizu, *World Bank*
Moeen Qureshi, *World Bank*
Visvanathan Rajagopalan, *World Bank*
Dani Rodrik, *Harvard University*
Abdel Senhadji-Semlali, *World Bank*
Murray A. Sherwin, *Executive Director, World Bank*
Lyn Squire, *World Bank*
Julie Stanton, *World Bank*
Ernest Stern, *World Bank*
Vinod Thomas, *World Bank*
James R. Tybout, *Georgetown University*
Larry E. Westphal, *Swarthmore College*
John Williamson, *Institute for International Economics*
Elaine Zuckerman, *World Bank*

Preface

THE GROWTH in the pace and scope of lending to developing countries for economic adjustment has raised many concerns and provoked much debate. The chief question is whether this instrument, designed essentially to provide support for the balance of payments, can effectively serve the broader objectives of policy and institutional reforms. Another important issue concerns conditionality and whether it can be designed to integrate short-term macroeconomic stabilization with longer-term reforms.

For the World Bank's report on adjustment lending, background papers were prepared on policy issues and country experiences, and a symposium was held at Bank headquarters on April 4–5, 1989, to discuss the background work. In the spirit of open debate, the symposium included commentary and reviews by some of the World Bank's practitioners and by outside critics of adjustment lending. This volume contains the statements, papers, and comments presented at the symposium, as well as two other papers commissioned after the conference—one to analyze loan conditionality (chapter 10) and the other to round out the case studies for the Asian region (chapter 17).

This book represents an assessment of nearly a decade of experience with lending to support adjustment programs. Although the effectiveness of structural adjustment and adjustment lending has varied considerably across countries and policy areas, the overall judgment is one of qualified optimism. Definitive conclusions are not yet possible, however, and efforts to evaluate the success of adjustment programs and adjustment lending must continue.

Opening this volume is an introductory statement to the symposium by Ernest Stern, one of the architects of adjustment lending. The remainder of the book is divided into four parts. The first covers major policy and sectoral issues related to structural adjustment, or what can be considered the content of adjustment programs. Part II is concerned with the evaluation, conditionality, and social consequences of adjustment operations. Case studies of the direct experience of nine countries with structural adjustment and adjustment lending are presented in Part III. Part IV contains the comments of various participants in the 1989 symposium and ties together many of the themes that are woven throughout the preceding text.

This book has benefited from contributions by Bela Balassa, Suman Bery, Fernando Clavijo, Simon Commander, Nadav Halevi, Arnold Harberger, Ishrat Husain, Donald Keesing, Enrique Lerdau, Robert Liebenthal, Dennis Mahar, Francis Ng, Peter Nicholas, Gerardo Sicat, Jose

Sokol, and William Steel, editing by Meta de Coquereaumont, and assistance from Karla Cabana and Rebecca Sugui. Valuable comments and suggestions were received from many people inside and outside the Bank as well as from participants in the symposium.

John A. Holsen
Director, Country Economics Department
The World Bank

1 *Evolution and Lessons of Adjustment Lending*

Ernest Stern

When the World Bank introduced the idea of structural adjustment lending in 1979, I think it is fair to say, neither Robert McNamara, the Bank president, nor I appreciated the full scope of the undertaking. McNamara made his first reference to structural adjustment in a speech to the U.N. Conference on Trade and Development (UNCTAD), and a brief paragraph in his 1979 address to the annual meeting of the World Bank proposed lending to help developing countries avoid balance of payments crises.

Coming in the aftermath of the second oil shock, the proposal reflected a great sense of frustration in the World Bank. Despite substantial lending, we had no real involvement with the major macroeconomic issues that our members faced. Clearly, our project lending was not an adequate tool. Our economic analysis, although it may have been as voluminous then as now, generally was not directly linked to operational decisions. We certainly did not have the kind of policy dialogue that has since emerged.

Starting Up

Initially our thinking focused on ways to help countries develop greater export capacity, given their need to deal with the tremendous drain of resources generated by the oil price increase. When we started, however, we were quite naive about just how profoundly distorted the development strategies of many of the developing countries were. (Even now, this issue is worth exploring at some depth.) The problem had been neglected not only in our own analysis but also in much of the economic literature of the time.

The oil shocks and subsequent occurrences in the 1980s revealed that many of the development strategies being pursued simply did not promise sustainable economic growth. That reality, although not yet fully comprehended, is still very much with us. It makes adjustment a subject of continuing great importance and great urgency.

Whether we will be able soon to put the debt crisis—one of the symptoms of these distortions—behind us, in part or in whole, really has nothing to do with the continuing need for developing countries to rethink their development strategies. They must begin to move from highly distorted price incentives and investment frameworks to something more stable, more oriented to the market system of prices, and more open and less protected.

In the early 1980s, we foresaw neither the full dimensions of the challenge nor the transformation that structural adjustment lending would impose on the World Bank. A look at the kinds of activities the Bank carried out in 1980, the demands on its staff, and its relationships with developing countries then reveals not only dramatic differences from the present but also that much of the change stems from the World Bank's operationally significant involvement in macroeconomic and sectoral adjustment issues. In retrospect, it is clear that we did not anticipate just how popular structural adjustment lending was going to become.

When we set out, it was a highly controversial subject. Indeed, our first proposals for adjustment lending met a great deal of opposition from the Board of Executive Directors and more generally, for a variety of reasons. First, many thought the problems we were seeking to address were short-term ones that did not require the attention of a long-term development institution. Second, members of the World Bank staff and of the Board felt strongly that we were essentially a project agency. They held that we should stick to what we knew and not venture into macroeconomic issues where we had no special competence.

Such involvement, it was said, would create all kinds of problems, among them, frictions between the World Bank and the International Monetary Fund (IMF). Some of these issues are still being argued, but perhaps not as vigorously as they were almost a decade ago. In the intervening years, in any event, we have learned a set of lessons that remain valid.

Lessons of Experience

The first lesson—a very important one that we learned fairly early—is that structural adjustment has to be seen in a countrywide context. Initially, and perhaps to some extent still today, we tended not to carry over into structural adjustment lending a truism about project lending: a soundly designed project in a poor economic environment will not yield expected results. In addition, we have at times been perhaps too complacent about the issues of comprehensiveness and sequencing, not recognizing that intermittent, partial, and gradual steps are insufficient in themselves; they must fit into a well-articulated, well-understood overall plan that has the full commitment of the government.

The second lesson concerns the great degree of economic dependence that the policies of the 1960s and 1970s had bred. The ample supply of capital, from both growing aid programs and the great liquidity created by oil price increases, led to a systemic failure. Developing countries as well as aid and export credit agencies—not to mention the World Bank—failed to insist on any reasonable standards of efficiency for investment capital and the management of economies.

The third lesson—and it became clear only gradually—was that adjustment postponed was pain compounded. This truth has been very hard to learn. It is still not fully understood. After all, most development economists—and certainly most of those in the World Bank—grew up believing that development could proceed in a fairly linear fashion and fairly painlessly. When we did, occasionally, deal with such problems as inequitable income distribution and the need for some drastic remedies, we still tended to perceive the process as a very gradual one and the pace of change as not very important.

We have learned since then that this approach is quite wrong. When distortions are serious—for example, if the prices of energy or food are only a fraction of world market prices—the longer adjustment is delayed, the more difficult it becomes politically. The more difficult politically, in turn, the more partial any adjustment is likely to be and the more likely it is to fail.

The fourth lesson, which emerged as we became more deeply involved with more and more countries in structural adjustment lending, was the very limited institutional capacity to manage economies flexibly. This is not to say that bureaucracies everywhere are inefficient or incapable, only that the strong vested interests they harbor did not change easily from a controlled administrative system or adapt readily to a more open system.

In general, it is fair to say, we grossly underestimated the institutional elements of adjustment at both the macro and the sectoral levels. Time and again the best of policy intentions, the best of policy letters solemnly agreed to and signed by the finance minister and the Bank, broke down. This often happened because of a lack of adequately trained people in the right places, the difficulty of changing bureaucratic structures, and the difficulty of laying people off as functions were reduced.

The fifth lesson, learned gradually in the course of adjustment lending, is the vital importance of macroeconomic flexibility. Adjustment lending, whether structural or sectoral, is not going to be very productive unless the country has a stable macroeconomic environment.

The arguments against this position can be very seductive politically. It is often suggested that one ought to start slowly and that the macroeconomic issues will take care of themselves in time. I myself am convinced that these are siren songs to which we listen at our peril. It is important as part of any liberalization effort, any adjustment effort, that the macroeconomic framework be sustainable. If it is not, we have learned time and again, the imbalances created tend to overwhelm whatever structural changes can be made at the sectoral level.

Finally, it is my personal conclusion—one which is certainly not universally shared—that structural adjustment lending ought to be anchored in balance of payments problems.

It is important to distinguish between the need for policy reform and the need for structural adjustment lending by the World Bank. They are not identical. People often ask, "Why get involved at all in structural adjustment lending? Why bribe governments to do what they ought to be doing anyway?" The answer obviously is that one cannot bribe governments to undertake basic adjustments. Any government that would agree to structural changes just because there is a loan at the end of the process does not understand the scope of the changes, is not committed to the endeavor, would not resist the political opposition reforms might generate, and will not ensure that the adjustment policies are sustainable.

In my view, the correct answer has to be that we provide quick-disbursing loans because the actions being undertaken by the government have some balance of payments impact, some additional costs that we can help to defray. To me, that justification has been and continues to be the basic anchor for structural adjustment lending.

This standard does not mean that there is no need for policy reform in sectors in which the costs are not in foreign exchange. Indeed, countries face major issues of reform in education and the other social sectors, in transport, infrastructure, the environment, and urban development. Although the World Bank should be an active participant in those policy reforms, and a source of financial support, I believe quick-disbursing assistance is not appropriate for these types of reforms.

Underestimating the Political Factor

Taken together, these lessons hold a moral for economists. It is that we at the World Bank—and everyone else, I believe—underestimated the political difficulty of protracted adjustment. Economists here and elsewhere often tend to believe that we need only do our analysis, reach our conclusions, and write a report; the rest will follow. We do not have much experience with the political processes of change. We fail to give full weight in our own thinking to the fact that structural adjustment means a major redistribution of economic power and hence of political power in many of the countries undergoing this process.

Such a shift is not neutral. It does not happen easily or by itself. The politics of change is one of the reasons adjustment has taken a great deal more time than expected in some countries and one of the reasons some adjustment efforts have not been sustained.

I do not believe that the World Bank can do very much about this process except to understand the problem. Hiring political scientists to tell us what will or will not work in a country is not the solution. Those judgments are properly the country's responsibility.

Nevertheless, in working out adjustment loans and time frames for policy change, we need to give due attention to the political difficulty of adjustment. We should not say that because the politics are difficult the time has to be very protracted. Rather, we should take the difficulty as part of the judgment to be made about the adequacy of both the government's commitment and its capacity to bring about the specific change and achieve its objectives in the time agreed. We need to recognize that either the commitment or the pace of its implementation may be less than required.

Some Unresolved Issues

There remain a number of very important issues still to be resolved. I will conclude by raising four of them.

First, we have not yet been able to define very well how to handle policy reform in countries without significant balance of payments problems. Quick-disbursing lending seems to appeal to everyone. But I believe that such loans must be justified by their contribution to the balance of payments costs that adjustments incur and that the country lacks the resources to meet—and this justification becomes weak if there is no immediate balance of payments problem.

This issue is only a subset of a larger question about the transition from adjustment lending to exclusively project-based lending in a country: how does the World Bank build on the present policy dialogue—clearly most effective, most intimate, and most operationally relevant in the adjusting countries—once the adjustment process is finished? Once we no longer see a need for structural adjustment loans, what are the means by which the World Bank will maintain a continuing discussion with governments on their macroeconomic or sectoral management in an operationally relevant way?

The second set of issues relates to the nature of this transition for the countries now receiving adjustment loans. Transitions do take place. Overwhelmed today by the great number of countries in deep difficulty, we tend to forget that some countries have come out of that trouble. Transitions have started or are well advanced in Chile and Turkey, for example.

Yet it is easy to see the pressure building to perpetuate today's practices indefinitely. Stopping adjustment lending, goes the argument, would be wrong because it would reduce net disbursements to a country sharply. The management of the World Bank's disbursement pipeline is absolutely central, no matter how the transition will take place. During the period of adjustment lending, project pipelines tend to dry up because investment declines. In these circumstances, it is hard to get the governments' attention, to get them to make the expenditures necessary to develop a project pipeline. The result is that when adjustment lending, or quick-disbursing lending, comes to a natural end, when most of the incentive framework at the sector or macroeconomic level has been broadly put to right, the country finds itself with a very sharp drop in disbursements from the World Bank.

This drop, depending on the scale, obviously can create a major financing problem. We and the governments involved need to pay attention early on to managing the financial side of this transition. Otherwise, we will find that the end of adjustment lending brings very serious financial problems requiring a continuation of quick-disbursing lending, but for very different and essentially inappropriate reasons.

A related issue is how to handle policy reform in sectors that have no direct impact on the balance of payments. How can the World Bank and other development agencies be of greater assistance to governments in supporting the reforms necessary in the social sectors, urban areas, environmental management, and other spheres where quick-disbursing assistance may not be the proper tool because the balance of payments impact is small or because the financial benefits of the loan do not go to the sector concerned? What kind of sectoral lending can we envisage that will be useful to developing countries, will be the basis for effective support for sectoral policy change, and yet will not simply finance general imports?

A final question also relates to the transition. How do we assess the appropriate balance between project lending and structural adjustment lending?

One of the reasons the World Bank has been very effective—and became effective very quickly—in structural adjustment lending at both the macroeconomic and the sectoral levels is its very extensive database, the profound knowledge accumulated from its project work and sectoral analysis in many countries over many years. Structural adjustment lending, however, has a tendency to dry up those sources of information. Policy reform by itself does not produce anything; it only makes more efficient production and innovation possible.

The supply response is obviously crucial. In country after country investment levels have been dropping and in some cases have reached maintenance levels only. Clearly project lending ought to be seen not simply as a residual activity nor only as a way to understand the economy, but rather as a major tool to help begin the vitally needed increase in investments. For countries that have made progress in reorienting their policies, project lending should become increasingly important both for World Bank financing and as a stimulus to resumed commercial financing.

We are grappling with a fascinating subject. The analyses and findings assembled for this symposium make a valuable contribution to our understanding of the issues involved in adjustment lending and should stimulate continuing, fruitful discussion.

PART I

Issues of Policy Reform

2 *Introduction to Part I*

"ADJUSTMENT" has acquired a wide variety of meanings and interpretations. For some people, it refers to stabilization of the economy through measures to reduce or remove external and internal imbalances. For others, it refers to measures to achieve structural changes that will contribute to economic recovery and growth. At one extreme are those who suggest that adjustment and sound policies for economic development are one and the same, since both involve a wide range of desirable changes in the economy. At the other extreme are the critics who associate adjustment with policies they consider undesirable for development. It is useful, therefore, to clarify some of these concepts and define how the term is used in this volume.

Although long-term structural changes are an inevitable part or, better still, an underlying determinant of economic development,[1] this is not quite the sense in which adjustment is discussed here. A more time-bound phenomenon is meant, which is best illustrated by the experience of the 1980s, when developing countries were hit with three major shocks and the curtailment of external funding that came with the debt crisis in 1982. The three shocks were the global recession of 1979–82, the increase in real interest rates to positive levels for countries that had become accustomed to cheap financing, and the decline in the terms of trade for producers of oil and primary commodities. These shocks led to large and growing internal and external imbalances just when external financing declined sharply because of the debt crisis.

Two types of policy response, both labeled "adjustment," were called for. The first was stabilization, or managed reductions in expenditures to bring about an orderly adjustment of domestic demand to the reduced level of external resources available to the country. The second was structural adjustment, or changes in relative prices and institutions designed to make the economy more efficient, more flexible, and better able to use resources and so to engineer sustainable long-term growth. It was envisioned that effective structural adjustment measures would reduce the necessary extent of stabilization.[2]

Thus, in most countries adjustment involved, first, a rapid reduction of the imbalances in the current account of the balance of payments and the fiscal deficit—that is, stabilization. In this sense, adjustment also aimed to reduce the rate of inflation to a sustainable level. But this was not enough to improve growth because the reduction of imbalances at current output levels implied a cut in living standards or a cut in investment. These cuts had adverse implications for future growth, best illustrated with the familiar national income identity.

$$Y + \text{NFI} = C + I + X - M + \text{NFI} \tag{2-1}$$

where Y denotes gross domestic product (GDP), C consumption, I investment, X exports, M imports, and NFI net factor income. A reduction in the external current account deficit (or an increase in the surplus $X - M + \text{NFI}$) therefore involved a reduction in consumption C or investment I for the same level of gross national product (GNP). The stabilization phase therefore involved a cut in the standard of living and represented the harsh aspect of adjustment. One way to ameliorate this was to bring about a change in the pattern of expenditure, that is, to rely more on expenditure switching (rather than simply on expenditure reduction). One channel was to switch expenditures and production incentives from nontraded goods to import substitutes and exports. The level of imports (M) was a function of both income (Y) and the real exchange rate (r), as shown in equation 2-2:

$$M = M(r, Y). \tag{2-2}$$

Import demand would be reduced by a real depreciation of the exchange rate, so that the entire burden of stabilization would not fall on expenditure reduction. Furthermore, the real depreciation of the exchange rate would also induce a higher supply of exports.

The way to avoid lower standards of living was also to focus on the growth aspects of adjustment, that is, on structural adjustment. Structural adjustment includes reforms of policies and institutions—microeconomic (such as taxes), macroeconomic (such as fiscal imbalance), and institutional (such as public sector inefficiencies). These changes can improve resource allocation, increase economic efficiency, expand growth potential, and increase resilience in response to future shocks. The economic distortions are interconnected. For example, an overvalued exchange rate is evidence of macroeconomic distortions, yet it also contributes to microeconomic distortions because producers of traded goods face a relative price disincentive. Similarly, public enterprise pricing often leads to microeconomic distortions when prices do not reflect costs, to institutional distortions in that managers have inadequate incentives to be efficient, and to macroeconomic distortions as deficits become large.

In a world where resources had become severely constrained, the reforms of the 1980s tried to improve efficiency through the reallocation of resources. Policies in this direction constituted the structural change aspects of adjustment. In most countries, they involved changes in key relative prices in the economy, such as the real exchange rate, the real interest rate, and the internal terms of trade between agriculture and industry. They also involved, among other things, the restructuring of government operations and expenditures to fit the reduced resources and to improve efficiency.

There was also a need for institutional changes, especially for a fundamental rethinking of the role of government in society. Past development strategies called for a major and growing role for government in the provision not only of public goods but also of a broad range of manufactured goods as well as services. There was a need to refocus government involvement in the economy in view of the poor performance of state enterprises in many countries. The rethinking extended to the regulatory framework and particularly to the objectives of regulation and control in developing countries.

In many countries, the past neglect of the agricultural sector had been very costly to economies. The important role of agriculture as a provider of resources, a market for goods, and a supplier of food had been forgotten. Restructuring therefore involved the restoration of the terms of trade in favor of agriculture. Such restructuring need not be anti-industry, as is often suggested, since industrial growth cannot be predicated on a squeezing out of agriculture.

In many cases there was also a need to rethink the inward-looking approach that had been the hallmark of the 1960s and 1970s. Achieving a reduction of imports during the stabilization phase was a short-run objective. In the long run the objective was to expand exports in order to increase imports and access to the technology needed to boost growth. Again, the real exchange rate was a key variable in this strategy. The successful export-oriented approach of the East Asian countries was a clear indication that closed economies were not only bearing high costs because of poor resource allocation, but—more fundamentally—were lagging behind in the technological changes taking place in the rest of the world. The most dramatic example of the failure of the inward-looking approach was the collapse of the existing political regimes in Eastern Europe.

These structural changes would obviously take time, since the changes envisioned were for both policies and institutions. There were short-run costs to be borne in return for longer-run benefits. If the goal was to restore growth, it could not be achieved if economies were starved of external financing. This was the rationale for the World Bank's adjustment lending, which is reviewed in this volume. The purpose was to provide medium-term financing over a finite period to help countries undertake needed economic restructuring. The restructuring may involve adjustment of both types—policies to achieve changes in internal and external balances and changes in the structure of incentives and institutions.

Part I of this volume explores the six policy areas that typically are featured in the design of adjustment programs: fiscal policy, trade, finance, public sector management, agriculture, and industry (see table 2-1 for a summary of findings). Each chapter in Part I is devoted to one of these policy areas and examines the design issues and other concerns of that area. In addition, these chapters touch on the broader issues of the overall design of adjustment programs and the interaction between various policy reforms. They do not provide sweeping conclusions on the adequacy of policy design, but they indicate areas of success and failure and suggest improvements in the future.

FISCAL POLICY. Less progress has been made in fiscal reform than in the external accounts, as is clearly brought out in chapter 3 by Ajay Chhibber and Javad Khalilzadeh-Shirazi. Some countries reduced their fiscal deficit primarily by cutting expenditures (particularly investment expenditures), rather than by increasing revenue, but the policy was not sustainable. In other countries, debt service payments rose sharply in the budget—both because interest rates were rising and because devaluations increased the domestic currency cost of foreign debt repayments. As a result, a widening gap between the fiscal deficit and the current account deficit put increasing pressure on the private sector to generate a net surplus. This led to cuts in private investment and growth, often accompanied by higher inflation.

Some success has been achieved in rationalizing public investment, with the help of the World Bank's investment reviews.[3] There has been much less progress in reforming taxes and reallocating current expenditures. Given the urgency of reducing fiscal deficits, near-term revenue measures have dominated initiatives to reform tax policy in most countries in recent years. Exceptions are Indonesia, Mexico, and Turkey, which have undertaken thorough tax reforms. Reforms to relieve the financial pressure on the private sector and to generate increased domestic savings and investments through growth-oriented fiscal policy have generally been insufficient.

TRADE AND EXCHANGE RATE POLICY. Recipients of adjustment loans have made considerable progress in achieving exchange rate flexibility and strengthening the incentives for exports, as Vinod Thomas shows in chapter 4. The domestic currencies of recipient countries depreciated in real terms by an average of about 22 percent between 1981–83 and 1985–87 compared with 2 percent for nonrecipients. The adjusting countries' export volumes grew substantially, although export values increased much less because of declining world prices for these exports.

Table 2-1. Assessment of Reforms in the Major Policy Areas Affected by Adjustment Programs, 1981–88

Policy area	*Extent of reform*	*Assessment*
Overall reforms	External adjustment rapid, internal adjustment often unsustained, institutional reforms slow	Policies have mattered a great deal, but constraints include conflicts in design (for example, between fiscal and trade policies)
Fiscal	Initial deficit reductions not sustained	Expenditure cuts could not be maintained
	Some success in rationalization of public investment (as in Pakistan and Turkey)	More careful scrutiny of current expenditure needed
	Tax reform not comprehensive and with limited success; Indonesia, Mexico, and Turkey are exceptions	Short-run revenue concerns have dominated
Trade	Progress in exchange rate flexibility and export incentives	Strong responses in export volume, but nonprice factors need greater emphasis (as in East Asia)
	Progress in replacement of quantitative restrictions by tariffs and in tariff reform, but import liberalization slower	Greater liberalization constrained by stabilization requirements and internal opposition; export response assists in import liberalization (as in Korea and Turkey)
Financial	Reforms initiated in only a few cases, but receiving greater attention	Reforms often protracted and require sound macro framework (as in Chile and Turkey)
Public sector management	Institutional reforms and divestiture slow, particularly in Sub-Saharan Africa	Introduced in almost every adjustment program
	Some reduction in enterprise losses	Gains more from price increases than from improvements in efficiency
Agriculture	Visible improvements in price policy	Improvements especially strong in Sub-Saharan Africa
	Reform of parastatals slower	Supply response to price constrained by institutional factors
Industry	Focus on trade policy and its impact on industry	Reforms specific to industrial sector not given sufficient attention

Chile, Korea, and Turkey have made spectacular progress in boosting export volume. Most countries, however, have barely begun to use the price and nonprice instruments at their disposal to increase exports.

On the import side, several countries have replaced quantitative restrictions with tariffs and have reformed their tariff structure. The structure of protection provided by import barriers, with its implicit bias against exports, has been more resistant to reform, however. The ten major trade adjustment borrowers have typically reduced the discrimination against exports more than have other countries from the same regions that were also studied. Liberalization efforts raise far fewer objections if exports are doing well and if the private sector believes that liberalization is a medium-term program that will be sustained. Economic analysis and country experience show that countries would benefit from replacing quantitative restrictions on imports with tariff protection, reducing tariff dispersion, and lowering protection. To improve a program's credibility and the private sector's responsiveness, the main features and goals of the program should be announced publicly and early.

FINANCIAL SECTOR. In the few countries that have undertaken financial reforms, such as Argentina, Chile, Indonesia, and Turkey, an appropriate macroeconomic policy framework has been critical to success. Large budget deficits make financial reform more difficult because they lead to high interest rates (as in Brazil and Turkey), a crowding out of the private sector, and a weakening of the quality of bank portfolios. Efforts to finance fiscal deficits have frequently created further problems for the financial sector, as chapter 5 by Alan Gelb and Patrick Honohan shows. Budget deficits financed through an "inflation tax" tend to increase the opportunity cost of holding money, which causes the monetary base to decline (as happened in Argentina). Some governments have increased revenue by raising reserve requirements; others have relied on the statutory sale of government bonds at low and often negative interest rates to mitigate the adverse budgetary impacts. Financial sector repression has often increased as external resources to finance budget deficits have declined.

In any event, financial reforms have tended to be protracted; the organized financial system in many developing countries is technically insolvent because of poor management, insufficient supervision of bank lending, and incorrect signals on lending as a result of financial repression. Much remains to be done in improving regulation and in financial sector restructuring. The impact will be limited, however, unless the financial repression that has accompanied the large fiscal deficits is reduced.

At the 1989 symposium on which this book is based, in the discussion of the World Bank's role in policy reforms in the areas of trade and finance, Vinod Dubey found the evidence encouraging. Progress in the implementation of conditionality in trade and finance was respectable. The evidence also suggested that adjustment lending is a useful tool in promoting reforms in these areas. The findings of the papers on trade and finance provide strong support for continuing to emphasize trade and financial sector reforms in adjustment lending, while at the same time addressing the constraints on better policy implementation.

PUBLIC SECTOR MANAGEMENT. Although almost every adjustment program has promoted institutional reforms of the public sector, these reforms have been almost uniformly slow, as John Nellis shows in chapter 6. There has been some success in slowing or even halting the creation of new enterprises and the growth of public enterprise employment. Some public enterprises have reduced their losses, although largely through price increases permitted by their monopoly position rather than through improvements in efficiency. Improving efficiency in utility companies, for example, has proved elusive, and their financial losses remain high. Few attempted reforms have had much impact on planning, policy analysis, or debt management in the public sector. After initial delays, several countries—Jamaica, Niger, Panama, and Togo among them—have made progress in divesting public enterprises; others, including Ghana, Senegal, and Turkey, have not. It is too early to evaluate the performance of enterprises since their privatization.

In the symposium discussion of reform of the public sector, Murray A. Sherwin drew on the New Zealand experience to underscore the importance of establishing clear commercial objectives for public enterprises. If public functions are to be performed by them, these functions should be clearly identified and their funding made visible. In the case of privatization it is essential to have a clear framework for monitoring and accountability so that management can be left with a fair degree of autonomy in its functions. The risks of privatizing into inefficient markets should be minimized by policies promoting competition.

AGRICULTURE. Efforts to reduce disincentives to agriculture have been significant in many countries, especially in Sub-Saharan Africa, as Odin Knudsen and John Nash show in chapter 7. Although pricing policy is a crucial element in the recovery of agriculture, supporting measures that are also needed include both institutional reform and the strengthening and improvement of government expenditure programs to reduce the constraints farmers face in responding to better prices. A number of studies show that public investment, carried out well, can be an effective complement to price policy in efforts to increase the response of farm production to changes in incentives.[4] In particular, when expenditure programs are being cut and government revenues from agriculture are falling as producer prices rise, it is essential to ensure the continued funding of critical public investments in agriculture.

Other problems affect the agricultural sector in the many developing countries in which public agencies monopolize commodity trade and input distribution. Often these agencies are costly and inefficient, discourage private trade, and tax farmers. One way to reduce inefficiencies is to eliminate government market interventions, and some success has been achieved in this area. When the immediate alternatives are limited, however, because of past discouragement of private sector involvement, it may not be advisable to dismantle public agencies quickly; instead, adjustment programs have addressed inefficiency and overhead costs in these agencies or have attempted to minimize the costs to farmers and private trade. One mechanism is to set pricing rules—for example, by linking farm prices to international prices—to avoid arbitrariness and increase the likelihood of more sustained reforms. Some of the World Bank's sectoral adjustment loans in agriculture, particularly in Mexico, have introduced such automatic pricing rules. Other measures seek to reduce overstaffing (Ghana), limit the scope of operations handled by individual agencies (Morocco and Tanzania), and break up large and unwieldy agencies into smaller and more specialized ones by, say, separating credit operations from the distribution of physical inputs (Colombia). Experience shows that such reforms are more difficult to implement but more lasting than those that merely realign prices periodically.

INDUSTRY. Adjustment issues in the industrial sector vary widely, depending mostly on the level of industrialization. In countries such as Chile, India, Mexico, and Turkey, complex industrial structures need to be made more competitive internationally. In Africa, however, the problems are much more basic, such as the extreme shortages of skilled labor and modern technology.

Some countries, in trying to achieve rapid industrialization, invested disproportionately and unwisely in heavy and chemical industries in the 1960s and 1970s; others established public enterprises in many areas or tried to foster industrialization through distorted incentive systems relying on heavy protection, subsidized credit, and other regulatory mechanisms. Frequently the industries thus promoted were viable only with continuing support. In those cases, adjustments in industry meant reducing losses, protection, and regulation so that a more efficient and sustainable industrial structure could develop. With the exception of Asian countries, adjustment operations for industry have generally emphasized trade and exchange rate policies. Measures have concentrated on restructuring, pricing policies, investment incentives, and the redirection of investment in manufacturing from the public to the private sector.[5]

In chapter 8, James R. Tybout uses demand-side decomposition of growth to study the changes in domestic demand and manufacturing trade flows during the 1980s. The countries with adjustment loans appear to have done slightly better than their respective regional averages in terms of growth in manufacturing value added during 1984–86, when most adjustment programs were under way. The same countries also performed better than their regional averages during the precrisis period of 1978–81. Tybout found weak evidence that, when loans featured conditionalities related to trade liberalization or devaluation, countries tended to exhibit increased import penetration during the adjustment period. Similarly, an emphasis on conditionalities related to export promotion policies and devaluation seems to have been associated with export expansion.

At the symposium, W. David Hopper and Visvanathan Rajagopalan emphasized sectoral and micro-level issues. Improvements are needed in three complementary areas: policies and regulations, institutions, and human resources. The review of agricultural performance indicates that improvements in productivity depend not only on introducing better policies but also on strengthening institutions and developing human resources. Adjustment lending is useful in supporting policy reform, but greater attention needs to be devoted to the complementary investments required for long-term development. These include the recovery and development of physical infrastructure, protection of the environment, and the provision of technology.

Notes

1. See Simon Kuznets, *Six Lectures on Economic Growth* (Glencoe, Ill.: Free Press, 1959).

2. It was always recognized that there was an overlap between stabilization and structural adjustment and that certain measures—exchange rate realignments, for example—played a role under both headings.

3. See Basil Kavalsky, "Reviewing Public Investment Programs," *Finance & Development*, March 1986.

4. These studies are surveyed in Ajay Chhibber, "The Aggregate Supply Response in Agriculture: A Survey," in Simon Commander, ed., *Structural Adjustment in Agriculture: Theory and Practice* (London: Overseas Development Institute, 1989).

5. These and other measures are covered in Gerald M. Meier and William F. Steel, eds., *Industrial Adjustment in Sub-Saharan Africa* (New York: Oxford University Press, 1989).

3 *Public Finance*

Ajay Chhibber
Javad Khalilzadeh-Shirazi

THIS CHAPTER examines fiscal reform in adjustment programs and draws major lessons for the design of reform and of conditionality in World Bank adjustment lending. Although the scope of the chapter is broad, coverage of the issues and countries is selective. The country references are illustrative rather than exhaustive, since Part III of this book presents detailed case studies. The main emphasis is on a group of thirteen developing countries that received three or more World Bank adjustment loans since the Bank began adjustment lending in 1979. These adjustment loan–intensive countries are sometimes compared with twelve countries that received fewer than three adjustment loans and with fifteen countries that received no adjustment loans from the World Bank.

The first part of the chapter focuses on the macroeconomic implications of fiscal deficits, the extent to which selected countries have managed to reduce these deficits, the relation between growth and the sustainability of fiscal policy, and the consistency of fiscal policy instruments with other policy instruments. The next two sections go into issues of expenditure and revenue. The section on expenditure policy relates in particular to the level and composition of recurrent outlays and public investment. This discussion is followed by an examination of tax systems and experience with their reform. The final section summarizes key conclusions and outlines the set of growth-oriented fiscal policies appropriate for inclusion in adjustment programs and lending.

Macroeconomic Aspects of Fiscal Adjustment

Fiscal crises, in the form of large budget deficits,[1] have been diagnosed as a primary feature of external disequilibria and macroeconomic instability in many developing countries. The massive flow of financial resources to developing countries in the 1970s (largely recycled oil exporters' deposits) helped finance—or, some may say, caused—these deficits. Foreign savings were used to cover shortfalls in public sector savings.[2] But after 1982 (see figure 3-1) these flows dried up as the enormity of the debt buildup was revealed, and the underlying unsus-

Figure 3-1. Current Account and Public Sector Deficit as a Percentage of GDP for Thirty-Three Developing Countries, 1980 and 1982–87

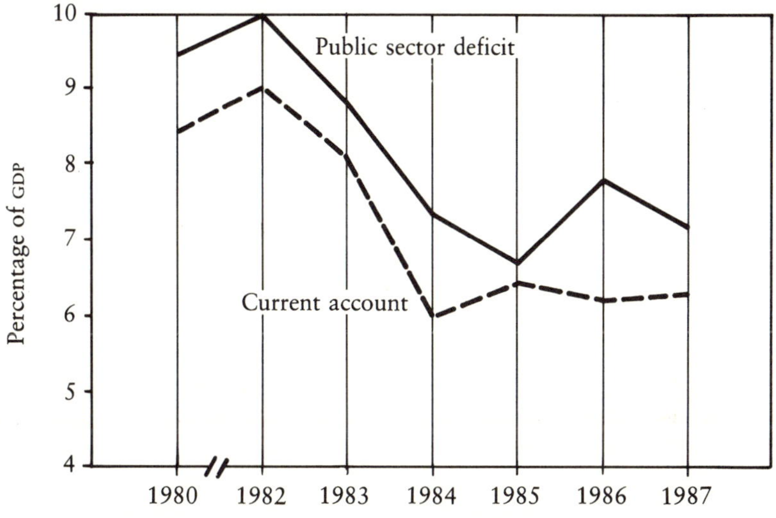

Source: World Bank data.

tainability of the fiscal deficits was exposed in a large number of developing countries. Moreover, external conditions deteriorated sharply; as real international interest rates rose dramatically, oil and commodity prices fell, and growth in industrial countries decelerated, demand for the exports of developing countries (and others) was reduced. These factors exacerbated fiscal problems and the deterioration in economic performance in developing countries. Heavy adjustments were required to redress the budget deficit; government expenditures had to be cut sharply.

Fiscal Crises

The need for adjustment gives rise to several questions: How much of adjustment should take place in the public sector as opposed to the private sector? How much should be in the form of restraint on aggregate demand, and how much should come from efforts to increase supply? When reducing aggregate demand, an obvious need is to reduce the budget deficit. One approach is to view fiscal policy as primarily an instrument for reducing expenditure and to rely on other instruments, such as the exchange rate and pricing, to shift expenditures and resources toward tradable goods—expenditure switching. But the manner in which the budget deficit is reduced, and by what amount, and the consistency of other policies with fiscal policy significantly affect the ability of the economy to increase output and thereby diminish the need to cut demand. Consequently, these factors affect as well the sustainability of fiscal changes. The availability of external finance to smooth the process of reform is, of course, a key factor.

Has fiscal adjustment been adequate considering the decline in external financing many developing countries have experienced in recent years? If not, how have budget deficits been financed, and what are the implications for the economy of alternative financing packages? Has fiscal policy "crowded in" or "crowded out" the private sector and thereby affected the sustainability of reform? A preliminary attempt is made to answer these questions in this section, which also includes a broad assessment of World Bank and International Monetary Fund (IMF) conditionality related to macroeconomic fiscal issues, and a discussion of the consistency of fiscal policy with other instruments of adjustment.

There is no doubt that excessive fiscal deficits were the proximate cause of economic crises in many developing countries, such as Argentina, Malawi, Mexico, Nigeria, and the Philippines (see table 3-1). Once the crisis occurred, the credit squeeze affected both the public and private sectors. In the case of Malawi and the Philippines, recent data show that the private sector was affected much more than the public sector by the credit squeeze. Countries such as Indonesia, Korea, and Pakistan that restrained the growth of credit to the public sector appear to have avoided this problem. Although both Indonesia and Korea had temporary problems in the early 1980s because of excessive expansion of credit to the government, both adjusted very quickly by, among other things, drastically cutting the growth of credit to the public sector.

A large budget deficit can therefore have adverse implications for three key macroeconomic targets: debt, inflation, and the growth rate of the economy (for a fuller discussion, see Buiter 1985; Anand, Chhibber, and van Wijnbergen, 1990; and World Bank 1988). The arithmetic for this goes as follows: The current account surplus is equal to net private savings (that is, private savings minus private investment) minus the public sector deficit. A fiscal deficit can be financed in one of three ways:[3] (1) external borrowing or grants, (2) domestic borrowing from the banking system, and (3) domestic borrowing from nonbank sources. Depending on the method of financing, a large fiscal deficit creates one or more macroeconomic problems. Large external borrowing creates a debt problem, financing through monetary creation leads to high inflation, and heavy domestic borrowing leads either to insufficient credit for the private sector (when credit is allocated by the government and the financial institutions it controls) or to high real interest rates and less private sector credit, which reduces private investment and future output growth.

Table 3-1. Growth of Real Domestic Credit in Selected Countries, by Sector and Timing of Economic Crisis, 1980–81 to 1985–86
(annual percentage rate of change)

Country[a]	*1980–81*	*1981–82*	*1982–83*	*1983–84*	*1984–85*	*1985–86*
Argentina (1982)						
Government	337.2	23.1	320.4	−135.9	−448.7	12.5
Public enterprise	98.2	895.4	−185.0	−174.9		
Private sector	58.4	27.1	−27.5	−100.8	−300.0	−6.4
Malawi (1981)						
Government	74.6	16.6	12.0	−5.9	9.2	23.0
Public enterprise	−7.4	−3.7	−13.0	14.4	20.0	−8.2
Private sector	−12.2	4.9	4.8	−23.9	−20.8	0.1
Mexico (1982)						
Government	22.8	113.1	−37.7	−30.1	35.8	n.a.
Public enterprise	33.5	92.1	18.5	9.5	−24.9	n.a.
Private sector	18.6	−36.5	−48.5	23.4	−1.3	n.a.
Nigeria (1983)						
Government	63.4	53.9	43.9	6.9	−7.0	n.a.
Public enterprise	16.2	−13.0	98.5	−34.6	−9.2	n.a.
Private sector	17.6	8.4	−1.1	−1.5	−1.2	n.a.
Philippines (1983)						
Government	51.3	74.9	14.7	−44.2	−27.5	69.2
Public enterprise	5.3	25.3	34.3	−19.4	10.0	−48.2
Private sector	10.7	5.1	15.3	−50.0	−35.2	−23.8
Indonesia (1981)						
Government	52.3	5.6	−18.1	51.4	6.6	n.a.
Public enterprise	−21.4	11.0	−14.0	−7.4	3.2	n.a.
Private sector	21.4	35.6	15.3	23.5	16.3	n.a.
Korea (1981)						
Government	69.5	18.1	−1.6	0.6	4.5	8.9
Public enterprise	21.5	20.5	17.4	−3.9	−4.0	−2.4
Private sector	10.8	18.6	13.7	10.3	15.0	12.7
Pakistan (1981)						
Government, public enterprise	−4.0	19.2	3.2	2.5	−1.4	9.5
Private sector	10.0	10.8	14.0	7.6	22.2	12.9

n.a. Not available.
a. Year of economic crisis in parentheses.
Source: IMF, *International Financial Statistics.*

Fiscal Deficits in Adjustment Loan–Intensive Countries

The evidence for the loan-intensive countries, the thirteen countries that received three or more World Bank adjustment loans, shows that the reduction in the budget deficit closely followed the decline in the current account balance from 1982 to 1985 (figure 3-2).[4] Until 1985 the loan-intensive countries reduced their fiscal deficit more than did countries that received no adjustment loans. Since 1985, however, the loan-intensive countries appear to be having greater difficulty than nonrecipients

Figure 3-2. Current Account and Public Sector Deficit as a Percentage of GDP for Thirteen Adjustment Loan–Intensive Countries, 1980 and 1982–87

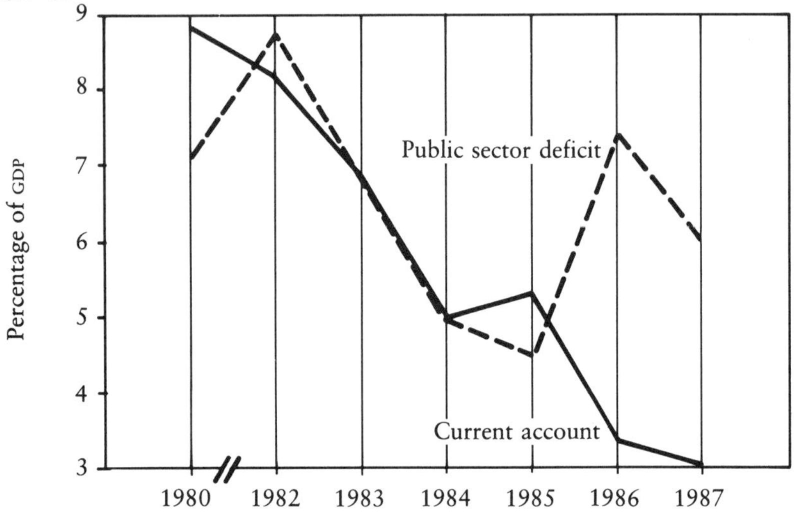

Source: World Bank data.

in controlling fiscal deficits (figure 3-3). The divergence between the public sector deficit and the current account balance has become substantial, which implies increased pressure on the private sector to generate a net savings surplus. Therefore domestic financing of the budget deficit rose sharply in a number of countries.[5] As a result, some countries such as Mexico and Zambia faced problems of high inflation, whereas others such as Turkey experienced high real interest rates.[6]

Why were the loan-intensive countries, all of which had World Bank–IMF adjustment programs with strong conditionality on fiscal deficits, not able to maintain a lower fiscal deficit as well as nonrecipient countries?[7] One possible reason is that loan-intensive countries suffered larger terms of trade shocks. A disaggregated look shows that among the loan-intensive countries, only five—Côte d'Ivoire, Malawi, Mexico, Philippines, and Zambia—suffered a deterioration in the fiscal deficit. In Côte d'Ivoire, Malawi, Mexico, and Zambia fiscal deficits deteriorated as worsening terms of trade led to falling revenues, while expenditure programs continued because they could not be easily cut. In the Philippines the increase in fiscal deficits was due largely to the increased losses of public sector financial institutions, which had provided loan guarantees under the Marcos regime. Since the loan-intensive countries suffered larger

Figure 3-3. Public Sector Deficit as a Percentage of GDP in Selected Country Groups, 1980 and 1982–87

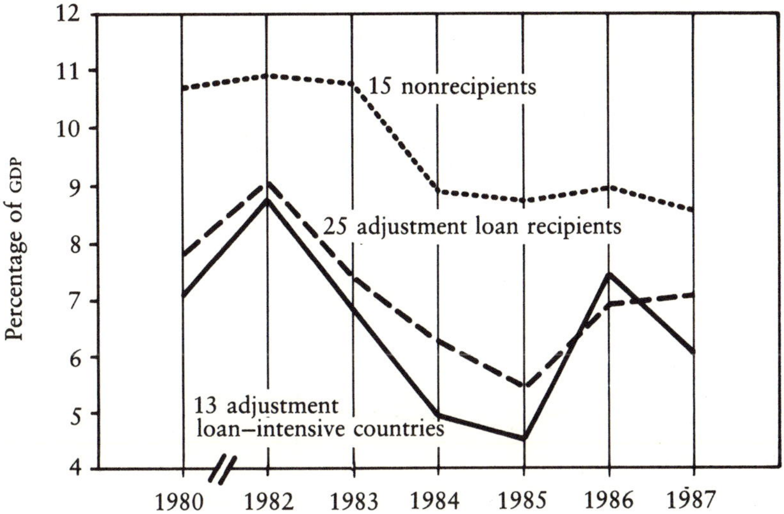

Source: World Bank data.

terms of trade shocks (see chapter 11) than did nonrecipient countries, they faced greater difficulty in reducing fiscal deficits as well.

The link between the fiscal deficit and the terms of trade, both in levels and changes, is verified by the following equations, which use pooled time-series and cross-country data for 1980–87 for twelve loan-intensive countries (*t* statistics in parentheses). The results show a significant negative relationship between the terms of trade index and the fiscal deficit. Expenditures rose when the terms of trade improved, but were difficult to cut quickly once terms of trade and consequently revenues fell (see also figure 3-4).

$$\text{PSD} = \underset{(3.06)}{12.1478} - \underset{(2.30)}{0.0891}\ \text{TOT} + \Sigma_i b_i D_i \qquad (3\text{-}1)$$

$$\bar{R}^2 = 0.52 \qquad \text{D.W.} = 1.24$$

$$\text{PSD} = \underset{(3.20)}{1.99} - \underset{(1.86)}{5.8135}\ \hat{\text{TOT}} + \underset{(8.63)}{0.6581}\ \text{PSD}(-1) \qquad (3\text{-}2)$$

$$\bar{R}^2 = 0.55 \qquad \text{D.W.} = 1.96$$

Figure 3-4. Expenditure and Revenue as a Percentage of GDP among the Thirteen Adjustment Loan–Intensive Countries, 1980 and 1982–87

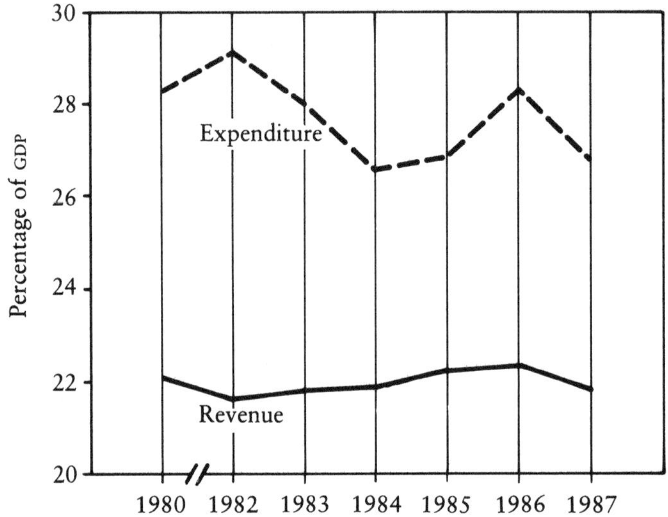

Source: World Bank data.

where PSD = public sector deficit as a percentage of GDP
TOT = terms of trade index (1980 = 100)
$\hat{\text{TOT}}$ = percentage change in the terms of trade index
D_i = country dummy variable.

Sustainable Fiscal Deficits and Growth

In the post-1982 adjustment period considered here, the adjustment to lower budget deficits has come primarily through expenditure cuts (figure 3-4). These expenditure reductions have cut heavily into public investments (which experienced the largest percentage of reductions) and the noninterest component of current expenditure (figure 3-5 and table 3-2). These cuts have affected social and economic services and subsidies and have important implications for future growth and equity that suggest the need for a careful consideration of alternative policies.[8] Because of a variety of social and political pressures on the government, the reduction in expenditure has not always been rational and efficient.

In choosing between a reduction in expenditure or an increase in revenue, some important macroeconomic implications need to be kept in mind. One is the possibility that an increase in revenue could lead to a

Figure 3-5. Capital and Current Expenditure as a Percentage of GDP for Thirteen Adjustment Loan–Intensive Countries, 1980 and 1982–86

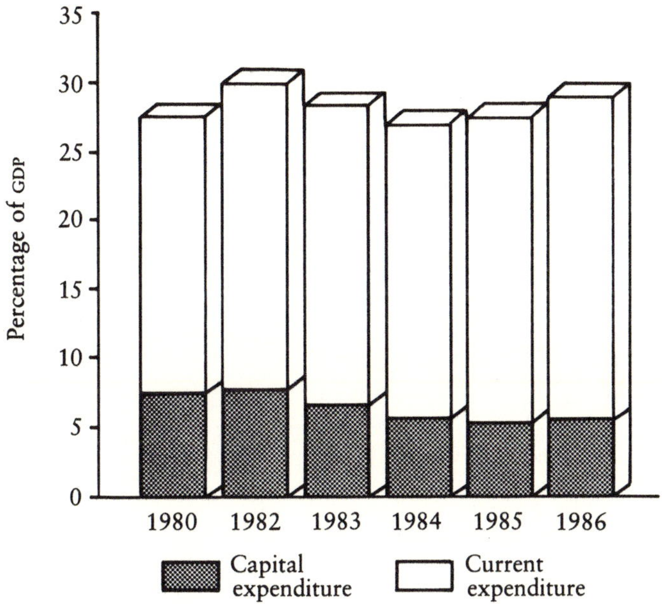

Source: World Bank data.

reduction in the aggregate savings rate of the economy. Known as the Please effect, this occurs when the public sector propensity to save is lower than that of the private sector (Please 1967; Chhibber 1985).[9] A recent study (Balassa 1988) has shown a negative correlation between growth and public consumption as a share of GDP. Many Asian economies, however, have raised taxes to finance public investment and have thereby raised savings and investment rates in the economy. The choices made in cutting expenditures or raising revenues also have wide-ranging effects on trade balances and income distribution. Who benefits and who loses from government expenditure and the manner in which expenditure choices are financed are key factors in the ability of the government to undertake reforms and address poverty and the social costs of adjustment (Cornia, Jolly, and Stewart 1988). These issues have been neglected or given insufficient attention in the design of adjustment programs.[10]

Although in general it is not difficult to identify when fiscal deficits are unsustainable—inflation accelerates, interest rates are high, and the private sector gets crowded out or external imbalances grow—it is less

Table 3-2. Change in Real Public Expenditure by Functional Category for Thirty-Four Randomly Selected Developing Countries, 1982–86
(unweighted average)

Account	*Percentage rate*
Capital account	−10.3
Current account	0.1
Goods and services	−4.3
Wages	−7.0
Interest	81.3
Subsidies	−1.7
Other	−1.2
Change in real total expenditure	−2.4
Current account (functional categories)	0.1
General	−5.3
Defense	−5.8
Education	−5.7
Health	−0.8
Social security	−4.9
Economic services	−7.7
Housing	4.4
Other social	10.8
Other (including interest)	41.9

Source: IMF, *Government Financial Statistics,* various years.

easy to decide what constitutes a sustainable level. This level depends, among other things, on how the private sector adjusts to changes in fiscal policy. If a reduction in the fiscal deficit leads to lower private savings, its effectiveness in lowering the current account deficit is reduced. Conversely, a country can run a higher budget deficit without adversely affecting the current account if the private sector is willing to generate additional net savings surpluses at reasonable rates of inflation and real interest rates, as happened in Malaysia and Thailand, for example.

Whether the improvement in the current account is brought about by a reduction in investment or an increase in savings is fundamental to the medium-term success of the adjustment program. It is in this area that potential conflicts arise between stabilization and adjustment. There is little merit in having a low budget deficit and a low external account deficit if the outcome is a low level of savings and investment in the economy. Thus the quality of fiscal adjustment is as important as the quantitative improvement in the deficit. The composition of public expenditures and the nature of the government's tax and credit policies are key factors determining the outcome of fiscal adjustment and are addressed in more detail in later sections of this chapter.

The sustainable level of the fiscal deficit, therefore, depends on such factors as the cost and availability of external and internal finance, the quality and composition of public resource mobilization and use, accompanying adjustment measures, and the behavioral responses of the rest of the economy. Turkey's adjustment experience provides an interesting example of the need to assess these factors carefully in judging the sustainability of fiscal policy.

Turkey repeatedly exceeded IMF fiscal targets in the early stages of its adjustment program. Undoubtedly, the financing needs commensurate with larger public sector deficits generated higher medium-term inflation and real interest rates. But the thrust of the program was growth-oriented, centering on export performance and on keeping savings and investment rates up. A key contributing factor was the substantial excess capacity resulting from the heavy investments in the 1970s, which allowed for a quick improvement in output and exports once the exchange rate was realigned. A recent study (Anand, Chhibber, and van Wijnbergen 1990) argues that in terms of forgone growth the cost of a more conservative fiscal policy might have been high in the early stages of the adjustment program. After 1985, however, as net external inflows declined, further increases in the fiscal deficit could not be sustained. This combination of higher fiscal deficits and lower external inflows has led, particularly since 1985, to high real interest rates and inflation. Thus the concept of sustainability requires careful case-by-case analysis and a focus on both the short- and long-term consequences of deficit financing.

Consistency between Fiscal Policy and Other Measures

Consistency among various components of an adjustment program is a major concern when designing such programs. Almost every component of an adjustment program has fiscal implications. In particular, exchange rate and trade policies, financial liberalization, and price liberalization in selected sectors have large effects on the budget. Unless these effects are anticipated and their influence incorporated into fiscal programming, they can be destabilizing and disruptive and possibly lead to a collapse of the program and to policy reversals.

EXCHANGE RATE POLICY. Consistency between fiscal and exchange rate policies is a major issue in the design of adjustment programs. In general, the need for coordination between the two is obvious. Devaluation is unlikely to be effective unless accompanied by appropriate demand management policies, including a tight budget, to reduce aggregate demand and imports and thereby decrease the pressure on the current account. Without appropriate fiscal restraint, inflation increases and the real effective devaluation is quickly eroded, with few effects on resource allocation.

The coordination of exchange rate and fiscal policies can become complex since changes in the exchange rate affect the size of the budget deficit through changes in revenue generated by customs duties and export taxes, foreign debt service, transfers to enterprises, and subsidies (see the appendix to this chapter for the case of Zimbabwe). The effect of devaluation on debt service costs can be seen in table 3-2, which breaks down real expenditures by category for thirty-four randomly selected developing countries. The table shows the large contribution of rising interest costs to fiscal problems. If the impact of devaluation on the budget is likely to be adverse, it may be counterproductive to recommend free floating of the currency (such as an exchange auction). Movements in the exchange rate and the budget deficit may reinforce each other in a destabilizing manner. This happened in Bolivia, Sierra Leone, and Zambia, where the fiscal situation deteriorated following the devaluation because of the loss of the black market premiums that had previously accrued to the government (Pinto 1987; Kharas and Pinto 1987). In such cases, a series of managed exchange rate changes programmed within an overall reduction in the budget deficit may be a much safer alternative, with some priority in sequencing given to deficit reduction.

TRADE POLICY. Important issues of consistency also arise with respect to trade policy. The first stage of the World Bank's recommendations for trade reform usually involves a shift from quantitative import restrictions to tariffs, which improves the fiscal position of the government. Subsequent reforms that call for reductions in the tariff rate, however, may require compensatory fiscal measures. Policy reversals may take place if governments do not implement such compensatory measures, as happened in Morocco.

PRICE POLICY. Sectoral price liberalization usually benefits the government budget. In many cases, the benefit comes from a decline in the losses of state enterprises. If a sector is a net taxpayer, however, price decontrols can have an adverse fiscal impact. This is often the case for the agricultural sector, where input subsidies are the rule and the prices received by farmers are kept low through export taxes and the payment of below-market procurement prices (see Chhibber 1985; Braverman and Hammer 1986). Thus price increases to the farm sector will adversely affect the budget unless they are compensated for by a reduction in input subsidies. Comprehensive price liberalization in several sectors often presents fewer problems because the government's fiscal losses in some sectors could be balanced by gains in others. Individual sectoral adjustment loans would, however, need to direct attention to this issue to ensure that there were no adverse effects on the government's fiscal position.

Some countries have imposed selective price controls in an attempt to control inflation, often in the mistaken belief that inflationary expectations alone had contributed to high inflation. In Brazil under the Cruzado Plan, price controls were put in place as a vigorous expenditure program was being undertaken. In this case, price controls in the face of an 8 percent increase in wages led to an increase in public enterprise deficits. A consumer boom eroded the trade surplus, and the program collapsed with much higher inflation than before (Cardoso and Dornbusch 1987). Recent studies (Cukierman 1988; Simonsen 1988) suggest, however, that even orthodox stabilization programs are insufficient to control inflation when inflationary expectations set in and, furthermore, that they are often accompanied by a prolonged recession with heavy social costs. The issue remains unsettled since the answer depends to a large extent on the somewhat nebulous concept of the "credibility" of policies and how best to attain it (Blejer and Cheasty 1988).

An issue of great concern to many governments is the short-run inflationary consequences of price liberalization—the release of repressed inflation (Feltenstein and Farhadian 1987). In this case the monetary overhang which often accompanies price controls must be gradually dissipated, and careful coordination of public enterprise price policy and fiscal policy is needed. The immediate burst in prices following decontrol and liberalization can lead to policy reversals if the eventual impact of deficit reduction on inflation takes effect over a longer period. This is what has led to the interruption in China's economic reforms and is a key issue in planning reforms in Algeria, Angola, and much of Eastern Europe.

Resource Allocation and Use in the Public Sector

The preceding section argued that stabilization and adjustment typically require considerable changes in government expenditure policy both to reduce unsustainable fiscal deficits and to enhance the impact of public spending on growth and income distribution. Thus adjustment programs have devoted considerable attention to four broad issues of public expenditure: (1) the level and composition of recurrent expenditures, (2) the size and allocation of public investment, (3) institutional processes and mechanisms for budgeting, and (4) the fiscal consequences of public enterprise operations. Each of these areas is discussed below.

Recurrent Expenditures

Table 3-2 shows the changes (unweighted averages) in real expenditures in different categories for thirty-four randomly selected developing countries during 1982–86. Cuts have been made in every category of expenditure except housing and other social services. Increasingly, concern is being expressed that budgetary allocations for operations and maintenance are inadequate. The World Bank, on the basis of its detailed sectoral knowledge, has at times set specific targets for increases in operations and maintenance expenditures in the belief that the payoff from such outlays would be high. In some cases, structural adjustment loans have stipulated a target for increased real spending on social sectors, even when the loan has also included a condition requiring a reduction in the overall deficit or in recurrent expenditures.

Because of the large amounts that are involved, subsidies—their effectiveness, relevance, and costs—are among the recurrent expenditure categories most often subject to scrutiny in adjustment programs (World Bank 1987). Both explicit and implicit subsidies are covered and involve a wide range of items, including foodstuffs. For most products, the eventual elimination of subsidies should be the goal. Where appropriate, subsidies and cost recovery ought to be handled jointly. For some items, particularly foodstuffs, however, the focus might justifiably be on better targeting of beneficiaries rather than on the complete elimination of subsidies, both to improve the distributional impact and to reduce or restrain budgetary outlays. Although World Bank adjustment lending often contains conditions related to a reduction in and rationalization of subsidies, reform has proved to be difficult in some cases, such as fertilizers.

Public Investment

In many developing countries the level, composition, and institutional processes of public investment are key aspects of fiscal adjustment. Resource constraints often dictate a relatively sharp cutback in the magnitude of public investment (see figure 3-5). Such cutbacks generally have a significant impact on the balance of payments because the import component of this spending generally exceeds the recurrent expenditures component. Within a reduced public investment program, priority is usually given to projects with shorter gestation and higher rates of return. Many developing countries lack a systematic process for evaluating public projects and for establishing multiyear budgeting requirements.

In the early phases of the adjustment process, the emphasis is generally on scaling down the size of the public investment program and shifting the focus from the manufacturing sector to infrastructure and social sectors. A core investment program consisting of a small number of projects that can be rapidly completed is often devised. In Pakistan and Turkey, for example, the governments have increased the emphasis on infrastructure, which has important complementary linkages with private sector productivity. Some structural adjustment loans, such as one for Turkey, contain highly specific quantitative conditions on public investment concerning, for example, the size of the gap between public investment and savings, a ceiling on the growth of public investment, and a reduction in the number of projects in the program. Generally, however, structural adjustment loans contain no explicit quantitative targets for public investment. Rather, conditionality takes the form of a requirement for review and agreement on the size and composition of the program at some future time.

As the process of adjustment and expenditure compression has progressed, concern has been expressed about the insufficiency of public investment, particularly for infrastructure and social sectors. Thus some recent adjustment loans have specified an increase in, or a minimum level of, public investment; those for Chile and Ghana are examples. Reducing the share of public investment allocated to the manufacturing sector in order to free resources for these other sectors has sometimes been a related feature of conditionality.

Budgetary reforms, particularly improvements in the process of investment planning and priority setting and in capital budgeting and control, are widely emphasized in adjustment programs and loans. For example, one for Ghana required implementation of the IMF technical assistance recommendations on budgeting and expenditure control and stipulated further measures for strengthening institutional capacity for budgeting. One for Côte d'Ivoire contained provisions for strengthening the capacity for project identification, economic evaluation, and supervision in technical ministries as well as the use of "agreed criteria" for appraisal of economic and social projects. This focus on institutional issues in the budget area arises from the belief that expenditure reforms are unlikely to be durable unless the related institutional capacity is strengthened. This type of institutional change is often difficult to effect given the shortage of skilled personnel and the low government pay scales in most developing countries. Accordingly, sufficient time must be allotted for the implementation of such changes.

Fiscal Consequences of Public Enterprise Operations

In many developing countries, the financial performance of public enterprises has a major bearing on the government budget and the allocation of resources between public and private sectors.[11] Budgetary transfers to finance the investment outlays of public enterprises or their operating losses are often a major drain on public finances. Accordingly, the reform of public enterprises, including investment size and financing, budgetary transfers, pricing, personnel, and divestiture, is an important component of fiscal reform and conditionality in structural loans.

Price and rate increases figure prominently in conditionalities related to public enterprises. The intent of such increases is gradually to phase out subsidies, which are particularly common for petroleum products, electricity, and fertilizers, and to bring the prices of petroleum products and other homogeneous tradables to international levels. Considerable progress has been made in raising petroleum prices, but phasing out fertilizer subsidies has proved to be more difficult, as the cases of Pakistan and Turkey show.

The financial performance of public enterprises, often measured relative to a targeted rate of return or level of self-financing, is a common conditionality. What seems often to be overlooked is the possibility that price or rate increases by public enterprises enjoying market power may actually work against improvements in efficiency. This issue arises particularly in the context of electric power utilities and other natural monopolies. Improvements in resource utilization among utility companies have proved elusive, for example, in Bangladesh, Colombia, and Indonesia, where rates of power loss remain very high despite efforts to stem the losses.

Reform of Taxation

In many developing countries the tax system distorts incentives by its influence on the relative prices of commodities and factors of production. Moreover, tax revenues are often insufficiently buoyant with respect to growth in output and income and do not adequately serve equity objectives. Typically, a large proportion of tax revenues is raised through taxes on international trade, particularly imports, and excise taxes. For example, 38 percent of tax revenues in low-income countries in 1985 originated from taxes on international trade and 13 percent from excise taxes (table 3-3).

Existing Structure of Taxation

Changes in tax systems that reduce distortions in production and improve incentives for investment and savings can go a long way toward promoting structural adjustment and economic growth. Moreover, the revenue elasticity and equity aspects of the tax system can be enhanced by changes that broaden the tax base, simplify the tax system, and strengthen tax administration. Thus adjustment programs have increasingly come to include elements of tax reform. In designing a tax reform package, however, tradeoffs among various objectives are inevitable. These objectives include revenue generation, efficiency, equity, and administrative simplicity. In addition, administrative constraints often significantly limit the overall design and pace of reform. Nevertheless, theoretical insights

Table 3-3. Composition of Tax Revenue for Sample Groups of Countries by Income Level, 1975 and 1983
(unweighted average)

	Low-income[b]		*Middle-income*[c]		*Industrial*[d]	
Tax category[a]	*1975*	*1985*	*1975*	*1985*	*1975*	*1985*
Domestic income	28	26	30	32	35	35
Individual	9	9	8	10	27	27
Corporate	18	15	17	17	7	7
Other direct taxes	5	4	18	18	33	34
Social security	1	1	12	11	29	31
Property	2	1	3	2	2	2
Domestic commodity	28	32	27	31	29	29
Sales, VAT, turnover	13	17	9	13	16	17
Excise	13	13	12	12	10	10
International trade	39	38	25	19	4	2
Import	25	28	20	17	4	2
Export	11	8	4	1	0	0

a. Figures for subcategories do not add up to the total given for each category because of the presence of small unallocated taxes.
b. Includes eleven countries.
c. Includes thirty-six countries.
d. Includes nineteen countries.
Source: World Bank (1988).

and experience provide broad guidelines for reforming tax systems. The desirable changes include:

- Shifting away from taxation of production to taxation of consumption in the form of a value added tax coupled with excise taxes on a few luxury items so as to achieve greater equity
- Broadening personal income taxation to include income from all sources, with a top marginal rate significantly below that found in many industrial and developing countries, and with very few exemptions and rates
- Simplifying and rationalizing corporate taxation so that there are very few rates, a relatively low marginal effective rate, and neutrality with respect to sectors, assets, and the financing composition of investment
- Eliminating the double taxation of dividends
- Introducing inflation accounting for both personal and corporate taxes
- Reducing and simplifying tariffs so that they are based on ad valorem rates and serve protective rather than revenue-raising purposes, and replacing high tariffs on luxury goods with excise taxes
- Strengthening the tax administration system overall.

Even though few countries have successfully carried out such comprehensive tax reforms, it nevertheless remains important that even partial reforms be based on a well-designed overall tax system. In particular, reform of international trade taxes needs to be closely coordinated with reform of domestic trade taxes.

Experience with Tax Reform in Adjustment Programs

Because of large and unsustainable fiscal deficits, many developing countries have allowed short-run considerations of revenue to temper their fundamental tax reform plans. Indeed, given the urgency of reducing the fiscal deficit, short-term revenue-enhancing measures have often dominated tax policy initiatives in recent years. These measures have frequently included an increase in excise and international trade taxes because of the relative ease of administering such taxes. Malawi, for example, increased import duties and excise taxes on selected goods in the early 1980s. Other countries with similar experiences include Argentina, Bangladesh, the Philippines, Thailand, and more recently Morocco, which increased a special surtax on imports. These ad hoc changes, however, further complicate the tax structure and, because of increased protection and cascading effects, have adverse implications for incentives.

Changes in categories of tax revenues as a percentage of GDP from 1982 to 1986 for a selected group of countries are shown in table 3-4. Few countries have significantly increased their tax/GDP ratio. This finding underscores the earlier observation that expenditures have borne the brunt of fiscal deficit reduction. Simply to maintain the tax/GDP ratio, many countries have introduced ad hoc measures, as noted above. The inelasticity of the tax systems in many developing countries has given rise to the need for frequent ad hoc changes in the tax rates or the tax base to ensure that tax revenues increase in line with GDP.

Reform of international trade taxes in the context of trade liberalization programs has been the most common tax change aimed at improving resource allocation. Generally, the emphasis has been on converting specific duties to ad valorem duties and reducing the level and dispersion of tariff rates. Converting quantitative restrictions to tariffs has typically been an accompanying measure. Virtually all structural adjustment loans and trade or industry sector adjustment loans have contained extensive conditionalities with respect to tariff regimes. By and large, significant progress has been made on this front. However, in some cases (for example, Kenya in 1983), trade liberalization has suffered setbacks in part because tariff reductions negatively affected revenue during a period when a foreign exchange shortage caused imports to decline. In cases such as Kenya, the reduction and rationalization of tariffs were initiated but compensatory revenue measures were not instituted. In other cases, such as the Philippines and Thailand, tariff reform was not undertaken because the negative effect on revenue was foreseen. Similarly,

Table 3-4. Broad Categories of Government Revenue as Percentage of GDP in Selected Countries, 1982 and 1986

Country	Domestic direct taxes	Domestic indirect taxes	International trade taxes	Total tax	Nontax	Total revenue
Chile						
1982	9.0	12.3	1.4	22.7	9.0	31.7
1986	6.3	14.1	3.0	23.4	5.6	28.9
Colombia						
1982	2.6	2.8	1.8	7.4	0.9	8.3
1986	3.3	3.5	2.2	9.6	0.5	10.1
Côte d'Ivoire						
1982	4.1	5.6	10.1	21.3	6.4	27.7
1986	3.7	5.7	9.6	20.3	11.4	31.7
Jamaica						
1982	11.9	8.9	3.0	23.9	0.9	24.8
1986	11.9	11.1	5.2	28.4	1.0	29.4
Kenya						
1982	6.5	8.2	5.0	19.7	3.4	23.1
1986	6.8	9.9	4.4	21.4	3.2	24.6
Malawi						
1982	6.4	5.9	4.2	16.7	2.9	19.6
1986	7.1	6.4	3.5	17.1	4.5	21.6
Mexico						
1983	10.5	5.6	0.5	16.8	1.0	17.8
1986	8.0	6.1	0.9	15.0	1.0	16.0
Morocco						
1982	4.6	8.7	6.4	20.1	2.6	22.7
1986	5.0	8.1	4.2	17.9	3.8	21.7
Pakistan						
1982	2.9	4.9	5.9	13.6	2.9	16.5
1986	2.2	5.8	5.8	13.8	3.7	17.5
Thailand						
1983	3.6	6.7	3.7	14.6	1.5	16.1
1986	3.4	7.9	3.5	15.6	1.5	17.1

Source: World Bank and IMF data.

the removal of export taxes on agriculture is sometimes impeded by the expected loss of revenue, particularly since imposition of a land tax to balance the loss encounters powerful political opposition (for example, in Argentina).

Reform of domestic indirect taxes has been less extensive than reform of tariffs. Several countries, including Indonesia, Korea, and Turkey, have recently introduced a value added tax (VAT) as the main instrument for rationalizing their system of indirect taxation. More than thirty developing countries now have some form of VAT. Some VATs apply to the manufacturing stage (for example, in Indonesia) while others extend to wholesale and retail stages (for example, in Korea and Turkey). Experience with the VAT has been favorable, even in the short-run generation of revenue. Although the IMF has long advocated the introduction of a VAT as the most desirable, broad-based, efficient form of commodity taxation, not until the mid-1980s did the World Bank take a more active role in advocating VATs. Until then, the World Bank had generally accorded only limited attention to the taxation of goods and services, except for tariffs, in its economic work and adjustment lending. An important exception was the explicit support in structural adjustment loans to Turkey for the introduction of a VAT as early as 1981.

Progress in reforming personal and corporate income taxation has been very limited. The inertia in streamlining income taxation derives from the low share of income taxes in overall tax revenues, the difficulty of enforcement, the opposition of powerful vested interests, and a genuine desire to influence savings and investment decisions. Two broad areas are particularly problematic in the income tax systems of most developing countries. First is the large number of exemptions and incentives, which are often intended to stimulate investment and savings or to serve other policy objectives. Such provisions reduce the tax base and revenues (to an often unknown extent), but there is very little empirical evidence that they produce socially desirable results, at least in the case of investment incentives, which are pervasive in some countries (for example, Morocco and Turkey). A second problem with income taxation, particularly in high-inflation countries, is the absence or inadequacy of indexation of income and assets for purposes of taxation. High inflation can have other negative impacts on revenue because collections lag or interest expenses are fully deductible.

Growth-Oriented Fiscal Programs: Lessons of Experience

Fiscal adjustment and reform programs are difficult to design and implement, given the complexity of underlying economic and institutional factors and the presence of social and political sensitivities. The discussion presented in this chapter points to several broad conclusions about the nature and extent of fiscal adjustment in developing countries in this decade:

- Fiscal policy reforms have often been triggered by actual or impending budgetary and balance of payment crises. Under such circumstances, short-run considerations have dominated the policy measures introduced.

- A number of countries have undergone considerable adjustment with respect to reductions in fiscal and external deficits, although several countries experienced a reversal on the budget side after 1985. As expected, the short-run impact of budgetary retrenchment has generally been recessionary, with a fall in investment and growth.
- Reduction of the fiscal deficit has been achieved primarily through cutbacks in expenditures relative to GDP, particularly in public investment. These cutbacks have been accompanied by more focused public investment programs, often a core set of projects and activities in high-priority areas such as infrastructure. The allocation of recurrent expenditures has also been improved, although the reduction and elimination of some subsidies (for example, on fertilizers) has proved to be more difficult.
- With a few exceptions, revenues have not been very significantly increased. Tax systems are not sufficiently elastic, and reductions in imports due to foreign exchange shortages have resulted in the loss of tariff revenues, a main component of tax receipts. Indeed, to maintain or modestly increase tax/GDP ratios, many countries have introduced ad hoc tax measures that adversely affect efficiency and incentives.
- Fundamental tax reform, except for tariffs, has not been a significant aspect of fiscal adjustment.

Growth-oriented adjustment programs go considerably beyond the traditional stabilization approach to fiscal reform, which emphasizes measures to reduce aggregate demand. By definition, fiscal policy changes aimed at augmenting aggregate supply, like other structural reforms, take longer to bring about the desired results. Consequently, adjustment policies accenting fundamental fiscal reform require a medium-term perspective. Countries suffering from a severe macroeconomic imbalance need to restore a reasonable degree of stability before structural measures can be expected to elicit the desired response. But what constitutes a reasonable degree of macroeconomic correction depends on a number of factors, including the availability of external finance to support an appropriate adjustment program. Countries committed to fundamental fiscal reform—as well as to reform in other key policy areas—should have access to the necessary financial support within a time frame that allows them to initiate and sustain the process of change.[12]

In the case of the World Bank, structural adjustment lending, because of its economywide approach, remains the most appropriate vehicle for supporting fiscal reform. In principle, there is no reason why a series of fiscal-based structural adjustment loans could not be designed for a country willing to undertake structural and institutional reforms in expenditure policy, public sector pricing, and taxation. Considerable preparation, in the form of policy studies, would need to precede such lending operations, however. The World Bank has in recent years prepared many reviews of public investment (expenditure), some of which have served as background for structural adjustment loans. More sharply focused studies of this type, including reviews of the revenue side, are needed to underpin adjustment programs and lending. Loan conditionality would need to be geared toward reform actions as opposed to necessarily short-run improvements in key macro targets (for example, the budget deficit). In countries with an acute stabilization problem, measures to reduce aggregate demand would also be needed. Finally, multiyear financing commitments would be required to help persuade governments to undertake and sustain the reforms (Fischer 1986).

Appendix: Exchange Rates, Inflation, and Fiscal Adjustment in Zimbabwe

Coordination of exchange rate and fiscal policies requires a careful assessment of the various linkages through which each affects the other. High fiscal deficits lead to high inflation. If the real exchange rate appreciates and trade balances deteriorate, there will be a need for increased foreign borrowing, a loss of foreign reserves, or import controls. Eventually, a country is forced into a devaluation in order to realign the real exchange rate. How effective the devaluation will be in bringing about a depreciation of the real exchange rate depends to a large extent on how it affects domestic inflation. A key factor, as shown in a recent empirical study on Zimbabwe (Chhibber and others 1989), is how the government adjusts fiscal policy.

In the model used for the Zimbabwe study depreciation of the exchange rate affects inflation in three ways. The first is a direct cost-push effect through increased import costs. On average, a 1 percent increase in import costs as a result of devaluation would raise domestic inflation by 0.2 percent. The second way is through the fiscal deficit: the change in the exchange rate affects various components of the budget, particularly foreign debt service, trade taxes, and import costs of public enterprises; and there is a second-round effect on the fiscal deficit from the initial increase in prices (Tanzi effect; see Tanzi 1977). The impact of these changes in the fiscal deficit on inflation depends at least in the medium term on how the budget deficit is financed. The third way is through the positive effect on output of depreciation of the real exchange rate; these changes in output then contribute to a reduction in inflationary pressures. The key parameter here is the magnitude and speed of the export response to changes in the real exchange rate.

On the assumption that 25 percent of the increase in the budget deficit due to a devaluation is monetized (this is the historical average), that the balance is financed by foreign and domestic borrowing, and that the export elasticity is around 0.2 in the short run and 1 in the long run, the Zimbabwe model shows that a 1 percent annual increase in the rate of devaluation raises domestic inflation by 0.4 percent each year. Given foreign inflation, the real exchange rate depreciates by 0.6 percent a year. Note that 0.2 percent of inflation comes from a direct cost-push effect, while the remaining 0.2 percent comes from linkages through the fiscal deficit and effects on real output.

If the option to borrow (foreign or domestic) is limited, the results change dramatically. When half instead of a quarter of the budget deficit is monetized, domestic inflation rises by 0.6 percent a year for a 1 percent annual increase in devaluation. This simulation shows one reason why adequate financing of an adjustment program is crucial and why devaluations erode quickly when they lead to higher budget deficits. The real effects of devaluation are completely eroded if adjustment lags on revenues are longer. For example, if customs duties are not collected ad valorem and other revenues adjust to inflation over four years instead of about two years, the higher fiscal deficit would completely erode the positive effects of the devaluation. There is no change in the real exchange rate.

Notes

John Brondolo and Reza Firuzabadi provided excellent research assistance. The authors are grateful to Bela Balassa, Francis Colaco, Jaime de Melo, Catherine Mann, William McCleary, Pradeep Mitra, and Vinod Thomas for comments on an early draft.

1. The term "budget deficit," unless stated otherwise, refers to the public sector borrowing requirement. There is a growing body of literature (see Tanzi, Blejer, and Teijeiro 1987) on different concepts of the fiscal deficit. Although these concepts are all useful in revealing the fiscal stance of the government, it is the public sector borrowing requirement that reflects the financing requirement.
2. The link between the growth of debt and the fiscal deficit has been empirically verified (Tanzi and Blejer 1986).
3. A fourth way is through the buildup of arrears, which has emerged in recent times as a significant fiscal issue. Arrears can be treated as forced borrowing by the government, but the accumulation of arrears can be only a temporary measure since it destroys the government's credibility.
4. The data for this section are from the World Bank country briefs and not from *International Financial Statistics* or from central World Bank data sources. Accurate information on the public sector deficit was available for only twenty-five adjustment loan recipients (those with one or more adjustment loans since 1980) and for fifteen nonrecipients. Of the twenty-five adjustment loan countries, thirteen received three or more adjustment loans and are referred to here as adjustment loan–intensive countries.
5. Results are available from the authors.
6. Turkey's inflation rate was also high, but not explosive, averaging 30 to 40 percent a year between 1980 and 1986. It has since accelerated to over 60 percent a year.

7. An important qualifier of this comparison is that many nonrecipient countries, and the less loan-intensive countries, had IMF programs in place.

8. In the thirteen adjustment loan–intensive countries considered here, negative growth in GDP per capita was observed in Chile, Côte d'Ivoire, Jamaica, Malawi, Mexico, the Philippines, and Zambia between 1980 and 1986. Only Korea, Pakistan, Thailand, Turkey, and Morocco (marginally) showed positive growth in GDP per capita.

9. For an empirical verification of the Please effect, see Chhibber (1985).

10. For details see chapter 12 by Elaine Zuckerman.

11. This discussion is limited to fiscal issues. Chapter 6 treats the issues related to public enterprise reform in more depth.

12. The World Bank and IMF (see Tanzi 1987) have increasingly recognized the need for refocusing fiscal reform packages to include supply-side measures. The World Bank is proposing a change in its policy in this direction, as evidenced in recent internal policy documents.

References

Anand, Ritu, Ajay Chhibber, and Sweder van Wijnbergen. 1990. "External Balance, Fiscal Policy and Growth in Turkey." In Torsun Aricanli and Dani Rodrik, eds., *The Political Economy of Turkey: Debt, Adjustment, and Sustainability*. London: Macmillan.

Balassa, Bela. 1988. "Public Finance and Economic Development." PPR Working Paper 31. Policy, Planning, and Research, World Bank, Washington, D.C.

Blejer, M. I., and Adreane Cheasty. 1988. "High Inflation and Heterodox Stabilization and Fiscal Policy." *World Development* 16 (8):867–81.

Braverman, Avishay, and Jeffrey Hammer. 1986. "Multi-Market Analysis of Agricultural Commodities." Agriculture Department, World Bank, Washington, D.C.

Buiter, W. 1985. "A Guide to Public Sector Debt and Deficits." *Economic Policy* 1 (November):13–19.

Cardoso, Eliana, and Rudiger Dornbusch. 1987. "Brazil's Tropical Plan." *American Economic Review* 77 (May).

Chhibber, Ajay. 1985. "Taxation and Aggregate Savings: An Econometric Analysis for Three Sub-Saharan African Countries." CPD Discussion Paper Series 1985-35. Country Policy Department, World Bank, Washington, D.C.

———. 1989. "The Aggregate Supply Response in Agriculture: A Survey." In Simon Commander, ed., *Structural Adjustment in Agriculture: Theory and Practice*. London: Overseas Development Institute.

Chhibber, Ajay, Joaquin Cottani, Reza Firuzabadi, and Michael Walton. 1989. "Inflation, Exchange Rates and Fiscal Policy in Zimbabwe." PPR Working Paper 192. Policy, Planning, and Research, World Bank, Washington, D.C.

Cornia, Giovannini, Richard Jolly, and Frances Stewart, eds. 1987. *Adjustment with a Human Face*. Oxford, U.K.: Clarendon Press for UNICEF.

Cukierman, Alex. 1988. "The End of High Israeli Inflation: An Experiment in Heterodox Stabilization." In Michael Bruno, Guido di Tella, Rudiger Dornbusch, and Stanley Fischer, eds., *Inflation Stabilization: The Experience of Israel, Argentina, Brazil, Bolivia, and Mexico.* Cambridge, Mass.: MIT Press.

Feltenstein, Andrew, and Ziba Farhadian. 1987. "Fiscal Policy, Monetary Targets, and the Price Level in a Centrally Controlled Economy: The Case of China." *Journal of Money, Credit, and Banking* 19 (2).

Fischer, Stanley. 1986. "Issues in Medium-Term Macroeconomic Adjustment." *World Bank Research Observer* 1 (2) July:163–82.

International Monetary Fund. Various years. *International Financial Statistics.* Washington, D.C.

Kharas, Homi, and Brian Pinto. 1987. "Exchange Rate Rules, Black Market Premia, and Fiscal Deficits: The Bolivian Hyperinflation." CPD Working Paper. Country Policy Department, World Bank, Washington, D.C.

Pinto, Brian. 1987. "Black Market Premia, Exchange Rate Unification, and Inflation in Sub-Saharan Africa." Country Policy Department, World Bank, Washington, D.C.

Please, Stanley. 1967. "Savings Through Taxation: Reality or Mirage." *Finance & Development.*

Simonsen, M. H. 1988. "Price Stabilization and Incomes Policies: Theory and the Brazilian Case Study." In Michael Bruno, Guido di Tella, Rudiger Dornbusch, and Stanley Fischer, eds., *Inflation Stabilization: The Experience of Israel, Argentina, Brazil, Bolivia, and Mexico.* Cambridge, Mass.: MIT Press.

Tanzi, Vito. 1977. "Inflation, Lags in Collection, and the Real Value of Tax Revenues." *IMF Staff Papers* 24.

———. 1987. "Fiscal Policy, Growth and Stabilization Programs." *Finance & Development* (June).

Tanzi, Vito, and M. I. Blejer. 1986. "Public Debt and Fiscal Policy in Developing Countries." IMF Working Paper WP/86/5. Washington, D.C.

Tanzi, Vito, M. I. Blejer, and M. O. Teijeiro. 1987. "Inflation and the Measurement of Fiscal Deficits." *IMF Staff Papers* 34 (4):711–38.

World Bank. 1987. "Bank Treatment of Subsidies." Country Policy Department, Washington, D.C.

———. 1988. *World Development Report 1988.* New York: Oxford University Press.

Comments

Peter S. Heller

IN THIS CHAPTER, Ajay Chhibber and Javad Khalilzadeh-Shirazi analyze the role of fiscal reform in adjustment programs. They initially discuss the macroeconomic links between fiscal reform and the adjustment process, arguing that the crises that engender adjustment programs have often been related to exogenous circumstances (for example, a collapse in world commodity prices, a surge in real interest rates, or weak export demand). Fiscal deficits that were previously viable have become unsustainable and have brought on some combination of excessive external borrowing, inflation, and constraints on credit to the private sector. The authors argue that stricter fiscal discipline is not a sufficient condition for sustainable adjustment, but that a comprehensive policy package is required to stimulate savings and investment. They then discuss public expenditure policy and tax reform in the adjustment process, arguing that fiscal adjustment has been accomplished primarily through expenditure cuts, since the scope for increasing revenue has been limited. The authors draw on a cross-country analysis to suggest a large number of stylized facts that are used as the basis for policy recommendations.

My comments fall into two broad categories, one relating to substantive issues and the other relating to the methodology of the study. On the substantive side, I have five points to raise. First, the authors argue that the quality of fiscal adjustment matters as much as, if not more than, the quantity of adjustment. This is a view that the IMF has also come to recognize and consider in the design of programs. A short-run emphasis on deficit-cutting measures may lead to the adoption of policies that in the medium run exacerbate rather than reduce the budget deficit, thus weakening the prospects for growth. The problem, of course, is that in the short run the adoption of important fiscal reforms or of a higher investment effort may be costly and, in the absence of additional budget financing, not feasible.

The authors seem to suggest that when additional investments can be financed with external funds on concessional terms a larger budgetary deficit may be acceptable within the framework of an adjustment program than would otherwise be the case. Yet even when additional investment can be financed fully from a highly concessional loan or grant there may be reasons to be cautious about accepting a higher budget deficit. In the medium term, can the government meet the higher operational and maintenance costs associated with the investment? What additional domestic outlays are needed to complement the investment? Will the government be able to meet the higher debt-servicing that may be required in the medium term?

Second, the authors seem to equate policies of adjustment with investment-led growth. They argue that "there is little merit in having a low budget deficit and a low external account deficit if the outcome is a low level of savings and investment in the economy." Certainly, adjustment ought to facilitate an economic environment that is supportive of higher medium-term growth. Such higher growth may derive from more investment, but it may also stem from a strengthening of the performance of markets, the more rapid introduction of technological change, a higher current expenditure on operations and maintenance, and so on. The temptation to opt for higher investment and to neglect operations and maintenance is one of the biases of an excessive emphasis on public savings and investment.

Third, in the case of Turkey, the authors seem to assert that the initially high deficit, in excess of IMF targets, was desirable because of its positive impact on growth but that it ultimately contributed to higher real interest rates and accelerating inflation. If the latter is true, then the cost of achieving the higher growth may in fact have been too high relative to its medium-term effects. The policy lessons that emerge from this example are unclear. If it is difficult for a country to fine-tune its fiscal policies, it may prove more sensible in the medium run to err on the conservative side in the initial policy stance.

Fourth, in discussing the adverse budgetary effects of a devaluation coupled with price liberalization, the authors fail to mention how detrimental, in the long run, artificial prices can be in eroding the tax base. To suggest that price liberalization for tax-paying sectors is likely to be bad for the budget neglects the fact that price liberalization in repressed sectors can lead to an improvement in public finances.

Fifth, the authors appear to treat the consequences of unsustainable deficits as separable, depending on how they are financed: inflation if financed through money creation, constrained credit to the private sector if through domestic debt creation, or excessive external debt if through external financing. However, the manner in which the deficit is financed is likely to be of less importance than the many consequences of the deficit (inflation, depreciation, and so on).

Methodologically, the authors rely heavily on cross-country analysis rather than on individual case studies. This approach has its limitations. For example, the fact that adjustment loan–intensive countries were able to maintain their cuts in the deficit relative to the experience of other countries does not really say much about the adjustment process. In many respects an approach using case studies would be more useful, since it would allow a coherent description of the fiscal experience of the countries in question and the possibility of a careful analysis of the relationships between the fiscal and overall adjustment processes. Similarly, rather than simply focusing on the postcrisis period, it would be useful to have a discussion of the events leading up to the crisis that precipitated the adjustment process. This discussion would allow the reader to better understand the way a country's fiscal policies help precipitate such crises and would, in turn, assist in an analysis of the appropriate fiscal response. This approach would also allow some assessment of the "counterfactual," that is, of what might have happened in a particular country in the absence of an adjustment program.

4 *Trade Policy Reform*

Vinod Thomas

DURING THE 1980s, many developing countries received financial and policy support from the World Bank and the International Monetary Fund (IMF) for trade reforms. This chapter evaluates these policy reforms using cross-country data and country studies. The analysis considers reforms in the forty countries that received trade adjustment loans during 1980–87 and assesses reform implementation in the twenty-four countries for which sufficient data are available.[1] The effect of reforms on incentives is also examined, as are changes in economic performance in countries that have received trade adjustment loans and have carried out reforms.

Extent of Reforms

Halevi (1989) considered the following restrictions in commercial policy in the forty countries: export impediments,[2] import impediments on inputs used in export production, quantitative restrictions[3] on both noncompetitive and competitive imports, and tariff rates[4] and rate dispersion. The countries were grouped into three categories according to judgments on the relative antiexport bias before reform for each country: low, medium, or high.[5] Chile and the Republic of Korea had a relatively low level of restrictions; 60 percent had a high level, and 35 percent had a medium level.

Degree of Restrictiveness

A comparison with the restrictiveness of industrial countries provides a perspective on that of developing countries. The weighted average *tariff rate* for fifty developing countries was 26 percent at the end of 1985 according to Erzan and others (1986). Adding other import charges raises the figure to 34 percent. For members of the Organisation for Economic Co-operation and Development (OECD), average tariffs on industrial goods were estimated to be about 5 percent according to a report of the General Agreement on Tariffs and Trade (GATT 1980) and Finger and Laird (1987) and are roughly of that order today. Erzan and others estimated the coverage of *nontariff barriers* in the same fifty developing countries to be 40 percent (unweighted) of import items corresponding to all tariff positions at the end of 1985. Finger and Laird provide a similar estimate for thirty-eight developing countries for 1982. They also estimated that 15 percent of the product categories of the eleven industrial countries were subject to nontariff barriers in 1984. Laird and Yeats (1988) provide a similar figure (15.9 percent) for all products in fourteen industrial countries in 1986.[6] These estimates indicate that developing countries have a much more restrictive trade regime than do industrial countries.

What Was Proposed

The intensity of reform proposals was also grouped into three categories: low, medium, or high. This intensity was considered as strong as the initial degree of restrictiveness in more than half the forty countries that received trade adjustment loans. Of the twenty-four countries with *high initial restrictiveness*, reform proposals were strong in twelve (for example, Ghana, Jamaica, Mexico, and Turkey), while in six they were only mild (for example, Brazil, Guyana, and Pakistan). Among the fourteen cases with *moderate initial restrictiveness*, nine had moderate or strong proposals. In general, the intensity of the proposals was commensurate with the initial degree of restrictiveness more frequently in export policy than in import policy.

The main components of trade policy proposals under adjustment lending are summarized in table 4-1. Although policy packages are not uniform there are common threads. One is a reduction in restrictions on exports and imports, and another is greater reliance on the price mechanism, that is, on exchange rate depreciation and the use of tariffs in place of quantitative restrictions.[7] The loan proposals were most consistent in their attempt to reduce direct impediments to exports and restrictions on imported inputs for export production. Reform of exchange rate policy was almost always a stated, or unwritten but important, goal. Almost all loans supported a greater use of price mechanisms, as well as reductions in the level and dispersion of tariff rates. Proposed reductions in quantitative restrictions on imports were large in some cases but modest on average in the case of items both competitive and noncompetitive with domestic production.

There has been less attention, however, to reforms that would promote greater internal competition. Because most proposals were put together quickly, as is usual in loans for direct balance of payments support, they often included plans for studies to identify needed future actions. Not much evidence is available for assessing progress on these studies. Proposals to reduce protection for import substitutes have been cautious.

Table 4-1. Intensity and Distribution of Proposals for Trade Policy Reform among Forty Countries Receiving Trade Adjustment Loans
(number of countries)

Area of reform	*Present*	*Not present*	*Strong*	*Moderate*	*Mild or absent*
Exchange rate[a]	38	2			
Export promotion[b]	33	7			
Protection studies	28	12			
Overall export policy			15	15	10
Imports for exports			17	15	8
Overall import policy			14	15	11
Nonprotective quantitative restrictions			14	16	10
Protective quantitative restrictions[c]			14	15	11
Tariff level[c]			7	21	12
Tariff dispersion			7	24	9
Schedule of future action			6	29	5
Overall reduction in antiexport bias			17	12	11

a. Often these were not explicit conditions, but understandings under the program.

b. Removal of restrictions and provision of export credits, insurance, guarantees, institutional development, and the like.

c. Where reforms include a replacement of quantitative restrictions, they are counted in both these lines.

Source: World Bank data.

Most programs envisioned that some level of effective protection would continue indefinitely. In some cases, particularly in Sub-Saharan Africa, additional incentives were introduced for import substitution—for example, higher duties on imported inputs that compete with domestic production. (Increasing the duties on imported inputs reduces the protection provided to finished goods that use them.)

Implementation Record

The twenty-four countries with data on implementation were ranked in five categories according to the degree of implementation of the reform proposals. Some examples are given below. The two countries that had a low level of restrictiveness (Chile) or antiexport bias (Republic of Korea) at the beginning of the 1980s were also assigned the highest ranking on implementation. Success in implementation for the eight countries judged to have a moderate level of restrictiveness covered the range from the lowest (Malawi), through the middle of the range (Panama), to the highest (Mauritius). Among the fourteen countries that initially had high levels of restrictiveness, six (of the nine countries with strong proposals for commercial policy reform) had the highest or next to highest ranking in implementation (Ghana, Madagascar, Mexico, Philippines, Senegal, and Turkey). Table 4-2 presents these examples in a three-way classification that takes into account both the intensity of proposals and the degree of compliance, that is, as a product of the constructed indices of proposals and of implementation.

Although implementation was swift in exchange rate adjustment and the removal of export restrictions, countries in the sample have been slow to liberalize imports. Overall, trade reforms were moderately significant. Substantial actions were taken in reducing export restrictions (licensing, prohibitions, and export taxes). Restrictions on imported inputs for exports have also been significantly reduced. On the import side, several countries (Jamaica, Mexico, Senegal, and Turkey) have made progress in switching from quantitative restrictions to tariffs. Many countries have adopted tariff reform programs. Progress has been most notable in reducing maximum tariff rates, limiting the number of tariff classes, establishing a (low) minimum tariff, and reducing tariff exemptions.

The lowering of protection, however, has been modest on average. Most trade regimes continue to maintain escalated tariff structures, with higher tariffs (and quantitative restrictions) on final goods than on capital goods and low rates (and exemptions) for intermediate and raw materials. Tariff dispersion has usually been reduced, but dispersion in effective protection is still large. This experience supports the conclusion of Papageorgiou, Michaely, and Choksi (forthcoming) that commercial liberalization is a drawn-out process. For instance, of the fourteen countries with highly restrictive trade regimes in the early 1980s, only four (Jamaica, Mexico, Senegal, and Turkey) had achieved a high degree of commercial liberalization by 1987–88.

Stronger reforms have been implemented in exchange rate policy than in commercial policy. There was a larger depreciation in the real exchange rate in most of the countries receiving trade adjustment loans than in most of the others. In part this was because of the higher debt and greater external shocks in the former, which required a larger depreciation, and in part because of exchange rate and macroeconomic reforms accompanied by some trade liberalization.[8] A real depreciation of the currency is an important liberalization measure. In the presence of binding quantitative restrictions on imports, it increases the price not only of tradables relative to nontradables but also of exportables relative to importables, thereby reducing antiexport bias. Moreover, a large depreciation can eventually make quantitative restrictions redundant and thereby result in a de facto liberalization of the import regime.

Table 4-2 shows the extent of exchange rate depreciation and the intensity of commercial policy reforms among the twenty-four countries. The latter summarizes the outcomes of policy changes—taking account of what was proposed and what was implemented—in three categories:

Table 4-2. Intensity of Reforms in Trade Regimes in Twenty-Four Sample Countries, 1980–87

Exchange rate depreciation[a]	Reduction in antiexport bias through commercial policy (export and import)		
	Mild	*Moderate*	*Substantial*
Mild (no depreciation or appreciation)	Guyana*	Côte d'Ivoire, Senegal	
Moderate (less than 20 percent)	Kenya, Malawi, Togo, Yugoslavia,* Zimbabwe*	Bangladesh, Madagascar, Morocco, Panama, Philippines, Thailand	Jamaica, Korea,[b] Mauritius
Substantial (20 percent or more)	Pakistan, Zambia*	Colombia, Ghana	Chile,[b] Mexico, Turkey

* Aborted, reversed, or no reform of commercial policy.

Note: The table indicates changes after reform compared with the prereform situation. In the case of commercial policy, the judgment of the prereform situation is derived from accounts in World Bank reports. In the case of the exchange rate, it is based on trends in purchasing power parity over the long term. Some important changes since 1987 are not captured in this table, such as improvements in Morocco and reversals in Turkey, but some major improvements that occurred in 1986–87 are emphasized (for example, Jamaica and Mexico in commercial policy). Some important reforms are not included in this sample because adjustment lending for trade policy was too recent (Indonesia, Uruguay) or because the reform was not in connection with adjustment lending (Bolivia, Haiti).

a. Based on a measure of the average change in real effective exchange rate during the period after the first loan compared with the period from 1965 to the year before the first loan.

b. Chile and Korea had already achieved substantial reforms by the early 1980s.

Sources: World Bank and IMF data.

mild, moderate, and substantial accomplishments. The table focuses on changes after the trade loan. But, by comparing these changes with the situation prior to the loan, it also gives a rough idea of how much of the problem was being addressed. However, the table does not fully capture the extent of the initial problem. For example, both Korea and the Philippines depreciated the real exchange rate moderately compared with their long-term levels, but the adequacy of the long-term levels in each case may have been different. Subject to this caveat, the table distinguishes strong reformers of commercial policy and reformers of exchange rate policy from weak reformers. (For a qualitative discussion of rankings according to both the initial problem and the reform, see table 13-3.)

Progress and Constraints to Implementation

The extent of implementation has varied greatly among countries and policy areas. Overall, price reforms have been relatively substantial under trade adjustment programs. Examples include removal of export taxes, introduction of duty drawback schemes for exporters, and more uniformity in tariffs. But there has been less success in institutionalizing and sustaining some of the price changes. By and large, institutional reform has been limited. There are many instances of abandonment, reversals, and flip-flops in price policies. Despite modest goals, Yugoslavia abandoned reforms, Côte d'Ivoire and Kenya made slow progress, Morocco and Thailand partially reversed their tariff policy reform, Argentina reversed its reform of quantitative restrictions, and Sierra Leone, Somalia, Uganda, and Zambia reversed their policies of exchange rate auctions. Unless changes appear to be sustainable, the credibility of actions and the supply response to them are likely to be limited (Rodrik 1988).

Four factors have constrained more thorough implementation and sustainability: weak macroeconomic performance, inadequate government commitment to reform, difficulties in implementation, and conflicts among policy reforms and weaknesses in design.

WEAK MACROECONOMIC PERFORMANCE. Economic instability and external imbalances are serious constraints to liberalization, while export growth makes liberalization easier. Recession, inability to address inflation, and real appreciation of the currency have inhibited trade reforms to varying degrees in Costa Rica, Jamaica, Mexico, and the Philippines. Balance of payments problems resulting from a fall in copper prices and faulty exchange rate management contributed to the reversal of reform policy in Zambia. Export performance and the availability of foreign exchange also offset the sustainability of reform. A strong and rapid supply response improves the sustainability of reforms by reducing their transition costs associated with the release of resources from previously highly protected sectors. Slow export expansion hurt Kenya's liberalization attempts. Export diversification is just beginning in Costa Rica and Côte d'Ivoire, which made more rapid progress in commercial policy reform but were also vulnerable to declining terms of trade. Even in Chile the rapid growth of exports and the availability of foreign exchange have been important in preventing policy reversals. In Jamaica the availability of financing has been crucial for maintaining the liberalization effort in the face of a worsening current account balance.

INADEQUATE GOVERNMENT COMMITMENT. In a number of cases in which the government has not been fully committed to the program (Kenya, Malawi, Zambia), implementation has been weak. The slow pace of reform has in turn sometimes hurt the credibility of the program for the private sector, thereby diminishing its sustainability. Inadequate commitment has limited the sustainability of reforms, particularly in the highly indebted countries and in Sub-Saharan Africa. Changes in political regimes and leadership have often compounded these problems and have led to policy reversals. A related constraint is internal opposition to reform. There are always winners and losers from policy changes. Resistance from losers, as in Zimbabwe, has delayed or reversed reductions in protection. In Yugoslavia, despite modest goals related to trade and the foreign exchange regime, political opposition (in addition to macroeconomic instability) led to a dilution or reversal of most elements of the program.

DIFFICULTIES IN IMPLEMENTATION. Sometimes a country's limited administrative capacity has been a critical constraint. Bangladesh and Côte d'Ivoire made slow progress in part because of administrative difficulties. The introduction of export tax rebates, duty drawback systems, and bonded warehouses has been subject to administrative delays in many cases. If changes in policy are to be successfully implemented, they often require changes in administrative arrangements and capabilities (for example, import administration may need to be reorganized to implement tariff reforms). Sometimes, policy changes were predicated on the completion of studies, which were delayed for various reasons in a number of the cases reviewed (for example, Colombia and Kenya). Inadequate capacity for medium-term policymaking is a common problem.

CONFLICTS AMONG POLICY REFORMS. Inadequate stabilization efforts have constrained trade reform in Pakistan and Panama. In contrast, stabilization and trade reforms in the 1980s have reinforced one another in Chile, Colombia, and Korea, where the ability to quickly regain stability in the external sector has helped to sustain trade reforms. The targets of structural adjustment and stabilization have at times conflicted.

For instance, the imposition of customs duties and tariff surtaxes to increase revenues for stabilization purposes in the Philippines has conflicted with attempts to liberalize imports. To increase revenue Morocco raised import tariffs, which had been reduced in an earlier phase of reform. These conflicts may sometimes be unavoidable. Trade taxes create distortions, so less-distorting, alternative sources of revenue are preferable. When a country has a weak tax system, however, some trade taxes may remain necessary in the short term to generate revenue.

Effects of Policy Changes

The previous section reviewed the main elements and intensity of changes in trade policy. In this section I survey the evidence on the effects of those changes.

Change in Incentives

REAL EXCHANGE RATE. An indicator of the incentives for the production of tradables relative to nontradables is the real exchange rate. Exchange rate misalignments were significant in the early 1980s for the recipients of trade adjustment loans. Subsequent adjustments were also substantial in a large number of cases. They involved a series of devaluations or institution of a crawling peg, supported by macroeconomic adjustments. Figure 4-1 compares changes in a trade-weighted multilateral real exchange rate relative to major trading partners for a group of twenty-one industrial countries, the forty recipients of trade adjustment loans, and forty-eight nonrecipients. The domestic currency depreciated in real terms by more than 22 percent between the periods 1981–83 and 1985–87 for the group of forty trade adjustment loan countries, in contrast to 2 percent in the nonrecipient countries and a slight appreciation in the industrial countries. This implies that the price of traded goods relative to that of nontraded goods increased on average in the trade adjustment loan countries.

Real exchange rate indices indicate the change in bias against tradable goods, but they seldom distinguish between exportable commodities and import substitutes.[9] To make that distinction, measures of changes in the levels of effective protection for the different sectors would be needed or measures of effective exchange rates for exporting activities as opposed to import-substituting activities. Individual country studies of effective protection and antiexport bias exist (for example, for Chile, Colombia, Kenya, Korea, Mexico, Morocco, Pakistan, Philippines, and Turkey), but the results are not comparable across countries. Comparisons of even nominal protection rates or the coverage of quantitative restrictions are difficult. In a few cases, changes in protection levels over time have also

Figure 4-1. Real Exchange Rate Indices for Selected Country Groups, 1978–88
(unweighted averages)

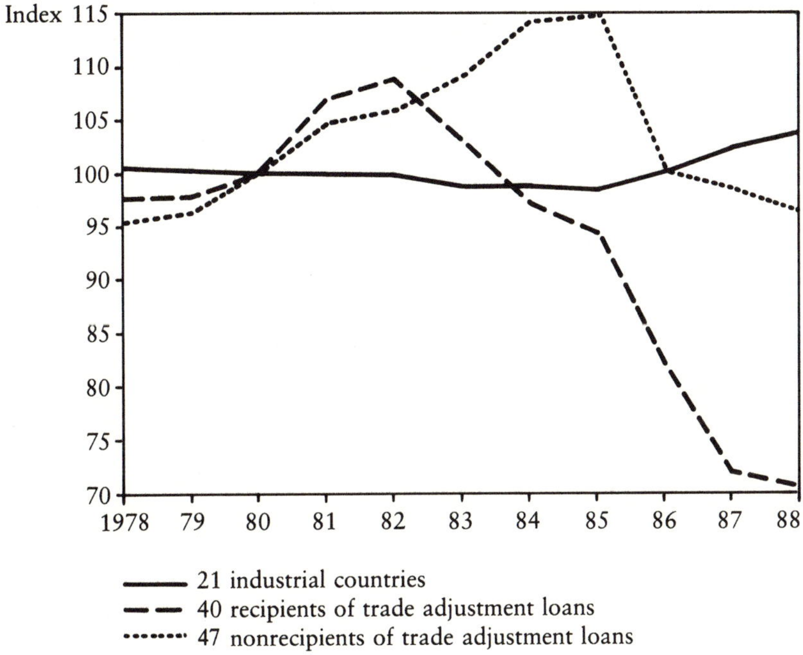

Note: An increase in the index indicates real appreciation. This figure does not indicate initial currency misalignments. For a discussion of "proper" levels of exchange rates, see Williamson (1985).

Source: The trade-weighted multilateral index of the real exchange rate for the various countries is based on IMF data.

been assessed, but intercountry comparisons of the changes are even more difficult than comparisons of the levels.

IMPORT LIBERALIZATION AND PROTECTION. Overall import/GDP ratios reflect the effects of the depreciation of the real exchange rate and the availability of financing in addition to import liberalization. During the 1980s import levels in developing countries declined (in current and constant prices) on average because of balance of payments problems, as did import/GDP ratios. The ratio of nonfuel imports to GDP declined as well, although the extent of the fall was less than for total imports. The reduction in the import/GDP ratio was significantly less, however, for coun-

Table 4-3. Imports of Goods and Nonfactor Services in Current Prices as a Percentage of GDP for Selected Country Groups, 1980–88
(unweighted averages)

Sample group	1980	1981	1982	1983	1984	1985	1986	1987	1988[a]	Percentage change 1984–86/1980–82	Percentage change 1985–87/1981–83
10 intensive trade loan recipients	32.7	33.3	29.4	30.1	31.1	32.0	29.5	31.1	33.1	−2.9*	−0.1*
26 trade loan recipients	34.3	34.7	31.0	29.7	30.5	30.9	29.2	31.7	30.7	−9.3*	−3.8*
40 trade loan recipients	33.0	33.4	31.6	30.3	30.7	30.8	29.0	30.3	30.6	−7.7*	−5.5*
47 nonrecipients	38.8	40.4	38.8	35.6	34.1	33.5	33.1	32.2	32.3	−14.6	−14.0
87 developing countries	36.1	37.2	35.5	33.2	32.5	32.3	31.2	31.3	31.4	−11.8†	−10.5†
21 industrial countries	35.5	35.7	35.1	34.5	36.5	36.9	33.2	32.6	31.5	0.3	−2.5

* The difference in means between the recipients and nonrecipients of trade adjustment loans is significant at the 5 percent confidence interval.
† The difference in means between the recipients and nonrecipients of trade adjustment loans is significant at the 10 percent confidence interval.
a. Preliminary estimates.
Source: World Bank estimates.

tries associated with trade reforms and adjustment lending. As indicated in table 4-3, the ratios declined systematically less among countries that received trade adjustment loans than in the other countries, and these differences were statistically very significant.

Direct examination of the conditions in trade adjustment loans and their implementation records suggest that import protection on average has fallen only modestly in most of these countries. By and large, tariff structures remain escalated, with the highest protection afforded to final goods. This seems consistent with the evidence on changes in the composition of nonfuel imports since 1980. If protection of the most protected goods (consumer goods) had been reduced substantially, they would have increased as a fraction of total imports while imports of intermediates used in their domestic production would have decreased as a share of the total. Instead, intermediate goods, and capital goods to a lesser extent, have increased relative to consumer goods in the total (table 4-4).

Individual countries show considerable variation in changes in impediments to imports. Chile, Korea, Mexico, the Philippines, and Turkey are among the countries that undertook import reform. Chile's import liberalization, which began in 1975, has been the most extensive in recent time. Quantitative restrictions were rapidly replaced by uniform tariff rates of 10 to 15 percent by mid-1979. Commercial policy reversals were corrected and coupled with a substantial devaluation during 1983–87, when the export/GDP ratio nearly doubled. In Mexico a major reduction in import restrictions in the mid-1980s substantially reduced antiexport bias and significantly increased exports. Korea is an example of sustained liberalization and export development over a long period. Turkey carried

Table 4-4. Composition of Nonfuel Imports at Current Prices in Countries with Trade Adjustment Loans 1980–87
(percentage share of total nonfuel imports)

Component	*1980*	*1982*	*1983*	*1984*	*1985*	*1986*	*1987*
Consumer goods	22.4	20.4	20.2	19.7	18.0	17.9	16.5
Capital goods	31.0	32.6	33.7	32.7	33.1	32.2	32.2
Intermediate goods	46.6	47.0	46.1	47.6	48.9	49.9	51.3
Total nonfuel imports	100.0	100.0	100.0	100.0	100.0	100.0	100.0
Average value (millions of U.S. dollars)	4,260	3,871	3,492	3,568	3,517	3,818	4,379

Note: Data are averages for the thirty-seven countries for which data were available.
Source: World Bank data.

out a major trade reform in the first half of the 1980s, transforming the economy from its inward orientation to a more outward-looking one and nearly tripling its export/GDP ratio during 1980–87. The Philippines began with a tariff reform in the early 1980s, followed by substantial reductions in quantitative restrictions in the mid-1980s.

Milder reform and even reversals of reform occurred in some cases. Colombia, whose trade regime has been characterized by stability over the past thirty years, undertook some export promotion along with modest import reform in the 1980s. Kenya and Pakistan, among many others, undertook only mild reforms, although their existing trade regimes were quite restrictive. In other cases—such as Yugoslavia and Zambia—policy improvements have been followed by abandonment or reversals of reforms. Estimates on the effects of incentives are available in a few cases (Colombia, Kenya, Korea, Mexico, Morocco, Pakistan, the Philippines). The estimates, however, are not comparable across countries. In general, the effect on antiexport bias has varied, ranging from very significant reduction in Mexico to little change in Pakistan.

Relative Performance Before and After Lending

Changes in performance indicators for recipients of trade adjustment loans compared with nonrecipients (the control group) are presented in table 4-5. To allow some time after the first loan to a country, only the twenty-six countries that received a trade adjustment loan before 1986 are considered. Average changes in indicators for trade loan recipients relative to nonrecipients are shown for 1985–87 compared with 1981–83, as well as average changes for the recipients for the three-year period following the first loan (excluding the year of the loan) compared with the three years before the loan relative to the changes over the same periods for nonrecipient comparators (see Balassa 1988). The numbers show how many recipient countries in each classification performed better on each indicator than their comparators after the start of trade adjustment lending. The plus and minus signs indicate an improvement or a worsening of the average value of an indicator for the trade adjustment loan group in comparison with the average value of the same indicator for the comparator group.[10]

There are important limitations to this type of comparison (see Khan 1988 for a discussion).[11] Most important, perhaps, is that the countries with adjustment loans are not necessarily selected randomly. Many factors affect performance other than the presence of this type of lending and reforms. Subject to these and other caveats, the trade indicators show that, on average, the change in performance between 1981–83 and 1985–87 was better for the loan recipients than for the forty-seven nonrecipients. The last three rows in the top half of the table show the total percentage of cases across all nine indicators in which those countries with trade adjustment loans (in three different classifications) did better than the others. The relative performance of the twenty-six countries three years after as opposed to three years before the loan is considered in the lower half of the table.

The relative improvements in the trade adjustment countries are most apparent in the indicators of trade and growth. These improvements are probably attributable to the additional financing provided by the loans, exchange rate adjustments, and improvement in the incentive regime. There was a relative worsening, however, of some debt indicators as well as investment ratios. This is not altogether surprising because these countries borrowed more heavily than the others, but since they also made major adjustments, the weak improvements in the debt indicators may have ramifications for the sustainability of the improvements.

Difference in Export Performance

Exports of developing countries expanded rapidly in the 1970s but growth decelerated in the 1980s to half that of the 1970s. Although overall export growth was weaker in the 1980s (3.6 percent average annual rate) than in the 1970s (6.8 percent), performance was stronger for recipient countries (4.5 percent) than for nonrecipients (2.8 percent) in the 1980s. About one-third of the trade loan recipients also managed to increase their exports in recent years (1982–88) compared with the longer-term trend (1965–81, figure 4-2). Among the ten intensive recipients (those that received three or more trade loans), more than half increased their shares in total exports to industrial countries from nonoil-exporting developing countries.

Manufacturing exports from developing countries grew at an average annual rate of 7.6 percent during 1982–87, while the rate of increase for all exports was only 3.1 percent. Particularly rapid rates of increase in manufacturing exports during 1982–87 were recorded by Turkey (29 percent a year), Mauritius and Mexico (25 percent), Thailand (20 percent), Korea and Zambia (around 15 percent), and Ghana and Morocco (10 percent). Growth in manufacturing exports was stronger in the countries with trade loans than in the other countries, even when calculated using unweighted averages (table 4-6). The annual growth rate for 1982–87 was 9 percent for the loan recipient group compared with 6 percent for the nonrecipient group. Although exports of primary products and services have been very important for some countries, over time the main contribution to export performance at the margin probably came from manufactured exports.

To improve performance in this area, a realistic exchange rate policy that yields competitive production costs, given the productivity of labor

Table 4-5. Indicators of Performance before and after Trade Adjustment Lending: Twenty-Six Recipients of Loans before 1986 and Forty-Eight Nonrecipients

Indicator	*Low-income*	*Middle-income*	*Low- and middle-income*	*Sub-Saharan Africa*	*Highly indebted*	*Exporters of manufactures*
Number of trade loan recipients	9	17	26	11	10	7
Number of nonrecipients	20	27	47	18	4	8
			1985–87 compared with 1981–83			
GDP growth	9+*	12+*	21	10+*	3−*	5+
Investment/GDP	5+	14+	19	9+	6−	7+
Real exchange rate	8+†	15+*	23	9+†	8+	7+
Manufacturing exports growth	7+*	12+	19	10+*	1−*	4−
Import growth	8+*	12+*	20	8+*	4−	6+
Resource balance/GDP	2−	12+	16	5+	10+*	1−
Inflation	8+†	14+	22	10+*	7−	1−
External debt/exports	6+	17+†	23	8+	10+*	6+
Debt service/exports	5+	10+	15	4−	3−	7+
Share showing improvement[a]	0.74	0.77	0.76	0.74	0.58	0.70
10 intensive recipients	0.83	0.72	0.74	0.78	0.53	0.56
All 40 recipients	0.63	0.74	0.71	0.68	0.58	0.56

			Three years after compared with three years before			
GDP growth	5+	13+	18	6+	5+	4+
Investment/GDP	4−	11+	15	5−	8+	4−
Real exchange rate	7+	16+	23	10+†	9+	7+
Manufacturing exports growth	7+	14+	21	9+	5−	4+
Import growth	6+	14+†	20	6+	5+*	7+†
Resource balance/GDP	5+	11+	16	8+	8+	2+
Inflation	7+	13+	20	9+	6+	4−
External debt/exports	5+	14+	19	7−	9+	5+
Debt service/exports	5−	9+	14	3−	5+	4+
Share showing improvement[a]	0.63	0.75	0.71	0.64	0.67	0.65
10 intensive recipients	0.78	0.69	0.71	0.71	0.71	0.78
All 40 recipients	0.58	0.70	0.64	0.62	0.63	0.54

* The change in means for the recipients between the two periods relative to the change for nonrecipients is significant at a 5 percent confidence interval.

† The change in means for the recipients between the two periods relative to the change for nonrecipients is significant at a 10 percent confidence interval.

Note: The numbers in the table show for each indicator the number of recipients in each classification that improved in the period after the trade adjustment loan compared with the period before the loan relative to the change over the same periods for nonrecipient comparators. The year of receipt of the first loan is excluded from the comparison in the lower half of the table. The plus and minus signs indicate an improvement or a worsening of the average value of an indicator for recipients compared with the change in average value for nonrecipients.

a. The share of the product of the number of variables and the number of countries showing improvement in the total.

Table 4-6. Average Annual Percentage Growth Rates of Export Volume and GDP for Selected Country Groups, 1980–88
(unweighted averages)

Indicator and country group	1980	1981	1982	1983	1984	1985	1986	1987	1988[a]	Percentage change 1984–86/1980–82	Percentage change 1985–87/1981–83
Merchandise exports											
87 developing countries	5.4	2.4	2.6	0.1	6.6	5.2	3.7	6.0	4.4	49.0*	19.2†
10 intensive trade loan recipients	12.1	7.5	7.8	−4.9	11.5	3.5	9.2	7.5	3.5	−11.7†	94.2
26 trade loan recipients	9.1	4.8	2.2	−2.9	7.3	3.6	8.3	7.8	5.1	19.3†	380.5†
40 trade loan recipients	7.6	4.7	−0.4	−1.2	6.8	5.0	6.8	5.7	4.1	56.3†	464.5†
47 nonrecipients	3.5	0.3	5.1	1.2	6.5	5.4	1.0	6.3	4.8	44.9	92.4
Manufacturing exports[b]											
87 developing countries	18.4	9.7	1.2	11.2	9.8	10.6	7.2	5.5	10.7	−5.8*	5.4†
10 intensive trade loan recipients	26.8	20.2	−3.8	15.6	11.9	9.5	10.2	13.7	17.2	−26.9*	4.5†
26 trade loan recipients	18.7	7.3	0.9	6.7	9.0	11.5	5.0	12.7	12.2	−5.2*	92.6†
40 trade loan recipients	25.6	6.5	0.6	10.3	7.4	14.1	11.6	9.9	13.7	1.2†	104.9†
47 nonrecipients	11.9	12.6	1.7	12.1	11.8	7.4	3.5	1.7	7.9	−13.4	−52.2

GDP											
87 developing countries	3.6	3.4	1.8	1.2	2.4	3.1	3.2	2.3	3.3	−0.9†	34.8†
10 intensive trade loan recipients	0.2	2.4	1.1	0.2	2.1	2.7	3.8	4.2	4.1	128.8†	188.7†
26 trade loan recipients	3.4	2.2	0.7	0.6	2.7	3.3	4.2	3.7	3.8	60.2†	214.1†
40 trade loan recipients	2.7	2.8	0.3	0.4	2.2	3.5	3.9	3.2	3.6	63.7†	198.2†
47 nonrecipients	4.4	3.8	3.1	1.9	2.6	2.7	2.6	1.6	3.0	−29.2	−20.5

* Differences in means between the recipients and nonrecipients of trade adjustment loans were significant at the 5 percent confidence interval.

† Differences in means between the recipients and nonrecipients of trade adjustment loans were significant at the 1 percent confidence interval.

a. Preliminary estimates.

b. The definition of manufactures is from the Foreign Trade Statistics, International Economics Department, World Bank; it includes line items of 5 + 6 + 7 + 8 − 68 in the Standard International Trade Classification (SITC).

Source: World Bank data.

Figure 4-2. Export Growth for Forty Countries with Trade Adjustment Loans
(percent)

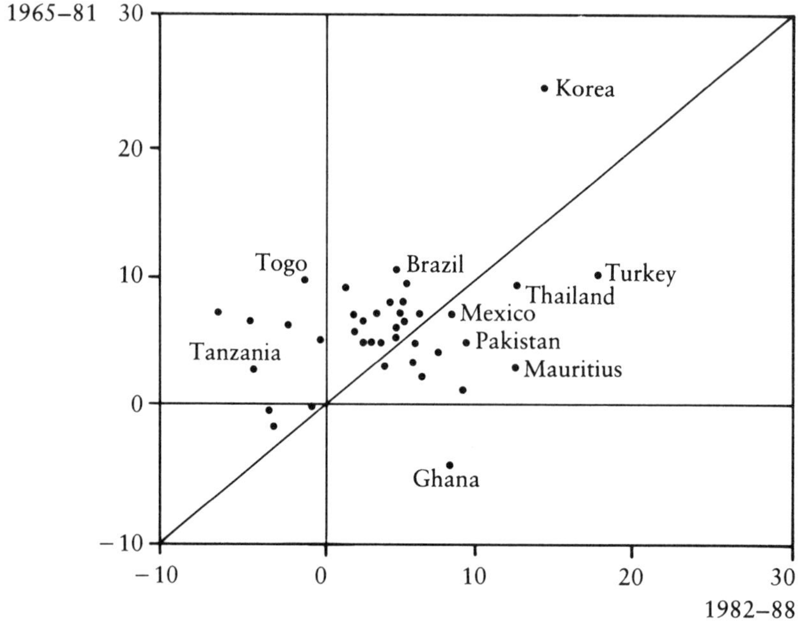

Source: World Bank data.

in each country, will continue to be essential, as will measures to enhance productivity. Exporters also need access to a growing range of domestically produced inputs at world prices and of world quality. Institutional and marketing support to export activities are also especially strong among successful exporters, while the opposite is true among the poor performers.

Some countries have introduced export incentives while maintaining protection in the import regime. But unless protection is reduced, the incentive to shift resources from production for a captive domestic market to a tough and competitive international market is likely to remain limited. And as long as import controls remain in place, there will be a need to introduce such things as duty drawback schemes, export processing zones, and bonded warehouses to ensure that exporters receive special access to imported inputs at world prices. In addition, the successful East Asian exporters have paid attention to easy access to foreign exchange for exporters, preshipment credit for working capital, labor costs, training, education, infrastructure, technology, and marketing (for a discus-

Figure 4-3. Change in Growth Rate of GDP and Imports for Countries with Trade Adjustment Loans

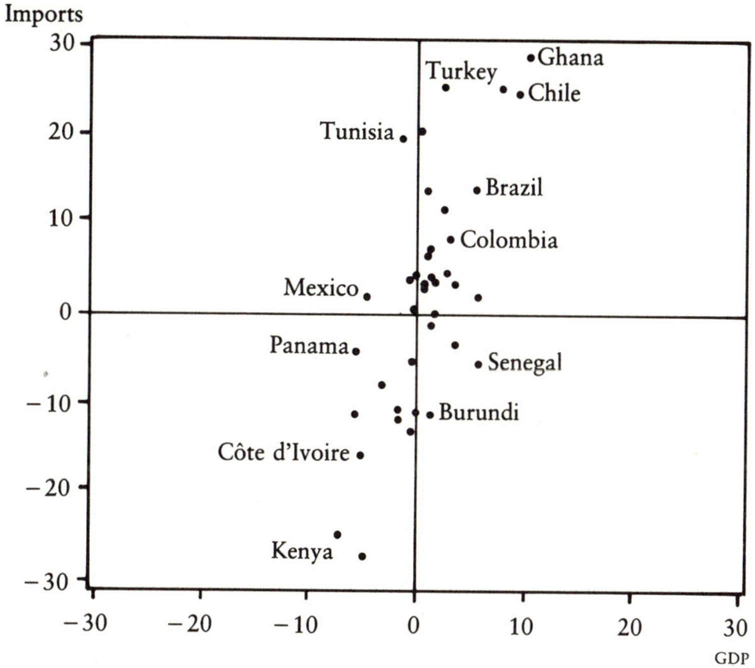

Note: The figure shows the percentage point improvement in the growth rate of GDP and imports three years after the first trade loan compared with three years before.

Source: World Bank data.

sion, see Keesing 1988). Their exports have also benefited from a favorable regulatory environment, support for enterprise development, and a forward-looking industrial policy. Furthermore, the East Asian countries have dealt successfully with protection abroad to maintain their prospects for market penetration.

Does Policy Matter?

In the first half of the 1980s, import compression was the dominant force behind a negative relation between changes in the trade balance and changes in GDP. Figure 4-3 shows the strong positive link between import growth and GDP growth. Some observers argue on this basis that the changes in the availability of external financing (affecting imports) were a powerful explanation of changes in GDP in this period. To be sure, starting from a situation in which domestic savings are not easily converted into foreign exchange to purchase imports, greater external financing and the relaxation of import controls, by permitting increased importation of raw materials and intermediate and capital goods, can contribute to higher GDP. Adjustment lending has facilitated additional financing for imports. It has also supported import liberalization, which together with real exchange rate adjustments was expected to boost GDP more than would the increased importation of inputs alone.

The possible effect of changes in commercial policy and in the real exchange rate is considered below in a framework that incorporates the effect of external financing and the effect of changes in the terms of trade. The short-term impact of increased financing on the growth of GDP is expected to be positive. An improvement in terms of trade is also expected to increase GDP growth. A depreciation of the real exchange rate would have a positive effect on GDP growth if the increase in tradable production more than offsets the decline in nontradable production. Commercial policy reform that reduces antiexport bias would increase GDP growth if the positive effect on exportables is larger than the negative effect on importables.

To illustrate these propositions, we consider changes between a period before reforms and after reforms as below:

$$\text{(4-1)} \quad \dot{\text{GDP}}_i = \beta_0 + \beta_1 \dot{F}_i + \beta_2 \dot{\text{TOT}}_i + \beta_3 \dot{\text{RER}}_i + \beta_4 P_i + \epsilon_i$$

where

β_0 = constant
$\beta_1, \beta_2, \beta_3, \beta_4$ = coefficients of the respective variables
F = financing
TOT = terms of trade
RER = real exchange rate
P = index for commercial policy reform
ϵ = the error term, assumed to be uncorrelated with the independent variables, and with zero mean and constant variance
i = each of the countries
$\dot{}$ = rate of change.

The four variables on the right-hand side are assumed to be related to $\dot{\text{GDP}}$ in a log linear fashion. Estimations were made for the forty countries with trade adjustment loans as opposed to forty-seven nonrecipients, with a dummy variable indicating the presence of a loan. Estimations were also made for a group of thirty-eight reform countries that excluded the four trade loan recipients with no progress or a reversal in commercial policy (table 4-2) plus Bolivia and Haiti (which carried out trade reforms without adjustment loans) as opposed to the remaining forty-nine nonreformers; a dummy variable indicated the presence of reforms. Finally, for the twenty-four countries with detailed implementation data, a variable was used to indicate the extent of policy change. This variable was, in turn, an index of policy change—obtained as the product of the indices of reform proposals—ranked 3, 2, 1—and the degree of fulfillment of what was proposed—ranked 80, 60, 40, 20, and 0 percent (based on Halevi 1989).

Table 4-7 provides the results of ordinary least squares estimations for the eighty-eight developing countries. Changes are considered during three years after the loan compared with three years before. Changes in financing and terms of trade generally have the expected effects. (Alternatively, changes in imports—as a proxy for financing, not shown in table 4-7—are found to be strongly and positively associated with changes in GDP growth.) The contribution to GDP growth of policy reform is positive and strong when reformers are compared with nonreformers, and when the extent of policy implementation is accounted for. The coefficient of $\dot{P}$ in the analysis of the twenty-four countries with data on implementation is extremely robust. The impact of real exchange rate depreciation (defined as a decrease) is positive and significant. In the absence of either RER or P, the other variable assumes much greater significance (not shown), presumably because of the high correlation between the two variables.

Conclusion

Overall, implementation of trade policy reform has been moderately significant in the sample of developing countries. Reforms in exchange rate policy and a reduction in impediments to export have occurred, as well as a reduction in impediments to the import of inputs needed by exporters. Although quantitative restrictions have been replaced by tariffs in many countries, success in lowering quantitative restrictions has been more modest in the face of foreign exchange constraints, except in selected cases (for instance, Chile, Korea, Mauritius, and Mexico). In some cases there has been a reduction in effective protection for importables and in antiexport bias (for example, Mexico, Morocco, and Philippines). Domestic reforms, however, have lagged even in some of the major trade reformers (for example, Mexico), and institutionalization of reforms and reductions in protection levels have been limited.

Given the strong emphasis on trade policy under adjustment lending, one might expect greater reforms of the trade regimes than actually occurred during this period. In particular, four factors have constrained reform: macroeconomic instability, inadequate conviction concerning the benefits of reform and vested interests against reform, weak capacity for implementation, and conflicts in design. Institutional reform has been found to be particularly slow, while price reforms have not always been sustained. These issues are important because sustainable price changes

Table 4-7. GDP Growth, External Factors, and Policy Reform

Equation	Constant	$\dot{F}$	$\dot{TOT}$	$\dot{RER}$	$\dot{P}$	R^2	F statistic	Number of observations
			Three years after compared with three years before[a]					
Dummy: 1 = 40 recipients	0.33	0.002	0.08	−0.05	0.32	0.18	3.3	66
0 = 47 nonrecipients	(0.42)	(0.32)	(2.55)	(−2.54)	(0.29)			
Dummy: 1 = 38 reformers[b]	−0.29	0.002	0.09	−0.04	1.78	0.22	4.2	66
0 = 49 nonreformers[c]	(−0.40)	(0.33)	(2.85)	(−2.43)	(1.67)			
Reform: Index of policy change	−3.09	0.02	0.09	−0.08	3.38	0.60	7.0	24
	(−2.09)	(1.70)	(1.92)	(−2.29)	(2.58)			

Note: t statistics are in parentheses. The dependent variable is $\dot{GDP}$. Changes and changes in growth between the periods give similar results.

a. The reference year 1984 is for nonrecipients.

b. Excluding Guyana, Yugoslavia, Zambia, and Zimbabwe from the group of forty trade loan recipients, but including the nonrecipient reformers Bolivia and Haiti.

c. Excluding Bolivia and Haiti from the group of forty-seven nonrecipients but including the four countries listed in footnote b.

and effective institutional support are vital to achieving meaningful supply responses.

On nine performance indicators, the strongest improvement of trade loan recipients over nonrecipients in the postloan period relative to the preloan period was in the growth in manufacturing exports and in imports. Less progress was made with respect to debt indicators. For the short period under review, the overall positive evidence is modest. In general, the more significant improvements concern middle-income countries. The evidence is also more favorable when early loan recipients are considered (especially when only the ten intensive trade loan recipients are considered) than when all forty recipients are included in the comparisons.

Regression analysis found the growth in output to be affected by proxies for external factors. At the same time, policy reform was found to have a positive impact on growth performance (see also Edwards 1989). The evidence of this policy impact is mild when all trade loan recipients are compared with nonrecipients but stronger when reformers are compared with nonreformers. Country studies corroborate this finding as well. The evidence supports the need for continued and stronger efforts to reform trade regimes.

Notes

I gratefully acknowledge the collaborative assistance of Bela Balassa, Mansoor Dailami, Jaime de Melo, Sebastian Edwards, Nadav Halevi, Ramon Lopez, Francis Ng, and Julie Stanton. The work benefited from comments from Ajay Chhibber, Patrick Conway, Faezeh Foroutan, Gene Grossman, Arnold Harberger, Ann Harrison, Thomas Hutcheson, Kazi Matin, John Nash, Arvind Panagariya, Dani Rodrik, James Tybout, John Williamson, Alan Winters, and Alexander Yeats. Rebecca Sugui prepared the paper.

1. The analysis in this chapter and several others is based on a review of eighty-one adjustment loans with a significant component for trade reform that were approved between 1979 and 1987. Of these eighty-one loans, forty-seven were structural adjustment loans (SALS), thirty-two were sectoral adjustment loans (SECALS), and two were program loans. Many included technical assistance components or were accompanied by technical assistance loans in support of trade reforms. Of the forty countries that received loans, detailed implementation data were available for only twenty-four in which sufficient time had elapsed since their first trade adjustment loans. Most of these twenty-four countries had received a trade loan before 1986, although a slightly different group of twenty-six countries constitutes the pre-1986 recipients. Among the forty countries, ten "intensive" adjusters received three or more trade adjustment loans.

Eighty-eight developing countries constitute the full sample. These are the ninety-five countries defined by the *World Development Report 1989* as low-income and middle-income countries, minus ten countries (Afghanistan, Bhutan, Iran, Iraq, Kampuchea, Lao People's Democratic Republic, Lebanon, Libya, Romania, Viet Nam) for which data were not available, plus three (Gambia, Guinea-Bissau, and Guyana) that had received adjustment loans but were not already included in the *World Development Report* definition because of their small populations. Forty-eight countries in the sample were middle-income countries and forty were low-income countries (GNP per capita of $480 or less in 1987).

2. Export restrictions have included prohibitions based on economic or safety grounds, restrictive licensing, export quotas, export taxes, and limitations on the retention of foreign exchange.

3. Quantitative restrictions have included import prohibitions, quotas, and restrictive licensing of various sorts. Other restrictions include licensing and controls for foreign exchange, requirements for advance deposits for imports, and restricted import channels (as in the case of a state trading monopoly).

4. In addition to customs duties, tariffs include customs surcharges, surtaxes, stamp taxes, and taxes on foreign exchange.

5. The judgments were based on recommendations for loans, country memoranda, country briefs, audit reports, mission reports, background work for World Bank (1988), IMF reports, and the Ford Foundation project on trade policy and the developing world. Sufficiently large differences were detected to permit such a broad classification.

6. When "secondary trade restrictive intent" is included, the figure rises to 27.2 percent; estimates for imports "affected," rather than covered, are higher still—48 percent.

7. These proposals are grounded in the conceptual and empirical work of many trade policy analysts; see, for example, Balassa (1988); Bhagwati (1978); Corden (1974); Krueger (1978); and Little, Scitovsky, and Scott (1970).

8. Although the achievement of a real depreciation clearly depended on macroeconomic adjustments (fiscal, monetary, and wage), this chapter focuses only on exchange rate policy identified under trade adjustment lending.

9. When quantitative restrictions are binding before and after the depreciation, however, the depreciation increases the price of exportables relative to importables.

10. For most indicators a positive change is an improvement. For resource balance/GDP, external debt/exports, and debt service/exports, a positive change is a worsening and is indicated in the table by a minus. For the real exchange rate, a greater real depreciation for recipients between periods than that for comparators is an improvement.

11. In particular, sample selectivity bias is likely to come into play here in that changes in performance attributed to the receipt of a loan may reflect conditions that systematically led to the receipt of the loan.

References

Balassa, Bela. 1988. "Quantitative Appraisal of Adjustment Lending." PPR Working Paper 79. Policy, Planning, and Research, World Bank, Washington, D.C.

Bhagwati, Jadgish. 1978. *Foreign Trade Regimes and Economic Development.* Cambridge, Mass.: National Bureau of Economic Research.

Corden, W. M. 1974. *Trade Policy and Economic Welfare.* Oxford: Clarendon Press.

Edwards, Sebastian. 1989. "Openness, Outward Orientation, Trade Liberalization, and Economic Performance in Developing Countries." Trade Policy Division, Country Economics Department, World Bank, Washington, D.C.

Erzan, R., H. Kuwahara, S. Marchese, and R. Vossenaar. 1986. "The Profile of Protection in Developing Countries." UNCTAD Discussion Paper 21. Geneva: U.N. Conference on Trade and Development.

Finger, Joseph M., and Samuel Laird. 1987. "Protection in Developed and Developing Countries—An Overview." *Journal of World Trade Law* 2 (6) December.

GATT. 1980. "The Tokyo Round of Multilateral Trade Negotiations—II, Supplementary Report." Geneva: General Agreement on Tariffs and Trade.

Halevi, Nadav. 1989. "Trade Liberalization in Adjustment Lending." Trade Policy Division, Country Economics Department, World Bank, Washington, D.C.

Keesing, Donald B. 1988. "Adjustment and Export Development." Trade Policy Division, Country Economics Department, World Bank, Washington, D.C.

Khan, Mohsin S. 1988. "The Macroeconomic Effects of Fund-Supported Adjustment Programs: An Empirical Assessment." International Monetary Fund, Washington, D.C.

Krueger, A. O. 1978. *Foreign Trade Regimes and Economic Development: Liberalization Attempts and Consequences.* Cambridge, Mass.: Ballinger.

Laird, Samuel, and Alexander Yeats. 1988. "Trends in Nontariff Barriers of Developed Countries, 1966–86." PPR Working Paper 137. Policy, Planning, and Research, World Bank, Washington, D.C.

Little, I. M. D., Tibor Scitovsky, and M. F. Scott. 1970. *Industry and Trade in Some Developing Countries: A Comparative Study.* New York and London: Oxford University Press.

Papageorgiou, Demetrios, Michael Michaely, and Armeane Choksi, eds. Forthcoming. *Liberalizing Foreign Trade.* Vol. 7, *Lessons of Experience in the Developing World.* Oxford, U.K.: Blackwell.

Rodrik, Dani. 1988. "Liberalization, Sustainability, and the Design of Structural Adjustment Programs." Trade Policy Division, Country Economics Department, World Bank, Washington, D.C.

Williamson, John. 1985. *The Exchange Rate System.* Rev. ed. Washington, D.C.: Institute for International Economics.

World Bank. 1988. *Adjustment Lending: An Evaluation of Ten Years of Experience.* Policy and Research Series 1. Washington, D.C.

———. 1989. *World Development Report 1989.* New York: Oxford University Press.

Comments

John Williamson

MY PRIMARY DUTY here is presumably to offer a verdict on whether the World Bank has been pursuing the right objectives in the trade conditions attached to adjustment loans and whether it has been achieving those objectives. Accordingly, I shall discuss first the objectives pursued by the World Bank and subsequently Thomas's attempt in this chapter to measure success.

The World Bank has sought through its trade adjustment loans to persuade developing countries to open up their economies and exploit rather than fight their comparative advantage. Had adjustment lending started twenty rather than ten years ago, I doubt whether opening up to the world economy would have been a central focus. The profession was converted by Little, Scitovsky, and Scott (1970), followed by the meticulous assembly of empirical evidence at the World Bank under the intellectual leadership of Bela Balassa, and reinforced by the dramatic and visible success of outwardly oriented policies in the East Asian newly industrialized countries. The benefits of outward orientation are now a staple component of Washington conventional wisdom, a belief that I share. Chapter 4 provides some modest additional support for this position, especially in the positive coefficient on the policy variable, although I doubt if it will convert many of the skeptics in the World Bank's client countries.[1]

A key ingredient of an outward-orientation policy is a "competitive" or "realistic" exchange rate. Figure 4-1 shows conventional International Monetary Fund (IMF) measures of real effective exchange rates as the relative prices of different nations' output, and this measure is used to generate the estimates shown in table 4-7. Thomas takes for granted that depreciation of the real exchange rate in that sense will increase the relative price of tradables in terms of nontradables, but this is a hypothesis that deserves testing. The empirical results would have been more interesting had they been based on the relative price of nontradables, which measures the supply-side incentive to produce exportables and so is a more interesting concept—although one that is more difficult to measure—than the real exchange rate in most developing countries.

My major concern with the treatment of exchange rates in this chapter is that exchange rate policy is judged by how much real depreciation was achieved rather than by whether misalignments were avoided. The problem is acknowledged, but the procedure is nonetheless misleading in principle: for example, it means that encouraging Korea to further devalue an already undervalued won is counted as a success. Any adequate evaluation of the World Bank's success in this field requires judgments on "proper" levels of exchange rates analogous to my fundamental equilibrium exchange rates (Williamson 1985). In the context of a developing country, however, one might want to modify the definition to refer to a rate that would be expected to limit current imbalances to a size that could be sustainably financed while promoting export growth adequate to buy the imports needed to exploit the economy's full growth potential.

I have the impression that, when the World Bank and the IMF have differed over their advice on exchange rates, the reason is that the World Bank has been basing its advice on a concept such as this while the IMF has employed the narrower criterion of financial viability. The World Bank was right to use the broader criterion and should not allow charges that the concept contains an element of subjectivity to prevent it from making its use explicit. The failure to measure the extent of overvaluation means, for example, that Thomas cannot emphasize the harm being done to Côte d'Ivoire and Senegal by the obstinate insistence on treating the fixed parity of the CFA franc as sacrosanct.

The other key element of an open economy is a commercial policy that roughly equalizes the domestic resource cost of earning or saving a unit of foreign exchange in all the various ways possible. Balassa's (1975) concept of outward orientation refers to the similarity of the domestic resource costs of exporting and of import substitution. The dispersion of effective protection rates measures variations in the domestic resource cost of saving foreign exchange by import substitution, and an analogous measure could obviously be constructed on the export side.

Like the fundamental equilibrium exchange rate, the dispersion of domestic resource costs is a sophisticated concept for which accurate measures are not available. I nevertheless hold the (quixotic?) view that a crude measure of a relevant concept is preferable to an accurate measure of a fundamentally irrelevant concept. It is rather disappointing to discover that the vast amount of empirical study undertaken in the World Bank could not be exploited to yield some rough estimates of how much progress in equalizing domestic resource costs has been accomplished by trade adjustment loans.

Reforms of most of the measures listed under "overall import policy" in table 4-1 seem likely to have helped equalize domestic resource costs. I have two reservations, however, about World Bank advice on commercial policy.

The first concerns the advice to reduce or preferably eliminate taxation of agricultural export crops. Every economist knows that, for a country with monopoly power in world trade, equalization of domestic resource costs would require an "optimum tariff," but the relevance of this principle for developing countries is usually denied on the grounds that they do not possess any significant monopoly power. Although that is true for individual countries, it is not true for developing countries collectively with respect to a few important products produced only in the tropics (most notably beverages). A common export tax on those commodities, by enabling low-income countries to redistribute income toward themselves at the expense of the rich, seems to me worthy of encouragement rather than the reverse (Williamson 1987).

The second reservation concerns the timing of import liberalization. As Thomas admits in passing, the liberalization of competitive imports can have a negative effect on domestic output, which can be important when the mobility of resources between sectors is low, as is often the case in the short run. This implies a low domestic resource cost from continuing to restrict imports until new investment is needed. Even if one cannot hope to synchronize tariff reductions with investment needs in any sophisticated way, a policy of announcing a tariff reduction well in advance (to discourage new investment in inefficient import-substituting industries) and then timing it to coincide with an easing of the payments position may be preferable to the rigid timetable of import liberalization seemingly urged (if not always enforced) by the World Bank. The former strategy is, after all, that adopted by Europe during its postwar recovery.

The measures of the success of the World Bank's trade adjustment loans are presented in tables 4-5 to 4-7. Table 4-5 does not present particularly persuasive evidence, partly because the margin of superior performance on the part of the countries receiving trade adjustment loans is less than overwhelming and partly because some of the superiority could be due to the import growth permitted by increased finance rather than to the policy changes that conditioned the loans. Table 4-7 provides some assurance that import growth from increased finance is not the entire story, since the policy variable is significant (and implies increased growth of as much as 2 percent a year) even after allowing separately for import growth.[2] And table 4-6 indicates that export growth has been stronger, to a marginally significant extent, in the countries with trade loans. Thus the evidence justifies a verdict of at least limited success.

Nevertheless, I wonder whether a better research strategy might not be possible. Rather than ask whether countries with trade loans had better performance, one could break the question down into two. The first would ask whether smaller exchange rate misalignments and lower domestic resource cost dispersion achieved superior performance, which would provide a direct test of whether those are indeed the policies the

World Bank should have been promoting. The second would then ask whether trade loans succeeded in reducing misalignments and the dispersion of domestic resource costs, which would provide a direct test of whether the World Bank had succeeded in promoting those policies. If both questions were answered in the affirmative, one would have a much stronger basis than that provided in the chapter for endorsing the World Bank's trade adjustment loan policy. This alternative approach would require at least crude measures of exchange rate misalignments and the dispersion of domestic resource costs, an admittedly difficult task. But I believe it would be worthwhile to make the effort.

Notes

1. A recent example that came across my desk argued as follows: "something should be done urgently to further protect our local industries. The area of policy focus to be addressed now is a discriminatory export policy with the sole aim of conserving the country's food and raw materials. If protectionism through import duty variations is informed by the need to protect local industries, then the government should not hesitate to balance the present tariff structure with the introduction of export quotas for food and raw materials. . . . Export quota is the practice in most market-oriented economies . . ." (*Monthly Business and Economic Digest*, United Bank for Africa, Lagos, January 1989, p. 1).

2. Average import propensities are typically around 0.2, so a finding that 5 percent import growth buys 1 percent output growth implies that a dollar of imports buys only a dollar of extra output (and hence $2 of extra supply of goods). It is perhaps surprising that extra imports buy as little growth as this, given that most of these countries were foreign-exchange constrained over the estimation period.

References

Balassa, Bela. 1975. "Reforming the System of Incentives in Developing Countries." *World Development*.

Little, I. M. D., Tibor Scitovsky, and M. F. Scott. 1970. *Industry and Trade in Some Developing Countries: A Comparative Study*. New York and London: Oxford University Press.

Williamson, John. 1985. *The Exchange Rate System*. Rev. ed. Washington, D.C.: Institute for International Economics.

———. 1987. "Exchange Rate Policy for Developing Countries." *Journal of Foreign Exchange and International Finance* 1 (1) January:39–46.

5 *Financial Sector Reform*

Alan Gelb
Patrick Honohan

THE RECENT UPSURGE of concern with financial policy in developing countries arises primarily from three characteristics of their financial systems. Many financial institutions are extremely unsound; control over interest rates and the direction of credit is often excessive and amounts to repression of the financial systems; and deposit money banks dominate the financial systems while the nonbank financial sector has been neglected.

To help developing countries address these problems, the World Bank introduced financial sector adjustment loans. By mid-1988, four such loans had been made: one each to Argentina (1988) and Ecuador (1988) and two to Turkey (1986 and 1988), with an additional trade and financial sector adjustment loan to Jamaica (1987; all fiscal years). Financial reform has also been a major component of a few structural adjustment loans, notably to Chile and to the Philippines. Changes in financial policies have also been incorporated in the World Bank's financial intermediation loans (which use financial institutions in borrowing countries to on-lend World Bank funds to final borrowers); these have a longer history, but the scope of policy reform has been more limited. Financial sector loans are now in preparation for Ghana, Hungary, Kenya, Nepal, and Nigeria, and others are being considered. The empirical evidence on the conception, implementation, and effects of such loans is still limited, however.

The Need for Reform

In perhaps the majority of developing countries, financial institutions covering a large part of the market are technically insolvent. In a smaller number of countries, many institutions have lost their capital several times over, a phenomenon observed in both publicly owned and private institutions, but especially in the former.

Soundness, Prudential Regulation, and Supervision

As with most bank failures in industrial countries, the poor quality of bank management—including fraud and insider abuse—has been evident in many failures in developing countries.[1] Management's problems have included undue concentration of risks in certain sectors or to certain individuals, lending to uncreditworthy clients at the behest of directors or the government, and close ownership links between banks and their borrowing clients (including public banks and their public clients).

Insolvency has also resulted from factors external to the financial system.[2] Unforeseen macroeconomic shocks that upset the calculations on which loans were based have left borrowers unable to service the loans. Large devaluations have sometimes created difficulties, particularly where many borrowers have been in import-related businesses or have incurred dollar debts or when a bank has held a foreign exchange exposure. Deflationary policies have generally resulted in a deterioration of the quality of bank loan portfolios. Trade liberalization measures have weakened the ability of those previously protected by trade barriers to repay their loans. Thus bank failures may accompany some aspects of desirable macroeconomic adjustment programs.

Although not all of these problems could have been forestalled by adequate supervision and prudential regulation, including adequate accounting and auditing standards, some could have been, and the cost of dealing with the problem promptly would have been far lower. Furthermore, a weak regulatory and supervisory framework is a barrier to effective financial liberalization, because liberalization places different, and in many respects heavier, demands on prudential regulation and supervision than does a directed credit system (Dooley and Mathieson 1987; Diaz Alejandro 1985). The skills required of banking institutions in liberalized financial markets are different from those needed where interest rates and credit flows are heavily controlled.

In most cases of a bank's collapse, the state has ultimately indemnified the losses to depositors because of the perceived importance of preserving confidence and avoiding a flight from deposits. But the consequences of bank insolvency go beyond the adverse impact on government budgets. Distressed banks and borrowers can impede the access to credit of good borrowers and sound investment projects. And, while bank difficulties go unrecognized, management continues to lend to nonperforming borrowers in the hope of some reversal of their fortunes. In a scramble for liquidity to support this unsustainable behavior, banks may bid up interest rates to levels well above the likely return on investments. New lending projects are not entertained by banks in these circumstances, and because of the liquidity squeeze not even worthwhile investment projects can raise finance outside the banking system at a reasonable cost. The repositioning of the economy's productive capacity to a new set of relative prices or to an export-oriented policy is thus inhibited. Meanwhile, the volume of "paper assets" and the government's potential liability mushroom.[3]

Correcting the insolvency problems of the banking system is thus an urgent task. Although the character of reform is more that of crisis management than of long-term development, the task must be accomplished with a view to the longer run if problems are not to recur. Certain "infrastructural" components are needed to restructure a banking system. For example, accounting and auditing standards must conform to generally accepted principles. A system for classifying loans by quality is necessary to allow for adjustments for the inadequacy of capital and early warning of problems. Adequate systems of prudential regulation and supervision must be installed to ensure the health of the restructured system. Implementing these reforms may require legal and institutional changes in the relationship between banks and their regulators and between lenders and borrowers.

Financial Sector Repression

Excessive regulation of interest rates, extensive direction of credit, and unduly heavy taxation of financial intermediation severely inhibit the effectiveness of financial systems in many developing countries. Such repressed financial systems may not be able to offer savers an asset that can be expected to retain its real value over time. In that case, financial intermediaries may be little used, and savers may rely instead on relatively unproductive assets or capital flight.[4]

The disposition of the funds that are made available to financial institutions may also be constrained. Intermediaries may not be able to expand credit to promising projects or to avoid lending to sectors and projects in which the risk of failure outweighs the likely returns. In many developing countries more than half of bank credit is directed. The productivity of aggregate investment in an economy may thus be seriously impaired, thereby wasting resources and slowing growth. By withholding responsibility from the financial institutions, directed credit also tends to weaken the process of loan recovery and can wreak havoc with the financial viability of intermediaries.

From certain perspectives, central direction of credit allocation might result in a good distribution of credit even though it does not take advantage of the informational gains offered by a decentralization of credit decisions (see Cho 1986). In the absence of such controls, however, and given a reasonable degree of macroeconomic stability, the financial sector could be performing the important role of assessing the relative potential of different projects. But because of the prevalence of credit direction, skills in credit assessment may not be developed anywhere in the economy.

Some regulations may have been instituted in order to avoid the risks of unduly vigorous competition or to ensure that favored borrowers were adequately served. But it is now quite generally recognized that these regulations have often been excessive and ultimately resulted in less credit, much of it misdirected, and in a new set of prudential risks. These regulations can prevent adequate diversification of bank portfolios and severely limit the spreads that are obtainable.

In most cases, financial sector repression has a pronounced fiscal dimension as well. The financial system has traditionally been an administratively convenient source of tax revenue. A zero or low rate of remuneration on high reserve requirements (often more than one-fifth of deposits and occasionally approaching two-thirds) has also contributed to the fiscal burden on financial intermediation and to the widening of the spread between borrowing and lending rates in many developing countries. The total tax burden levied on financial systems in developing countries is often as high as 2 to 3 percent of GDP and sometimes as high as 7 or 8 percent.

The Nonbank Financial Sector

In most developing countries, the financial system is dominated by banks; nonbank financial intermediation has been comparatively neglected. If not too heavily regulated, banks can perform many of the most important functions within a financial system: they can provide a safe and liquid repository for savings, operate an efficient payments mechanism, and provide the necessary financing for trade. When it comes to other financial services, however, such as the financing of long-term industrial development (by debt or equity) or the provision of high-yielding long-term savings media, the performance of banks has often been questioned.[5] It is widely believed that other types of institutions are needed to complete the picture and ensure the maximum contribution of the financial sector to economic development—as well as to stimulate the banks by competing with them.

The World Bank's main focus in this area has been on the development of capital and money markets. Capital markets give investors access to long-term funds and equity. Long-term loans are suitable for financing investments with long gestation periods and returns that will materialize only over a long period. Equity capital is desirable for financing risky investments; it allows investors to go through a bad period without fear of bankruptcy. From the saver's point of view, equity and long-term investments can offer a higher expected return and maturities matched to the saver's needs. An effective capital market can thus result in greater resource mobilization and more productive investment. But banks in most countries are reluctant to commit themselves to long-term lending or equity investment (or are forbidden by law to do so) since their own liabilities are fixed and generally short term. There is also concern that industrial equity in many developing countries is insufficient to provide a robust basis for long-term growth.[6]

Money markets represent the short-term end of capital markets. Their development allows large firms and institutions to satisfy their needs for short-term borrowing and lending without the intermediation of banks, thereby improving efficiency and cutting costs.

The emergence of a successful capital market requires not only reasonable macroeconomic stability but also an adequate regulatory framework that will prevent fraud and conflicts of interest and ensure adequate disclosure. Without this framework, savers will distrust the market because they are individually unable to assess the probity and creditworthiness of borrowers. The establishment of an adequate regulatory framework is thus primarily an institution-building activity.

Financial Intermediation Loans

The World Bank's involvement in financial sectors has not been confined to adjustment lending. Of quantitatively greater importance have been operations involving the use of domestic financial institutions to on-lend World Bank funds to final borrowers. The first loans of this type were channeled through specialized development finance institutions (DFIS), some of which were established specifically or primarily for this purpose, often with World Bank involvement. More than 150 DFIS around the world have been used by the World Bank for lending in industrial sectors alone. Over time a larger share of loans has been channeled through the commercial banking sector via such "apex" institutions as the central bank.

This lending responded to a deficiency in the provision of long-term finance and was seen as the only way to reach smaller, private borrowers in the industrial and agricultural sectors. During the past few years industrial lending through financial intermediaries has averaged about US$2 billion annually, and this type of lending is likely to increase.

Unfortunately, many of the loans made by the DFIS did not perform satisfactorily, and by the start of the 1980s the parlous financial state of many of them had become apparent. As many as one-third had severe portfolio problems because of a variety of elements in the macro and sectoral environments and poor lending procedures. A review in 1985 concluded that about half the DFIS were in reasonable condition but that only about ten to fifteen were sufficiently profitable to turn to the market for financing (World Bank 1985).

The expansion of World Bank lending activities to include a wider range of intermediaries (notably the commercial banks) was an attempt to reach a wider range of clients. But it also sidestepped the serious portfolio problems in many of the development banks. The doubts about the soundness of many banking systems raise questions about the allocation of resources intermediated by the commercial banks as well as about the ability of these banks to assess credit risk.

To the extent that World Bank lending for financial intermediation has included conditions related to general financial policy, the conditions have been confined largely to reforms to raise interest rates on subsidized lines of credit. This focus has often reflected concern that other, heavily subsidized lines of credit would undercut demand for World Bank–financed credit lines and prevent the loans from being disbursed. As the prevalence of repeat loans to intermediaries with poor loan recovery records suggests, the solvency of intermediaries, their managerial capabilities, and their credit processes have often received little attention, although these aspects have now begun to be addressed more seriously.

The Content of Adjustment Policy Packages

Reform of a country's financial policy will often be directed toward restoring the solvency of the banks, freeing up the financial system, and developing a capital market.

The Prudential Framework and Bank Restructuring

Three elements of policy are typically required to restore financial systems to a solvent state. First are measures to determine the state of bank portfolios and the necessary provisions and write-offs. These measures include the strengthening of accounting and auditing systems and skills, implementation of external audits, and classification of the portfolio according to loan quality. Legal changes to facilitate the intervention of regulators may also be needed. Second are measures to implement provisioning rules for less severely affected banks and to require weaker banks to clean up their loan portfolios and install new management. Some banks will need to recapitalize and reduce costs, merge (if a satisfactory business plan can be developed), or be liquidated. Third are measures to improve bank supervision and regulation for the system as a whole to ensure timely provisioning against losses and provide information for both bank management and regulators.

This third measure will usually require an overhaul of the accounting and auditing rules and systems and of the rules for portfolio classification and the treatment of unpaid interest. Measures to permit a credible, flexible response by regulators may also be needed. For example, the introduction of "cease and desist" orders would permit a graduated tightening of conditions, or the creation of a deposit insurance corporation would insure depositors and free the central bank from the need to intervene in failing banks, which is extraneous to its main policy function. Changes may also be needed in the laws affecting loan recovery.

These three measures, prosaic as they may seem, constitute a vital part of the restoration process. They may almost amount to a cultural revolution in the way the financial system and the corporate sector interact. Adequate accounting and auditing constitute the information infrastructure needed for financial markets to operate well, in the sense of enabling claims on real assets to be properly valued. In most developing countries, this infrastructure is sadly lacking.

Why not simply allow insolvent banks to fail? First, if depositors do not have confidence in the banking system, resource mobilization will be severely curtailed and gains in efficiency and convenience will be diminished accordingly. Second, a wave of nervousness among depositors may lead to a bank run. Runs that force the liquidation of bank assets can severely disrupt the economy and significantly set back growth. Even if a bank run is forestalled by bank closure, this in itself impedes the operation of the payments system and disrupts economic activity.

In the case of insolvent state-owned banks, some people have argued that immediate action to reveal the poor quality of the loan portfolio and to clean up the balance sheet may be unnecessary and imprudent. Unnecessary because the threat of a bank run may not be great in the case of state-owned banks and because changing the management may be sufficient to avoid a recurrence of the poor lending policies. Imprudent because announcement of the insolvency may damage business confidence, diminish the chances of good recovery on doubtful loans, and present the government with a budgetary commitment it can ill afford to absorb in the short run. The choice between the orthodox and dissenting views here hinges on the likely success of an attempt to cover up the insolvency and on the likely effectiveness of a bank management encumbered with a balance sheet so bad as to make profitability unattainable for years.

Most governments, however, consider it important to preserve the confidence of depositors and have arranged for at least some depositors to be indemnified from loss when banks fail. In most cases indemnification has been after the fact, but in several cases an explicit deposit insurance scheme has been proposed in preference to an implicit guarantee by the state.

Not everyone agrees on the desirability of formal deposit insurance schemes, while others argue about what form they should take and whether they should be compulsory. Those opposed claim that deposit insurance schemes eliminate the incentive for depositors to select a financial institution according to criteria for prudential management and make them indifferent even to reckless management behavior. An insurance fund is rarely sufficient to meet major calls upon it, and efforts to limit insurance to small deposits are routinely sidestepped by such practices as deposit splitting. Alternative approaches that might restore incentives, such as relating the insurance premium to the regulator's perception of the risk of the portfolio, are not easily effected, especially in developing countries. The main response to this line of criticism is that, since ex post indemnification of depositors has been widespread, moral hazard already exists and that explicit insurance is preferable to implicit, not least because it provides a mechanism for regulation.

A related controversial issue is the extent to which a financial system can be made self-regulating by mandating extensive disclosure of information and relying on depositors to police the banks. For various reasons, such an approach is not generally thought to be robust. It does, however, form the philosophical basis of the most comprehensive banking reform undertaken in a developing country, that of Chile, although the Chilean system also mandates an active role for the bank superintendency.

Where establishment of a deposit insurance scheme has formed part of an adjustment program, the insurance agency has had functions beyond paying out to depositors of failed banks.[7] In such cases, the agency can also intervene in banks identified as in serious difficulties; this allows the central bank, which might otherwise be the only agency equipped to undertake the work, to concentrate on policy as it affects the continuing banks.

The task of the intervening agency, whatever its nature, is to decide whether the failed banks should be liquidated or restarted with an injection of capital. A restart can be contemplated only in the context of a carefully worked-out business plan probably involving considerable reforms to the internal procedures and policies of the bank. New management is essential; in the initial, transition phase managers might come from the intervening agency, but they should be replaced by outsiders as soon as possible. The next stage is to identify nonperforming parts of the portfolio and separate them from the remainder of the banks' assets. If this job is left to bank management, a successful restart of the banks' operations could be jeopardized. Invariably, a substantial reduction in staff and branch expenses will be required. It may be quite some time before the rehabilitated banks are in a position to operate independently (in the case of publicly owned banks) or be bought by private interests. The financial restructuring should not include anything for the former shareholders: it is banks (or their depositors) that are being bailed out, not the bankers.[8]

Whether liquidation or rehabilitation is chosen, the protection of depositors is costly. Even in countries that already have a deposit insurance scheme, the fund built up with insurance premiums is rarely sufficient to meet the deficits that emerge in a major crisis. In most cases, the cost falls directly or indirectly on the government. A cost borne by the central bank eventually tends to fall back on the budget and must be managed and spread over time to prevent an inflationary expansion of domestic credit. Part of the counterpart funds generated by a policy-based loan disbursed against general imports can be earmarked for capitalization of the insurance scheme, as was done in Turkey under its second financial sector adjustment loan.

To avoid a recurrence of bank failures, prudential regulation and supervision need to be strengthened. Adjustment programs typically recognize this by proposing an increase in the number and quality of bank inspectors to review bank management and portfolios and an improvement in the procedures for off-site review and analysis by bank regulators of returns made by banks. Many problems could have been avoided by strict adherence to formal procedures for the diversification and classification of loans, nonaccrual of interest, and provisioning of nonperforming loans.

Freeing Up the Financial System

The policy agenda for dismantling controls on interest rates and credit allocation includes some or all of the following features: removing all interest rate controls on deposits, withdrawing interest subsidies and cross-subsidies, reducing the complexity of sectoral credit targets and their deviation from uncontrolled levels, removing credit ceilings in favor of broad instruments of monetary control, allowing commercial banks to engage in underwriting or to invest in private corporate securities, limiting entry barriers to those required by prudence (which can sometimes include an increase in capital),[9] reducing fiscal or quasi-fiscal burdens on the financial sector (such as those caused by low remuneration of heavy reserve requirements), and liberalizing foreign exchange controls.

All these measures have the general objective of using broad market signals wherever possible to improve the effectiveness of the financial sector in mobilizing and allocating resources. In practice, and for a variety of reasons, however, most countries choose to retain some degree of control over financial resource allocation and some degree of subsidy in their financial systems. World Bank programs often focus on reducing the most egregious deviations from a market configuration, such as the prevalence of credit at negative real interest rates or at rates below those available on deposits (which encourages the substitution of borrowed for one's own funds). As noted below, the timing of liberalization and its extent are sometimes debatable, especially when financial reforms interact with other policy reforms or macroeconomic imbalances.[10] Still disputed is the extent to which one can rely on market signals to meet development needs for credit in otherwise suboptimal environments (although it may be argued that the allocation of resources to desirable uses is better dealt with by fiscal means than by credit allocation).

There is no uniform approach to an ideal regime of taxation of financial intermediation. Such taxes add to the wedge between borrowing and lending rates, thereby contributing to inefficiency in the allocation of resources. Where capital shortage is a major constraint to development, distortions of this type may be more severe than in capital-rich countries. For this reason, a reduction in financial sector taxation is often a priority in financial reform. Excessive zeal in eliminating fiscal burdens on the financial sector, however, could result in undue taxation elsewhere in the economy. In inflation-prone countries, the tax should not be linked to nominal interest receipts because, if inflation and nominal interest rates rise sharply, the tax could grow quickly in importance and the spread of interest rates could severely widen.[11]

The taxation, explicit and implicit, of financial intermediation could be used to offset the adverse effects of cartelization and monopoly power in the banking system. The authorities, faced with a situation in which banks are able to unduly depress deposit rates and increase lending rates, can make skillful use of unremunerated reserve requirements to offset these distortions.[12] Although the ideal long-run solution is to encourage greater competition through liberal (although prudent) entry policies, the results of such a program may be slow, and to the extent that economies of scale exist in financial intermediation (itself a much-debated issue), some degree of monopoly power may remain even when entry is free.

Development of Capital Markets

The development of a capital market typically involves four main areas of policy. First, legislation is needed to establish an adequate regulatory framework for both primary and secondary markets so that a variety of securities can be sold. The framework should include adequate requirements for systematic accounting and disclosure of accounts and protection of minority interests.[13] Second, taxation reform is needed to reduce disparities in the effective rate of taxation of different types of security in order to reduce fiscal disincentives, especially to the use of equity and long-term debt.[14] Third, technical assistance and training are needed for the establishment of necessary institutions and intermediaries. Fourth, an appropriate framework is needed for providing adequate liquidity to the market. This might, for example, include increased authority for banks to participate in securities markets (a measure that poses problems of both prudential regulation and potential conflicts of interest, however).[15]

Problems and Issues of Financial Reform

Adjustment of the financial sector may be unsuccessful or even counterproductive if not supported by appropriate macroeconomic policies. Despite the close connection between the macroeconomic situation and the health of the financial sector, financial policy loans have been made to countries in which the macroeconomic situation was less than satisfactory.[16] Although a review of experience suggests that countries have generally complied with the specific conditions for financial policy contained in such loans, some analysts argue that it is unrealistic to expect a favorable result when macroeconomic stability is not being achieved.[17] They believe that financial sector reforms should be deferred until a more stable macroeconomic environment can be ensured.

Interaction with Other Adjustment Programs

Indeed, the phasing of financial sector reforms in relation to other reforms has become an important policy issue. Macroeconomic and trade policy adjustment measures can have undesirable side effects for the financial sector, notably by worsening the condition of bank portfolios.[18] Conversely, distortions caused by unduly rigid financial regulation can be much greater in the absence of macroeconomic balance. High inflation, for example, can cause a fixed nominal interest rate to diverge even more from the market-clearing level and result in a deterioration of resource allocation and a worsening of credit rationing.[19]

This interactive nature of reforms raises difficult issues of the phasing and sequencing of various reforms. Some considerations argue for delay in the liberalization of financial markets until other aspects of reform have been implemented. Because of the increased speed and magnitude of the response of a liberalized financial sector to changes in the policy environment, some firms and financial institutions that might have survived under a more controlled regime will fail if the system is subjected to a significant shock to macroeconomic, trade, or fiscal policy.[20]

Abrupt liberalization of the financial sector can itself generate undesirable side effects. For example, if all interest rates are deregulated at once, the (generally) shorter maturity of deposits than of loans will imply a severe squeeze on the profitability of banks.[21] Unless the low interest rates on loans can be renegotiated, permanent increases in interest rates may require some form of state subvention if depositors are to be protected. Similarly, reforms that seek to ease the tax burden on the financial system will generally result in pressure on the budget. This in turn may manifest itself in a distorting tax imposed elsewhere in the economy, in inflation, or in the explosive issue of public debt. An increase in public debt further raises interest rates and contributes to financial instability, as Turkey's experience has shown.

Although the consensus is that full-blown financial sector liberalization is best introduced at a time of macroeconomic and policy stability, it must be recognized that every delay in eliminating distortions represents a real loss to the economy (via the adverse effect on resource allocation). Delay may also be accompanied by a buildup of off-balance-sheet government liabilities. Furthermore, some reform steps can be taken at an early stage without the same risk entailed in other reforms. This applies particularly to the correction of serious problems of insolvency and to institution-building. The interest rate structure can be rationalized by eliminating preferential and subsidized rates even if it is not yet fully liberalized. Measures to promote competition, such as announcing (with adequate lead time) an opening of the system to foreign banks, might be needed to induce reform in an oligopolistic domestic financial system.

Concern about the fragility of the financial system should not be used as an excuse to delay reform indefinitely. Rather, it should spur reform efforts that are sufficiently thoroughgoing to result in robust institutions. In practice, the timing of financial reforms will probably follow "windows of opportunity" (as, for example, in Argentina), and the shocks that might arise in the course of other likely reforms will need to be factored in.

Dissenting Voices

As is the case with most issues of economic policy, some people believe that conventional advice concerning financial sector reform neglects important institutional considerations. Some of these arguments are presented here.

Some commentators argue that the higher interest rates that result from liberalization are likely to reduce growth and increase inflation, at least in the short run.[22] This is an empirical issue that has not yet been fully resolved, although the evidence is currently against this dissenting view, at least in the long-run context. The experience of the Southern Cone countries in Latin America, especially Chile, in the late 1970s is often mentioned in this connection.[23] Although it is true that real interest rates soared in Chile, with real bank lending rates averaging 74 percent in 1975–78, isolating the role of interest rate liberalization in a period of extensive policy changes is difficult. Not only were there tariff reforms and an opening of the capital account during the same period as liberalization of the financial sector, but inadequate supervision of financial institutions and an unsustainable exchange rate policy also influenced events. Despite the rapid growth experienced by Chile in the years immediately following the reforms, the financial instability that ensued remains a specter that is hard to exorcise and that haunts discussions of financial liberalization in other countries.

Another area of disagreement relates to the potential conflict between short- and long-term objectives arising from the use of monetary policy to combat inflation. Structural changes that substitute market-based monetary policy instruments for bank-by-bank credit ceilings pose potential short-term risks for monetary control. Although it should in principle be possible to neutralize any undesired side effects of the change on macroeconomic conditions, lack of experience in the operation of the new (mostly indirect) system could cause problems. Some policymakers wish to retain certain features of the unreformed system (such as credit ceilings) despite their structural inefficiency because they perceive that the features make monetary control easier. This perception may make reform programs less ambitious than they might otherwise be.

A closely related argument is based on the controversial theory that, in a liberalized financial system, monetary restraint might be comparatively ineffective (or even counterproductive) in restoring balance in current account payments and the macroeconomy in general. According to this neostructuralist view, monetary restraint might choke off production as much as, or even more than, it does demand, whereas in a system of directed credit, monetary restraint could be confined mainly to less productive sectors or to consumer spending. This line of argument is particularly relevant to the short run, and it is weakened if fiscal policy instruments more appropriate to achieving macroeconomic balance are available.

More generally, it is sometimes held that the financial system will not on its own channel funds to the most socially, as opposed to privately, productive sectors, so that some degree of directed credit is needed. In particular, it is argued, a "sound and totally liberalized" financial system may not always be the most desirable for development. Some situations lend themselves to second-best considerations, for example, where a poor legal framework in a volatile economy leads the formal sector to consider only short-term, heavily collateralized lending and inhibits equity markets.[24]

A conventional response to this point is that the divergence between social and private valuations is best met with explicit tax or subsidy measures because using directed credit can conceal a very large implicit subsidy that may well be far in excess of the difference between social and private valuations. In addition, the use of subsidized credit frequently involves high leakages because of fungibility. This is only a partial response, however. To the extent that the discrepancy being identified is the result of an institutional failure, such as the absence of certain financial instruments, it may well be that the best cure lies partly in policy interventions in the financial sector. This does not necessarily argue, however, for programs and institutions of the types common at present.

Frequently discussion and disagreement center on the institutional arrangements for adequately implementing monetary policy and prudential regulations and for dealing with failed banks. Should these functions be united under one institution—say, the central bank—or is a separation of functions desirable? Also, should insurance intermediaries and securities markets have their own regulators, or does the need for coordination argue for a single regulatory body?

Country experience on this issue varies, given the varying degree of complexity of financial systems and the resources that are available to implement financial policy. Many countries accept the importance of a degree of independence of the monetary policy authority from other aspects of government, although the degree of independence varies.[25] The responsibility for bank supervision is given sometimes to the central bank, sometimes to a government ministry, and sometimes to a separate superintendency of banks. A separate superintendency can have merit to the extent that it is needed to ensure that sufficient attention is devoted to prudential supervision in the face of competing demands on the attention of senior central bank or ministry officials. But whatever institutional arrangement is preferred, it is essential that the bank supervision function be adequately funded and that there be an adequate two-way flow of information between the supervisors and those responsible for monetary policy.

Another debate concerns universal banking. Although the introduction of universal banking has been recommended in some World Bank programs (an early example was in the Philippines), some analysts believe that allowing banks to become involved in corporate securities weakens prudential safeguards and obstructs the development of autonomous capital markets. This conflict mirrors the longstanding debate between adherents of the traditional Japanese and German approach to banking and those supporting the approach of the United Kingdom and the United States. By now, however, it seems clear that attempts to retain rigid barriers between segments of the financial sector can have, at best, a finite lifetime.

All in all, these and other dissenting voices call attention to the need to think through reforms carefully and to take account of the specific institutional features of each country.

Winners and Losers

Achieving consensus on financial sector reforms is usually difficult because of the powerful special interests that are affected.[26] A highly regulated banking system is typically a cartelized and potentially profitable one. Opening the system up to competition will erode high profits and allow new institutions and markets to flourish at the expense of the old. In anticipation of such effects, therefore, there will be strong lobbying against liberalization.

There are losers as well from the establishment of tighter prudential regulation. Uncreditworthy borrowers who received loans from badly managed banks will no longer have access to credit. That they have received loans in the past, however, suggests that they will form a powerful lobby against reform. In most developing countries, extensive ties exist between major banks and borrowers; moving them to an "arms-length" relationship attacks the basis of the economic power structure and is therefore a slow and difficult process.

It is often asserted that financial liberalization will improve income distribution and reduce the concentration of economic power. There is probably something to this assertion, although the evidence is not conclusive. Credit allocation is normally more concentrated than are deposit holdings and tends to follow the distribution of assets available for collateral.[27] Many examples suggest that subsidized credit is in practice available mostly to the larger or more prosperous segments of the targeted sectors. Small savers benefit from the liberalization of deposit rates. The very poor have little or no access to formal credit, however; their interests lie in the improvement of economic growth and employment that may be expected to flow from reform. Reform may also end the artificial stimulus to capital-intensive production that severely negative interest rates provide.

Drastic changes in interest rates can have very large distributional effects, however, to the extent that they affect long-term loans. This effect is especially important with respect to housing credit, which is heavily subsidized in many countries. Middle-class borrowers may have entered into long-term commitments wholly unaware that interest rates would be much higher without the subsidies. Even though these borrowers have gained substantially from the subsidy, they might be unable to meet their commitments at the unsubsidized rate. In practice, both equity and political considerations may call for partial compensation of long-term borrowers who are severely affected by a change in the interest rate regime. But such compensation schemes must be strictly circumscribed if the benefits of the reform are not to be dissipated. Certainly the new interest rates must apply to all new borrowing, and the scheme of compensation should be simple, open, and preferably funded out of fiscal resources.

Given the sensitivity of the issues addressed, governments and the World Bank sometimes prefer not to state explicitly in loan documents some of the steps that may need to be taken, but let them be implied by other requirements. As with other policy-based loans, full implementation of a financial sector adjustment loan is most likely when the government is firmly committed to reform and may even have already taken some preparatory steps prior to the loan.

The Success of Financial Adjustment Policies

The ultimate objective of financial sector reform is to achieve a higher rate of sustained economic growth. Attempts to measure the success of reform in these terms, however, are compromised by the multitude of other factors that contribute to economic growth. The effectiveness of financial sector reforms also needs to be examined in terms of intermediate objectives. For example, has the liberalization of interest rates contributed to a higher savings rate, to a higher rate of monetization, or to reduced capital outflow? Has the removal of sectoral credit controls led to more productive investment choices? Has the removal of bank-by-bank credit restrictions reduced bank margins? Have the rehabilitation and improved supervision of banks resulted in a sound and energetic banking system? Has the elimination of directed credit resulted in reduced loan delinquencies? Have structural improvements in capital markets led to increased recourse to the capital market?

In most cases, the financial adjustment programs supported by the World Bank have not been in effect long enough to provide definitive answers to these questions. On the basis of the cases that have been reviewed, it seems that countries have complied with most of the conditions of the programs. But financial sector reforms, being part of quick-disbursing, policy-based operations, have sometimes been introduced in problematic macroeconomic circumstances, and in some cases the poor macroeconomic environment has continued throughout the period of loan implementation.[28]

More generally, the degree to which an efficient financial system can contribute to the process of economic growth has not been precisely established. Certainly, a well-performing financial system is no remedy for policy weakness elsewhere in the economy. Nevertheless, when things go seriously wrong in the financial system, such as hyperinflation or widespread bank failures, the impact on the economy can be sudden, dramatic, and long-lived. Recent research on the depression in the United States in the 1930s attaches considerable importance to the impact of bank failures on the availability of credit (independent of the deflationary effect of monetary contraction). In some episodes of financial insolvency in developing countries, cause and effect have been difficult to disentangle because the insolvency of the banks became evident only at the time of recession.

Some indirect evidence of the influence of financial reform on economic growth may be obtained by an examination of countries whose financial sectors vary from very repressed to close to the ideal of liberalization programs. The relative contribution of liberalized and repressed financial systems to economic growth has also been considered in a number of statistical studies (Fry 1988; Gonzales Arrieta 1988). In a review of twenty-one countries during 1971–80 (IMF 1983), the six countries with positive real interest rates grew more rapidly than the ten with moderately negative rates, which in turn had average growth rates well above those of the five with severely negative rates. A recent study of this issue (Gelb 1989) using 1965–84 data for thirty-four countries also finds a positive impact of interest rates on growth.[29]

Evidence on the impact of distortions caused by directed credit is even less easily quantified, essentially because of fungibility, which makes it difficult to assess what would have happened in the absence of directed credit. Few, if any, studies conclusively attribute favorable results to programs of directed credit. In many countries, institutions implementing directed credit programs have faced serious problems with the quality of loans, which suggests poor credit allocation. To the extent that directed and subsidized credit diverts funds from still more worthwhile projects, it may cause social losses even if it is profitable for the financial intermediary.[30]

The Form of Financial Sector Loans

A policy-based loan has the effect of financing part of the borrowing country's international payments deficit, as well as supporting the budget through the provision of counterpart funds.[31] A typical loan for financial policy reform might be disbursed against general imports over a period of two years in two tranches. Counterpart domestic funds are generated as importers turn in domestic currency for foreign exchange; what happens then depends on how the government uses these payments.

The major fiscal costs of financial sector reforms are of two types. One results from a financial liberalization that substantially removes the financial system from the tax base. In a repressed financial system, high, unremunerated reserve requirements may yield the government the annual equivalent of 2 to 3 percent of GDP, and lowered debt-servicing charges from repressed interest rates on public debt may amount to a further percentage point or two. Liberalization may therefore have an appreciable fiscal cost, especially in terms of present value. There may also be some fiscal cost in compensating for the elimination of interest cross-subsidization.[32] A second fiscal cost attends financial restructuring as depositors and debtors are bailed out. This cost can represent as much as 20 to 30 percent of one year's GDP, as the experience of Chile and the Philippines suggests, but it can be spread out over time.[33] For example, the government can provide intermediaries with interest-bearing paper in exchange for the bad portfolio to enable intermediaries to continue to serve depositors.

Compared with these two components, the fiscal costs of institutional changes, such as introducing external auditing, are naturally small. The major cost of such actions can be political, inasmuch as they affect powerful interest groups. Financial sector reforms of the type being discussed do not typically have important direct foreign exchange costs.[34]

The amount of counterpart funds generated by World Bank loans for financial reforms is not usually closely related to the fiscal costs of those reforms nor to the time profile of such costs. Depending on the size of the loan and the nature of the policy reforms, such loans may cover only a part of the fiscal costs (Chile, Ghana, Philippines) or more than the fiscal costs (Turkey). The loans will generally far exceed any direct foreign exchange costs of the reforms.

Inasmuch as balance of payments considerations have substantial weight in determining loan amounts, it seems that, by their nature, financial reforms do not provide a good yardstick for judging the appropriate size of policy-based loans. Should loans therefore be designed to establish a tighter link between disbursements and fiscal costs? For financial sector reforms, this would mean severely reducing the size of tranches linked to the reform of accounting and auditing practices; linking disbursements to market liberalization (but only to ease adjustment to a better fiscal system; there is little point in reducing taxes on financial transactions only to raise them in other distorting ways, such as on exports); and establishing a link between disbursement and the fiscal costs incurred in the process of financial restructuring.[35] This would have implications for the speed of disbursement and would require major changes in the type of loan. Major disbursements would be linked to the adjustment costs of fiscal reforms and of restructuring only, with small technical assistance components for reforming the financial infrastructure. It would perhaps be necessary to supplement this by an explicit balance of payments component, with its own appropriate conditionality.

The disbursement of financial intermediation loans, by contrast, depends on the speed of disbursement of the corresponding credit lines to final borrowers, even when such loans include policy reform as a condition.[36] As noted, the policy content of financial intermediation loans has typically been limited to the raising of subsidized interest rates. Raising these interest rates is often necessary so that lines of credit disbursed on terms acceptable to the World Bank will not be undercut by cheaper domestic lines. This introduces a link between policy reform and disbursement, but it is implicit rather than explicit.

It may not be realistic to expect the "real" economy to be reformed prior to undertaking the reform of a financial sector, but financial policy loans must be part of a viable package. They must be designed in the context of an adequate macroeconomic policy framework if they are not to misfire or result in a deferral of needed macroeconomic adjustment. Adherence to specified macroeconomic conditionality should be required for the disbursement of financial adjustment loans to ensure that the recipients of such large and quick-disbursing loans do not defer or slow the implementation of other measures needed to ensure lasting macroeconomic adjustment.

In cases where the financial infrastructure is deficient, is it realistic to expect rapid results from reforms? Banks may never have had to develop the credit processes appropriate for a market economy, and deep institutional reforms take time. How soon can we expect a change in the banking culture of a country? It takes at least five years to train a bank examiner. Legal reforms also take time, especially in countries with a division of executive and legislative powers. The experience of Chile and the Philippines shows how slow and difficult it can be to dissolve ownership links between banks and firms. In these circumstances, quick-disbursing policy-based operations may not be appropriate. A more effective approach might be to combine smaller technical assistance packages that disburse over periods of about five years with complementary larger, quick-disbursing loans provided at the time of financial restructuring.

In planning such policy reform operations, the adverse consequences for bank portfolios of adjustment measures to redirect flows of factors and goods (notably exchange rate adjustments and trade liberalization) are not sufficiently taken into account. They should be anticipated and measures taken to prepare for them. For example, bank regulation and supervision could be addressed at an early stage, rather than waiting until problems multiply.

Other questions need to be answered. Given the poor financial condition of banking systems in many countries (and the adverse implications for resource allocation that follow), should the volume of financial intermediation loans increase rapidly? Is there a danger of further weakening the system by piling still more debt onto undercapitalized borrowers? Given the poor history of directed credit, at least in terms of repayments, is debt the right instrument to foster development? Can equity or pseudo-equity contracts be used instead to strengthen capital structures? How would such a move be compatible with the lending policies of the World Bank?

What kind of financial system are we trying to achieve with restructuring? In particular, what role should development banks play in the more liberalized systems of the future? If these questions are not considered carefully, the restructured banks may face a long-run earnings problem that leads them quickly back to a distressed condition.[37]

Conclusion

The typical package for financial sector reform involves policy changes to increase the power of centralized decisionmaking in some areas and to reduce it in others. In the area of prudential regulation and supervision, reforms seek strengthened information systems, stronger and more detailed regulations, and closer central supervision. At the level of the intermediaries, reforms seek improved procedures, some of which (such as credit policies, loan review, and management information systems) are natural complements to improvements at the central level. In regard to the relative cost and availability of credit, the typical reform program calls for a reduction in government control and tries to broaden the range of options for finance.

The internal consistency of policy packages of this type follows from certain assumptions underlying the market-economy model, in particular the assumption that the qualities of goods and services will be reasonably apparent to participants in the market so they can formulate appropriate plans for production and spending. Liberalizing the financial market without also ensuring a correspondence between financial contracts and the values and productivity of the real assets underlying them does not help strengthen market mechanisms. It may even undermine them, as indicated by the experience of more than one country.

It is also possible, of course, for the reform pendulum to swing too far—and in several directions. If carried too far, prudential regulation can strangle financial innovation. A drive focused exclusively on privatization can cause much-needed public sector reforms to be neglected. In general, however, given the starting positions of the financial systems in most developing countries, financial reforms in the indicated directions are vital for strengthening the role of the market in allocating resources, both internally and internationally. They will also be needed if developing countries are to take advantage of the internationalization of finance that is currently under way.

How should financial sector operations evolve? Many needed financial reforms are institutional and infrastructural and require the acquisition of scarce skills. They take time to become effective, and it is not clear that a quick-disbursing policy-based operation is the best medium for effecting them. It might be better to formulate medium-term, lower-intensity operations for certain components of financial sector reform. Given the close links between financial policies and performance and the macroeconomic situation, the macroeconomy needs to be taken into account when planning reforms, especially when they have fiscal implications. The implications for the financial system of other reforms, such as reform of the trade regime, need to be considered at an earlier stage than they have been. Disbursement of financial reform loans could be tied in more closely to the costs of the reforms, which are primarily those related to restructuring and fiscal adjustment. And, as with other reforms, if financial reforms are not embraced intellectually by the government of the adjusting country, they will be adopted reluctantly and will surely fail.

Notes

1. For an assessment of the causes of bank failure in the United States, see U.S. Government (1988).

2. It is difficult to assign relative weights to internal and external causes of failures among financial institutions. Macroeconomic disturbances often hasten the demise of weak financial institutions and may be mistaken for the underlying causes. Conversely, an institution weakened by external shocks may be particularly prone to experience a deterioration in the quality of management (see De Juan 1987).

3. For a discussion of the consequences of widespread insolvency, see Hinds (1988).

4. There is some evidence that countries with repressed financial systems grow more slowly and that their output/capital ratios are low (see Gelb 1989).

5. Among the financial instruments that the World Bank has frequently sought to expand in developing countries are long-term loans. But how important is the provision of long-term loans? If they were vital, the long-term resources made available from World Bank funds, for example, could be expected to command much higher interest rates than do short-term loans. Top-grade borrowers feel reasonably confident of being able to roll over short-term bank loans and so are unwilling to pay much of a premium for long-term funds. It seems likely, instead, that unsatisfied demand for long-term loans has come mainly from less creditworthy clients. Willingness to pay a maturity premium thus could signal low creditworthiness, which could make a competitive banking system reluctant to make long-term loans to a broader spectrum of clients, even at a premium. The advantages to a bank of being able to review and recall loans at regular intervals should not be minimized. With early evidence of a borrower's deteriorating position, prompt action can possibly turn the position around, whereas the holder of a long-term claim may have no comparable sanction.

6. Corporations in developing countries often have higher debt/equity ratios than those in developed countries, apparently because of low retention of profits.

7. In the case of a structural adjustment loan to Chile, for example, a separate superintendency of banks already existed, but there was no formal deposit insurance system.

8. In some cases, debt-relief programs may also assist borrowers. In Chile loans were reprogrammed to reduce interest rates and extend terms, and preferential exchange rates were introduced after devaluation. Such debt-relief programs for borrowers may be introduced to avoid a massive sale of assets, which would further reduce their prices and add to the burden of bailing out the system.

9. Reducing entry barriers can strengthen a banking system when it has been dominated by industrial-financial groups that have relied too much on within-group lending, as in Chile, the Philippines, and Turkey. In 1980 the Philippines offered universal status to banks with sufficiently diversified ownership and encouraged the entry of foreign shareholding partners. The success of this measure can be debated; ownership of many Philippine banks remains dominated by

family groups, although the leavening of outside shareholders may have had beneficial effects. The procedures for the restructuring or liquidation of insolvent banks can be viewed as constituting a parallel reduction in the barriers to exit.

10. Some theorists have observed that partial liberalization of a formal banking system may even worsen the supply of credit to the productive sector to the extent that it diverts deposits from a curb market that was more efficient in channeling deposit resources to that sector. This argument seems to be based mainly on experience in Korea, where curb markets are extensive and, unlike formal sector banks, are not subject to reserve requirements. It is not evident that curb markets are generally more efficient than the formal banking system, which might give this point broader application; furthermore, the use of unregulated intermediaries increases the risks of crisis (see, for example, Sheng 1988).

11. This happened, for example, in the Philippines where, without any change in tax rates, the burden of the tax on gross receipts of financial institutions approximately tripled in 1984. The remuneration of large reserve requirements at low fixed rates has a similar impact as market rates increase.

12. In Ghana, for instance, banks were able to command a very high spread between borrowing and lending rates because of the interaction of credit ceilings and an inflow of funds from abroad.

13. In Turkey enactment of a Capital Market Law (in 1981) and establishment of a Capital Market Board (1982) were among the conditions of structural adjustment lending. Unfortunately, macroeconomic conditions did not favor the growth of the market, and its role in financing private investment remained minor.

14. In Chile, Jamaica, and Malaysia, for example, bank deposits have been exempt from the withholding tax that applies to securities. This discriminatory taxation discouraged the holding of corporate debt and the development of the capital market in general.

15. There is no consensus on the optimal structure of financial intermediation and its relationship with capital markets. Some developed countries, notably the Federal Republic of Germany and Japan, have done well with "bank-based" systems in which banks and business firms have close relationships; in others, the system is "market-based," with banks and firms more at arms-length. In some countries, banks are "universal"; in others, financial institutions are more specialized. How the various elements of a financial system perform is probably far more important than the precise configuration of the system.

16. Argentina and Turkey faced major macroeconomic imbalances during implementation of financial sector reforms. After floods and a disastrous earthquake in Ecuador during early 1987 the fiscal deficit expanded and inflation accelerated. Implementation of financial sector reform in such a sharply worsened environment was clearly going to be more difficult. The major problems with the experiments of the 1970s with financial liberalization in the Southern Cone countries may be attributed mainly to inappropriate macroeconomic policies (especially exchange rate policy), although inadequate prudential supervision and regulation were also to blame.

17. Some governments have even taken measures that exceeded the loan requirements, as in Argentina and Ecuador. But there have also been cases in which reforms have subsequently been partially reversed; the financial transactions tax in Turkey, for example, was initially reduced from 15 to 3 percent, but was subsequently increased. Furthermore, continuing high budgetary deficits in Turkey have kept real interest rates high and inhibited recovery of the financial sector despite the sectoral adjustment measures. For a discussion of the consequences, see Atiyas (1989).

18. It could be argued that the emergence of this problem in Turkey in the early 1980s could have been anticipated far earlier in the structural adjustment program. Perhaps more should have been done to improve auditing and bank supervision so that the problem could at least have been monitored. By the time actions of this type were introduced in financial sector loans, the damage to the banks' portfolios was already serious.

19. For example, fixed rates on rural lending in Brazil resulted in large losses on official credit lines as inflation soared following the breakdown of the cruzado.

20. In Chile, for example, liberalizing the capital account of the balance of payments in an environment of market-determined interest rates resulted in a surge in the external value of the currency, overborrowing, and the puncturing of the speculative boom in real assets.

21. The problem is particularly acute in the case of housing loans. In Hungary, for example, a very high proportion of the portfolio of the financial system is in the form of long-term fixed-interest housing loans, which are now well below market levels.

22. There are two separate issues here: first, whether real interest rates "overshoot" or rise to unduly high levels following liberalization, and second, whether the higher interest rates actually depress economic activity and worsen inflation.

23. McKinnon (1988) compares financial sector reforms in Chile with those in other countries, notably in Asia.

24. This point has been much discussed in the context of the celebrated Dewey Dee affair in the Philippines, in which investors' confidence was badly jolted when a prominent financier suddenly absconded, leaving large money market debts behind him. It is to fill this perceived gap in the financial system that many see the proper role of DFIS, not only in the Philippines but in many other countries as well, notably in Sub-Saharan Africa. If the gap is an imaginary one, then both the role and the viability of DFIS are placed in question.

25. Perhaps the greatest degree of independence is provided by adherence to a multicountry currency zone, such as the CFA zone in Africa, where the central banks, being international institutions, are not answerable to any one government.

26. This is true for all policy reforms; spurred on by massive insolvency, some financial reforms have been more easily accomplished than, for example, tariff reforms.

27. For an interesting analysis of the impact of collateral on credit allocation and hence of efficiency, see Feder and others (1988).

28. Further examination of the Chilean case suggests that financial sector reform can have the beneficent effects suggested above if the macroeconomic situation is kept under control. Real interest rates and bank spreads have moderated and the real volume of deposits and bank credit has grown since the reforms, all of which support the rapid growth of output.

29. This study identifies a causal chain from higher interest rates, through greater mobilization of savings by the financial system, to increased efficiency of investment, and thereby to growth. Analyses also suggest that high interest rates on deposits encourage additional saving in developing countries (notably in Asia), but that the effect is very small. There are also a number of clear-cut examples of the effect of real interest rate increases on monetization; often this seems to have been attributable to a reflow of funds previously held outside the country.

30. Korea is sometimes mentioned as a country that experienced rapid growth even though a selective credit policy was in operation. But rapid growth in the

uncontrolled financial curb market substantially offset the impact of this policy on the overall distribution of credit there. A more conventional story is that of Indonesia, which introduced a system of administrative allocation of credit in 1974 (and abandoned it in 1983). Despite the higher rate of investment in Indonesia after 1974, the growth rate of output actually declined, which suggests that investment had not been especially well directed.

31. For a discussion of counterpart funds and the relationship with monetary policy, see Roemer (1988).

32. This has been a notable factor in the case of Turkey. In the Philippines, by contrast, the higher interest rates of 1984 probably contributed to government revenue.

33. Of course, in the absence of restructuring, a government would also incur costs (as well as the buildup of claims due to weakening institutions) because subsidies would be needed to maintain the liquidity of insolvent intermediaries.

34. It might be argued, however, that if depositors were to suffer losses they would reduce their spending on imports as well as on domestic output. If so, recapitalization of the banking system, which protects deposits, could have indirect foreign exchange costs.

35. The second financial sector adjustment loan to Turkey contained a component specifically for restructuring, which linked disbursements with the cost of system reform.

36. The terms of World Bank loans are typically far longer than the terms of the loans offered to final users of funds, and there may be no requirement that domestic repayments be relent again up to the term of the bank loan. In such cases, the World Bank loan initially funds the private sector, but later it funds the government.

37. This issue is now being faced by at least one large institution restructured according to a World Bank program.

References

Atiyas, Izak. 1989. "The Private Sector's Response to Financial Liberalization in Turkey: 1980–82." PPR Working Paper 147. Policy, Planning, and Research, World Bank, Washington, D.C.

Cho, Yoon Je. 1986. "Inefficiencies from Financial Liberalization in the Absence of Well-Functioning Equity Markets." *Journal of Money, Credit and Banking* 18 (2) May:191–94.

De Juan, A. 1987. "From Good Bankers to Bad Bankers: Ineffective Supervision and Management Deterioration as Major Elements in Banking Crises." Financial Policy Division, Country Economics Department, World Bank, Washington, D.C.

Diaz Alejandro, Carlos F. 1985. "Good-Bye Financial Repression, Hello Financial Crash." *Journal of Development Economics* 19 (September-October):1–24.

Dooley, M. P., and Mathieson D. J. 1987. "Financial Liberalization and Stability in Developing Countries." WP/87/19. International Monetary Fund, Washington, D.C.

Feder, Gershon, Tongroj Onchan, Yongyuth Chalamwong, and Chira Hongladarom. 1988. *Land Policies and Farm Productivity in Thailand.* Baltimore, Md.: Johns Hopkins University Press.

Fry, Maxwell J. 1988. *Money, Interest, and Banking in Economic Development.* Baltimore, Md.: Johns Hopkins University Press.

Gelb, Alan. 1989. "Financial Reforms and Economic Performance." Financial Policy Division, Country Economics Department, World Bank, Washington, D.C.

Gonzales Arrieta, C. M. 1988. "Interest Rates, Savings, and Growth in LDCS: An Assessment of Recent Empirical Research." *World Development* 16 (5):589–605.

Hinds, Manuel E. 1988. "Economic Effects of Financial Crisis." PPR Working Paper 104. Policy, Planning, and Research, World Bank, Washington, D.C.

IMF. 1983. *Interest Rate Policies in Developing Economies.* Occasional Paper 22. Washington, D.C.: International Monetary Fund.

McKinnon, R. I. 1988. *Financial Liberalization and Economic Development: A Reassessment of Interest Rate Policies in Asia and Latin America.* International Centre for Economic Growth Occasional Paper. San Francisco, Calif.

Roemer, Michael. 1988. *The Macroeconomics of Counterpart Funds.* Discussion Paper 262. Cambridge, Mass.: Harvard University, Institute for International Development.

Sheng, Andrew. 1988. "Financial Adjustment in a Period of Disinflation: The Case of Malaysia." Financial Policy Division, Country Economics Department, World Bank, Washington, D.C.

U.S. Government, Office of Comptroller of the Currency. 1988. *Bank Failure: An Evaluation of the Factors Contributing to the Failure of National Banks.* Washington, D.C.

World Bank. 1985. "Financial Intermediation Policy Paper." Industry Department, World Bank, Washington, D.C.

Comments

Maxwell J. Fry

ALAN GELB and Patrick Honohan provide a concise summary of the components of World Bank adjustment programs that address the reform of financial sectors in developing countries. The basic principles they propound appear entirely reasonable. The authors recognize, however, that precise measurement of the effects of such reforms is impossible; financial reforms invariably come as part of a larger package of policy measures. Furthermore, World Bank loans specifically for financial sector adjustment are in their infancy. In my view, the main danger is expecting too much, too soon.

If, as Gelb and Honohan state (and I concur; Fry 1988), the three main problems that plague the financial sectors of developing countries are massive insolvency, excessive controls on interest rates, and domination by commercial banks, a question immediately arises concerning the appropriateness of using short-term adjustment lending to solve them. Although excessive interest rate controls can be removed rapidly, the problems of insolvency and domination by commercial banks require more time. Even in the case of interest rate reform, however, there is now ample evidence that the deregulation of interest rates can produce perverse effects in the absence of at least a modicum of macroeconomic stability, adequate prudential supervision of the financial system, and a reasonable degree of competition.

If the financial sector is important in the development process, a short-run adjustment plan is not sufficient to ensure its health; a program for long-run financial development is clearly needed as well. By itself, a short-term adjustment program may remove excessive interest rate controls and may shore up some insolvent financial institutions, but it cannot tackle the underlying problems of insolvency and commercial bank domination. Nor can it relieve what is perhaps the most severe constraint on the financial sector of many developing countries: the lack of adequate accounting and audit skills, both for prudential supervision and for internal management. To tackle these problems, a much longer time frame is needed.

Gelb and Honohan point out that insolvency and excessive control of interest rates and the direction of credit are linked. It also appears from the experience of some Latin American countries that insolvency and a laissez-faire policy are linked. The paradox is resolved, as both Long (1983) and the present authors recognize, by understanding that more rather than less prudential supervision is a prerequisite for successful financial liberalization. Veneroso (1986) concluded that all cases of extraordinarily high real interest rates were caused by distress borrowing in conjunction with deposit insurance. The lack of adequate regulation of banking practices led to undue risk taking on the part of the banks, while deposit insurance enabled them to acquire risky assets without provoking the withdrawal of deposits. When the level of nonperforming assets rose, banks raised deposit rates to attract more funds to pay the interest on existing deposits. This false demand for credit by distress borrowers put upward pressure on interest rates, which in turn dragged down more firms.

Although there is no evidence that banking is necessarily more costly in developing countries than in countries of the Organisation for Economic Co-operation and Development (OECD) (Hanson and Rocha 1986), spreads tend to be substantially wider nonetheless. Other things being equal, one would expect to find no significant difference in the spreads between average deposit and loan rates in the two groups of countries. Other things, however, are not equal. Specifically, developing country banking systems are less competitive, are more heavily taxed, and suffer higher rates of loss than banks in OECD countries. In Uruguay, for example, because of the oligopolistic structure of the banking system, the spread between average deposit and loan rates remained more than 15 percentage points until June 1981, despite reduced required reserve ratios (Hanson and de Melo 1985).

Hanson and Rocha (1986) also find high operating costs for banks in developing countries with high inflation rates and little or no competition. Financial repression, which is intensified as inflation rises, raises banks' cost ratios by reducing the real size of the banking system and at the same time encouraging nonprice competition, such as the proliferation of bank branches. Implementing selective credit policies also involves substantial administrative costs for the banks (Morris 1985).

Almost all developing countries possess specialized financial institutions in the form of development finance institutions (DFIs) or development banks. A major problem inherent in virtually all specialized financial institutions in developing countries springs from the fact that they are established to lend to borrowers that existing financial institutions—the commercial banks—have avoided. By and large, commercial banks choose not to lend when the perceived risks are too high, so specialized financial institutions have been set up deliberately to lend to high-risk borrowers. They are not, however, compensated with higher loan rates for assuming higher risks. Invariably, therefore, the specialized financial institution set up to support a problem sector of the economy itself becomes a problem institution.

Very few DFIs have become self-supporting, autonomous financial institutions capable of mobilizing resources entirely on commercial terms. First, DFIs have often been required to make loans at low rates of interest, frequently negative in real terms. Second, DFIs have financed projects that have been evaluated as economically viable (often by the World Bank) but which are not financially viable. About one-third of the DFIs in developing countries are now in serious financial difficulties, mainly because of their large percentage of nonperforming loans. The problem of arrears increased substantially with the worldwide recession and deteriorating terms of trade for developing countries in the early 1980s (World Bank 1985).

Uncompetitive financial markets have been another side effect of governments' selective credit policies. In many developing countries, specialized financial institutions have been established as a result of government decrees, with exclusive franchises for particular financial activities or particular sectors of the economy. Not only has specialization produced in this manner generally raised intermediation costs and destroyed any actual or potential competition, it has also failed to achieve the goal of an adequate and efficient distribution of credit. All too often, specialized banks have expropriated scarce resources to finance large and inefficient investments, while small investment projects have been starved of funds. In most developing countries, less specialization and compartmentalization are prerequisites for an efficient and aggressive financial sector.

Initially, the World Bank lent to specialized financial institutions through its financial intermediation loans to DFIS. Since 1975, however, when it decided to increase its lending to small and medium-size enterprises, the World Bank has found commercial banks to be more effective than DFIS in channeling funds to wider groups of enterprises (Levitsky 1986). Specifically, these programs have worked best when all financial institutions have had access to World Bank funds through a rediscount mechanism with an apex institution rather than when funds have been earmarked for specific lending institutions.

Now Gelb and Honohan conclude that the dubiousness of many banking systems raises questions about the allocation of resources intermediated by the commercial banks as well. Despite a voluminous body of literature (much of it produced in the World Bank) criticizing directed credit programs, the World Bank continued its selective credit policy in lending to small and medium-size enterprises. These resources might better have been used to improve commercial bank lending in general rather than to compound the problem of dubious loans in commercial bank portfolios.

The World Bank's policy stance on financial sector issues has changed dramatically over the past two decades. World Bank reports on the financial sectors of developing countries in the late 1970s and early 1980s tended to focus on macroeconomic and sectoral issues. At the institutional level, the reports favored deregulation and sometimes advocated the adoption of universal banking.[1]

During the 1980s the World Bank shifted its emphasis from institution building, often within a nationalized framework, toward greater reliance on market forces within a systemwide approach to finance. Since 1978 the World Bank has commissioned many comparative studies of financial systems in developing countries with the objective of developing broader-based lending programs. Toward the end of the 1970s and during the 1980s, therefore, the World Bank began to replace project loans with apex and structural adjustment loans aimed at development of the financial sector.

The first wave of World Bank financial sector reports of the late 1970s and early 1980s stressed macroeconomic and sectoral issues. These issues included price stability, abolition of interest rate ceilings, and rationalization or elimination of directed credit programs and discriminatory taxation of financial intermediation, whether directly through taxes on transactions and on loan and deposit rates or indirectly through reserve requirements, forced investments in low-yielding government bonds, and minimum requirements for providing subsidized credit to priority (high-risk) sectors (see Hanson and Neal 1985). Reports gave only very brief attention to the institutional aspects of the financial sectors being analyzed. Although these early reports often stated that bank regulations and supervision needed improvement, that was about as far as the recommendations went.

After the disastrous results of the experiments with financial liberalization in Latin America and the increasing financial fragility worldwide, the second wave of World Bank financial sector reports from about 1983 on has devoted much more attention to microeconomic, institutional, and regulatory issues. There is also more recognition of macroeconomic stability, particularly fiscal responsibility, as a prerequisite for successful financial development (Hanson and Neal 1985). However, there has been virtually no discussion of the second-best dilemma that arises when controls in some areas, such as interest rate ceilings, are dismantled but controls in other areas, such as limitations on asset portfolios, are strengthened. Indeed, Chile may have been following the only set of policies with any theoretical underpinnings when it abolished virtually all controls over every financial activity. Unfortunately, the Chilean government was unable to persuade the private sector that its hands-off policy also implied no bailouts, and credibility in this regard was destroyed when the government stepped in to rescue a failing bank as early as 1977 (Diaz Alejandro 1985).

Recent experience with financial reform and liberalization indicates just how important market structure and regulation are in determining the outcome of such programs. In particular, cartelized or highly concentrated banking systems have not responded as anticipated to the abolition of interest rate ceilings. Bank associations simply assume responsibility for establishing appropriate interest rates for their members when governments relinquish this function. Financially repressed markets tend to be cartelized or highly oligopolistic in the first place.

In summing up the experience with liberalization policies in the Southern Cone countries of South America, Blejer (1983) concluded that many domestic markets, but particularly the financial markets, given their size, organization, and high degree of segmentation, reacted in an oligopolistic manner to the opening of the economy. Since not all financial agents had the same access to international borrowing, borrowers without direct access to international markets had to obtain credit from domestic financial intermediaries that could borrow abroad. Under these conditions, the domestic interest rate is determined not solely by the foreign interest rate, the expected rate of change in the exchange rate, and any risk premium, but also by domestic market conditions, including the domestic demand for and supply of credit, the structure of the domestic financial system, and the state of inflationary expectations.

The only part of Gelb and Honohan's chapter with which I disagree is its apparent belief that capital markets can be developed under adjustment lending programs. Although an effective capital market may indeed result in greater mobilization of resources and more productive investment, the World Bank has yet to demonstrate that it has the key to developing such a market.

Not only is the developing world littered with insolvent DFIs, it has all too few successful capital markets: markets in which interest rates are freely determined by the interaction of supply and demand are few and far between. To establish such markets, a logical progression in financial development programs is crucial. The monetary authority can support the market determination of interest rates in a few easy stages. It is important to start the process by introducing short-term financial assets with no risk other than a small amount of interest risk. Prices must be determined in the market through the free interplay of demand and supply. A good place to start is with the establishment of a treasury bill market, a market for central bank negotiable certificates of deposit, and interbank money markets. Only after experience has been gained in these simple, low-risk, open markets does it make some sense to turn to the development of equity markets.

It strikes me that the World Bank, in its early and ongoing concern with equity markets in developing countries, has been guilty at times of encouraging financial sectors to run before they can walk. Surely, equity markets require the most diligent prudential supervision of all. Possibly the greatest challenge is to identify what can be done in the absence of adequate accounting and auditing skills. Given the enormous cost of hiring multinational accounting firms to audit financial institutions on a case-by-case basis, more concern with the training of counterparts seems vital.[2]

Efforts to reform financial sectors have focused mainly on liabilities. More attention needs to be given to increasing assets. The repatriation of funds needs to be encouraged; policies are also needed that will help keep money at home. Innovative methods are needed to improve the health of financial institutions. Perhaps some version of debt/equity swaps can be brought down to the local level. Financial adjustment loans might best be used to help developing country governments remove the most deleterious of the discriminatory taxes that have resulted in negative effective protection of financial intermediation (see Fry 1989). Although Gelb and Honohan point out that a reduction in financial sector taxation is often a priority in financial reform, they say little more about this subject. The World Bank is now providing fiscal support for such reforms in its new financial sector adjustment lending program. Perhaps recent World Bank initiatives in this direction will be more successful than some past efforts.

Notes

1. For example, a report prepared jointly by the International Monetary Fund and the World Bank recommends universal banking for the Philippines (World Bank 1980).
2. In an earlier search for a temporary remedy to this problem, I suggested that the Belgian external audit system warranted serious consideration.

References

Blejer, M. I. 1983. "Liberalization and Stabilization Policies in the Southern Cone Countries: An Introduction." *Journal of Interamerican Studies and World Affairs* 25 (4) November:431–44.

Diaz Alejandro, Carlos F. 1985. "Good-Bye Financial Repression, Hello Financial Crash." *Journal of Development Economics* 19 (September-October):1–24.

Fry, Maxwell J. 1988. *Money, Interest, and Banking in Economic Development.* Baltimore, Md.: Johns Hopkins University Press.

———. 1989. "Managing Deficit Finance." Economic Development Institute, World Bank, Washington, D.C.

Hanson, James A., and Jaime de Melo. 1985. "External Shocks, Financial Reforms, and Stabilization Attempts in Uruguay during 1974–83." *World Development* 13 (8) August:917–39.

Hanson, James A., and Craig R. Neal. 1985. *Interest Rate Policies in Selected Developing Countries, 1970–1982.* World Bank Staff Working Paper 753. Washington, D.C.

Hanson, James A., and Roberto de Rezende Rocha. 1986. "High Interest Rates, Spreads, and the Costs of Intermediation: Two Studies." Industry and Finance Paper 18. World Bank, Washington, D.C.

Levitsky, Jacob. 1986. "World Bank Lending to Small Enterprises: A Review." Industry and Finance Paper 16. World Bank, Washington, D.C.

Long, Millard. 1983. "Review of Financial Sector Work." Industry Department, Financial Development Unit, World Bank, Washington, D.C.

Morris, Felipe. 1985. *India's Financial System: An Overview of Its Principal Structural Features.* World Bank Staff Working Paper 739. Washington, D.C.

Veneroso, Frank. 1986. "New Patterns of Financial Instability." Industry Department, World Bank, Washington, D.C.

World Bank. 1980. "The Philippines: Aspects of the Financial Sector." Washington, D.C.

———. 1985. "Financial Intermediation Policy Paper." Industry Department, World Bank, Washington, D.C.

6 *Reform of Public Enterprises*

John R. Nellis

THE PERFORMANCE of public enterprises in developing countries has not generally lived up to the expectations of their creators or funders. Public enterprises have not generated the anticipated rates of return on equity invested. Nor, all too often, have they attained their noncommercial objectives—with regard to employment generation, technology transfers, or regional development, for example. Nor, frequently, has performance reached the anticipated levels of economic productivity and efficiency. Performance varies considerably from region to region, with public enterprises in Asian countries showing fewer problems than those in Latin America, which, in turn, generally perform better than enterprises in Sub-Saharan Africa. Every country possesses a number of profitable enterprises (although many are exploiting a protected or monopoly position), and some of these enterprises are sound even when measured by the strictest economic criteria. But there are still too many money-losing, inefficient public enterprises in developing countries.

In the case of individual enterprises, the details of poor performance have been known for some time. Numerous attempts have been made to resolve problems, frequently in conjunction with World Bank project lending. Despite perceptible improvements in many firms in technology, training, and managerial procedures, however, performance levels—measured by the traditional criteria of profitability, or rate of return on investment, and self-financing ratios—have all too often stagnated or worsened.

Reviews of project lending for public enterprise reform have concluded that many of the factors contributing to poor performance were external to the firm and so outside the control of management: deficient macroeconomic policy, uneconomic pricing regimes, lack of clearly defined objectives for individual enterprises or subsectors of enterprises, conflicts and shortcomings in the legal and regulatory framework, too easy access to the banking and credit system, weak financial structures, ineffective or interfering monitoring systems, and chaotic budgetary relations. Given these common circumstances, even dynamic and competent management, working with high-quality equipment, may be incapable of generating reasonable returns.[1] Conversely, good financial returns are sometimes a function of distortions and are not due to the efforts of management.[2] These realizations constituted the fundamental justification for the inclusion of public enterprise sectors in adjustment operations. Since piecemeal and particularistic reforms had proven to be insufficient, the logical alternative was to attempt systemic revision of policy and procedures.

Reforms Attempted through Adjustment Programs

The first World Bank–sponsored attempt to reform public enterprises in a systemic, cross-sectoral manner was the Senegal parapublic project, which became effective in 1978, three years before the first Senegal structural adjustment loan (SAL). Between 1982 and 1984 a few other World Bank–assisted reforms of public enterprises took the form of loans to fund technical assistance outside the framework of a structural or sectoral adjustment operation. These programs were in the Republic of Congo, Madagascar, Mali, Mauritania, and Peru. All other cases have been an integral part of, or closely associated with, adjustment lending. As of March 1988, the number of adjustment-related operations totaled 101—51 in SALs and 50 in sectoral adjustment loans (SECALs).[3] Public enterprise reforms have been an element of almost every adjustment operation, structural or sectoral.

In keeping with perceived deficiencies in performance, there have been many more actions in Sub-Saharan Africa than elsewhere: through 1988, twenty-six SALs in seventeen different countries. All twenty-six had public enterprise components.

The situation for SECALs is more complicated. Those specifically and uniquely devoted to public enterprise reform have been approved in seven countries: Benin, Jamaica, Mauritania, Morocco, Niger, the Philippines, and Tunisia. Similar projects, commonly referred to as PERLs (public enterprise restructuring loans), are in preparation in at least six more countries. But public enterprise reforms—of policy, pricing, relations between the state and the public enterprises, staffing, training, and the financial and managerial structure of individual firms—have also figured in a large percentage of the other forty-four SECALs approved between 1980 and March 1988. In many of these loans, especially those to the agricultural and industrial sectors, the public enterprise components have been prominent.

The reform packages have some basic similarities.[4] Cross-sectoral improvement activities have fallen under three general headings: (1) reforms of the macroeconomic policy and financial frameworks affecting public enterprise performance; (2) reforms of the institutional framework (the ways in which the government guides, supervises, and evaluates public enterprises); and (3) issues of divestiture.

In addition, more than half of all public enterprise components of adjustment loans have contained elements aimed at the restructuring and improvement of specific enterprises. By bringing some of the most important and sensitive reforms of individual enterprises into a large and visible adjustment operation, it was hoped to increase the likelihood that painful reforms—such as staff reductions, financial restructurings, plant closures, and price increases—would actually be implemented. Including enterprise-level reforms as conditions of an adjustment operation appeals to World Bank project officers and frustrated government staff alike, but the practice does add to the number and complexity of conditions. Improvements in specific enterprises have figured in more than forty operations; in many of the more recent and important ones the resources devoted to rehabilitating enterprises have been equal to or greater than the funds spent on cross-sectoral reforms.

Reform of the Policy Framework

An adjustment operation, especially one with a public enterprise component, inevitably raises questions of the proper role, or the redefinition of the role, of the state. Most public enterprise–related adjustment programs, and all those approved after 1984, propose some actions—often backed up by conditionality—related to this broad policy issue. Actions have included (1) analyzing and clarifying which economic activities are appropriate for state involvement; (2) classifying enterprises on the basis of whether they should be retained, restructured, sold, or closed; and (3) identifying specific enterprises to be sold or closed, subsectors in which privatization will take place, and measures to facilitate or support the sale of enterprises. Countries with reform programs range from those which are still undertaking studies and policy reform preparatory to divestiture (Morocco and Turkey, for example) to those which have moved into the action stage of sale and liquidation (Guinea, Jamaica, Niger, Panama, and Togo, for example).

A modest number of adjustment operations have addressed the elimination of monopolies and monopsonies in public enterprises. This has been the subject of conditionality in ten SALs and six SECALs. More rare have been attempts to place public and private enterprises on an equal regulatory footing, although the Niger SAL abolished tax exemptions for public enterprises. Trade liberalization measures are much more commonly advocated; they are present in about half the SALs with public enterprise components and are either directed toward or have an effect on industrial and manufacturing public enterprises. Another general policy area is that of legal and legislative reform, which has figured in the public enterprise adjustment operations in Turkey and throughout francophone Africa. The main tasks are to clarify the juridical framework, decrease the number of legal types of enterprises, change decrees to eliminate or lighten control procedures and increase managerial autonomy, create the legal texts necessary to implement privatization, and rationalize the usually cluttered scene with regard to supervisory agencies.

Public enterprise components of adjustment operations in Benin, Ghana, Madagascar, Morocco, Panama, Senegal, and Turkey and in most other countries have set pricing formulas that, in most instances, are aimed at rationalizing the way prices are set and periodically adjusted. In six francophone countries pricing issues have been addressed through support of contract plans that specify the mutual obligations and rights of the owner—the state—and the enterprise for a three- to five-year period and usually specify pricing arrangements for the firm.[5] Loan conditionalities often call for studies on procedures of price setting in the natural monopoly, service-providing public enterprises; on methods and timing for price adjustments; and on mechanisms to improve billing and collection procedures.

Labor policies have featured prominently in the public enterprise components of adjustment operations. Excess staffing is a common problem in public enterprises. Substantial layoffs can cut costs considerably, and the resulting savings in the wage bill can provide resources to motivate the remaining work force. Reductions in staff and changes in employment rules are conditions in twelve SALs and in a larger number of SECALs. Most countries have approached work force reductions with caution, however, because of concern about the welfare of affected employees and the fear of provoking labor unrest or organized political resistance. In response to these legitimate concerns, several recent reform programs—in Benin, Congo, Ghana, and Mali (and several in preparation)—have created training and redeployment funds or supported forms of severance pay.

Reforms in financial policy have also become prominent in public enterprise components of adjustment operations. Many governments have tried to reduce the burden of public enterprises on their budgets by simply declaring an end to direct subventions from the state. In many cases the public enterprises then had to resort to the national and international credit systems, which, in turn, began to suffer from holding the nonperforming debts of those enterprises. Congo and Senegal have attempted to analyze this situation, to propose reforms, and to improve the analyses by domestic banks or reviewing ministries of investment proposals by public enterprises; similar steps are under consideration in most proposed public enterprise reform operations in Africa. Strengthening the scrutiny of public enterprise expenditure and borrowing, increasing interest rates on loans to public enterprises to market levels (or at least to the rates paid by the domestic private sector), and reducing automatic access to credit are reform measures in at least fifteen SALs and as many sector operations in all four regions of the developing world.

Another major financial problem is that of cross-debts and arrears. Settlement of arrears, and the installation of mechanisms to prevent their recurrence, is the key issue in the Moroccan PERL. An emphasis on clarification, settlement, and prevention of future cross-debts between public enterprises and government and among public enterprises themselves is a cornerstone of most adjustment loans and credits in Sub-Saharan Africa; examples can be seen in Congo, Ghana, and Niger. A related issue is the strengthening of the budgeting forecast and allocation system to allow governments to rationally assess and meet their financial commitments to public enterprises; this is a continuing theme of adjustment reform in Senegal and elsewhere—again particularly in Africa.

Reform of the Institutional Framework and Rehabilitation of Enterprises

Relations between the public enterprises and the state have received a great deal of attention in every PERL and in most SALs as well. A large number of SECALs have also addressed this issue. This general theme has been disaggregated into many parts.

More than twenty-five public enterprise operations have dealt with the creation or improvement of control and guidance agencies in the central managing organization (the president's or prime minister's office, the ministry of finance or of planning, or the central bank); in the technical ministries, particularly industry and agriculture; or in holding companies. Although several African countries have created ministries of state enterprises during the period of World Bank–assisted reform, this has not been at the request of the Bank or a requirement of the adjustment loan except in the case of Togo. Indeed, the World Bank has generally opposed the creation of specific ministries of this nature on the grounds that, in the ministerial competition for resources, these entities become uncritical defenders of public enterprises rather than stimulators and evaluators of their performance. Training programs for government supervisors and evaluators of public enterprise operations, in both the technical and central ministries, are often included in public enterprise operations.

Closely related is the creation or strengthening of information and monitoring systems to provide the data on public enterprises needed to guide and evaluate their performance. This is done both at the level of the firm, to improve internal management, and at the subsectoral or national level, to provide essential information for holding companies or ministerial reviewers. Many of the more than twenty-five operations that attempt to deal with this issue are also working to improve state guidance and control agencies.

A common reform is to enhance the power and autonomy of the boards of directors. Efforts focus partly on enlarging a board's legal powers and responsibilities and partly on changing its composition from a majority of civil servants to a majority of independent individuals, preferably representatives of the private sector, creditor agencies, user groups, chief suppliers, technical experts, and other interested groups.

One very important issue has been addressed more through studies than through direct action. Performance evaluation that is based on a comparison of results with the initial objectives is often mentioned and is consistently regarded as desirable. But performance evaluation of this type requires that information systems and competent monitors be largely in place. Thus, activities in this field have been mainly of a preparatory nature, except in Gambia, Ghana, Korea (where an innovative performance evaluation system was supported in the single adjustment operation), and in seven francophone countries where performance contracts have been or are being installed.

Rehabilitation of individual public enterprises has been equally multifaceted. A more or less standard package of diagnosis and prescription has emerged that can be applied in all developing regions. Diagnostic studies of the problems of a key enterprise, group of enterprises, or the sector as a whole have been attempted in more than fifteen operations. Management and financial audits frequently follow the diagnostic studies (in a slightly smaller number of operations), followed in turn by recovery plans or rehabilitation programs. (These actions have been called for directly in the adjustment operations, or they have been included in accompanying technical assistance loans.) A common theme among countries and regions is the weakness of accounting practices within firms; adjustment operations or the projects that parallel them propose training or technical assistance in many instances. In francophone countries, and increasingly in anglophone Africa and Latin America, contract plans, or performance agreements, are being initiated and installed in public enterprises working in largely noncompetitive markets. Training for the personnel of firms has been featured in sixteen adjustment operations and is a prominent part of most of the public enterprise restructuring loans in preparation. Finally, capital support and restructuring has been advanced in only five operations, four in Sub-Saharan Africa and one in Turkey.

Divestiture

Divestiture refers to the full range of mechanisms by which the state reduces its direct involvement in the economy: the full or partial sale or transfer of ownership, the sale of assets, leasing arrangements, contracting out, and liquidation (in its various forms). Close to forty adjustment operations have contained divestiture elements, which in most cases concentrate on the full or partial sale of ownership. The sale of a specifically named enterprise or set of enterprises has been clearly set out in loan or credit conditions in only five adjustment cases: Ghana, Guinea, Jamaica, Panama, and Senegal. The closure and liquidation of specific public enterprises has been a subject for conditionality in seven countries, six of them in Sub-Saharan Africa: Benin, Burundi, Central African Republic, Guinea, Niger, Panama, and Senegal.

A more common conditionality for divestiture is that governments prepare, and discuss with the World Bank, studies or action plans on the classification of enterprises and the future of problem enterprises. The best course of action is frequently a matter of dispute, with the World Bank generally favoring divestiture and the government favoring restructuring. Adjustment operation conditions often require investigation of or progress on privatization, but not the sale of a particular enterprise. Recurring phrases state that the government "will initiate a divestiture program"; "will agree with the International Development Association on a strategy for rationalization and disengagement of the state enterprise sector"; "will implement a divestiture program"; "will accelerate its program on divestiture"; and that the government's progress on divestiture "will be satisfactory to the Bank." Such phrases—almost always in the future or conditional tense—are common, occurring in the documents for at least twenty-five adjustment operations, roughly half of them in Sub-Saharan Africa. The intention, of course, is that the future tense will change to the present as the scheduled divestitures occur. (There are several sound financial and economic reasons for this vagueness, which are discussed below.) Hard conditionality on divestiture is concentrated in the smaller and poorer countries of Africa.

Other divestiture actions have been scattered; they include leasing arrangements (prominent in Togo) and management contracts (common in hotel sectors). There has been relatively little experimentation in adjustment operations with such changes as the contracting out to private suppliers of services performed by public enterprises, although such steps are often suggested in consultants' reports prepared in the early stages.

Assessment of Results

Public enterprise aspects of adjustment lending pose at least two problems for the evaluator. First, many of the objectives of these reforms, particularly those in the institutional realm, are qualitative and not easily subject to precise measurement. Second, even in cases in which the desired outcome can be precisely stated, several years of effort and implementation will be required before any assessment of achievement can be meaningful. There are also elements that are both qualitative in nature *and* long term. With regard to the qualitative objectives, one is thrown back on impressionistic assessments of whether progress has been satisfactory. Although these judgments can be of some benefit, they are obviously less than ideal. The problem of assessing the long-term objectives is equally intractable; not many of the public enterprise–related adjustment operations have been in place long enough to permit a judgment concerning which targets have been hit and which missed.

Therefore, in this chapter, an attempt is made to assess the experience of nine countries that meet the following criteria: (1) public enterprise reforms have figured prominently in adjustment operations, (2) the reforms have been in place long enough to produce at least some discussable (if not always measurable) results, and (3) the results have been reviewed by World Bank staff. These countries are Côte d'Ivoire, Ghana, Jamaica, Morocco, Niger, Panama, Senegal, Togo, and Turkey. This list also is representative of public enterprise–related adjustment operations: just over half the countries are in Sub-Saharan Africa, and most are small countries.

Types of Reform Attempted

The type and frequency of public enterprise reforms attempted in the thirty-one adjustment operations in the nine countries are presented in table 6-1. The figures require some interpretation. With regard to divestiture, the twenty-nine operations do not equate to twenty-nine different programs. Privatization actions started by the first adjustment loan in Togo, for example, were pursued and deepened by later loans, and the same is the case for Jamaica, Niger, and Senegal, all of which have had at least two adjustment operations. These countries needed subsequent adjustment operations to reinforce initial efforts, to actually launch a divestiture after initial preparation, or—commonly because of an overambitious original timetable—to provide additional time to prepare and complete the arrangements. This said, it is still true that divestiture reforms were far and away the most common efforts in these thirty-one operations.[6] They were followed, in roughly equal measure, by pricing reforms, institutional strengthening, and rehabilitation of specific enterprises.

Table 6-1 lists the same wide range of reform activities reviewed earlier in this chapter. But whereas the overall review indicated that the emphasis was more often on preparation for divestiture than on actual sales or closures, in the smaller sample the opposite is clearly the case: implementation actions are almost three times more numerous than preparatory activities. Moreover, the conditionality called for in the divestitures in the sample tends to be precise and action oriented, in particular in Jamaica, Niger, Panama, and Togo. In addition, many of the public enterprise reforms initiated in this particular group of countries tend to be concrete, measurable, and monitorable. Enterprises are either sold or

Table 6-1. Type and Frequency of Public Enterprise Reforms in Adjustment Operations in Nine Sample Countries

Reform	*Number of operations in which reform is stressed*
Divestiture	
Implement full or partial sale, lease, or liquidate	21
Examine cases, classify, set policy, prepare	8
Pricing	15
Institutional framework	15
Rehabilitation and restructuring in specific firms	15
Reduction in work force	12
Financial audits of troubled firms	11
Preparation of policy statements	10
Settlement of cross-debts and arrears	9
Contract plans	7
Reduction in transfers and subventions	6
Management audits of troubled firms	4
Financial restructuring	*
Training	*
Export promotion	*
Elimination of monopolies	*
Revision of legal framework	*
Specification of rate of return on assets	*
Preparation of corporate plans	*
Reform of management pay scales	*
Increase in competition	*
Subsidies and credit	*

* Mentioned in three or fewer adjustment operations.
Source: World Bank data.

closed or they are not; prices are either increased by the assigned date and by the stipulated percentage or they are not; workers are either dismissed from an enterprise or they are not (although whether they stay dismissed is another matter); and the same is true for the completion of financial audits, contract plans, rehabilitation plans, and the like. Thus, the operations in this sample provide a relatively tangible record for review.

Results of Reform Efforts

DIVESTITURE. Reforms related to the privatization and liquidation of public enterprises or to the preparation for divestiture were featured in adjustment operations in eight of the nine countries. Adjustment loans signed in Turkey did not deal directly with divestiture (the energy SECAL contained a minor reference to the process), but large-scale privatization was the leading element in a PERL, the three-year preparations for which were halted at the request of the Turkish government—without any enterprise having been sold. In contrast, in Jamaica, Niger, Panama, and Togo all of the divestiture programs either stipulated or suggested have been carried out or are in an active stage of preparation.

In Panama, for example, even though the disbursement of the second tranche of the second structural adjustment loan was canceled at the request of the government, five of the scheduled seven divestitures were completed. In Jamaica the government was committed under the public enterprise restructuring loans to divest its public enterprise portfolio by a value of 150 million Jamaican dollars by December 1987; it far exceeded the goal by divesting to the value of 500 million Jamaican dollars. Thirty-two of the forty-five firms on the list for divestiture were fully or partially privatized, leased, or dissolved by November 1987. In Togo four public enterprises were leased to private operators. The best known of these four was the STS steel mill, a financial and political success but a dubious economic proposition. The management of a clothing firm was handed over to a Togolese in the private sector—one of the first examples of a management contract being given to an African entrepreneur. Two public textile firms were merged and a sale was negotiated with a Korean-American group, but the sale was seriously delayed at the last moment. Five other public enterprises were liquidated and their assets sold. Almost twenty other commercial and industrial public enterprises are on the sales block; arrangements for several are quite far advanced. In Niger, as of December 1987, three public enterprises had been fully privatized, eight partially privatized, and four liquidated, while divestiture work was under way for eight others. In many of the cases cited there were financial and economic drawbacks, some of which are reviewed below. With regard to the divestiture conditions of adjustment agreements with these four countries, however, the conclusion is that the conditions have substantially been met.

In Ghana a loan condition was that divestiture be initiated in at least ten public enterprises, one of which was specified by name. The objective was to put five companies on the market and to prepare five inactive public enterprises for liquidation. A March 1988 World Bank report notes that some preparatory work has been completed but that "no decisions have yet been taken." In a statement that could easily be applied to a number of countries and divestiture cases, the report argues: "This slow progress need not be construed as lack of commitment or effort on the part of the Government, but rather as reflecting the inherent difficulties associated with the implementation of such a program."

In Morocco the PERL and various SECALs have emphasized studies and preparation rather than overt action (although the agricultural SECAL required some action on a liquidation, the status of which is unknown).

In the case of the PERL, the World Bank reasoned that the policy framework and the openness of public enterprise operations needed to be improved first. Only after demonstrating that its concern was with efficiency and that ownership issues were secondary (as one of many mechanisms to improve efficiency) would the Bank broach the issue of divestiture. The Moroccan PERL thus called for consideration, studies and classifications, and a draft law on privatization, all of which were achieved on schedule. (The king of Morocco, in his speech opening Parliament on April 8, 1988, announced a major privatization initiative, and a law proposing the sale of most Moroccan public enterprises is now being debated.) The divestiture question will receive more concrete attention in the proposed second PERL.

Senegal has moved very slowly on divestiture, exhibiting the full range of difficulties in the privatization process: reluctance to sell to foreigners, fear of a concentration of ownership of divested firms, difficulty reconciling market value with book value, and problems finding an appropriate and open sales mechanism in the absence of an adequate equities market. Thus, although studies and preparation for divestiture have figured in adjustment lending to Senegal since 1980, not until 1987–88 was more demanding conditionality introduced. Results have been modest. In October 1987 the Special Commission on the Disengagement of the State published a list of ten public enterprises in which the share of state ownership was to be reduced through the sale of stock issues. In only two of the ten would ownership pass from a public majority to a private majority; in the rest, the government already had only a minority share, which was to be reduced or eliminated. The accompanying explanations left many technical and mechanical questions unanswered. In early 1988 the government published a list of ten additional firms that were to be put up for sale. But the authorities removed from the first list two of the larger firms, stating that they needed to be restructured prior to sale. No buyers have yet been found for any of the enterprises on either list. The government has managed to liquidate seven small enterprises (that in total accounted for 1 percent of government equity in nonfinancial public enterprises) but has not fulfilled its commitment to identify a second list of public enterprises to be closed. The conclusion is that Senegal is creeping forward on this issue without enthusiasm, at a pace far slower than anticipated.

In Côte d'Ivoire, conditionality was met by the liquidation of two of the six sugar firms.

The first lesson learned from these experiences is that the divestiture process takes longer than anticipated. Divestiture cannot be easily synchronized with rapid loan disbursement. Trying to do so usually only makes matters worse. For example, specifying a date by which a particular enterprise must be sold can be counterproductive. The announcement provides an incentive for purchasers to wait until the deadline nears and then offer a low price, while governments will feel obliged to accept either a low price or an offer contingent on the granting of protection or competition-reducing distortions. (This was the case in the privatization of a group of firms in Guinea, a country not included in the sample reviewed here. In that divestiture program, which was a matter of strong conditionality in the loan, five of the fourteen companies sold were transferred as monopolies, and another company was given the exclusive right to import fuel oil, duty free, for fifteen years.)

The second lesson is that although most governments are complying, albeit with varying degrees of speed and enthusiasm, with the conditions and suggestions for divestiture, there is as yet little information on the postprivatization performance of the entities sold. A small feeder airline privatized in Panama has expanded its fleet and opened new routes. Private traders allowed to compete with a food-distributing public enterprise in Niger are providing more goods at lower prices to a greater number of outlets, while the public enterprise itself, faced with competition, has cut costs and is now making a profit. In countries where divestiture and monopoly-breaking has taken place, there are a fair number of encouraging anecdotes of this nature. But anecdotes, no matter how consistent with the tenets of neoclassical economics, do not amount to a conclusive demonstration of a generalized superior capability of the private sector to put resources to efficient use. Future review work must concentrate on this essential issue.[7]

A third lesson is that the World Bank has not proven to be particularly adept at advising governments on the timing or detailed mechanics of privatization ventures. For example, when Togo received two offers for its textile enterprises, the Ministry of State Enterprises asked for advice in selecting the better offer. The World Bank provided a detailed report on the pros and cons of the two offers. The report was circumspect but clearly favored the offer that proposed to bring in more restructuring capital, create more jobs in Togo, and produce for export rather than for the protected domestic market. From an economic point of view, that offer was clearly superior to the other one, and it was duly accepted by the government. But the foreign investors proved unable to raise the stipulated amount of restructuring capital, and the sale was delayed. This led some Togolese to think that the other, smaller, more traditional offer—which would undoubtedly have gone through more rapidly—should have been taken. The point is not that the World Bank's economic advice was bad; on the contrary, it was good. The issue, rather, is that economic analysis is only part of the deal-making process.

The fourth and final lesson is an obvious one: liberalization should precede, or at a minimum parallel, privatization. Above all, privatization must not become an obstacle to liberalization (this could happen when new, protected, and powerful private owners take steps to prevent further liberalization). The point is simple: divesting into uncompetitive markets may do more harm than good. In practical terms, this means taking more time at the beginning of or during adjustment operations to reform the policy and regulatory environment and encourage competitive forces so that privatization can produce the needed benefits of efficiency and productivity. Recent actions of the Togolese government, which is in the forefront of privatizers, are illustrative. The government has become concerned about the nature and pace of the divestiture arrangements so far concluded and has announced a pause in privatization actions. The World Bank has supported this pause for evaluation and consolidation and is now concentrating more on eliminating the remaining policy distortions and reforming the industrial incentive system than on setting numbers and dates for the sale of public enterprises.

PRICING, POLICY REFORM, AND REHABILITATION. Pricing issues have featured prominently in about half the operations under review. In the vast majority of cases—Côte d'Ivoire, Jamaica, Morocco, Niger, Togo, and Turkey—the called-for price increases have been achieved. Compliance has not generally been a problem. Contrary to usual practice, action has proven easier than contemplation; pricing studies in several countries have taken much longer to mount and review than anticipated. (It may well be that calling for a study is the way the World Bank and the borrower government agree to resolve disputes over particularly contentious pricing issues, which would account for the slow pace of these actions.)

The lengthy and well-studied Turkish experience is particularly interesting in regard to price issues. The Turkish government's primary goal in public enterprise reform was to reduce the burden on the budget posed by resource-consuming enterprises. A variety of price adjustments and increases was enacted, and the financial position of the enterprises improved while government transfers remained even and then declined. But it has been argued in a World Bank evaluation report that financial improvements came about because monopoly public enterprises were allowed to raise prices and that no gains in efficiency can be observed in the utility enterprises in question, or indeed in the sector as a whole.

In Jamaica the loss-making railway raised its tariffs, laid off a substantial number of workers, and closed several uneconomic lines, all in the framework of various SALs. The cases in Jamaica and Turkey are but two instances in which the financial positions of firms were improved through pricing revisions but the gains in efficiency are unknown or unobserved. In the Jamaican railway cost-cutting measures such as staff reductions and line closures presumably also contributed in the long run to the return to profitability. But it is not possible on the basis of available data to sort out which element accounted for the greater percentage of the variance.

The degree of compliance with requirements and requests for staff reduction has been high, indeed surprisingly so given the politically sensitive nature of the issue. Ghana is the outstanding case. In a two-year period, the infamously overstaffed cocoa board lost 54,013 names from its staff list: 25,000 "ghost," or nonexistent, workers were dropped from the payroll, and a further 29,013 staff were laid off. This action was taken in response to a loan conditionality that "excess labor" be identified and eliminated. Early SALs in Turkey had requested or required the same sort of program; 30,000 workers were laid off from public enterprises during 1979–82. Staff reductions of a significant if less dramatic nature have also taken place in Côte d'Ivoire, Jamaica, Niger, Panama, and Togo. (The labor issue was not addressed in the Morocco PERL.) The layoff program in Ghana is at present running into difficulties, however, not because political will is exhausted but because of a lack of funds for the generous severance payments previously agreed to by the public enterprises.

The pace and impact of the rehabilitation and restructuring of individual enterprises vary greatly from country to country. Improvements in management and financial performance are reported in five key public enterprises in Côte d'Ivoire, in several formerly troubled firms in Jamaica, and across the board in Turkey. In the Jamaican case the assertions of progress are backed by data on the physical and financial improvements; in the Turkish case the improved macrofinancial situation is taken as a proxy for improvements within firms. In Sub-Saharan Africa much of the rehabilitation work has been diagnostic and preparatory: financial and management audits, consultants' reports and proposals, improvements in the capacity to review investment proposals, training programs, and the like. As with many other reform measures, particularly in Africa, the proposed schedules for rehabilitation and restructuring activities have consistently underestimated the time needed—further confirmation of the poor fit between the time frame required to make improvements in efficiency and the disbursement schedules for adjustment loans.

Inasmuch as World Bank–supported public enterprise reform has been under way for ten years in Senegal, there is a clear record to evaluate, and indeed one can point to improvements associated with adjustment operations: in financial and management information systems, in setting objectives (through contract plans, discussed below), in pricing policies, and especially in accounting and auditing. But the economic impact of these reforms is less easy to discern. The sector continues to accrue financial losses, and the trend is downward. In 1982–84 the sector lost an average of 4 billion CFA francs a year; in 1986 public enterprises lost 7.8 billion CFA francs. (A significant part of the loss is due to price supports to farmers paid through public enterprises for rural development and so cannot necessarily be attributed to operating inefficiencies.) Presumably, the counterfactual argument applies: losses would have been greater without the adjustment-associated reforms. There are more encouraging signs as well: debts of the public enterprises have declined over the past few years, and operating subsidies to public enterprises have been reduced—by 5 percent in 1986 and by a further 15 percent in the 1987–88 budget.

Senegal has had extensive experience with the performance agreement, or contract plan. The results have been less than encouraging. Goals have been set, the mutual responsibilities and commitments of the two contracting parties clearly set out, and performance measures clearly established. In the financial field, pricing regimes have been specified, investment programs stated, noncommercial operations costed out and compensation arranged for, and operating subsidies set. But in case after case the government has proven unable or unwilling to honor the financial commitments agreed upon, and the agreements have had to be repeatedly and extensively revised or have fallen into abeyance. Experience with the device in other countries (Côte d'Ivoire, Niger, and Togo) has been too short to permit an assessment. The first months of experience with the contract plans negotiated in Morocco (their signing was a condition of the PERL) have been positive, however, and for the first time in years the government has honored financial commitments to two key firms.

Some progress has been made in reducing transfers and subventions. A direct approach was pioneered in Turkey, where a structural adjustment loan specified that in 1983 investments in public enterprises were to be held to 6.5 percent of GNP and that overall the financing of public enterprises was not to exceed 5.9 percent of GNP. The actual figures were 7.2 and 6.4 percent, respectively. Nonetheless, overall transfers were substantially reduced from previous levels. To meet its loan conditions, Senegal managed to reduce operating subsidies to public enterprises by simply decreeing that total subsidies in year *X* would be *Y* percent less than the previous year.

INSTITUTIONAL REFORM. Reform of the policymaking, supervisory, and evaluating institutions has absorbed considerable attention and resources in all the countries in the sample. In Côte d'Ivoire, Ghana, Niger, Togo, and particularly in Morocco and Senegal, World Bank–supported efforts are under way to strengthen the data base and the monitoring and managerial capacity of the central institutions guiding public enterprises. A central goal of reform is to shift governmental methods of supervision away from extensive and rigid controls and approvals and toward a smaller number of more flexible mechanisms for evaluating performance.

Introducing contract plans, reforming boards of directors, lightening financial review procedures, increasing both management's latitude and the competence and capacity of government supervisors, introducing legal changes that place more enterprises in the more lightly supervised categories—these are but some of the institutional changes being introduced. For countries other than Senegal, about all that one can reasonably say at this stage is that the process has been launched and that the first signs are encouraging.

For example, in Morocco the PERL-supported Directorate of Public Enterprises (within the Ministry of Finance) is supervising the preparation of the contract plan and ensuring that the Treasury honors its financial commitments, drafting legislation on divestiture procedures, hiring consultants to build a sectoral data base and management information system, advising a central policymaking committee on public enterprise strategy in general, coordinating a training program for government and enterprise staff, supervising the complicated process of clearing arrears, and conducting studies on relevant questions such as the optimal powers and composition of boards of directors. Serious and numerous obstacles remain, but in general the directorate is tackling the problems with dynamism and commitment and is disseminating a changed and positive attitude regarding the need for efficiency within public enterprises. Preparations for the PERL and the conditionality associated with it have helped improve the directorate's position, and resources furnished under the PERL provided consultants and training.

Roughly similar strengthening measures are being supported in Ghana, Niger, and Togo; early SALs did the same in Turkey, with modestly positive results. In Senegal SALs and related technical assistance loans to the Court of Public Enterprise Accounts have turned that body into an effective, respected organization. The main agency supervising public enterprises in Senegal, however, has not so far played its anticipated role—despite considerable input from the World Bank. Problems have included rapid turnover in its leadership, the junior status and lack of experience of its cadre, and its inability to change the budgeting system to better reconcile government commitments with revenues (the government's failure to honor contract plans reveals the need for such change). Of course, one small agency cannot reasonably be expected to overcome singlehandedly the poverty and deficiencies of an entire system; moreover, recent changes in the organization's management and personnel are expected to lead to improvements in performance.

Conclusions

Adjustment operations affecting public enterprises have required or requested reforms in many areas: divestiture (in all its many forms); policy changes, particularly with regard to pricing; measures to improve management of the resources used by the enterprises, including labor; better guidance and evaluation by the state; and restructuring and rehabilitation of firms. So far there has been a variable but generally acceptable degree of compliance with conditionality. Adjustment operations have underlined both the importance and the intractability of the institutional issues in public enterprise reform: management, guidance, and evaluation of performance. Progress in these fields is slow and subject to wide variation from country to country. Across the board, but especially in the institutional realm, much remains to be done. There is little information on the performance of firms after they have been divested and disturbingly little evidence that gains in efficiency have been responsible for the perceived improvement in the financial situation of many enterprises (improvement seems attributable largely to across-the-board cuts in investment and price increases in monopolies). Nonetheless, in the context of adjustment operations many governments have succeeded in reducing the flow of resources into poorly performing public enterprises.

More specifically, in the nine countries reviewed in detail (and there is no reason to believe that this is an unrepresentative sample), the following reforms are discernible over the adjustment period:

- A freeze on new hiring in public enterprises and, in several instances, a reduction in the number of employees, a sometimes substantial one
- A freeze on the creation of public enterprises and, in many instances, a reduction in their number through divestiture and amalgamation into the regular line administrations
- A general but not universal reduction in the budgetary burden of public enterprises (mainly through price increases, investment cuts, and staff layoffs)
- Considerable increases in the quantity, quality, and availability of information on the physical, financial, and economic performance of public enterprises
- Widespread experimentation with institutional mechanisms to better monitor and manage state enterprises
- Equally widespread experimentation with private sectors as alternate users of the resources previously invested in public enterprises.

These are not dramatic advances, but they are steps forward.

Much of the public enterprise reform now being instituted through adjustment operations can be regarded as preliminary or "brush-clearing" steps; that is, difficult, tedious, and time-consuming measures that do not individually or immediately turn the firms around but that set the scene for more dramatic improvements. The complexity and slow pace of the reform packages being implemented are regrettable but probably unavoidable. Getting prices right and selling off the industrial and commercial public enterprises that are not natural monopolies were once viewed as "simple" solutions; they have proven to be either not so simple or only partial solutions, although both are, and will continue to be, of critical importance.

The public enterprise reform packages proposed and implemented under adjustment operations have been based on "best practice," that is, on the prevailing economic and managerial wisdom and on international experience with improving performance.[8] As expected, these reforms have brought macroeconomic benefits, as measured by a reduction in the flow of funds from governments to public enterprises, in many countries (Jamaica, Turkey, and more recently Ghana and Niger) but not yet in others (Senegal and, surprisingly, Togo, despite its lead role in privatization). But a reduction of the burden on the budget, no matter how important in the short run, is not the ultimate justification for reform. In the long run, the value of the reforms will be measured by the extent to which they promote efficiency. On this crucial issue, the data are not yet sufficient to allow a conclusion.

The World Bank, in its conditions for adjustment lending, should continue to move away from specifying the number of public enterprises to be sold by a particular date; this approach is counterproductive. The loan to Jamaica that specifies divestiture of a stated dollar amount of the state portfolio is worth further examination by those who favor concrete goal setting. But in general the divestiture process is too uncertain to allow the setting of a deadline, especially in the short term. Furthermore, it appears unwise to make purely institutional reforms a matter of hard conditionality because the time frame for their design and implementation exceeds that of even several sequential SALs.

Institutional development projects, running parallel to adjustment operations, may be one solution to this perplexing problem. Some of the factors involved in meeting such conditionality lie outside the control of governments; moreover, it is unlikely that institutional reform will make or break an adjustment operation. Indeed, the World Bank might consider establishing two levels of conditions. Primary conditions would include a few key, clear, easily monitored objectives, for which lack of complete compliance would be automatic grounds for bringing an operation to a halt. Secondary conditions would include most institutional reforms and most public enterprise reforms in general, but nonfulfillment would provoke milder sanctions that would not halt the program.

Notes

1. The most succinct review of the economic and organizational obstacles to good performance of public enterprises is found in Shirley (1983). For an analysis of problems specific to public enterprises in Sub-Saharan Africa, see Nellis (1986).

2. For discussions of this point, see Jones (1982).

3. Since many countries have had several adjustment loans or credits affecting the public enterprise sector, the total number of borrowers is less than 100. Moreover, counts vary according to how reform activities are classified; in April 1989 the World Bank's Industry Department concluded that eighty-three operations contained public enterprise actions.

4. This chapter deals with public enterprise reform under adjustment lending; for a thorough study of the World Bank's experience with public enterprise reform as a whole, see Shirley (1989b).

5. For a review of contract plans, see Nellis (1989).

6. This confirms the conclusions of Shirley and Kikeri (1987), which listed divestiture as the issue most often tackled in World Bank operations to develop the private sector.

7. A World Bank research project titled "Ex-Post Performance of Divested State-Owned Enterprises" was launched in August 1989. The study will measure changes in economic efficiency and fiscal incidence in a sample of eight public enterprises, six of them in developing countries. It will analyze the factors that led to perceived changes in performance (if any) and draw lessons for future divestiture programs. For a preliminary statement on why the World Bank has sponsored privatization efforts, and with what results to date, see Nellis and Kikeri (1989).

8. The best survey of issues and reform measures is found in Shirley (1989b). For case studies of performance evaluation and improvement mechanisms, see Park (1986) on Korea, and Shirley (1989a) on Pakistan.

References

Jones, Leroy P. 1982. *Public Enterprise in Less Developed Countries.* Cambridge, U.K.: Cambridge University Press.

Nellis, John R. 1986. *Public Enterprises in Sub-Saharan Africa.* World Bank Discussion Paper 1. Washington, D.C.

———. 1989. *Contract Plans and Public Enterprise Performance.* World Bank Discussion Paper 48. Washington, D.C.

Nellis, John R., and Sunita Kikeri. 1989. "Public Enterprise Reform: Privatization and the World Bank." *World Development* 17 (5):659–72.

Park, Y. C. 1986. *A System for Evaluating the Performance of Government-Invested Enterprises in the Republic of Korea.* World Bank Discussion Paper 3. Washington, D.C.

Shirley, Mary M. 1983. *Managing State-Owned Enterprises.* World Bank Staff Working Paper 577. Washington, D.C.

———. 1989a. "Evaluating the Performance of Public Enterprises in Pakistan." PPR Working Paper 160. Policy, Planning, and Research, World Bank, Washington, D.C.

———. 1989b. *The Reform of State-Owned Enterprise: Lessons from World Bank Lending.* Policy and Research Report 4. Washington, D.C.: World Bank.

Shirley, Mary M., and Sunita Kikeri. 1987. "Survey of the Work of the World Bank Group on Private Sector Development." Country Economics Department, World Bank, Washington, D.C.

Comments

Leroy P. Jones

As an economist from academia commenting on a paper by a political scientist from the World Bank, I take it my task is to oversimplify. Accordingly, I first collapse John Nellis's fully nuanced and documented statements into a few bold propositions. Then I attempt to identify underlying causal patterns.

At one level, the chapter gives an exceptionally useful description of the World Bank's involvement in more than 100 public enterprise reform efforts. Given the nature and magnitude of the problems in the World Bank's client countries, this is not a remarkable level of activity. It is, however, a dramatic change from just ten years ago, when there was debate over whether public enterprise was even a useful unit of observation for World Bank work. The Marris (1979) report's conclusion that it was a potentially fruitful area correlates with the beginning of serious World Bank work in the area, although no outsider should attempt to attribute causation in such a complex organism as the World Bank. In any event, a great deal has been accomplished since then, and Nellis's chapter superbly documents public enterprise reform embodied in adjustment loans.

At another level, the chapter frankly admits the difficulties of trying to act as a change agent on a sensitive and complex reform in a foreign country. If I read it correctly, three messages are among the more important ones.

First, a decade ago we learned that problems observed in individual public enterprises often originated at the higher level of controlling bodies. Accordingly, effective reforms had to be pursued not only through project lending but also through policy reform at the sector level via adjustment lending. This policy work was essential for creating an environment in which enterprise work could be effective. For example, the reform of a steel mill is difficult if the manager lacks the autonomy to hire the right people and reward them for a job well done.

Second, after a decade of working at the sectoral level, we have learned that many public enterprise problems do not have their genesis within the sector alone but are rooted in broader imperfections in markets and political systems in which the sector functions. To return to the example of the steel mill, it is not necessarily an improvement to give the mill manager hiring autonomy in a political system that encourages him to hire politically well-connected individuals (or those who can otherwise make the manager better off without making the company better off) and in an economic system with protected markets that allows the manager leeway to indulge such costly behavior.

Third, the most important—or at least the most common—area of reform has been divestiture, but results to date have not been dramatic, to say the least. Among the nine countries Nellis selected for intensive study, Jamaica sold enterprises worth 500 million Jamaican dollars; Togo leased four public enterprises, shut down five, and has twenty on the block; Niger privatized three companies fully and eight partially; and Panama sold off five public firms. These are the successes. Considerably less happened in the other five countries. Even the successes represented only a small fraction of the total number of public enterprises in the country and an even smaller fraction of total sales or value added. The success of reforms other than divestiture is harder to quantify, but the impression is one of less than outstanding results.

I will concentrate my comments on the divestiture issue. Given the limited successes, we need first to determine whether the World Bank has been doing the wrong things, doing the right things poorly, or doing the right things well but in a difficult arena in which success necessarily has a long gestation period.

A clue to what is going on is provided by the observation that success in divestiture appears to be a positive function of per capita income. That is, divestiture has gone furthest and fastest in developed countries (Western Europe, New Zealand, and Japan) and slowest in developing countries, with some newly industrialized developing countries or middle-income countries in between (Chile, Korea, and Mexico). The correlation is very far from perfect but is perhaps strong enough to attribute some explanatory power to the following hypotheses:

- Divesting into competitive markets is unambiguously good. Divesting into monopoly or otherwise imperfectly competitive markets entails a tradeoff: one may get the desired improvements in efficiency but at some loss of market power or bureaucratic and regulatory power. Letting the private sector exploit a monopoly position is an economic evil that is not eliminated (although its manifestations are certainly changed) by either regulation or public ownership. The issue is that of choosing the lesser evil here—and a legitimate case can be made for any of the options.
- Market imperfections are, tautologically, far more widespread in developing countries than in developed countries. This is true in the sense that enterprises not only sell in imperfect product markets, but also acquire fundamental inputs in imperfect factor markets: stock markets

are thin or nonexistent, and credit and foreign exchange are allocated by other than competitive forces, as are a variety of other government permits and protections.

- Therefore, divestiture is liable to be a much slower process in developing countries. This is so because there is less scope for unambiguous gains and because it takes time to construct necessary safeguards in the intermediate cases. Furthermore, legitimate concerns about divestiture have an exponential impact on the gestation period because they provide a comfortable cloak for illegitimate opposition.

In sum, to paraphrase Adam Smith, the extent of divestiture is limited by the scope of the market.

Although divestiture in developing countries could and should be used as an opportunity to reduce some of these market imperfection, it can often work in the opposite direction. An all too typical story of divestiture runs as follows: visit country X and be told that enterprise Y is a divestiture success story with vastly enhanced profitability; visit company Y and be shown how costs have been reduced and demand increased by a variety of impressive management reforms; visit the political opposition and be told that profits were turned around primarily because of a side-condition of divestiture that competing imports be banned for five years. Was this divestiture a success from the public point of view? Clearly tradeoffs were involved, and we need a detailed quantitative study (a commodity, incidentally, which is also in lamentably short supply).

The alternative to divestiture is reform of enterprises within the public sector. Here again obstacles are substantial, and once again they are, at least to some extent, larger in developing countries. A common feature of public enterprise reform is to assign greater autonomy to managers. If the enterprise faces competitive markets, however, what is really happening is that one form of control is traded for another: the manager is more subject to the discipline of market forces and less subject to bureaucratic forces. If, however, the enterprise faces imperfect markets, then lessened bureaucratic control is not countered by increased market discipline and the manager or enterprise may be left free to pursue individual interests rather than the interests of the nation. Granting borrowing autonomy to public enterprises whose lenders know (or think they know) that the resources of the state ultimately guarantee the loan is at best a mixed blessing, as the Latin American debt crisis has shown.

Once again, the point is not that increased autonomy is not a desirable goal. Rather, it is that in developing countries progress toward that goal may be slow and may vary from decision area to decision area. And sometimes increased autonomy in one area is accompanied by increased control (for example, over results) in others. Or, to paraphrase Smith again, the extent of autonomy is limited by the scope of the market.

The conclusion, then, is that the slow progress reported by Nellis is largely explicable as a concomitant of attempting reforms that necessarily have a long gestation period in developing countries. Furthermore, the obstacles to reform are in part a function of the scope of markets, and these obstacles will not disappear as long as developing countries are developing countries. It may be salutary to recall the words of the late Senator Estes Kefauver, describing the U.S. aid program: "We are fighting twenty-year problems with five-year plans, two-year people, and one-year money."

Reference

Marris, Richard. 1979. *Survey and Critique of World Bank–Supported Research on International Comparisons of Real Product.* World Bank Staff Working Paper 365. Washington, D.C.

7 *Agricultural Policy*

Odin Knudsen
John Nash

IN THE EARLY to mid-twentieth century, agriculture led many countries into relative prosperity, based on natural comparative advantage and export-led growth. Beginning in the 1950s, however, industrial development was financed through taxation of agriculture, pricing policies that depressed food and agricultural commodity prices so that wages could be kept low, overvalued exchange rates and commercial policy that discriminated against exports, establishment of parastatal agencies to carry out government policies in all sectors, and heavy borrowing from abroad. The inflow of foreign capital, invested to a large extent in the industrial sector, led to further overvaluation of the real exchange rate and shifted the internal terms of trade against agriculture.

As a result, by the late 1970s many developing countries had large foreign debts to service, little potential for growth because industrial sectors had failed to develop as planned, and agricultural sectors that were functioning poorly after years of hostile policies. In low-income Sub-Saharan Africa, for example, the agricultural growth rate fell from 2.6 percent a year in 1965–73 to 1.4 percent in 1973–84 (World Bank 1986).

It soon became clear that World Bank project lending in this distorted policy environment further discouraged agricultural growth by perpetuating overvaluation through the provision of foreign exchange and by indirectly sanctioning the continuation of antiagricultural policies. To foster macro-level and sectoral reforms while providing countries with the foreign exchange they urgently needed to carry out these reforms, the World Bank developed new loan instruments: the structural adjustment loan and structural adjustment credit (hereafter collectively called SALs) and, after 1983, the sectoral adjustment loans (SECALs). Although not aimed only at agricultural policies, the early SALs contained conditions that were intended to correct the policy bias against agriculture. Agricultural SECALs, however, generally included conditions related solely to the agricultural sector and generally followed measures for macroeconomic stabilization.

This chapter reviews the experience with and lessons of these policy-based loans. The first section summarizes the types of conditions related to agriculture in SALs and agricultural SECALs. The following sections draw out policy lessons for the design of agricultural reform programs and examine issues relevant to the future of lending directed toward agricultural policy.

Policy Reforms in Agricultural Adjustment Loans

Agricultural conditions accounted for about 10 percent of all conditions in the sample of adjustment loans and for 9 percent of all legal requirements.[1] This distribution varied little by region except in the case of Latin America and the Caribbean, where the figures were 5 percent and 6 percent. The importance of these conditions was about proportionate to their distribution, with 11 percent judged critical to the success of the loan. The following subsections examine the main policy areas covered by agricultural conditions (see also tables 7-1 and 7-2).

Pricing

Since prices are the main determinant of incentives for agriculture, pricing has received special attention in adjustment loans. Almost 60 percent of SALs and all but one agricultural SECAL have included agricultural pricing conditions. In Africa 80 percent of SALs and SECALs have contained such conditions. Input and output pricing conditions have been about equally common. Almost one-third of the pricing conditions have been judged to be critical to the loan's success. Implementation of agricultural pricing conditions has been successful in about 68 percent of the cases, which is somewhat below the average of 73 percent for all conditions. The success rate is only 44 percent for Latin America and the Caribbean, however, which may be related to the unstable macroeconomic environment in which the price reforms were carried out.

PRODUCER PRICES. Conditions related to producer prices have generally concerned the need to increase them.[2] Some adjustment loans have required that producer prices be set at specific levels agreed to with the World Bank. The agricultural SECAL to Mexico linked official domestic prices for some crops to international prices via a price band. This mechanism, if used for all official prices and if complemented by measures to reduce industrial protection, would ensure both that the prices for agriculture as a whole are approximately correct and that relative prices within the sector are appropriate. Other adjustment loans, for example, to Morocco and Jamaica, have required changes in the mechanisms or formulas for establishing prices. By improving the pricing strategy rather than merely setting new prices, this kind of condition offers greater hope for sustained reform.

Because of the reluctance of governments to relinquish control of agricultural markets, only four of the twenty-one SECALs have required the abdication of the official price-setting authority and withdrawal of the government from the market. Madagascar was required to refrain from setting an official price for rice and from procuring rice domestically, although it was allowed to operate a buffer stock using imported rice to prevent prices from rising above a trigger level. Ecuador was required to cease procurement activities directed at establishing minimum prices.

CONSUMER PRICES. Only the agricultural SECAL to Ecuador and some SALs in Africa have required decontrol of consumer prices. Some others (for example, in Mexico) have required that global subsidies administered via low consumer prices be reduced or not be expanded.

INPUT PRICES. Fifteen of the twenty-one agricultural SECALs have included conditions related to input pricing. These loans have required increased prices (or reduced subsidies) for the three most important inputs—fertilizer, water, and credit. A few (for example, in Kenya) have had conditions related to certified seeds, although most of these have been of a nonprice, institutional nature. None of the loans has required decontrol of input prices or disengagement of the state from these input markets, even though sectoral analysis has often identified state involvement as a problem.

TRADE LIBERALIZATION. Since policies that cause domestic prices to diverge from their international levels must be reinforced by international trade controls, many loans (eight of the twenty-one agricultural SECALs and forty-nine of the seventy-nine SALs and SECALs) have required some liberalization of trade. Of the eight SECALs requiring trade liberalization, all but two were linked to pricing reforms. Loan conditions have usually involved removing restrictions (or reducing taxes) on exports of agricultural products or imports of agricultural inputs. Some loans, in the interest of reducing all barriers to trade, have required reductions in barriers to imports of agricultural products (for example, in Mexico and Ecuador). Taken alone, these steps would exacerbate the antiagricultural bias by removing trade protection for agriculture while leaving industrial protection in place. But as part of a comprehensive effort that includes a reduction of trade barriers in the industrial sector and devaluation of overvalued exchange rates, these measures can open the economy to trade opportunities. Conditions intended to liberalize trade in inputs have been rare (only three of twenty-one SECALs).

Institutional Reform

Conditions related to institutional reform appear in 71 percent of the seventy-nine SALs and SECALs in table 7-1 and constitute the largest single

Table 7-1. Conditions for Agricultural Policy in Seventy-Nine Structural Adjustment and Sectoral Adjustment Loans, by Region and Policy Area, Fiscal 1980–87

	Africa		Asia		Europe, Middle East, North Africa		Latin America and Caribbean		Total	
Agricultural policy	*Number*	*Percent*	*Number*	*Percent*	*Number*	*Percent*	*Number*	*Percent*	*Number*	*Percent*
Agricultural pricing (input and output)[a]	30	80	3	27	3	33	9	39	45	57
Trade	16	44	6	55	5	56	23	100	49	62
Institutional reform	29	81	5	45	7	78	15	65	56	71
Credit and banking[b]	11	31	3	27	1	11	9	39	24	30
Macroeconomic	20	56	2	18	6	67	10	43	38	48
Public investment budget	21	58	1	9	5	56	10	43	37	47
Environment	3	8	1	9	1	11	2	9	7	9
Total loans evaluated	36		11		9		23		79	
Number of countries	23		5		3		12		43	

a. Includes interest rate subsidies.
b. Excludes interest rate subsidies.
Source: An internal Word Bank study by Nelson Ridley and Colleen Roberts of seventy-nine SALS and SECALS in fiscal 1980–87 that contained agricultural conditions.

category of agricultural sector conditionalities. The two main subcategories of institutional reform are privatization and deregulation of markets.

PRIVATIZATION. Most analyses of agricultural policies have noted two problems with the operation of government-owned companies or public enterprises. First, the legal monopoly power enjoyed by these companies usually leads to inefficient operation and large fiscal losses. Second, they are the instrument through which the state carries out the pricing and regulatory policies that have done so much harm.

Only the first problem has been addressed through adjustment lending. Seven SECALs have required either that the private sector be allowed to compete with the public enterprises in a particular market or that some public enterprises be divested or closed. Four of these conditions covered product markets and three covered input markets. Some loans, especially SALs in Africa, have required reorganizing the public enterprises so that they operate more efficiently. Twelve (all but two of them in Africa) of a sample of twenty-nine adjustment loans required some divestiture. For the seven loans for which implementation data were available, implementation was generally found to be successful.

Virtually no adjustment loans, however, have required that public enterprises be abolished or completely privatized or that they withdraw from direct participation in the market. Because private institutions are weak in some countries, especially in Africa (partly because their development has been suppressed by the public enterprises), public enterprises cannot be withdrawn precipitately from the market. With few exceptions, however, withdrawal of public enterprises does not appear even to have been considered as an explicit long-term objective. Two exceptions were Ecuador, where the crop-marketing public enterprise was required to withdraw completely from procurement activities, and Panama, where the agricultural marketing public enterprise was limited to providing market information and managing warehouses.

DEREGULATION. Three of twenty-one SECALs have contained conditions for the removal of regulatory constraints on markets. Tanzania had to abolish permits for internal movements of grains. Morocco was required to dismantle an elaborate system for regulating upstream flour marketing, including licenses that limited market access and fixed allowances for distribution margins.

MACROECONOMIC. Macroeconomic policies, particularly exchange rate policy, have been as important as direct agricultural policies in depressing the sector. Most agricultural adjustment programs, therefore, have required exchange rate reform of some kind. Forty-eight percent of the seventy-nine SALs and SECALs had conditionalities for macroeconomic policy related to agriculture. World Bank President's Reports on twelve SECALs cite progress on the macroeconomic front preceding the loan. The most common requirement has been for more rapid devaluations. Some adjustment loans have also been preceded by other measures to correct antiagricultural biases in the trade regime. This has usually been done through SALs or trade policy loans rather than directly through agricultural SECALs (Colombia is the main exception).

Other Policy Areas

Two other policy areas occasionally mentioned in adjustment loan conditionalities are the environment and the alleviation of poverty. A few loans have required regulation of pesticide use; in Jamaica one required measures to control erosion, and another required the sale or lease of government-owned land to improve land use. In general, however, despite the impact of agricultural policies on the environment, environmental issues have been ignored in adjustment lending.

Poverty alleviation, too, has been relatively neglected. From fiscal 1980 to fiscal 1987 only one loan (to Ghana in 1984) included a poverty alleviation program. In fiscal 1988, however, two adjustment loans (to Mexico and Morocco) included such programs. A loan to Colombia addressed this issue by targeting counterpart funds for investment in regions where incomes would fall during adjustment.

Issues for the Design of Agricultural Reform Programs

The World Bank's experience in promoting agricultural reform has been too short to permit firm conclusions about what does and does not work. Only one agricultural sector adjustment operation has had a completion report. Nonetheless, this experience and the general literature on agricultural development suggest some broad guidelines for future loans.

One caveat is particularly important: adjustment is a long-term process. Experience with agricultural adjustment has shown mixed results in the short run. The evidence on the relation between adjustment operations and agricultural growth is ambiguous. Countries that received adjustment loans increased the average annual growth rate of their agricultural production from 1.6 percent to 2.8 percent in the three years following the loan, with a further increase of 3.2 percent in the years until 1987. Agricultural growth also increased more in these recipient countries than in comparable groups of nonrecipient countries. But these averages are deceptive. Of twenty-nine recipient countries, thirteen showed lower agricultural growth rates between the loan year and 1987 than for the three years before the loan (Balassa 1988b).

Chile's experience with agricultural reform suggests that the sequencing and pace of reforms are important to their effectiveness in the long term. In late 1973 Chile began, with some World Bank involvement in the early stages, a long-term program of general economic and agricultural reforms that now appears to have been successful (Knudsen and Yotopoulos 1985). Before the military takeover in 1973, the government had administered the agricultural sector through direct ownership of important production, distribution, and financial enterprises. It also had employed a multitude of controls and subsidies, including price controls, quantitative restrictions, interest rate controls, and tariff preferences.

Starting in late 1973 the government introduced changes based on free-market principles. It deregulated prices, divested itself of state land and of marketing, distribution, and agroindustrial processing enterprises; reduced technical assistance and public expenditures; and attempted to rationalize the budget, exchange rates, and banking. These sudden and extensive changes led to pronounced instability in the agricultural sector in the short term. Agriculture became decapitalized, agricultural debt accumulated and many loans became nonperforming, and the land planted to the fourteen main traditional crops declined from 1.2 million to 0.87 million hectares by 1983. Many farmers who had acquired their land through agrarian reform lost it.

Beginning in 1983, the government attempted to stabilize agricultural prices through variable tariffs and government procurement of some commodities. Retrenchment was not complete, and the government's role remained limited. The measures taken were successful, and in a period of continuing macroeconomic stability, the agricultural sector rebounded and stabilized. Fifteen years after the commencement of the agricultural reform, the sector is booming, with rapid growth (7.1 percent a year from 1984 to 1986) of both traditional crops for domestic consumption and fruits for export.

Chile's experience shows that agricultural reform takes years, that too much change too quickly can lead to instability, and that temporary retrenchments may be necessary. Despite a profound commitment to laissez-faire, the government considered it necessary to give agriculture special consideration through price stabilization measures and through protection for wheat, oilseeds, sugar, and milk—markets it viewed as artificially depressed and unstable because of the policies of developed countries.

Price and Nonprice Factors in Agricultural Growth

A consistent goal of conditions in World Bank loans for agriculture has been to move crop and input prices toward their international levels. Except in cases where initial distortions are severe, however, price reform alone cannot produce major gains in sectoral or national growth rates in the short run.[3] They must be complemented by nonprice policy measures, and even then the growth rate will respond only in the medium to long term.

PRICE REFORMS. In the short run price reforms will improve efficiency but not growth rates. Because the supply response is high for individual crops, "getting the prices right" causes a rapid adjustment in relative production between crops in favor of those that can be produced most efficiently. Long-run supply responses of individual crops in developing countries are greater still and have been estimated at ten times or more the short-run response (World Bank 1986). These production shifts between crops provide gains in allocative efficiency and increase the economic value of production in a step-like fashion.[4]

But such correction of relative prices alone will not lead to sustained increases in agricultural growth. First, the aggregate supply response in agriculture is much lower than the response of individual crops, even in the longer run, since the supply of land, a major factor of production, is relatively inelastic in many countries (Binswanger and others 1987). Even Argentina, which until recently had a fairly elastic supply of land and well-developed infrastructure, has an estimated aggregate supply elasticity of between 0.21 and 0.35 for the short run, although it may be close to 0.8 for the long run. Countries with less developed infrastructure have a much lower aggregate supply elasticity, for example, between 0.2 and 0.3 in the short and long run for India, about 0.1 in the short run and 0.16 in the long run in Kenya (Chhibber 1988).

Second, the price adjustment is often comparatively small. A study of nineteen developing countries (Krueger, Schiff, and Valdes 1988) found that domestic prices for export crops averaged only 11 percent below their international equivalents in 1975–84. This study also found that domestic prices were actually higher than their international counterparts in the case of crops whose domestic supplies were in part imported.[5] Third, aggregate response to price changes is limited to crops grown by producers who market their crops or use purchased inputs; the changes have virtually no impact on the production of large numbers of subsistence farmers.

Of course, if the reduction of price distortions causes production to shift to outputs with high income elasticities, such as livestock or fresh fruits and vegetables, it may improve growth rates. The switch to fruits and vegetables contributed to the growth of Chilean agriculture, for example. But with the exception of livestock in some countries, such as Argentina and Uruguay, these products are not heavily taxed by direct pricing policies.

NONPRICE FACTORS. Public goods such as roads, irrigation, and research and extension have been shown to be extremely important in sustaining agricultural growth (for a survey of related studies, see Lele and Mellor 1988). Chhibber (1988) found that, on average, a 1 percent increase in irrigation infrastructure increased output by 1 percent in the countries studied. Other studies show a significant response of output to increased density of rural roads as well (Binswanger 1989). Although such findings might lead one to ask whether price or nonprice factors are more important, a more useful approach is to view them as complementary. Investment in irrigation or drainage expands the fixed factor of production, land, and gives farmers a greater choice of crops. Improved transportation makes it profitable for farmers to produce some outputs, such as perishables, that could not be marketed before. Nonprice factors lower the cost of adjusting to changes in relative prices and increase responsiveness to these changes.

Price and nonprice factors are complementary in another, longer-run sense as well. Recent research has emphasized the importance of relative prices in guiding the direction of technological change in agriculture (Hayami and Ruttan 1985; Mundlak 1988). Where one input is relatively expensive, technological change will proceed so as to economize on its use. Beyond this, decisions affecting both public and private investment in physical infrastructure and human capital, research and extension activities, and the adoption of new varieties or techniques by farmers are all guided by relative prices. Where prices are close to their opportunity costs, investment and technological change are more efficient. This is particularly true of intersectoral pricing. A study (Cavallo and Mundlak 1982) that included technological change induced by changes in intersectoral prices estimated a higher aggregate long-run supply elasticity than have other studies.

Since public goods such as roads, irrigation systems, and research and extension services take many years to develop and yield returns, their beneficial effects on agricultural growth become apparent only in the long term. Meanwhile, the austerity in public expenditures required by structural and macroeconomic adjustment may initially slow growth, despite the increase in agricultural prices that results from adjustment measures. There is thus a danger that the sustainability of the reforms will be threatened as the government and farmers become discouraged with the slow, painful process.

The Chilean experience with agricultural reform over many years, with some periods of retrenchment before the effects on growth were felt, together with what is known generally about the determinants of agricultural growth, suggest certain lessons for agricultural reform and adjustment lending. In planning the first agricultural SECAL to any country, the World Bank and the government should agree on a series of adjustment operations to take place over at least five years. Some of these operations could include hybrid loans that combine fast-disbursing adjustment loan funds with slower-disbursing project or program funds. The first operation should not be too ambitious or politically painful. What is important is to secure a clear commitment to the longer-term objective and see that precedents are set. Ideally, there should be a public commitment by the government to the basic elements of a long-term program. Loan effectiveness should be judged according to the implementation of policy reforms rather than an immediate improvement in agricultural growth and trade balances. Some retrenchment should be anticipated so that temporary adjustments can be made when unforeseen events occur or reforms do not work as expected. Only after the program is well advanced—perhaps after five to ten years—can its effectiveness in increasing output be assessed.

The experience with price and nonprice factors and long-term agricultural growth also demonstrates the importance of maintaining public and private investment. Because of fiscal austerity, public investment programs have suffered, particularly in agriculture. In Mexico, where fiscal constraints are particularly severe, public investment in agriculture dropped from US$1,824 million in 1982 to less than US$500 million in 1987. In many countries a tremendous potential exists for switching some current expenditures to investment while still reducing overall expenditures. For example, although credit programs have been found to be ineffective in encouraging agricultural growth (Binswanger 1989), credit subsidies accounted for 4 to 99 percent of total government spending for agriculture in a sample of six Latin American countries in 1970 and 1980 (Elias 1985). In most countries under adjustment, however, funds released as a result of lower expenditures for salaries and input subsidies have not been used to augment investment budgets. In Morocco, agriculture's share of public investment fell from 15 percent in 1984 to 7 percent in 1986, despite substantial fiscal savings from reductions in input subsidies. Net investment in agriculture has probably been negative, with depreciation in agricultural and rural infrastructure outweighing the small amounts of investment that have continued.

Sector loans have rarely addressed both the quality and the specific level of funding of the public sector investment portfolio. About 50 percent of SECALs contain conditions related to a satisfactory investment budget (see table 7-2), but frequently the emphasis is on stopping "white elephant" projects rather than on a thorough review of the investment portfolio or of government procedures for project selection. The Mexico agricultural SECAL is the only loan to specify a minimum level of funding for agricultural investments. Future adjustment loans should require that at least part of the savings produced by a reduction in current expenditure be converted to investments. Also, to protect investment budgets and

Table 7-2. Conditions in Twenty-One Agricultural Sectoral Adjustment Loans (SECALs), Fiscal 1980–88

	Number of agricultural SECALS	
Condition	*Reforms preceding loan*	*Conditions in loan*
Product price	17	15
Decontrol consumer price	2	4
Decontrol producer price	3	1
Change official consumer price	5	1
Change official producer price	7	5
Reduce subsidies	2	2
Liberalize trade	9	8
Conduct studies	3	7
Input price	14	15
Decontrol or set at world level	1	1
Raise official price	10	12
Lower official price	0	0
Liberalize trade	4	3
Conduct studies	1	3
Privatization	10	9
Product distribution	7	5
Input distribution	3	3
Conduct studies	0	1
Institutional reform	10	17
Deregulation	0	3
Other	9	14
Conduct studies	1	6
Macroeconomic	12	3
Exchange rate	12	1
Deficit	4	1
Other	2	3
Public investment	4	10
Environment	0	2
Poverty alleviation	2	2

Source: Authors' examination of World Bank President's Reports on twenty-one agricultural SECALS (virtually all those through fiscal 1987 and one for Mexico in 1988).

encourage a more efficient allocation of government-provided goods and services, both current and capital government expenditures for agriculture should be increasingly financed by farmers through user fees and other cost-recovery measures. The design of administrative structures to permit this cost recovery should be part of World Bank financing. By exerting stronger pressure to reduce current spending and recover costs, the World Bank could ensure the survival of investment budgets without compromising the macroeconomic objective of deficit reduction.

Price Stabilization and Food Policy

Almost all developing countries have programs for price stabilization and food subsidies. The international prices of food staples are volatile, and this volatility is magnified in domestic markets by the erratic devaluations typical of countries with macroeconomic imbalances. Almost all governments, whatever their views on the role of the public sector, attempt to stabilize the prices of important agricultural crops. Since food constitutes a large part of the total expenditure of the populace, especially the poor, programs to correct price volatility and alleviate its effects receive high priority. Given these aspects of food policy in developing countries, reform options in this area are relatively constrained. To be sustainable, reforms should be based not on the abandonment of these objectives but rather on the development of more efficient and less intrusive mechanisms for stabilizing food prices and protecting food consumption.

The mechanisms used to stabilize prices vary widely, ranging from domestic procurement or importation schemes directed toward a specific commodity to financial schemes such as buffer funds, which are financed through variable taxes. Whatever the mechanism, the result has usually been to tax producers. Although the effect of price instability on production plays a part in government thinking, the welfare of urban consumers is a prime concern. Indeed, governments often go beyond price stabilization and subsidize consumption through price controls or general subsidies. (General subsidies are those that are available to all consumers of a product.) Fear of political unrest produced by sudden increases in basic food prices reinforces this tendency. Exchange rate instability also accentuates the desire to stabilize commodity prices. When governments devalue as part of an adjustment program, they usually want to tax the windfall gains to producers and holders of commodity stocks in order to keep consumer prices down. The use of export taxes to partly offset movements in the exchange rate is well documented for Uruguay (Jarvis and Medero 1988) and Argentina (Sturzenegger forthcoming).

Stabilization of commodity prices may also help attain macroeconomic objectives. Large movements in commodity export earnings that constitute a significant part of aggregate foreign exchange earnings can destabilize the economy through effects on the money supply or "Dutch disease" effects (see, for example, Pinto 1987). When governments are unable to institute countervailing fiscal and monetary programs because of general macroeconomic instability, export taxes can exert a stabilizing effect on the economy. For this to happen, however, the increased revenue from the taxes that are imposed when export earnings are high must be used to reduce the creation of domestic credit, not to increase spending.

Used in this way, export taxes sterilize part of the change in the flow of foreign exchange.

The extensive theoretical debate on price stabilization has not produced any clear conclusions about whether a theoretically well-designed stabilization mechanism increases or decreases the welfare of producers and consumers. Price stabilization schemes in practice, however, clearly impose enormous costs. Price supports reinforced by trade controls not only insulate producers from short-term fluctuations in world prices but also divorce domestic prices from long-term trends in border prices, thereby perpetuating inefficient patterns of production. Public enterprises preempt private sector participation in the procurement, storage, transport, processing, and sale of basic foods, while their purchases are subsidized by fiscal transfers or low producer prices. Huge financial losses and economic inefficiency are the results (Knudsen and Nash forthcoming a and b).

Experience with sector operations shows that most governments will not completely abandon the objectives of stabilizing prices and subsidizing consumption. Thus, for example, if a public enterprise is the mechanism used to implement this goal, the government will be unwilling to privatize or abolish it before having a viable alternative for stabilizing prices. The attempt to remove the government from procurement activities in Ecuador failed because no viable alternative was specified.

What is the lesson for agricultural adjustment lending? The desire of governments to stabilize prices or other macroeconomic variables should be recognized, but more efficient means should be sought to achieve these objectives. Government intervention should be limited to a small number of commodities and should not involve direct handling of the commodity. Ideally, the intervention should be based on publicly announced pricing rules and prices linked to international prices. If the exchange rate is unstable, then an ad hoc price stabilization scheme may be needed until the macroeconomic situation is under control. When the concern is to stabilize prices to avoid macroeconomic fluctuations, an alternative to ad hoc export taxes deserve consideration, such as the revenue stabilization fund for copper that is used in Chile or the buffer funds that are used for agricultural exports in Papua New Guinea.[6]

Consumer price controls and subsidies on important foods are also unlikely to be entirely removed. General subsidies, however, should be replaced by a targeted food system for the poor, as recent World Bank operations have attempted to do. The Mexico agricultural SECAL limited the maximum level of global subsidies, while also requiring a minimum level of funding for direct, targeted subsidies to cushion the impact on the poor. The team preparing the Venezuela SAL is aware of this tradeoff and is focusing on the development of indirectly and directly targeted food subsidies.

Food stamps are a cost-effective method of targeting subsidies, but the system cannot be developed overnight. Much administrative work is required to minimize abuses and keep down costs. The food stamp system in Mexico took more than a year to design and begin implementation—and even then serious errors were made.

In designing alternative subsidization schemes, it should be recognized that leakages are inevitable and may even be used to broaden support for the alternative system and thus contribute to its sustainability. In Mexico, for example, food stamps were provided to unions as part of a political bargain when removing global food subsidies. To limit the program's costs and to avoid creating strong incentives for rural-urban migration, the subsidy should not be open-ended. Furthermore, the price of the stamps should be linked to the price of the food product to prevent program costs from ballooning quickly in a period of rapid inflation, as happened in Mexico. (Food stamps redeemable for a given physical quantity of food had a fixed price unrelated to the food's actual price.)

The impact on the income of the target population of price rises resulting from the adjustment program should be estimated and measures taken to ensure the transfer of approximately equivalent resources to this population through the targeted subsidy program. The Mexico agricultural SECAL required targeted food programs to redress the estimated US$225 million reduction in the purchasing power of the poorest 20 percent of the population that would occur as a result of food price adjustments once general subsidies were eliminated. Obviously, decisions on levels of funding for direct subsidies must be balanced by macroeconomic and fiscal considerations.

Trade Liberalization

One of the most common objectives of agricultural adjustment loans has been trade liberalization (see table 7-1). The success of such trade reforms is determined by a number of factors, however, including macroeconomic considerations, pricing objectives (including stabilization), and trade incentives in other sectors. This section discusses some of these connections and their implications for policy reform.

The most significant discrimination against agriculture has occurred through protection of industry and overvaluation of the exchange rate. A study of agricultural incentives in sixteen developing countries found that the "disprotection" of agriculture resulting from overvaluation and industrial policy was 25 to 29 percent; that is, farmers received real prices that were 25 to 29 percent lower than they would have been in the absence of such policies. This discrimination generally overwhelmed the advantage received from various input subsidies to producers or direct protection from restrictions or taxes on imports (Krueger, Schiff, and Valdes

1988). Liberalization of agricultural trade should therefore be preceded or accompanied by a general trade liberalization program for other commodities, including adjustment of the exchange rate to realistic levels. This has in general been done in most programs.

The agricultural trade regime cannot be treated independently of the agricultural pricing policy. If, for example, quantitative restrictions are to be removed from a commodity for which minimum price or other price stabilization measures are in effect, the replacement regime must be able to fulfill the same objective. A variable tariff might appear to be an adequate substitute that will provide the same degree of protection, but in practice it may not be able to do so. Nominal exchange rate movements may overwhelm even a variable tariff, and adjusting the tariff to exchange rate fluctuations may prove administratively difficult, especially in the presence of parallel exchange markets and capital controls. In addition, the stated or invoice price on which the tariff is calculated may be false or may not take into account other favorable terms, such as credit concessions. Also, when capital controls are in effect, it may pay to import agricultural goods at a loss, thereby permitting false invoicing and providing a mechanism for moving capital abroad.

If, under a minimum price scheme, the government is committed to purchase all available supplies at a fixed price, the budgetary repercussions of undercutting trade protection may be serious; the government may find itself paying the support price for domestic production that is displaced by a flood of imports. Under these circumstances, it will be difficult to obtain government cooperation in converting quantitative restrictions to tariffs. If variable tariffs are put in place when the exchange rate is unstable, the government should not try to enforce a minimum price rigidly. Price movements below this price are inevitable as exchange rate movements undercut prices.

Because of these connections between direct procurement schemes and trade controls, other means must be found to stabilize prices. On the premise that a well-functioning storage market will best stabilize prices, the Madagascar agricultural SECAL introduced a staged process for building up private capabilities for rice procurement and storage. As a first step, the government withdrew from domestic procurement but operated a buffer stock of imported rice, and it applied a pricing mechanism that sought to avoid large price increases from speculation while allowing a profit to those engaged in private trading and storage. This scheme worked well in establishing the private sector in these activities. The next step is to be government withdrawal from running the buffer stock as all storage functions are taken over by the private sector.

Because of import barriers that indirectly create disincentives to export, some governments have attempted to promote exports. Measures have included reduced export taxes, tax or duty drawback schemes, duty-free zones, special credit lines, insurance or other special subsidies for exporters, and the creation of government agencies to promote exports in other ways. Often poorly designed for correcting antiexport distortions, these measures may turn out to be as costly and inefficient as overzealous import protection. A study of export promotion through subsidized credit and insurance found the schemes to be ineffective and socially costly (Fitzgerald and Monson 1989). These programs seldom include primary agriculture, although they often include agroindustry, and they adversely affect agriculture through their effect on the exchange rate and through higher taxation of the sector to support the export promotion activities (Nogués 1989). An alternative approach that relies on technical assistance to governmental trade promotion organizations has almost never been successful because of problems inherent in such a role for the public sector. The only exception found (by Keesing and Singer 1989) was the official trade promotion organization in Chile, which was marginally helpful in promoting exports of grapes and salmon.

Evidence from Africa suggests that the best way to promote exports (including agricultural exports) may simply be to follow a realistic exchange rate policy and to reduce government interference in markets. Balassa (1988a) compared the export performance of nineteen Sub-Saharan African countries in 1974–78. He found that, on average, those following market-oriented policies gained 15 percent in export market share, while those following interventionist policies lost 24 percent, with intermediate countries losing 10 percent.

The Deepening of Reforms

The strategy behind policy-based lending is to make basic economic reforms under the auspices of a SAL or a broad-based SECAL and then, once the economy has been sufficiently stabilized, to introduce deeper and broader reforms. Reforms undertaken in this way are considered more likely to be institutionalized and so to become permanent. Thus, for example, Mexico's commitments upon joining the General Agreement on Tariffs and Trade (GATT) institutionalized, or "deepened," its trade reform process. This deepening of reforms is essential to a program's success because the private sector will not make the desired investment decisions unless the reforms are viewed as permanent (Rodrik 1988).

Most adjustments undertaken previous to or as conditions of SECALS have not helped to deepen reform. Experience with product pricing provides an example of why this is so. Although measures were introduced to raise the levels of controlled consumer prices or official producer prices, the institutional apparatus for determining prices was usually left intact and thus subject to the same political forces that had caused prices to be set low to begin with. This failure to dismantle the old apparatus is especially troublesome because as inflation erodes the price increases the political battles need to be fought over and over again to ensure that price increases are maintained in real terms.

In a few cases the mechanisms used to set official prices have been altered rather than the specific price levels, for example, by creating a link with world prices. This approach alleviates some political pressure. But in only four of the twenty-one SECALs examined has the real structural problem been addressed by eliminating controls on both trade and consumer prices (see table 7-2). Given the ease with which superficial price changes can be reversed, the private sector will be reluctant to base long-term investment decisions on these reforms.

The situation is similar with respect to inputs, an area in which reforms are generally superficial and do not affect the basic structure of the defective system. In the case of fertilizer, for example, instead of removing the government from the business of manufacturing and distributing fertilizer, reforms have raised the official price in order to reduce the heavy subsidies required by the fertilizer sector, which is frequently a government monopoly. It is doubtful, however, whether the pressure to allow prices to lag behind inflation can be resisted once the government's pressing budgetary problems are ameliorated.

Most reforms directed at the privatization of state enterprises have also been quite superficial. Many loans have required that the legal monopoly of certain parastatals be eliminated, but only one loan has required that the government actually withdraw from a market. Simply eliminating the legal monopoly of the government has not generally been sufficient to overcome the private sector's reluctance to enter a market, given the threat of unfair competition from a public enterprise with unlimited resources and the power of government at its disposal. (In Mexico, for example, the private sector did not respond quickly when a public enterprise's monopoly in grain imports was abolished.) In many cases World Bank lending has supported the same publicly owned marketing organizations that were specifically designed to suppress the small traders, who, according to a recent review of agricultural marketing projects, "are often best placed to meet the needs of small farmers" (World Bank 1988). Criticizing this pattern, the review concluded it resulted from unwarranted assumptions that private traders are inefficient or exploitative and that strategic crops should be marketed by state monopolies.

The legal regulatory framework is another problem that has not really been touched. In most developing countries the regulatory environments impede change and thwart the objectives of trade liberalization. Although these obstacles are usually not a direct burden on the agricultural sector, they are of special concern to agroindustries, many of which expand in response to changes in the trade regime or other adjustments. But only three of the twenty-one SECALs acted to alleviate regulatory burdens, and none required action on this issue before the loan (see table 7-2).

It is not difficult to understand why this pattern of superficial reform has emerged. A deepening of reforms requires very detailed and complete information on the legal framework in each country. In addition, governments are reluctant to make changes that are not easily reversed. Nonetheless, now that the adjustment process is supposed to be well advanced in many countries, the World Bank should put more emphasis on the legal framework, and governments, if they are truly committed to adjustment, should be more willing to relinquish controls in ways that cannot readily be reversed. Privatization of state enterprises, while not a guarantee of continuity, certainly raises the cost of reversal. The GATT, an international forum for making trade reform binding, can exert direct pressure that raises the costs of reversal and makes reform more durable: under GATT accords, reversal of trade reductions in tariffs or other restrictions can invite retaliation from other member countries.

Because of the political difficulty of some institutional reforms, the World Bank should be prepared to accept that reforms may be gradual. Nonetheless, a basic condition of initial lending should be the government's willingness to commit itself to significant long-term institutional reforms by policy declarations and precedent-setting dismantling or sales of at least some public enterprises.

The World Bank review of structural adjustment lending raised the question of whether sectoral adjustment lending can proceed before macroeconomic stabilization has been achieved (World Bank 1989). Although progress on agricultural reform may be possible in an unstable macroeconomic situation, it is rare, especially in the case of pricing and trade policy. With inflation or unstable exchange rates, not only are relative prices and trade unlikely to respond quickly to uncertain signals but also the political will for change deteriorates. Agricultural SECALs in Argentina and Ecuador failed in large part not because the designs were faulty or too ambitious, but because the macroeconomic situation was so unstable that the political will to act was eroded.

The Future

What does the future hold? Have the World Bank and its borrowers learned the lessons of the early 1980s on adjustment lending?

The answer is mixed. A certain fatigue is evident. New agricultural SECALs are not planned for 1988–92 for twelve of the twenty-one countries that previously received such loans (Burkina Faso, Central African Republic, Colombia, Ecuador, Madagascar, Morocco, Nigeria, Sierra Leone, Sudan, Uruguay, Yugoslavia, and Zambia). Only four countries that received such loans in 1986 or 1987 are currently expected to receive follow-up loans during the next five-year period, and even in these cases the lags are often as long as three to four years. Although this does not mean that reform will halt in many of these countries, it does imply that the World Bank's role will be limited. Furthermore, it raises doubts about whether reforms will stick or be deepened.[7]

On the positive side is evidence that the World Bank has begun in recent loans to address some problems in innovative ways that may give momentum to the reform process. One area in which this has been occurring is price stabilization in the context of agricultural trade liberalization. An agricultural SECAL for Morocco has assisted in building a variable tariff system to replace trade controls, and one for Mexico initiated a study on the feasibility of implementing a similar system. The Madagascar adjustment loan is exploring the use of buffer stocks to stabilize prices. These schemes are still in the experimental stage, and in-depth evaluations will not be possible for some time.

The situation is similar with respect to food subsidy programs. Although recent adjustment loans (to Mexico and Morocco, for example) have recognized the need for cushioning price adjustments with targeted subsidies for the poor, the World Bank operational staff is just beginning to build up the specialized knowledge needed to deal with food programs.

The World Bank and developing countries are learning from the difficult process of agricultural reform. It is a new process that has yet to become self-sustaining, and the World Bank's participation will continue to be necessary. With the Uruguay Round of Multilateral Trade Negotiations in its last phases, it may be that agricultural reform efforts in developing countries will be complemented by global reform so that markets rather than governments will guide agricultural development in the 1990s.

Notes

We wish to thank Bela Balassa, Ajay Chhibber, and Jaime de Melo for very thoughtful comments on early drafts of this chapter. Remaining errors are our responsibility.

1. The discussion in this section is based on an analysis of a sample of adjustment loans by the World Bank's Industry Development Division and on tables 7-1 and 7-2. The true contribution of agricultural conditions to adjustment loans is probably understated here, since agricultural SECALs are underrepresented in the Industry Development Division's sample.

2. A few loans, such as those to Colombia and Morocco, have put a ceiling on producer prices or required that they be reduced. For some other countries, such as Burkina Faso, Côte d'Ivoire, Ecuador, Ghana, the Philippines, and Uganda, the conditions have concerned improving relative prices so as to encourage diversification in the sector.

3. That is, increasing allocative efficiency (eliminating the classical "triangle" losses in traditional welfare analysis) shifts GDP to a higher plane but does not by itself raise the underlying growth rate of the economy.

4. The agricultural reform in China is an interesting example. Although output of several crops increased at unprecedented rates (grains at 5 percent, cotton at 17 percent) from 1979 to 1983, output slowed considerably after 1984 (to 1.1 percent and 1.2 percent, respectively) as the effect of the initial price and institutional reforms dissipated. Even the growth between 1980 and 1983 was attributable largely to nonprice factors such as institutional reform. An econometric study found that 60 percent of the expansion was due to institutional reform, 25 percent to input use and technology changes, and only 15 percent to price changes (Lin 1987).

5. Indirect taxation through overvalued exchange rates and other measures, however, was found to be quite substantial, overwhelming even positive price differences between domestic and international prices. These distortions are not ameliorated by reducing the differences between domestic and border prices.

6. These funds not only partially neutralize the macroeconomic consequences of export earnings instability, but they do so in a way that does not tax the agricultural products in the long run (see Knudsen and Nash forthcoming a).

7. We are indebted to Anandarup Ray for making this point in an internal World Bank memorandum to Randolph Harris, March 8, 1989.

References

Balassa, Bela. 1988a. "Incentive Policies and Agricultural Performance in Sub-Saharan Africa." PPR Working Paper 77. Policy, Planning, and Research, World Bank, Washington, D.C.

———. 1988b. "Quantitative Appraisal of Adjustment Lending." PPR Working Paper 79. Policy, Planning, and Research, World Bank, Washington, D.C.

Binswanger, Hans P. 1989. "How Agricultural Producers Respond to Prices and Government Investments." Paper presented at First Annual World Bank Conference on Development Economics, April 27–28, Washington, D.C.

Binswanger, Hans P., Maw-Cheng Yang, Alan Bowers, and Yair Mundlak. 1987. "On the Determinants of Cross-Country Aggregate Agricultural Supply." *Journal of Econometrics* 36:111–31.

Cavallo, Domingo, and Yair Mundlak. 1982. *Agriculture and Economic Growth in an Open Economy: the Case of Argentina.* Research Report 36. Washington, D.C.: International Food Policy Research Institute.

Chhibber, Ajay. 1988. "Raising Agricultural Output: Price and Nonprice Factors." *Finance & Development* June:44–47.

Elias, V. V. 1985. *Government Expenditures on Agriculture and Agricultural Growth in Latin America.* Washington, D.C.: International Food Policy Research Institute.

Fitzgerald, Bruce, and Terry Monson. 1989. "Preferential Credit and Insurance as Means to Promote Exports." *World Bank Research Observer* 4 (January):89–114.

Hayami, Yujiro, and Vernon Ruttan. 1985. *Agricultural Development: An International Perspective.* Baltimore, Md.: Johns Hopkins University Press.

Jarvis, Lowell, and Maria del Rosario Medero. 1988. "Domestic Beef Price Stabilization in a Beef Exporting Country: Uruguay, 1961–86." Paper presented at the Twentieth Conference of the International Agricultural Economics Association, Buenos Aires, Argentina, August 24–31.

Keesing, Donald B., and Andrew Singer. 1989. "Experience of the World Bank in Support and Assistance for Export Marketing." Trade Policy Division, Country Economics Department, World Bank, Washington, D.C.

Knudsen, Odin, and John Nash. Forthcoming a. "Agricultural Price Stabilization and Risk Reduction in Developing Countries." In Alberto Valdes and Romeo Bautista, eds., *Trade and Macroeconomic Policies' Impact on Agriculture.* Washington, D.C.: International Food Policy Research Institute.

———. Forthcoming b. "Domestic Price Stabilization Schemes in Developing Countries." *Economic Development and Cultural Change.*

Knudsen, Odin, and P. A. Yotopoulos. 1985. "Agriculture in the Process of Trade Liberalization and Retrenchment: The Case of Chile." Agriculture Department, World Bank, Washington, D.C.

Krueger, A. O., Maurice Schiff, and Alberto Valdes. 1988. "Agricultural Incentives in Developing Countries: Measuring the Effect of Sectoral and Economywide Policies." *World Bank Economic Review* 2 (3) September:255–71.

Lele, Uma, and John W. Mellor. 1988. "Agricultural Growth, Its Determinants, and Their Relationship to World Development: An Overview." Paper prepared for the Twentieth Conference of the International Agricultural Economics Association, Buenos Aires, Argentina, August 24–31. (Revised September 23, 1988.)

Lin, Justin Yifu. 1987. "Household Farms, Cooperative Farms and Efficiency: Evidence from Rural De-Collectivization in China." Discussion Paper 91. Department of Economics, University of Hong Kong.

Mundlak, Yair. 1988. "Capital Accumulation, the Choice of Techniques, and Agricultural Output." In John W. Mellor and Raisuddin Ahmed, eds., *Price Policy.* Baltimore, Md.: Johns Hopkins University Press.

Nogués, Julio. 1989. "Latin America's Experience with Export Subsidies." PPR Working Paper 182. Policy, Planning, and Research, World Bank, Washington, D.C.

Pinto, Brian. 1987. "Nigeria During and After the Oil Boom: A Policy Comparison with Indonesia." *World Bank Economic Review* 1 (May):419–46.

Rodrik, Dani. 1988. "Liberalization, Sustainability, and the Design of Structural Adjustment Programs." Trade Policy Division, Country Economics Department, World Bank, Washington, D.C.

Sturzenegger, Adolpho. Forthcoming. "The Political Economy of Price Discrimination in the Argentine Pampas." In A. O. Krueger, Maurice Schiff, and Alberto Valdes, eds., *The Political Economy of Agricultural Pricing Policy: Latin America.* Baltimore, Md.: Johns Hopkins University Press.

World Bank. 1986. *World Development Report 1986.* New York: Oxford University Press.

———. 1988. "Agricultural Marketing: The World Bank's Experience." Operations Evaluation Department, World Bank, Washington, D.C.

———. 1989. *Adjustment Lending: An Evaluation of Ten Years of Experience.* Policy and Research Series 1. Washington, D.C.

Comments

Nurul Islam

My comments touch on several of the issues discussed by Odin Knudsen and John Nash: the influence of price and nonprice factors; the relationship among prices, aggregate supply response, and growth; input subsidies and government expenditures on agriculture; price stabilization; protecting the poor during adjustment; agricultural protectionism; and the sustainability of reform.

Reforms of agricultural pricing policies, including those affecting the level and stability of prices, liberalization of agricultural trade, and reduction in government involvement in the marketing and distribution of agricultural outputs and inputs, have been among the most widely discussed and controversial aspects of agricultural structural adjustment programs. The analysis of Knudsen and Nash deals more with policy recommendations in the World Bank's agricultural adjustment lending than with the impact of such reforms on performance. Still urgently needed is an empirical analysis of how the reforms were actually implemented and what their impact was on the agricultural sector.

Extensive research has quantified the extent to which economywide policies such as those dealing with trade and the exchange rate affect relative prices not only within agriculture but in other sectors as well. Research has also shown that the effects of these policies dominate those of sector-specific pricing policies implemented through subsidies and taxes or public intervention. For reforms of price policy to be effective, they must be combined with or even preceded by macroeconomic policy reforms, especially in the areas of trade and the exchange rate. High inflation or volatile exchange rates can soon erode or offset reforms of government support prices or agricultural taxes and subsidies.

Although some years ago experts considered "getting the prices right" to be the most effective way of generating efficient growth, opinion today seems to be shifting toward the belief that both *price and nonprice factors* are important. Experience with structural adjustment programs may have contributed to this pragmatic conclusion. Controversy persists, however, on two issues: (1) the relative importance of price and nonprice factors and (2) the sequencing of corrective measures on these two fronts.

The relative priority that should be attached to price and nonprice factors depends on the particular circumstances of each country. If price distortions are severe and long-standing, pricing policy reforms may greatly improve efficiency and growth even if nonprice factors are inadequate. It would be a one-shot improvement, however, unless nonprice factors were significantly strengthened. In other cases, the strengthening of nonprice factors may be the dominant consideration, partly because, as Knudsen and Nash point out, the aggregate supply response to price changes is itself a function of nonprice factors.

The interrelations between price and nonprice factors can be illustrated in a number of cases. For example, despite favorable coffee and tea prices in Kenya, productivity per hectare increased little among smallholders, primarily because of inadequate access to research and extension services, credit, and inputs; in contrast, productivity increased on large estates because of more ample access to these nonprice factors. In Cameroon, despite lower cotton prices than in Kenya, Malawi, and Nigeria (both in nominal terms and in purchasing power parity) and despite a fall in the price of cotton relative to the price of maize, yields per hectare were larger than in other countries because Cameroonian farmers had access to improved technology and extension services. Similarly, in Nigeria new technology and organizational efficiency increased cocoa production despite low returns from exports due to an overvalued exchange rate (Lele and Mellor 1988).

In the view of many developing countries, the recent heavy emphasis of international development agencies on pricing policy reforms, without commensurate attention to nonprice factors, is an excuse for inadequate assistance and inaction on nonprice issues. Everyone recognizes that improving nonprice factors requires substantial resources in both the short and long runs. The supply response is not only higher in the long run than in the short run, but it is also higher in the presence of improved nonprice factors such as infrastructure. Achieving this response requires a long-term commitment from both lenders and borrowers.

Another issue discussed by Knudsen and Nash is the *relationship among prices, aggregate supply response, and growth.* As they mention, aggregate supply elasticities in agriculture are rather modest, frequently 0.6 or less. The higher estimates of price responses that are obtained in a general equilibrium framework come only after a period of ten to fifteen years and are based on models of technological change and capital accumulation that include intersectoral capital flows and labor migration. These models seem to suggest that favorable price changes in agriculture are the principal engine of growth. Such price changes set in motion technological progress, which is incorporated in physical and human capital on the basis of farmers' selection of the most appropriate technologies from among a wide set of those readily available. This model, however, tends to ignore or underplay the role of public action in the field of technology, institutions, and infrastructure. Empirical verification of these models, including their implicit assumptions, is still limited and requires further research (Mundlak 1989; Cavallo and Mundlak 1982; IFPRI 1988).

In this connection, the controversy regarding the relationship between relative price changes in agriculture and the generation of technology needs some clarification. First, it is generally agreed that price incentives accelerate the diffusion of technological innovations once they are available; what is being debated is the generation of technology in response to price incentives. Second, the relevant policies and organizations differ for basic or fundamental research and applied and adaptive research. Third, no distinction is made between changes in relative prices within agriculture and changes in agricultural prices relative to nonagricultural prices, or between the effects of short- and long-term price changes on the generation of technology. Systematic analysis and clarification of the various aspects of the process of technological innovation and their interrelations are needed. For example, although the emphasis of private research may be affected by relative price changes within agriculture, it is unlikely that aggregate government research expenditures on agriculture or basic science are affected to any significant extent.

In the context of adjustment lending, government expenditures on agriculture, particularly *input subsidies*, have received much attention in recent years. Loans for agricultural adjustment programs have usually included the condition that input subsidies be reduced or eliminated.

Among input subsidies, the most controversial is the one for fertilizer—the most important ingredient in the Green Revolution. Several arguments have been advanced in favor of a fertilizer subsidy: it compensates for imperfections in the capital market and for the risks associated with adopting a new technology with high cash costs; it is required to stimulate the process of trial and error needed initially to determine the optimum uses of fertilizer; and it is needed temporarily to offset high costs of distribution and transportation in the early stages of fertilizer use, when the volume of sales is low and the unit cost of distribution is high.

The importance of these considerations depends on the circumstances of each country and the effect of fertilizer use on output relative to the prevailing ratio of fertilizer price to output price. Although it is often argued that, however justified, temporary subsidies are inadvisable because they tend to become permanent, several countries have shown that subsidies can be reduced or even eliminated over time. It has also been argued that the resources spent on subsidies would be better spent on agricultural investments with higher returns such as research, extension, infrastructure, and so on, and that such expenditures would in turn help increase returns from the use of fertilizer. Experience with structural adjustment programs in many countries demonstrates, however, that the reduction of subsidies is often accompanied by a reduction rather than an increase in public investment in agriculture, with adverse effects on growth and employment in agriculture.

Economists continue to debate whether the *stabilization of agricultural prices* has a desirable impact on consumer and producer welfare. Some argue that substantial benefits may accrue from price stabilization if macroeconomic and dynamic considerations are taken into account. Price instability adversely affects investment not only by farmers but also by those engaged in marketing, distribution, and processing. Moreover, consumers, especially poor consumers, incur high transaction costs every time prices change because they need to reallocate their expenditures in order to fulfill their minimum nutritional requirements (Timmer 1988; Ahmed 1989). Furthermore, the very poor—who in many countries constitute a large part of the population and have almost no access to credit—cannot hold back sufficiently on consumption when prices are low to save enough to avoid hunger when prices are high. Even farmers who do not produce enough food for their own needs must sell some of their output immediately after harvest when prices are low to meet urgent cash requirements and must buy more during other times when prices are higher.

Most governments, in both developing and developed countries and whatever their position on the role of markets, intervene to achieve some price stability. Governments are unwilling to stand idle and let people go hungry when world prices have risen, even if their action may worsen the problem at some time in the future; nor do they allow their farmers to go bankrupt and join the urban unemployed if prices collapse in the short run, even if the commodities they produce have limited markets in the long run. Policymakers therefore need a mechanism for addressing price fluctuations. Analytical studies and practical measures are needed so that a cost-effective method for stabilizing prices can be designed.

Prices are affected not only by fluctuations in world prices and exchange rates but also by variations in domestic production due to the weather or the availability of inputs and technological innovations. Knudsen and Nash concentrate on price instability arising from external causes rather than from fluctuations in domestic production. This emphasis naturally leads to a discussion of taxes and subsidies on foreign trade as the principal mechanism for stabilizing domestic prices. Experience, however, is very limited in this respect, and the subject requires further study. In addition, countries differ widely in their capacity to formulate and implement such taxes and subsidies.

The fluctuations in domestic output and prices can be reduced by varying exports and imports, by varying domestic stocks, or by doing both. For countries that are not consistent exporters or importers, an exclusive reliance on trade adjustment mechanisms for stabilizing prices is not necessarily the most effective approach. Occasional exporters cannot sell their surplus output in the world market except at a considerable loss, while occasional importers cannot import a small amount at short notice to offset shortfalls in domestic production without incurring delays and high costs. Furthermore, a country's staple food products may not commonly be traded in international markets. These considerations support the case for using domestic stocks, in appropriate combination with variations in exports and imports, wherever feasible as a method for stabilizing domestic prices.

What is needed is to analyze for a given country the tradeoffs among (1) the degree of price stability being sought, (2) the size and cost of stocks, and (3) the degree of reliance on imports. The narrower the price band (the margin between ceiling and floor prices) within which stability is sought, the larger the size of the necessary stocks and the larger the cost of stabilization. For example, a study in Kenya found that holding the producer price of maize between US$129 and US$151 per ton would cost between US$1.0 million and US$1.5 million more annually than would holding prices between US$125 and US$155 per ton (Pinckney 1989). Even a moderate degree of flexibility in response to changes in world prices or domestic production can considerably reduce the costs of price stabilization. In the Kenyan example, a policy that translates a US$10.00 change in the world price to a US$1.00 change in the domestic price would save about US$350,000 annually on average, while a policy that allows the official price to increase by 6 percent when production falls by 10 percent would save about US$600,000 annually (Pinckney 1989).

A narrow price band that does not meet the costs of private traders for marketing, distribution, and processing will discourage private stock holding and so increase the amount of public stocks required. In view of the high cost of stabilizing prices through the management of domestic stocks, such efforts should be confined to a very few vital commodities. It is unlikely, however, that a public stock policy for price stabilization can be carried out without some control over imports and exports. If exports and imports are unregulated while domestic prices are held within a band, the cost of holding stocks will be enormous. The actual importing and exporting can be undertaken by private traders under a system of licensing, and domestic trading in food grains can also be left to private traders, with occasional intervention by the public stock-holding agency.

At least in the early stages of the adjustment process, the need to *protect and compensate the poor* is increasingly being recognized—for example, when food prices rise after the elimination of subsidies or employment and income fall at least in part because of a reduction in government expenditures. Targeting subsidies to the poor is easier said than done, however. It confronts not only the political opposition of those excluded from the subsidy but also the problems of logistics and inadequate information about the target group. If the very poor constitute a high proportion of households, marketwide subsidies may be more cost-effective than narrowly targeted schemes that are subject to large leakages. A recent study by the International Food Policy Research Institute found, for example, that the total cost (the amount of subsidy plus administrative costs and leakages) of transferring US$1.00 to the target groups in an economically depressed rural area in the Philippines was US$1.19 if all households received subsidies, US$1.60 if only households consuming less than 80 percent of their calorie requirements were targeted, and US$3.61 if only households with malnourished preschool children were targeted. The major reason for the differences in costs was leakages to nontargeted groups in the latter two cases (IFPRI 1988).

The discussion by Knudsen and Nash of *agricultural protectionism* in developing countries makes it appear stronger and more pervasive than it is. It is true that agricultural protectionism is on the rise in the middle-income developing countries, particularly for import-competing food products. In other developing countries, however, usually only one or two commodities have domestic prices that are higher than world prices at the official exchange rate. The current depression in world prices has contributed in several instances to an improvement in the relative price of import-competing agricultural commodities in domestic markets. In some cases, exchange rate adjustments have led to a rise in domestic prices. This emphasizes once again that trade reforms cannot be divorced from exchange rate reforms.

The reform of protectionist policies in agriculture or of trade policies generally should take place within a framework of overall trade liberalization so that intersectoral discrimination does not persist. One forum for reciprocal trade liberalization is the Uruguay Round of Multilateral Trade Negotiations. In the Uruguay Round, developing countries, especially high-income developing countries, will be requested to grant reciprocity in trade concessions. In this context, they should receive credit for unilateral trade liberalization undertaken under structural adjustment programs. Furthermore, as Knudsen and Nash emphasize, the incorporation within the GATT framework of concessions already given by developing countries is likely to improve their durability and reduce the likelihood of policy reversal.

To contend that the only way to deepen and broaden recent policy reforms in agriculture is to dismantle all government undertakings or public enterprises in the agricultural sector seems an extreme position.

Recent experience confirms two major risks or difficulties of rapid and wholesale privatization: (1) the public monopoly may be replaced by a private monopoly or oligopoly, with government failures replaced by market failures of a greater magnitude, and (2) the public marketing and distribution system may collapse before a viable private one can be developed. Examples of such outcomes abound. International development agencies need to maintain a nonideological approach on this matter so that efforts can be made both to improve the efficiency of public enterprises and to encourage competition between public and private enterprises. The *durability of agricultural policy reforms* depends less on the dismantling of all government institutions capable of interfering with the market mechanism and more on each country's conviction concerning the desirability and extent of policy changes. Such reforms should be based on a reasoned analysis undertaken by the recipient countries in an atmosphere of open debate in which dialogue with the lending agencies is only one input. This process requires a national capability for analyzing and formulating policy. Assistance by international organizations in building up such a capability will make an important contribution to the sustainability of policy reforms.

References

Ahmed, Raisuddin. 1989. *Rice Price Fluctuations and an Approach to Price Stabilization in Bangladesh.* IFPRI Research Report 72. Washington, D.C.: International Food Policy Research Institute.

Cavallo, Domingo, and Yair Mundlak. 1982. *Agricultural and Economic Growth in an Open Economy: The Case of Argentina.* IFPRI Research Report 36. Washington, D.C.: International Food Policy Research Institute.

IFPRI. 1988. "Commentary: Achieving Growth with Equity Through Appropriate Agricultural Pricing Policy." IFPRI Report 2. Washington, D.C.: International Food Policy Research Institute.

Lele, Uma, and John W. Mellor. 1988. "Agricultural Growth, Its Determinants and Their Relationship to World Development: An Overview." Paper prepared for the Twentieth Conference of the International Agricultural Economics Association, Buenos Aires, Argentina, August 24–31.

Mundlak, Yair. 1989. *Intersectoral Factor Mobility and Agricultural Growth.* IFPRI Research Report. Washington, D.C.: International Food Policy Research Institute.

Pinckney, T. C. 1989. *Storage, Trade, and Price Policy under Production Instability: Maize in Kenya.* IFPRI Research Report 71. Washington, D.C.: International Food Policy Research Institute.

Timmer, Peter C. 1988. *Agricultural Pricing and Stabilization Policy.* Cambridge, Mass.: Harvard Institute for International Development.

8 *Industrial Performance: Some Stylized Facts*

James R. Tybout

ROUGHLY A DECADE AGO, external shocks in the form of oil price increases, world recession, deterioration in the terms of trade, and high interest rates began to create major adjustment problems for developing countries. In many cases these problems were exacerbated by excessive public spending, overvalued exchange rates, and various stopgap policies designed to maintain macroeconomic stability or external balance. By the early 1980s some combination of adverse external shocks and unwise domestic policies had placed a number of countries on the brink of economic crisis.

Either voluntarily or as a condition for external assistance, many countries began a process of policy reform. The new policies, which amounted largely to devaluation and trade promotion, had two basic objectives: (1) to restore stability and external balance without distortionary interventions and (2) to lay the foundation for a new era of sustained growth.

This chapter analyzes the performance of the manufacturing sector during the adjustment process in a sample of fifteen countries that were heavily involved in adjustment programs and had received adjustment loans from the World Bank.[1] The analysis focuses on short-run patterns of growth and trade. The first part of the chapter briefly reviews the consequences for the industrial sector of external and policy-induced shocks and the conditionalities of World Bank adjustment loans and then examines the performance of the country sample. These countries' growth rates are juxtaposed with average growth rates for their respective regions during three periods: precrisis, crisis, and adjustment. Next, a decomposition of the demand-side sources of growth is used to study the changes in domestic demand and manufacturing trade flows that have accompanied changes in growth. Intertemporal and regional comparisons are made once again. In the second part of the chapter, an attempt is made to associate loan conditions with patterns of manufacturing growth and trade among the sample countries.

Performance of the Manufacturing Sector

Just as trade regimes typically favor industry at the expense of agriculture, policymakers typically attempt to minimize the adjustment burden imposed on industrial firms during periods of adverse external shocks and contractionary macroeconomic policies. There are several reasons for this concern. Successful industrial development is often viewed as a critical prerequisite for rapid growth in productivity and gross national product (GNP). Industrial technology is subject to scale economies and rapid technological advance; similarly, the industrial sector is an incubator for entrepreneurial development and the accumulation of human capital.[2] Because capital is concentrated in the industrial sector, a large fraction of national savings originates there; for the same reason, the sector is an important tax base.

Failure to maintain stable market conditions for industrial producers can also create short-run problems. One obvious consequence of industrial malaise is urban unemployment; another, perhaps more insidious consequence is general financial distress. When austerity programs, high interest rates, or overvalued exchange rates cut industrial profits, liquidity falls, business failures increase, and the quality of banks' loan portfolios deteriorates. Especially where financial regulation has been wanting, the situation can quickly deteriorate into runs, financial crises, and expensive government bailouts (Tybout 1986).

Unfortunately, it has probably been especially difficult for policymakers in countries with structural adjustment loans (SALs) to insulate industrial producers, given the shocks they have experienced. First, the industrial sector relies heavily on imported materials and capital equipment, so foreign exchange shortages have probably constrained current industrial production, fixed investment, and technical efficiency. Second, because a substantial fraction of industrial goods are tradable, the overvalued exchange rates in the early 1980s typically caused significant reductions in the demand for the output of manufacturing industries. Third, many industrial products, particularly consumer durables and capital equipment, are relatively sensitive to the effects of demand fluctuations. Industrial sectors thus tend to produce goods that are sensitive to national income contractions. Fourth, in addition to these inherent characteristics of industry, there is evidence that financial structures in the industrial sector were generally at greater risk in the early 1980s than they had been in the 1970s.[3] Hence the sector was already fragile before the reforms began, a situation that was exacerbated by the growing reluctance of international creditors to provide new funds. The balance of this chapter is concerned with whether the SAL countries *did* manage to insulate their industrial sectors from radical adjustment, how they attempted to do so, and the role of World Bank conditionality in shaping these policies.

Three Phases of Performance

To examine the short-run costs of crisis and adjustment for industrial producers, several indicators of performance will be constructed by country and by broadly defined region.[4] The indicators will be calculated for three periods, each chosen to approximate an era in world economic conditions. The first period, 1979–81, spans a time of moderate growth in the industrial countries and relatively easy access to private credit in world capital markets. The second, 1982–83, is characterized by recession in the industrial countries and a scarcity of private external credit for developing countries. It corresponds to the advent of serious crises in a number of the countries studied in this chapter. The third period, 1984–86, is characterized by recovery among the industrial countries and increased adjustment lending to developing countries. These periods are of course crude approximations to the turning points in specific countries, and their interpretation is further confounded by unpredictable lags in adjustment. Nonetheless, it will be seen that clear patterns emerge.

A brief elaboration of conditions in the SAL countries during each period provides useful background for later sections. During the precrisis years (1979–81) these countries were surprisingly similar. First, trade protection was typically substantial. Except in Chile, import-competing producers enjoyed considerable protection through both nontariff and tariff barriers. Second, except in Kenya, Korea, and Malawi, this protection was at least partly offset by overvalued currencies. Third, the SAL countries were generally suffering from the second oil-price shock (Mexico excepted), and their terms of trade problems were typically compounded by deteriorating world prices for their exports.[5] Fourth, significant price controls were in force in Morocco, Pakistan, the Philippines, Turkey, and many of the African countries. Fifth, these same countries tended to have a large public sector and state ownership of industrial enterprises.

The combination of overvalued exchange rates, terms of trade shocks, protection, and state intervention made the SAL countries relatively susceptible to balance of payments problems. These materialized when international credit markets tightened and the world moved into recession. The crises did not occur simultaneously in all countries, but it is generally reasonable to describe 1982–83 as the period when the greatest impact was felt. In roughly half the sample the crises were exacerbated by further terms of trade shocks.[6] Two initial policy reactions typified the stopgap attempts of SAL countries to deal with foreign exchange shortages: overvalued exchange rates were abandoned and trade protection was increased.[7]

As countries tried to regain their economic footing, a process of structural adjustment ensued. World Bank adjustment lending helped ease the foreign exchange shortage, which by 1984 was severely exacerbated by high debt-service obligations and the unavailability of private external funds. World Bank loan agreements included various conditions, especially with respect to exchange rates and trade policy. In part because of this conditionality, the structural adjustment period saw further devaluations and some dismantling of the new trade barriers that had been instituted during the crisis years.

Conditionality

Loan conditionality has spanned the entire policy spectrum from macroeconomic policies to those for trade, finance, and the productive sectors. For industry, these sectoral policies pertain to pricing, entry and exit, subsector planning and restructuring, investment incentives, technology, marketing, and various others (see table 8-1).

Several patterns of conditionality during fiscal 1982–87 merit mention. First, "firm" policy conditions have pertained most frequently to trade and exchange rate policies; firm policy conditions specific to the industrial sector have been relatively less common.[8] Second, when specific to industry, conditions have most frequently concerned subsector restructuring, followed by investment incentives and pricing policies (see table 8-1). Other industrial policy areas have been mentioned relatively infrequently (none of them has been at issue in more than 10 percent of the loan packages in the SAL country data base). Third, about 53 percent of industrial policy conditions have been fully implemented, which is almost identical to the implementation rate for *all* provisions for conditionality.

Although regional variations in conditionality are limited, some patterns do emerge. Subsector restructuring and pricing policy reforms are relatively common in Africa. In Latin America and the Caribbean concrete conditionality was relatively limited, with most of the emphasis on quantitative restrictions, export regimes, and exchange rate policies. Public investment and export policies appeared relatively frequently among the less concrete measures. The relative emphasis in Europe, the Middle East, and North Africa (EMENA) has been on export promotion; some trade liberalization has also been required. Macroeconomic and financial sector conditionality has been relatively light, emphasizing tax policy and interest rate reform respectively. Industrial conditionality has also been relatively light in this region. Conditionality in Asia has been heaviest in the areas of import duties and tariffs, although industrial policy has also figured rather prominently, particularly with respect to issues of entry and exit, technology, and subsector restructuring. Macroeconomic and financial conditions have been less common.[9]

Manufacturing Growth

Before discussing the manufacturing growth of SAL countries in each period, a note of caution is in order. It is not yet possible to assess these countries' success in realizing the long-run goals of adjustment pro-

Table 8-1. *Conditionality and Implementation Affecting Industry in Fifteen SAL Countries*

Policy area	*Number of conditions*	*Percentage of all industrial sector conditions*	*Percentage of all adjustment conditions*	*Industrial conditions fully implemented*[a]	
				Percent	*Number*
Pricing and subsidies	10	13.0	0.7	80.0	5
Entry and exit of firms	4	5.2	0.3	0.0	3
Other regulatory	7	9.1	0.5	60.0	5
Restructuring of subsector and firms	29	37.7	2.1	65.2	23
Investment promotion and incentives	17	22.1	1.3	53.9	13
Technology	2	2.6	0.2	0.0	2
Subsector planning (supply and demand)	1	1.3	0.1	0.0	1
Marketing	0	0.0	0.0	0.0	0
Other sector-specific policies	7	9.1	0.5	0.0	3

Note: Figures are constructed from the ALCID data base of the World Bank's Industry Development Division. For a fuller discussion of their interpretation, see Coogan (1989).

a. Implementation data were not available for all of the conditions. The number of conditions on which the percentages are based is given in the last column.

grams.[10] Short-run growth rates, however, as William Steel has stressed in an internal World Bank paper, reflect largely the extent of capacity utilization and the associated adjustment costs. They should *not* be viewed as reflecting success in adjusting for two basic reasons. First, the longer-run objectives of adjustment programs—that is, sustained growth and efficient production—can run counter to short-run objectives related to easing adjustment costs, especially when major stabilization attempts are necessary. Second, despite the common elements of SAL country experiences, adjustment has meant different things in different countries. Some countries have simply been recovering from transitory shocks, such as world recession and borrowing constraints. Others have been attempting to accommodate more permanent problems, such as secular deterioration in their terms of trade. And still others have been adopting new development strategies altogether—typically ones more oriented toward exploitation of their comparative advantage. Accordingly, different growth paths must be expected, especially in the short run. All that is known with certainty is the *extent* of output fluctuations and the short-run adjustment burden that such fluctuations imply.

REGIONAL PATTERNS. Table 8-2 presents annualized growth rates for the fifteen SAL countries by region. The regional figures are averages of real growth rates by country weighted by base-year country size (see the appendix for details and countries used in the regional calculations). To get a crude indication of how well insulated industrial producers were from macroeconomic fluctuations, I begin with a general examination of the relation between the growth of gross domestic product (GDP) and that of industrial value added.

One way to judge the performance of the industrial sector, or its "insulation" from shocks, is to compare manufacturing growth rates with GDP growth rates. By this yardstick, the most drastic reductions in GDP and manufacturing growth took place in Africa during 1982–86. Moreover, African manufacturing contracted more rapidly than GDP, despite the fact that African countries are generally at an early stage of development and should be undergoing relatively rapid industrialization. "Deindustrialization" also took place in Latin America during 1978–81 but was reversed during the adjustment years, so in this region manufacturing went from being a lagging to a leading sector. In EMENA, by contrast, industry was a leading sector during all periods under review. Asia showed balanced growth until the 1984–86 adjustment period, when manufacturing emerged as a leading sector. Thus regional performance overall suggests that manufacturing producers in Asia and EMENA were somewhat protected from macroeconomic contractions, while producers in Latin America were less protected and those in Africa were the least protected.

Table 8-2. Average Annual Growth Rates of Manufacturing Value Added and GDP for Fifteen SAL Countries, 1979–81, 1982–83, and 1984–86

Region and country	1979–81		1982–83		1984–86	
	GDP	Manufacturing	GDP	Manufacturing	GDP	Manufacturing
Africa	−0.01	0.02	−0.04	−0.06	−0.02	−0.05
Côte d'Ivoire	−0.04	0.00	0.00	0.15	0.03	0.06
Ghana	−0.12	−0.22	−0.03	−0.23	0.13	n.a.
Kenya	0.02	0.03	−0.03	−0.04	0.04	0.03
Malawi	−0.02	n.a.	0.02	n.a.	−0.02	n.a.
Zambia	0.03	0.04	−0.06	−0.05	0.01	0.01
Latin America	0.05	0.00	−0.02	0.02	0.00	0.03
Chile	0.07	0.06	−0.06	−0.10	0.04	0.06[a]
Colombia	0.03	0.06	0.02	0.01	0.07	0.06
Jamaica	−0.09	−0.10	0.05	0.16	0.01	0.05
Mexico	0.10	0.08	−0.05	−0.04	−0.02	0.02
Asia	0.07	0.07	0.04	0.03	0.04	0.07
Korea	0.02	0.03	0.08	0.07	0.10	0.12
Philippines	0.03	0.03	0.01	0.01	−0.05	−0.05
Thailand	0.04	0.06	0.04	0.01	0.04	0.07
EMENA	0.03	0.06	0.02	0.03	0.04	0.05
Morocco	0.01	0.02	0.02	0.01	0.03	0.04
Pakistan	0.06	0.09	0.06	0.08	0.07	0.07
Turkey	0.05	0.09	0.01	0.06	0.05	0.06

n.a. Not available.

Note: Regional growth rates are weighted averages of real growth rates (denominated in domestic currency) for all countries (see appendix for list of countries) in the region for which data were available for all three periods. The weights are shares in regional GDP or regional manufacturing value added, depending on which aggregate is being studied.

a. This growth rate is calculated by using a production (rather than value added) growth rate to infer the data for 1986.

Source: See appendix.

SAMPLE PERFORMANCE. How did the fifteen SAL countries fare? There are several ways to evaluate their performance on the basis of the data presented in table 8-2. One possibility is to compare each country's manufacturing growth with the regional average. Such comparisons show that only half the SAL countries had growth rates above regional norms during both the 1978–81 reference period and the 1982–83 crisis period. However, ten of the thirteen SAL countries with observable data registered growth rates above the regional norms during the 1984–86 recovery period. This pattern is weakly supportive of the view that the manufacturing sector was better able to rebound from recession and crisis in the SAL countries than elsewhere.

A more subtle observation can be made if individual SAL countries are followed through time. Four countries were above their regional norms in all periods (Kenya and Zambia, Pakistan and Turkey); three were below their region in the first period and above it thereafter (Côte d'Ivoire, Jamaica, and Korea); and three were below their region in the second period but above it thereafter (Chile, Colombia, and Thailand). So six of the ten SAL countries showed positive turnarounds relative to their regions. If adjustment lending were unrelated to country turnaround, there should also have been about six countries that started above regional norms and fell below them. Only Mexico did this, however, and even that was a marginal case.[11]

An alternative way to judge the performance of SAL countries is to compare manufacturing growth rates with GDP growth rates. Since the industrial sector typically grows faster than GDP in developing countries (see, for example, Chenery, Robinson, and Syrquin 1986), the difference between manufacturing and GDP growth in each region can be taken to indicate the "normal" amount of industrialization taking place. A comparison of industrialization in the SAL countries with their respective regional norms shows that of the thirteen countries with available data, only five (Chile, Colombia, Korea, Pakistan, and Philippines) failed at least to match the regional rate of industrialization during 1984–86. During the precrisis period, however, this was the case for a different, larger set of SAL countries (only Ghana, Kenya, Morocco, and Zambia failed to match their regional average rates of industrialization). Put differently, the SAL countries did manage to industrialize relatively rapidly, but this was true both before and after adjustment programs were instituted.

Sources of Manufacturing Growth

Adjustment programs are likely to affect the growth of industrial output through several channels. First, to the extent that real expenditure is constrained by an adjustment program, the contraction of aggregate demand should reduce industrial capacity utilization across the board. Second, and counter to this force, to the extent that an adjustment program eases a foreign exchange constraint, the resultant increased availability of imported inputs may allow industrial expansion. The foreign exchange effect can dominate the aggregate demand effect if prices are rigid and there is substantial excess demand for industrial products.[12] Third, if an adjustment program involves real devaluation, the effects of expenditure-switching in product markets should help both exporters and import-competing producers. Devaluation also increases the price of imported inputs, however, and so can hurt manufacturing producers.

To gain a better understanding of the roles played by these basic forces, it is helpful to employ algebraic decompositions of gross manufacturing output by demand source: domestic market expansion, import substitution (given domestic market size), and export expansion. The expression used is

$$(8\text{-}1)\qquad \Delta Q_t = \Delta D_t(1 - \overline{m}_t) - \Delta m_t\overline{D}_t + \Delta X_t$$

where Q_t is gross manufacturing output in period t, D_t is domestic demand for manufacturing output (for both intermediate and final use), m_t is the share of domestic demand supplied by imports, and X_t is the amount of manufacturing output exported. Bars denote averages of period t and period $t - 1$ values.[13]

The first term is the portion of output expansion attributable to domestic market expansion, assuming that the import penetration rate, m, remains constant. This term should pick up general aggregate demand effects. The second term reflects the effect of changing import penetration rates on output expansion—note that *reductions* in import penetration rates amount to positive import substitution and contribute positively to output growth. If manufactured intermediate and capital goods are important components of manufactured imports, however, import substitution may reflect foreign exchange rationing and associated *constraints* on output. (When this happens, domestic demand or exports, or both, should be falling as import substitution rises.) The last term simply reflects export expansion. In the presentation of results (see tables 8-3 and 8-4), these three components of output expansion are expressed as ratios to beginning-of-period output, so they will always sum to the cumulative rate of output growth for the period:

$$(8\text{-}2)\qquad \Delta Q/Q = (\Delta D/Q)(1 - m) - (\Delta \overline{m}/Q)D + \Delta X/\overline{Q}.$$

Contrasts across periods for a given country will reveal how domestic and world market conditions contributed to expansion (or contraction) of the industrial sectors (see table 8-4). In particular, it should be apparent whether the industrial sector's net contribution to the current account improved or worsened, whether this change was due to export expansion

Table 8-3. Sources-of-Growth Decomposition for the Manufacturing Sector, by Region, 1979–81, 1982–83, and 1984–86

	Summary statistics			*Contribution to total output growth*		
Region and period	*Output growth* $\Delta Q/Q$	*Import share* $\overline{m}$	*Export share* $\overline{X}/\overline{D}$	*Domestic market expansion* $(\Delta D/Q)(1-\overline{m})$	*Import substitution* $-(\Delta m/Q)\overline{D}$	*Export expansion* $\Delta X/Q$
Africa						
1979–81	0.21	0.40	0.03	0.11	0.10	−0.01
1982–83	−0.12	0.33	0.02	−0.23	0.11	−0.01
1984–86	0.06	0.27	0.02	−0.03	0.08	0.00
Latin America						
1979–81	0.11	0.16	0.03	0.15	−0.04	−0.00
1982–83	−0.04	0.14	0.03	−0.13	0.09	−0.01
1984–86	0.06	0.10	0.03	0.06	−0.01	0.01
Asia						
1979–81	0.22	0.21	0.14	0.17	0.00	0.04
1982–83	0.11	0.20	0.14	0.08	0.02	0.01
1984–86	0.19	0.18	0.14	0.14	0.02	0.03

EMENA						
1979–81	0.03	0.18	0.06	−0.02	0.03	0.03
1982–83	0.06	0.16	0.07	0.02	0.03	0.01
1984–86	0.13	0.16	0.08	0.15	−0.04	0.02
All regions						
1979–81	0.15	0.20	0.08	0.14	−0.01	0.02
1982–83	0.03	0.18	0.08	−0.03	0.06	0.00
1984–86	0.12	0.15	0.08	0.09	0.01	0.02
Sample countries						
1979–81	0.18	0.17	0.09	0.17	−0.01	0.02
1982–83	0.04	0.15	0.09	−0.03	0.06	0.01
1984–86	0.13	0.13	0.09	0.12	−0.01	0.02

Note: Growth rates (gross output) are cumulative over the periods indicated. (For example, figures for 1979–81 reflect a comparison of 1978 and 1981 values.) Reported figures are weighted averages of country-by-country figures; the weights are the respective country's share in total manufacturing value added for the group. Further details are provided in the appendix.

Source: See appendix.

Table 8-4. Sources-of-Growth Decomposition for the Manufacturing Sector for Fifteen SAL Countries, 1979–81, 1982–83, and 1984–86

Country and period	Summary statistics: Output growth $\Delta Q/Q$	Summary statistics: Import share $\overline{m}$	Summary statistics: Export share $\overline{X}/\overline{D}$	Contribution to total output growth: Domestic market expansion $(\Delta D/Q)(1-\overline{m})$	Contribution to total output growth: Import substitution $-(\Delta m/Q)\overline{D}$	Contribution to total output growth: Export expansion $\Delta X/Q$
Chile						
1979–81	0.14	0.24	0.02	0.22	−0.08	−0.01
1982–83	−0.11	0.21	0.02	−0.24	0.13	−0.00
1984–86	0.19	0.15	0.02	0.18	0.01	0.00
Colombia						
1979–81	0.12	0.17	0.04	0.13	−0.02	0.01
1982–83	−0.02	0.17	0.03	−0.02	0.02	−0.02
1984–86	0.15	0.14	0.03	0.09	0.05	0.02
Côte d'Ivoire						
1979–81	0.24	0.31	0.04	−0.04	0.27	0.01
1982–83	0.08	0.20	0.04	0.01	0.08	−0.01
1984–86	0.21	0.18	0.03	0.23	−0.02	0.00
Ghana						
1979–81	−0.13	0.30	0.01	−0.18	0.06	−0.01
1982–83	−0.18	0.23	0.01	−0.28	0.11	−0.00
1984–86	0.35	0.19	0.01	0.36	−0.01	0.00

Jamaica						
1979–81	−0.15	0.45	0.45	−0.07	−0.11	0.02
1982–83	0.05	0.46	0.38	0.12	0.11	−0.18
1984–86	−0.03	0.37	0.24	−0.04	0.08	−0.07
Kenya						
1979–81	0.19	0.42	0.05	−0.05	0.27	−0.03
1982–83	0.06	0.28	0.04	−0.09	0.16	−0.02
1984–86	0.15	0.25	0.04	0.21	−0.08	0.02
Korea						
1979–81	0.25	0.18	0.28	0.14	0.05	0.06
1982–83	0.21	0.16	0.26	0.18	0.02	0.01
1984–86	0.31	0.15	0.24	0.25	−0.00	0.07
Malawi						
1979–81	0.12	0.44	0.04	−0.15	0.24	0.03
1982–83	0.09	0.34	0.04	0.01	0.10	−0.02
1984–86	−0.01	0.30	0.04	−0.06	0.02	0.02
Mexico						
1979–81	0.27	0.13	0.02	0.35	−0.08	0.00
1982–83	−0.10	0.11	0.03	−0.21	0.11	0.00
1984–86	0.04	0.07	0.03	0.05	−0.02	0.01
Morocco						
1979–81	0.05	0.25	0.07	−0.05	0.08	0.03
1982–83	0.10	0.20	0.09	0.03	0.05	0.01
1984–86	0.05	0.19	0.10	0.05	−0.03	0.03

(Table continues on the following page.)

Table 8-4 (continued)

Country and period	Summary statistics: Output growth $\Delta Q/Q$	Summary statistics: Import share $\overline{m}$	Summary statistics: Export share $\overline{X}/\overline{D}$	Contribution to total output growth: Domestic market expansion $(\Delta D/Q)(1 - \overline{m})$	Contribution to total output growth: Import substitution $-(\Delta m/Q)\overline{D}$	Contribution to total output growth: Export expansion $\Delta X/Q$
Pakistan						
1979–81	0.29	0.29	0.15	0.21	0.04	0.04
1982–83	0.23	0.24	0.15	0.13	0.07	0.04
1984–86	0.25	0.20	0.14	0.21	0.03	0.01
Philippines						
1979–81	0.12	0.24	0.10	0.06	0.00	0.06
1982–83	0.05	0.22	0.12	0.02	0.04	−0.01
1984–86	−0.08	0.19	0.12	−0.11	0.03	0.00
Thailand						
1979–81	0.23	0.16	0.05	0.20	0.00	0.02
1982–83	0.12	0.15	0.05	0.11	0.01	−0.00
1984–86	0.15	0.14	0.06	0.09	0.02	0.03
Turkey						
1979–81	−0.03	0.11	0.03	−0.04	−0.01	0.03
1982–83	0.11	0.10	0.06	0.06	0.02	0.03
1984–86	0.21	0.11	0.07	0.23	−0.04	0.02
Zambia						
1979–81	−0.02	0.28	0.00	0.04	−0.06	−0.00
1982–83	0.08	0.25	0.00	−0.07	0.15	−0.00
1984–86	0.05	0.19	0.01	0.04	0.00	0.01

Source: See appendix.

or import substitution, and whether industrial output was closely tied to domestic demand conditions. Contrasts with average regional patterns (table 8-3) should also indicate which countries were doing well relative to other countries in similar circumstances. Finally, once each country's industrial performance has been assessed, a crude attempt can be made to associate policy reforms with outcomes.

Since the real exchange rate has fluctuated considerably in a number of the countries in the sample, it makes a difference whether exports, imports, and production are expressed in terms of real value (as is typically done) or as indices of physical volume. For example, real devaluation increases the domestic currency value of imports and exports relative to goods produced and consumed at home. Hence, if the decomposition is done in value terms, export expansion and increased import penetration will appear to accompany real devaluation even if physical trade flows (and the dollar-denominated manufacturing trade balance) remain unaffected. Because the primary interest here is in changes in physical resource allocation, not in the valuation effects of exchange rate changes, I depart from tradition and use indices of physical volume to implement equation 8-1 (see appendix for details).[14]

Annualizing the manufacturing growth rates in tables 8-3 and 8-4 would not yield exactly the same growth rates as in table 8-2. The reason is that in tables 8-3 and 8-4 the figures are growth rates of gross output, whereas in table 8-2 the figures refer to value added. Qualitatively, however, the patterns are similar for most countries, but for Côte d'Ivoire, Kenya, Turkey, and Zambia there are substantial contrasts. These contrasts imply either that physical input-output relationships changed or that the relative prices of inputs and outputs changed. Given Africa's heavy reliance on imported inputs, it is not surprising that most of the growth discrepancies are found in that region.

General patterns. Several patterns emerge clearly from the results for all fifty countries included in the regional totals in table 8-3 (see table 8-6 for the list of countries). First, as is typically the case, the expansion of domestic markets has generally been the most important source of expanded demand for manufactured products. Second, and more interesting, rapid import substitution took place during the crisis years 1982–83 when domestic demand contracted. So developing countries generally responded to the debt crisis and world recession with large cutbacks in manufactured imports, thereby conserving foreign exchange. This response softened the strong contractionary effects of falling domestic demand in countries where recessionary forces were strong, but it probably meant production bottlenecks in countries where imported inputs were key. (This issue is picked up again later when regional and SAL country patterns are examined.)

Third, during 1984–86 import penetration rates remained at the reduced levels of the 1982–83 period. (Recall that reductions in protection during 1984–86 were often accompanied by offsetting devaluations.) This is probably the most striking structural adjustment to emerge from the aggregate figures. If it reflected either ongoing foreign exchange shortages or attempts to generate product market demand, the consequences have most likely been damaging: imported inputs were in short supply, and protection of product markets tended to generate the familiar collection of inefficiencies.[15] Fourth, the expansion of manufactured exports has not been a major source of growth in demand among the fifty countries. After dropping to near zero during the 1982–83 period, export expansion rebounded to precrisis levels of about 2 percent.

Surprisingly, the sample of fifteen SAL countries heavily involved in World Bank adjustment programs performed almost identically to the full comparator group of fifty developing countries in all periods. Although the SAL countries consistently grew slightly more rapidly than the comparator group because of more expansion of domestic markets and experienced slight increases in import penetration during 1984–86, these contrasts are very minor. Part of the explanation for the close similarity in performance lies in the fact that the SAL countries are part of the comparator group, but the similarity and its invariance with respect to period is nonetheless surprising. One interpretation is that World Bank lending and conditionality have served to maintain the economic position of recipient countries in the developing world.

REGIONAL PATTERNS. The regional weighted averages show more diversity (table 8-3). First, the import substitution that was apparent in the overall figures took place mainly in Africa (during all periods) and in Latin America (during 1982–83). In Asia and the EMENA region import substitution during 1982–83 took place on a much more limited scale. There are several plausible explanations for this pattern. First, the effects of domestic market contraction were most severe in Africa and Latin America, so the pressure was greater to generate demand for industrial output through protectionism.[16] Second, the debt crisis was most severe in these two regions, so relatively severe foreign exchange shortages probably forced cutbacks in imported inputs. During 1984–86 the import substitution of 1982–83 was actually undone in the EMENA region, perhaps because of reductions in barriers to trade in Morocco and Turkey. But Africa continued to scale down the domestic market share of its imports at a rapid clip.

Expansion of manufactured exports has been less important than import substitution in generating foreign exchange and demand. Nonetheless, there are clear cross-regional contrasts in export performance. In Latin America and Africa the export expansion of 1984–86 essentially made up the ground lost to export contraction during 1982–83. In contrast, the effect of growing export markets was positive and somewhat more significant during both periods in Asia and the EMENA region. Nonetheless, no region gives evidence of a structural shift toward a heavier reliance on manufactured exports when its experience is compared with that of the precrisis period.

SAMPLE COUNTRIES VERSUS REGIONAL NORMS. In Africa all sample countries showed the same strong pattern of import substitution during 1982–83 that appears in the regional average. They also showed a positive but small role for exports in the expansion of output during the adjustment period. However, the African SAL countries did deviate in several significant ways from the regional norm.[17] First, except in Malawi, output expanded in all African sample countries during 1984–86 by servicing a growing domestic market for manufactured products. (The regional average shows a shrinking domestic market.) Second, except in Malawi, import substitution was not significant during 1984–86. Indeed, substantial import penetration took place in Kenya. One hypothesis is that World Bank adjustment lending allowed these countries to resume importing intermediate goods, thereby releasing a constraint on capacity utilization. (In Côte d'Ivoire, Ghana, and Kenya import penetration was accompanied by relatively rapid expansion of output.) Another possibility is that adjustment lending allowed (or forced) these countries to forgo additional increases in protection. Still another explanation is that these countries had already done as much import substitution as was feasible by 1984. The relative merits of these perspectives cannot be assessed without additional empirical work; each, however, seems to have an element of truth.

In Latin America both Chile and Colombia appear to have followed the regional pattern rather closely. A contraction associated with falling domestic demand during 1982–83 was offset by import substitution. Recovery took place during 1984–86, with import penetration rates remaining stable. Mexico also followed the regional pattern in 1982–83, but during 1984–86 it showed increased import penetration and significant export expansion. So Mexico, more than Colombia and Chile, appears to have opened up during 1984–86. Jamaica differed from the regional pattern during both periods. In 1982–83 Jamaica underwent a large drop in manufactured exports, yet output expanded because of strong domestic markets and import substitution. Import substitution continued during 1984–86, but its effects were more than offset by reductions in exports and domestic demand, and output fell.

In Asia both Korea and Thailand followed the regional pattern: relatively rapid output growth, mild import substitution during 1982–86, and significant export expansion (with a dip in 1982–83). The Philippines, by contrast, deviated considerably from the regional norm with substantial import substitution during the 1982–86 period and a large contraction in output in the adjustment years, 1984–86. Hence this country's reduced reliance on imports reflected either the effects of foreign exchange scarcity on intermediate imports or an expenditure-switching policy that was insufficient to prevent domestic recession.

Among the SAL countries in the EMENA region, Morocco and Turkey followed the regional pattern fairly closely. They both exhibited rapid export growth coupled with domestic market contraction during the precrisis period of 1978–81, shifted to import substitution during 1982–83, and experienced a domestic market recovery and export expansion in 1984–86 that more than offset import penetration. The only notable distinction between these two countries' performances and the regional norms is that Turkey showed considerable import penetration during the precrisis years. Pakistan, however, deviated somewhat from regional norms by expanding domestic demand during the precrisis years and continuing gradual import substitution through all three periods.

In summary, the SAL countries whose manufacturing sectors followed regional patterns were Chile and Colombia in Latin America, Korea and Thailand in Asia, and Morocco and Turkey in the EMENA region. African SAL countries deviated from the regional norm by showing much less import substitution and more demand expansion during 1984–86. The other countries that deviated from regional norms did so by showing more import substitution (Jamaica and Pakistan) and/or substantially lower growth in domestic markets (Jamaica and Philippines), except for Mexico, which showed increased import penetration and export expansion.

A Link between Conditionality and Performance?

The remaining question is whether any obvious patterns emerge that link loan conditionality to the performance measures reviewed in the previous section. Identifying such linkages is a daunting task and one that at best yields merely suggestive conclusions. In the turbulent environments that have characterized countries undergoing adjustment, diverse forces have acted on industrial producers simultaneously. Fiscal and monetary policies, the real exchange rate, commercial policy, credit market conditions, price controls, and world market conditions have all influenced the volume of domestic production and the fraction of this production that was exported. These same forces have also helped to determine the volume of imported industrial products and so the contribution of the industrial sector to the current account deficit or surplus. Isolating the effects of specific loan conditions, particularly ones that are designed to effect gradual, long-run changes, is not a simple task.

To further complicate matters, the industrial sector has in turn affected the rest of the economy. For example, in instances where inordinate financial stress has been placed on firms, widespread problems of illiquidity or insolvency have rendered much of the financial sector's portfolio nonperforming. Financial crises, capital flight, and abandonment of adjustment efforts have sometimes resulted. Less dramatically, when the industrial sector has been insufficiently responsive to export incentives, current account problems have helped to undermine efforts to restore external balance without protection.

If it is difficult to link policies and performances, it is even more challenging to link certain policy mixes with World Bank loan conditionality. First, it is impossible to gauge the extent of many types of reform. (For example, how binding were quotas or price controls before they were relaxed?) Second, it is difficult to say what impact conditionality has had on the policymaking process. In cases where the political will to reform has been weak but loan conditionality has been explicit and enforceable, the impact may have been considerable. In other cases, recommended changes may have gone largely ignored. In still other instances, policymakers may have undertaken major reforms regardless of whether they were conditions of World Bank or International Monetary Fund (IMF) lending. For all these reasons, this section evaluates the effects of actual policies, rather than conditionality, on industrial performance.

A crude categorization of reforms in the sample countries is attempted in table 8-5. The policy reforms that are most important for the manufacturing sector's performance are assumed to pertain to protection, export promotion, the exchange rate, and industrial policies (as described earlier). Countries are classified according to whether these policy areas have been significant dimensions of their reform programs. Performance is measured according to import penetration (whether negative import substitution took place) and export expansion (whether exports accounted for more growth during the adjustment period than during the precrisis reference period); performance on both indicators is taken from the analysis of sources of growth in the previous section.

As already discussed, import penetration can reflect many things and may be good or bad. When accompanied by output expansion, increased import penetration probably reflects relaxation of a foreign exchange constraint and improved efficiency. By contrast, increases in import penetration that are accompanied by little or no output growth may reflect a worsening of conditions, either because of an overvalued currency or (less probably) because of trade liberalization without export promotion or a compensating devaluation.[18] The analysis of import penetration that follows is therefore limited to an appraisal of this variable's responsiveness to policy reforms; judgments regarding the desirability of responses are not attempted.

Table 8-5. Policy Reforms and Manufacturing Trade Flows for Fifteen SAL Countries

	Emphasis of reforms				*Performance*	
Country	*Trade reform*	*Export promotion*	*Devaluation*	*Industrial policy*	*Import penetration*	*Export expansion*
Chile	X	X	X			X
Colombia	X		X			X
Côte d'Ivoire	X				X	
Ghana	X		X		X	
Jamaica	X	X	X			
Kenya	X				X	X
Korea	X	X	X	X		X
Malawi			X			
Mexico	X	X	X		X	X
Morocco	X				X	
Pakistan		X	X			
Philippines	X			X		
Thailand	X	X	X	X		X
Turkey	X	X	X		X	
Zambia			X			X
Total	12	7	11	3	6	7

Source: Reform classifications are based on World Bank country briefs and country studies prepared for a report on adjustment lending (World Bank 1988).

Several patterns emerge. First, in all six countries in which import penetration increased, trade liberalization was an important dimension of the reform package. Moreover, three of these countries did not exhibit significant real devaluation. If patterns were random, one would expect to find that only 4.8 countries had liberalized trade and only 1.6 had not devalued. Although the sample size is too small for these deviations to be statistically significant, they suggest that trade liberalization was real and that it tended to increase import penetration. Similarly, one is tempted to infer that countries avoiding devaluation tended to experience more import penetration.

Although very weak, there is also some evidence that export promotion policies and devaluations have encouraged export expansion. Of the seven countries that expanded exports, four had promotion programs; the expected number under the assumption that encouragement had no effect is 3.3. Similarly, six of the seven countries with significant export expansion devalued, while one would have expected 5.1 countries to have devalued in the absence of any association between exports and the exchange rate. One reason these associations are statistically weak is obviously the small size of the sample. However, several economic forces may also have been at work. First, since expansion of manufactured exports requires reallocation of productive capacity, lack of confidence in the long-term policy may have inhibited entrepreneurs from reacting. Second, the policy reforms themselves may not have been very dramatic. Third, export performance may have largely reflected world market conditions in the short run.

Summary

Policymakers in developing countries typically view expansion of the industrial sector as the key to development. The sector also receives careful attention because industrial contraction can lead to urban unemployment and financial disruptions in the short run. So, when external shocks combined with domestic problems to create economic crises for many developing countries, policymakers had strong incentives to pursue adjustment programs that insulated industrial producers as much as possible from adverse conditions. This chapter has been concerned with how successful they have been, what policies they have employed, and what role World Bank adjustment lending has played in this process.

In a sample of fifty developing countries, growth in manufacturing value added dropped during 1982–83 with the advent of the debt crisis and world recession. Nonetheless, the manufacturing sector did not shrink relative to the rest of the economy, so in this sense the adjustment costs for manufacturers were contained. The exception was in Africa, where rapid deindustrialization took place. Overall, manufacturing value added rebounded in 1984–86, but in Africa recovery was very slight and growth rates remained negative.

A subsample of countries that received substantial adjustment lending from the World Bank had somewhat better than average growth in manufacturing value added during the period when most adjustment programs were under way (1984–86). Four of the thirteen SAL countries with complete data outperformed their respective regions in all periods analyzed, and another six went from being below average before the adjustment period to being above average during the adjustment years. (Only one SAL country went from above regional norms to below norms.) With respect to rates of industrialization, the sample tended to outpace regional averages both before and after 1982–83.

A demand-side sources-of-growth decomposition showed that, overall, developing countries reacted to world recession and the debt crisis with substantial reductions in the domestic market's share of manufactured imports. This probably reflected some combination of product market demand switching (induced by devaluation and increases in protection) and reduced use of imported inputs. Regional analysis revealed that this import-substitution process was most important in Latin America and

Africa, where domestic markets for manufactured goods contracted most dramatically and shortages of imported input may have limited capacity utilization. Especially rapid import substitution began in Africa during the 1982–83 crisis period. Although import substitution continued into 1984–86 in Africa as domestic markets for manufactured products remained stagnant, it was reversed in Latin America as growth resumed in domestic markets.

Many SAL countries followed the regional patterns. The five African SAL countries, however, did not exhibit continued import substitution during 1984–86. Moreover, domestic markets in three of the five countries grew considerably faster than the regional norm (Côte d'Ivoire, Ghana, and Kenya). One possible explanation is that World Bank lending released a constraint on imported inputs.

A final issue examined was the role of conditionality in shaping policies and performance in SAL countries. Among conditions directly affecting the industrial sector, those relating to trade liberalization and exchange rate devaluation were stressed relatively frequently; subsector restructuring conditions were also fairly common, especially in Africa. Although it is unclear what the SAL countries would have done in the absence of this conditionality, most did devalue and liberalize trade somewhat. Indicators of industrial performance were examined for possible correlation with these changes in the policy regime. Weak evidence was found that countries in which trade liberalization or devaluations have been important also tended to exhibit increased import penetration during the adjustment period.

Appendix

Calculating Growth Rates

All data on GDP and manufacturing value added were taken from the World Bank Andrex data base and valued in current domestic prices. Data were converted to constant prices with the use of the domestic consumer price index (CPI), the only deflator consistently available for all countries and periods. Once converted to real terms, the annualized growth rates covering the period t to $t + k$ were constructed for country i as follows:

$$g^{z}_{it,t+k} = (Z_{it+k}/Z_{it})^{1/k} - 1 \qquad \text{(8-3)}$$

where Z is the variable of interest (GDP or value added).

Growth rates are constructed country by country by using the methodology described above. To get regional growth rates, G_R, a weighted

Table 8-6. Countries Included in Average Growth Calculations, by Region

Africa	*Latin America*	*Asia*	EMENA
Benin	Argentina	Bangladesh	Cyprus
Central African Republic	Barbados	Fiji	Greece
Côte d'Ivoire	Bolivia	India	Jordan
Gambia	Chile	Indonesia	Morocco
Ghana	Colombia	Korea	Pakistan
Kenya	Dominican Republic	Malaysia	Tunisia
Liberia	Ecuador	Myanmar	Turkey
Malawi	El Salvador	Philippines	
Niger	Honduras	Singapore	
Nigeria	Jamaica	Sri Lanka	
Senegal	Mexico	Thailand	
Sierra Leone	Panama		
Togo	Paraguay		
Zaire	Trinidad and Tobago		
Zambia	Uruguay		
Zimbabwe	Venezuela		

average of country-specific growth rates, is constructed using base-year shares in total GDP or manufacturing value added as weights:

$$G^{z}_{Rt,t+k} = \sum_{i \in R} \alpha^{z}_{i0} g^{z}_{it,t+k} \tag{8-4}$$

where R is the set of countries in the region, and $\alpha^{z}_{i0} = Z_{i0}/(\sum_{j \in R} Z_{j0})$. The countries included in regional growth rate calculations are listed in table 8-6.

Sources-of-Growth Decompositions

Several issues arise when implementing the sources-of-growth decomposition presented in the text. The first has to do with the treatment of real exchange rate fluctuations. Specifically, output series are recorded in domestic currency, while trade flows are in dollars—one must somehow put these in comparable units and adjust for inflation. The usual procedure is to convert trade flows to domestic currency and to infer a domestic currency value for domestic demand. Or, defining q, d, x, and m to be physical quantities of gross manufacturing production, domestic demand, exports, and imports, respectively, one infers the nominal value of domestic demand as:

$$P^d d = \pi P^{\$} m - \pi P^{\$} x + \bar{P} q \tag{8-5}$$

where

$$P^d = \left(\frac{q}{q + m - x}\right) P + \left(\frac{m - x}{q + m - x}\right) \pi P^{\$}.$$

Here P^d is the average price paid by domestic users of manufactured goods, π is the exchange rate (units of local currency per dollar), $\bar{P}$ is the average price received by producers of domestic manufactured goods, and $\bar{P}^{\$}$ is the world price of manufactured goods expressed in dollars.

All terms in equation 8-5 are then deflated with a domestic price deflator to obtain the variables necessary to implement equation 8-2 of the text: $M = (\pi P^{\$}/P^d)m$; $X = (\pi P^{\$}/P^d)x$; $Q = (\bar{P}/P^d)q$; and $D = d = (\pi P^{\$}/P^d)m - (\pi P^{\$}/P^d)x + (\bar{P}/P^d)q$. This procedure is acceptable if relative prices remain fairly stable. But major devaluations can cause large changes in the real exchange rate (proxied by $\pi P^{\$}/P^d$), so that the magnitude of measured exports and imports (X and M) expands relative to domestic demand and production. In other words, export expansion and import penetration are automatically generated by a devaluation in this accounting framework, even if the physical flow of goods is unaffected.

To look only at changes in physical flows, the present study employs an alternative approach. Specifically, measured values for imports, exports, and production are deflated by their own price indices, and then used to calculate the variables in equation 8-2: $M = (P^{\$}m)/P^w$; $X = (P^{\$}x)/P^w$; $Q = (\bar{P}q)/P^c$; and $D = (P^{\$}m)/P^w - (P^{\$}x)/P^w + (\bar{P}q)/P^c$.

Here P^w is an index of the average world price (expressed in dollars) for traded manufactured goods, and P^c is a domestic manufacturing price index. All price indices except the exchange rate are initialized to a value of 1.0 in the base year (1978).

Regional and Aggregate Sources of Growth

To construct regional and aggregate sources of growth, the decomposition described above was done for each country and period. Then, for a given period (say, period $t - k$ to t), each term in equation 8-2 was weighted by the country's base-year (1978) share in regional manufacturing value added (α_i), and summed over all countries in the relevant group. The weighted average sources-of-growth decomposition was thus:

$$\begin{aligned} \Sigma\, \alpha_i(\Delta Q_{it}/Q_{it-k}) &= \Sigma\, \alpha_i(\Delta D_{it}/Q_{it-k})(1 - \overline{m}_{it}) \\ &\quad - \Sigma\, \alpha_i(\Delta m_{it}\overline{D}_{it}/Q_{it-k}) + \Sigma\, \alpha_i(\Delta X_{it}/Q_{it-k}). \end{aligned} \tag{8-6}$$

A sources-of-growth decomposition could not be constructed for several of the countries listed in table 8-6, although it was possible to construct one for several countries not listed there. So the set of countries used in calculating equation 8-6 differs slightly from the set of countries listed in table 8-6 by the exclusion of Benin, Liberia, and Panama and the inclusion of Egypt, Guatemala, and Portugal.

Data Sources

The first data problem encountered is that Andrex does not include gross manufacturing production data. The World Bank's economic and social data base (BESD) does provide gross manufacturing production data for most countries, but the series does not extend to 1986 and is often based on establishments above a certain size (for example, with more than fifty workers) and does not correspond closely to production indices directly available from the countries. The BESD series was thus used only to get an approximation to the base-year (1978) domestic currency value of production.[19] The base-year production series was then used to generate a series on real manufacturing production for 1978–86, with the use of the manufacturing production index available from Andrex. (In several spot checks, this series looked very close to the series available directly from the countries.) The only problem with this approach was that the production index stopped in 1984 or 1985 in some countries. When this occurred, it was brought forward to 1986 with the use of manufacturing value added growth rates for the missing years. When value added was itself not available through 1986, the country was left out of the analysis.

The second problem was that manufacturing price deflators were generally not available for individual countries, nor was there a world (dollar-denominated) price index for manufactured goods. The former was approximated with domestic CPIs, the latter with the U.S. CPI.

The final data problem was one of consistency between trade and production data. Trade data are collected according to the Standard International Trade Classification (SITC) system, while production and value added data are available only by the International Standard Industrial Classification (ISIC) system. Differences in the systems make it impossible to get a strictly conformable set of production and trade flow statistics.[20]

Several solutions to this problem were tried. First, detailed (five-digit) SITC data were taken directly from the Geneva System and aggregated to get an approximation to the ISIC definition of manufactured products. This approach had the most appeal conceptually; unfortunately, trade data on certain products were missing for some countries for recent years. So the approach worked well in certain countries but was unacceptable as a general procedure. Next, data on manufacturing trade were taken from the Andrex data bank. (These data originated in the Geneva System, but their "holes" have been filled with extrapolations based on regional trends.) The main problem with this approach is that Andrex defines manufacturing more narrowly than does the ISIC system for purposes of trade statistics.[21] Hence the Andrex trade data do not suffer from sudden drops because of missing data, but neither do they conform to the definition of manufacturing used for the available production series. In an attempt to get the best of both systems, Andrex trade data were augmented by data taken directly from the Geneva System on the manufacturing categories not included in the Andrex system. This hybrid system yielded figures of the correct order of magnitude and was less sensitive to problems of missing data. Like the pure Geneva data, however, the resultant figures were subject to holes in certain cases and proved unacceptable for comparative exercises.

Since it was necessary to work with Andrex trade data, the reasonableness of these figures was examined for a sample of countries for which all three options could be tried (that is, where missing data did not appear to be a problem). It was found that although exports are understated considerably by the omission of food and mineral products, trends are generally correct. Imports were much less problematic because developing countries import few primary products (except oil), processed or otherwise, and other manufactured products are captured by the narrow Andrex definition.

Notes

I wish to thank Bela Balassa, Jaime de Melo, Mieko Nishimizu, and especially William Steel for many helpful comments on early drafts. I am also indebted to Julie Stanton for excellent research assistance and to Diane Coogan for generous assistance in preparing the conditionality data reported herein. Any remaining errors are naturally my own responsibility.

1. These fifteen countries are Chile, Colombia, Côte d'Ivoire, Ghana, Jamaica, Kenya, Korea, Malawi, Mexico, Morocco, Pakistan, the Philippines, Thailand, Turkey, and Zambia.
2. In developing countries, growth in industrial productivity tends to outpace that of the rest of the economy (see, for example, Chenery, Robinson, and Syrquin 1986). This assertion does not appear to hold for the developed countries.
3. In almost all developing countries for which data are readily available, corporate leverage grew and liquidity fell between 1975 and 1981.
4. These indicators are specific to manufacturing. Ideally, the analysis would include the nonmanufacturing industries, mining and construction, but these sectors are quite distinct from manufacturing and would require separate treatment. The scope is therefore limited to manufacturing, which is typically the target of attempts to promote changes in product mix, volume of output, and trade flows.
5. There are a few exceptions. For example, in Morocco phosphate prices were beginning to improve in 1980.
6. Chile, Ghana, Jamaica, Kenya, Pakistan, the Philippines, and Zambia endured further deterioration in their terms of trade.

7. Chile, Ghana, Kenya, Mexico, Morocco, Pakistan, the Philippines, and Zambia had significant real devaluations; only Colombia and Thailand registered significant revaluations. Exceptions to increased protectionism were Kenya, Korea, and Turkey, which underwent significant trade liberalization.

8. A "firm" condition is one that is quantifiable or can be evaluated objectively. The characterization of exchange rate policy as one of the policies most frequently covered by conditionality requires some clarification. In looking at World Bank loan data alone, exchange rate conditionality does not appear to be very common. But, as the 1988 World Bank report on adjustment lending explains, as a "result of the IMF's responsibility for exchange rates, [conditionality] figures understate the importance given by the World Bank to movements in exchange rates. In the context of adjustment programs, governments are usually expected to establish and maintain exchange rates that are competitive internationally, but in only a few cases (such as Chile, Colombia, and Ghana) has there been explicit conditionality" (World Bank 1988).

9. The infrequency of macroeconomic and financial conditions in Asia has been interpreted to reflect the absence of problems rather than shortcomings of the lending process (World Bank 1988). In Africa, however, it has been argued that more might have been done to deal with high wages and low productivity. In general, it has been suggested that there was insufficient attention to industrial policy (pricing, regulations, incentives, and technology) and to the financial sector (World Bank 1988).

10. Such an exercise would involve detailed microeconomic analysis of investment patterns, industrial productivity, and competitiveness. Several research projects are now under way at the World Bank that focus on these issues.

11. Mexico came very close to the "normal" growth rate for Latin America during the recovery years. It might be objected that this type of comparative exercise is invalid because the countries that received adjustment assistance were not randomly selected from their respective regions. If the inferences discussed above are to be invalidated, however, it must be argued that the World Bank, wittingly or not, systematically chose to lend to countries with the best prospects for accelerating their growth. I am unaware of convincing evidence that this occurred.

12. This type of effect is formalized in the fix-price temporary disequilibrium literature (for example, Gunning 1983 and Standaert 1985).

13. This expression, known as a direct decomposition, is based on the identity $Q = D(1 - m) + X$.

14. For purposes of comparison, demand-side decompositions based on real domestic currency values were also done. Generally, the effects of devaluation on the relative magnitudes of domestic production and trade flows tended to influence the findings heavily.

15. There is, of course, the possibility that sustained import substitution represented displacement of foreign producers by efficient domestic producers—some have argued that this happened in the Chilean textile industry, for example. On average, however, the evidence suggests that import substitution leads to lower growth in factor productivity than other forms of demand expansion (Nishimizu and Robinson 1984) and disperses productivity growth much more across sectors (Nishimizu and Page 1987).

16. There was a notable twist in the composition of imports away from consumer goods during 1980–86 in a sample of thirty-seven countries receiving World Bank lending for trade reforms (see chapter 4, table 4-4). Although comparable data have not been compiled for the SAL countries in this study, it is reasonable to suppose they followed a similar trend.

17. One reason might be that Nigeria, which accounts for about 50 percent of manufacturing value added in the region, heavily influences this average pattern.

18. I am grateful to Bela Balassa for stressing the ambiguities of import penetration as a performance measure.

19. When even this was not possible, base-year manufacturing value added from Andrex was multiplied by 2.5 to get an approximate base-year production figure, since the ratio of value added to production was very close to 0.4 in countries where both were observable.

20. For example, foods are considered manufacturing in the ISIC system if they have been processed. But some detailed SITC categories include both processed and unprocessed varieties of certain foods, which makes it impossible to isolate manufactured food exports. Similar problems arise with other primary products, such as copper and wood.

21. For example, Andrex excludes processed food products.

References

Chenery, Hollis, Sherman Robinson, and Moshe Syrquin. 1986. *Industrialization and Growth*. New York: Oxford University Press.

Coogan, Diane. 1989. "Conditionality and Implementation Data from Adjustment Loans: An Analytical Guide to the ALCID." Industry Development Division, Industry and Energy Department, World Bank, Washington, D.C.

Gunning, J. W. 1983. "Rationing in an Open Economy: Fix-Price Equilibrium and Two-Gap Models." *European Economic Review* 23 (1):71–98.

Nishimizu, Mieko, and John Page. 1987. "Economic Policies and Productivity Change in Industry: An International Comparison." Industry Department, World Bank, Washington, D.C.

Nishimizu, Mieko, and Sherman Robinson. 1984. "Trade Policies and Productivity Change in Semi-Industrialized Countries." *Journal of Development Economics* 16 (1 and 2):177–206.

Standaert, Stan. 1985. "The Foreign Exchange Constraint, Suppression of the Trade Deficit, and the Shadow Price of Foreign Exchange in a Fix-Price Economy." *Journal of Development Economics* 18 (1):37–50.

Tybout, James R. 1986. "A Firm-Level Chronicle of Financial Crises in the Southern Cone." *Journal of Development Economics* 24 (2):371–400.

World Bank. 1988. *Adjustment Lending: An Evaluation of Ten Years of Experience*. Policy and Research Series 1. Washington, D.C.

Comments

Mieko Nishimizu

THOSE WHO HAVE WORKED on policy conditionalities have probably learned that one must write words down very precisely and, if possible, quantify them. James Tybout's chapter focuses on two terms—"industrial performance" and "structural adjustment"—and I am not certain whether the author and I understand these terms in exactly the same way.

First, the term "industrial performance." In answer to the question, "What is industrial performance?" any manager of an industrial company will respond, "To make the best and the cheapest." A little more honest answer would be, "Well, sometimes to make the best, sometimes to cut unit cost, sometimes both." In economic terms this means productivity change, or in economic jargon it means total factor productivity change, if quantity and quality changes can be measured accurately. So industrial performance is a dynamic concept. Tybout's study, however, uses demand-side sources-of-growth decomposition to represent performance. This methodology is a static one and hence limits the analysis substantially.

Second, the term "structural adjustment." I am not sure about Tybout's time horizon with respect to structural adjustment, so I will exaggerate to make the point. In the short run there are quasi-fixed inputs, so that short-run industrial performance depends on capacity utilization, whatever the cause. If demand is the cause, business managers would have to find new markets, including exports. With the right financing or financial leveraging to tide a business over, it would survive. Otherwise, the company would go under. The supply-side phenomenon of more firms performing and surviving instead of going under is an important part of the stabilization-with-growth or short-run adjustment-with-growth scenario at the microeconomic level. Of course, one must keep in mind that there are causes other than domestic absorption for varying capacity utilization in industry, particularly in developing countries.

In the long run all inputs are variable, and technology changes as well. Industrial performance, reflected (one hopes) in profits, is then part of the long-term transformation of the structure of production. It is part of the natural process of shifting resources from less productive to more productive activities, along with all the alterations in taste and composition of demand that accompany rising income. The good performance of fast-growing firms continuously redefines the comparative advantages of the economy over time—the process by which the industrial sector of developing countries catches up with the rest of the world. But there are obstacles preventing this natural process from occurring—inadequate economic policies being among the most important ones.

I mention these points because Tybout's chapter asks a very important question: Do policies matter for industrial performance and structural adjustment? The chapter focuses primarily on trade policy, which has both short- and long-term implications, and the policy discussion suffers from the ambiguous time frame concerning structural adjustment. Although the chapter is quite indecisive about whether polices do make a difference, from the perspective of the battlefield of industry there is no question that policies matter. The important question is how.

In the development literature a number of arguments have been advanced concerning the relationships among development policies, growth, and productivity change. A substantial body of literature addresses the appropriate use of trade policy to increase growth and productivity. Perhaps equal attention has been given to the role of market mechanisms in guiding the allocation of resources and providing incentives for disciplining costs and improving productivity.

One obvious link between trade policy and productivity is the positive association between output growth and productivity change. In developing countries the size of the market has long been viewed as an important determinant of growth and structural transformation. The existence of economies of scale implies that a widening of the market through trade should lead to reductions in real production costs. In the context of an outward-oriented (or export-led) development strategy, this argument is usually cast in terms of the benefits of increased demand through expansion of exports, but it applies equally to import substitution in large domestic markets.

The literature on foreign exchange constraints suggests a second link between trade policy and productivity. This link exists because in many developing countries imported intermediate and capital goods are not easily substituted by domestically produced ones. Policies that limit the availability of these goods reduce the potential for domestic producers to utilize capacity fully and therefore reduce productivity in the short to medium term. The increased availability of foreign exchange, however, can raise capacity utilization and lead to short-term increases in total factor productivity.

A different type of trade policy argument is related to the effects of international competition on the efficiency of domestic producers. It is possible that the "challenge-response" mechanism implied by international trade forces domestic industries to adopt new technologies, to improve efficiency, and generally to reduce costs and improve quality wherever possible. According to this argument, both export rivalry and import competition are beneficial to productivity. Although an import liberalization policy may restrict the demand for domestic goods, such a policy also raises competition and therefore improves production efficiency. The counterargument is also widely asserted: protectionist policies designed to promote import substitution can have dynamic negative effects on efficiency (beyond the allocative losses) arising from reductions in competitiveness and increased inefficiency in production.

Care must be taken, however, not to overstate these arguments regarding the benefits of international competition. Excessive response to export promotion policies, for example, may distort incentives and lead to rising inefficiency in export production. There is also the infant industry argument for according protection to high-cost industries that cannot compete immediately but are expected to become internationally competitive.

With regard to the loss in efficiency caused by protectionist policies, however, there is logical clarity on one issue: the *instruments* by which protection is afforded to domestic industries can affect productivity quite apart from the *levels* of protection granted. Quantitative restrictions on imports break the link between domestic and international prices and thus insulate domestic producers from *movements* in international prices. Such an import regime will permit rising costs to be passed forward in a fashion that is not possible under a system based on equivalent tariff protection. Changes in international prices convey substantial information on productivity trends in the rest of the world, but instruments that interfere with the transmission of these prices can make the productivity performance of competitors irrelevant and can lead over time to a deterioration in comparative advantage.

Moreover, the relationship between resource allocation and productivity performance depends on the nature of the planning and regulatory practices that are applied in such economies. Theoretically, it is possible for the planners or regulators to "simulate the market" so that the distribution of productivity growth rates will be very like that in a market economy. In practice, however, it is humanly impossible for planners or regulators to have ideal information or models that continuously replicate market solutions, particularly in large and complex economies. As such, planned or highly regulated economies tend to generate incentives related to averages that are easily observed as opposed to marginals that are more difficult to see. Thus nonmarket economies may differ significantly from market economies in both the level and distribution of their productivity growth rates.

The policy arguments discussed above are not mutually exclusive, however. Nor are the postulated effects of policy choices on productivity performance independent of each other. In the real world one observes the net effect of a combination of these phenomena simultaneously, so that discriminating among policies and their consequences is difficult. In addition, one must always be cautious in implying the direction of causality from a statistical association.

Perhaps with a more careful distinction between short and long term and more attention to the nature of the reforms in each country, this chapter would have presented a more convincing argument about associations—at best—between policy changes and industrial performance. This brings me to my penultimate point.

Before asking whether policies mattered, the chapter does not examine exhaustively whether the reforms in the countries with adjustment loans were good ones. Such an examination of the design of policies that formed the various reform packages would have benefited the study, as would a more systematic investigation of the appropriateness of the macroeconomic framework in each country and the sequencing of reforms.

A last point: it is a fact of life in industry at the microeconomic level that improving performance is essentially a highly complex and multifaceted *management* problem. How companies transfer and master technology, how managers train workers and engineers, how maintenance functions are performed, how the company's financial programming and planning are conducted, and similar practices are all important parts of productivity performance, and they ultimately boil down to the quality of human capital called "good managers." Good managers, in turn, are scarce human resources indeed in many developing countries. Therefore good policies may be necessary to challenge industry to perform, but they need not be sufficient to induce supply response.

PART II

Evaluation of Adjustment Programs

9 *Introduction to Part II*

THE EVALUATION of adjustment lending operations would be relatively straightforward if the objective were simply to determine the extent to which agreed-on policy actions had been implemented. The task would involve consideration and assessment of a few key loan conditions—say, four or five—within the monitorable component of the action program. Since these conditions refer to policy intentions or actions rather than to performance, the task could, at least in principle, be more easily undertaken for World Bank adjustment loans than for International Monetary Fund (IMF) operations. In evaluating IMF operations one cannot avoid the vexatious problem of how to disentangle the influence of program and nonprogram factors.

Such an evaluation, however, would fail to address the broader and fundamental question of how effective adjustment lending operations have been in enabling the World Bank to assist developing countries in attaining long-term growth and development. Support of these objectives has, of course, always been a major part of the World Bank's mandate. To execute this mandate throughout the 1950s, 1960s, and 1970s, the World Bank financed development projects. In the 1980s it gradually added fast-disbursing financing through its adjustment lending facilities, both in support of balance of payments needs and as a catalyst for policy and institutional reforms. The acute deterioration of the external payments position of many developing countries in the early 1980s was the main rationale and impetus for the introduction of adjustment lending. Since then, however, there has been a growing awareness of the compelling need for policy and institutional reforms at both the macroeconomic and sectoral levels as a means of adjusting to the changed global environment of the 1980s and of resuming long-term sustained growth. Thus adjustment lending operations have become the main vehicle of policy dialogue between the World Bank and its developing country members.

The chapters in Part II evaluate three distinct but related aspects of adjustment programs: (1) the degree of policy change that has been associated with conditionality in the loan agreements, (2) the link between policy reforms and macroeconomic performance, and (3) the social consequences of adjustment programs. These are not the only relevant aspects of adjustment lending operations, nor does the discussion touch on the broader issue of the evolution of the role of the World Bank in the process of global adjustment and intermediation. The chapters cover the major areas of current concern and debate, however, and provide a useful starting point.

The tradeoffs inherent in the adjustment process pose some important questions for the World Bank. How should loan conditionality be formulated so as to cover both macroeconomic and structural aspects in view of the fact that the underlying structure of the economy is an object of reform?[1] Should loan conditions be tied to policy intentions or to performance? How can conditions related to short-term macroeconomic requirements be integrated with those related to institutional and policy reforms, which are by nature long-term processes?

In chapter 10, William McCleary assesses the nature of the conditions attached to adjustment loans and their implementation record. Although his data for the sample of fifteen countries with adjustment loans do not permit him to determine whether conditionality was well designed, they do permit him to describe the kind of policy measures that were agreed on and to assess the extent to which they were implemented. This information allows several conclusions about the conditions that have been the most successfully implemented and those that have been the most difficult to carry out. An important conclusion is that future adjustment operations would probably benefit from reducing the number of conditions in loan agreements.

In chapter 11 Riccardo Faini and associates undertake a cross-country analysis to evaluate the macroeconomic impact of adjustment programs. They employ the familiar "before-after" and "control-group" methodology that has also been intensively applied in the evaluation of IMF-supported programs.[2] In addition, they provide quantitative information regarding the macroeconomic impacts of World Bank–supported adjustment lending programs. Together with the information provided by the previous studies of IMF programs, these results should provide a useful basis for evaluating the joint impact of the Bretton Woods institutions on the economic performance of loan recipients.

The authors draw on a large set of data gathered from ninety-three developing countries, especially the thirty countries that received their first adjustment loan before 1985. This large sample gives them several years of observations and a conveniently large group of comparator countries against which to assess the performance of loan recipients. Their findings, however, are affected by several methodological and statistical pitfalls inherent in this type of exercise.

First, because the set of adjustment loan recipients is not a random sample, the estimated coefficients of the impact of adjustment lending in recipient countries relative to changes in nonrecipient countries are statistically biased.[3] Second, macroeconomic performance may reflect the influence not only of reforms stipulated in adjustment programs but of other factors as well. For example, the positive effect of reform may be muted by a negative external shock, or a country's performance may improve without any policy change in the presence of a positive shock. Third, countries are likely to exhibit different degrees of responsiveness to policy measures, with responsiveness itself often being a function of policy reform. The supply response to policy change has been found to be less strong in low-income countries than in middle-income countries, for example. Fourth, the reliability of macroeconomic indicators, that is, of their informational content, is in question when the underlying structure, policy, rules, and regimes are themselves the focus of and subject to change. Most traditional analyses of macroeconomic policy are based on the implicit assumption that the underlying structure is given. The complexity of evaluating adjustment programs lies in the fact that the underlying macroeconomic structure can also be the focus of change under the program and so may be continually changing.

At a more fundamental level, adjustment processes involving policy reform and institutional change inevitably have implications for both intertemporal resource allocation and sociopolitical factors. First is the tradeoff between present costs and future benefits, which needs to be understood and taken into account. This distinction, however, is seldom made explicitly. Second is the potential for social conflict and a shift in income distribution, which needs to be resolved both politically and economically.

The social cost of adjustment is receiving increasing attention in the design and implementation of adjustment lending operations, as Elaine Zuckerman demonstrates in chapter 12. She provides a general analysis of the distributional implications of adjustment programs. After examining the experience of adjustment programs in which little was done explicitly to direct social expenditures toward the poor, Zuckerman concludes that more attention should be placed on alleviating the adverse impact of adjustment programs on the poor. What actions should be undertaken, however, will remain controversial for a long time not only because it is difficult to identify the poor accurately by occupation and socioeconomic characteristics, but also because little is known about the effectiveness of special targeting of services and programs.

Nevertheless, the distributional implications of adjustment programs will remain a key issue in the design of adjustment programs, if only because sustainability is likely to be jeopardized if the distributional implications are too severe. Since the benefits of adjustment programs are often slow in appearing, other ways must be found to ensure that the program is sustained. Closely considering the distributional implications of the proposed measures is one way to support sustainability or at least to avoid undermining it.

Notes

1. For an insightful and historical discussion of these issues in the context of IMF conditionality, see Sidney Dell, *On Being Grandmotherly: The Evolution of IMF Conditionality*, Princeton Essays in International Finance 144 (Princeton, N.J.: Princeton University, 1981).
2. For a discussion of this issue, see Morris Goldstein and Peter J. Montiel, "Evaluating Fund Stabilization Programs with Multi-Country Data: Some Methodological Pitfalls," *IMF Staff Papers* (June 1986):344–64.
3. For an excellent recent survey of literature on evaluating IMF-supported programs, see Mohsin S. Khan, "The Macroeconomic Effects of Fund-Supported Adjustment Programs: An Empirical Assessment," IMF Working Paper WP/88/113 (Washington, D.C.: International Monetary Fund, 1989).

10 *The Design and Implementation of Conditionality*

William A. McCleary

BETWEEN 1980 AND 1987 the World Bank made adjustment loans totaling US$15 billion to fifty-one countries. Of this total, fifty-one structural adjustment loans (SALs) accounted for US$5.90 billion and seventy sectoral adjustment loans (SECALs) for US$9.35 billion. Almost half the number of loans and credits for adjustment went to Sub-Saharan African countries, but because of the relatively small size of individual operations in Africa, the total amounts lent to countries in Latin America and the Caribbean and in Europe, the Middle East, and North Africa (the EMENA region) were larger.

Throughout the period of adjustment lending, the World Bank has conducted internal reviews to evaluate how well adjustment programs were working and to draw lessons from the experience. Relatively informal progress reports were prepared in 1982, 1984, and 1986. Also in 1986 the World Bank's Operations Evaluation Department conducted a more substantial examination of fifteen SALs for which audit reports had been completed (World Bank 1986), and in 1988 the Strategic Planning and Review Department surveyed experience to date (World Bank 1988b) and posed some questions for consideration in the report on adjustment lending that was completed later that year (World Bank 1988a). Virtually all these reviews complained that not enough time had passed to allow an evaluation of the full effects of adjustment programs, that it was difficult to disentangle policy changes arising from adjustment loans from those stemming from other sources, and that the effectiveness of programs was hard to judge when countries were being subjected to external exogenous shocks, such as slow world growth or drought.

Having acknowledged these difficulties, the evaluation reports were still able to reach a number of broad conclusions:

- Implementation performance for adjustment loans was generally satisfactory but ranged from successful (for example, Côte d'Ivoire, Ghana, Korea, Thailand, and Turkey) to moderately successful (for example, Pakistan, Philippines, and Senegal) to outright failure (for example, Bolivia, Guyana, and Zambia).

- In early adjustment loans the World Bank was often guilty of over-optimism with respect to government commitment and capacity to implement; loans were too complex and took longer to implement than expected.
- Government commitment to an adjustment program was more important to implementation than was external pressure.
- Providing greater attention to institutional reforms in order to build up government capacity took time and required specialists with expertise that differed from that required to supervise policy reforms. Institutional support was likely to be better handled through free-standing projects than in the context of adjustment loans.
- Reforms would be more likely to be sustained and the commitment of government would be more likely to be manifested if adjustment loans were given more on the basis of action already taken and less on promises of future actions.

This chapter attempts to push the work of the previous reviews a bit further by providing more precise answers to three questions. How well has conditionally been implemented? Does performance in implementing conditions vary substantially across the various policy areas? What are the most important determinants of this performance? Each of these questions is addressed in turn after a brief discussion of the structure of World Bank–supported adjustment programs and of the important differences in programs, especially those for countries in Africa and for highly indebted countries. The chapter draws on evidence on implementation for fifty-one adjustment loans in fifteen countries.

The Nature of Adjustment Programs

Both SALs and SECALs are used in support of adjustment objectives. SALs have generally supported programs to increase domestic resource mobilization and improve efficiency. They do this through reforms of trade policy, changes in prices and regulations in key productive sectors, increases in government revenues, and changes in the size and composition of government expenditures. SECALs, though more narrowly focused, normally support the same broad objectives with measures that can have considerable macroeconomic impact. These measures include reforms of trade policy or the financial sector; reforms of sectoral pricing, institutions, and the composition of public expenditure; and still more narrowly focused measures such as those affecting input pricing (elimination of fertilizer subsidies, for example). Both SALs and SECALs have also supported institutional changes to strengthen a government's capacity to plan and implement reforms, for example, through programs to improve project evaluation, tax administration, or the monitoring of public enterprises. SALs are distinguished from SECALs more by the breadth of policy and institutional reforms in a particular operation than by the nature of the reforms themselves.

Government programs supported by adjustment lending have tended to have three distinct elements. First, the programs set out the broad objectives to be achieved in the medium term. These include targets for the key macroeconomic variables (such as savings rates, current account deficits, or aggregate or sectoral growth rates) and for important sectoral variables (such as crop diversification and the development of export industries or domestic sources of energy). Second, the programs lay out a broad set of measures to be introduced in the medium term (including those that might be supported by future SALs or SECALs) in support of these objectives. Examples are measures to increase the scope of taxation or cost recovery or to improve incentives for exports or agricultural products. Third, the programs detail a set of specific actions that the government plans to take over twelve to eighteen months and that the World Bank will monitor.

To facilitate monitoring and ensure that progress is appropriate, the loans generally are disbursed in tranches. Disbursements depend on satisfactory compliance with key conditions and with implementation of the program in general. The World Bank is increasingly relying on more specific tranche conditions rather than more general statements of intentions. All SALs and 87 percent of SECALs were tranched (included tranche-release conditions) in fiscal 1986–88, whereas 83 percent of SALs and 8 percent of SECALs were tranched during fiscal 1979–83. The SECALs that have not been tranched in recent years have tended to be small repeat operations or those in which conditionality has been "up front," or "front-loaded"; that is, countries are required to undertake most of the conditionality before the first disbursement of the loan.

Differences in Adjustment Programs among Countries

It was clear from the outset of adjustment lending that programs would vary among countries because the problems differ. The need for stabilization, the relative importance of various sectors, and the nature and degree of distortions are different. In addition, political considerations and institutional constraints affect the types of reform that can be attempted and the speed with which they can be planned and implemented. Moreover, the World Bank's knowledge and preparation, and so the status of its dialogue with governments, varies substantially among countries and even between sectors in the same country.

Differences in country programs are illustrated by the two sets of countries that have absorbed the bulk of World Bank adjustment lending: the Sub-Saharan African countries and the highly indebted middle-income countries. Although these two groups share several characteristics, including severe macroeconomic imbalances, heavy debt-servicing burdens, and stagnating or falling per capita consumption, the differences between them are more important than the commonalities.

In the 1980s the Sub-Saharan countries saw an intensification of longstanding difficulties in finding a workable development strategy. Central to their problems were a bias against agriculture, inefficient state enterprises, unproductive government investment, a tendency to emphasize public service employment over expenditures for maintenance and rehabilitation, and severe shortages in qualified manpower. Combined with rapid population growth, these constraints reduced or even reversed improvements in living standards. With the onslaught of drought, sharply declining commodity prices, and higher oil prices in the 1980s, painful adjustments became inevitable.

In the highly indebted countries the crisis was more sudden and unexpected. For a long period extending through the 1970s, these countries enjoyed rising living standards, expanding modern industry and services, and growing public services, financed in part by large overseas borrowing. Then a crisis erupted in the early 1980s with the sharp fall in the terms of trade, higher real interest rates, and greatly reduced voluntary lending by commercial banks. Slower growth and increasing protectionism in industrial countries compounded their problems. Countries such as Mexico and Nigeria, which overexpanded their public sector expenditures in response to initial gains from higher petroleum prices, found themselves in need of structural adjustment.

The structure of loan conditionality, defined by the percentage of conditions falling into each major policy area, is shown in table 10-1 for Sub-Saharan countries, highly indebted countries, other developing countries, and all three groups together. Table 10-2 shows the proportion of total loans in the sample containing conditions related to a specific policy area. Adjustment programs for all groups have emphasized fiscal and budgetary policies to reduce domestic absorption, and trade and exchange rate policy to provide appropriate incentives for the production of tradable goods.

In the Sub-Saharan countries the focus of adjustment has been on reforming agriculture and public institutions. Because of the dominant role of agriculture and the promising potential for agricultural exports, emphasis has been on raising producer prices, reducing the taxation of farmers through the high profits or low efficiency of state marketing boards, and improving the quality of public services in such areas as extension and research. Programs for public enterprises and agencies have emphasized improving profitability by raising prices and efficiency, reducing overstaffing, restructuring activities and finances, and divesting some enterprises. The World Bank recognized that progress in Sub-Saharan coun-

Table 10-1. The Structure of Conditionality in World Bank Adjustment Loans, 1980–88
(percentage of all conditions by region)

Policy area	*Sub-Saharan African countries*[a]	*Highly indebted countries*[b]	*Other developing countries*[c]	*All countries*
Exchange rate[d]	4	2	0	2
Trade	25	32	25	28
Fiscal	8	11	15	11
Budget and public expenditure	12	9	10	10
Public enterprises	19	17	12	16
Finance	4	13	13	11
Industry	7	2	2	3
Energy	2	3	15	6
Agriculture	17	10	7	11
Other	2	1	2	2
Total	100	100	100	100

Note: Data are based on an analysis of fifty-one SALS and SECALS in fifteen developing countries. There were a total of 504 legal conditions in those fifty-one loans. Figures may not total 100 because of rounding.

a. Includes Ghana, Kenya, Malawi, and Zambia.

b. Includes Chile, Colombia, Côte d'Ivoire, Jamaica, Mexico, Morocco, and the Philippines.

c. Includes Korea, Pakistan, Thailand, and Turkey.

d. Because of the IMF's responsibility for exchange rates, these figures understate the importance given by the World Bank to alignment of exchange rates. In the context of adjustment programs, governments are usually expected to establish and maintain exchange rates that are competitive internationally, but only in a few cases (such as Chile, Colombia, and Ghana) has there been explicit conditionality to this effect.

Source: World Bank data (supervision reports, tranche-release reports, and performance audits).

tries would likely be slower than elsewhere because of their shortage of trained manpower and weak institutional support, and correspondingly greater effort would be needed to obtain lasting results.

In the highly indebted countries adjustment programs have stressed trade and financial policies. Trade policies have emphasized improving the incentive structure for exports while progressively liberalizing imports through reductions in quantitative restrictions and tariffs. Changes in the financial sector have emphasized decontrolling interest rates and credit allocation, developing new capital market instruments, and, where needed, strengthening the portfolios of lending institutions through financial restructuring and improved auditing and supervision. Adjustment programs for the "other" developing countries in the sample more closely resemble those of the highly indebted countries than those of Sub-Saharan countries, but with somewhat less emphasis on trade policy and more on energy policy.

Table 10-2. The Content of World Bank Adjustment Loans, 1980–88
(percentage of sample loans containing conditions in each policy area)

Policy area	*Sub-Saharan African countries*[a]	*Highly indebted countries*[b]	*Other developing countries*[c]	*All countries*
Exchange rate	31	18	0	16
Trade	77	91	63	78
Fiscal	62	73	56	65
Budget and public expenditure	69	50	38	51
Public enterprises	62	55	44	53
Finance	39	36	44	39
Industry	54	9	25	26
Energy	8	14	50	24
Agriculture	77	41	38	49
Other	23	9	13	14
Number of loans	13	22	16	51

a. Includes Ghana, Kenya, Malawi, and Zambia.
b. Includes Chile, Colombia, Côte d'Ivoire, Jamaica, Mexico, Morocco, and the Philippines.
c. Includes Korea, Pakistan, Thailand, and Turkey.
Source: World Bank data (supervision reports, tranche-release reports, and performance audits).

The Implementation of Conditionality

The following analysis of experience in implementing conditionality is based on data from supervision reports, tranche-release reports, and, where available, performance audits done by the World Bank after completion of a loan. These sources were supplemented by economic reports and information supplied orally by persons with expert knowledge of the countries. Data were reviewed on fifty-one SALS and SECALS in fifteen developing countries to determine progress in implementing each item of conditionality during the period of the loan.[1] Implementation success was graded according to a five-point scale: (1) little or no progress, (2) moderate progress (some steps taken but not much progress), (3) significant progress (substantial steps taken—more than halfway to goal), (4) implementation fulfilled, and (5) implementation more than fulfilled. These assessments were summed across policy areas and across countries.

This grading process naturally has limitations. First, it obviously involves judgment: the appropriate grade was not always clear. Second, although full implementation is a desirable objective beforehand, it may not always remain desirable or reasonable. Economic circumstances can change unexpectedly, political resistance can be greater than anticipated, and errors can be made in estimating how long it takes to implement particular policy changes. Moreover, conditions differ in the difficulties they pose for implementation, their impact on the economy, and the pain they may inflict on various segments of the population. Striving for perfect implementation of a relatively large number of conditions could lead the World Bank to be unnecessarily inflexible. It might also have the undesirable side effect of leading World Bank staff to frame conditionality so that it could more easily be fulfilled. Plainly, any grading system must be supplemented by analyses of country performance such as those that appear in other chapters of this book, especially the case studies in Part III.

The results of this grading of the implementation of conditionality (table 10-3) support several generalizations:

- About 60 percent of the conditions in SALs and SECALs have been implemented fully or more than fully.
- This rate increases to more than 80 percent if conditions on which progress has been substantial are included.
- Progress varies considerably among policy areas, with implementation of conditions of energy policy (especially energy pricing) being the strongest and export finance and tax reforms being the weakest.
- Conditionality has been more successfully implemented in SALs than in SECALs, but this difference disappears if the conditions on which there has been substantial progress are included.
- Performance in implementing conditionality does not vary sharply among groups of countries, but highly indebted countries are somewhat more successful than Sub-Saharan countries and "other" developing countries. The observed differences probably reflect differences in the composition of conditionality and random factors rather than any systematic differences in performance among the three groups of countries.

Variations in Implementation among Policy Areas

What stands out in this analysis of implementation progress is the variation in outcomes by policy area. Policy changes have clearly been implemented successfully in some areas, such as exchange rate management, the energy sector (especially pricing), agricultural pricing, the financial sector, and budgetary and public expenditure policy. Policy change has equally clearly been slower or less successful in the industrial sector, taxation, and some aspects of public enterprises. There also are variations within policy areas. In trade, for example, reductions in tariffs and quantitative restrictions have been more fully implemented than improvements in export financing. The reason is not that the former are more politically palatable than the latter—the reverse is almost certainly the case. Rather, the reason is that export finance often involves institutional changes that

Table 10-3. Extent of Implementation of Conditionality by Policy Area during and after the Loan Period, 1980–88

	During the loan period		*Current situation*[a]	
Policy area	*Conditions fully implemented (1)*	*(1) plus substantial progress (2)*	*Conditions fully implemented (3)*	*(3) plus substantial progress (4)*
Exchange rate	70	90	63	88
Trade	55	84	63	89
Quantitative restrictions	63	93	69	90
Import duties	62	77	73	82
Import and export finance	20	80	43	86
Export incentives	61	82	63	92
Other trade policies	33	76	41	94
Fiscal	53	78	70	95
Tax policy	46	54	87	100
Budget and public expenditure	68	78	72	85
Public enterprises (including restructuring)	61	87	70	90
Finance	71	86	74	90
Industry (excluding restructuring)	53	93	43	86
Energy	79	83	83	89
Energy pricing	85	85	100	100
Agriculture	57	82	58	84
Agricultural pricing	64	86	62	81
All conditions	60	83	68	89
All SAL conditions	68	84	74	92
All SECAL conditions	61	83	60	85
Sub-Saharan countries	52	85	62	87
Highly indebted countries	67	89	73	91
Other developing countries	53	80	56	84

Note: Based on an analysis of fifty-one SALS and SECALS in fifteen countries.
a. Based on most recent data available (generally 1987 but sometimes 1988).
Source: Authors' assessments based on World Bank data.

are more difficult and take more time to implement than do many other types of change. The case is similar for export incentives: it has been easier to remove disincentives to exports such as taxes or quotas than to establish effective duty drawback or bonded manufacturing systems, which are technically difficult to set up and have been implemented very slowly.

Among reforms of industrial policy there has been substantial success in reducing price controls (as in Ghana, Malawi, Morocco, and Pakistan) but not much progress in rationalizing industrial tax incentives (as in Kenya, Korea, Philippines, and Thailand). For public enterprises, what works relatively well are covenants on pricing, financial targets, improvements in information systems and monitoring, and reductions in overstaffing, including even fairly large reductions, as in Ghana and Turkey. What works more slowly are improvements in management and operations, the restructuring of firms or subsectors, and, slowest of all, liquidation and divestiture. Thus Ghana, Mexico, and Pakistan have taken preparatory steps but have made little progress in closing or selling off public enterprises. But targets were more than met in Jamaica, and progress was substantial in Côte d'Ivoire. Liquidation and privatization programs often face considerable political opposition, and privatization is often delayed by difficulties in valuing assets and finding suitable buyers.

The policy areas in which implementation has been most successful are those involving changes in prices, such as exchange rates, interest rates, or agricultural and energy prices; those in which political considerations are the least sensitive, as for most restructuring of government expenditure; and those that do not require institutional changes, such as changes in staffing, training, procedures, laws, and regulations.

Continued Progress with the Passage of Time

Because policy change is continuous and because full implementation of many institutional reforms can follow adjustment loans only with a considerable lag, it is important that the reforms supported by adjustment lending continue after loan disbursement ceases. Currently the implementation of conditionality shows continuing modest progress (table 10-3). Today 68 percent of all conditions could be considered fully implemented, compared with 60 percent during the loan disbursement period. Most striking are tax reforms implemented after an unforeseen lag (for example, in Turkey, institution of a value added tax, indexing of rates, and improvements in collection procedures; in the Philippines, indirect tax reforms). Progress has also continued in areas involving the management and restructuring of public enterprises. Examples include restructuring of a major holding company in Malawi, subsector restructuring in the Philippines, and rehabilitation of a number of public enterprises in Côte d'Ivoire. Similarly, in the period after disbursement, further progress was made in establishing or improving export credit and insurance schemes in Côte d'Ivoire and Mexico.

Although there has been some retrogression in implementation since the loan disbursement period, in no policy areas has backsliding been substantial. Instead, most backsliding has been piecemeal. Tariff reform has stalled in Kenya because of foreign exchange shortages and in Thailand because of a potential loss of government revenue. Measures to free up market entry and to alter incentives favoring capital intensity lagged in the Philippines, as did measures to rationalize incentives for new industry in Kenya. Public sector price increases were abandoned in Thailand because of political opposition. The only example of large-scale policy reversal is in Zambia, which overturned important reform efforts in foreign exchange auctioning, import licensing, and consumer subsidies.

The Importance of Key Conditions

Among the various conditions attached to any adjustment lending operation usually four or five might be called key conditions. Although their legal status is no different from that of other conditions, they deserve to be singled out because government officials and World Bank staff designing the loan operation put particular emphasis on them or because they were expected to make a significant contribution to stabilization or adjustment in a short time.

Such conditions are expected within one or two years to have an impact on, for example, savings, the level and composition of investment, budget deficits, or the production of tradable goods. These key conditions span the range of stabilization and adjustment policies but fall most heavily in trade policy (35 percent), public expenditure and fiscal policy (19 percent), public enterprise reforms (14 percent), and pricing, with agricultural and energy pricing together accounting for 14 percent. Specific examples of key conditions include measures to achieve public sector savings targets of 4.5 to 4.7 percent of GDP in Chile, agreement on the 1988–90 public investment program (with protection for twenty-one key projects) and reductions in price and distribution controls in Ghana, and phased reductions in quantitative restrictions and tariffs in Turkey.

The key conditions in the fifty-one adjustment loan operations were isolated and analyzed for performance. On balance, performance on key conditions was better than performance on all conditions: 68 percent of key conditions were fully implemented within the loan period (table 10-4) compared with 60 percent of all conditions (table 10-3). And in public enterprise reform, tariff changes, and industrial policy, the performance is strikingly better for key conditions. By contrast, progress in tax reform and export finance is little affected by key-condition status.

Factors Affecting Implementation

This investigation of the implementation of conditionality in fifteen countries has revealed the importance of macroeconomic policies, tranche-

Table 10-4. Extent of Implementation of Key Conditions in Adjustment Loans during the Loan Period, 1980–88
(percent)

Policy area	*Successful implementation*	*Distribution of key conditions*
Exchange rate	100	4
Trade	59	35
Quantitative restrictions	59	16
Import duties	77	8
Import and export finance	0	2
Export incentives	62	8
Other trade policies	0	1
Fiscal	64	7
Tax policy	40	3
Budget and public expenditure	71	13
Public enterprises	78	14
Finance	79	8
Industry	80	3
Energy	90	6
Energy pricing	88	5
Agriculture	56	11
Agricultural pricing	60	9
Other policies	0	0
All key conditions	68	100

Source: Authors' assessments based on World Bank data.

release conditions, government commitment, the quality of World Bank advice, and the economic environment. Each of these factors is discussed below.

The Macroeconomic Policy Framework

The evidence shows that appropriate macroeconomic policies are essential to the success of sectoral reforms. Otherwise, appreciating real exchange rates, excessively high real interest rates, and general inflation can threaten the viability of reforms. This is particularly the case for reforms whose success depends on such factors as better incentives for the production of tradable goods, the right choice of production techniques, and the correct assessment of relative profitability. Therefore the World Bank has generally agreed to support sectoral reform programs only when a stabilization program supported by the International Monetary Fund (IMF) is in place to handle the macroeconomic issues or when the World Bank is assured that the government is pursuing a program that addresses short-term stabilization issues as well as medium-term development objectives. In Ghana, for example, a strong IMF-supported stabilization program provided the appropriate environment for five successful sectoral adjustment operations. Similarly, in Morocco an IMF standby arrangement and an extended Fund facility provided an umbrella under which five sectoral loans could proceed. At first, budgetary constraints slowed the implementation of trade liberalization, but later efforts to mobilize public resources made possible considerable progress in trade reform.

Despite the World Bank's general intention that sectoral reforms be supported by appropriate stabilization programs, there have been some worrisome exceptions. Turkey achieved remarkable adjustment during five years of SALs and IMF standby arrangements. Subsequently, however, Turkey received three sectoral loans despite growing budget deficits and high real interest rates, which dampened private investment in tradable goods and threatened the viability of firms and financial institutions. A number of financial sector and agricultural sector loans have been given to countries without the macroeconomic framework to ensure the real exchange rates, interest rate and credit conditions, and price stability needed for the program's success (for example, Argentina, Ecuador, Kenya, Mexico, and Turkey). The case of Mexico illustrates the problems of trying to achieve stabilization and structural adjustment objectives simultaneously. Although the heterodox anti-inflationary policy adopted in December 1987 reflected the government's pragmatism, the use of price controls created a dilemma because distorted relative prices will still have to be corrected when controls are lifted.

Tranche-Release Conditions

The trend throughout the World Bank toward greater use of tranche-release conditions shows up in the fifteen-country sample as well. All SALs have included tranche-release conditions except for those in Thailand. The only SECALs not tranched in recent years have been the export development loans for Mexico (two) and Pakistan, which have been small or repeat operations. SALs have averaged eleven or twelve conditions per loan, 91 percent of which were tranche-release conditions (the remainder were other dated or undated covenants). SECALs have averaged nine to ten conditions, only 75 percent of which were tranche-release conditions. Thus, on average, the number of conditions in SALs and SECALs does not appear to have been excessive, although in some cases a considerably larger number of conditions has been specified (for example, Chile, Côte d'Ivoire, Jamaica, and Philippines).

Although there appears to be no general movement toward greater use of first-tranche conditions in the fifteen countries, such front-loading has shown up in loans for Colombia (trade and export diversification, 1985), Ghana (imports for reconstruction, 1985, and the industrial sector, 1986), Pakistan (the energy sector, 1985), and Zambia (agricultural rehabilitation, 1985, industrial reorientation, 1986, and recovery credit, 1986; all fiscal years).

The importance that the World Bank places on the implementation of tranche conditions is attested to by the fact that tranche-release delays have occurred in nearly three-quarters of all adjustment loans as a result of insufficient progress in fulfilling conditions, although almost all tranches have eventually been released. These delays reflect the difficulties in implementing complex and politically sensitive reforms and the World Bank's expectation that borrowers will achieve a reasonable record of compliance. The importance of tranche conditions is also reflected in implementation progress on the loans for the fifteen countries: full implementation for 71 percent of first-tranche conditions, 62 percent of second- (and third-) tranche conditions, and 43 percent of other legal conditions.[2] Despite the seriousness with which the World Bank views tranche conditions, several tranche releases have been granted after rather questionable performance. Examples are the SALs for Bolivia, Costa Rica, Guyana, and Yugoslavia. The second SAL for Kenya is an example of tranche-release despite little or no progress toward freeing up grain marketing or liberalizing the trade regime—both important conditions.

Nonetheless, the message is clear: implementation is better for a small number of key conditions in each loan, and it is better for tranche conditions than for other conditions. Any improvement in implementation is likely to depend on greater selectivity in setting conditions and on greater care in monitoring progress. This would involve increased reliance on tranche-release conditions, limiting conditions to a reasonable number of key concerns, setting realistic schedules for implementation, and then taking a stricter attitude about fulfillment. There would still need to be some flexibility to waive or alter conditions in light of unforeseen changes in economic or political circumstances, however.

Greater consideration of actions already taken by governments appears desirable, whether actions are taken before disbursement or as a condition of presenting the loan to the World Bank's Board of Executive Directors for approval. For governments, such conditionality, especially relating to prior actions, reduces their vulnerability to charges of yielding to outside pressure. For the World Bank, such actions dispel uncertainty by demonstrating a government's commitment and capacity to implement the loan. Increased reliance on front-loading would be particularly desirable in countries where there are vocal opposition parties or no track record of success. Limiting conditionality to a small number of agreed-on concerns also seems essential if the World Bank is to take a stricter position on fulfillment. The gains from requiring strict adherence to conditionalities should outweigh by a large margin any losses resulting from shortening the list of conditions. When the list of conditions is long, it has proved difficult to delay tranche disbursements when most conditions have been fulfilled, even though some of the missing conditions have supported objectives essential to the program.

Assessment of Government Commitment

Programs have been better implemented where the government has played the leading role in analyzing the issues, designing the program, and formulating the actions. Nonetheless, there is often a need for substantial World Bank assistance in the design of adjustment programs, and the Bank's experience with programs in other countries can almost always be of help. Serious problems arise, however, if an adjustment program is viewed as the World Bank's rather than the country's program. Progress in implementation has been stronger where governments have "owned" the program and hence were committed to carrying it through. The ownership of and commitment to any economic reform program appear to depend on several factors:

- An understanding and acceptance of the program by political leaders, senior officials, and technical experts
- A clear assignment of responsibilities to various implementing agencies
- An institutional capacity to carry out the program
- An institutional capacity for economic and financial analysis and the formulation of policy advice
- A longer-term program (say, three to five years) of economic objectives and policy goals that provides the context for the adjustment measures supported by a particular SAL or SECAL.

The first three factors determine the will and the capacity to implement the program; the last two affect the sustainability of the adjustment effort. Since adjustment is a continuing process, sustaining policy changes depends on the ability to make midcourse corrections and to place those changes in an appropriate context of continuing medium-term adjustment. Because the extent to which these factors apply in a particular country varies significantly, the relative roles of governments and the World Bank, and of technical assistance and country economic and sector work, have also varied.

The degree of involvement of the government and the World Bank (and usually the IMF) in the design of adjustment programs has varied by region as well. The government's role has tended to be greatest in Asia and Latin America, somewhat less in the EMENA region, and weakest in Sub-Saharan Africa. Government involvement also tends to be weakest at the beginning of adjustment, when time pressures are the heaviest. Typically the country is in urgent need of resources, and specific knowledge of what reforms are both desirable and feasible is often poor. In these circumstances there has been a tendency to accept commitments to actions that are undesirably vague and inadequately thought through. If the government is really to own the program, more time will have to be allowed for the policy dialogue, for the careful design of measures to fit local conditions, and for the formation of a consensus among the nation's political leaders and officials.

As the adjustment proceeds, and especially if enough progress is generated to justify a series of loans, this problem is likely to be reduced by a continuing dialogue, supplemented by increased policy work within the country (aided by technical assistance, as needed) and by a better focused World Bank program for economic and sectoral work. Among the most successful adjusting countries (Chile, Korea, Thailand, and Turkey), substantial progress was possible from the inception because governments had their own ongoing programs and medium-term frameworks. In Thailand this was aided by a well-designed and relevant economic and sectoral work program that contributed quickly to the design of action programs. In other countries studies in the context of the early adjustment loans and a redirection of economic and sectoral work were needed to assist in the design of many policies (as, for example, in Côte d'Ivoire, Ghana, and Pakistan).

That this dialogue in the context of adjustment lending works is evidenced by the growing consensus among Sub-Saharan countries and the World Bank about the essential problems and specific remedies. Issues that were contentious at the start of the 1980s, such as exchange rates, agricultural price reforms, tax policies, and the respective roles of the public and private sectors, have become decidedly less so. But this process takes time and a willingness of World Bank staff and government officials to learn from experience and adopt a pragmatic, open-minded approach. What is still needed for Sub-Saharan Africa is greater sensitivity in the World Bank to the possibility of slow supply responses to price changes, to the importance of nonprice factors in resource allocation, and to conflicts between the objectives of changing exchange rates and reducing budget deficits (as, for example, in Zambia). It is also evident that the emphasis on building institutions in Sub-Saharan Africa is justified, given the need to implement and sustain policy reform over the longer term.

The Quality of World Bank Advice

The World Bank has now had considerable experience with adjustment lending. Since 1980 it has learned a great deal about the formulation of advice, appropriate coverage, the need for accurate assessment of government commitment, realistic timetables for implementation, and the desirability of flexibility in designing conditionality and interpreting its implementation. This experience has allowed the World Bank to improve its advice.

Some early SALs caught the World Bank quite unprepared to give specific advice. For example, the first Pakistan SAL called for tariff reform but without specifying what was to be done or what the effects might be on government revenues, production, and imports. The government was unwilling to adopt a tariff reform program without a clearer understanding of its likely effects in these areas. Later, as the result of a program of economic and sectoral work, the World Bank was able to give more concrete suggestions about export incentives and quantitative restrictions, which the government accepted. In Malawi progress in reducing the taxation of agricultural export crops was spotty early on, picking up momentum only after a method was introduced for analyzing the effects of price changes on the production of food and export crops.

The number of conditions in adjustment loans has varied considerably, and many loans have been heavily loaded with actions to be carried out by governments. This has often led to a lack of focus and excessive complexity and has caused difficulties in implementation, even in successful adjusting countries such as Korea and Thailand. Also evident has been a tendency to set unrealistic timetables, especially for operations involving institutional change or political processes, such as tax reforms and the restructuring, liquidation, or divestiture of public enterprises.

The Economic Environment

Although there can be short-term tradeoffs between stabilization and growth, the two reinforce each other in the long run. Desirable adjustment measures are likely to be sustained and effective only if reasonable economic growth is maintained. A favorable economic environment makes the implementation of adjustment programs easier for several reasons. In an expanding economy it is easier to generate resources for financing investment, government expenditures, and imports. Private investment is likely to be more responsive to changes in market signals. Resources are likely to flow more smoothly and quickly between sectors. More generally, the desired reallocation of resources must be accompanied by new investments, which are unlikely in an environment of economic recession and pessimistic expectations. Painful policy changes are likely to be more acceptable if people think the pain will not last long. And governments can devote more attention to medium-term structural adjustment efforts if they do not have to dissipate their energies fighting such short-run problems as severe foreign exchange shortages, budget imbalances, or runaway money supplies.

Several countries have survived the crises of the 1980s with very respectable growth rates—examples are Korea, Pakistan, Thailand, and Turkey. Each of these countries quickly restored favorable export growth rates through changes in exchange rates and other export incentives. Pakistan and Turkey were also helped, at least in the early years, by large inflows of foreign capital and remittances from migrant workers. All four countries implemented extensive reform programs. Even so, there were notable lapses, including continuing large budget deficits in Turkey and Pakistan, and a failure to complete import liberalization programs in Pakistan and Thailand.

For countries that began from a position of stagnation and massive distortions, the implementation of adjustment programs has been more difficult. Zambia's adjustment program followed a prolonged period of stagnation and a record of poor economic management. Inflows of IMF and World Bank resources could not offset the hardships inflicted by the end of price controls and subsidies and the introduction of a foreign exchange auction. The failure of the program to generate any visible benefits quickly allowed political opposition to overwhelm it. Reforms in Ghana also followed a long period of falling incomes, mismanaged budgets and public enterprises, and badly distorted price incentives. The Economic Recovery Program, announced in April 1983, emphasized substantial cuts in budgetary deficits through both expenditure reduction and revenue mobilization, a massive realignment of the exchange rate with a view toward eventually establishing a foreign exchange auction, and a phased removal of price controls. Complementing these reforms, which emphasized reduced absorption and increased domestic production, was a large inflow of resources from the IMF and World Bank to provide the necessary inputs to increase production. Positive results, produced fairly quickly, inspired confidence in the government's management and were important to the program's success.

Summary and Conclusions

First, about 60 percent of the conditions in SALS and SECALS have been fully implemented. Extending the review beyond the loan disbursement period yields a somewhat higher rate of success in implementation. This suggests that reversals of policy have been relatively minor and that progress continues to be made after loan completion in implementing changes that take more time. Second, implementation varies significantly among policy areas: it is best for price changes and the reallocation of public expenditure and worst for institutional reforms. Third, implementation performance is better for a small number of key conditions (about four or five) in adjustment loans than for conditions overall. (Key conditions are expected to have a large impact on stabilization or adjustment within a short period.) Fourth, the major factors affecting implementation appear to be the overall macroeconomic policy framework, tranche-release conditions, government commitment, the quality of World Bank advice, and the economic environment.

Given the high economic and social costs of rapid adjustment to external shocks, quick-disbursing adjustment loans are likely to remain an important part of World Bank lending for the foreseeable future. Learning from experience and adapting and changing structural adjustment procedures to increase their effectiveness thus continue to be essential. The analysis in this chapter gives important indications of what works and what does not, of what needs changing and what should not even be attempted in the context of adjustment lending. More broadly, it shows a greater need for selectivity in adjustment lending to ensure that loans will be effective and that they do not serve merely to postpone adjustment by relieving resource constraints.

Greater selectivity has a number of dimensions:

- More concern with developing a consensus within governments about the appropriate reform strategy and with ensuring government commitment to that strategy
- More time spent ensuring that external and internal financing for the adjustment program are adequate and that programs will not have to be abandoned because of lack of resources
- More careful selection of a small set of important conditions that are likely to have a major impact on adjustment within a short time.

In all, greater selectivity would assist the World Bank by increasing the effectiveness of its programs and reducing the risk to its portfolio. It will also assist developing countries by ensuring realistic levels of external and internal financing in support of their adjustment efforts.

Notes

1. See notes to table 10-1 for country groupings and the countries included in each group. These fifty-one loans constitute 42 percent of the number and 60 percent of the value of SALS and SECALS approved during fiscal 1980–87. The conditions examined were those legally required as part of agreements with the World Bank.

2. If the conditions on which progress was substantial are added to the total, the figures become 88 percent of first-tranche conditions, 85 percent of second-tranche conditions, and 73 percent of other legal conditions.

References

World Bank. 1986. "Structural Adjustment Lending: A First Review of Experience." Report 6409. Operations Evaluation Department, World Bank, Washington, D.C.

———. 1988a. *Adjustment Lending: An Evaluation of Ten Years of Experience.* Policy and Research Series 1. Washington, D.C.

———. 1988b. "Interim Report on Adjustment Lending." Report R88-15. Washington, D.C.

Comments

Elliot Berg

The effectiveness of policy-based lending can be evaluated by three kinds of criteria: process (the quality of the dialogue), implementation (meeting conditions and other proposed reforms), and results in meeting either intermediate targets (such as for investment rates, exports, and deregulation of markets) or ultimate goals (such as for output and income distribution). Judgments about the effectiveness of policy reforms in any of these dimensions are always difficult because of problems of definition and measurement. In these comments I define successful implementation as the induced adoption of policy reforms that are both durable and additional (in other words, beyond what would have been adopted anyway).

William McCleary focuses on the second type of criteria—success in implementation. His chapter provides a detailed and yet admirably concise overview of the content of conditionality in World Bank adjustment loans and assesses the degree to which loan conditions have been implemented. He notes that implementation has been slow in reforms of the industrial sector, taxes, and public enterprises and mentions that tranche disbursements were delayed in three out of four loans because of inadequate progress in meeting conditions. The overall assessment, however, is strongly positive. Implementation has been generally satisfactory and improves over time. Backsliding is apparently not much of a problem. Implementation is even better for key conditions than it is overall.

That the explicit conditionality in the World Bank's adjustment lending has been so effectively implemented is a rather surprising finding. Compliance with International Monetary Fund (IMF) performance criteria has been much less impressive; according to some counts, the compliance rate in the early 1980s was something like 20 percent (see, for example,

Spraos 1986). Moreover, successful implementation is not what earlier episodes in conditional lending lead us to expect.

The main effort in conditioned policy lending occurred in Latin America in the 1960s under the Alliance for Progress. Most of the conditionality involved stabilization measures familiar in IMF standby agreements. Few traces of the exercise in conditionality were visible by the end of the decade. One recent assessment offers the following observation: "the Alliance assumption that the offer of external assistance can provide an effective inducement for a country to adopt basic policy changes and reforms still appears to retain considerable vitality in U.S. assistance strategies and negotiations. Since the Alliance experience can be interpreted as an overwhelming repudiation of the general efficacy of this assumption, its continued vitality is striking" (Heller and Wionczek 1988).

Some attempts at policy-based lending also took place in South Asia in the 1960s; the United States and the World Bank tried to condition aid to India on reforms in agriculture and liberalization of the trade regime, including a devaluation of the rupee. One participant-observer argues that at least the timing of the devaluation was affected by the conditioned policy loan and that the tilt of long-term trade policy was thereafter in the direction of liberalization (Lewis 1989). This is a debatable conclusion, and in any case the experience was marked by misunderstandings on all sides and caused much bitterness among Indians; policy-based lending was never tried in India again.

In Pakistan the U.S government, between 1963 and 1966, gave conditioned loans tied to import liberalization. For various reasons the implementation was on-again, off-again until 1967, when it was finally abandoned. The trade regime was more restrictive in 1967 than it had been in 1963. These and other experiences with explicit conditionality (including the World Bank's own experience with covenants and conditions in project lending) indicate a generally poor track record.

In addition to the sparsity of historical precedent for effective conditionality, there is a more important reason why the good results reported by McCleary are surprising. The general environment within which conditions are set and monitored and the kind of behavior that they inspire are such that highly imperfect implementation is to be expected.

Before taking up this point in detail, one methodological point is worth making. Of the more than fifty countries that had received adjustment loans by 1989, fifteen are analyzed by McCleary. Of these, five are from Sub-Saharan Africa, four each from Asia and Latin America, and two from the Middle East and North Africa. But the proportion of total adjustment loans (in number) going to Sub-Saharan Africa—about half—is much greater than the proportion in the study sample. It is not certain that this makes much difference in the experience with conditionality, but it is possible, even likely, that it does. Adjustment programs in Sub-Saharan Africa tend to be less home grown, more heavily conditioned, and more heavily laden with institutional conditionality than is usual in other regions. African economies are more open and more commodity dependent. All of this should make programs there at once more difficult and more fragile than in other regions. The bias in the sample may therefore yield a more upbeat assessment of the effectiveness of conditionality than reality warrants.

Intuition, fed by experience, suggests that explicit conditionality is a highly implausible instrument of policy reform and adjustment from which little should be expected. This is due to the nature of the environment in which the conditioned lending takes place. The relevant elements in this environment are well known.

1. Many of the intellectual or analytical underpinnings of 1980s-style adjustment lending are contested—such fundamentals as the feasibility of export-led growth, the efficacy and beneficence of deregulated markets, and the desirability of market-determined interest rates or exchange rates. It is true, as McCleary notes, that there is more consensus on these ideas now than there was ten years ago. But as indicated by the Economic Commission for Africa's recent attack on liberalization ideas, profound disagreements remain. Similar disagreements also exist on less cosmic matters, such as the size and timing of exchange rate adjustments, the desirability of border pricing for basic foods, and the degree and the speed of reducing protection for the industrial sector. Since consensus is lacking in many countries on important loan conditions, implementation will tend to lack conviction and programs will be easily diluted or derailed.

2. Political and bureaucratic consensus is even more uncommon than intellectual or analytical agreement. Agreements negotiated and signed by ministers of finance or planning are implemented by sectoral ministries. Sometimes these ministries are only perfunctorily consulted; often they are in deep disagreement with the spirit and the particulars of the reform program. This seems to be especially likely for ministries of agriculture.

3. Conditions related to institutional reforms are almost sure to lag and are in any case prone to cosmetic compliance. This may have something to do with lack of commitment or political will, but more often it is a simple result of administrative failures that are due to limited capacity, that is, to factors inherent in underdevelopment.

4. Explicit conditionality coexists uneasily and may indeed be incompatible with the notion of local "ownership" of adjustment programs—that is, with a government's responsibility for and commitment to adjustment.

5. Monitoring is difficult. There are multiple conditions, many more than the ten or so that are sometimes regarded as "legal" (those found in loan agreements). Many—especially the "process" conditions—are so imprecise as to be essentially unmonitorable. Moreover, in developing countries the administrative systems are normally diffuse and opaque. Combined with infrequent and sometimes hurried supervision, this means that it is often difficult for lenders to know whether or in what sense implementation has in fact occurred. Deliberate or accidental slippage is possible at every stage. The World Bank's capacity to supervise all this is extremely limited. Administrative opacity may even prevent confirmation that conditions for effectiveness have been satisfied, as happened in one West African country recently when lack of implementation was not discovered until months after disbursement had begun.

6. The threat of loan suspension, rarely very credible to begin with, is likely to diminish rather quickly. Both parties are anxious to continue disbursement, performance is rarely all bad, and assessment of good and bad implementation is usually subjective. Nowadays, adjustment loans are usually part of an exercise to close the resource gap, with the IMF frequently in the wings making ominous noises about the need to continue spending if the program is not to unravel. In some countries, programs seem to continue in the face of repeated foot-dragging and surface compliance with conditions. The low and diminishing credibility of the threat of program cancellation should encourage the reduction of reform efforts.

Given the circumstances outlined above, one should expect implementation of explicit conditionality to be often perfunctory and superficial. This does not mean that governments will try to avoid implementing the whole slate of conditions. In fact, many of the conditions are superfluous in the sense that the government in question would have taken the actions even without conditionality. It does mean, however, that probably in a substantial number of cases conditionality is acceptably implemented only at the expense of watering down the original requirements or because the World Bank accepts pro forma compliance. Thus, for example, a condition for tranche release may be the adoption of an action plan for reforming public enterprises. If implementation is nil or partial, World Bank staff will settle for the completion of terms of reference for a study to recommend an action plan. Or tranche release may require economic evaluation of a certain number of projects in the public investment program. But delays and risks of nonperformance induce World Bank staff and management to accept perfunctory reviews of projects as meeting the condition.

The fact that such dilution of content and pro forma compliance may be common raises the question of how to interpret the figures on implementation assembled by McCleary. The observation that 60 percent of conditions are fully implemented and more than 80 percent "substantially" implemented takes on a different meaning if the yardstick for measuring compliance is rubbery and if many conditions are superfluous. Given not only the ability but the strong incentive to bend the yardstick, one should hesitate to conclude that a 60 percent implementation rate indicates success. When the superfluity of many conditions is also taken into account, the 60 percent compliance rate looks even less impressive.

One should also hesitate to interpret the delays in tranche release as evidence of "the importance that the World Bank places on the implementation of tranche conditions." It is at least as plausible to interpret it as evidence that weak compliance is widespread and as an indicator that the World Bank and its partners needed time to work out a mutually acceptable combination of improved performance, softening of content, and surface compliance.

Thus far the effectiveness of conditionality has been considered only in terms of the implementation record and its interpretation. There is another side of the question that is much more important: the propensity for explicit conditionality to undermine the quality of policy dialogue and the durability of policy reforms.

First of all, conditionality gives the impression of being imposed from outside, even when it is not. It causes liberalization ideas and policies to be identified with outsiders. Local critics attack the "World Bank's austerity program" or the "World Bank's liberalization scheme"; foreign reporters write about it the same way. This may have a slight facilitating effect since the authorities know they can blame the World Bank or IMF if things go wrong. But the overall effect is to discourage the growth of local "ownership," discredit the policy ideas at issue, and delay the growth of political responsibility.

More important, explicit conditionality tends to distort the policy dialogue and can poison it altogether. It tends to replace the joint search for acceptable policies, which is what the dialogue should be about, with a process of game playing aimed at signing an agreement and completing disbursements. To address the real obstacles to reform—for example, local skepticism about the technical suitability of proposed reforms, or concern that minority groups may benefit excessively, or aversion to political risk—the policy dialogue should be conducive to joint problem solving and friendly persuasion, rather than simply to document signing. Effective dialogue of this kind requires open and experimental attitudes, a noncontentious environment, and extensive opportunity for genuine exchange of ideas and consensus building around specific issues and proposals.

No doubt in some cases the policy dialogue in adjustment lending approaches this ideal. But the conditionality factor discourages effective dialogue. Instead, it tends to encourage a game in which differences are reconciled more on paper than in reality and agreements are framed so as to meet conflicting needs—the country's need for understated, flexible conditions that will not involve rigid, risky, or excessively difficult commitments, and the World Bank's desire for conditionality that is as firm and explicit as possible. This does not necessarily rule out true dialogue and spirited debate over substantive issues; there has been more such debate in the past decade than ever before, stimulated by policy lending. But in terms of solving problems and changing minds the impact is much diluted by the conditionality-ridden atmosphere.

To the extent that explicit conditionality leads to this kind of game playing, it is counterproductive. It diverts attention and energy from real problem solving to contract maintenance. Along with the related matter of the rubbery yardstick for evaluating the extent of implementation, it implies a considerably less sanguine view of the effectiveness of explicit conditionality than that put forward by McCleary—and by the authors of the earlier report on adjustment lending (World Bank 1988).

Of course, the validity of this view depends on how widespread have been the tendencies to dilute conditionality and distort the dialogue. My view is that these tendencies are common and probably dominant. But this could easily be wrong because it is based on observation that is too distant or biased, in the sense of being based on too few or too unrepresentative a sample of countries. There is nonetheless enough evidence to suggest that the tendencies in question are not rare and could be widespread. The recommendations presented by McCleary—to reduce the number of conditions, to front-load more of them, to build more internal consensus, to take more time, to monitor conditionality more closely, and to take a firmer line on compliance—are a recognition that problems of the sort outlined above do exist. Just how general or pervasive they are will not be known until there are more in-depth country case studies. In any case, to neglect these seamier sides of the conditionality process, as do McCleary's chapter and the World Bank's 1988 report on adjustment lending, may encourage unwarranted complacency.

Even if it were granted that explicit conditionality has proved to be inappropriate, ineffective, and counterproductive, better alternatives would have to be found before explicit conditionality could be abandoned. To consider the options here would take this discussion too far afield. But the search for alternatives is not likely to be vigorous so long as it is generally believed that there is not much basically wrong with the way explicit conditionality works in adjustment lending. The first task should be to take a hard look at that belief.

References

Heller, Jack, and M. S. Wionczek. 1988. "The Assumptions of the Alliance." In L. R. Scheman, ed., *The Alliance for Progress: A Retrospective.* New York: Praeger.

Lewis, John. 1989. "Policy Based Assistance: An Historical Perspective on AID's Experience and Operations in India/Asia in a Bilateral and Multilateral Context." Washington, D.C.: U.S. Agency for International Development.

Spraos, John. 1986. *IMF Conditionality: Ineffectual, Inefficient, Mistargeted.* Princeton Essays in International Finance 166. Princeton, N.J.: Princeton University.

World Bank. 1988. *Adjustment Lending: An Evaluation of Ten Years of Experience.* Policy and Research Series 1. Washington, D.C.

11 *Macro Performance under Adjustment Lending*

Riccardo Faini
Jaime de Melo
Abdel Senhadji-Semlali
Julie Stanton

THE PROMOTION of both stabilization and growth represents a significant challenge for the design of adjustment policies. Despite the relatively short time that has elapsed since the advent of adjustment programs, an evaluation of them is clearly important—but it is fraught with difficulties. To begin with, any assessment of World Bank–supported adjustment programs must recognize that most of them were undertaken jointly with the International Monetary Fund (IMF). Any assessment must also recognize that performance will be influenced by the external environment: countries that faced a more unfavorable environment would be expected to show less improvement than other countries. Furthermore, it would be desirable to control for the adjustment policies that might have been undertaken in the absence of World Bank and IMF adjustment lending. Finally, one should recognize that participation in World Bank and IMF programs is not independent of a country's own policies.

Taking into account all these difficulties with the quantitative assessment of adjustment lending is well beyond the scope of the preliminary study undertaken here, which focuses on a simple statistical analysis of macroeconomic performance. In a companion paper we attempt to tackle some of these difficulties by postulating a simple but specific model of how World Bank and IMF lending and the external environment interact (Faini and others forthcoming). Here, we rely on a simpler control-group analysis, which is more restrictive in its assumptions and therefore less satisfactory in controlling for the methodological problems mentioned above. We use several approaches to check for the robustness of our results, however.

In the following section we briefly discuss the pitfalls of alternative statistical approaches in assessing the effectiveness of adjustment programs. This discussion indicates the limitations of our statistical evaluation. Next we provide summary statistical evidence on the environment under which adjustment lending took place, emphasizing the relative roles of commercial and official multilateral funds and the size of external shocks. The following sections present our statistical analyses. A first-cut statistical evaluation compares the relative performance of countries that received a high amount of World Bank and IMF adjustment loans with countries that received a low amount. Then thirty countries that received their first World Bank–supported adjustment loan by 1984 are compared with sixty-three countries that had not. Finally, we look at tradeoffs between growth and improvement in the balance of resources for the same group of thirty recipient countries and compare these tradeoffs with those for nonrecipient countries.

Limitations and Implementation of the Methodology

Two issues in any assessment of adjustment lending are the choice of evaluation method and the choice of indicators. A discussion of the selection of method is necessary because none of the available methods provides a good prediction of the counterfactual, that is, of what policies would have taken place and consequently what the performance would have been in the absence of adjustment lending. A discussion of the choice of indicators is useful since the intermediate objectives of adjustment lending are many, and there are interactions between indicators.

Alternative Approaches and Selection of Indicators

Adjustment effectiveness can be measured in several ways.[1] One way, the before-after approach, defines the effectiveness of adjustment as the difference in the values of a set of indicators before and after adjustment was initiated. Another way (which is often used by the Operations Evaluation Department of the World Bank) measures effectiveness in terms of the difference between the target values specified in the adjustment programs and the values that are realized.

Each approach has its advantages and disadvantages. The before-after approach is simple to apply, but it is subject to serious biases because it assumes that all factors (besides the adjustment program) that affect performance, such as terms of trade variations and movements in interest rates, do not change between the pre- and postadjustment periods. In the actual-versus-target approach, one gets no information about how adjustment lending affects a country's performance. Furthermore, just as the situation prevailing before a country enters into an adjustment lending program is not likely to be a good predictor of what would have happened in the absence of an adjustment loan, so too loan targets may be achieved because of favorable exogenous developments, irrespective of the policies adopted. Thus neither of the two approaches provides an adequate view of the costs and benefits of the adopted policy course.

The control-group approach, with its several variants, is designed to overcome the shortcomings described above. The simplest variant assumes that adjustment loan recipients and nonrecipient comparators face the same exogenous factors and the same initial conditions. The performance of the nonrecipient group serves as an estimate of what the performance of the adjustment loan group would have been in the absence of adjustment programs. Because of its simplicity and ease of application, this is the approach we use in the statistical analysis of performance indicators for adjustment loan recipients.

This control-group approach still does not provide a good basis for the counterfactual, however. It does not take into account the fact that changes in the external environment may not be the same for both groups of countries. Nor does it identify what the policy choices would have been in the absence of adjustment lending. In our companion paper (Faini and others forthcoming) we recognize these complications and use a modified control-group approach in which we postulate a simple reaction function that policy choice in the absence of adjustment lending depends on initial conditions.

Moreover, it may be argued that changes in performance attributed to an adjustment lending program may reflect the country-specific conditions that led countries to participate in the program.[2] For example, countries with large external disequilibria had to cut public investment expenditures and also had a greater probability of entering into an adjustment lending program. This possibility is not usually adequately captured in statistical evaluations of effectiveness. As shown by Goldstein and Montiel (1986), if macroeconomic performance is positively correlated with the country-specific conditions that led countries to participate in an adjustment lending program (sample-selectivity bias), then the control-group estimate of the effects of adjustment lending will overstate the true effects of the program.

Other issues arise because of the choice of indicators for measuring performance. We used nine indicators in four areas: growth, external balance, internal balance, and external debt. Growth indicators are average real growth rates for gross domestic product (GDP) and exports, and the investment/GDP ratio. Indicators of external balance are average values of the real effective exchange rate index (an increase in the value of the index signifies a real devaluation) and the current account deficit as a fraction of GDP. Indicators of internal balance are the government budget surplus or deficit as a fraction of GDP, and inflation. Indicators of external debt are gross external debt and total debt-service payments (interest and principal); both are given as fractions of exports of goods and nonfactor services.

Obviously there are interdependencies among this group of indicators. To take these interdependencies into account one would have to specify an appropriate structural model as given in Khan and Knight (1981) or Bourguignon, Branson, and de Melo (1989). Such an approach would lend itself to counterfactual simulation analysis but would be more demanding of the data, especially for a large sample of heterogeneous countries. Furthermore, the nine indicators selected here do not assess the full set of targets under adjustment lending (for example, public sector and financial sector reforms are not covered). The choice of indicators was dictated by the desire to have indicator values for as large a group of countries as possible. Because of this focus on breadth rather than depth, the results presented here are best viewed as complements to the more thorough country studies of the effectiveness of adjustment lending (see Part III of this volume).

Implementation

Subject to these caveats, our objective was to assess the effects of adjustment lending programs on macro performance. Of the forty-eight countries that received World Bank structural adjustment loans or sectoral adjustment loans, only thirty received their first adjustment loan before 1985. Our evaluation covers this subgroup of thirty recipients for which two to three years of data are generally available after receipt of the first adjustment loan. This group of thirty countries is compared with a control group of sixty-three countries that had not received their first adjustment loan before 1985, that participated in IMF adjustment programs only, or that did not participate in adjustment programs supported by either the IMF or the World Bank. We also rely on a two-way classification of countries by income level (low income and middle income) to control for the influence of institutional characteristics on program effectiveness.

Obviously this definition of the control group of nonrecipients of adjustment lending is not very satisfactory. Furthermore, most of the thirty countries that participated in World Bank–supported adjustment programs also participated in IMF-supported adjustment programs.[3] We therefore decided to evaluate both the effectiveness of World Bank–supported adjustment programs and the joint effectiveness of World Bank–IMF–supported adjustment programs. In this regard, it was not easy to decide on a before-after cutoff point when World Bank and IMF programs were not initiated in the same year. We selected 1982 as the cutoff point, that is, as the first year for the assessment of World Bank–IMF programs, because this was the year in which adjustment lending intensified.

In our examination of the joint effectiveness of World Bank–IMF adjustment programs, we assess countries that received a nonnegligible amount of World Bank and IMF financial support. In a first-round evaluation, we look for robustness by defining the control group as low-credit (LC) recipient countries. This control group is constructed so that it includes one-third of the ninety-three countries in our sample. Values of performance indicators for low-credit countries are then compared with the corresponding values for high-credit (HC) recipients, also defined so as to include one-third of the countries in the sample. Slicing the sample into terciles and omitting from the comparisons the middle tier is a crude way to add some robustness to the comparisons of the average value of indicators before and after adjustment lending. The first-round evaluation relies on nonparametric statistics (the number of countries in the high-credit group that improved their performance relative to themselves and to the low-credit control group) and is therefore similar to previous assessments (for example, Balassa 1988).

The second-round evaluation relies on tests of significance of changes in mean values (corrected for unequal variances and differences in sample size). Two tests are performed. The first is for change in mean performance among high-credit recipients after adjustment lending. For each of the nine indicators, x, we test the null hypothesis $\mu_{x,1}^{HC} = \mu_{x,2}^{HC}$ where subscripts 1 and 2 refer to the before and after periods. The second test is for effectiveness, and for indicator x we test the null hypothesis

$$\mu_{x,2}^{HC} - \mu_{x,1}^{HC} = \mu_{x,2}^{LC} - \mu_{x,1}^{LC}.$$

In assessing the effectiveness of only World Bank–supported lending for the group of thirty countries defined above, we use the same set of performance indicators and the same combination of nonparametric and parametric statistics. The main difference in these tests is that the cutoff point is now endogenous, that is, it is determined individually for each country according to the year of its first adjustment loan.

The External Environment

In this section we ask two questions: (1) Was adjustment assistance under IMF and World Bank auspices directed mostly to countries that faced a more unfavorable external environment? (2) Was there complementarity or substitutability between commercial bank lending and IMF and World Bank lending? The relative importance of private and official funds was examined to determine whether official lending served as a catalyst for private funding, which is one of its objectives.

To measure the significance of the deterioration in the external environment, we quantify the impact of the external disturbances associated with declining terms of trade and rising real interest rates. External disturbances are measured over the adjustment loan period of 1982–86, while 1976–81 is taken as the base period.[4] The formula for computing the welfare costs of external disturbances is as follows:[5]

$$\Delta w/w = -(\overline{R}_2 - \overline{R}_1)(\overline{D/Y})_1 + (\overline{PX}_2/\overline{PX}_1 - 1)(\overline{X/Y})_1 - (\overline{PM}_2/\overline{PM}_1 - 1)(\overline{M/Y})_1 = -\text{RIR} + \text{TOT} \quad (11\text{-}1)$$

where subscripts 2 and 1 refer to the periods 1982–86 and 1976–81, respectively, a bar over a variable means an average value over the relevant period, and the variables are defined as follows:

$\overline{R}$ = average real interest rate (the deflator is the U.S. GDP deflator and the nominal interest rate is the weighted interest on concessional and commercial debt)
$\overline{Y}$ = average real GDP measured in dollars
$\overline{PX}$, $\overline{PM}$ = export and import price indices measured in dollars and deflated by the U.S. GDP deflator
X, M = exports, imports
D = gross outstanding debt, net of reserves
RIR = real interest rate index
TOT = terms of trade index.

In equation 11-1 the first term measures the welfare effect of higher-than-expected interest payments, and the remaining terms measure the effect of changes in the terms of trade. The choice of periods implies that the welfare measure is expressed as a percentage of the average value of GDP during 1976–81. Because cutoff points for the measurement of external shocks are debatable, however, we also report calculations that use 1978–81 as the base period.

Estimates of the size of the external shock are shown in table 11-1.[6] The choice of base period does not significantly affect the estimated impact of higher real interest rates, but use of the base period 1976–81 results in a significantly higher estimate for the impact of declining terms of trade than does use of the base period 1978–81. In general, the estimated magnitude of external shocks is greater for recipients of World Bank adjustment loans than for the control group.

When countries are classified by intensity of World Bank–IMF lending (high- and low-credit groups), the terms of trade shock is higher for low-credit countries. The measure of World Bank–IMF lending intensity is the average net IMF credit plus World Bank structural and sectoral adjustment loans during 1982–86, expressed as a percentage of average 1982–86 GDP. The cutoff points for high-credit and low-credit countries are chosen so that the sample of ninety-three countries is divided into three groups. The cutoff points are World Bank–IMF credit of more than 0.7 percent of GDP for the high-credit group and less than 0.02 percent for the low-credit group. Countries that fall in the middle are excluded from the comparisons.

Table 11-1. External Shocks as Percentages of Average GDP for Sample Groups of Countries, 1978–81 and 1976–81

	+ RIR[a]		− TOT[b]	
Country group (number)	*1978–81*	*1976–81*	*1978–81*	*1976–81*
All recipients (30)	0.011	0.010	0.036	0.052
All intensive recipients (12)[c]	0.011	0.010	0.045	0.065
Nonrecipients (63)	0.006	0.006	0.033	0.049
High-credit (31)	0.012	0.010	0.022	0.037
Low-credit (31)	0.003	0.003	0.042	0.063
Low-income[d]				
Recipients (12)	0.015	0.012	0.067	0.091
Nonrecipients (24)	0.010	0.008	0.016	0.037
Middle-income				
Recipients (18)	0.009	0.009	0.017	0.028
Nonrecipients (39)	0.004	0.004	0.041	0.054

Note: A positive value indicates a worsening of the external environment in 1982–86 compared with the base period. Number in parentheses indicates the number of countries in each category. See table 11-6 for country classifications.

a. RIR: real interest rate, as measured by $(\overline{R}_2 - \overline{R}_1)(\overline{D/Y})_1$, the first term of equation 11-1.

b. TOT: terms of trade index as measured by $(\overline{PM}_2/\overline{PM}_1 - 1)(\overline{M/Y})_1 - (\overline{PX}_2/\overline{PX}_1 - 1)(\overline{X/Y})_1$, the third and second terms respectively of equation 11-1 (reversed to show a sign change). Note that the column heading has a negative sign. The numbers are reported as positive ratios to GDP whereas equation 11-1 defines a deteriorating external environment as a negative number.

c. Intensive recipients are countries that received three or more adjustment loans (see table 11-6).

d. For definitions of low- and middle-income, see World Bank (1989), chap. 2.

Source: World Bank data.

The correlation between the estimated size of the external shocks and the availability of World Bank, IMF, and private credit is shown in table 11-2. The correlation between the size of the external shock and the intensity of World Bank and IMF credit is in all three cases insignificant, which suggests that World Bank and IMF lending was not targeted to countries facing the most unfavorable external environment. As expected, there is a strong positive correlation between World Bank and IMF credit, reflecting the fact that much of World Bank adjustment lending took place simultaneously with IMF stabilization programs. The significantly negative correlation between World Bank and IMF adjustment lending and net private credit supports the widely held view that World Bank and IMF credit served as a substitute for rather than a supplement to private credit. This result suggests that the joint involvement of both institutions was not sufficient to serve as a catalyst for inducing commercial bank lending.

Table 11-2. Correlation Matrix of External Shocks and External Financing, 1982–86: Pearson Correlation Coefficients
(credit flows as a ratio of average GDP for the period)

	IMF[a]	World Bank[b]	World Bank and IMF	Net private credit
External shocks[c]				
Number of observations	91	91	91	91
Correlation coefficient	−0.06	0.03	−0.01	−0.05
Significance level	0.56	0.75	0.90	0.62
IMF financing				
Number of observations		93	93	93
Correlation coefficient		0.29	0.78	−0.19
Significance level		0.005	0.0001	0.06
World Bank financing				
Number of observations			93	93
Correlation coefficient			0.83	−0.23
Significance level			0.0001	0.03
World Bank and IMF financing				
Number of observations				93
Correlation coefficient				−0.26
Significance level				0.01

Note: Mean values of variables:

Net private credit	−0.002
External shock	0.05
Net IMF credit	0.003
World Bank credit	0.003
World Bank–IMF credit	0.006

a. Net IMF credit.
b. Structural and sectoral adjustment loans.
c. Calculated and expressed as in table 11-1 (+RIR −TOT).
Source: World Bank data.

Indicators of Performance

The relative performance of high-credit and low-credit countries in each income group (low and middle income) is summarized in table 11-3. The measure of relative performance is the change in performance in high-credit countries in 1982–86 compared with 1978–81 relative to the change in performance in low-credit countries between the same two periods. For example, the entry "10+" in the third row under the column heading "Low income" indicates that ten of sixteen high-credit countries in the low-income classification improved their GDP growth when compared with the change for the low-credit control group. The plus sign

Table 11-3. *Performance Indicators for Recipients of World Bank and IMF Adjustment Loans Relative to Nonrecipients, by Income Group*

Indicator	Low-income			Middle-income			
	Number	*Relative to own performance*[a]	*Relative to nonrecipients*[b]	*Number*	*Relative to own performance*	*Relative to nonrecipients*[b]	*Row sum*
High-credit countries (HC)	16			15			31
Low-credit countries (LC)	10			21			31
GDP growth	10+	—	—	10+	*	—	20
Investment/GDP	5−	—	—	2−	*	*	7
Export growth	14+	—	*	9+	—	—	23
Real exchange rate	12+	—	—	13+	*	*	25
Current account surplus/GDP	12+	—	*	11+	*	*	23
Budget surplus/GDP	7−	—	—	8+	—	—	15
Inflation	10−	—	—	10−	—	—	20
External debt/exports	9−	—	—	6−	*	—	15
Debt service/exports	11+	—	*	10+	—	—	21
Share showing improvement	0.63			0.59			

* Denotes 10 percent (or more) significance level of test of equality of means.

— Denotes statistical insignificance.

Note: The numbers in the table show for each indicator how many high-credit recipient countries in each classification improved during 1982–86 compared with 1978–81. The plus and minus signs show the direction of change of the average value of an indicator in comparison with the average value of the same indicator for the low-credit comparators. For five indicators—GDP growth, investment/GDP, export growth, current account surplus/GDP, and overall budget surplus/GDP—a positive difference is an improvement (shown by a plus sign). For example, if the average GDP growth of high-credit recipients in a subgroup was 0.2 percentage points less than that of low-credit countries during 1978–81 and 0.1 percentage points less during 1982–86, the difference (0.1) is positive, and the relative performance of high-credit recipients improved. For three indicators—inflation, external debt/exports, and debt service/exports—a positive difference is a worsening (shown by a minus sign). For the real exchange rate, a greater real depreciation between periods than that of the comparators is an improvement.

a. $\mu_{x,1}^{HC} \neq \mu_{x,2}^{HC}$ (see the discussion under "Implementation" in the text).

b. $\mu_{x,2}^{HC} - \mu_{x,1}^{HC} \neq \mu_{x,2}^{LC} - \mu_{x,1}^{LC}$ (see the discussion under "Implementation" in the text).

Source: World Bank data.

indicates that change in GDP growth was on average higher in the high-credit group during 1982–86 than during 1978–81 relative to the change for the low-credit group.

The nonparametric statistics in table 11-3 suggest a mild improvement in the performance of high-credit countries relative to that of low-credit countries. If an equal weight is given to each indicator, 63 percent of high-credit countries in the low-income classification and 59 percent in the middle-income classification improved when compared with corresponding countries in the low-credit group. Interestingly, the pattern is very similar across indicators for both income classifications.

On the positive side, the patterns suggest relative improvements in high-credit countries in GDP growth, the current account and exports (via a larger real exchange rate devaluation than in low-credit countries), and debt service. On the negative side, the patterns suggest relative worsening in the ratio of real investment to real GDP and of the budget deficit to GDP.[7] Although the worsening fiscal position is an unambiguous sign of a deteriorating situation that was unintended by the adjustment programs, it could be argued that the falling share of investment in GDP was intended and reflects a cut in overly ambitious public investment programs. Unfortunately, the available data do not allow for a breakdown of investment into its public and private components.

Even though the value of each performance indicator represents an average over several years, there is much variance in the calculated means, especially among low-income countries. As the second column in table 11-3 indicates, none of the changes in means is significant for the high-credit recipients in the low-income classification. Since most of the countries in this classification are Sub-Saharan African countries, in which performance varied considerably and for which data are unreliable, this should come as no surprise. For the middle-income countries, however, the changes in performance are statistically significant for approximately half the indicators. Note the significant improvement in GDP growth during 1982–86 compared with 1978–81 and the worsening investment performance.

Relative to low-credit comparators, high-credit recipients among low-income countries significantly improved their performance in terms of export growth, debt service, and the current account. This relative improvement may not be a sign of sustainable recovery, however, since investment dropped. High-credit recipients among middle-income countries improved upon their own earlier performance for half the indicators. Relative to low-credit comparators, however, their performance showed no significant improvement (except for the current account and real exchange rate) and a significant worsening for investment. Here, too, in spite of a mild relative improvement, there are no signs of a sustainable recovery.

As mentioned previously, this simple control-group approach suffers from several shortcomings. In the companion paper using the same data set (Faini and others forthcoming), we specify a simple statistical model for a subset of the indicators used here. We postulate that changes in the value of indicator i for country j, y_{ij}, depends on a vector of (unobservable) autonomous policy changes, x_i, on changes in the external environment, SH_i, and on participation ($\text{CON}_j = 1$ if participation, otherwise zero). Specifying autonomous policies as an adjustment process toward the long-run values of the dependent variable allows us to write the model as:

$$\text{(11-2)} \qquad \Delta y_{ij} = \beta_{0j} + (y'_{i-1})\beta_{1j} + SH_i\beta_{2j} + \text{CON}\ \beta_{3j} + \epsilon_{ij}.$$

In equation 11-2 Δ refers to the difference between the post- and preadjustment periods, and y'_{i-1} is a vector of first-period averages of selected indicators. In our sample, the control group is composed of thirty-two countries that did not receive any IMF or World Bank loan during 1982–86 and nine countries that received their first adjustment loan only in 1985 or 1986. This gives forty-one countries in the control group and fifty-two countries that received IMF and World Bank adjustment lending. In the latter group, only two countries received their first adjustment credit in 1984, so that the statistical results relate to the performance of fifty countries which received adjustment credits before 1984 and hence were carrying out policy reforms whose performance-enhancing effects were supposed to last throughout the period (until 1986).

Equation 11-2 was estimated for four indicators (GDP growth, investment share in GDP, inflation, and the current account) for the same sample of countries as in this paper. In the estimation, period averages were for 1978–81 and 1982–86. The main results of Faini and others (forthcoming) can be summarized as follows:

- Countries that faced the most unfavorable external environment fared worse on each of the four indicators.
- Countries that participated in World Bank–IMF programs had a loss in growth similar to that of the control group.
- Controlling for autonomous policy changes and for the external environment, countries that participated in World Bank–IMF programs had investment rates similar to those of the control group.
- The current account of countries that participated in World Bank–IMF programs improved more than the current account of the control group (a result similar to one in Khan 1990).

Thus when one controls for the external environment and for autonomous policies that would have been pursued in the absence of adjustment programs, one finds that growth performance was not statistically different for countries that participated in World Bank–IMF adjustment programs. Since the comparisons are for 1982–86 as opposed to 1978–81, program effects are measured for a period of up to five years. This result contrasts with the negative effect of IMF adjustment programs found by Khan (1990), who used a similar methodology but allowed for program effects to last only two years. Since structural adjustment is a long-run proposition and adjustment lending is a short-run tool, it should come as no surprise that when relevant factors are taken into account, growth is not higher in countries with adjustment loans.

Performance of Adjustment Loan Recipients

The remainder of the chapter examines the interactions between World Bank and IMF adjustment programs. The analysis therefore deals only with the group of thirty countries that received World Bank structural or sectoral adjustment loans before 1985. For this group of thirty countries, enough time has elapsed for a preliminary before-and-after analysis. The focus here is on how the thirty recipients of adjustment loans compare with nonrecipient countries. Nonrecipient countries are now defined as countries that did not receive an adjustment loan from the World Bank before 1985. We use the same low-income and middle-income classifications as before, but we do not control for IMF participation or for lending intensity. We use the same set of indicators as before and the same averaging method, but the average values for each performance indicator are now taken over the three years preceding and the three years following receipt of the first World Bank adjustment loan. As in Balassa (1988), the year of receipt of the first loan is excluded from the comparisons.

Although we are not controlling for IMF participation, we do note that the thirty countries that received World Bank adjustment loans before 1985 account for about 84 percent of IMF adjustment loan commitments and 59 percent of net IMF credit disbursements through 1986. The comparisons presented here should therefore be viewed as complementary to, and a check for, the comparisons reported previously for combined World Bank–IMF adjustment lending.

Table 11-4 gives the average value of the performance indicators for the group of thirty recipient countries and the comparator group of sixty-three nonrecipient countries. Both groups are further divided into the low-income and middle-income classifications used earlier. Comparing the average values for the indicators for the recipient and nonrecipient groups generally reveals poorer performance for loan recipients in the years preceding adjustment lending. With the exception of exports, the growth indicators, on average, show no improvement. As before, there is a marked decline in investment as a share of GDP. The indicators of external balance show an improvement, however, which reflects the fact

Table 11-4. *Average Values of Performance Indicators for Recipient and Nonrecipient Countries*

	Low-income[a]				Middle-income[b]			
	Three years before		Three years after		Three years before		Three years after	
Indicator	Loan recipients	Non-recipients	Loan recipients	Non-recipients	Loan recipients	Non-recipients	Loan recipients	Non-recipients
GDP growth	0.030	0.032	0.023	0.029	0.023	0.046	0.022	0.024
Investment/GDP	0.19	0.21	0.18	0.19	0.25	0.28	0.19	0.25
Export growth	−0.02	0.06	−0.00	0.01	0.03	0.05	0.06	0.03
Real exchange rate	1.06	1.00	1.94	1.04	1.02	1.00	1.09	1.01
Current account surplus/GDP	−0.09	−0.08	−0.07	−0.07	−0.07	−0.05	−0.05	−0.05
Budget surplus/GDP	−0.08	−0.04	−0.08	−0.04	−0.06	−0.06	−0.06	−0.06
Inflation	0.26	0.14	0.33	0.13	0.26	0.20	0.38	0.32
External debt/exports	3.96	2.03	4.45	3.03	1.35	1.06	2.10	1.68
Debt service/exports	0.21	0.10	0.23	0.16	0.28	0.17	0.31	0.22

Note: The year of receipt of the first loan is excluded from the calculations, which are for three-year periods preceding and following the year of receipt of the first loan.

a. Twelve recipients of adjustment loans and twenty-four nonrecipients.

b. Eighteen recipients of adjustment loans and thirty-nine nonrecipients.

Source: World Bank data.

that loan recipient countries generated the necessary noninterest current account surplus to service the larger interest payments on their external debt.

As has been analyzed elsewhere (for example, Cohen 1988 and Rodrik 1988), the burden of external debt servicing has been accompanied by a deterioration (inflation) or stagnation (budget deficit) in the indicators of internal balance. And for both low-income and middle-income adjustment loan recipients, external debt indicators deteriorated. The combination of stagnating or deteriorating indicators for internal balance and external debt raises questions about the long-run sustainability of the achievements of adjustment programs to date.

Table 11-5 reports values of performance indicators for adjustment loan recipients in the same format as table 11-3. A comparison of the two tables shows similar results for middle-income countries. For low-income countries, however, four of the nine indicators have different signs in the two tables. As in table 11-3, tests of the changes in means for a country's own performance show that the changes are insignificant for low-income recipients. When the same comparisons are made for countries that received three or more adjustment loans, the share of indicators showing improvement rises from 53 percent to 62 percent for the low-income group and from 55 percent to 67 percent for the middle-income group.

Tradeoffs between Growth and External Adjustment

For most countries, foreign borrowing was closed off after 1981, which implied that the gap between absorption and income had to be reduced. Corden (1989) refers to the resulting reduction in absorption as the primary (or inevitable) cost of reducing a current account deficit. The goal of adjustment lending in the medium term was to raise capacity utilization and to shift resources into the production of tradables at levels higher than would have been attainable in the absence of adjustment lending. This goal was to be achieved, in particular, through institutional reforms and reforms of incentive structures, which would reduce the extent of relative price rigidities. Since relative price rigidities cause a secondary cost of adjustment, one can say that adjustment lending was intended to reduce the secondary cost component of adjustment by increasing supply responsiveness.[8]

In this section we look for evidence of whether the adjustment loan recipients were able to achieve external adjustment at a lower cost of forgone growth than did nonrecipients; that is, whether the change in growth and the change in the current account are different for adjustment

Table 11-5. Performance Indicators for Recipients of World Bank Adjustment Loans Relative to Nonrecipients, by Income Group

Indicator	Low-income			Middle-income				
	Number	Relative to own performance[a]	Intensive recipients[b]	Number	Relative to own performance[a]	Intensive recipients[b]	Row sum	Row sum for intensive recipients
Loan recipients (AL)	12		5	18		7	30	12
Nonrecipients (NAL)	24		24	39		39	63	63
GDP growth	5 −	—	3	11 +	—	5	16	8
Investment/GDP	5 +	—	2	6 −	*	2	11	4
Export growth	8 +	—	4	9 +	—	5	17	9
Real exchange rate	9 +	—	5	11 +	—	6	20	11
Current account surplus/GDP	6 +	—	3	15 +	—	6	21	9
Budget surplus/GDP	6 +	—	3	6 +	—	4	12	7
Inflation	3 −	—	1	13 −	—	6	16	7
External debt/exports	7 +	—	4	9 −	*	3	16	7
Debt service/exports	8 +	—	3	9 +	—	5	17	8
Share showing improvement	0.53		0.62	0.55		0.67	0.54	0.65

* Denotes 10 percent (or more) significance level of a test of equality of means for the recipient and nonrecipient results.

— Denotes statistical insignificance.

Note: The numbers in the table show for each indicator how many recipient countries in each classification improved relative to nonrecipient comparators in the three-year period of the first loan compared with the three-year period before the loan. The year of receipt of the first loan is excluded from the calculations. The plus and minus signs show the direction of change in the average value of an indicator for recipients compared with its average value for the nonrecipient comparators (a plus sign indicates an improvement). Indicators and interpretation of results are the same as in table 11-3.

a. Only the test $\mu_{x,1}^{AL} \neq \mu_{x,2}^{AL}$ is reported here; the test for effectiveness cannot be performed because averaging over the control group (nonrecipient countries) is done repeatedly.

b. Refers to the twelve countries that received three or more adjustment loans (see table 11-6).

Source: World Bank data.

loan recipients. To test this hypothesis we estimated the following reduced form equation:

$$\text{(11-3)} \qquad \Delta\text{GDPK}_1 = \alpha_0 + \alpha_1 D + \alpha_2\,\Delta(\text{RESBAL/GDPK})_i + \alpha_3 D\,\Delta(\text{RESBAL/GDPK})_i + \epsilon_i$$

where Δ is the percentage change between the three-year average after receipt of the first adjustment loan and the three-year average before receipt of the loan, Δ GDPK is the change in real GDP, $i = 1, \ldots 93$ countries, $D = 1$ for the thirty adjustment loan recipients (AL) and 0 for the sixty-three nonrecipient countries (NAL), and Δ (RESBAL/GDP) is the terms-of-trade–adjusted change in the resource balance over GDP. The estimation is for the data appearing in figure 11-1. For countries that did not receive a World Bank adjustment loan, 1982 was selected as the year marking the break in three-year periods for measuring the change in GDP.

After correcting for heteroskedasticity, the results are as follows (*t* values in parentheses):

$$\text{(11-4)} \qquad \begin{aligned} \Delta\text{GDPK}_i = \; & \underset{(-2.69)}{-0.01} + \underset{(1.94)}{0.02\ D} \underset{(-3.03)}{-0.19\ \Delta\text{RESBAL}_i} \\ & \underset{(-0.31)}{-0.71\ D} \cdot \Delta\text{RESBAL}_i. \end{aligned}$$

$$F = 10.8$$

The intercept dummy is of the expected sign (an upward shift for recipient countries). The slope dummy, however, is of the wrong sign (that is, a steeper resource balance to GDP tradeoff for recipient countries) but insignificant.

Because of suspected multicollinearity between the slope and intercept dummies, we exclude the slope dummy, which results in a further improvement:

$$\text{(11-5)} \qquad \Delta\text{GDPK}_i = \underset{(-2.71)}{-0.01} + \underset{(2.13)}{0.02\,D} - \underset{(-3.50)}{0.20\,\Delta\text{RESBAL}_i}.$$

$$F = 14.5$$

The regression results do not directly support the hypothesis that adjustment lending helped reduce the secondary burdens of adjustment since the tradeoff between growth and improvement in the external balance is the same for both groups of countries. However, the greater improvement in the trade balance among recipients of World Bank adjustment loans is consistent with the results in table 11-4, which shows these countries had a higher initial debt burden and consequently a need for greater improvement in their current account. And the higher growth among

Figure 11-1. Tradeoff between GDP and Resource Balance for Recipient and Nonrecipient Countries

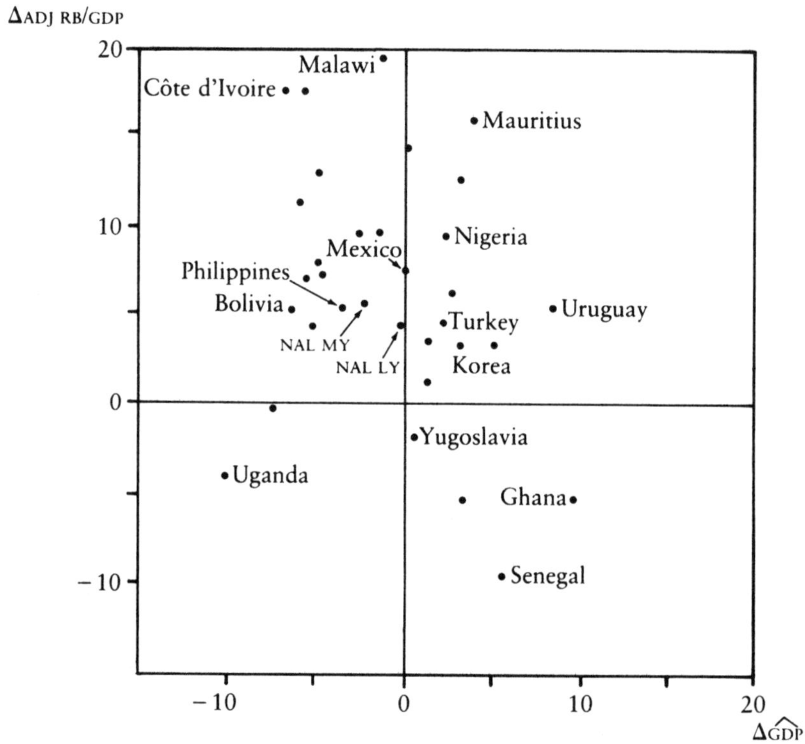

$\Delta\widehat{GDP}$ = Percentage point improvement in the GDP growth rate three years after the loan compared with three years before.

ΔADJ RB/GDP = Percentage point improvement in terms-of-trade–adjusted resource balance as a fraction of GDP three years after the loan compared with three years before.

NAL LY = Average for low-income countries that did not receive adjustment loans.

NAL MY = Average for middle-income countries that did not receive adjustment loans.

Source: World Bank data.

loan recipients is consistent with an increased availability of foreign funds, which reduces the foreign exchange constraint.

Conclusions

In this chapter we used a simple control-group approach to assess quantitatively the economic performance of countries that received adjustment lending from the World Bank and the IMF. The statistical evaluation addressed three questions: (1) Was there complementarity between World Bank–IMF lending and private lending? (2) Did recipients of adjustment loans improve their performance relative to their own past performance? (3) Did recipients improve their performance relative to a control group of nonrecipients?

With respect to the first question, there was a negative correlation between the intensity of World Bank–IMF lending and private lending during 1982–86. World Bank–IMF lending thus appears to have been a substitute for rather than a complement to private lending.

With respect to their own past performance, countries with adjustment loans improved their external position, a reflection of the fact that they generated a sufficient surplus in their trade balance to service their external debt. Fiscal (and inflation) indicators deteriorated, however, indicating that macroeconomic imbalances remained and casting some doubt on the sustainability of adjustment. Growth rates also fell, a reflection of deteriorating terms of trade and the difficulties in achieving the required reduction in absorption.

With respect to performance relative to comparators, nonparametric statistics for the selected group of nine economic indicators show that, overall, adjustment loan recipients improved relative to nonrecipients. However, the percentage of indicators showing an improvement (the average of the number of countries showing improvement in all indicators) varied between 53 and 63 percent depending on classification. For the group of twelve countries that received three or more adjustment loans, the share of indicators showing an improvement varies between 62 percent for the low-income group and 67 percent for the middle-income group. Statistical tests of difference of means for individual indicators suggest that these improvements were often statistically insignificant. In sum, the evidence suggests that some mild relative improvement occurred.

Appendix: Data Sources and Country Classification

All data were extracted from the World Bank's economic and social data base (BESD) and Andrex data base. Data in constant dollars were obtained by using the exchange rate conversion factor from the World Bank's

Table 11-6. Classification of the Ninety-Three Sample Countries

Credit intensity	*Country*	*Credit intensity*	*Country*
L	Algeria	H	Madagascar
H	Argentina	H	Malawi (1981, 4)
	Bangladesh	L	Malaysia
	Barbados	H	Mali
L	Benin	L	Malta
	Bolivia (1980, 2)	H	Mauritania
L	Botswana	H	Mauritius (1981, 2)
	Brazil (1983, 3)		Mexico (1983, 2)
	Burkina Faso	H	Morocco (1984, 4)
	Burundi	L	Myanmar
L	Cameroon	L	Nepal
H	Central African Republic	L	Nicaragua
L	Chad	H	Niger
H	Chile		Nigeria (1983, 2)
L	China		Pakistan (1980, 4)
	Colombia	H	Panama (1983, 2)
	Congo	L	Papua New Guinea
H	Costa Rica (1983, 2)	L	Paraguay
H	Côte d'Ivoire (1981, 3)		Peru
L	Cyprus		Philippines (1980, 3)
H	Dominican Republic		Portugal
H	Ecuador	L	Rwanda
L	Egypt	H	Senegal (1980, 2)
L	El Salvador	L	Seychelles
L	Ethiopia		Sierra Leone (1984, 1)
	Fiji	L	Singapore
	Gabon	H	Somalia
	Gambia	L	South Africa
H	Ghana (1983, 5)	L	Sri Lanka
L	Greece		Sudan (1980, 2)
L	Guatemala	L	Syria
H	Guinea		Tanzania (1981, 2)
H	Guinea-Bissau (1984, 1)		Thailand (1982, 2)
L	Guyana (1981, 1)	H	Togo (1983, 2)
	Haiti	L	Trinidad and Tobago
	Honduras	H	Tunisia
L	Hong Kong		Turkey (1980, 8)
H	Hungary	H	Uganda (1983, 1)
	India	H	Uruguay (1984, 1)
	Indonesia	L	Venezuela
L	Israel		Yemen Arab Republic
H	Jamaica (1979, 6)		Yemen, People's Dem. Rep.
	Jordan		Yugoslavia (1983, 2)
H	Kenya (1980, 3)	H	Zaire
	Korea (1981, 3)	H	Zambia (1984, 4)
L	Lesotho	H	Zimbabwe (1983, 1)
H	Liberia		

H = high-credit; L = low-credit.

Note: Numbers in parentheses are the date of the first World Bank adjustment loan and number of adjustment loans; countries with three or more loans are the intensive recipients.

annual *Atlas*. In the calculation of external shocks (equation 11-1), terms of trade indices were obtained by dividing the current values of exports and imports (expressed in dollars) by the constant values. Similar results were obtained when the terms of trade indices were calculated from current and constant local currency values from national accounts data.

To calculate the effective interest rate on external debt, we applied the London interbank offer rate (LIBOR) + 1 to the share of total nonconcessional debt and the implicit interest rate from interest payments on concessional debt. For World Bank–IMF lending, we constructed two variables, one based on gross IMF credit, another on net IMF credit (IMF purchases less IMF repurchases). In both cases, World Bank adjustment loan credits are the sum of structural and sectoral adjustment loan commitments. Results based on gross IMF credit are not reported because they are extremely close to those obtained for net credit.

Table 11-6 describes the sample of ninety-three countries and the classifications used in the text (low- and middle-income classifications are from World Bank 1989, chap. 2). For the thirty World Bank adjustment loan recipients, the year of receipt of the first loan is indicated in parentheses, followed by the total number of adjustment loans received. The subset of intensive recipients consists of twelve countries that received three or more adjustment loans.

Notes

1. The following discussion draws on Faini and others (forthcoming).
2. This is known as sample-selectivity bias. For a further discussion, see Goldstein and Montiel (1986), Khan (1990), and Faini and others (forthcoming).
3. The group of thirty adjustment loan recipients accounts for 84 percent of the commitments of adjustment lending and for 59 percent of net IMF credit disbursements through 1986.
4. The year 1982 is chosen as the breakpoint to correspond with the breakpoint selected for measuring performance.
5. The formula is derived from a two-period maximization by firms and households under assumptions of perfect competition and wage-price flexibility (see Dornbusch 1986, pp. 354–56).
6. Note that the definitions of both RIR and TOT are dependent on the signs used. Specifically, RIR is interpreted as a worsening if it is positive (higher interest rates) and an improvement if negative. Conversely, for TOT, which is defined as $X - M$, a positive number indicates improvement and a negative number a worsening. Thus in equation 11-1 improvement in the external environment is a positive number and a worsening is a negative number, whereas for convenience the opposite sign convention is used in table 11-1.
7. It should be noted, however, that the fiscal data are very weak and sparse.
8. Orthodox stabilization programs usually concentrated on expenditure-reducing policies to reduce external imbalances. By contrast, the World Bank–IMF–supported programs initiated in the early 1980s have placed greater emphasis on expenditure-switching and, particularly, on output-augmenting policies as a component of adjustment. Hence the characterization of these programs as "ad-

justment with growth." World Bank–IMF–supported adjustment programs were supposed to increase the responsiveness of demand and supply to relative price shifts so as to increase the effectiveness of expenditure-switching policies. This objective was to be achieved by greater reliance on the price mechanism and by a reduction in distortions.

References

Balassa, Bela. 1988. "Quantitative Appraisal of Adjustment Lending." PPR Working Paper 79. Policy, Planning, and Research, World Bank, Washington, D.C.

Bourguignon, François, William H. Branson, and Jaime de Melo. 1989. *Macroeconomic Adjustment and Income Distribution.* OECD Development Center Technical Paper 1. Paris: Organisation for Economic Co-operation and Development.

Cohen, Daniel. 1988. "The Management of the Developing Countries' Debt: Guidelines and Applications to Brazil." *World Bank Economic Review* 2 (1) January:77–104.

Corden, W. Max. 1989. "Macroeconomic Adjustment in Developing Countries." *World Bank Research Observer* 4 (1):51–64.

Dornbusch, Rudiger. 1986. *The Effects of OECD Macroeconomic Policies on Non-Oil Developing Countries.* World Bank Staff Working Paper 793. Washington, D.C.

Faini, Riccardo, Jaime de Melo, Abdel Senhadji-Semlali, and Julie Stanton. Forthcoming. "Growth-Oriented Adjustment Programs: A Statistical Analysis." *World Development.*

Genberg, Hans, and Alexander K. Swoboda. 1987. "The Medium-Term Relationship between Performance Indicators and Policy: A Cross Section Approach." EPD Discussion Paper EPD-01. Economic Projections Department, World Bank, Washington, D.C.

Goldstein, Morris, and Peter J. Montiel. 1986. "Evaluating Fund Stabilization Programs with Multicountry Data: Some Methodological Pitfalls." *IMF Staff Papers* 33 (2) June:314–44.

Khan, Mohsin S. 1990. "The Macroeconomic Effects of Fund-Supported Adjustment Programs: An Empirical Assessment." *IMF Staff Papers* 37 (2) June:195–231.

Khan, Mohsin S., and Malcolm Knight. 1981. "Stabilization Programs in Developing Countries: A Formal Framework." *IMF Staff Papers* 28 (1):1–53.

Rodrik, Dani. 1988. *The Welfare Economics of Debt Service.* NBER Discussion Paper 2655. Cambridge, Mass.: National Bureau for Economic Research.

World Bank. 1989. *Adjustment Lending: An Evaluation of Ten Years of Experience.* Policy and Research Series 1. Washington, D.C.

Comments

Peter J. Montiel

THERE IS A LONG TRADITION of using multicountry samples to assess the macroeconomic effects of International Monetary Fund (IMF) financial programs. The most recent survey I have seen is in a paper by Mohsin Khan (1990). This chapter by Riccardo Faini and associates is the first I have seen that attempts to apply methodologies from this literature to an analysis of the macroeconomic effects of World Bank adjustment lending, and I agree with the authors that this is a useful complement to country studies.

Since my previous work in this area concerned the methodological pitfalls of using multicountry samples to assess the macroeconomic effects of IMF-supported financial programs (Goldstein and Montiel 1986), my comments on this chapter will focus on this set of issues. I will take the specific questions addressed by the authors one at a time and provide alternative interpretations of the evidence, based largely on methodological quibbles.

Faini and his associates construct a data set consisting of eleven years (1976–86) of observations on nine macroeconomic variables for a group of ninety-three developing countries. They then divide this sample in two ways. First they rank the countries according to their use of World Bank and IMF adjustment loans (relative to GDP) during 1982–86 and classify the upper tercile into a group denoted the high-credit (HC) countries and the lower tercile into a group denoted the low-credit (LC) group. The former is the "treatment" group while the latter is the control group. A second grouping of thirty countries that entered into World Bank adjustment loan arrangements before 1985 is the treatment group, while the remaining sixty-three countries represent the control group.

The authors pose two questions as they begin their analysis: (1) Did high-credit countries face a worse external environment than low-credit countries during the 1982–86 period? (2) Were World Bank and IMF loans complementary to commercial bank loans during this period? The reason for the first question seems clear: the authors want to measure the effects of adjustment lending by comparing pre- and post-1982 macroeconomic outcomes, so they want to make sure that external factors are not responsible for any observed differences in performance between high-credit and low-credit countries. The second question relates to the authors' first exercise in measuring the effects of loans—in other words, the response of commercial lending is one of the macroeconomic outcomes they are interested in.

To answer the first question, the authors use a measure of external shocks that seems a reasonable approximation of the welfare effects on developing countries of changes in real interest rates and the terms of trade:

$$\Delta w/w = -(\overline{R}_2 - \overline{R}_1)(\overline{D/Y})_1 + (\overline{PX}_2/\overline{PX}_1 - 1)(\overline{X/Y})_1 - (\overline{PM}_2/\overline{PM}_1 - 1)(\overline{M/Y})_1 = -\text{RIR} + \text{TOT}$$

where the variables are defined in chapter 11. Does the measure $\Delta w/w$ adequately summarize changes in the external environment? I suspect not. Most economists would undoubtedly agree that the most significant shock to the external environment facing developing countries in 1982 was the debt crisis. The changed availability of external financing is not represented in this equation, which contains no mechanism to capture the effect of credit rationing. Unfortunately, this means that, contrary to the authors' conclusion, the external environment may well have been systematically different for high- and low-credit countries.

With regard to the second question, the authors find a negative (although not significant) correlation between World Bank–IMF lending and net private credit and conclude that adjustment lending from these institutions did not serve as a catalyst for private lending during the 1982–86 period. This is surprising since this period was precisely the heyday of the active involvement of the Bretton Woods institutions in securing private lending in support of adjustment programs. I think the problem could be the use of cross-section tests. For example, low-income countries tend to rely more on official financing than on private lending relative to middle-income countries, and this country-specific characteristic could account for the negative correlation observed in cross-section. Since a number of countries would tend to rely preponderantly on either official or private lending, these two variables would tend to be negatively correlated across countries. As shown in table 11-3, for example, half of the high-credit countries proved to be in the low-income group while only a third of the low-credit countries were in that group.

In the main part of the chapter the macroeconomic experience of countries that received adjustment lending is evaluated with the use of both simple before-after and control-group approaches. The main conclusion is that adjustment lending seemed to improve growth, but at the expense of lower investment and a somewhat worse fiscal situation. The interpretation offered is that growth may have improved because of the greater availability of imports and that lower investment may have been due to the weeding out of inefficient investment.

Although I am in strong agreement with the authors that the availability of imports may have been an important contribution to the positive short-run impact of adjustment lending on growth, particularly in the credit-rationed 1982–86 period, in my role as devil's advocate I would like to offer an alternative interpretation based on sample-selectivity bias. Sample-selectivity bias can occur in control-group studies such as this whenever the criterion for selection into the treatment group (high credit in this case) and control group (low credit) is nonrandom. Given nonrandom selection, sample-selectivity bias will exist if the criterion that determines selection is related to the determinants of post-treatment performance. Bias results because the differences in post-treatment performance that are due to the way the groups were chosen will tend to be wrongly attributed to the treatment itself.

Is there reason to suspect nonrandom selection of countries to the treatment and control groups in this case? A priori, I would say yes. I would expect two kinds of countries to appear in the high-credit group during the 1976–86 period. First would be low-income countries that never had much access to commercial financing and have always been heavy official borrowers. Some evidence on this was mentioned above. Second would be countries that relied quite heavily on market borrowing before 1982 but then became active IMF and World Bank borrowers because of the debt crisis.

These speculations are borne out by the numbers. Using *World Economic Outlook* (IMF 1988) classifications, I found the composition of the high-credit and low-credit groups shown in table 11C-1, which indeed seems to suggest that selection was nonrandom, as one would expect.

Next, is there reason to believe that the criterion of selection for the treatment group was related to post-1981 economic performance? Again I would have to say yes. As I mentioned earlier, the main external shock confronting these countries during the treatment period (post-1981) was the debt crisis itself. This shock had a very severe effect on the highly indebted countries but relatively little effect on small, low-income official borrowers with no access to the private international capital market. As

Table 11C-1. Composition of the High-Credit and Low-Credit Groups by Financial Criteria

Criterion	*High-credit*	*Low-credit*
Highly indebted countries	6	1
Market borrowers	2	10
Diversified borrowers	6	9
Official borrowers	17	11
Small, low-income countries	12	5

Table 11C-2. Growth and Investment of Alternative Developing Country Groups, before and after the Debt Crisis

Group and indicator	Before 1982	1982–86	Difference
All developing countries			
Growth	5.2	3.1	−2.1
Investment/GDP	26.5	23.8	−2.7
Highly indebted countries			
Growth	5.4	1.3	−4.1
Investment/GDP	24.3	18.1	−6.2
Small, low-income countries			
Growth	3.4	3.1	−0.3
Investment/GDP	20.2	17.2	−3.0

Note: All figures are unweighted arithmetic averages. The pre-1982 figures cover 1970–81 in the case of growth, and 1980–81 for investment.
Source: IMF (1988).

is well known, the highly indebted countries suffered a sharp slowdown in growth after 1981 and an even more severe collapse in investment. Growth and investment in the small low-income countries did not move nearly as much. Table 11C-2 provides the numbers.

Rather than adjustment lending resulting in relatively better growth despite the relatively poorer performance of investment, my alternative interpretation is the following: the criterion for selection was such that the treatment group (the high-credit countries) contained many small, low-income official borrowers for which the debt crisis resulted in relatively better growth and a smaller number of highly indebted countries for which the debt crisis meant a much worse investment performance than average. Thus *average* growth was better for the high-credit countries as a group, and a number of countries in this group showed relatively better performance on this criterion than the low-credit group. *Average* investment was relatively worse for this group, however, because of the magnitude of the investment collapses among the highly indebted countries.

References

Goldstein, Morris, and Peter J. Montiel. 1986. "Evaluating Fund Stabilization Programs with Multi-Country Data: Some Methodological Pitfalls." *IMF Staff Papers* 33 (2) June:314–44.

IMF. 1988. *World Economic Outlook.* Washington, D.C.: International Monetary Fund.

Khan, Mohsin S. 1990. "The Macroeconomic Effects of Fund-Supported Adjustment Programs: An Empirical Assessment." *IMF Staff Papers* 37 (2) June:195–231.

12 *The Social Costs of Adjustment*

Elaine Zuckerman

UNTIL RECENTLY, World Bank–supported adjustment programs have focused narrowly on economic problems, with little attention given to social consequences. They have emphasized short-term restoration of balance of payments equilibrium and financial stability (as have International Monetary Fund stabilization programs). Their objectives have also included improvements in the incentive system and restoration of medium- to long-term aggregate growth. They have fallen short of expectations in stimulating growth (World Bank 1988a), however, generally because many adjusting countries, burdened by overwhelming debt, have had to implement austerity measures that leave little room for growth (Fischer 1986).[1]

By the mid-1980s it was recognized that adjustment experiences, combined with the legacy of inappropriate past policies, were negatively affecting human welfare.[2] UNICEF's seminal book *Adjustment with a Human Face* (Cornia, Jolly, and Stewart 1987) raised the development community's consciousness about the need to cushion the poor from the fiscal cutbacks under adjustment.[3] The data needed to demonstrate that social welfare is deteriorating are scarce, but it has become evident that many countries with adjustment programs have reduced public expenditure on social services, cut back staffing in the public sector, and experienced higher unemployment. Real wages have eroded dramatically in many adjusting countries, and social welfare has suffered.[4] Today, adjustment programs are gradually being broadened to emphasize concerns with growth and equity. But more needs to be done.

Poverty Groups at Risk

Since 1987, World Bank staff guidelines concerning adjustment lending and social welfare have required that policy framework papers for low-income countries include "a brief description and assessment . . . of the social impact of the government's intended adjustment program" and that the president's report on structural adjustment loans and credits (SALs) analyze the "short-term impact of the adjustment programs on the urban and rural poor, and measures proposed to alleviate negative effects." An increasing number of these reports now estimate the expected impact on the "new poor"—those impoverished by adjustment programs in the short term, such as retrenched public sector employees. Many SALs require compensation for the new poor, such as severance payments or retraining, as a condition of loan disbursement. A few recent SAL reports have gone even further, analyzing the social impact on both the new and the old poor and requiring measures to counter the negative effects of adjustment operations on both groups (for example, in Chile).[5] With lenders' assistance, some countries (for example, Bolivia and Ghana) have initiated programs to alleviate adverse impacts on the poor during the adjustment process through complementary compensatory operations. Although not all adjustment programs incorporate measures to protect the poor or undertake systematic analysis of the likely impact, there is an accelerating trend in this direction.

Recent World Bank symposiums on poverty and adjustment and adjustment lending have shown that confusion and controversy surround the question of which category of the "poor" should be considered during adjustment.[6] Three broad groups are candidates. (Note that females tend to be overrepresented in all of these groups.[7])

First are the new poor—the direct victims of adjustment, such as retrenched civil servants and public and private enterprise employees who were laid off because of austerity measures or shifts in production. They include former middle-class professionals who were better off before the adjustment and who, although they have become poorer, are not necessarily poor (although some of them may be).

Second are the borderline poor—low-income, vulnerable groups that are most affected by changes in the availability and price of major items of consumption, especially food, and by cutbacks in social programs. Recessions and adjustment hit these groups severely. The borderline poor tend to include some of the elderly, infants, landless and poor farmers, and lactating and pregnant women.

Third are the extreme or structural poor.[8] Some members of this group are directly affected by adjustment, such as those in cities who are subject to increased food prices, while others, usually those in rural areas, are little affected because they live outside the influence of production forces and public services. This is particularly the case in Africa and parts of Asia, where 80 to 90 percent of the poor live in rural areas, producing much of what they consume, and seldom benefiting from government services. This is less true of Latin America, where large portions of the poor are urban dwellers who receive some subsidies and services.

In general, the poorest 10 to 20 percent of a population often reside in rural areas and suffer from malnutrition, illiteracy, disease, short life expectancy, and high infant mortality rates (Lipton 1988). Traditional investment projects have seldom reached them, either because they are too weak and poor to contribute the required energy and assets or because projects were not directed to them. Since most of the extreme poor in developing countries are potentially productive, singling them out for special assistance during adjustment programs, by increasing their access to employment and assets, could contribute to economic growth.[9]

Following much debate at a 1988 symposium on poverty and adjustment, developing country administrators reached a strong consensus that measures to help the poor under adjustment should cover all the poor, not just the new or borderline poor (World Bank 1988c). Some development agency officials felt, however, that the complexity of adjustment programs precludes attention to issues such as long-term structural poverty.

Data Approaches and Methodologies for Measuring Social Welfare

Little hard data exist yet to demonstrate that adjustment adversely affects the poor or other socioeconomic groups. Still, an emerging literature, pioneered by Cornia, Jolly, and Stewart (1987), compassionately argues that the poor are worse off because of adjustment. For several reasons, the arguments so far are based largely on anecdotal evidence. First, many adjustment programs are still in the early stages and their medium- and long-term effects cannot yet be determined. Second, in trying to account for the primary causes of deteriorating social welfare, it is difficult to separate the influence of adjustment measures from the negative legacy of inappropriate past policies. Third, accurate longitudinal data on welfare distribution are woefully inadequate.

What data can be used to assess the impact of adjustment on social welfare? A variety of biological and socioeconomic measures are employed, but they must be viewed cautiously. Most lack a sufficient level of disaggregation, and differences among and within income groups are obscured by the presentation of only national per capita averages. Methods of data collection may be suspect, and even relatively reliable country data may not be comparable across countries. All these caveats should be kept in mind during the following description of popular data approaches.

Basic Indicators

Time-series data covering nutrition, infant and child mortality rates, life expectancy, disease, anthropometry, school enrollment, and poverty cutoff lines are popularly used to measure poverty. The accompanying tables present cross-country data for per capita caloric intake as a percentage of daily requirement (1970–85) and infant mortality rates and life expectancy data (1970–87) for the twenty-three countries reviewed for an earlier report on adjustment lending (World Bank 1988a).

Data on per capita caloric intake as a percentage of daily requirement (table 12-1) are available only through 1985, but interesting trends are observable. (Annual fluctuations of a few percentage points are normal in all countries.) Overall, standards for caloric intake were maintained or increased everywhere over the entire period except in five of the twenty-three sample countries, where significant drops occurred (Ghana, Guinea, Peru, Zaire, and Zambia; Zambia began and ended the period at 92 percent of the required caloric intake, but it had improved to 102 percent in 1977 before dropping back to 92 percent). These countries either postponed adjustment indefinitely (Peru), began undertaking it only after protracted delays (Ghana and Guinea), or failed to sustain it (Zaire and Zambia). In addition, Kenya's per capita caloric intake dipped slightly from 97 percent to 95 percent of daily requirement, dropping further below a nutritionally acceptable level. Except for these countries plus Bolivia, Guinea-Bissau, and Pakistan, all the other adjustment countries studied achieved nutritionally adequate levels of per capita caloric intake. The latter three countries improved their intake over the period but still remained below the accepted standard. Sub-Saharan Africa as a whole fared worse than other regions. Thus per capita caloric intake appears to reflect both the state of the economy and the government's degree of commitment to sustained macroeconomic adjustment.

All countries made steady overall progress in reducing infant mortality rates and increasing life expectancy (tables 12-2 and 12-3). Although progress has been gradual for some and more dramatic for others, recessions and adjustment did not impede it. These gains are attributable largely to medical advances. The level of achievement differs vastly from country to country, however. Of the twenty-three countries surveyed, Costa Rica and Jamaica scored best, both with an infant mortality rate of 18 per thousand in 1987 (down from 60 and 40, respectively, in 1970) and a life expectancy of 74 years (up from 67 years in both countries in 1970). Malawi had the worst infant mortality rate (150, down from 193), despite steady progress, and Guinea and Guinea-Bissau had the lowest life expectancy at 43 and 40 years, respectively (up from 36 years for both). No correlation exists between achievements on these two indicators and per capita caloric intake as a percentage of daily requirement. Malawi, for example, made excellent progress in increasing caloric consumption, reaching 104 percent of intake in 1987. Regionally, Sub-Saharan Africa again lags seriously behind in both these indicators.

To conclude, per capita caloric intake declined during adjustment, but the other two most popular basic health indicators, infant mortality rate and life expectancy, improved notably despite recession and adjustment. This is because nutritional status is more sensitive to economic changes

Table 12-1. Per Capita Caloric Intake as a Percentage of Daily Requirement in Twenty-Three Developing Countries, 1970–85

Country	*1970*	*1971*	*1972*	*1973*	*1974*	*1975*	*1976*	*1977*	*1978*	*1979*	*1980*	*1981*	*1982*	*1983*	*1984*	*1985*
Bolivia	83.2	82.9	83.6	81.5	83.2	84.4	85.4	85.4	85.5	86.4	87.1	88.2	90.2	84.7	89.8	90.8
Brazil	102.8	104.0	103.0	102.9	104.3	104.2	105.0	105.3	105.9	109.5	110.3	109.5	110.5	109.6	110.2	111.2
Chile	109.5	109.9	112.4	106.1	109.1	103.7	104.7	103.6	105.5	107.6	107.8	109.4	107.9	107.4	106.6	104.3
Colombia	92.4	95.6	96.1	97.8	98.2	100.2	105.0	106.0	105.9	105.2	108.5	110.3	109.7	110.9	110.9	111.6
Costa Rica	107.2	109.9	110.6	111.6	111.8	115.0	116.3	116.3	115.8	116.8	117.0	117.2	118.5	120.8	125.1	125.3
Côte d'Ivoire	103.4	102.6	101.5	99.7	100.4	99.6	100.0	101.1	105.2	108.1	113.1	112.4	112.6	109.5	108.4	99.9
Ghana	96.4	96.5	94.8	95.6	95.6	94.0	92.9	85.5	84.2	80.4	78.1	74.3	69.7	65.4	76.0	77.6
Guinea	84.8	80.4	79.4	83.3	85.1	83.9	82.1	82.5	83.7	78.4	76.9	74.3	75.7	74.2	74.8	74.9
Guinea-Bissau	83.7	82.2	79.7	79.5	76.8	78.2	77.9	76.4	78.1	78.2	80.0	86.3	85.5	83.1	84.2	89.7
Jamaica	113.4	117.7	119.6	115.2	116.4	119.6	120.3	118.9	119.4	115.0	115.4	114.1	112.7	114.6	115.4	115.1
Kenya	96.9	95.7	98.5	97.3	97.2	96.2	97.5	97.5	97.1	95.1	94.7	93.7	94.3	91.4	92.7	95.4
Korea	108.5	109.4	112.9	115.1	114.9	118.7	118.3	117.7	120.4	121.4	119.6	119.4	120.6	120.0	120.9	119.4
Malawi	99.9	104.4	101.6	106.4	105.6	106.3	108.5	108.6	109.9	106.8	105.7	107.2	105.4	104.4	105.5	104.1
Mexico	116.3	115.6	117.3	119.0	119.9	122.7	121.3	123.2	126.0	128.2	131.2	133.7	134.6	134.7	136.4	134.2
Morocco	100.2	101.7	105.0	105.3	105.3	105.9	107.8	112.4	112.7	113.6	112.9	111.7	113.3	109.7	110.7	112.8
Pakistan	87.8	88.6	88.4	87.4	89.7	90.3	94.2	92.9	92.4	95.8	94.8	97.8	98.2	96.0	93.5	94.4
Peru	97.8	98.7	96.2	95.3	97.4	96.7	96.0	94.0	93.1	93.2	92.1	92.9	94.3	91.1	92.4	90.2
Philippines	91.5	90.8	89.3	90.7	94.4	92.8	96.3	99.0	100.8	104.6	104.3	103.7	103.1	103.4	103.6	100.0
Senegal	98.9	97.4	95.9	94.0	95.3	95.1	95.5	98.5	95.8	100.1	100.6	100.5	99.1	94.9	98.4	101.6
Thailand	101.8	101.8	101.9	105.1	106.8	107.0	107.5	106.9	108.0	108.5	107.0	109.5	108.6	110.8	110.9	108.1
Turkey	111.9	113.7	115.0	114.7	115.0	117.6	118.8	119.2	121.6	122.7	123.1	123.7	124.9	125.2	125.7	127.7
Zaire	102.8	101.7	102.3	103.7	103.4	103.1	103.1	101.0	96.2	95.3	95.7	96.5	97.5	97.1	97.0	96.9
Zambia	92.2	97.1	98.3	95.3	98.7	101.0	101.6	101.8	96.1	96.6	96.4	93.2	91.4	91.1	92.5	92.0

Source: World Bank data.

Table 12-2. Infant Mortality Rates in Twenty-Two Developing Countries, 1970–87
(deaths per thousand live births)

Country	*1970*	*1971*	*1972*	*1973*	*1974*	*1975*	*1976*	*1977*	*1978*	*1979*	*1980*	*1981*	*1982*	*1983*	*1984*	*1985*[a]	*1986*[b]	*1987*
Bolivia	153.4	152.2	151.0	148.4	145.8	143.2	140.6	138.0	135.2	132.4	129.6	126.8	124.0	121.2	118.4	115.6	112.8	110.0
Brazil	94.6	92.8	91.0	88.6	86.2	83.8	81.4	79.0	77.4	75.8	74.2	72.6	71.0	69.4	67.8	66.2	64.6	63.0
Chile	82.2	73.9	76.5	65.8	65.2	57.5	56.6	50.1	40.0	37.8	33.0	26.9	23.5	21.6	19.6	19.5	19.8	20.0
Colombia	79.0	77.0	75.0	72.0	69.0	66.0	64.5	63.0	61.3	59.7	58.0	55.5	53.0	51.6	50.2	48.8	47.4	46.0
Costa Rica	61.5	56.6	54.4	44.8	37.5	37.8	33.1	27.9	23.8	23.2	20.1	17.9	19.3	18.6	18.9	18.6	18.3	18.0
Côte d'Ivoire	134.6	131.8	129.0	126.4	123.8	121.2	118.6	116.0	113.8	111.6	109.4	107.2	105.0	102.8	100.6	98.4	96.2	94.0
Ghana	110.0	108.5	107.0	106.0	105.0	104.0	103.0	102.0	101.2	100.4	99.6	98.8	98.0	95.8	93.6	91.4	89.2	87.0
Guinea	185.4	183.2	181.0	179.0	177.0	175.0	173.0	171.0	168.6	166.2	163.8	161.4	159.0	156.2	153.4	150.6	147.8	145.0
Jamaica	39.6	37.8	36.0	33.8	31.6	29.4	27.2	25.0	24.2	23.4	22.6	21.8	21.0	20.4	19.8	19.2	18.6	18.0
Kenya	102.0	100.0	98.0	96.0	94.0	92.0	90.0	88.0	86.4	84.8	83.2	81.6	80.0	78.4	76.8	75.2	73.6	72.0
Korea	51.4	49.2	47.0	44.6	42.2	39.8	37.4	35.0	34.0	33.0	32.0	31.0	30.0	n.a.	n.a.	27.0	25.0	n.a.
Malawi	193.4	192.2	191.0	188.2	185.4	182.6	179.8	177.0	174.2	171.4	168.6	165.8	163.0	160.4	157.8	155.2	152.6	150.0
Mexico	73.0	71.0	69.0	67.2	65.4	63.6	61.8	60.0	58.6	57.2	55.8	54.4	53.0	51.8	50.6	49.4	48.2	47.0
Morocco	128.4	125.2	122.0	119.6	117.2	114.8	112.4	110.0	107.4	104.8	102.2	99.6	97.0	n.a.	n.a.	90.0	85.0	n.a.
Pakistan	142.4	141.2	140.0	138.2	136.5	134.7	133.0	131.2	129.0	126.7	124.5	122.3	120.1	117.8	115.6	115.0	111.0	n.a.
Peru	116.4	113.2	110.0	109.0	108.0	107.0	106.0	105.0	103.8	102.6	101.4	100.2	99.0	96.8	94.6	92.4	90.2	88.0
Philippines	66.4	65.2	64.0	62.0	60.0	54.0	56.0	54.0	53.4	52.8	52.2	51.6	51.0	n.a.	n.a.	48.0	46.0	n.a.
Senegal	164.4	163.2	162.0	160.4	158.8	157.2	155.6	154.0	151.6	149.2	146.8	144.4	142.0	139.0	136.0	133.0	130.0	127.0
Thailand	88.0[c]	n.a.	n.a.	n.a.	n.a.	n.a.	n.a.	n.a.	n.a.	n.a.	n.a.	n.a.	n.a.	n.a.	n.a.	43.0	41.0	n.a.
Turkey	133.6	133.8	134.0	n.a.	n.a.	n.a.	n.a.	n.a.	n.a.	n.a.	n.a.	n.a.	n.a.	n.a.	n.a.	84.0	79.0	n.a.
Zaire	131.0	129.0	127.0	125.0	123.0	121.0	119.0	117.0	115.0	113.0	111.0	109.0	107.0	105.2	103.4	101.6	99.8	98.0
Zambia	106.0	103.0	100.0	98.8	97.6	96.4	95.2	94.0	92.8	91.6	90.4	89.2	88.0	86.4	84.8	83.2	81.6	80.0

n.a. Not available.
a. Data for Korea, Morocco, Philippines, Thailand, and Turkey from World Bank (1987).
b. Data for Korea, Morocco, Pakistan, Philippines, Thailand, and Turkey from World Bank (1988d).
c. Data are for 1964 (World Bank 1987).
Source: World Bank data.

Table 12-3. Life Expectancy in Twenty-Three Developing Countries, 1970–87
(years)

Country	*1970*	*1971*	*1972*	*1973*	*1974*	*1975*	*1976*	*1977*	*1978*	*1979*	*1980*	*1981*	*1982*	*1983*	*1984*	*1985*	*1986*	*1987*
Bolivia	46.1	46.4	46.7	47.1	47.5	47.9	48.3	48.6	49.1	49.5	49.9	50.3	50.7	51.4	52.1	52.7	53.4	54.0
Brazil	59.0	59.4	59.8	60.2	60.6	61.0	61.4	61.8	62.1	62.5	62.8	63.1	63.4	63.8	64.1	64.5	64.9	65.3
Chile	62.4	63.0	63.6	64.3	65.0	65.7	66.4	67.2	67.9	68.7	69.5	70.2	71.0	71.1	71.2	71.3	71.5	71.6
Colombia	59.1	59.4	59.8	60.2	60.6	61.0	61.4	61.8	62.2	62.6	63.1	63.5	64.0	64.3	64.7	65.0	65.4	65.7
Costa Rica	67.1	67.6	68.1	68.4	68.7	69.0	69.4	69.7	70.4	71.0	71.7	72.4	73.0	73.2	73.3	73.4	73.5	73.7
Côte d'Ivoire	44.5	45.0	45.5	46.0	46.5	47.0	47.5	48.0	48.5	49.0	49.5	50.0	50.5	50.9	51.4	51.8	52.3	52.7
Chana	49.4	49.7	50.0	50.2	50.4	50.6	50.8	51.0	51.2	51.4	51.6	51.8	52.0	52.5	52.9	53.4	53.9	54.3
Guinea	36.2	36.5	36.9	37.2	37.6	37.9	38.2	38.6	38.9	39.2	39.6	39.9	40.2	40.7	41.2	41.7	42.3	42.8
Guinea-Bissau	35.5	35.5	35.6	35.7	35.8	35.8	35.9	36.0	36.3	36.7	37.0	37.3	37.7	38.0	38.4	38.7	39.0	39.4
Jamaica	67.2	67.5	67.8	68.0	68.3	68.5	68.7	69.0	69.7	70.5	71.3	72.1	72.9	73.1	73.2	73.3	73.4	73.6
Kenya	50.0	50.5	51.0	51.5	52.0	52.5	53.0	53.5	53.9	54.4	54.9	55.4	55.9	56.3	56.7	57.1	57.5	57.9
Korea	59.9	60.7	61.4	62.3	63.1	63.9	64.7	65.5	66.0	66.4	66.8	67.3	67.7	68.1	68.4	68.8	69.1	69.5
Malawi	40.4	40.7	41.0	41.3	41.6	41.9	42.1	42.4	42.8	43.1	43.4	43.7	44.1	44.4	44.8	45.1	45.4	45.8
Mexico	61.7	62.2	62.6	63.2	63.7	64.3	64.8	65.4	65.8	66.2	66.6	67.0	67.4	67.6	67.9	68.1	68.4	68.6
Morocco	51.9	52.4	52.9	53.5	54.1	54.6	55.2	55.8	56.2	56.7	57.2	57.7	58.2	58.6	59.0	59.5	59.9	60.4
Pakistan	46.1	46.3	46.5	46.8	47.1	47.4	47.7	48.0	48.4	48.8	49.2	49.6	50.0	50.4	50.8	51.2	51.5	51.9
Peru	53.9	54.7	55.6	55.8	56.1	56.4	56.7	57.0	57.3	57.6	57.9	58.3	58.6	59.1	59.5	60.0	60.4	60.9
Philippines	57.2	57.5	57.9	58.3	58.7	59.1	59.5	59.9	60.2	60.6	61.0	61.4	61.8	62.2	62.6	63.1	63.5	63.9
Senegal	42.6	42.9	43.2	43.5	43.9	44.2	44.6	44.9	45.0	45.1	45.2	45.2	45.3	45.8	46.2	46.7	47.1	47.6
Thailand	58.4	59.0	59.6	59.9	60.2	60.6	60.9	61.2	61.5	61.9	62.2	62.5	62.9	63.2	63.5	63.8	64.1	64.4
Turkey	56.2	56.8	57.5	58.1	58.7	59.3	59.9	60.5	61.0	61.5	62.0	62.5	63.0	63.4	63.8	64.2	64.6	64.9
Zaire	45.2	45.6	46.0	46.4	46.8	47.2	47.6	48.0	48.4	48.8	49.2	49.6	50.0	50.5	51.0	51.5	52.0	52.6
Zambia	46.5	46.9	47.3	47.7	48.1	48.5	48.9	49.3	49.6	49.8	50.1	50.3	50.6	51.1	51.6	52.1	52.6	53.1

Source: World Bank data.

than are infant mortality and life expectancy and is therefore the most important indicator of social welfare (Carlson 1988).[10] Nevertheless, as national averages these basic indicators mask inequalities among and within income groups just as do per capita GDP data.

Public Sector Expenditures

Some commentators believe that a country's commitment to improving basic needs is demonstrated by its expenditures on health, education, housing, water supply, and other amenities. These expenditures are frequently regressive, however (that is, they are spent on sophisticated urban hospitals, higher education, and other services largely for higher-income groups), and therefore they need to be disaggregated by beneficiary group before their impact on the poor can be evaluated. Of the World Bank reviews of public expenditure and investment, which often precede or accompany adjustment operations, only a handful have examined the effects on income distribution, although most have examined social sector expenditures.[11]

In 1988 equity issues were more systematically addressed in reviews of public social expenditures in Argentina, Brazil, Jamaica, and the Philippines. They confirm that (except in Jamaica, which has relatively equitable spending) expenditures are grossly mistargeted to higher-income and urban groups and that social sector bureaucracies have excessively high administrative costs. Public social expenditures in these countries in 1985–87 ranged from 18 percent of GNP in Brazil to 13 percent in Jamaica to only 3.6 percent in Argentina and the Philippines.[12] The World Bank is preparing public social expenditure reviews for other borrowing countries as well. These reviews are a valuable source of information on income distribution and provide a rationale for countries with budgetary constraints to redirect inequitable spending toward the poor. What is more, they have demonstrated that social bureaucracies are extremely inefficient and wasteful. Each of the 1988 reviews of social expenditure will be followed up with World Bank loans for projects and policy reform to help the countries achieve greater equity and efficiency in their social expenditures.

Household Surveys

The most promising data approach relies on household surveys, which disaggregate data to the household level, thereby differentiating among income groups. It must be cautioned, however, that past household surveys have not adequately captured intrahousehold consumption patterns (Glewwe and van der Gaag 1988).[13] In many countries women and children, especially girls, are fed less nourishing food than men, girls receive less education than boys, and women have less access than men to health care and productive assets within the same household (Dwyer and Bruce 1988). Such inequitable distribution within the household is not captured by the traditional nondisaggregated household model (Gillespie 1989). Given intrahousehold inequalities, individuals rather than households should be the recipients of economic outlays (Dwyer and Bruce 1988). Some household surveys are being refined to account for gender and for other intrahousehold differences in consumption. Since it is unlikely that nutritional status within the family could be captured directly, anthropometric studies serve as a proxy.

Fairly comprehensive household surveys such as the World Bank Living Standards Measurement Study (LSMS) collect data on consumption, income, anthropometric measures, basic needs, and other aspects. They furnish basic social indicators on consumption (nonfood, food, home-produced, purchased, prices), employment (self or wage), income, assets, transport, education (enrollment, attainment), health (status, use of medical care), nutrition, water supply, fertility, migration, and so on. Much of the expenditure data are disaggregated to the individual level, as are anthropometric data.

Ideally, the longitudinal data of these surveys would be analyzed before, during, and after adjustment in order to monitor the impact on income groups. This is already being attempted for Côte d'Ivoire (Kanbur 1988a, Glewwe and de Tray 1988) and hypothetically (in that little adjustment has occurred) for Peru (Glewwe 1988b and 1988c), based on the LSMS data available for these countries (see appendixes A and B to this chapter). Data from other household surveys have also been used to estimate the impact of adjustment on poverty, including a recent study on South Asia (Srinivasan and Bardhan 1988) and one on the Philippines (Blejer and Guerrero 1988). LSMS data are becoming available for Bolivia, Ghana, Jamaica, and Mauritania. LSMS surveys are also being launched in other countries.

In a few years, the Social Dimensions of Adjustment project in Sub-Saharan Africa will start yielding LSMS-type data for some twenty-five participating countries. The project questionnaires are being designed to capture intrahousehold gender differences.

Analytical Methodologies

Mapping the impact of adjustment programs on social welfare is difficult. Some feel that reliable analytical methodologies to do so have yet to be formulated. Kanbur (1988a) has attempted to quantify the impact of adjustment on income groups with the use of a household survey. A variety of other methodologies employ household and other available data. Another approach uses economywide models such as computable general equilibrium models, which simulate the distributional impact of adjustment (de Melo and Robinson 1982; Bourguignon, Branson, and de Melo 1989; Narayana, Parikh, and Srinivasan 1987), and input-output models such as social accounting matrices (Pyatt and Round 1985), which claim not only to organize data but to analyze the distribution of social welfare as well.[14] A useful complement to economywide models is partial analysis, which can be used to evaluate specific target groups, regions, and sectors.

Although much sectoral analysis has been undertaken, evaluation of experience with targeted programs, asset distribution, rural public works, and other schemes is still needed for many countries. All of the above methodologies can be used complementarily to contribute to our understanding. Furthermore, judgments concerning the political economy are essential for all countries.

Adjustment Measures Affecting Social Welfare

Several common features of adjustment programs particularly affect the distribution of social welfare, some positively, others negatively. These features and their distributional consequences are listed below.[15]

1. *Currency devaluation and export promotion.* These measures increase the price of tradable goods relative to nontradable goods and thus generally benefit exporters, including farmers, processors, and manufacturers. As the price of nontradable goods falls in relative terms, farmers growing nonexportable crops and others engaged in nontradable activities (such as construction, utilities, services, and informal sector activities) are hurt. Consumers, including many of the poor, are hit with higher prices for food and other goods.

2. *Liberalization of prices and lifting of subsidies.* The impact of these measures on the poor is severe if the general subsidies on food, public transport, energy, water, or other goods they consume disappear. Similarly, the removal of subsidies on farmers' inputs such as fertilizer may hit the rural poor. The removal of other subsidies, such as those on gasoline or middle-class housing, will affect the nonpoor more and the poor less. If the poor do consume such "luxury" items as gasoline or electricity, however, they may spend a larger portion of their budget on them. To the extent that poor farmers are engaged in the production of tradables and not merely in subsistence agriculture, they would benefit from increased producer prices.

3. *Reduction of public sector staffing and cuts in public sector salaries.* Civil servants and public enterprise employees who find themselves out of work and income as a result of staffing cutbacks or liquidation of public enterprises tend not to be destitute, and many may well earn income from other sources. An increasing number of adjustment loans

include compensation for this group. It may take the form of full or partial salary for a fixed term (usually six months to two years), retraining programs, job creation schemes such as emergency work and food-for-work, or, occasionally, resettlement incentives to relocate in rural areas (this is being tried in Guinea-Bissau and Mauritania, for example), a difficult transition for most urbanites. Assessing the impact of adjustment on laid-off employees who find new jobs (for example, in the informal sector) requires comparing their new net income with their old. Salary cuts, although not as drastic as job loss, also lower the standard of living.

4. *Cuts in public sector social services or an increase in cost-recovery measures.* All income groups may be hit by such measures, but especially the poor beneficiaries who lack the savings to pay for their own health, education, and other services. Expenditure cuts particularly constrain operation and maintenance budgets. Since recurrent costs usually constitute the bulk of social sector spending, the poor suffer most to the extent that they cannot afford alternative services.

5. *Targeted social sector expenditures to protect and assist the poor.* Such measures are a rare feature within structural adjustment programs (a SAL to Chile for health and social security is a rare example) but several sectoral adjustment loans (SECALS) target the poor (education SECALS in Ghana and Morocco and an agricultural SECAL in Mexico are examples). In the future, there are likely to be more social sector SECALS and more investment loans associated with SALS and directed toward the poor.

Solutions to Protect the Poor

Adjustment programs can further impoverish various income groups, but there is considerable scope for policies and programs that benefit the poor without undermining adjustment. Adjustment programs should be designed to ensure that, at least in the short and medium term, the incomes and standard of living of the poor do not deteriorate further. In the long term, the poor should be brought into the growth process by redistributing assets, generating employment, and developing human resources.

It is also important to keep in mind that some adjustment measures alleviate poverty for some groups while exacerbating it for others. For example, deregulating producer prices on agricultural products benefits the farmers who market their crops, while it worsens the position of the landless and poor urban dwellers who must pay the resultant increased food prices. The interests of net sellers and net purchasers of food are diametrically opposed, and there is a tradeoff between producer poverty groups and consumer poverty groups (Besley and Kanbur 1987). More generally, adjustment policies benefit those engaged in tradable activities while those engaged in nontradable activities suffer. In the ideal long-term scenario, the dislocated would switch jobs and benefit from adjustment.

Short-Term Measures

Short-term measures, although no substitute for more important and fundamental long-term antipoverty measures, are needed to ease the hardship temporarily during adjustment. They include measures to ensure the continued output of subsistence crops (rather than the single-minded promotion of export crops) and to protect outlays to the poor in social sectors such as primary education, health care, nutrition, and slum upgrading. Adjustment programs typically raise agricultural producer prices and reduce food subsidies, thereby causing higher food prices that hurt the urban poor and rural landless. These groups can be partly protected in several ways. Producer prices for certain food crops can be increased more slowly. Carefully targeted food subsidies can be introduced or can replace existing general or mistargeted subsidies. Such solutions entail both a budgetary cost and an efficiency cost (because of the "underpricing" of the targeted subsidized commodity). The efficiency cost may be justified by the social welfare benefits, while the budgetary problem is not necessarily insuperable. There might be scope for raising taxes among the better-off as a means of paying for popular poverty programs. For example, when Tunisia attempted to reduce public expenditures on food subsidies by doubling the price of wheat products, widespread protests that began in one of the poorest regions of the country forced a change in approach. The government decided instead both to introduce the price increase gradually (partly by halving the size of subsidized bread loaves) and to recoup the budgetary outlay through additional excise taxes. Options that target food subsidies specifically to the poor are also being considered.[16] Mexico, for example, has eliminated global food subsidies in favor of targeted programs for the poor based on nutritionally superior but socially inferior foodstuffs; Morocco is attempting to do the same. Neither country could sustain the cost of global subsidies.[17]

For the new and existing poor, short-term solutions include transitory compensatory measures such as emergency public works or food-for-work programs that provide temporary employment. Severance pay for retrenched workers is becoming a common feature of adjustment programs. Targeted food programs based on food stamps or rations are also recommended to guarantee a minimal nutritional level. These compensatory programs are designed to ensure that the basic needs of the new poor are maintained.

Multisectoral, quick-disbursing compensatory programs are also becoming popular (these are discussed in detail in Zuckerman 1989). Examples are Bolivia's Emergency Social Fund, Chad's proposed Social Development Action Program, Ghana's Program of Actions to Mitigate the Social Costs of Adjustment, Guinea's Socioeconomic Development Support Project, Guinea-Bissau's proposed Social and Infrastructure Relief Project, Guyana's proposed Social Impact Amelioration Programme, Haiti's proposed Economic and Social Fund Project, and Madagascar's Economic Management and Social Action Project. These programs suggest that labor-intensive, community-executed public works projects to rehabilitate or create social infrastructure may constitute appropriate types of intervention, but they need testing over time. These compensatory programs were originally designed as temporary measures (for example, Bolivia's is a three-year program and Ghana's a two-year program) on the assumption that the beneficiaries will be absorbed into the sectors that are spurred into new growth by the reallocation of resources that accompanies adjustment. Given the protracted experience with adjustment in most cases, however, it is clear that temporary compensatory solutions are insufficient to protect and assist the vulnerable and extreme poor. Some of these programs will need to be extended or made permanent.

For the borderline poor and extreme poor, it is recognized that greater public social expenditures are required in both the short and long runs. Even when budgetary constraints require that total social expenditure be cut back, programs for the vulnerable and poor must be protected through better targeting. For example, in Korea subsidized health programs aimed at the poor were expanded during the adjustment period and other poverty programs were maintained. Unlike many other countries, Korea managed to alleviate poverty even during adjustment. In many countries, however, social expenditures are not well targeted; they reach the better-off (for example, through expenditures for higher education and curative health care) and fail to benefit the poor. This mistargeting has exacerbated already highly regressive income distribution patterns in many countries.

Even under conditions of severely constrained resources, savings could be realized that would help to free resources for use in programs to assist the poor during adjustment. Three methods are described briefly here.

First, targeting available resources to the poor provides enormous potential for improving the equity of social expenditures without the need for additional resources. Two complementary methods to accomplish this are cost recovery and the shift of some service supply functions to the private sector; both are based on the principle that those who can afford to pay should do so. If at least some of the costs of public social services that are provided to the better-off could be recovered, these resources could be used to fund social services directed specifically to the poor. Reducing and redirecting public expenditures is, of course, an administratively and politically complex effort and may need to be undertaken gradually to avoid serious social unrest. A different approach is to shift the provision of social services for the better-off from the public to the private sector, thereby enabling more public expenditures to be directed specifically to the poor. Jamaica, for example, is privatizing some hospital services while maintaining essential public health services for the needy. Another advantage to this approach, as experience has shown, is the efficiency gains that can be realized from the increased use of private services among those who can afford them.

Second, administrative reform of social services can reap important gains in efficiency. Most social sector bureaucracies in developing countries are extremely inefficient. If these operations were streamlined and improved, considerable savings could be realized and applied to programs for the poor. Social security reform is a special need of Latin American countries, where expensive, unsustainable programs drain resources.

Third, taxation reform, a typical adjustment measure, could be designed to assist the poor. Equity objectives, which should be central to taxation reforms, are usually neglected. Progressive taxation can be instituted through more effective tax collection and revision of the tax code (often done to eliminate exemptions).[18] In Haiti and the Philippines, for example, poor administrative and collection practices result in regressive taxation. Underreporting and evasion are common in numerous countries. If supported by strong political will, tax reform can play a role in redistributing income; for example, China's central government redistributes nationally collected taxes to the poorest regions (although there is inevitable leakage to the rich within those regions).

Long-Term Measures

Over the long term, the focus must be on bringing the vulnerable and extreme poor into the production system as contributors to growth. Adjustment programs must be designed from the outset to restructure policies in the productive and social sectors so that they will reach the poor. The adjustment process in most countries has proved to be longer and more arduous than anticipated, often necessitating follow-up operations to maintain the reform momentum. Thus it is not sufficient to think simply in terms of short-term transitional measures.

Experience highlights that participation by poverty groups at the local community level is a crucial ingredient for success (Lewis 1988). The human capital of the poor should continue to be nurtured through the targeted provision of education, training, clean water, health care, family planning services, and social security. Their physical capital should be developed through special credit schemes, such as the Grameen (Rural) Bank program in Bangladesh; a reduction in regulatory barriers in the informal sector, where the poor often find employment; and the redistribution of assets such as land, livestock, and tools in rural areas and of jobs in urban areas. As the poor become more self-supporting, their need for secondary income transfers is reduced (Addison and Demery 1988). Only policies that involve the poor in the process of economic growth by increasing their access to productive assets and employment will reduce poverty.

In summary, it is clear that there is technical scope for governments to promote policies and programs to protect and assist the poor without undermining adjustment. Both short- and long-term measures are necessary. Short-term compensatory schemes, which are designed as an addition to adjustment programs, alleviate hardship only temporarily. What is also needed is to design adjustment programs from the outset that aim to increase the incomes, employment, and productivity of the poor.

Institutional Constraints

Programs targeted to the poor require strong institutions and staff with strong administrative skills. In many developing countries, weak institutions are a greater constraint on such programs than is a lack of funds. Indeed, donors are eager to finance compensatory programs as a way of assisting the poor during adjustment, but weak institutions impede the implementation of programs. The delay in implementing the Ghanaian Program of Actions to Mitigate the Social Costs of Adjustment was attributable mainly to weak institutions. Bolivia's short-term Emergency Social Fund established a separate organization to circumvent the cumbersome functioning of its normal bureaucracy. This may not be a suitable option for other countries, however, particularly for those that urgently need to strengthen their institutions and make them more sustainable.

Not all countries have the technical skills for the data collection and monitoring required to identify those who qualify for targeted programs. Socioeconomic information on all the poor is especially difficult to collect and update because the poor population tends to shift. To simplify this process one can target economically distressed areas (rather than particular individuals) with social services and subsidize foods that are consumed primarily by the poor and considered to be inferior goods by the rich.[19] Targeting programs too narrowly should be avoided, however, because of higher administrative costs and greater leakages (Kanbur 1988b).

Political Sustainability

Although lending agencies and academics should continue to insist on protecting the poor during adjustment, only strong and sustained political commitment on the part of policymakers will effect lasting changes. Key measures to assist the poor during adjustment include shifting public spending on social services away from the rich and middle classes to the poor and improving the efficiency of social expenditures. These are highly controversial measures in all countries because the middle classes tend to dominate the political process while the poor have little political clout. These political facts limit the scope and speed of reform.

Political opposition or support may make or break an adjustment program. For example, during the Zambian attempt at structural adjustment the removal of general food subsidies caused hardship to many more people than expected. Not only did political support erode as the anticipated benefits of reforms failed to materialize, but also social unrest and riots undermined the program. Attempts to remove food subsidies also led to riots in Algeria, Egypt, Morocco, Sri Lanka, and Tunisia. By contrast, a fairly stable political situation coupled with positive economic growth rates in Pakistan during the 1980s permitted a more successful implementation of adjustment measures. In Chile the military junta, which has been in power longer than any regime in the country's modern history, has been able both to implement and to reverse adjustment reforms. In addition, Chile has targeted social programs since the 1920s, and this long tradition facilitated the retargeting of resources to the poor under the budgetary constraints of adjustment and made these programs politically acceptable.

Popular social programs to protect the poor during adjustment also contribute to the sustainability of adjustment programs, as Bolivia's experience with the Emergency Social Fund is proving. Many community-based and grass-roots organizations have participated in and supported the program, as well as other recent compensatory schemes. To gain popular support for adjustment programs, some countries have mounted propaganda efforts. Guinea-Bissau's president and cabinet tour the countryside to explain the rationale for reforms and short-term sacrifices, and Guyana's political leaders convene rallies and distribute literature to drum up popular support for the Economic Recovery Program.

Lending Instruments

Several types of World Bank lending instruments are available to assist the poor during adjustment. Poverty alleviation measures can be incorporated into SAL operations; for example, a SAL in Chile includes conditions for social sector reform, while many other SALs include provisions for severance pay and retraining of retrenched workers. Sectoral adjustment lending operations such as education SECALs in Ghana and Morocco and the agricultural SECAL in Mexico can also incorporate measures to alleviate poverty. Several adjustment loans for human resources or social sectors are under consideration for countries such as Brazil, Jamaica, Senegal, and Venezuela. Some of these SECALs are hybrid loans combining features of both investment and adjustment operations. Another approach is through parallel sector investment projects, such as Bolivia's Emergency Social Fund and Ghana's Program of Actions to Mitigate the Social Costs of Adjustment, which provide quick responses. Complementary technical assistance operations such as Argentina's Social Sector Management Technical Assistance Project are another way to assist the poor during adjustment.

Each country's circumstances and needs should govern the selection of the appropriate option. Some argue that SALs are inappropriate for most countries because they tend to load too many reforms onto one adjustment operation (the "Christmas tree" approach). Chile, because of its long tradition of targeted social programs, could more readily incorporate poverty alleviation measures into its adjustment program than could most developing countries. Other countries might be better assisted through pure or hybrid SECALs or investment loans that do not involve competing policy reforms in the same package, as does a SAL. Although it is doubtful that quick-disbursing SECALs can directly alleviate long-term poverty, they can be a catalyst (for example, by accelerating expenditure shifts toward the poor), and they can mitigate the social costs of adjustment. Whatever the option selected, all SAL policy reforms should be designed so as to protect the poor from bearing the costs of adjustment and to assist them in becoming productive participants in the nation's economy.

Conclusions

It has become clear that the poverty-related aspects of adjustment are not simply a short-term problem. Adjustment programs have taken longer to implement and have proved far more arduous than originally expected. Ideally, adjustment will eventually spur long-term growth and an improved standard of living for the poor.[20] In the meantime, however, adjustment programs must be designed to protect and assist the poor. Measures to mitigate the social costs of adjustment are feasible and need not dilute the main objectives of adjustment.

Short-term, targeted interventions can ensure that the social welfare of needy groups is maintained at an acceptable standard. Public expenditures on social sectors should be redirected from the better-off to the poor. Private social services and programs with greater cost recovery are options for those who can afford to pay. Social bureaucracies need to be made more efficient in order to achieve needed savings. Compensatory programs are desirable complements to adjustment programs to mitigate their social costs, but they are insufficient to ensure sustained benefits for the poor. Some adjustment measures, such as less contractionary policies and progressive taxation, can also help the poor in the short term. In the long term, however, the extremely poor must become involved in the growth process through employment generation, human resource development, and the redistribution of assets such as land. These measures would contribute to adjustment's principal objective of realizing long-term growth and obviate the need for program targeting, which should be used only in the short term. Involving the poor in the growth process will also make adjustment more sustainable.[21]

Appendix A. Côte d'Ivoire: A "Factual" Case

A prerequisite to an analysis of the impact of adjustment on the poor in any country is an understanding of its poverty groups. Kanbur (1988a) used LSMS data for Côte d'Ivoire to disaggregate households into five occupational types, for each of which he constructed a poverty profile. According to his results, growers of food crops had the highest incidence of poverty (49.5 percent of them were poor), followed by export croppers (households that devote at least half their area to major export crops; 36.4 percent), those employed in the informal sector (19.3 percent), those in the formal sector (6.1 percent), and finally those in the government sector (3 percent). Conversely, government employees had the highest per capita expenditures and food croppers the lowest.

Kanbur also established a poverty line based on per capita household income. About 30 percent of Ivoirians fell below this line, and another, "hard core" poverty line cut off the poorest 10 percent of the population. He disaggregated his poverty groups into five regions: Abidjan, other urban areas, west forest, east forest, and the savanna. He distributed the sample households by ratio of agricultural to nonagricultural income, by area cropped, and by type of crop; he crossed these with the socioeconomic groupings listed above. Kanbur classified these categories by status of the household head. The incidence of poverty in the savanna was over 60 percent, whereas in Abidjan it was only around 5 percent. Per capita income and expenditure data support this finding. As for the hard-core poor, 26 percent of those in the savanna and none in Abidjan ranked in this group. Over 80 percent of the savanna population were food croppers.

Kanbur used data from Glewwe (1988a) to examine some basic needs: education, health, and housing were disaggregated by region and socioeconomic group. He found that the poorest groups were also worse off in basic needs. For example, literacy and school attendance rates were lowest in the savanna (11 percent) and highest in Abidjan (62 percent); the percentage of sick people who consulted health personnel was significantly lower for the poor than for the nonpoor; and although most poor owned their housing, they had less access to toilets, piped water, electricity, and other amenities.

Next, Kanbur examined the three Côte d'Ivoire structural adjustment loans of 1981, 1983, and 1986 to analyze the effects on poverty of macroeconomic adjustments during the 1980s. None of these SALs explicitly considered the potential effect on income distribution in any detail. The only major reform of social policy was the elimination of the urban housing subsidies, which had gone primarily to the better-off. The following were implications of the adjustment reforms:

- Many government sector employees were retrenched and lost their income.
- Increased prices for tradables benefited export croppers and those employed in the formal private sector to process and manufacture for export.
- Food croppers and informal and government workers were adversely affected because they were involved in nontradable activities. To the extent that demand for food increased on the part of the gainers from adjustment, food croppers earned extra income; but this increase may have been offset by the reduced expenditures of losers.
- One SAL recommended raising the domestic price of rice to international levels. This would have had a positive effect on rice farmers who are poorer than average but would not have affected other poverty groups very much because little rice is consumed by the poor.

After analyzing patterns of income distribution from 1980 to 1985, Kanbur found that real per capita income fell by 2.6 percent a year. This dramatic decline understates the corresponding increases in poverty, which rose by 4.8 percent a year, and in hard-core poverty, which rose by 7.9 percent a year. He also examined shifts in sectoral output and found that tradables gained, particularly in processing, while services, construction, and utilities declined in value added. He concluded that food crop farmers, already the poorest group, were hit hardest by the relative drop in the price of domestic goods, while export crop farmers, poorer than average, did best although their incomes also declined. Among food croppers the incidence of absolute poverty increased from 42 percent to 50 percent during this period and hard-core poverty increased from 13 percent to 20 percent.

Kanbur recommended that (1) food croppers receive compensatory protection during the adjustment of prices in favor of traded goods, (2) proposals to cut producer prices for exports in order to augment government revenue be reconsidered because export croppers are still very poor, (3) housing subsidies be removed as proposed in the SALs since they do not benefit the poor, and (4) the government direct expenditures on housing, health, education, and other amenities to the poor.

Appendix B. Peru: A Counterfactual Case

In April 1988 the Ghanaian undersecretary for finance and economic planning remarked that "adjustment is necessary to mitigate the cost of not adjusting." He concluded that adjustment, with all its welfare and other costs, is inevitable sooner or later for all countries, and that if later rather than sooner, the costs will have escalated substantially.

What are the social costs for a country that delays adjusting? The case of Peru, a nonadjuster, is considered here.[22] Peru was selected, first, because it has persisted in delaying adjustment even though many countries with similar problems are undertaking adjustment programs and, second, because the Peru Living Standards Survey (part of the World Bank's Living Standards Measurement Study) has already yielded data.[23]

Peru's recent macroeconomic situation has shown worsening fiscal and external imbalances. Its macroeconomic policies have been characterized by the application of selective price controls, overvalued and multiple exchange rates, restrictions on manufactured imports, agricultural subsidies, subsidized credit, negative real interest rates, unilateral limitation of debt-service payments, fiscal stimulation of consumption, and broad-scale state economic intervention.[24]

Problematic sectoral policies in Peru are not unlike those in countries with adjustment programs; Peru, however, is doing less to push the economy back on track. Sectoral policies with social welfare consequences in Peru have included disincentives to the production of tradables, particularly the country's key exports (mining and petroleum products, which accounted for 64 percent of exports in 1984); ill-advised public investments, such as massive irrigation projects with low returns that resulted in a 16 percent decline in agricultural GDP per capita during 1970–84; underinvestment in education, an inefficient education bureaucracy, and poor educational services, which contributed to rising dropout and repeat ratios, particularly at the primary level and in rural areas; and, until recently, expenditures on public health weighted heavily toward urban, curative, hospital-based health care at the expense of primary health care (which in 1984 received only 5 percent of the recurrent budget), despite the fact that in 1982 children less than five years old accounted for 47 percent of all deaths in Peru.

To assess how the poor have fared without adjustment in Peru, Glewwe (1988b) first identified the Peruvian poor. At the time of his study they resided primarily in rural areas: although 44 percent of all Peruvians lived in rural areas, 70 percent of the poorest 30 percent of the population were found there, and 83 percent of the poorest 10 percent. Land reform in the 1970s eliminated most large-scale private agriculture but did not improve the lot of most of the rural population. Most farmers, as well as the urban poor, were worse off in the 1980s than in the 1960s (Webb forthcoming). Although this was true in most Latin American countries as a result of the depression of the early 1980s (World Bank 1986), regardless of whether adjustment was undertaken, extreme poverty and inequality were particularly widespread in Peru. Of twelve countries examined in Latin America, Asia, and Africa during the 1960s and 1970s, Glewwe found that Peru had the highest Gini coefficient (that is, the most unequal per capita income distribution). Although it is difficult to establish a correlation between poverty and the absence of adjustment in Peru, its deteriorating nutritional record may well reflect such a relationship.

Glewwe (1988c) hypothesized the effects on the poor if adjustment policies were implemented. He estimated that adjustment measures would include a currency devaluation, which would raise producer prices for exports such as coffee that is grown by poor farmers and the price of imported food such as rice; reductions in social service expenditures, which would hit the poor's education and health care; and increased charges for utilities, such as electricity and water services, public transport, and petroleum products, which would be regressive (although the poor have less access to utilities than the rich, they spend a much larger proportion of their total budget on them, as is also the case with public transport and petroleum products). Even if Peru were to undertake adjustment, many of the poor would suffer from such cutbacks in expenditure. Glewwe therefore recommended targeted programs to protect the poor.

Notes

1. It may be too early to assess the long-term impact on growth since adjustment programs are still in their early stages.
2. Recession, economic mismanagement, lack of effective social policies, and external shocks are some of the other influences that are responsible for deteriorating social welfare.
3. This new concern also extends to the IMF. A review of the implications for poverty of IMF-supported adjustment programs argues that stabilization and adjustment have important short-run distributional implications, including negative effects on certain vulnerable groups (Heller and others 1988). It recommends that compensatory measures to protect these groups become part of IMF stabilization packages.
4. The country studies prepared for the World Bank adjustment lending report show that wages dropped significantly in some countries (World Bank 1988a).
5. Chile's six-decade-long tradition of social welfare interventions has been the impetus for its antipoverty interventions during adjustment.
6. This controversy is reflected in the literature: for example, Huang and Nicholas (1987), on the one hand, favor the new poor while Cornia, Jolly, Stewart (1987), on the other, favor the old as well as the new poor.
7. Lack of data makes it difficult to illustrate the share of the adjustment burden borne by females. The same applies to other vulnerable groups within

the household, such as children and the elderly. Intrahousehold disaggregation of data is needed to enable an analysis of adjustment's impact on the social welfare of these groups. Appropriate policy responses could then be designed for individuals, not just income groups.

8. The extreme or structural poor are also known in the literature as the chronic and ultrapoor (Lipton 1988). In this chapter the term extreme poor is generally used.

9. Lipton (1988) distinguishes between the poorest 10 percent of the population in developing countries, who are a potential resource, and the same decile in developed countries—the old, ill, handicapped, and drug and alcohol addicted—who are not potentially productive.

10. Lipton (1988) uses nutritional status to define the poor. He distinguishes between the "ultrapoor"—those at significant risk of income-induced undernutrition—and the "poor"—those with sufficiently low income to be at risk of hunger but not of undernutrition.

11. Before 1988, only the 1985 review of Ecuador's public investment disaggregated social sector expenditures by income group (de Melo 1988). These reviews generally cover a multitude of sectors, such as agriculture, industry, energy, transport, telecommunications, housing, water, education, and health.

12. Including the private sector, Brazil spent 25 percent of GNP on social expenditures in 1986. Brazil still has strikingly low social welfare indicators, however.

13. Deaton (1987) attempted to use the results of the Living Standards Measurement Study in Côte d'Ivoire to isolate gender differences. He found that the allocation of adult goods is heavily biased toward adult males and that women, old men, and particularly old women appear to have much less access to goods.

14. Social accounting matrices will be one of the methodologies employed for some of the countries in the Social Dimensions of Adjustment project to track income distribution changes before, during, and after adjustment in Sub-Saharan countries.

15. This list was compiled by examining SAL documents and a systematic summary of conditionality by William Steel.

16. Tunisian food subsidies are not targeted specifically to poor groups. Although they benefit all sections of the population including the poor, it is the middle- and upper-income groups and the urban population that benefit most. There is scope for specifically targeting the Tunisian poor if political and administrative constraints can be surmounted.

17. The limited successful experiences with reducing food subsidies indicates that geographical and commodity targeting, with their inevitable leakages, work better than screening programs based on income or nutrition level. Many attempts to reduce food subsidies have resulted in riots and political instability. These aspects of targeting food subsidies are discussed in detail in Berg (1987) and Pinstrup-Andersen (1988).

18. Bela Balassa has pointed out to me that there are tradeoffs in instituting progressive taxation: it may have adverse effects on efficiency and may lead to the emigration of professional, skilled, and technical workers.

19. In some countries it may be difficult to identify inferior but nutritionally adequate food consumed by the poor and disdained by the rich. For example, this was possible in Morocco, but it might be difficult in West Africa.

20. The standard of living of the poor will improve with growth only to the extent that the benefits of growth trickle down to them. Even so, it is now recognized that growth and its trickle-down effects alone are insufficient to eliminate poverty (World Bank 1988b).

21. It has been argued that adjustment programs in several countries have not been sustained at least in part because of the social costs (World Bank 1988a).

22. A recent IMF paper (Heller and others 1988) concluded that the counterfactual case can be an elusive and possibly misleading yardstick for comparison. It prefers a before-after approach for countries that have tried adjusting.

23. Data from the Peru Living Standards Survey became available in the fall of 1986. It is uncertain when the survey will be repeated, but the intention is to do so about every three years.

24. Although these policies contribute to macroeconomic imbalances, those that assist the poor could be selectively maintained and redirected through careful targeting, such as subsidized credit, within the context of overall trimming.

References

Addison, Tony, and Lionel Demery. 1988. "The Economics of Poverty Alleviation under Adjustment." Paper prepared for the World Bank Symposium on Poverty and Adjustment. Overseas Development Institute, London.

Berg, Alan. 1987. *Malnutrition: What Can Be Done?* Baltimore, Md.: Johns Hopkins University Press.

Besley, Timothy, and S. M. Ravi Kanbur. 1987. "Food Subsidies and Poverty Alleviation." All Souls College, Oxford University, and University of Warwick, United Kingdom.

Blejer, Mario I., and Isabel Guerrero. 1988. "The Impact of Macroeconomic Policies on Income Distribution: An Empirical Study." IMF Working Paper WP/88/57. International Monetary Fund, Washington, D.C.

Bourguignon, François, William H. Branson, and Jaime de Melo. 1989. *Macroeconomic Adjustment and Income Distribution.* OECD Development Center Technical Paper 1. Paris: Organisation for Economic Co-operation and Development.

Carlson, B. A. 1988. *Monitoring Human and Social Indicators in the Adjustment Process.* New York: UNICEF.

Cornia, G. A., Richard Jolly, and Frances Stewart, eds. 1987. *Adjustment with a Human Face.* Oxford, U.K.: Clarendon Press for UNICEF.

Deaton, Angus. 1987. *The Allocation of Goods within the Household: Adults, Children, and Gender.* LSMS Working Paper 39. Washington, D.C.: World Bank.

de Melo, Jaime, and Sherman Robinson. 1982. "Trade Adjustment Policies and Income Distribution in Three Archetype Developing Economies." World Bank Reprint Series 271. Washington, D.C.: World Bank.

de Melo, Martha. 1988. "Public Investment/Expenditure Reviews: The Bank's Experience." Public Economics Division, Country Economics Department, World Bank, Washington, D.C.

Dwyer, Daisy Hilse, and Judith Bruce. 1988. *A Home Divided: Women and Income in the Third World.* Stanford, Calif.: Stanford University Press.

Fischer, Stanley. 1986. "Issues in Medium-Term Macroeconomic Adjustment." *World Bank Research Observer* 1 (2) July.

Gillespie, Nancy. 1989. "Women in Development Issues for Economic and Sector Analysis." Women in Development Division, World Bank, Washington, D.C.

Glewwe, Paul. 1988a. *The Distribution of Welfare in Côte d'Ivoire in 1985.* LSMS Working Paper 29. Washington, D.C.: World Bank.

———. 1988b. *The Distribution of Welfare in Peru in 1985–86.* LSMS Working Paper 42. Washington, D.C.: World Bank.

———. 1988c. *The Poor in Latin America during Adjustment: A Case Study of Peru.* LSMS Working Paper 56. World Bank, Washington, D.C.

Glewwe, Paul, and Dennis de Tray. 1988. *The Poor during Adjustment: A Case Study of Côte d'Ivoire.* LSMS Working Paper 47. Washington, D.C.: World Bank.

Glewwe, Paul, and Jacques van der Gaag. 1988. *Confronting Poverty in Developing Countries: Definitions, Information, and Policies.* LSMS Working Paper 48. Washington, D.C.: World Bank.

Heller, Peter S., A. Lans Bovenberg, Thanos Catsambas, Ke-Young Chu, and Parthasarathi Shome. 1988. *The Implications of Fund-Supported Adjustment Programs for Poverty: Experiences in Selected Countries.* Washington, D.C.: International Monetary Fund.

Huang, Yukon, and Peter Nicholas. 1987. *Protecting the Poor during Periods of Adjustment.* Development Committee Pamphlet 13. Washington, D.C.: World Bank.

Kanbur, S. M. Ravi. 1988a. "Poverty and the Social Dimensions of Structural Adjustment in Côte d'Ivoire." World Bank, Washington, D.C.

———. 1988b. "The Principles of Targeting." Paper prepared for the World Bank Symposium on Poverty and Adjustment. Warwick, U.K.: Development Economics Research Center, University of Warwick.

Lewis, John Prior, and Norman Thomas Uphoff, eds. 1988. *Strengthening the Poor: What Have We Learned?* New Brunswick, N.J.: Transaction Books.

Lipton, Michael. 1988. *The Poor and the Poorest: Some Interim Findings.* World Bank Discussion Paper 25. Washington, D.C.: World Bank.

Narayana, N. S. S., K. S. Parikh, and T. N. Srinivasan. 1987. "Policies and Impacts (Pandits): Analysis with a General Equilibrium Model for India." Indira Gandhi Institute of Development Research, Bombay, India.

Pinstrup-Andersen, Per. 1988. *Food Subsidies in Developing Countries: Costs, Benefits, and Policy Options.* Baltimore, Md.: Johns Hopkins University Press.

Pyatt, Graham, and Jeffery I. Round, eds. 1985. *Social Accounting Matrices: A Basis for Planning.* Washington, D.C.: World Bank.

Srinivasan, T. N., and P. K. Bardhan, eds. 1988. *Rural Poverty in South Asia.* New York: Columbia University Press.

Webb, Richard Charles. Forthcoming. "The Political Economy of Poverty, Equity and Growth: Peru 1947–85."

World Bank. 1986. *Poverty in Latin America: The Impact of Depression.* Washington, D.C.: World Bank.

———. 1987. *World Development Report 1987.* New York: Oxford University Press.

———. 1988a. *Adjustment Lending: An Evaluation of Ten Years of Experience.* Policy and Research Series 1. Washington, D.C.

———. 1988b. "Report of the Task Force on Poverty Alleviation." Report R88-183. World Bank, Washington, D.C.

———. 1988c. *Targeted Programs for the Poor during Structural Adjustment: A Summary of a Symposium on Poverty and Adjustment, April 1988.* Washington, D.C.

———. 1988d. *World Development Report 1988.* New York: Oxford University Press.

Zuckerman, Elaine. 1989. "Compensatory Programs: Redressing Social Costs of Adjustment." Country Economics Department, World Bank, Washington, D.C.

Comments

Dennis de Tray

THE WELFARE CONSEQUENCES of adjustment programs have generated considerable debate. Elaine Zuckerman adds to this discussion by setting out the issues related to poverty and adjustment and by presenting some of the findings of country studies that review adjustment programs and their distributional impacts. Since these country studies are vignettes, often of programs that are still developing, I will restrict my comments to general issues of adjustment and the poor.

Breaking down the topics discussed in chapter 12 in the following three overlapping but quite distinct sets of issues helps to focus and clarify the discussion:

- Reduction of structural poverty—especially issues related to reducing poverty over the long term
- Protection of the poor during adjustment—ensuring that those who are least able to weather the economic fluctuations that may be part of the adjustment process are somehow protected
- Sharing of the social burden—providing a "soft landing" for the nonpoor who are affected by adjustment policies.

Two other issues covered in this chapter would also benefit from greater clarity of analysis: the questions of whether changes in the welfare of the poor are the consequences of adjustment programs or the legacy of past failures to adjust, and regional differences in the nature of poverty, especially as they relate to adjustment, in Sub-Saharan Africa and Latin America.

Clarity in discussing these different aspects of poverty is especially important in a policy context. First, different policies are needed to deal with each of the three sets of issues listed above. Second, conclusions about the social costs of adjustment may be quite different, depending on how blame is distributed between initial conditions (the consequences of past policies) and the adjustment policies themselves.

Reducing structural poverty—increasing the capacity of individuals, especially the poor, to earn income—is a central mandate of the World Bank. In this sense, a concern for the poor underlies many World Bank lending operations, both policy-based loans and project loans. It is debatable, however, whether reducing structural poverty ought to figure prominently in a discussion of adjustment policies. Improving a country's ability to address structural poverty in the future through a healthier, faster growing economy may be one of the main motivations for adjustment, but reducing structural poverty is seldom in itself a driving force in getting countries to adjust in the first place.

Countries under adjustment are often short of resources and of the capacity to implement programs. Asking them to add to the already large demands on their economic systems the task of developing programs to reduce poverty permanently may be very dangerous indeed. Pressure to develop such programs may endanger the adjustment process and produce little sustained improvement in the welfare of the poor.

One useful way of deciding whether a particular poverty-reduction issue belongs in a discussion of adjustment policies is to determine whether the poverty is to be reduced through consumption transfers or through programs to enhance productivity. Although temporary transfer programs may be needed under adjustment, it is difficult to argue that, in the context of *adjustment lending*, countries should focus more attention than usual on the longer-run issue of enhancing the earning capacity of the poor. This is not to argue that these longer-run issues are unimportant. They are, as I said, at the top of the World Bank's list of concerns. In the design of adjustment programs, however, the emphasis should be on the immediate problems associated with adjustment and the poor and not on longer-run issues associated with reducing structural poverty.

The second element of this three-part taxonomy—and the one that I believe is in most people's minds when they discuss issues of adjustment and welfare—is protecting the poor during adjustment. In thinking about the consequences of adjustment policies for the poor, it is useful to distinguish the immediate effects from medium- and long-term effects.

The immediate effects depend mainly on what the poor have been doing during the preadjustment period. What were they consuming? Were they working, and if so, at what? How much of their consumption was self-produced and how much was purchased through the market? How much of their consumption was subsidized and how much was purchased at market prices? What use were they making of government-provided goods and services? In the past, rhetoric has often outstripped fact in assessing the immediate consequences of adjustment programs or policies for the poor. As this chapter points out, however, in a small but growing number of countries, household surveys are producing information that provides a good starting point for determining when and where special programs are needed to offset the harmful effects of adjustment on the poor.

These first-round effects of adjustment policies on the poor differ significantly by region. For prototypical African countries, one fact dominates the assessment: the overwhelming majority of the poor in most African countries live in rural areas. Rural households in Africa tend to produce much of what they consume. Furthermore, most government services and subsidies in Africa are consumed by or benefit an urban middle class. Thus adjustment programs that cut subsidies, reduce government services, or increase user fees for water and electricity and the like often will not directly affect the majority of the poor. By contrast, in Latin America substantially larger portions of the poor live in urban areas, although even there the negative consequences of adjustment for the poor are often overstated.

Whether in Africa or Latin America, however, there can be no denying that adjustment policies generally hit the urban poor the hardest. This fact carries with it an important, optimistic message for the design of poverty-related adjustment polices: there is some hope of being able to deal with the problem since well-targeted programs to reach the urban poor are administratively more feasible and much less costly than programs aimed more generally at the poor.

What of the medium- and long-term effects of adjustment programs on the poor? These are much more contentious and problematic issues—and indeed the subject of considerable ongoing research. Often at the crux of the issue is the change in relative prices of tradables and nontradables and the extent to which the poor are involved in the consumption and production of tradables and nontradables. In Côte d'Ivoire, for example, adjustment policies have increased rural incomes by increasing the earnings of rural export crop producers. This change has increased the *relative* income disparity between export crop producers and the poor food crop producers. I believe, however, that eventually the result will be a richer rural community that benefits, in absolute terms, even the rural poor who do not produce cash crops.

The third category of welfare-related issues, sharing the social burden, concerns those who are the victims of government efforts to reduce fiscal deficits by reducing the size of the public sector and aggregate demand. Although the effects of these actions are certainly a function of the adjustment program, they are not a poverty problem in the conventional sense. The experience of several countries has shown, however, that the costs associated with this aspect of adjustment are often large enough to bring adjustment programs to a halt.

What is required for this group is a "soft landing" in recognition of the need for (and obligation of) society to distribute adjustment costs broadly. The key characteristic of policies addressing this problem is that they should ease the cost without stopping the process of adjustment. These are short-run costs, and the programs to deal with them must be temporary. If the programs are allowed to drag on, they will exacerbate the very problems the adjustment program was designed to solve. Since protests from this group of middle-income (and sometimes lower-middle-income) individuals often topple adjustment programs, there can be no disagreement that this is an important policy issue. But for real adjustment to take place, those earning rents from a highly distorted economy must eventually "lose."

The distinctions implied by this taxonomy of adjustment issues related to the poor are important for focusing policies correctly. It is all too easy to mislay the blame for the long-standing problems of the poor at the feet of adjustment policies. In many countries with active adjustment programs the subsidies and employment policies of the government were in any case not sustainable. Without adjustment, the existing system would have collapsed, through either runaway inflation or a complete breakdown of the economic system. At issue here is the counterfactual. Adjustment policies may be implemented during a period of declining well-being for the poor, but it is quite another matter to argue that the two are causally related. This debate is more than semantic. To judge the distributional impacts of adjustment programs and, therefore, to assign blame for declines in the well-being of different segments of society, one must have some sense of the negative pull of long-standing but ultimately unsustainable policies.

As I have already indicated, it is important in discussing adjustment and the poor to limit generalities, or at least to qualify them geographically. For most of the African continent, the issues of poverty are dominated by medium- and long-term development issues. The question is how best to increase the productivity and earning power of the poor—through investment in human capital or through improved access to income-generating assets? In Latin America the major issue concerns the overall decline in public subsidies and the provision of public sector goods and services and how to shift the composition of the remaining expenditures toward more targeted, more efficient programs for the really poor.

In thinking about adjustment and the poor it helps to divide the issues along the lines described above; appropriate policies differ for each of the subcategories, as do the effects on the poor and the links to adjustment. Clear thinking about adjustment and the poor as distinct from debates about broad poverty-related issues will, in the end, produce better focused, more efficient, and more sustainable policies for dealing with the poor during episodes of adjustment. Focusing on adjustment-related poverty will also give a more realistic sense of the implications for both the administration and the financing of programs. Many very competent people are challenging the barriers to knowledge in this area, and I am confident that we will soon be on much firmer factual ground than we now are when we discuss the welfare effects of adjustment programs.

PART III

Country Experience with Adjustment Lending in the 1980s

13 Introduction to Part III

PART III EXAMINES the experiences of nine countries in the four operational regions of the World Bank: Côte d'Ivoire, Ghana, and Zambia (Africa); Indonesia and the Republic of Korea (Asia); Pakistan and Turkey (Europe, Middle East, and North Africa); and Chile and Mexico (Latin America). All these countries except Indonesia have received two or more adjustment loans from the World Bank since 1986.

Tables 13-1 and 13-2 present selected economic indicators for eighty-eight developing countries and for the nine countries whose experience is reviewed in the following chapters. As a group, the countries selected for detailed review shared the deterioration in economic performance that the group of eighty-eight developing countries also experienced in the 1980s. The turnaround by the mid-1980s, however, was stronger for the nine countries than for the rest. The broad conclusion of the analysis of comparative behavior presented in chapter 11 was that adjustment lending was marginally successful overall. The positive outcome associated with adjustment lending was even stronger when the focus was narrowed to only those countries that were intensely involved in adjustment lending. The World Bank's 1988 report on adjustment lending also suggested that the positive association between performance and adjustment lending increases from mild to strong when the focus shifts from all loan recipients to the intensive recipients.[1]

What are some of the findings or implications of the case studies as a group? First, externally funded programs, whether by the World Bank or the IMF, are sometimes seen as inflexible and unresponsive to local conditions. Lack of government commitment to reforms may spring from inappropriate design. A government may grudgingly accept the program in order to get access to the external resources, but there may not be true commitment to the program. Nonetheless, the studies show that several adjusting countries, including Ghana, Korea, and Turkey, have to varying degrees been able to adapt and improve externally funded programs to meet their specific needs.

This issue touches on the "ownership" of the program. Ownership appears to require an enthusiasm for or at least a recognition of the need

Table 13-1. Selected Economic Indicators for Eighty-Eight Developing Countries, 1965–72 to 1987
(unweighted average percent)

	Period average				Recent experience						
Indicator	*1965–72*	*1973–77*	*1978–81*	*1982–88*[a]	*1982*	*1983*	*1984*	*1985*	*1986*	*1987*	*1988*[a]
Growth rate (constant prices)											
GDP (market prices)	5.4	5.1	3.8	2.5	1.8	1.2	2.4	3.1	3.2	2.3	3.3
Exports (goods and nonfactor services)	7.4	5.2	6.4	3.4	−1.8	3.5	6.0	1.4	4.0	5.3	5.5
Imports (goods and nonfactor services)	6.6	8.8	6.2	0.7	−3.7	−4.5	1.3	3.7	0.2	4.0	4.2
Share of GDP (current prices)											
Exports (goods and nonfactor services)	21.9	24.9	25.6	24.8	24.4	24.7	26.0	25.7	24.5	24.3	24.2
Imports (goods and nonfactor services)	25.5	31.9	35.5	32.5	35.5	33.2	32.5	32.3	31.2	31.3	31.4
Resource balance[b]	−3.6	−7.0	−9.9	−7.7	−11.1	−8.5	−6.5	−6.6	−6.7	−7.0	−7.2
Debt ratio[c]											
External debt/exports (goods and services)	106.3	107.7	143.4	277.6	199.6	230.3	234.5	282.6	333.3	341.7	321.2
Debt service/exports (goods and services)	11.6	11.5	15.1	21.8	18.4	19.1	19.1	22.0	24.5	22.9	26.5
Prices											
Consumer prices (percentage change)	5.9	21.4	19.5	28.7	20.9	28.1	29.3	32.9	24.9	26.5	38.5
Real exchange rate[d] (1980 = 100)	n.a.	n.a.	99.8	97.6	107.4	106.1	105.7	104.5	91.2	85.2	83.4
Terms of trade[e] (1980 = 100)	130.4	120.4	102.1	92.1	89.3	92.0	93.3	90.1	95.5	89.2	95.1

n.a. Not available.
a. Preliminary estimates.
b. Resource balance is the difference between exports and imports of goods and nonfactor services.
c. Public and private, medium- and long-term debt outstanding and disbursed; data for 1965–72 refer to 1970–72 only.
d. Increase indicates real appreciation.
e. Ratio of export to import price indices of merchandise goods; increase indicates an improvement.
Source: World Bank and IMF data.

Table 13-2. Selected Economic Indicators for the Nine Case Study Countries, 1965–72 to 1988
(unweighted average percent)

	Period average				Recent experience						
Indicator	*1965–72*	*1973–77*	*1978–81*	*1982–88[a]*	*1982*	*1983*	*1984*	*1985*	*1986*	*1987*	*1988[a]*
Growth rate (constant price)											
GDP (market prices)	6.0	4.6	4.9	3.2	−0.9	1.1	4.7	4.2	4.7	4.3	4.0
Export (goods and nonfactor services)	8.5	6.5	6.1	7.2	10.0	1.8	5.7	1.0	13.0	15.4	3.2
Import (goods and nonfactor services)	8.2	8.3	6.6	2.3	−15.1	−4.1	5.6	4.9	4.1	15.0	5.8
Share of GDP (current prices)											
Export (goods and nonfactor services)	18.3	22.4	21.0	25.0	20.7	23.1	25.1	25.3	26.7	27.5	26.3
Import (goods and nonfactor services)	19.0	23.6	24.4	24.6	23.6	24.4	23.9	24.3	26.0	25.7	24.4
Resource balance[b]	−0.7	−1.2	−3.4	0.4	−2.9	−1.3	1.2	1.0	0.7	1.8	1.9
Current account balance	−2.3	−3.9	−5.8	−3.8	−6.5	−4.7	−2.7	−4.1	−3.7	−1.6	−3.0
Gross domestic investment	18.8	21.0	21.7	18.4	19.0	18.2	17.7	18.5	18.1	18.7	18.9
Debt ratio[c]											
External debt/GDP	26.8	31.2	33.6	62.9	42.7	51.5	55.8	66.7	77.6	80.7	65.4
External debt/exports (goods and services)	201.6	170.2	182.4	243.2	199.4	227.9	219.8	251.0	282.8	278.9	242.8
Debt service/exports (goods and services)	19.0	18.3	26.1	29.8	28.4	30.1	27.7	30.0	31.3	30.2	30.6
Interest/exports (goods and services)	5.8	6.6	10.1	14.8	15.1	15.0	15.6	15.2	15.4	13.4	13.5
Prices											
Consumer prices (percentage change)	9.3	53.2	29.1	28.3	18.3	36.9	24.1	21.8	26.1	34.5	36.8
Real exchange rate[d] (1980 = 100)	n.a.	n.a.	104.0	81.6	118.9	100.6	86.4	80.2	63.1	58.9	63.0
Terms of trade[e] (1980 = 100)	139.7	114.7	101.8	89.6	89.4	92.7	92.6	90.4	86.8	86.9	88.1

n.a. Not available.
a. Preliminary estimates.
b. Resource balance is the difference between exports and imports of goods and nonfactor services.
c. Public and private, medium- and long-term debt outstanding and disbursed; data for 1965–72 refer to 1970–72 only.
d. Increase indicates real appreciation.
e. Ratio of export to import price indices of merchandise goods; increase indicates an improvement.
Source: World Bank and IMF data.

for the adjustment program on the part of key members of the government and the public at large. The programs in Ghana and Turkey were ambitious, but in both countries economic deterioration had induced a consensus on the need for change. Although opposition was not totally avoided, in both countries the programs were clearly seen as the only way out of economic chaos, a position that is particularly evident in Chad Leechor's study on Ghana (chapter 15). The same consensus never developed in the case of Zambia, which eventually reversed its reforms (chapter 16).

Second, the adequacy of financing also influences the effectivenss of adjustment policies since it affects society's ability to sustain programs that may have significant short-term costs. Adequate financing can provide the time and resources needed for an orderly transition to adjustment, although care must be taken to ensure that external financing does not lead to indefinite postponement of needed reforms. Inadequate financing, by contrast, can force a country to make demanding adjustments at a pace that is not politically and economically feasible and so lead to a program's collapse. Mohsen Fardi's chapter on Zambia shows quite clearly that inadequate funding contributed significantly to the collapse of the program in 1987.

Countries that have been willing to undertake comprehensive programs, such as Indonesia, Korea, and Turkey, have been able to attract substantial external financing, including commercial financing. Ghana provides a good example of the extent of external noncommercial financing available to a country for a rigorous program of adjustment. The World Bank, the IMF, and bilateral donors have assisted Ghana heavily and continue to do so.

Ghana's needs for external financing were relatively easy to address because it had not acquired a large stock of debt and interest payments were therefore not a problem for the adjustment program. For many other countries, however, debt servicing takes up a substantial portion of the foreign exchange earnings. The debt overhang emerged as a key factor in the financing package for Mexico, as John Nash discusses in chapter 22. This is an important issue because it affects the flexibility with which a country can handle its exchange rate policy. (Devaluation leads to larger real income losses because the stock of foreign debt is revalued.) With hindsight, and in light of recent debt initiatives, it is evident that timely debt relief would have helped avoid some of the up-down, stop-go features that adjustment programs have exhibited.

Third, the better performers—Indonesia, Korea, and Turkey—followed relatively sound policies over the long term and promptly adjusted to shocks. Unlike many other oil-exporting countries, Indonesia managed its oil resources well and largely succeeded in avoiding the "Dutch disease," as chapter 17 by Sadiq Ahmed shows. Korea followed a long-run program of macroeconomic stability and, as Mansoor Dailami explains in chapter 18, adjusted very quickly to stabilize the economy when economic conditions appeared to be getting out of hand in the late 1970s. Turkey's early successes are now threatened by growing macroeconomic instability, but Turkey has nevertheless stuck to a policy of economic liberalization for nearly a decade. In chapter 20, both Faezeh Foroutan and the commentary by Dani Rodrik underline the dangers to the entire program posed by the lack of fiscal discipline in recent years.

Fourth, the speed of the supply response is closely associated with sustainability. A strong export response, based on a substantial depreciation of the real exchange rate, few rigidities in labor markets and wages, and the presence of unutilized capacity helped Korea, Turkey, and, more recently, Indonesia continue their reforms. A powerful lobby in favor of reform emerged quickly. By contrast, Zambia reversed its policy in part because of lags in export growth. As exports continued to stagnate, foreign exchange became scarce while the exchange auctions caused the exchange rate to rise rapidly, and thus uncertainty and instability increased. The institutionalization of reforms also affects the supply response by giving the program credibility in the eyes of investors. Reasonable macroeconomic stability is also necessary for a good supply response, but it is not always easy to know just how much stability is needed for structural reforms to be effective. Korea's experience, as shown in chapter 18, illustrates the complementarity between macroeconomic stabilization and structural reform.

A fifth issue, which is related to the credibility of reform, is that of political and social stability. Reform, of course, involves change, but as Shahid Husain points out in his summary remarks, the Latin American countries that have pursued structural adjustment—Chile and Mexico—have had both a relatively stable political structure and an institutional framework that supported reform. Even in these two countries, however, the process has been slow and painful. Indeed, the reform process is likely to prove much more time consuming and arduous than anticipated, and the World Bank needs to gear its adjustment lending operations to a longer time frame.

Sixth, the country studies often show that insufficient attention has been paid to the social costs of adjustment.[2] For example, real wages often decline during adjustment as resources shift toward tradables and away from nontradables. The dilemma is how to design policies that bring this resource shift about without a sharp drop in consumption or in real wages for the poor. Is the targeting of subsidies a desirable approach, and if so, how can the targeting best be done? In the case of Turkey, for example, the potential impact of adjustment on the poor was barely addressed in the program design even though it was clear that real wages would have to decline to effect adjustment. Real wages fell sharply in Chile too, as Cristian Moran shows in chapter 21. Although attempts were made to direct expenditures toward the poorer groups and children, Moran argues that these measures were insufficient. In Ghana the issue was how to protect the urban poor rather than the poor in general, since farmers, poor and rich, on the whole benefited from the reform. Ghana's response was to set up the short-term compensatory Program of Actions to Mitigate the Social Costs of Adjustment. But except in these two cases, efforts to address the social costs of adjustment have been limited.

The countries studied in the chapters that follow have been categorized according to the relative influence of adjustment lending on performance (table 13-3). (No effort has been made to separate the effects of World Bank adjustment lending and of IMF programs.) Although this appraisal is unavoidably subjective, it is based on the individual country studies and the multicountry studies reported in this volume.

A low impact from adjustment lending can be found in both the successful and the not so successful cases of adjustment. For example, Korea, a successful adjuster, did not seem to be significantly affected by World Bank adjustment lending; having decided on its own to adjust, Korea would probably have done much the same thing without the adjustment loans. In Zambia, an unsuccessful adjuster, adjustment lending also did not affect performance. In contrast, adjustment lending seems to have had a major positive impact on performance in five countries. Chile and Indonesia benefited from the external resources provided. Adjustment lending had a favorable impact on stabilization and exchange rate policies in Indonesia (in the absence of a formal IMF standby) and on exchange rate and structural reforms in Turkey and Ghana. In Mexico the positive effect has been on recent trade policies. The positive impact was more modest, although it varied considerably, in the remainder of the nine countries. The strength of the positive impact is generally sensitive to the period examined; thus, for example, positive results were greater during an early period in Turkey and a later one in Mexico.

The country studies highlight the diversity of experience with adjustment lending. They do not lead to any simple conclusions on the effect of policy on performance, and they indicate both the strengths and weaknesses of adjustment lending as a means of supporting reform. Overall, the country experiences show that when a determined effort is made, when the technical groundwork has been carefully prepared, and when the political will and broad general consensus exist or can

Table 13-3. Terms of Trade Shocks, Performance, and Effects of Adjustment Lending in the Nine Case Study Countries

	Influence		
Indicator	*Low*	*Medium*	*High*
Terms of trade[a]	Ghana	Chile, Korea, Zambia	Côte d'Ivoire, Indonesia, Mexico, Pakistan, Turkey
Improvement in GDP growth[b]	Côte d'Ivoire, Mexico, Zambia	Chile	Ghana, Indonesia, Korea, Pakistan, Turkey
Reduction in trade balance[c] (exports minus imports of goods and nonfactor services as percentage of GDP)	Ghana, Pakistan	Turkey, Zambia	Chile, Côte d'Ivoire, Indonesia, Korea, Mexico
Incremental positive effect of adjustment lending on policy or financing[d]	Korea, Zambia	Côte d'Ivoire, Pakistan	Chile, Ghana, Indonesia, Mexico, Turkey

a. High means relatively adverse terms of trade shocks.

b. Rating is based both on an improvement during three years after adjustment lending compared with three years before and on the level of GDP growth in 1982–86. Low indicates a decline in the growth rate *and* growth of less than 3 percent. Medium indicates a decline in the growth rate but growth of more than 3 percent, *or* growth less than 1 percent despite an increase in the rate. High indicates an increase in the growth rate *and* growth of more than 1 percent.

c. Rating is based both on the reduction in the trade balance (three years after adjustment lending compared with three years before) and on the level of the deficit in 1982–86. Low indicates an increase in the deficit *or* a deficit of more than 10 percent despite a reduction. Medium indicates a reduction in the deficit by up to 10 percentage points *or* a deficit between 1 and 10 percent. High indicates a reduction in the deficit by more than 10 percentage points *and* a deficit of less than 1 percent.

d. Low indicates little effect of adjustment lending itself or an unsuccessful effort.

Source: World Bank (1988) and the studies presented in this volume.

be developed, adjustment programs can work—to the lasting benefit of the country.

Notes

1. World Bank, *Adjustment Lending: An Evaluation of Ten Years of Experience*, Policy and Research Series 1 (Washington, D.C., 1988).
2. This finding confirms the results of a recent study by G. A. Cornia, Richard Jolly, and Frances Stewart, *Adjustment with a Human Face* (Oxford, U.K.: Clarendon Press for UNICEF, 1987).

14 *Côte d'Ivoire: The Failure of Structural Adjustment*

Christophe Chamley

FROM 1965 TO 1975 economic performance in Côte d'Ivoire was impressive, with real growth over the period averaging 8 percent a year and never falling below 4 percent. This smooth pattern was disrupted by the cocoa and coffee boom in 1976, when prices rose more than threefold as a result of a frost in Brazil. The windfall revenue from the boom was captured by the government. Producer prices remained stable while the stabilization fund for coffee and cocoa accumulated a surplus equal to 16 percent of GDP in 1977 at the peak of the boom. These resources were used by the government to launch a vast investment program.

Although there was no indication that a permanent change had occurred in world coffee and cocoa markets that would prolong the price increases, the government continued to pursue its expenditure programs as though such a change had taken place, even after prices began to fall. Between 1977 and 1980 prices fell by 30 percent. Current expenditure, particularly civil service salaries, increased as a share of GDP. Investment was accelerated at a rate that strained the absorptive capacity of the economy, and the marginal profitability of new investments was low.

Two legacies of the commodity boom have been particularly detrimental to the Ivoirian economy. The first was the fiscal deficit, an outcome, in part, of the belief that the "fair" level of coffee and cocoa prices was above the preboom level. This belief seems to persist even today and makes implementation of reforms more difficult. The second was the increase in domestic prices that began during the boom and was accompanied by an equivalent expansion of the money supply. There are two standard explanations for the inflation in Côte d'Ivoire between 1975 and 1980. One emphasizes the impact of government spending on domestic demand (similar to the "Dutch disease"), and the second stresses the influence of monetary expansion. The first explanation may be closer to the truth because Côte d'Ivoire, as a member of the West African Monetary Union, has a fixed exchange rate with free capital movements. As a result Côte d'Ivoire does not have independent control over its monetary policy. Whatever the cause, the higher price level induced an appreciation of the real exchange rate. The macroeconomic policy pursued by Côte d'Ivoire during the 1980s did not reverse the increase in the price level.

For three years after the commodity boom was over, no significant adjustment took place. Thus by 1981 the budget deficit equaled 12 percent of GDP and the current account deficit equaled 17 percent of GDP, while the ratio of foreign debt to GDP had reached 35 percent. It became clear that the path being followed by the economy was unsustainable.

The Adjustment Program

The Ivoirian authorities launched a structural adjustment program at the end of 1981, which was supported by the World Bank with three structural adjustment loans (SALs) (1981, 1983, and 1986) and by the International Monetary Fund (IMF) through a multiyear arrangement under the Extended Fund Facility (1981–83) and two one-year standby arrangements (1984 and 1985).[1] The goals of the program were (1) to restore internal equilibrium by reducing public expenditures and instituting administrative reforms for the control of the budgetary process and (2) to restore external equilibrium in the short term by reducing the fiscal gap and in the medium to long term by introducing economic incentives for the diversification of the economy away from its main cash crops. It is useful to divide the period into three phases.

1. *The persistent fiscal gap (SAL I, 1981–83).* At this stage, the adjustment program was not very well defined. Lending seems mainly to have been a mechanism for policy dialogue. Since a "persistent oil boom" was anticipated because of the recent discovery of oil, the seriousness of the fiscal situation was greatly underestimated. Consequently, no significant reform was implemented. Minor improvements in the budget process had only a small positive impact on the fiscal balance, and these gains were offset by a drought that reduced agricultural output and by the rise in world interest rates. By 1983 the budget and external deficits were about the same as in 1980, before the start of the adjustment program.

2. *Partial restoration of equilibrium (SAL II, 1984–86).* During this second phase, a reduction in government investment expenditure from 15 percent to 7.6 percent of GDP had an equal impact on the deficit. These reductions were accompanied by a positive external shock—the end of the drought and a temporary increase in coffee and cocoa prices. The two effects contributed in roughly equal measure to restoration of the short-run macroeconomic balances. The situation was transitory, however, because the prices of coffee and cocoa were well above their trend; they fell again at the end of 1986.

3. *The economic crisis (SAL III, 1986–88).* The level of coffee and cocoa prices hit a historic low. This led to macroeconomic imbalances similar to those observed at the beginning of the adjustment program, but with

a much larger stock of outstanding debt. Interest payments were suspended in the spring of 1987, and since then the foreign debt to GDP ratio has been about 90 percent.

The First Phase: 1981–83

PROGRAM AND CONDITIONS. The adjustment process began in the fall of 1980 and led to the structural adjustment program supported by the Extended Fund Facility of the IMF and the first World Bank SAL. From the beginning the IMF took the lead in establishing and monitoring the broad macroeconomic targets, and the World Bank, while supporting these targets, concentrated on microeconomic issues such as the budget process, restructuring of public enterprises, choice of investment projects, and incentives for the diversification of the economy. (Table 14-1 presents loan conditions for each SAL.)

The program established a set of policy actions that included administrative reforms, a large number of studies, and specific economic policy measures. Very few of these policy actions were specified as conditions for disbursement. In general, the first SAL was a "soft" program that set the basis for continuing policy dialogue. All parties involved were conscious that the agreement was to be the first in a series.

The structural adjustment program recognized the main imbalances and identified the policies needed to address them. The seriousness of the situation was grossly underestimated, however, because the postboom prices of cocoa and coffee were considered to be temporary, and the recent discovery of oil in Côte d'Ivoire raised expectations of a new source of revenue. Thus, for example, the structural adjustment program was expected to introduce a pricing system (which remained unspecified) for the agricultural sector that would adjust the producer prices of officially supported crops sufficiently to offset the possible inflationary effect of a prolonged period of high oil revenue while maintaining the country's competitiveness in exports and import substitutes. What was expected was a prolonged oil boom!

FISCAL POLICY. Government capital expenditure as a share of GDP was reduced from 18 percent in 1980 to about 15 percent in 1981 and 1982, but the level of current expenditure remained largely unchanged (table 14-2). (The reduction in current expenditure in 1981 was offset by an equally significant increase in 1982; this variation may have been due to payment delays.) On the revenue side, the receipts from cocoa and coffee were relatively small because of low international prices and drought-reduced output. The net surplus of the stabilization fund was between 2 and 3 percent of GDP (compared with 16 percent in 1977).

Table 14-1. Main Conditions of the Three World Bank Structural Adjustment Loans to Côte d'Ivoire

Category	*SAL I*	*SAL II*	*SAL III*
Public sector			
Administration	Improvement of budgetary accounting, the centralization of public finance, and the general efficiency of the public sector Draft of a three-year plan (*schema-directeur*) to be translated into a three-year rolling public investment program (*loi-programme*) Integration of oil surpluses into the budget	Continuation of improvements in administrative efficiency and the unification of the budget process initiated in SAL I through (1) extension of the *schema-directeur* to the sectoral level, (2) a quarterly system of reporting for important investments, (3) standardization and generalization of the economic appraisal process, (4) reinforcement of programming and evaluation units in technical ministries, and (5) integration of public enterprises (resource transfers and investment budget), resources of the marketing board, and oil revenue in the budget process	
Expenditure	Ceiling of 5 percent in the growth of the level of nominal public expenditures in 1981 Specific first-year performance conditions for new foreign borrowing, growth in domestic assets of the banking system, interest rates Satisfactory reviews of investment and financial decisions, and the approval of the 1982 investment budget with its associated *loi-programme*	As in SAL I, overall macro-targets were set and monitored in the framework of the Extended Fund Facility with the IMF. (Adoption of a financial program for 1984 acceptable to the World Bank as a condition for the second tranche.)	

Revenue	No action on tax reform or on the revenue side of the budget	No evaluation of the tax system because it was thoroughly reviewed by the IMF	
Public enterprises		Introduction of synoptic tables in the transport and telecommunications sectors to determine performance targets for basic financial data and key indicators of management efficiency and enterprise productivity Extension of this system to the thirty-one most important public enterprises Program of management audits (conducted with some delays)	Extended actions already taken under SAL II: (1) reduction in real transfers to public enterprises, (2) disaggregation of the system of synoptic table for the thirty-one enterprises, (3) rehabilitation of five enterprises, audits of three, improvement of supervisory procedures of four
Agriculture	Restructuring of the Ministry of Agriculture Review of the budget of regional development agencies Financial restructuring of the regional development agencies (with a 1982 plan as a condition for a second tranche) Increase in some producer prices for nontraditional agricultural exports Removal of some subsidies and phasing out of some inefficient projects (sugar)	Closing of the two least efficient (of six) government sugar complexes Some reduction in personnel of the agricultural agencies World Bank review of some of the agencies Increase in producer prices of agricultural products, particularly nontraditional exports. The price of some products (rubber) was based on world prices. Support for a special pruning program for coffee[a]	Diversification of export crops Phasing out of export taxes and application of the value added tax for significant agricultural products (palm oil, sugar, cotton, rubber, coconut, coprah, and fresh pineapple) Extension of the export subsidy scheme to agricultural exports (begun in the middle of 1987 and only partially implemented) Further rehabilitation of the sugar industry through a comprehensive program Elimination of subsidies on food crop seeds Financial restructuring of national agricultural bank

(Table continues on the following page.)

Table 14-1 (continued)

Category	SAL I	SAL II	SAL III
Industry	Commission of studies; no specific action	Uniform tariff levels toward 40 percent (on 60 percent of industrial value added for fertilizers and agroindustries, with the exception of coffee and cocoa processing, chemicals, plastics, and engineering industries) Removal of quantitative restrictions (replaced by an important surcharge and five-year phaseout of a list representing 40 percent of local value added) Introduction of an export subsidy scheme at the rate of 20 percent on the domestic value added (which suffered considerable delays)[b] Acceleration of value added tax refunds for exports Proposal for a preferential interest rate for export activities, which was rejected by West Africa Monetary Union	Removal of quantitative restrictions Partial application of the export premium for non-CFA countries

	Revision of the investment code, reform of agencies in charge of promoting small and medium-size enterprises, creation of an investment promotion agency[c]
Housing	Sale of some subsidized units,[d] increases in rents, introduction of management audits

a. As in SAL I, the World Bank was aware that the prospects for coffee were better than for cocoa and that the Ivoirian policy of equal prices for the two crops should be replaced by a price differential favoring coffee. The policy included in SAL II, however, fell short of this action.

b. Although 1984 implementation was clearly intended, explicit conditionality required only submission to the national assembly. The review for the second tranche states that the subsidy should be in place by the end of 1985. First payments were made only in August 1986, however, and the program was still not completely implemented in 1988.

c. The effects of these reforms were either dubious or difficult to evaluate.

d. The public housing program catered essentially to civil servants with middle to high income and was heavily subsidized (to the tune of more than 1 percent of GDP by 1982). Following the actions under SAL II, urban public expenditure dropped by 45 percent between 1982 and 1985.

Source: World Bank.

Table 14-2. Consolidated Public Sector Finance in Côte d'Ivoire, 1980–87
(percentage share of GDP)

Budget item	*1980*	*1981*	*1982*	*1983*	*1984*	*1985*	*1986*	*1987*[a]
Total revenue	28.5	27.8	27.7	29.2	34.0	36.6	31.7	28.0
Tax revenue	20.4	22.1	21.3	20.8	20.5	19.8	20.3	23.1
Coffee and cocoa stabilization fund	3.9	1.3	2.7	3.7	9.2	10.0	4.3	−1.7
Public enterprise surplus	0.7	0.2	0.5	0.7	0.3	2.6	2.6	2.9
Social security	1.4	1.2	1.3	1.3	1.0	1.1	1.3	1.2
Other revenue	2.2	2.9	1.8	2.7	3.0	3.1	3.2	2.5
Total expenditure	40.7	35.6	43.8	40.9	35.7	34.6	34.0	35.5
Current	22.6	20.6	28.6	29.6	28.1	27.4	27.7	29.2
Treasury	15.1	13.4	18.2	18.0	16.5	16.1	17.7	18.7
Wages	8.3	9.4	9.5	10.0	8.8	8.0	8.3	9.3
Materials	4.1	4.1	3.7	3.0	2.5	2.4	2.7	2.9
Subsidies	n.a.	n.a.	3.7	3.6	3.5	3.1	3.1	3.8
Unclassified	n.a.	n.a.	1.2	1.4	1.7	2.6	3.5	2.7
Interest on debt	3.2	4.8	7.2	8.2	8.5	8.4	7.2	7.4
Domestic	n.a.	n.a.	1.0	1.4	1.3	1.1	0.7	1.0
External	n.a.	n.a.	6.1	6.9	7.2	7.4	6.5	6.4
Other	4.3	2.4	3.2	3.3	3.1	2.9	2.8	3.1
Capital	18.1	14.9	15.2	11.3	7.6	7.2	6.3	6.3
Central government	n.a.	n.a.	9.9	6.9	4.1	4.6	3.0	3.7
Public enterprises	n.a.	n.a.	5.4	4.4	3.5	2.5	3.3	2.6
Surplus (pay basis)	−12.2	−7.8	−16.1	−11.7	−1.7	2.0	−2.4	−7.6

n.a. Not available.
a. Preliminary data.
Source: Ivoirian authorities and World Bank staff estimates.

The increase in international interest rates imposed an additional burden on the budget. Interest rates on new commitments reached a peak of 12 to 13 percent in 1981–82. As a consequence, interest payments on the debt increased from 3.2 percent of GDP in 1980 to 7.2 percent in 1982.

The 3 percentage point reduction in capital expenditure from 1980 to the levels in 1981 and 1982 was insufficient to reduce the deficit, given the low revenues from cocoa and coffee and the increase in international interest rates. A further reduction in capital expenditure (by 4 percent of GDP) was implemented in 1983, but overoptimistic projections of revenue delayed the implementation of sufficiently austere fiscal measures. Thus by the end of 1983 the government deficit constituted about the same share of GDP (12 percent) as it had before the adjustment program.

Ivoirian compliance with the conditions of SAL I was judged to be good, mainly because the conditions applied to broad and soft overall targets for the budget of 1982 and the assessment was made in the middle of 1982. At this very early stage of the first adjustment loan period the failure of the economy to adjust was not yet apparent. The pressure of the fiscal gap became obvious later with the large expansion of credit by the Central Bank. The expansion of credit overtook the targets set with the IMF, and the last tranche of the Extended Fund Facility was not released.

The Second Phase: 1984–86

During the period of SAL II three positive shocks affected the economy of Côte d'Ivoire: the drought ended, the value of the dollar increased by 24 percent in 1984, and the international prices of cocoa and coffee recovered. The CFA prices of cocoa and coffee increased by about 75 percent between 1982 and 1984. Government expenditures were cut simultaneously. Internal and external balance was restored, but the recession that had been initiated by the first expenditure cuts in 1983 deepened. Real GDP fell by 2.5 percent in 1983 and by 2 percent in 1984. A brief economic recovery in 1985 ended with the fall of cocoa and coffee prices at the end of 1986.

PROGRAM AND CONDITIONS. The second SAL was intended to strengthen the structural adjustment process that SAL I had begun. This follow-up had been anticipated from the beginning, but by the time of SAL II the situation in Côte d'Ivoire had worsened. Interest rates on foreign debt were higher than in 1982–83, coffee and cocoa prices were low, and cocoa output fell 30 percent from the 1981 level because of drought. Furthermore, the expected oil boom did not materialize.

Although SAL II addressed the same issues as SAL I, the urgency of undertaking fundamental reforms was now very apparent, and the program of reforms was considerably more comprehensive and detailed. In addition to the four main areas covered by SAL I, SAL II provided for reforms in public housing, particularly the subsidization of housing for public sector employees. The restructuring and management of public enterprises also received special emphasis. Always important in the Ivoirian economy, in 1977 public enterprises employed about one-third of the formal labor force, produced 27 percent of value added, and were responsible for 68 percent of capital formation. But they lacked a clear definition of their roles, their supervisory mechanisms were inadequate, and their mediocre economic and financial performance strained the government budget. By 1985, however, the reorganization of the public enterprise sector had led to efficiency gains that were reflected in new surpluses in operating funds.

Tariff reform was another important element of the adjustment program, particularly the substitution of tariffs for quantitative restrictions. Under SAL II the tariff rate was brought to a uniform value of 40 percent. Although the need for the tariff reform had been identified at the beginning of the adjustment program and in the studies undertaken in SAL I, no practical reform measures had been taken before SAL II.

All of these policy measures contributed significantly to the restoration of internal and external balance in the short term. The program had one important shortcoming, however: it did not succeed in introducing a set of incentives to diversify the economy.

FISCAL POLICY. The transition from the first to the second phase was marked by further reductions in government capital expenditure in 1983 and 1984 to 7 percent of GDP, a level that has been maintained since that time. Current expenditure was also reduced slightly by an amount equal to about 1.5 percent of GDP. Thus the total reduction in expenditures was about 5 to 6 percent of GDP (table 14-2).

The recovery of cocoa and coffee prices and the end of the drought had a strong impact on the revenue of the stabilization fund. Its surplus as a percentage of GDP was 5.5 percentage points higher in 1984 than in 1983. Standard taxes as a share of GDP remained unchanged at about 20 percent, their level since 1975, so taxes made no additional contribution to revenue. The fiscal gap, which had been equal to 12 percent of GDP at the end of the first phase in 1983, was thus met in roughly equal parts by the reduction in expenditure and the increase in cocoa and coffee revenues.[2]

By 1985 the numerous measures for reorganizing public enterprises began to bear fruit, and the operating surplus of public enterprises as a proportion of GDP increased by 2 percentage points. That same year the budget showed a surplus for the first time (equivalent to 2 percent of GDP). In 1986, however, the budget was again in deficit (2.4 percent of GDP) because of the fall in world cocoa prices at the end of the year.

THE ECONOMY: RECESSION AND PARTIAL RECOVERY. In the first phase of the structural adjustment program the level of real output stagnated and output per capita fell. This recession was deepened by the drought in 1983 and by the large reduction in government investment expenditure in 1984. The change in real output per capita from 1980 to 1987 is shown in figure 14-1. To exclude the contribution of the coffee and cocoa sector, the value of output net of exports is also shown. (This is a rough measure since there are induced effects between this sector and the others. Exports other than coffee and cocoa were small and stagnant as a share of GDP.)

Figure 14-1. Change in Real Output Per Capita in Côte d'Ivoire, 1980–87

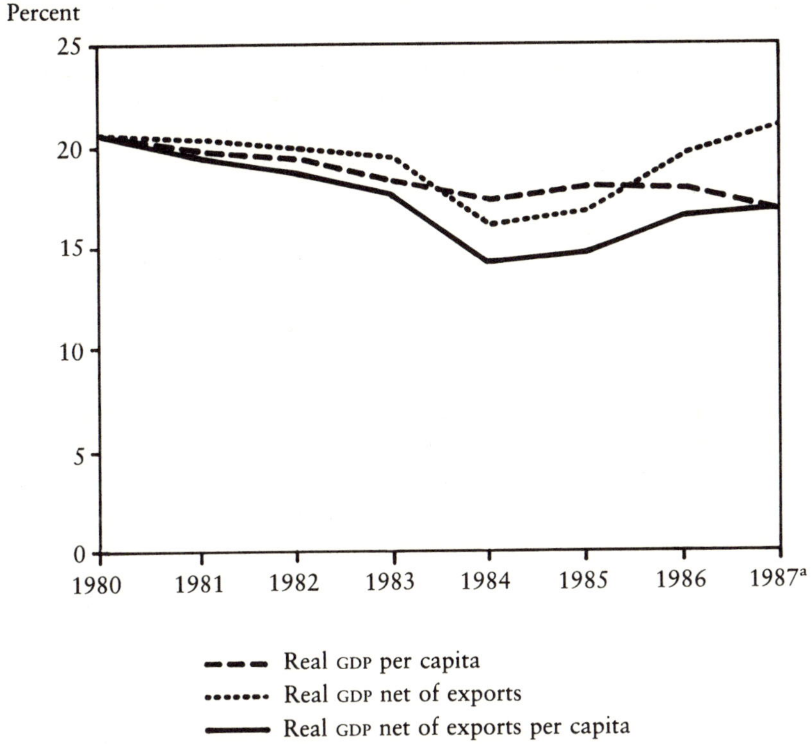

a. Estimated.
Source: World Bank data.

As real GDP increased by 5 percent in 1985 and then by 3 percent in 1986, a brief economic recovery occurred even though real government expenditure remained stable.[3] The recovery was very weak, however. An increase in indirect taxes accounted for 2 percentage points of the growth of measured real GDP. This contribution is only a statistical artifact and does not represent any increase in the production of goods and services. Thus the increase in production over the two years 1985 and 1986 was only about 6 percent, which was barely sufficient to keep pace with the population growth. In 1986 (for which there are detailed accounts), real growth was led by expenditures of public entities while real output decreased by 7 percent in the textile and leather sector and by 9 percent in construction.

The Third Phase: 1987–88

SAL III began in February 1985. The drought had finally ended, and the economy was entering its 1985–86 recovery phase. Internal and external economic balance had been restored, and the decline in output had been arrested. Although the structural problems of the economy had not been solved, the lack of pressure in the short term generated complacency and contributed to the two-year lag between the initiation of SAL III and its effect on the economy.

The fall in cocoa and coffee prices at the end of 1986 marked the beginning of a new crisis, which led to the conclusion of the negotiating process. Coffee and cocoa prices continued to fall and reached their lowest level in recent history. In 1987, for the first time, the price stabilization fund registered a deficit (of 1.7 percent of GDP).

PROGRAM AND CONDITIONS. Despite the progress in the first five years of the adjustment program, the fundamental issues remained the same under SAL III. The general purpose of SAL III was to extend and broaden the changes begun in the previous years. The government's fiscal policy program included detailed administrative reforms and changes in the composition of expenditures, which resembled the fiscal program under SAL II. Since reforms in the housing sector had been satisfactory, they were dropped from SAL III and replaced by policy reforms for the energy sector.

The major reform under SAL III was the establishment of an export premium program to offset the overvaluation of the real exchange rate, since devaluation was not an option for Côte d'Ivoire as a member of the CFA community. The misalignment of the exchange rate had been discussed since the beginning of the structural adjustment program in 1981, but no action had been taken to resolve the problem. The premium, which was to be financed through an import tariff, was to be applied at a rate of 20 percent to nontraditional exports directed to non-CFA countries. The policy was, in effect, a simulated exchange rate adjustment.

The premium was first extended to nontraditional agricultural exports in the fall of 1986. Its implementation was limited, however, because it excluded cotton and pineapple. Pineapple was excluded under the pretext of a temporary lack of quality control in the industry, but since pineapple represented almost half the agricultural exports that were eligible for the premium, it is likely that the exclusion was based on the added cost. Even for eligible goods, some payments were delayed because of the budget crisis. The premium was extended in the fall of 1987 to nonagricultural exports. Some payment delays occurred again in 1988.

No specific price policy for coffee and cocoa was set under the SAL program. The World Bank and the Ivoirian authorities could not agree on specific measures. There was only "a plan to arrest the projected decline in coffee output," which was included as a condition for the second tranche. A shift in the incentive structure from cocoa to coffee had been identified as a goal under SAL I, but even this vague condition was abandoned as the prices of coffee and cocoa dropped dramatically at the end of 1986.

FISCAL POLICY. Since public sector capital expenditure had been reduced from 18 percent of GDP in 1980 to a little over 6 percent in 1986, its level was no longer a problem for Côte d'Ivoire, so no expenditure-cutting targets were set. The program merely set standard goals for the project selection process, without specifying particular policy measures. Current expenditure was treated in the same way.

The fall in cocoa and coffee prices at the end of 1986 generated a revenue shortfall of about 6 percent with respect to the "standard" expected surplus of 4 percent of GDP. Since current and capital expenditures had not increased, the deficit for 1987, estimated at 7.6 percent of GDP, was due entirely to this shortfall. The situation worsened as a result of a further fall in commodity prices at the beginning of 1988, and in 1989 the prospects for a price recovery in the near future were still not good. Interest payments on foreign debt were suspended in April 1987. Since these payments represent a large fraction of GDP (see table 14-2), their suspension provided needed breathing space for the Ivoirian authorities, at least in the short term.

Macroeconomic Issues

Most of the conditions in the SALs addressed issues of microeconomic management and did not emphasize an economywide approach to structural adjustment. The World Bank was restricted in this respect by at least three factors. First, the IMF has responsibility for determining and monitoring the overall level of revenue, spending, and credit. Second, the nominal exchange rate is a rigid institutional constraint; any change in the nominal rate is ruled out because it would raise a set of complex issues with the other countries of the CFA zone. Third, Ivoirian authorities resisted any suggestions for changes in some key prices (coffee and cocoa, civil service wages). Despite these limitations, the serious macroeconomic problems facing the authorities in Côte d'Ivoire must be considered in any discussion of structural adjustment.

Fiscal Policy

REVENUE. The structure of public sector revenue and expenditure is an essential element of the economic crisis in Côte d'Ivoire. The two main sources of revenue are taxes on income, trade, and value added, and taxes on coffee and cocoa (the stabilization fund). The share of revenue from these two sources is presented in table 14-2.

Revenue from taxes on income, trade, and value added has remained remarkably stable at between 20 and 23 percent of GDP since 1975. It is unlikely that this ratio can be increased significantly, even with considerable effort, because an increase in the tax burden would induce a shift of activities toward the informal sector while an increase in tariffs would lead to an increase in smuggling.

The second component of revenue is highly variable and arises from the margin between the world prices of coffee and cocoa (net of processing costs) and the producer prices. This component of revenue represented 16 percent of GDP at the peak of the boom in 1976, decreased to less than 3 percent during 1981–82, increased again to more than 10 percent in 1985, began to fall after 1986, and became negative in 1987.

Since the beginning of the commodity boom in 1976, the prices of coffee and cocoa have been adjusted to maintain parity between them and to keep their real value with respect to the consumer price index at a constant level. The stated policy (still in place) has been to provide a "stable price" to producers and to insulate them from the fluctuations in international prices. The government has thus captured the windfall gains of the commodity booms. The producer prices of coffee and cocoa have been increased only gradually, at about the same pace as the domestic price level. They have never been decreased, and any such move would be considered a strong signal by the government. Until 1987, producer prices were below the international prices (net of processing costs), and the margin constituted a tax on producers. At present, however, international prices are so low that the margin has become negative and producers are being subsidized.

This policy provided some protection to the agricultural sector from the recession that was caused by the sudden decline in government expenditures (this is partially illustrated in figure 14-1). Indeed, the rural sector may have suffered less in Côte d'Ivoire than in other countries from the adjustment measures.

Agricultural pricing and taxation policy has been an important element of the structural adjustment debate in Côte d'Ivoire. Following trends in the world market, the World Bank has consistently recommended an increase in the price of coffee relative to cocoa. These recommendations have led to only minor incentive programs for coffee, such as encouragement of pruning. At the then world prices, Ivoirian producers of coffee and cocoa were being subsidized, and this situation was untenable from a fiscal point of view. A lowering of producer prices seemed to be in order, but the move was opposed by the Ivoirian authorities and by producers, and for good reason. Because prices in the rest of the economy were rigid, a reduction in producer prices would have lowered the welfare of the agricultural sector and reduced the incentive for exports.

A partial solution to this problem would be to lower the price of cocoa and possibly coffee in order to finance an additional premium on nontraditional agricultural exports. But the revenue generated from lower coffee and cocoa prices would be insufficient to provide a meaningful premium. Furthermore, this policy would not restore the "equilibrium" values of the relative prices of agricultural products (including coffee and cocoa) and nontradable goods in the economy. In other words, the fixed nominal exchange rate and the apparent downward rigidity of the price level impose severe constraints on agricultural tax policy.

EXPENDITURE. Government expenditure represents a very large fraction of GDP (between 35 and 45 percent). Two changes in the pattern of expenditure have characterized the adjustment period: a decrease in capital expenditure and an increase in current expenditure. Capital expenditure was kept at a high level (more than 15 percent of GDP) until 1982. It was reduced to 7 percent of GDP from 1983 to 1984 and has been maintained at that level since then (table 14-2). Changes in capital expenditure constituted the dominant mode of policy adjustment in the 1980s.

Current expenditure actually increased during the adjustment period. It is remarkable that the wage bill, one of the two major components of current expenditure, increased as a share of GDP until 1983, decreased slightly in 1984 and 1985, then increased again in 1986 and 1987 and by 1987 was at a higher level than at the beginning of the adjustment process in 1980. This increase represents an important failure of the adjustment program: a sound principle of public finance is that the level of current expenditure be geared to the long-run revenue capacity of the government. This capacity, measured in terms of shares of GDP, was smaller at the end of the 1980s than it was before the commodity boom in 1975. Until the pattern of current government expenditure is altered, a major component of structural adjustment will be missing.

The second major component of current expenditures is interest on the debt. Most of the government debt is foreign debt because rules of the West African Monetary Union prevent the government from borrowing domestically. Interest payments as a share of GDP increased from 3 percent to 9 percent between 1980 and 1984 because of the rise in international interest rates. Although world rates have fallen since then, the interest burden as a share of GDP has remained almost at the same level because of the increase in the stock of the debt from 35 percent of GDP in 1980 to about 90 percent of GDP in 1989.

Because government expenditures represent such a large fraction of GDP, the composition of these expenditures on goods and services affects the allocation of resources between tradables and nontradables and so may affect the orientation of the economy toward foreign markets. The major links between fiscal policy and the allocation of resources are through wage policy and the impact of fiscal policy on the composition of aggregate demand.

Wage Policy and the Labor Market

The public sector is an important player in the labor market. Many analysts believe that it contributes to the rigidity of the domestic price level by ignoring macroeconomic conditions in the setting of wages. The government wage bill increased both as a share of GDP (see table 14-2) and in real terms during the first period of adjustment between 1980 and 1983, when the recession was gradually deepening. Only in 1984, when the fiscal crunch became acute, did the absolute level of the real wage bill decrease. Estimates for 1987 indicate that these cuts may have been only temporary.

The average wage in the public sector has an impact on the average wage in the economy. Wages in the public sector are not determined by conditions in the labor market but are a policy instrument, and current policy rules out any decrease in nominal wages in the public sector. The issue here is not whether wages are high in the public sector—although casual evidence shows that they are much higher in CFA countries than in non-CFA countries. The issue is whether the wage policy contributes to the rigidity of nominal wages and prices throughout the economy and, in addition, whether this rigidity prevents an adjustment of the real exchange rate. Given the fixed nominal exchange rate, this is an important issue that needs to be examined. Although there have been some studies of wage determination in Côte d'Ivoire (Levy and Newman 1988; van der Gaag and Vijverberg 1988), there have been no studies on the impact of public sector wages on the labor market.

Resource Allocation and Impact on the Real Exchange Rate

Fiscal policy instruments such as the level of government expenditure or the taxation of cash crops are important determinants of the real exchange rate, which should be taken into account in policy analysis. Devarajan and de Melo (1987) emphasize the importance of this effect when a large fraction of government expenditure goes to nontradables. An increase in government expenditure then induces an increase in the supply of nontradables and therefore a decrease in the supply of tradables. This induces a movement along the economy's production frontier and a decrease in the real exchange rate, which is determined by the marginal rate of transformation along the production frontier.

This argument is correct, but it is not particularly useful for policy analysis. An increase in expenditure on nontradables results in a shift of resources because of the crowding out of domestic resources by the government. The impact on the production of tradables depends on the concavity of the production frontier (that is, on the possibilities of substitution in the economy). If the degree of substitution is large (small), government expenditures have a large (small) impact on the production of tradables. Therefore, it is useful to focus directly on the composition of the crowding out of resources by the government.

The application of the Devarajan–de Melo analysis to the taxation of cash crops is misleading because it does not focus on the actual link between fiscal policy and the allocation of real resources. Thus government taxation of cash crops to finance expenditures on foreign goods would induce a shift of resources away from the tradables sector if a fraction of the taxable revenue is spent on nontradable goods. The measurement of the impact of fiscal policy on the allocation of resources depends on the composition of expenditures and on the degree of substitutability in the economy. Thus the first task in an analysis of the impact of government expenditure in Côte d'Ivoire is to break down expenditures by tradables and nontradables.

Savings, Investment, and External Equilibrium

Net savings by the government decreased after 1980 and became negative by the end of the decade: capital expenditure was reduced from 18 percent to 6 percent of GDP while the deficit was reduced only from 12 percent to 8 percent. Without a drastic adjustment in expenditure or revenue, or both, government net dissaving will prevent a resumption of growth. As in other heavily indebted countries, rising interest on the foreign debt has had a strong impact on the net savings rate. Most of the decrease in the net savings rate has been due to the increase in interest payments on the foreign debt. (This calculation assumes that interest payments of 7.4 percent of GDP are made; this has not been the case since April 1987, when arrears began to accumulate, but the general analysis nonetheless applies.)

The level of private savings has been remarkably stable, with the exception of the usual fluctuations due to recessions. The reason for this stability, however, is that the government, through its fiscal policy, has absorbed most of the external shocks to the economy. Devarajan and de Melo (1987) show a correlation between the budget deficit and the external deficit.

Conclusion

Although the structural adjustment program resulted in some improvements in the efficiency of the public sector, it did not achieve the main objective of establishing the conditions for a resumption of growth. After ten years, the price structure of the economy did not change to favor diversification. Thus the economy remained heavily dependent on two cash crops with bleak future prospects. Attempts to diversify the economy toward nontraditional exports were a failure: nontraditional exports remained at 5 percent of GDP since 1980. The policy measures that were taken were too little and too late. The needed adjustments in current expenditure and long-term revenue of the government and in the prices of coffee and cocoa were not made, while the export premium was introduced too late and at a time when deterioration in the government budget prevented effective implementation.

The fixed exchange rate has constituted an important institutional constraint. Although it has provided price stability in CFA countries relative to non-CFA countries in Africa, there have been costs associated with this policy. The combination of rigidities in the price system and the policy stance of the Ivoirian authorities has prevented a significant readjustment of the real exchange rate. Current economic policy prevents adjustments of relative prices within the agricultural sector, between the agricultural sector and the rest of the economy, and between the tradable and nontradable sectors. Furthermore, the lack of price adjustment contributes to the budget deficit. This worsening macroeconomic situation illustrates that microeconomic policy actions alone are insufficient. Côte d'Ivoire's suspension of interest payments has delayed the day of reckoning, but this is an unstable condition that will have to end soon.

Notes

1. This chapter describes the World Bank structural adjustment program in Côte d'Ivoire and discusses its contribution to the Ivoirian economy. It does not discuss the IMF program. Although additional analyses and counterfactual simulations would no doubt provide interesting additional insights, they could not be undertaken here because of space limitations and because a significant part of the design of the program was left to the IMF. The purpose here was simply to describe the macroeconomic adjustment of the Ivoirian economy and discuss the main issues.

2. This attribution of shares to external and internal factors is particularly simple and does not require a structural model for determining the endogenous supply response because the output of coffee and cocoa is inelastic in the short run. Thus an increase in world prices would have no effect on output. This analysis also ignores the induced effect on revenue of the 1985 recession brought on by the sharp reduction in government expenditure. These induced effects are very much smaller than the initial expenditure shock and are not necessary in this approximation of effects.

3. Treasury expenditures increased by 80 billion 1985 CFA francs, most of them unclassified payments that may have been in arrears; the government wage bill increased by only 6 billion CFA francs.

References

Devarajan, Shantayanan, and Jaime de Melo. 1987. "Adjustment with a Fixed Exchange Rate: Cameroon, Côte d'Ivoire, and Senegal." *World Bank Economic Review* 1 (May):447–87.

Levy, Victor, and John Newman. 1988. "Labor Market Adjustment during a Recession: The Micro and Macro Evidence." World Bank, Washington, D.C.

van der Gaag, Jacques, and Wim Vijverberg. 1988. *Wage Determinants in Côte d'Ivoire.* LSMS Working Paper 33. Washington, D.C.: World Bank.

Comments

Shantayanan Devarajan

CHRISTOPHE CHAMLEY'S chapter documents one of the saddest stories of the 1980s. After achieving an average annual GDP growth rate of 8 percent in 1965–75, Côte d'Ivoire's economy slowed to a grinding halt in the 1980s. The growth rate at the end of the 1980s averaged a little over 1 percent. Moreover, this slowdown was caused not by an adverse external shock but by a favorable shock: the coffee and cocoa boom of the mid-1970s. The windfall revenue from this boom was spent on an investment program. When the boom ended, the government continued spending, which led to unsustainable current account deficits, a debt overhang, and a secular decline in competitiveness. Worse still, this favorable terms of trade shock was known to be temporary at the outset, since it was caused by a frost in Brazil.

In his case study Chamley divides Côte d'Ivoire's adjustment experience into three phases: (1) an initial phase, when a structural adjustment loan was issued with only mild conditionality; (2) a second loan, with stricter conditionality, which was able to be met in part because of a favorable turn in coffee prices during the same period; and (3) a third phase, up to the end of the 1980s, in which the economy continued to perform poorly and many of the original structural adjustment issues continued to be discussed. Chamley further divides the policy measures into those dealing with internal and external balance, price incentives, and administrative reform. His overall conclusion on Côte d'Ivoire's structural adjustment experience can be summarized by the words "too little, too late." I will focus on the first two policy areas and on his overall conclusion.

On the subject of internal and external balance the most important point, not sufficiently emphasized by Chamley, is that in Côte d'Ivoire there is very little difference between internal and external balance. First, when the government fixes the producer price of the two major export crops (coffee and cocoa), changes in world prices will affect the fiscal deficit and current account deficit symmetrically. Second, in Côte d'Ivoire the fiscal deficit was financed by foreign borrowing (which is the mirror image of the current account deficit). This was necessary because, on the one hand, the country's membership in the CFA zone essentially prevents financing its deficit through seigniorage revenue and, on the other hand, the weakness of the domestic capital market makes government borrowing from the private sector virtually impossible. Third, a quick look at the facts shows that the current account and fiscal deficits were roughly the same percentage of GDP throughout the adjustment period.

The link between the two deficits has implications for the setting of price incentives in Côte d'Ivoire. For example, it may be thought that raising producer prices for coffee and cocoa would increase export incentives and thereby cut the current account deficit. But this would also increase the fiscal deficit (if expenditure is held constant). Furthermore, the fiscal deficit is financed by foreign borrowing, and the real appreciation associated with the inflow of foreign capital may act as a disincentive to export, with the end result being lower exports. By separating price incentives from the discussion of internal and external balance, Chamley fails to draw this connection between the two.

As for expenditure policy, Chamley points out clearly how this is both the cause of and possibly the solution to Côte d'Ivoire's problems. When coffee and cocoa prices fell in the late 1970s, government expenditure continued to rise, leading to an increased foreign debt and large current account deficits. In adjusting to this crisis, too, expenditure policy may be one of the few instruments available. As Chamley shows, the tax/GDP ratio in Côte d'Ivoire (leaving out the revenue from the price stabilization fund) stayed constant throughout the 1980s. The produce marketing board's revenue fluctuates with world prices and hence is procyclical. Thus the only way to address the twin deficits is to cut expenditure. It should be added that Côte d'Ivoire did undertake major expenditure cuts beginning in 1983. Capital expenditure fell from 18 percent of GDP in 1980 to 6 percent in 1986. Total government expenditure was reduced from 41 to 34 percent of GDP in the three-year period 1983–86. Chamley does not say why more could not have been achieved on the revenue side. He states that the World Bank decided to defer to the IMF on this issue. If this strategy has failed to yield the desired results, perhaps the

World Bank should consider an alternative strategy. For example, the value added tax may be used as a revenue-enhancing instrument.

Almost all the discussion about price incentives in Côte d'Ivoire is related to the country's membership in the CFA zone. Although lowering export taxes may provide price incentives, this may be counterproductive in the end. The most important price incentive for adjustment, however, is the real exchange rate, or the relative price of tradables to nontradables. In the CFA zone, with the nominal exchange rate fixed and world prices exogenous, the main means of affecting the real exchange rate is via the price of nontradables. This is linked to wages, which are in turn linked to the operation of the labor market in Côte d'Ivoire. It would have been helpful to learn more about this, especially about what steps are being taken to depreciate the real exchange rate.

Under the second SAL an attempt was made to simulate a devaluation by imposing a uniform tariff and subsidy scheme. First, quantitative restrictions were removed and a uniform import tariff of 40 percent was introduced; then an export subsidy of about 30 percent was established. The intent was to raise the price of tradables relative to that of nontradables and thereby achieve a real depreciation. Unfortunately, two factors prevented this outcome. First, the import tariff gave rise to smuggling, which undermined the collection of revenue from the tariff. Second, to cut costs the government stopped paying the export subsidies. Exporters were then worse off than before because the harmonization of the tariff and subsidy scheme led to higher tariffs on intermediate goods.

One final point about price incentives deserves mention. There is a temptation during the structural adjustment process to try to get as many prices as possible "right." There also appears to be a belief, implicit in Chamley's chapter and more explicit in other documents, that prices in Côte d'Ivoire are far from "right." Yet, even with such distortions, how did the economy manage to grow at 8 percent a year in the past? Was it luck, foreign aid, or some dynamic internal forces in the economy? Put another way, if only the internal and external balance of the country is restored, will the economy resume rapid growth?

Chamley describes two kinds of institutional reform that were introduced as part of the structural adjustment process: improvements in the selection of public projects and new methods of budgeting. Although these are useful reforms, why does nothing appear to have been done about tax administration? After all, if the problem was the fiscal deficit, it should be attacked from both the revenue and the expenditure sides.

Chamley's conclusion that adjustment in Côte d'Ivoire was a case of "too little, too late" should be qualified by asking what could have been done differently, given the institutional constraints in the country. Plainly, devaluing the exchange rate was not an option. It is true that some earlier cutbacks in government expenditure might have helped, although the expenditure/GDP ratio did fall significantly. Another option would have been to increase the tax/GDP ratio, whose obdurateness remains a puzzle.

Of course, to answer this question properly would require, as Chamley notes, some counterfactual simulations. He says that this would call for more analytical work. Nevertheless, he attributes the success of the second SAL to good luck (high coffee and cocoa prices) and good policy in equal proportions. This *is* a counterfactual simulation, although we are not sure what analytical framework he used.

More generally, there are several analytical frameworks being used both directly and indirectly as part of the SAL appraisal process. It is worth asking what counterfactuals were performed as part of the appraisal and what could be performed today with these models.

Some perspective on the constraints on Côte d'Ivoire's adjustment experience can be obtained by comparing its performance with that of Ghana, an economy that is similar in many ways but with one crucial difference: Ghana is not a member of the CFA zone and hence can use the nominal exchange rate as an instrument of adjustment. During the 1980s Côte d'Ivoire had consistently lower inflation than Ghana. In fact, the highest annual rate in Côte d'Ivoire was lower than the lowest observed in Ghana. But at the end of the period Côte d'Ivoire had a much higher foreign debt: 125 percent of GDP, as opposed to Ghana's 40 percent of GDP.

This contrast illustrates the tradeoff involved in belonging to the CFA zone: by relinquishing the seigniorage tax as a means of raising revenue, countries maintain lower inflation rates. However, they may have to rely to a greater degree on foreign borrowing, which may leave them with serious long-term problems.

15 *Ghana: Ending Chaos*

Chad Leechor

At the lowest point of the economic crisis in Ghana in 1982 and 1983, the country was a scene of devastation. Power systems had ceased to function, even in Accra, the capital city. Communication, postal, and railroad services had broken down. Tax collection had fallen to about 5 percent of GDP. Investment had fallen below the level needed to maintain the capital stock. Foreign exchange reserves had been nearly depleted. Real income per capita, which had been falling for almost a decade, was by 1983 a third below the level reached in the early 1970s (figure 15-1).

The main cause of the crisis was a failure of economic policy. Fiscal discipline was weak as the government pursued extensive industrialization and public sector employment without commensurate efforts to increase revenue. Budgetary deficits were financed mainly through monetary expansion, which accelerated inflation. Because the official exchange rate was virtually unchanged for a decade, it created substantial overvaluation of the local currency. Domestic production was inhibited by extensive controls on prices and distribution. Exports were depressed by cumbersome regulations, explicit export taxes, and hidden taxes in the form of low producer prices and overvaluation of the exchange rate.

Although these policies led to economic decline, the severity of the crisis was also attributable to several shocks beyond the control of the government. First, a protracted drought ravaged Sub-Saharan Africa, and Ghana was not immune to its destructive effects. Agriculture, the largest sector, was particularly hard hit, and the repercussions were felt throughout the economy. Second, the world price of cocoa, Ghana's predominant export crop, had taken a sharp turn downward, while the price of crude oil, Ghana's major import, had gone up significantly. Third, about a million Ghanaian workers returned home from Nigeria. Ghana was thus deprived of a customary source of foreign exchange from remittances, while its unemployment rose. External debt had little to do with the crisis, however, as the stock of debt was only about US$1 billion in 1982 (4 percent of GDP at the official exchange rate or 20 percent at a more realistic rate) and the debt service ratio was about 15 percent.

Before 1983 the Ghanaian authorities had progressively increased control over the economy. As inflation rose, there was a tendency to step

Figure 15-1. Index of Per Capita Income in Ghana, 1957–87

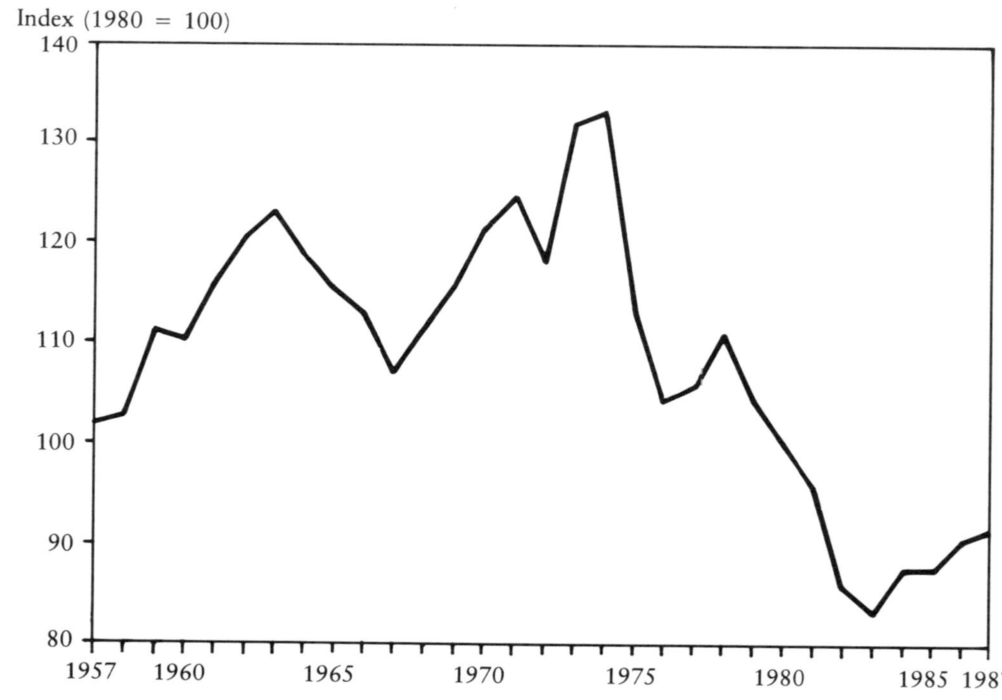

Sources: IMF, *International Financial Statistics*, various issues; Roemer (1984).

up enforcement of price controls. As trade deficits widened, imports were increasingly restricted through licensing requirements and foreign exchange allocation. As foreign exchange reserves dwindled, efforts were made to limit the number of exporters and to administer export prices, both with the objective of stopping foreign exchange leakages. Much attention was devoted to alleviating undesirable economic symptoms, while the more fundamental causes were seldom addressed. The cedi (¢) was devalued twice between 1974 and 1983, raising the exchange rate from ¢1.15 to ¢2.75 to the U.S. dollar. But the adjustment was insignificant in relation to the forty-six-fold increase in the domestic price level that had occurred in the intervening years.

Adjustment policies had been deliberately avoided since 1971, when an early experiment was prematurely aborted. At that time, in response to a balance of payments crisis, the Busia administration devalued the cedi sharply, by 82 percent against the U.S. dollar. The measure proved divisive; although cocoa farmers and rural workers generally welcomed it, urban consumers were vehemently opposed. A military coup was carried out with little resistance, and the new administration quickly reversed the exchange rate policy and set the cedi at its original level. Subsequent administrations appeared to regard the episode as a warning against adjustment policies in general.

The Adjustment Program

A far-reaching policy reform, the Economic Recovery Program (ERP), was announced in April 1983. It called for increased fiscal discipline; more realistic pricing of goods, factors, and foreign exchange; and a determined, if gradual, shift away from administrative control toward more reliance on markets. In almost three decades of Ghana's independence, this approach to policymaking had never taken hold, so at its onset it seemed fraught with dangers. It was feared that those who would be adversely affected might try to derail the reform process through economic or political means. Structural rigidities threatened to slow and diminish the supply response. In spite of these apparent risks, the ERP was launched and sustained through a very difficult initial stage. As it turned out, the program was successfully implemented over four years and was followed by a more comprehensive plan designed to build on the initial gains and to facilitate broader structural adjustments.

The ERP was conceived by the government of Ghana in collaboration with the World Bank and the International Monetary Fund (IMF). Support from the IMF was critical in the initial stage, which involved primarily stabilization measures to restore internal and external balances. The role of the World Bank was more prominent in a subsequent stage, when the government, having demonstrated its commitment to stabilization, attempted to rehabilitate the economy and restore growth.

Stabilization Measures

The ERP gave high priority to fighting inflation at home and securing a sustainable external balance with an adequate flow of imports. To curb inflation, which had been rising through the 1970s and had exceeded 100 percent a year in the early 1980s, efforts were made to improve fiscal control and thereby to restrain monetary expansion. Initially, fiscal control was achieved mainly through a substantial cut in government expenditure from 10.2 percent of GDP in 1982 to 8.6 percent in 1983. The cut was implemented across the board and encompassed reductions in real wages and operating expenditures as well as in development outlays. Subsequently the emphasis shifted to resource mobilization, particularly increased tax revenue, to support an expansion in public services and infrastructure. Government revenue (inclusive of grants) rose steadily from 5.6 percent of GDP in 1983 to 13 percent in 1986 (figure 15-2). Budget deficits were reduced from about 7.5 percent of GDP during the economic downturn in 1979–82 to 2.7 percent of GDP in 1983 and well below 2 percent of GDP thereafter.

In working to achieve external balance, the Ghanaian authorities did not want to rely on compression of imports, as had been done in the past. But at the onset of the ERP, prospects for earning foreign exchange were grim because the exchange rate had been misaligned for more than a decade. The combination of high domestic inflation and little change in the nominal exchange rate had made the cedi one of the most overvalued currencies in the world. Since the required adjustment was extremely large, the government chose to undertake periodic devaluations over several years. In 1983 the exchange rate was devalued from ¢2.75 to the U.S. dollar to ¢30, a magnitude seldom seen elsewhere. Further devaluations brought the exchange rate to ¢50 to the U.S. dollar in 1984, ¢60 in 1985, and ¢90 in 1986 (figure 15-3). Since 1987 the exchange rate has been determined by foreign exchange auctions.

Before adequate foreign exchange earnings were secured, however, essential imports had to be procured to maintain domestic production and to meet local demand. Although Ghana's external debt was moderate in size, the fact that its payments were in arrears had blocked its access to external resources. The IMF provided a sizable bridging fund, which allowed Ghana to pay off a large part of its external arrears and thereby improve its ability to borrow abroad to finance its imports.

Adjustment Measures

To assist recovery and encourage growth, adjustment measures under the ERP attempted to shift away from administrative control of allocative

Figure 15-2. Government Revenue and Expenditure as a Percentage of GDP in Ghana, 1978–87

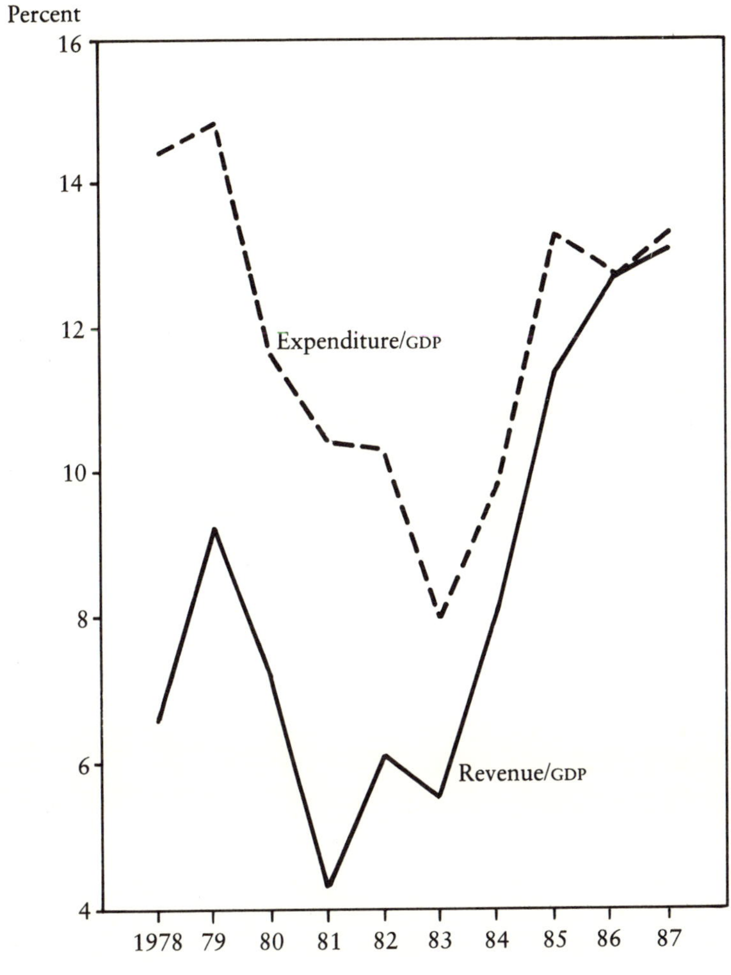

Source: IMF, *International Financial Statistics*, various issues.

mechanisms and move toward greater reliance on markets. The shift was meant to be selective and gradual, however, because the magnitude of existing distortions was overwhelming. Moreover, the depleted infrastructure severely constrained production and distribution, while the resources available were extremely limited. Too abrupt a change might have entailed excessive economic and social costs. Firms might not have

Figure 15-3. Nominal and Real Cedi Exchange Rate Relative to the U.S. Dollar, Annual Average, 1978–87

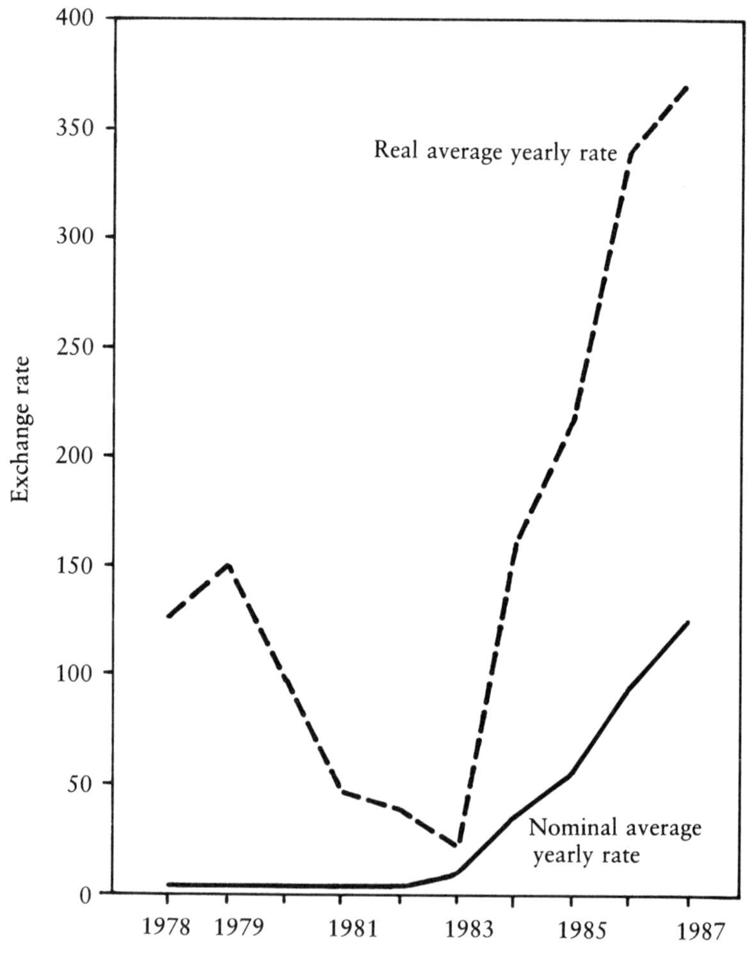

Source: IMF, *International Financial Statistics*, various issues.

survived the transition period, and vulnerable groups might have experienced undue hardship. The World Bank played an active role in supporting this transition, assisting in the design of the adjustment program and providing resources for removing the most serious obstacles on the path to recovery.

Given the environment in which the ERP was launched, extensive reforms were needed. A full description would be tedious and not particularly instructive, so the following discussion concentrates on the major reforms, grouped according to broad objectives.

THE EXTERNAL SECTOR. The first and probably most important measure under the ERP was to correct the massive misalignment of the exchange rate. The series of devaluations begun in April 1983 effected a large real depreciation. By early 1987 the exchange rate had reached the level of ¢160 to the U.S. dollar, compared with the rate of ¢2.75 prevailing in early 1983. The process of adjustment was somewhat convoluted, consisting of multiple rates initially, followed by unification and a few large devaluations. Finally, the official rate was left to be determined in a weekly auction.

On trade policy, the ERP attempted to increase exports and trade flows overall, rather than relying on import restrictions to reduce external imbalances. The exchange rate policy was a primary instrument for providing incentives to actual and potential exporters. In addition, foreign exchange was allocated to ensure the rehabilitation and recovery of traditional exports. In the interim phase, a foreign exchange retention scheme was introduced to reduce the remaining bias against exports. The scheme was gradually phased out as the exchange rate moved toward a sustainable level. Export procedures were simplified, and administrative price setting was abolished. The World Bank assisted the export promotion efforts through three adjustment loans. The first one was for the rehabilitation of traditional exports; foreign exchange and local currency funds were provided to revive the cocoa, timber, gold, and diamond sectors. The other two, an industrial sector adjustment loan and a structural adjustment loan, attempted among other things to promote nontraditional exports through incentives, access to foreign exchange, and relief from indirect taxes.

Although import controls were extensive at the time the ERP was launched, an immediate shift to a tariff-based import regime was considered too risky in the presence of remaining exchange rate overvaluation and foreign exchange shortages. Instead, the licensing system was streamlined, mainly by establishing priorities in the annual import program and integrating import and foreign exchange licenses. In addition, no restrictions were placed on imports unless foreign exchange was requested from the government. Subsequently, a foreign exchange auction was introduced as an allocative mechanism, and an open general license was granted for the foreign exchange acquired. Import tariffs were reduced and simplified. The World Bank played a major role in this process of gradual trade liberalization, supporting the adjustment measures through a structural adjustment credit and two reconstruction import credits.

Apart from trade, the government significantly reduced its arrears in external payments from more than US$200 million in 1983 to less than US$20 million in 1985. Ghana's improved credit standing and its efforts in seeking external assistance, both financial and technical, enabled it to draw on external capital during the economic reconstruction.

PUBLIC FINANCE. Improved fiscal discipline was a major objective of the ERP. The strategy adopted was to restrain expenditure sharply at the outset and then to allow some increase in expenditure as more revenue was raised. Much attention was devoted to the structures of the tax system and the expenditure program to minimize the adverse impact of individual measures.

Revenue gains came primarily from the devaluations, which increased the duties collected on imports. A temporary import surcharge was also applied to mop up scarcity rents resulting from quantitative restrictions. Export taxes, with the exception of the cocoa tax, were phased out. Personal income taxes had become highly punitive under protracted inflation since deductions lost their real value and tax brackets became small in real terms. Gradual reforms were introduced. Another important change was in tax administration, which was upgraded by layoffs of incompetent staff, recruitment of a new managerial and professional team, improved compensation, and ultimately reorganization of the tax bureau. Administrative fees, which had declined in real value after many years of high inflation, were raised across the board. The World Bank and the IMF collaborated in providing technical assistance for the reform of tax policy and administration.

Expenditures were severely restrained initially, despite obvious deficiencies in infrastructure and civil service salaries. As revenue rose, however, remedial actions were quickly undertaken. In 1984 and 1985 civil service wages and salaries were raised substantially. By 1985 the gains in revenue were sufficient to permit a significant increase in development expenditures as well, much of which was for rehabilitating transport facilities. In 1986, however, the introduction of an overambitious pay scale caused fiscal control to deteriorate. The overall fiscal balance for the year was eventually restored, however, as the new pay scale was revised downward and development expenditures were reduced.

The World Bank supported the process of rationalizing expenditures initially with two import credits for measures to curtail subsidies, particularly for fertilizer, and to increase accountability for public investment. Subsequently, greater financial discipline was imposed on public enterprises to limit their losses and the need for budgetary transfers. These measures were supported in part by an industrial sector adjustment credit and a structural adjustment credit.

DEREGULATION. At the inception of the ERP, the domestic economy was a fifth below the peak reached in the 1970s. Much of the capital stock was in disrepair. Intermediate goods were unavailable because of foreign exchange shortages. Moreover, many producers had terminated or scaled down production as a result of pervasive controls on prices and distribution.

A prominent feature of the ERP was its reliance on incentives and competition as stimuli for production. This approach deviated sharply from the previous reliance on price and distribution controls, which had depressed profits and led to smuggling and shortages. The government moved with caution, however, lifting controls gradually, and for some products no deregulation was attempted.

Prices of consumer goods were decontrolled first. The number of goods subject to price control was reduced from twenty-three to thirteen in 1984 and to eight in 1985. Price controls remained for sensitive inputs, including petroleum products, cotton, tobacco, and cocoa. The objective of price setting changed, however, from limiting consumer costs to stimulating producer responses. Producer prices for cocoa, for example, were raised well in excess of the devaluations; as a result, the ratio of producer prices to border prices rose from about 20 percent in 1982 to about 50 percent in 1985. Similar increases were also granted for petroleum products, cotton, and tobacco.

Changes in distribution controls followed a similar pattern. State-owned monopolies were progressively eliminated along with price controls. In some cases, only prices remained subject to control while production and distribution were open to competition. Cocoa, however, was subject to both price and distribution controls because of its strategic role in generating foreign exchange and government revenue. But some improvements were made in efficiency by liquidating estate holdings, cutting the work force, and streamlining operations.

INSTITUTIONAL REFORMS. The civil service and state-owned enterprises were extensively restructured to contain operating costs and enhance productivity. Staffs were widely cut in the public sector, and compensation was upgraded for those remaining. (In 1986, for instance, the cocoa board took 25,000 "ghost" workers off the payroll.) The management and operating procedures in many major state-owned enterprises, including the cocoa board and the gold mine, were reviewed with the assistance of local and foreign experts.

Economic Performance

Following implementation of the ERP, aggregate production rose by more than 6 percent annually in constant prices for three years, compared with a 3 percent annual decline in the three years preceding the ERP. Domestic savings and investment also rose significantly, their respective shares in GDP nearly doubling. The largest gains came in 1984, the first full year after the ERP was announced and implemented. In later years growth was more moderate, but still significant.

Economic Responses and Recovery

The response was most dramatic in the industrial sector, where capacity utilization had been very low. Imports of intermediate goods and spare parts, made possible initially by the injection of foreign exchange from the IMF and the World Bank, allowed manufacturing firms to expand production rapidly. After the introduction of the ERP, real manufactured output rose at an annual rate of 14 percent. The remaining industrial subsectors showed some recovery, although not as much as manufactures. For the industrial sector as a whole, real output rose by 11 percent a year during the adjustment period, compared with a decline of about the same magnitude before adjustment.

Agricultural response was also strong. In particular, food crop production rose by about 80 percent in 1984 and by about 10 percent thereafter. This expansion, however, cannot be attributed to policy change alone. The return of normal rains after a protracted period of drought helped make the turnaround possible. The value of output in forestry and logging grew by about 3 percent a year in constant prices. The agricultural sector as a whole grew by more than 5 percent a year. Exports of cocoa rose in foreign exchange value by 43 percent and timber by nearly 100 percent within two years of the introduction of the ERP.

The upsurge of activities in agriculture and industry was accompanied by significant growth in the services sector. As expected, the transport and trading subsectors, which had the most extensive linkages to agriculture and manufacturing, grew the fastest. The entire service sector grew at an annual rate of 6 percent after the introduction of the ERP, in contrast to its downward trend before 1983.

Along with production, savings and investment also recovered even though they were not of immediate priority under the ERP. The rate of fixed capital formation rose from a low 4.5 percent of GDP before the ERP to 8.3 percent thereafter. Private saving was largely unchanged after the introduction of the ERP, but dissaving by the public sector was cut substantially so that net domestic savings rose from 4.2 percent of GDP to about 7.2 percent. Despite this recovery, however, the level of savings and investment remained low by international standards. This outcome may have been anticipated by the authorities, who had emphasized rehabilitation and increased utilization of existing productive capacity under the ERP. The second phase of the ERP, which was launched in 1987, appears to have moved toward a greater emphasis on resource mobilization and capital formation.

One casualty of the economic crisis was the financial sector. Inflation and general economic deterioration substantially eroded public confidence. Domestic financial assets lost their real value over time. Savers turned to assets less susceptible to inflationary erosion, including foreign currency (such as the CFA franc) and real assets. The considerable financial depth that Ghana had attained by the mid-1970s was lost in the process, as the ratio of bank deposits to GDP fell from 27 percent in 1977 to about 10 percent in 1983 and 1984. Some progress was made thereafter, as nominal deposit rates were raised to achieve positive real returns, and the deposits to GDP ratio rose slightly to about 14 percent in 1986. The financial sector still has a long way to go to achieve full recovery, however.

Macroeconomic Balance

A major achievement of the ERP has been improved fiscal control. Budgetary deficits were substantially reduced over the adjustment period, from an average annual rate of about 8.8 percent of GDP in the decade preceding the ERP to an average of 1.6 percent from 1983 to 1986. This improvement was not accompanied by comparable credit and monetary discipline, however, and inflation remained a serious issue throughout the adjustment period.

In each year after the introduction of the ERP, the central bank extended far more new credit to the public sector than it needed for deficit financing (see table 15-1).[1] This lending was the main cause of the rapid growth in high-powered money (monetary base), which averaged about 50 percent a year from 1983 to 1986. With the money multiplier remaining unchanged over the period, the money supply grew by the same rate as the monetary base. Such rapid monetary expansion put considerable pressure on prices, even when scarcity rents fell as a result of increased production and imports. The consumer price index rose by an annual rate of 25 percent between 1983 and 1986, which was much lower than before the crisis (about 60 percent), but quite high in view of the considerable success in deficit reduction.

External Balance

Before the adjustment program, import and foreign exchange controls had been the main instruments for balancing external payments. The resulting shortages of imports had constrained production and consumption and lowered the overall volume of international trade. Import

Table 15-1. Selected Monetary Aggregates for Ghana, 1983–88
(billions of cedis)

Aggregate	*1983*	*1984*	*1985*	*1986*
Central bank credit to public sector	24.5	38.6	57.5	94.5
Government	24.3	35.1	45.0	78.0
Parastatals	0.2	3.5	12.5	15.9
Increase in public sector credit	—	14.2	18.8	37.0
Monetary base	14.6	21.8	29.6	47.3
Increase in monctary base	—	7.2	7.8	17.7
Money supply (M1)	16.7	26.8	38.3	55.2
Increase in M1	—	10.1	11.5	16.9
Government deficits	4.9	4.8	7.2	−0.3

Source: Bank of Ghana and World Bank staff estimates.

restrictions had usually been retained until a favorable exogenous shift occurred in the terms of trade.

A new approach was pursued under the ERP. Instead of relying on import restraints, the authorities attempted to create three conditions consistent with a sustainable external balance. They wanted to (1) increase production, (2) reduce absorption, primarily by controlling government expenditures, and (3) increase external demand for domestic goods (expenditure switching) by eliminating overvaluation of the cedi. This new approach allowed imports to rise substantially, from about US$539 million in 1983 to US$780 million in 1986. Exports, stimulated by devaluation of the exchange rate, increased even more. Thus the trade gaps were narrowed during the recovery without any sacrifice in domestic consumption or production, and the volume of international trade was expanded.

The new approach also inspired confidence in the government's economic management. As a result, the prospects for foreign investment and external assistance improved, and the problem of capital flight became less serious. During the recovery period the net capital account balance shifted significantly in the country's favor, complementing the improved trade balance (see table 15-2). The strengthened external position allowed the country to pay off a large part of its external arrears and to replenish its foreign exchange reserves.

A Long-Term Perspective on the Recovery

Clearly, the economic recovery since the inception of the ERP has been impressive. The standard of living for the average Ghanaian has improved

Table 15-2. Balance of Payments in Ghana, 1979–86
(millions of U.S. dollars)

Item	*1979*	*1980*	*1981*	*1982*	*1983*	*1984*	*1985*	*1986*
Current account								
Merchandise	184	132	−310	10	−100	−115	−95	−7
Exports (f.o.b.)	1,066	1,104	711	641	439	566	632	773
Imports (c.i.f.)	−882	−972	−1021	−631	−539	−681	−727	−780
Nonfactor services	−95	−104	−113	−85	−65	−91	−110	−130
Resource balance	89	28	−423	−75	−165	−206	−204	−137
Net factor income	−46	−80	−81	−82	−82	−81	−111	−105
Private transfers (net)	−3	−3	−4	−1	17	73	33	49
Current account balance	40	−55	−508	−158	−230	−215	−283	−193
Capital account								
Grants (official transfers)	82	83	87	84	72	141	93	115
Official long-term loans (net)	108	96	49	16	15	131	108	213
Official medium-term loans (net)	−14	−13	42	97	13	−42	−70	−102
Trust fund	34	0	0	0	0	−1	−7	−11
Direct foreign investment	−3	16	16	16	2	2	6	4
Private capital (net)	−5	0	−13	−5	12	−14	5	18
IDA allocation[a]	14	14	14	0	0	0	0	0
Capital[b]	−26	12	0	13	61	−85	15	−18
Errors and omissions	−105	−141	63	−36	−187	−38	16	−18
Net capital account	85	67	258	185	−13	94	165	138
Overall balance	125	12	−250	27	−243	−121	−117	−56

a. From the International Development Association of the World Bank.
b. Not elsewhere specified.
Source: Bank of Ghana and World Bank staff estimates.

considerably since 1983. Policymaking has improved as well. Its success has made Ghana something of a model for other African countries and earned praise from the world media and the international community.

A more cautious observer, however, would look at the recent recovery not only in the light of the crisis that preceded it but also in the context of longer-term development. At the depth of the crisis, per capita income had fallen by more than one-sixth of its level at independence. By the end of 1987, four full years after the adjustment program started, Ghana's real per capita income was still one-third below the peak level reached in the mid-1970s and one-tenth below the level prevailing at independence in 1956 (see figure 15-1). There has been no real gain in the average standard of living after three decades. Although economic output more than doubled in the postindependence period, population grew even faster, leaving the average person with less income than at independence.

Thus Ghana has lost considerable ground in terms of development. Once one of the most prosperous developing countries, Ghana is today among the poorest. Since Ghana's independence, developing countries as a whole have experienced an average annual growth rate in per capita income of 3 percent, while African countries averaged 1.7 percent. In this period per capita income therefore rose by 109 percent in developing countries as a whole and by about 53 percent in African countries, while it declined by about 10 percent in Ghana. Ghana's record since the adjustment program started has been much better, however, and compares favorably with trends in the rest of the world. In the five-year period 1983–88 the economy maintained an average growth rate of 5 percent a year.

Assessment of Conditionality

What was the role of the World Bank in Ghana's adjustment process, and what was Ghana's record of compliance with adjustment loan conditionality between 1983 and 1986? In answering these questions, only the conditions made in the context of adjustment loans extended by the World Bank between 1983 and 1986 are examined. The following analysis does not review the ERP as a whole, the conditionality set by the IMF, or traditional World Bank project operations. Also excluded is the structural adjustment credit that became effective in fiscal 1986, since it is too early to draw any firm conclusions about it. Through this process of elimination, four adjustment loans are left for the present review: the first reconstruction import credit, an export rehabilitation credit, the second reconstruction import credit, and the industrial sector adjustment credit.

Before presenting the results of this analysis, several caveats must be stated. First, the assessment reflects judgments based on partial information. There are gaps in information about the deviation of actual measures from required conditions, sometimes because no indicators for measuring progress were specified. The conclusions reached are necessarily tentative. Second, the conditions set for the loans do not necessarily reflect the full role of the World Bank in the adjustment process. Many actions considered desirable by the World Bank may not appear explicitly as loan conditions. The government may not have been willing to endorse them or, conversely, it may have been ready to implement them without prompting from the World Bank. In other cases, a provision might not be included if it were already covered in an agreement with the IMF. Thus the conditions reviewed in this section cover only a small fraction of the common ground between the World Bank and the government.

Scope of Conditionality

The scope of World Bank conditionality varied in the course of Ghana's economic recovery. Initially, when the country was still in the depth of the economic crisis, the World Bank set conditions mainly for emergency relief. As the country recovered and the World Bank acquired experience in policy-based lending, the focus shifted to rehabilitation and capacity utilization. Finally, in 1986 and 1987 the questions of growth and the quality of investment were tackled through industrial sector and structural adjustment credits. As the objectives grew more complex, the number of conditions expanded from ten per loan in 1983 to sixteen in 1985 and thirty-nine in 1987.

The conditions under these loans were generally clearly stated. Assessing compliance is not straightforward, however. In some cases no indicators were specified for measuring progress and no targets or dates were identified. For instance, one loan required reinstatement of the duty drawback program before release of the second tranche, but no indicators were specified. Reinstatement of the duty drawback program in itself would have served no useful purpose, however; what needed to be demonstrated was that the duty drawback program had been of benefit to exporters. And it was virtually impossible to monitor compliance or to determine whether any progress had been made in the case of conditions that simply called for the establishment of a task force or study group to resolve specific problems (such as divestiture of public enterprises or dissolution of the cocoa marketing mechanisms). Clearly the mere existence of such teams served no relevant purpose, but no method was specified for determining whether the intended work was being done.

Implementation

Ghana's record of policy implementation is nonetheless very good, perhaps exceptional. The core conditions for all the adjustment loans were

Table 15-3. Ghana's Implementation of Conditionalities under World Bank Adjustment Loans

Satisfactory implementation	*Partial implementation*	*Little or no progress*
Exchange rate policy	Civil service compensation	Cocoa marketing arrangements
Foreign exchange allocation	Financial management reform (cocoa board)	Monetary and credit discipline
Import liberalization	Divestiture of public enterprises	Prudential management and regulatory framework for the financial sector
Resource mobilization	Petroleum products	Duty drawback scheme
Decontrol of prices and distribution	Domestic indirect taxation	
Pricing of agricultural products	Income tax policy	
Pricing of freight and utilities	Import taxation	
Institutional reforms in civil service and mining	Export taxation	
Commercialization of fertilizer sector		

Source: World Bank reports.

implemented to a satisfactory degree. This record is particularly remarkable given the depth of the original crisis and therefore the difficulty of meeting the adjustment conditions. Exchange rate adjustment provides an illustration; the cedi was devalued from ¢2.75 to ¢90.0 to the U.S. dollar in just three years, a change so drastic that it has seldom been matched elsewhere. Resource mobilization is another example; the ratio of revenue to GDP rose from 5.6 percent in 1983 to 13 percent in 1986, another rare achievement. A summary of Ghana's record of compliance with conditionalities is presented in table 15-3.

Implementation of loan conditions has generally been successful when the government has endorsed the actions to be taken and when timetables and indicators of progress have been clearly specified. Political difficulty did not appear to impede progress when these two conditions were satisfied. Devaluations and tax increases are clearly among the most politically sensitive matters, yet they were successfully implemented.

A lack of strong government endorsement has usually precluded subsequent progress. In the case of the cocoa procurement system, for example, the government consistently resisted the use of alternative marketing mechanisms, although it allowed limited institutional reforms of the existing monopoly. Proposals made by the World Bank under various adjustment loans were modified along the way and appeared in much weaker forms as legal conditions. The duty drawback scheme also lacked strong government endorsement. Decisionmakers appeared not to fully appreciate its significance, while working-level officials were concerned more with protecting revenue than with implementing the duty drawback scheme. As a result, little was achieved in either of these areas.

A firm endorsement does not in itself guarantee successful implementation, however. Problems may arise because of technical difficulties (due possibly to limited capacity) or the absence of any indicators of progress. Inadequate control of monetary and credit aggregates is an important example of a technical constraint to implementation. In the case of Ghana the government was clearly committed to fighting inflation, but the thinness of the bond market (for deficit financing) and the massive devaluations that were undertaken impeded full implementation of monetary and credit controls. Civil service compensation is another area in which there was agreement on the merit of action but implementation was less than satisfactory. The inadequacy of the data prevented the World Bank from providing appropriate guidance on the size and timing of salary increases. As a result, the pay scale implemented by the government in 1986, although consistent with the World Bank's condition, turned out to be too costly and had to be canceled.

Sustainability

Since 1983 the government of Ghana has generally been receptive to the World Bank's approach to economic management. Progress has been substantial, and the economic gains have been widely shared. The government is likely to stay the course rather than revert to the policies that led to the crisis. In this general sense the World Bank's approach, as represented by its loan conditionality, appears to be sustainable. Moreover, through the adjustment loans, the World Bank has contributed to institution building and an internalization of essential skills, which should prevent some of the implementation problems and reversals observed in the past.

The risks of reversal appear to be manageable. Unlike the case in many countries where external debts represent a crushing burden, Ghana's debts are of recent vintage and have been actively managed. Domestic resistance to adjustment policies is limited to specific, uncoordinated interest groups, with no threat of escalating to alarming proportions. The economy's weak spots are mainly the continuing heavy dependence on the cocoa sector and the slow emergence of new exports. Reforms are also needed to prevent the financial sector from becoming a serious obstacle to structural change and growth. In particular, it is necessary to restructure the nonperforming assets of the banking sector and to build up a system of prudential regulations.

Tranching

The World Bank made extensive use of conditions for the release of tranches in the four adjustment credits reviewed here and used the timing of actions to achieve a variety of purposes. Under an early adjustment loan prepared at the depth of the crisis, quick disbursement was deemed essential, and many conditions were required before the appraisal. The other early loans also had "up front" conditionality. When it would take time to implement a particular condition (such as institutional reform, training, and drafting of proposals) or when no government endorsement was evident (as with retrenchment of the work force and increases in utility rates), a tranche-release provision or dated covenant was used. Conditions in this category were the most numerous. A large and increasing number of actions were recommended but not mandatory. This category covered measures that were desirable but not strictly essential and measures that were essential but politically difficult to implement.

Social Implications of Adjustment

The adjustment program brought considerable gains to many traditionally vulnerable groups. The largest group of beneficiaries was perhaps the rural workers engaged in the production of traditional export items, particularly cocoa and timber, who accounted for more than half the work force. As producer prices were raised, real wages in rural areas went up accordingly. The economic recovery also improved the circumstances of the rural population as the unemployed were rehired or found new jobs. The working poor in urban areas benefited from large increases in the minimum wage. In addition, improved resource mobilization by the government enabled an increase in social services and improvement of infrastructure.

The distribution of the economic gains of the adjustment program was perhaps uneven and was certainly not universal, however. People who had had access to unrealistically cheap foreign exchange lost out under the new regime. A large number of workers in the civil service and in public enterprises were laid off, although the impact of the layoffs was mitigated by severance payments and retraining. And the large proportion of the population that remained outside the organized and monetized economy was unable to share fully in the gains made under the adjustment program. The government was aware of this problem and in 1987 launched a major poverty-alleviation effort with the support of the World Bank (Program of Actions to Mitigate the Social Costs of Adjustment, or PAMSCAD).

Conclusions and Lessons

Several lessons may be derived from Ghana's experience with adjustment and economic recovery.

First, for all the praise lavished on Ghana's performance, four years of recovery have not brought the country back to where it was four years before the crisis. Per capita income today is lower than it was at independence three decades ago and far below the peak level reached a decade earlier. But given the length and depth of the country's economic decline, a long consolidation period may be needed. Confidence, once lost, is not easily restored. Private sector responses to current policies may therefore be slow although they may not yet have been exhausted.

Second, the experience of Ghana shows that fiscal restraint does not necessarily rule out substantial recovery. Contrary to common apprehension, the economy rebounded at a time when government spending was sharply reduced. Expenditure cuts often removed waste, as with the termination of payments to "ghost" workers in civil service and state enterprises.

Third, and also rather unsettling to conventional wisdom, fiscal control in a developing country does not automatically produce monetary control or price stability. In addition to fiscal control, other causes of credit and monetary growth must be taken into account. In the case of Ghana, the massive devaluations and the substantial primary price increases, which increased the costs of state-owned marketing boards, appeared to have contributed to the inflationary pressure.

Fourth, when external debt service obligations are small, devaluations can provide incentives for the private sector and raise revenue for the government at the same time. Of course, this outcome was made possible in Ghana by its particular economic structure. The devaluations' stimulatory effects on export production (in the primary sector) outweighed their contractionary effects on imported inputs (in the industrial sector) and consumer goods. Tariff revenue increased as the import bill grew in terms of domestic currency. This result makes exchange rate adjustment a more attractive instrument than tax increases.

Fifth, there are no clear indications that Ghana's experience can be transferred to other countries. Some of the uncertainties arise from the difficulties of making large exchange rate adjustments and sharp expenditure cuts and mobilizing substantial revenue. The Ghanaians had been through so much economic trouble for so long that they were willing to put up with extraordinary hardship during the adjustment period. Moreover, the Ghanaian leaders had an unusual strength of political will, particularly during the first two years of adjustment when difficult measures had to be undertaken before any benefits of recovery were visible. These two critical factors may not be present in other countries.

Note

1. This excess borrowing from the central bank is a curious phenomenon. Other instruments were also available for deficit financing (sale of government bonds or borrowing from commercial banks, for example), and even if these alternatives were not used the government could have limited its borrowing from the central bank to an amount equal to the deficits. Why the government borrowed so much more than it needed is an interesting question, but it lies beyond the scope of this paper.

References

IMF. Various years. *International Financial Statistics.* Washington, D.C.: International Monetary Fund.

Roemer, Michael. 1984. "Ghana 1950–1980: Missed Opportunities." In A. C. Harberger, *World Economic Growth.* San Francisco: Institute for Contemporary Studies.

Comments

Lyn Squire

CHAD LEECHOR has presented a very thorough survey of the adjustment process in Ghana, and I am in broad agreement with his assessment of the policy measures that have been taken. My comments go beyond his analysis in two ways. First, I discuss some of the noneconomic factors that lie behind the policy measures and that are essential for a successful adjustment program. Second, I examine whether the adjustment process in Ghana has yet reached the point of self-sustaining growth.

Two noneconomic factors are especially important: political leadership and administrative capacity. Changing a country's basic approach to economic development is a major task; maintaining commitment to a new approach is an even more difficult one, while implementing the program requires a certain level of administrative capacity.

Ghana's ability to chart a new course and stick to it has been remarkable and is attributable mainly to the outstanding leadership of Chairman Rawlings. Passive support for an adjustment program is not sufficient—the aborted effort in Sierra Leone, for example, and the subsequent failure to provide a new direction to economic policy are direct consequences of indecisive leadership. The Ghanaian government has made its commitment to the program absolutely clear, and at least part of its continued success must be attributed to the clear signals and unqualified endorsement of the reform effort provided by Ghana's top political leadership.

The second factor is the administrative capacity needed to implement a program successfully. Managing an auction for foreign exchange, conducting a review of public expenditures, and dismantling a system of controls are just some of the tasks that place a heavy burden on the civil service. In the case of Ghana, the civil service had undoubtedly suffered as a result of the economic decline of the 1970s—salaries had fallen drastically in real terms, morale was low, and retaining qualified staff proved difficult. In this respect Ghana, like many other countries in Africa, was probably not well placed to implement a reform program. And, indeed, part of the program now includes reform of the civil service. Nevertheless, Ghana was able to overcome these difficulties by drawing on the skills and dedication of a few key members of government, whose energy and enthusiasm kept a large program on track. Although stretched to the limit, administrative capacity proved adequate in the end.

The importance of such a core team also emerges from the experience of other countries. Guinea-Bissau's reform effort, for example, has benefited from the presence of an economic team to implement its reform program. In Nigeria, by contrast, despite its more developed administrative capacity, progress has been less smooth in the absence of a well-knit team responsible for implementing the program.

In reviewing the Ghanaian experience, therefore, I see two important lessons for other countries. First, passive support for adjustment is not sufficient. The demonstrated commitment of the political leadership is essential. Second, potential problems arising from a relatively weak administrative capacity can be overcome provided there is a well-coordinated economic core team with clear responsibility for implementation.

Next I would like to assess whether Ghana has yet achieved self-sustaining growth. For the purposes of this discussion, I assume that self-sustaining growth requires a rate of investment of at least 20 percent of GDP and a rate of national savings of at least 15 percent. These numbers are based on the experience of fourteen countries in Sub-Saharan Africa that achieved an average rate of growth in GDP of 4 percent or more a year for at least four years. In 1988 Ghana was investing only 12 percent of GDP and had a national savings rate of only 6 percent, while its average annual GDP growth rate in 1985–88 was 5.4 percent. The implication of these figures is that Ghana's excellent growth performance in recent years can be attributed, at least in part, to better utilization of the existing stock of capital and to a significant inflow of concessional assistance well above the Sub-Saharan average.

As an illustration of the importance of these factors, consider the effect of a smaller inflow of concessional assistance. Assuming that concessional assistance to Ghana grew at the same rate as it did in the rest of Sub-Saharan Africa and that consumption and the incremental capital-output ratio (ICOR) remained unchanged, GDP growth in 1985–88 would have averaged 4.4 percent a year compared with an observed rate of 5.4 percent, that is, a reduction in the growth rate of one percentage point. Clearly, this is a very rough calculation, but it indicates the role played by concessional assistance. This calculation, together with the advantage provided by a temporarily low ICOR, suggests that Ghana's recent high growth rate is not an indication that self-sustaining growth has been realized.

What are the prospects for achieving self-sustaining growth? In the immediate future Ghana will have to increase its investment rate to offset a rising ICOR. In addition, since foreign savings are unlikely to constitute as large a share of total savings as they have in the recent past, financing that higher rate of investment will require an increased rate of national savings. According to the World Bank's most recent set of projections, Ghana's investment and national savings rates will rise to my minimum required levels of 20 and 15 percent, respectively, by 1994. Compared with current levels, these are ambitious but not impossible targets, so self-sustaining growth seems feasible.

What is critical to the achievement of these targets, however, is the significant distributional change that occurs within aggregate investment and savings. For both investment and savings the role of the private sector is expected to increase relative to that of the public sector. Consider the case of investment. Although the urgent need to restore the economic and social infrastructure implied a prominent role for the public sector in capital formation during the first phase of the reform program, the engine of growth and hence the main source of investment in the long run is expected to be the private sector. This, in fact, is an important objective of the adjustment program. But private sector investment has been very slow to respond to the new incentive structure, and at present it accounts for only about one-third of total investment. By 1995 it will have to account for nearly half of a much larger total.

The recent disappointing performance in Ghana notwithstanding, there are signs of improvement: cocoa is being replanted, investment has picked up in the gold and forestry sectors, and foreign investors are beginning to explore possibilities in manufacturing. Nevertheless, the basic lesson for other countries is that the response of private investors is likely to take some time to emerge, especially if the previous policy regime was clearly opposed to the private sector. For Ghana, the critical issue is whether current indications of an upturn will indeed develop into a period of growth led by the private sector. The evidence of the next two years will determine the final assessment of Ghana's reform program.

The issue is similar for savings. The rate of private savings is projected to increase from about 3 percent of GDP in 1988 to almost 9 percent by 1995. Whether current efforts to restructure the banking system, liberalize interest rates, and mobilize deposits will be sufficient to achieve the desired rate of savings remains to be seen.

These remarks lead to an important general conclusion. For countries such as Ghana that have successfully completed the first stage of adjustment, the determinants of private savings and investment become increasingly important. But our understanding of investment and savings behavior in developing countries in general and in Africa in particular is weak. Assuming that more and more countries will be reaching this second stage, the World Bank should make sure that it is in a position to offer the best possible policy advice on these matters. The important lesson for the World Bank, therefore, is that the determinants of private savings and investment should be seen as a priority area for economic and sector work and for the research program.

16 *Zambia: Reform and Reversal*

Mohsen A. Fardi

THIS CHAPTER EXAMINES Zambia's attempts at stabilization and structural adjustment during the 1980s, although the country's efforts in this direction go back to at least 1972 when it obtained a program loan from the World Bank. The first section summarizes the causes and origins of the economic crisis in Zambia and early efforts at adjustment. The following sections discuss the policy content of recent stabilization and adjustment operations, the outcome of these programs, and the extent of compliance with loan conditions. Conclusions and lessons derived from Zambia's experience are presented at the end of the chapter.

Causes and Origins of the Crisis

Zambia began its structural adjustment program after years of low to negative economic growth rates. Average annual real GDP growth rates before 1980 (2.4 percent during 1965–72 and 0.3 percent during 1973–80) were much below the average for developing countries. GDP in Zambia declined an average of 0.1 percent a year from 1980 through the years of the stabilization and adjustment programs.

The slight growth before 1978 resulted from copper production and exports, which increased annually by a rate of about 2.6 percent, and agriculture, which grew by less than 2 percent annually. The government's agricultural policies, including price controls, food subsidies, and inadequate export incentives, have prevented the country from achieving its potential for agricultural development, which is considered quite high since less than a quarter of arable land is now under cultivation (Jansen 1988).

Zambia's export earnings come almost exclusively (95 percent) from copper. Since 1976, export earnings have been declining continuously primarily because of falling copper reserves and production and, until 1987, declining copper prices. Copper production and export were hindered by inadequate maintenance, a shortage of foreign exchange, management inefficiency, and transport difficulties. Since Zambia's production costs for copper are among the highest in the world, the decline in copper prices has had an immediate impact on the profitability of the industry and on Zambia's terms of trade.[1] The deterioration in the terms of trade also contributed to a large decline in national income and to the depressed state of the economy. The terms of trade index declined by 72 percent during 1969–80 (from 353 to 100).

Although the terms of trade were deteriorating, the exchange rate was not allowed to adjust, which led to an effective real appreciation of the domestic currency. The fixed exchange rate was maintained through an import licensing system that was based on a priority list of goods and services. Despite government efforts to control imports in line with available foreign exchange, commercial payments began to be in arrears in 1975. As proceeds from copper exports declined and foreign exchange became more scarce, the effective exchange rate became more overvalued, restrictions on import licenses became more severe, and arrears increased. The difference between the official and the black market exchange rates widened, inefficiencies in the distribution of scarce foreign exchange increased, and graft and corruption emerged.

Consumer prices and nominal interest rates were also subject to government control until 1984. The average annual increase in consumer prices was 14.5 percent during 1973–80. The interest rate on bank deposits ranged between 4 and 7 percent during 1965–83.

After independence the Zambian government took over a number of key enterprises that had been established by foreign interests, including the copper mining companies. The government also took an active role in the economy by investing in import-substituting manufacturing enterprises during the copper boom years and by increasing recurrent expenditure to expand programs for free public health and educational services and to provide consumer subsidies. In 1982–83 the public sector accounted for about 72 percent of formal sector employment (World Bank 1987b). Public expenditure ranged between 10 and 25 percent of GDP during 1975–82.

Until recently Zambia continued to import more than it exported by borrowing externally and by accumulating arrears. On the strength of its future earnings from copper exports, the country was able to attract finance from commercial and official bilateral and multilateral sources. With the exception of 1979, Zambia has had a significant current account deficit every year since 1975. By 1980 the current account deficit was 14 percent of GDP.

To sum up, the roots of the economic crisis facing Zambia in the 1980s lay in the need for a rigidly structured economy to adjust to a rapid decline in per capita income because of a rapid decline in the terms of trade. Maintaining a fixed rate of exchange, low agricultural prices, and extensive price controls created a strong bias against noncopper exports and increased the import intensity and capital intensity of domestic production. The public sector was overextended because of the government's unsustainable support of a large number of public enterprises and its effort to provide free public services for a rapidly growing urban population. As copper exports and the national economy declined, the government relied on large-scale foreign borrowing, including International Monetary Fund (IMF) resources, and the growth in arrears to stave off the need for retrenchment and restructuring. Since structural adjustment had to take place eventually, this delay simply made it even more difficult.

The Adjustment Program

The stabilization and adjustment program in Zambia had three parts: an IMF-supported program, a World Bank–supported program, and debt relief through reschedulings of debt by official and private creditors.

The IMF-Supported Program

Zambia has received the support of the IMF several times since 1976. A review of these arrangements shows an unchanging pattern of objectives and an unwavering optimism in expecting a resurgence in copper prices and exports and a turnaround in government management of its fiscal affairs.

The IMF-supported programs endeavored to reduce the unsustainable deficits in the fiscal budget and the current account and to create an environment favorable to the development and diversification of exports and a reduction in inflationary pressures. The policy measures that were to bring about the desired changes were depreciation of the exchange rate, unification of tariff rates, a reduction in restrictive economic and trade regulations, an increase in interest rates, removal of price controls and consumer subsidies, limitations on domestic financing of the fiscal deficit, an increase in tax revenue, and limitations on any increase in the public sector wage bill.

Despite some improvements in the policy environment, almost all agreements with the IMF were suspended or canceled because of an inability to meet the targets for the current account and fiscal budget deficits, the accumulation of external arrears, and insufficient control over domestic credit. These repeated interruptions, suspensions, and cancellations severely reduced the credibility of the stabilization program. The government appears to have lacked sufficient control over the program to maintain a consistent policy course.

The World Bank–Supported Program

Although the objectives supported by the IMF and the World Bank overlapped, the IMF-supported program focused on improving macroeconomic stability, while the World Bank's support initially had a sectoral orientation. As management of the macroeconomic policies became more critical, however, the World Bank–supported program focused more on issues such as the foreign exchange auction market.

In January 1983 the government committed itself to three objectives that would set the stage for renewed expansion: (1) adequate economic incentives for the production of agricultural and manufactured exports, (2) increased international competitiveness of the economy, and (3) the allocation of resources in line with the first two objectives. Annual GDP growth was projected at 2 to 2.5 percent for the next ten years, which was an implicit acceptance of a continued decline in per capita income.

The World Bank supported Zambia's adjustment program by granting a sectoral adjustment loan for rehabilitating the mining sector and two sectoral adjustment credits for rehabilitating the agricultural and manufacturing sectors. Growth in these sectors was expected to develop new exports, reverse economic decline, and create the basis for sustained long-term growth.[2] The sectoral adjustment loans were to finance imports required for the rehabilitation of the sectors concerned. None of these operations was designed as quick-disbursing support for the balance of payments. As economic conditions deteriorated and the need for policy reform became more urgent, however, these operations acquired the quick-disbursement feature. A fourth operation, the Economic Recovery Credit, was designed to reinforce policy measures adopted under the previous three sectoral operations. The adjustment strategy was based on an expected increase in copper exports and in funds from external sources.[3]

Structural Adjustment Policies

FISCAL POLICY. The government's critical tasks were to reduce public sector expenditures, to increase public revenue, and to limit financing of the budget deficit to the amount of net external borrowing. Tight fiscal and monetary policies, accompanied by positive interest rates and depreciation of the exchange rate, were expected to reduce the size of aggregate demand (expenditure reduction) and change the orientation of the economy toward tradable goods (expenditure switching). Expenditures were to be reduced by cutting subsidies and imposing limits on public sector employment and wage hikes. Revenue was to be increased through the mineral export tax, rationalization of import tariff rates, and new excise taxes.

Beginning with the 1984 budget, recurrent expenditures were tied to each ministry's development priorities. Allocations for agriculture were increased from an average of 6 percent of total public expenditure in the years before 1984 to 9 percent in 1984. Priority was placed on finishing existing projects in line with development objectives. Representatives of external lending agencies were invited to review the government's plans and the status of ongoing projects. The World Bank conducted a review of public expenditure in 1986 and made recommendations that the Zambian government accepted in principle. Preparations were made to implement a three-year rolling fiscal plan, and a study of the tax structure was undertaken with World Bank and IMF assistance. The recommendations emanating from the public expenditure review and the tax study were to be implemented in the 1987 and 1988 budgets.

MONETARY POLICY. A tight monetary policy to reduce inflation was an important element of the reform program. One condition for the release of the second tranche of the Industrial Reorientation Project was decontrol of interest rates. Accordingly, the government introduced a daily auction market for treasury bills in September 1985, which led to an immediate increase in the open market rate from 9.5 percent to 24 percent. Commercial bank lending and time deposit rates were also raised.

During 1983–85 the growth of the money supply was controlled and the money supply contracted relative to GDP. In 1986, however, the financing of large budget deficits through domestic borrowing led to a 66 percent increase in the money supply, excess liquidity, and rapid depreciation of the kwacha. Although the commercial bank rate was increased to 30 percent in 1986, it was still much below the inflation rate (the wholesale price index increased 64 percent in 1985 and 74 percent in 1986). In the absence of sufficient control over the money supply and complementary fiscal adjustment, the interest rate remained negative in real terms.

THE EXCHANGE RATE SYSTEM. Before 1985 Zambia followed a fixed exchange rate system with occasional adjustments. From 1976 to July 1983 the kwacha was devalued three times: 20 percent in 1976, 10 percent in 1978, and 20 percent in January 1983. In July 1983 Zambia adopted an adjustable rate system pegged to the trade-weighted average value of the currencies of five major trading partners. After considerable examination of alternatives, the government settled on an auction market to allocate foreign exchange and to establish a more realistic exchange rate. With this mechanism the government also hoped to avoid the misallocation of scarce foreign exchange and to eliminate the graft associated with the existing administrative system.

Despite some reservations about the feasibility of an auction market for Zambia, the prevailing view within the World Bank was that the auction system would be the most efficient way to allocate scarce foreign exchange, would provide guidance on the real value of the currency, and would serve as an incentive to exporters. Zambia's aid consortium also strongly endorsed the introduction of the auction system, although some members were concerned about its effects on equity and domestic prices.

When the auction market opened on October 1, 1985, the value of the kwacha fell as was expected, from 2.2 to 5 kwacha to the U.S. dollar. During the next eight months the value depreciated gradually to 8 kwacha to the U.S. dollar, but in the second half of 1986 it fell rapidly to 19 kwacha to the U.S. dollar, which was equal to a real effective depreciation of 60 percent of its value in 1980. Government attempts to stabilize the exchange rate by increasing restrictions or by increasing the amounts available for auction failed to arrest the rapid depreciation. Accumulating arrears and delays of up to ten weeks in delivering foreign exchange led to a loss of confidence in the system. By the end of April 1987, when the kwacha had depreciated to 22 kwacha to the U.S. dollar, the auction system was abandoned and a fixed exchange rate regime was reinstated.

TRADE POLICY. With the introduction of the foreign exchange auction, import licensing and import prohibitions that had been established for protective purposes were eliminated. Instead, a registration system was put into effect to assist with the management of external payments. As part of a tariff reform, import duties on industrial capital equipment were raised to 15 percent and a minimum tariff of 10 percent was imposed on previously duty-free imports of intermediate goods. Foreign trade regulations were streamlined by eliminating exemptions and rebates of import duties on a large number of inputs. A uniform sales tax of 15 percent was imposed on domestically produced goods to reduce the effective protection of domestic production. Duty drawbacks were simplified for exporters.

PRICES AND INCOMES POLICY. Until December 1982 the prices of essential consumer goods were subject to government control at wholesale and retail levels. This practice led to inefficiencies in production and distribution, disincentives to expand output, and the emergence of black markets and smuggling in the border areas. In late 1982 it was decided to set the retail prices for most consumer goods in line with border prices. As a result, the prices of most consumer goods were decontrolled, although changes in the prices of some goods remained subject to government approval.

The extent of the price liberalization became apparent after the opening of the foreign exchange auction market. The depreciation of the exchange rate had an immediate and significant impact on domestic prices. The price of refined petroleum products jumped by 150 percent, public utility rates by 80 percent, bread by 100 percent, sugar by 49 percent, maize by 40 to 50 percent, and fertilizer by 77 percent. For some services, such as telecommunications, that were denominated in U.S. dollars, prices increased by the full extent of the exchange rate depreciation.

The government tried to control aggregate demand by imposing limits on public employment and wages. Nominal wages were increased by less than 10 percent annually, well below the inflation rate. The freeze on employment was not very effective, however, because the hiring of temporary workers and contract employees continued to expand overall public employment.

DEBT RELIEF. Zambia's debt is one of the highest in the world. Debt per capita in 1986 was US$840, or 3.6 times GNP and 7.2 times exports of goods and services. Zambia accumulated its foreign debt when it was considered a middle-income country, so the terms were too hard for it to meet in the 1980s. A high proportion of Zambia's foreign debt is short term, nonconcessional, and not subject to rescheduling; about 20 percent of outstanding debt has been rescheduled at least once. Given the large share of debt not subject to rescheduling and Zambia's high debt service obligations, rescheduling has provided only short-term relief. Although rescheduling lowered debt service in absolute amounts, external debt and debt to the IMF increased from US$3.9 billion in 1984 to US$6.4 billion at the end of 1987. By 1985 the scheduled debt service exceeded 80 percent of exports of goods and services. Zambia could not meet its obligations under the rescheduling arrangements reached in 1983–84 and 1986, and arrears continued to accumulate, growing to twice the value of exports at the end of 1987.

Economic Performance

GDP, which had grown by only 0.3 percent a year during the 1970s, did not respond positively to the policy changes of the 1980s. In fact, as a result of continued deterioration in the terms of trade, gross national income declined by 2.4 percent annually during 1980–86, with most of the decline occurring in 1986 when gross national income fell by 17 percent. (Table 16-1 shows changes in macroeconomic indicators for Zambia from 1965 to 1987.)

Domestic supply responded much more slowly than expected to the incentives provided by the price and exchange rate adjustments. The volume of copper production continued to decline despite efforts to rehabilitate and improve management of the industry. Refined copper production declined from 610,000 tons in 1980 to 460,000 tons in 1986, while the price fell by 48 percent in nominal terms (World Bank 1986 and 1988). Despite optimistic expectations of an imminent reversal in the price trend, world copper prices continued to decline. Capacity utilization in manufacturing remained low because shortages of foreign ex-

Table 16-1. Macroeconomic Indicators for Zambia, 1965–73 to 1987
(average annual growth rates based on constant prices)

Indicator	*1965–73*	*1973–80*	*1980–86*	*1986*	*1987*
Gross domestic product	2.4	0.3	−0.1	0.4	−0.2
Gross domestic income	2.2	−6.0	−0.3	−4.7	3.8
Gross national product	2.4	0.8	−2.0	−11.0	1.3
Gross national income	2.2	−6.0	−2.4	−17.1	6.5
Agriculture	2.0	1.6	3.1	9.0	−1.0
Industry	2.7	−0.3	−0.8	−1.6	0.7
Manufacturing	9.8	0.5	0.6	0.4	0.6
Services	2.3	0.4	−0.6	−0.9	−0.6
Total consumption	1.1	1.9	−0.3	−1.7	4.3
Private consumption	−1.9	3.1	1.0	−4.6	6.1
General government	10.4	−0.6	−3.3	6.3	0.0
Gross domestic investment	6.2	−16.5	−8.2	6.0	−33.8
Fixed investment	n.a.	−15.4	−11.6	−8.8	17.3
Total expenditures	3.0	−4.1	−1.8	−0.6	−1.5
Gross domestic savings	3.2	−18.8	1.3	−20.4	0.6
Exports[a]	2.5	−0.1	−4.4	8.0	11.3
Imports[a]	3.4	−8.5	−9.7	−13.2	9.1
Capacity to import	2.1	−11.2	−5.7	−26.3	33.7

n.a. Not available.
a. Goods and nonfactor services.
Source: World Bank IEC data base, November 1988.

change limited access to needed imports. Value added in the industrial sector declined during 1980–86. The basic problem in the industrial sector remained the insufficient participation of the private sector. The only relatively bright spot was agricultural production, which was helped by higher producer prices and favorable weather.

Internal Balance

The government's efforts to establish internal balance were only partially effective in the first phase of the adjustment program. Although consumption in the public sector was reduced in real terms from 1980 to 1986 (annual real rate of change of −3.3 percent), general government expenditure as a share of GDP remained at around 25 percent.[4]

With the rapid decline in per capita income and the strong resistance of urban consumers to reducing their consumption, private consumption increased by 1 percent annually in real terms during 1980–86 and its share in GDP increased from 55 percent to 66 percent. Thus the burden of adjustment in domestic absorption fell primarily on domestic investment, which declined by 8.2 percent a year (on a gross basis) during 1980–86 (after falling an average of 16.5 percent a year during 1973–80). The fall was precipitated by the rapid economic decline, the existence of excess capacity, the shortage of foreign exchange for imports of capital goods, and the falling rate of private and public savings.

External Trade Balance

Exports continued to decline during the adjustment years, mainly because of the decline in copper exports. Although exports of nontraditional goods increased somewhat, the amounts remained insignificant. As a result, merchandise exports declined by 53 percent (from US$1,457 million in 1980 to US$681 million in 1986). Imports of goods and nonfactor services declined from US$1,765 million in 1980 to US$809 million in 1986—an annual decline of 9.7 percent on average (26.3 percent in 1986), which came on top of an average decline of 8.5 percent during the 1970s. This drastic cut in imports aggravated an already very difficult economic situation.

Despite the shortfall in exports, the trade balance improved from a deficit of US$157 million in 1980 to a surplus of US$20 million in 1986. However, the current accounts deficit, which had improved from US$761 million (19 percent of GDP) in 1981 to US$153 million (5.5 percent of GDP) in 1984, increased to US$345 million (21 percent of GDP) in 1986.[5]

Public Revenue and Expenditure

Between 1981 and 1985 total government expenditure declined in real terms by 18 percent. All expenditure categories except interest payments declined: capital expenditures by 30 percent, wages and salaries by 16 percent, and subsidies by 25 percent. The budget deficit also was cut by 18 percent during that period. Total revenue increased from 23.5 percent of GDP in 1984 to 26.5 percent of GDP in 1986. The depreciation of the kwacha had a positive effect on government revenue from foreign trade (mineral export tax, import duties, and excise taxes). Rescheduling of the major part of the interest due on external debt in 1983 and 1984 helped to limit interest payments on external debt to about 1.3 percent of GDP and domestic finance of the deficit to about 3 percent of GDP. Inflation, although relatively high at about 20 percent a year, was not alarming and was considered a temporary result of the lifting of price controls and reductions in consumer subsidies. Thus it appears that until the end of 1985 the government succeeded in containing the budget deficit despite some shortcomings in its approach.[6] From about the fourth quarter of 1985 until the adjustment program unraveled in 1987, the government went through a severe fiscal crisis and ultimately lost the

Table 16-2. Central Government Budget as a Percentage of GDP in Zambia, 1981–86
(current prices)

Item	*1981*	*1982*	*1983*	*1984*	*1985*	*1986*
Revenue	24.45	24.14	25.57	23.54	22.41	26.50
Expenditure	39.84	40.90	34.49	32.87	36.86	63.83
Current	35.30	34.56	29.75	27.48	33.24	55.79
Interest	3.38	4.16	4.64	4.38	9.69	19.34
Foreign	1.35	2.07	1.11	1.46	6.11	13.78[a]
Domestic	2.03	2.09	3.53	2.93	3.58	5.56
Wages and salaries	8.02	8.13	7.25	6.96	7.61	5.46
Subsidies	3.17	3.49	1.97	1.80	2.67	4.71
Other	22.76	20.87	19.43	17.26	13.26	26.27[b]
Capital	4.54	6.34	4.74	5.39	3.62	8.05
Overall deficit	−15.39	−16.76	−8.92	−9.33	−14.44	−37.33
Source of finance						
Foreign	7.98	3.12	2.42	1.20	6.03	21.81
Domestic	4.82	13.60	2.75	3.83	8.55	15.52

a. Interest on external debt in 1986 on accrual basis.
b. "Other" expenditure in 1986 includes the following:

	Percentage of GDP
Transfers for IMF charges	6.8
Transfers for foreign exchange losses	3.8
Transfers and pensions	3.3
Recurrent departmental charges	4.7
Other constitutional and statutory expenses	7.2

Source: World Bank data.

gains made in earlier years. During this period the government lost control of the budget. As shown in table 16-2, the overall deficit, on an accrual basis, increased from about 9 percent of GDP in 1983 and 1984, the two years preceding the reform program, to 37 percent in 1986. Although a more elaborate analysis is necessary to establish causality, it can be observed that the jump in interest rates and the depreciation of the exchange rate were concurrent with unprecedented increases in wholesale and retail prices, the level of public expenditure, the budget deficit, and the money supply.

Whether the government had the will or the latitude to reduce its discretionary expenditures to offset the impact of increased interest and exchange rates is debatable. Given the protracted decline in national income and real public expenditures, and the large budget share of nondiscretionary expenditures, there was little that the government could do in the short term to reduce the fiscal deficit. Since the transfer of external resources was insufficient, the fiscal deficit was accommodated by expanding the money supply and accumulating large external and domestic arrears.

Net Flow of External Resources

Was the net inflow of external resources in support of Zambia's stabilization and adjustment program sufficient, particularly in light of the continuous decline in export earnings? Could a larger inflow of external resources have reduced the fall in imports, domestic investment, and the growth of per capita income?

Although definitive answers to these questions cannot be provided in the context of this review, data do show a wide gap between planned and actual transfers of external resources. The adjustment program was based on expected improvements in copper prices and export volume that never materialized. Yet even though export performance consistently fell short of expectations, the program's assumptions and design were never reexamined. Underlying this inaction was an overoptimistic belief in Zambia's ability to export, based on expectations of high copper prices.

Four major sources of external finance were expected when the program was designed: earnings from copper exports, bilateral assistance, IMF standby arrangements, and adjustment credit from the World Bank. All four fell severely short of expectations. Exports fell repeatedly below even the most conservative estimates. Multilateral donors were unable to provide sufficient resources to help Zambia, despite assurances that, unlike in the past, the resources would be put to good use. Zambia could not draw on the IMF's facilities because it had not met its previous commitments and was in arrears as well. In addition, because Zambia had no standby agreement with the IMF, debt rescheduling could not take place in 1985. As a result, accumulated arrears reached US$586 million in 1985, including US$125 million to the IMF.

Net transfers from all long-term sources declined from a peak of US$450 million in 1981 to US$1 million in 1987 (table 16-3). Net transfers from the World Bank were negative until 1985; in that year and the following, however, sectoral adjustment credits from the International Development Association (IDA) increased net transfers from the World Bank to an average of US$63 million.[7] The World Bank also accelerated disbursements from the existing sectoral adjustment operations in light of Zambia's liquidity crisis. Bridge finance from commercial banks was also sought in 1985 to pay Zambia's arrears to the IMF and so to pave the way for a new standby agreement. All these efforts were insufficient, however, and the external finance gap widened rapidly.

Assessment of the Program

Zambia's restructuring program began in 1983 and lasted for about four years. Implementation began to suffer after April 1986 when the eco-

Table 16-3. Net Transfers to Zambia from All Sources, 1980–87
(millions of U.S. dollars)

Source	*1980*	*1981*	*1982*	*1983*	*1984*	*1985*	*1986*	*1987*
World Bank[a]	−19.3	−22.9	−15.9	−19.2	−12.8	66.6	62.1	22.0
IBRD	−20.8	−25.0	−23.3	−28.4	−28.0	4.0	−15.7	−19.0
IDA	1.5	2.1	7.4	9.2	15.2	62.6	77.8	41.0
IMF	−18.2	336.9	−111.4	10.7	21.9	−43.4	−98.0	n.a.
Purchases	65.1	423.7	37.5	185.7	151.2	0.0	121.8	n.a.
Repurchases	57.3	57.0	95.2	121.4	73.0	19.0	143.9	n.a.
Net purchases	7.8	366.7	−57.7	64.3	78.2	−19.0	−22.1	n.a.
Interest	26.0	29.8	53.7	53.6	56.3	24.4	75.9	n.a.
Other sources	360.9	136.1	188.1	81.2	161.8	140.4	104.2	−21.0
Net transfers	323.4	450.1	60.8	72.7	170.9	163.6	68.3	1.0

n.a. Not available.
a. The World Bank includes both the International Bank for Reconstruction and Development (IBRD) and the International Development Association (IDA).
Source: World Bank (1987a) and the World Bank *World Debt Tables* data base.

nomic management team was changed and critics of the reform program were put in charge of implementing it. They continued efforts to implement some elements until May 1, 1987, when the program was abruptly abandoned.

During the adjustment period Zambia adopted policies for rationalizing the trade and exchange rate regimes and for rehabilitating the mining sector. Consumer prices were decontrolled and agricultural producer prices were raised. A substantial real depreciation in the effective rate of exchange took place. Interest rates were raised in nominal terms although real rates remained negative.

Scope and Implementation of Conditionality

Zambia received three sectoral adjustment loans and a structural adjustment credit from the World Bank. An export rehabilitation project in 1984 was designed to halt the decline in copper production and enhance the efficiency and profitability of the mining sector. Among the policy conditions to be met prior to the release of the second tranche were satisfactory progress in carrying out production and investment plans for the government-owned mining company, allocation of the foreign exchange needed to rehabilitate the company, and establishment of a uniform tariff system with a minimum and maximum rate. Although foreign exchange allocations fell 30 percent short of the government's commitments, progress in other areas was deemed sufficient to allow the release of the second tranche.

An agricultural rehabilitation project in 1985 financed imports of farm implements and consultant services. Among the conditions for release of the second tranche were full cost recovery for state enterprises that were marketing maize and fertilizer within a regionally differentiated price structure, improved efficiency of the enterprises, adoption of a mechanism for linking producer prices to border prices, and the opening of maize and fertilizer marketing to private traders.

The second tranche was released although compliance was only partial: a study of fertilizer usage was completed, a study of maize and fertilizer marketing was begun, and maize and fertilizer subsidies were reduced in accordance with a three-year plan for phased reduction. After the adoption of a foreign exchange auction, disbursement procedures for this project were modified so that the foreign exchange provided for the purchase of eligible imports was sold in the auction market. Although no data are available on individual sales, bids by farmers and suppliers of agricultural machinery were generally not successful.

Another sectoral loan in 1985 supported the auction market and industrial and trade policy reforms. Conditions for disbursement included adoption of the foreign exchange auction system, conversion from an import licensing to an import registration system, elimination of import prohibitions, and a reduction in maximum tariff rates from 150 to 100 percent. Conditions to be met before release of the second tranche included decontrol of interest rates, enactment of a new investment code, establishment of a minimum 10 percent tariff on remaining duty-free items, simplification of the export duty drawback system, and implementation of an action program to improve forecasting and budgeting for foreign exchange.

Again, the second tranche was released. The government attempted to comply with loan conditions by introducing a daily auction for treasury bills, which led to an increase in nominal interest rates although real rates remained negative; passing a new investment act (with parliamentary approval but not the presidential signature); rationalizing import tariffs; and simplifying duty drawback procedures.

In contrast to the three sectoral loans, the Recovery Program Credit of 1986 was a quick-disbursing policy-based credit. It was designed to provide the minimum level of imports needed for Zambia's recovery program. When the credit agreement was presented to the World Bank's Executive Directors in June 1986, four major problems were observed. First, the deficit in the current account was larger than agreed to because of falling exports, shortfalls in aid flows, slow disbursement of existing bilateral commitments, and larger than expected sales in the foreign exchange auction. Second, the government had failed to control the money supply. Third, the budget deficit was much larger than expected because of revenue shortfalls (resulting in part from unexpectedly low external

Table 16-4. Number of Major Policy Conditions in Zambia's Adjustment Operations by Policy Area

	Adjustment operation				
Policy area	*Export*	*Agricultural*	*Industrial*	*Economic*	*All programs*
Trade and foreign exchange	0	0	8	4	12
Agriculture	1	5	0	5	11
Public enterprise reform	0	0	5	1	6
Mining	3	0	0	2	5
Fiscal	0	1	0	4	5
Monetary	0	0	1	0	1
Social impact	0	0	0	1	1
Total	4	6	14	17	41

Source: World Bank data.

aid and growing losses among public enterprises arising from changes in the exchange rate). Fourth, the government was unable to handle the economic management of a tough stabilization and adjustment program.

This situation, which had already jeopardized Zambia's standby agreement with the IMF, led the World Bank to postpone signing the credit agreement until Zambia reestablished its eligibility for drawings under the standby arrangement. As a result, the Recovery Program Credit did not become effective until December 1986, and the second tranche was never released because of the policy reversals after the first tranche. The credit was canceled when the government abandoned the adjustment program in May 1987.

Although some marginal gains were achieved, little if any significant structural change took place in the Zambian economy during the relatively brief period in which adjustment policies were in effect.[8] Despite this lack of real structural reform, however, Zambia's progress in carrying out its policy commitments was deemed sufficient to permit release of the second tranche for the three sectoral adjustment operations. In retrospect, it appears that the World Bank may have gone too far in accommodating Zambia with the maximum amount of resources available, perhaps influenced by the Bank's strong desire to see Zambia succeed in its enormous adjustment efforts.[9] Table 16-4 shows the number of policy conditions in each major policy area for the four adjustment operations.

Sustainability and Policy Reversals

Overall, the adjustment program in Zambia was not sustainable and was reversed in late 1986 and early 1987. Although some controls were lifted from the exchange rate, the interest rate, and major producer and many consumer prices, high inflation during 1985 and 1986 nullified the economic impact of the price changes. Furthermore, the price liberalization measures were not institutionalized, and so prices remained subject to overt or effective administrative controls. At the end of 1986 the foreign exchange system was still subject to administrative controls and the auction market lacked stability, fuel prices did not reflect import costs and remained subject to government control, the price of fertilizer was below domestic cost, and interest rates remained negative in real terms.

Under some pressure from external lenders and with little planning, the government in December 1986 removed the subsidy on high-quality maize meal while maintaining it on the lower-quality maize consumed mainly by low-income groups. Although the objective was to target the subsidy to the poorer groups, the program did not work because the subsidized maize immediately disappeared from the shops. Riots and civil unrest followed in urban and mining areas. In response, the government reinstated the maize subsidy and took over the milling plants. Similarly, an attempt to raise fuel prices by 70 percent on April 20, 1987, collapsed in response to riots and protests.

Since abandoning the reform program on May 1, 1987, the government has tried to implement its own restructuring program, which has the spirit of the previous reform program but little of its content. It abandoned the foreign exchange auction market and reinstated the administered allocation of foreign exchange and a fixed exchange rate. The exchange rate was initially set at 8 kwacha to the U.S. dollar and adjusted to 13 kwacha in October 1988 (the final auction rate had been 21 kwacha to the U.S. dollar). A large degree of excess demand exists for imports at the fixed rate of exchange, as indicated by the open market exchange rate of up to 40 kwacha per U.S. dollar. Debt service payments were limited to 10 percent of export receipts less payments for imports of petroleum and fertilizer and imports for the mining sector.

Continuing high inflation since the fixing of the exchange rate has given rise to a large effective appreciation of the kwacha. A general price freeze on all commodities was replaced by price control of twenty-one essential groups of commodities (Republic of Zambia 1987). The price control system did not reduce the high inflation rate, which accelerated as a general shortage of basic goods emerged.

Future Agenda

The agenda for Zambia remains the same as before: to stop the decline in per capita income, to diversify the economy's production base, to improve the management of public resources, and to resolve the external debt problem. Diversification of domestic production and exports is particularly critical. Zambia has only about ten years of copper reserves remaining, and as reserves are drawn down, average production cost is expected to rise and profitability to fall. (Zambia is already a high-cost copper producer.) Clearly, Zambia cannot rely in the long run on its copper exports to generate foreign exchange, public revenue, employment, and growth.

Zambia's large external debt and debt service requirements are another critical problem. Zambia has been in noncompliance with its major creditors since May 1987. External debt, including short-term obligations and debt to the IMF, was estimated at US$6.4 billion at the end of 1987—3.4 times the size of GNP or 6.7 times the value of exports of goods and services—while external debt arrears were twice the value of exports. To resolve the present impasse Zambia must find innovative ways of reducing the external debt to a manageable size and get back on an economic reform track that is workable, politically feasible, and acceptable to international lenders.

Conclusions and Lessons

Zambia's performance under structural adjustment was at best mixed during the three years it was pursued. Marginal reductions were made in the current account deficit. The decline in GDP was arrested. Capacity utilization (which was as low as 40 percent) in the industrial sector improved slightly with the increase in imports of intermediate goods. There was a substantial depreciation in the real effective exchange rate, which would have helped to allocate scarce foreign exchange more efficiently had it been sustained longer. Nominal interest rates, as well as the prices of a large number of consumer and producer goods, were also raised.

On the negative side, management of the macroeconomy deteriorated rapidly after 1985 because of the inflationary effects of the exchange rate depreciation, a continuous decline in copper exports, and the accumulation of external arrears. Although some public expenditures were cut, increased government reliance on domestic banking to finance rapidly rising current expenditures, particularly for interest payments, and the depreciation of the kwacha contributed to a budget deficit exceeding 35 percent of GDP in 1986. Rapid declines in real wages and the standard of living and increasing unemployment led to social unrest and the erosion of political support for the adjustment program. The government's failure to modify some elements of the reform program and still comply with the terms of the IMF and the World Bank and its inability to meet rapidly accumulating debt service obligations finally led it to abandon the reform program.

Why did the reform program fail in Zambia? Some preliminary conclusions emerge from this brief review.

Program Design

The program placed too much emphasis on short-term adjustment of the balance of payments and fiscal budget deficits through the reduction of aggregate demand, which had already been falling since 1975. Not enough emphasis was placed on expanding domestic supply and arresting the decline in per capita income. Although World Bank–supported sectoral restructuring programs were designed to increase supply, there was a lag in the sectoral response, and stabilization policies could not buy enough time for the supply response to manifest itself before conditions had deteriorated.

No comprehensive assessment of the probable macroeconomic response to the adjustment policies was made before the program was designed. In particular, the requirement that Zambia adopt a foreign exchange auction failed to take into account Zambia's ability to address the fiscal deficit. Since Zambia had gone through years of significant decline in per capita income, the public sector's ability to reduce the fiscal deficit in the short to medium term was very limited. It was unlikely that expenditures could be cut to any significant extent, particularly since they had already been declining in real terms and nondiscretionary items, such as interest payments and defense, constituted a large part of the total.

The current account deficit was easier to control than the fiscal deficit because the availability of external finance set the maximum limit on the size of the current account deficit. On the domestic side, however, the government has a freer hand in financing its deficit by borrowing and expanding the money supply. When exports are falling and external finance is increasingly scarce, the burden of external adjustment is on the domestic side. In Zambia this resulted in a high rate of inflation and an unmanageable fiscal deficit.

External economic conditions also worked against Zambia. The anticipated improvement in the price of copper never materialized. An increase in the value of copper exports would have gone a long way toward consolidating the government's achievements and attracting further political support for the program. But when this failed to happen, no contingency plans were in place to allow for the necessary adjustment.

A more realistic assessment of Zambia's problems and capacities and of the future prospects for copper exports might have significantly improved the design and sustainability of the adjustment program. For example, a more concerted effort could have been made to reduce nondiscretionary recurrent expenditures, the program could have been extended over a longer time, a longer grace period could have been allowed for rescheduled debt, and the World Bank could have monitored the program more closely, to permit greater flexibility in responding to conditions in Zambia.

ADEQUACY OF RESOURCES. The net flow of external resources proved to be much less than expected. External assistance, although vital for the adjustment program while it lasted, fell short of Zambia's requirements. The net flow of long-term capital was also limited because of Zambia's lack of creditworthiness and the general decline in international lending to developing countries. Direct foreign investment in Zambia was negligible. The government's ability to mobilize external assistance was linked to its success in carrying out its reform commitments, while performance was to a great extent dependent on the timing and availability of sufficient concessional external assistance. Keeping up the flow of external resources was vital to the survival of the adjustment program, but it did not happen.

In retrospect, it is apparent that the government and World Bank staff were overoptimistic in assessing the availability of real resources, the expansion of copper exports, the capability of public administrators to execute the reform program, and the extent of the supply response to the foreign exchange rate and other price adjustments. Revenue from exports of copper continued to decline and export diversification failed to materialize.

PROGRAM TIMING AND DURATION. The social and economic problems of countries such as Zambia originated long before they became independent nations. Imbalances that have been created over a long time cannot be redressed overnight. The responses of productive sectors to more favorable incentives take time to emerge. The development of nontraditional exports and a reduction in import dependency also may take more time than is allocated within the framework of structural adjustment lending.

Zambia began its structural adjustment program at a time of severe economic and financial crisis. Per capita income had been declining for more than a decade. Not enough had been done when the economy had more strength to withstand the secondary shocks of adjustment, and too much was attempted after it had exhausted its strength. Perhaps Zambia tried to correct in too short a time the damage inflicted on the economy by years of inappropriate policies.

Political Will

Insufficient political support has been cited as a major reason for the failure of the reform. An opposing viewpoint expressed by some members of the World Bank and the Zambian government is that the reform package was enthusiastically "bought" by an influential minority in the government. Within the ruling party, however, support for the program was weak from the beginning, since the party stood to lose political influence and access to financial resources as a result of the reforms. In the political struggle that ensued in April 1986, the critics of the reform program were put in charge of its implementation, a factor that certainly contributed to its abandonment soon after.

Zambia's experience indicates that it is not sufficient for some members of the government to "buy" a reform package. The managers of the adjustment program and those who support it must be able to stay in power long enough to execute the reforms. For the program to be sustainable, it must provide adequate incentives for the political base of the government in power to continue to support it until restructuring begins to have some positive impacts.

Social Impact

Conspicuously missing from Zambia's reform program was any meaningful attention to the impact of the adjustment program on social welfare. This might have been because of the sectoral orientation of the reform program, and had the adjustment program continued more attention might have been given to improving social conditions. In any case, it was felt that Zambia had no alternative to adjustment and that without adjustment the standard of living would continue to fall.

Although the expected gains from adjustment were substantial, the hardship faced by many people during the transition was immense. The consumer price index for low-income groups increased by 72 percent from October 1985 to February 1987. Unemployment was very high, with as many as 2 million of a working population of 3.5 million reported to be unemployed. The removal of subsidies after a long period of decline in real incomes and widespread unemployment caused far stronger protests than was expected.

Structural adjustment entails a redistribution of resources and thus changes in the returns to factors of production. It further involves reductions in unearned income, subsidies, and administrative interventions. There are many tradeoffs between present costs and probable returns in the future. Although ultimately the gains from adjustment will be widespread, there must be some short-term rewards to induce those who bear the cost to continue to participate in the process. In Zambia it appears that the present cost of adjustment for a significant portion of society became greater than its discounted future value. Although Zambia has terminated its externally supported adjustment program, its need for external assistance remains as critical as ever.

Notes

1. For comparative international costs, see Takeuchi, Strongman, and Maeda (1986).

2. Zambia had received two program loans from the Bank in 1972 and 1976. The concern then, as in later years, was with declining copper production and prices, deterioration in the fiscal budget, the balance of payments position, efficiency of public investment projects, and the slow growth of the agricultural sector.

3. World Bank staff were aware of the critical role of external assistance for the survival of the reform program. A 1984 World Bank document stated that if at least US$350 million of new commitments annually and $200 million of additional resources could not be mobilized (on top of debt rescheduling), the adjustment program had virtually no chance of success.

4. The difference in the share of government consumption in GDP (about 25 percent) and the share of current government expenditure in GDP as shown in the fiscal data (56 percent in table 16-2) is due to large interest and transfer payments.

5. These data are from the World Bank International Economics Department Standard Tables of March 1988. More recent data (December 1988 Country Brief) show the current account deficit for 1986 to have been US$434 million, or 24.5 percent of GNP, larger than previously indicated.

6. In real terms, total government expenditures declined after 1970. In 1979 they constituted only 58 percent of the 1970 total, and in 1984 only 46 percent (see Jansen 1988).

7. Since 1956 the World Bank has granted twenty-eight loans and twenty-three credits to Zambia, totaling about US$951.4 million (1988 Country Brief). Because of budgetary problems, the implementation of World Bank–assisted projects in Zambia deteriorated in the 1980s. Serious delays in project implementation, particularly in the agricultural sector, led to slow disbursements of loans and credits.

8. In 1981 it was foreseen that Zambia's structural inflexibility would take many years to overcome, while its economy would remain vulnerable to terms of trade fluctuations (World Bank 1981).

9. An example of such action is the World Bank's agreement to release the proceeds of the agricultural sector credit to support the auction market.

References

Jansen, Doris J. 1988. *Trade, Exchange Rate, and Agricultural Pricing Policies in Zambia*. World Bank Comparative Study. Washington, D.C.

Republic of Zambia. 1987. "New Economic Recovery Programme: Progress Report No. 1 on the Implications of the Interim National Development Plan." Lusaka.

Takeuchi, Kenji, John E. Strongman, and Shunichi Maeda. 1986. *World Copper Industry: Its Changing Structure and Future Prospects*. Commodity Working Paper 15. Washington, D.C.: World Bank.

World Bank. 1981. *World Development Report 1981*. New York: Oxford University Press.

———. 1986 and 1988. *Commodity Trade and Price Trends*. Baltimore, Md.: Johns Hopkins University Press.
———. 1987a. *World Debt Tables*. Washington, D.C.
———. 1987b. "Zambia, Public Expenditure Review." Washington, D.C.

Comments

Ben King

MOHSEN FARDI'S chapter is a careful, comprehensive, and sober account of what happened in Zambia. His account ends with five reflections, to which I will return later. I have a few picky comments to make, but my main criticism is that his account is understated. So in a reversal of roles I will compensate by overstating.

At my station of life, one is usually permitted (on sufferance) the luxury of reminiscence. So I will begin by indulging—not entirely irrelevantly, but perhaps somewhat irreverently. In the summer of 1952 I went on my first operational mission for the World Bank: to Zambia, Zimbabwe, and Malawi, then Northern and Southern Rhodesia and Nyasaland. That was not only preindependence; it was prefederation.

We spent the most time in Zambia, or Northern Rhodesia, preparing a loan to that country to be on-lent to the railways. The original request to the World Bank was for 10 million pounds (then US$28 million), which we reduced to 5 million pounds. At this distance in time, it is legitimate to speculate how much this reduction was due to common prudence and how much to tit for tat. I shall not try to answer, but our justification at the time alluded to the fact that the production of copper had gone up over 50 percent in six years and that the price had quadrupled. Wages and incomes had risen sharply, and government revenue, which was approximately one-third of mineral output the year before, had increased by a factor of more than seven. Typically, it was being spent on the boomtowns of the copper belt and countryside. The government could easily have found the 5 million pound difference and come back to the World Bank when times were tougher.

Other themes at the time were the need for a countercyclical reserve fund, the predictable consequences of suppressing public utility prices, the burden of maize and wheat subsidies, the growing capital intensity of production, and the neglect of agriculture. Many of these criticisms had been made in a Colonial Office report fourteen years earlier, and most were repeated in an internal World Bank paper nineteen years later. Not much has changed, except that there will be no more copper booms in Zambia.

I am indulging in these autobiographical trivia to place the structural adjustment in Zambia in a historical context: not only Zambia's but the World Bank's too. In that vein I will quote from the appendix to a little book based on the Clayton lectures at Tufts University given in 1960 by Eugene Black: "The Bank has been at least equally concerned with the economic environment in which its loans are to be put to work. In loan discussions, it has as a matter of course consistently urged attempts . . . to put economic and fiscal policies on a sound footing." In other words, lending and what we turgidly call policy advice were mutually reinforcing, not mutually exclusive. But as is obvious from the book's title, *The Diplomacy of Economic Development*, policy discussion was supposed to take place in a diplomatic environment; it was intended as a means of "illuminating choices rather than imposing solutions."

Ten years later things had changed. In the World Bank's annual report for 1970 is a map of Africa covered with red and green dots representing agricultural projects: green for the entire period before 1968 and red for the two fiscal years after 1968. There are twenty green dots and twenty-five red ones. Their message is clear. We now know what happened to the red dots and their successors; the story can be found in several reports by the World Bank's Operations Evaluation Department (OED) and interim papers from the research project on Managing Agricultural Development in Africa (MADIA). On that map, Zambia has three red dots and no green ones. One of the three was a forestry project. The two agricultural projects proper did not fare well. One never got off the ground and was canceled. The second had a negative rate of return, as did a third that followed soon after. Price policy was at least partly to blame.

During fiscal 1966 to 1977, roughly the first twelve years after Zambia's independence, the World Bank lent Zambia US$463 million (gross, before cancellations). The three agricultural projects were only a small fraction of this total. Nearly US$200 million was invested in hydroelectric power. There were two program loans of US$30 million each, one of which was partially canceled. This flow of funds occurred despite repeated strong criticism of economic and fiscal policy in Zambia—in particular, the neglect of agriculture and the growth of the government's payroll. The new government managed to emulate most of its predecessor's substantial policies and to add a few of its own. It is hard to excuse the World Bank—and other lenders—from being party to these excesses.

During this time, the World Bank became hostage to its own lending program. Diplomacy was hard to practice when it became divorced from lending. Indeed, it became an article of faith that diplomacy could not be practiced in the context of project loans. As a consequence, project loans suffered from their environment. OED audits of Zambian projects reveal the effect of the price structure on many projects, the high investment cost per job, the shortage of staff and recurrent funds, and, when there was staff, the frequency of its turnover. For far too long on one agricultural project, the World Bank accepted assurances that something would be done to turn it around. Program loans were an occasional, but not very effective, vehicle for reform.

Expansion came to an end in 1975 when copper prices collapsed. They never again returned in real terms to their previous high levels. Gross domestic income per capita, which in 1969 had been 40 percent higher than in 1965, fell to a level close to 20 percent lower than in 1965. It was the beginning of a continuous decline. Government revenue dropped by 30 percent in 1975. For the first time, there was a substantial deficit on the recurrent budget. A deep cut was made in capital expenditures, and operating expenditures were cut in real terms. At the same time, personal emoluments rose. But the greatest causes of increased expenditure were subsidies, defense, and interest payments.

Staff resources devoted by the World Bank to the study of the Zambian economy were greatly increased at that time. In the fall of 1974 a large mission went to Zambia to prepare a report on the agricultural sector. This was followed in 1975 by a mission that produced a Basic Economic Report incorporating the findings of the agricultural mission and spelling out its prescription for changes in policy and practice. The report made a reasonably hopeful projection of Zambia's future, predicated on changes in policy. But it pointed out that its projections were highly sensitive to the price of copper.

In 1976 the World Bank made its second program loan to Zambia and the IMF its second standby credit. The World Bank's objectives included agreement on the broad outlines of an agricultural action program and a letter of intent to the effect that the government would finally establish a development equalization account. But the account came too late; there has been nothing to put in it.

In the following six years the World Bank's lending activities were rather low key. Zambia was now considered eligible for financing on concessional terms from the International Development Association. Loans and credits were smaller on average than in the previous twelve years. During this period the IMF's involvement was greater than the World Bank's; use of its credits rose from SDR95 million at the end of 1976 to SDR576 million at the end of 1982.[1] In 1978 the government asked for a third program loan and the consultative group of multilateral and bilateral lenders to Zambia held its first meeting. But little came of it because the World Bank considered Zambia's Third National Development Plan to be unrealistic. In its appraisal of the proposed loan, which was never made, the World Bank probed more deeply into additional aspects of the pricing system (uniform prices) and the inefficiencies of the marketing system. There was discussion of a structural adjustment loan in 1980, but it was felt that conditions that would be acceptable to the World Bank would not be acceptable to Zambia.

By 1982 the groundwork was being laid for reform in Zambia. The World Bank's representative in Lusaka prepared a paper entitled "Accelerated Development in Zambia: An Agenda for Action," which again stressed the now familiar strictures about the economy. It also made the prophetic observation that measures to curb consumption "will be much less painful if they are taken in an environment of economic growth." The government, on its side, drafted a memorandum that represented a break with past policies. In fact, it was the first of a series of documents in the next three years or so in which the Zambian government became its own most severe critic. They are so persuasive that it is hard not to sympathize with those who were working on Zambia in the World Bank; in a context in which the chosen instrument for reform was an adjustment loan, the series of credits that followed must have seemed a reasonable gamble. One must ask not only why things went wrong, but whether it was reasonable to expect this in advance. One must also ask whether there was any other feasible approach.

Fardi classifies the reasons for breakdown under five headings. I wish to comment on only a few, the first being the supply response. It is quite true that the supply response was insufficient, although there were a number of promising responses in the early days of the foreign exchange auction. But in agriculture, the sector that is the main hope for Zambia's future, the seeds of unresponsiveness had been sown years earlier through the almost complete neglect of the smallholder sector and the prevalence of incentives to consume agricultural produce and disincentives to produce it. Although there had been some response in some crops to intermittent improvements in prices resulting from devaluation or other measures, price policy is only a necessary, but not a sufficient, condition for growth.

Thus those responsible at the World Bank had been dealt a hand with very few honors by their predecessors. If the World Bank had taken a long view of the Zambian economy, it would have insisted on a better allocation of resources to agriculture as a condition for lending—any kind of lending—during the 1970s; the case had been very well documented by that time. But if it was assumed, when a US$100 million loan for power was under discussion, that matters vital to the economy could not also be discussed, then of course such insistence would have been difficult. That assumption ought now to be rejected. A comment on aid to Tanzania (from a book published in Sweden, where aid is not usually regarded with disfavor) appears, in retrospect, to be equally true of Zambia: "A lower level of aid allocated in a better manner would have been more useful. . . . The assistance was part of the making of the crisis."

Fardi suggests that there was not much the government could do by this time. On one, perhaps theoretical, level, this can be questioned. Reform of the agricultural sector was still the most neglected. Uniform prices were never removed, and marketing arrangements were not clarified. Producer and consumer prices of maize were out of step, controlled by different ministries. It was this that led to the December riots. The foreign exchange auction was never really given a chance. It lasted only six months under sympathetic leadership. From then on, manipulation doomed it. According to the World Bank's report on public expenditure, there was still room for reducing or switching expenditures.

Too much is made of the burden of interest payments on the budget. The reason they increased so much as a percentage of GDP is arithmetic; the kwacha depreciated, and interest denominated in foreign currency necessarily increased as a percentage of GDP, but this did not in any real sense constitute a greater burden on the economy than before. One could also say the same thing about the incoming aid on the other side of the ledger. Whether reduction of Zambia's huge debt would have been a more appropriate form of aid is another and a pertinent question.

As for domestic interest rates, one reason, if not the main one, for their increase was the freeing of interest rates. And here one may question whether a free capital market has any useful allocative effect when the government is the borrower of first resort. If the fiscal deficit cannot be brought under control, there is a case for rationing the remaining credit to priority customers. (It was alleged, for example, that high interest rates discouraged farmers.) One should really look separately at the primary deficit, exclusive of interest payments, and the cost of interest payments.

Nonetheless, on a realistic rather than theoretical level, the judgment that there was little the government could do may well be right. Even if the auction had continued under sympathetic management, would the government machinery have had the reflexes needed to manage an economy going through such a transition? A long history of protection from market forces and the conviction that profits were evidence of profiteering rather than of market response might have suggested otherwise. Subsequent events bore this out. When one talks of political will, much depends on expectations. Other countries have committed themselves to progressive devaluation, with all its discomforts, because they expected the benefits to outweigh the discomforts. This expectation was always weak in Zambia, and since both a quick and a large supply response was unlikely, whatever support there was evaporated. History cannot easily be expunged. As we now know, you cannot exorcise the ghost of Peron with a few sprinkles of holy water.

Fardi refers to a tradeoff between costs now and returns in the future. If there were costs to the economy attributable purely to the adjustment process rather than to events, they would be hard to identify. But no doubt the phrase refers only to social costs. With adjustment there are losers and winners. Even if one finds the figure of 2 million unemployed hard to credit (it suggests that almost everyone not employed by the government was unemployed), it would be reasonable to suppose that some of the losers would have been losers anyway and some would not. For the most part, they would have been urban; nearly half the population is urban, an extraordinarily high figure in Sub-Saharan Africa. In the rural areas people have been losers for years. It is doubtful that they had anything more to lose from the adjustment process; they might even have gained if consumer goods became available at prices lower than previous black market prices—or at any price if they had not been available at all before. This is not to deny that it would have been morally right and politically wise to afford some protection for those hardest hit, but the fact that they had no alternative occupation to turn to underlines the point about supply response.

A final point should be made about underfunding. To be sure, in relation to the expectations of the foreign exchange likely to be available, there was underfunding. As the chapter points out, this was due partly to disappointment among the external lenders, but much more to lower copper prices. What should be done in a world where prices do not always live up to expectations? Would the aid community have underwritten a worst-case scenario for the price of copper? Exactly who should bear the risk? These are not easy questions to answer. They do suggest that "underfunding" is not a term to be used in an absolute sense. Underfunding in relation to what?

The suggestion that "Zambia had exhausted its strength" may be true; if so, it implies that it was too late for a structural adjustment loan. But earlier the time was not ripe. When was the right time? One school of thought holds that the kind of wholesale reform a structural adjustment loan calls for is, in some countries at least, unlikely to be undertaken except in desperation, when economic breakdown has reached such a level that the costs of not adjusting have become unbearable. If this is so, one must really ask whether there are alternatives to structural adjustment as presently conceived.

Structural adjustment lending was born in 1980 in the wake of the oil shocks and the subsequent worldwide recession. It was originally conceived as an instrument to help developing countries over a perfectly genuine adjustment hump by supplying what amounted to working capital. However, to the World Bank's Executive Directors, who asked why project loans could not be used for this purpose, it was also presented as "a fundamental instrument for dialogue" between the World Bank and the country. When the Baker Plan came along in 1985, adjustment loans were seen as the obvious instrument for moving it off its pedestal. They have become the most favored notion of the 1980s, much as poverty lending was in the 1970s. In neither case can the objective be criticized; bringing about economic order and growth on the one hand and tightening up income distribution on the other are worthy goals. But rigidity of format is another matter. There may be times when it is necessary to concentrate on a few essentials for a long time, to accept second-best solutions, and to be patient.

Note

1. IMF funds are denominated in SDR (special drawing rights), which are based on a basket of currencies.

Comments on Africa

Edward V. K. Jaycox

THE AFRICAN CASES presented above were well chosen for their implications for the adjustment process. The cases of Ghana and Zambia show a similar degree of distortions present at the beginning of the programs, as well as a similar degree of dependency on single products. These cases and the difficulties of Côte d'Ivoire present valuable lessons for our reflection.

As the person now responsible for these operations in the World Bank, however, I find something missing from the discussion of Zambia. Zambia's was a terribly underfunded program. We overestimated copper revenue, overestimated aid flows, and did everything we could to paint a picture of an internally consistent financing plan based on the resources that we and others could bring to bear. If the case had been looked at more closely or more skeptically, the plan's lack of realism would have become apparent. Certainly this is clear with hindsight. A great number of shocks took place as the adjustment process went along: copper prices went down or stayed at the same level when they were expected to go up, aid that was expected did not arrive, deals with the Paris Club that were normative were made less liberal when the aid was increased. At one point, the actual financing was US$200 million less than had been expected in net capital inflows.

What happens in a very weak administrative situation like this is that the government resorts to the budget—to the creation of money—to meet vital needs in the economy, and to short-term borrowing at high interest rates. I do believe, however, that the end of the unraveling string in the Zambian case was the underfunding of that program. Even though the string goes all the way back to the 1940s, my real interest now is in what happened in the period of formal structural adjustment. In sum, the Zambian program was administered in a very chaotic way, and the chaos resulted in part from the inadequacy of financing and unrealistic financing projections.

The case of Côte d'Ivoire shows that attempting to undertake structural adjustment with both hands tied behind the back—that is, not able to use the exchange rate as a policy variable and not able politically to adjust nominal wages and prices downward—is not workable. The best solution for this economy would have been to lower the cost structure, which had gotten out of line. But that was not feasible politically in 1981, nor has it proved to be politically feasible since then. Nominal wages have to go down and real wages have to go down even faster in a zero or very low inflation situation—a very, very difficult task. Since the use of the exchange rate was not a policy option, what has been called the second-best solution was used: the simulated exchange rate adjustment. As a matter of fact, that is probably the second-worst solution because, as pointed out by Shantayanan Devarajan in his comments on the chapter on Côte d'Ivoire, both revenue and discipline in the economy were lost at the same time. That approach did not work and, in my view, it is not going to work. Furthermore, the program in Côte d'Ivoire was also underfunded. Lack of access to concessional finance, problems of creditworthiness and limits on creditors' exposure, lack of agreed arrangements for the reduction of debt or debt service, and the resulting very limited new or net flows of capital to Côte d'Ivoire, coupled with the policy constraints I have mentioned, make this a most difficult case.

In the case of Ghana, there is the more happy circumstance of adequate funding matched by resolute implementation of reforms. This type of program should be sustainable throughout Sub-Saharan Africa supported by the kind of efforts that have been made by the aid community as a whole. We have managed to mobilize a large amount of quick-disbursing grant money and money at very concessional terms—International Development Association (IDA) terms or better. For poor African countries that are debt-distressed, we have mobilized some US$6.4 billion, matching the funds of IDA, to support structural adjustment.

The process of structural adjustment will require a long time. In the case of Zambia, we knew it would be a fifteen-year effort. We knew this was not a little hump; it was a long haul. Indeed, if we had had at the beginning the kind of money we have today and had applied it to Zambia, I believe the results would have been far different. The prospects of actually making that long haul are good, but this will require considerable discipline and considerable management capacity. I firmly believe it is a feasible and a necessary thing to do.

17 *Indonesia: Stabilization and Structural Change*

Sadiq Ahmed

UNLIKE MANY other oil-exporting countries, Indonesia has managed its oil resources well and has largely succeeded in protecting the commodity-producing sectors (agriculture and manufacturing) and preventing them from lagging behind the rest of the economy (Gelb and associates 1988). During the 1970s Indonesia experienced a rapid growth in income, consumption, and investment. In addition, important social gains brought about a substantial reduction in the incidence of poverty.[1] Nevertheless, some structural problems remained at the end of the decade. These resulted chiefly from the complexities of the government's regulatory framework, which had intensified the adjustment challenges posed by a series of external shocks beginning in 1981. In response to these shocks the government implemented a broad range of adjustment measures and structural policy reforms that significantly reduced the macroeconomic imbalances while allowing economic growth to remain positive in per capita terms. Although some short-term social costs have been incurred, Indonesia's long-term growth prospects would undoubtedly have been severely jeopardized had these necessary adjustments not been implemented.

This chapter examines Indonesia's adjustment to a series of external shocks since 1981. The first section discusses the nature and magnitude of these external shocks. The following sections review Indonesia's policy response, analyze the role of the various policy instruments in the process of stabilization and structural change, and evaluate Indonesia's economic performance. The last section examines the World Bank's role in the adjustment process.

Nature and Magnitude of External Shocks

Indonesia's external terms of trade fell by about 38 percent between 1981 and 1989. Oil prices accounted for the major part of this decline. Indonesia's average crude oil export price of US$15 a barrel in 1989 was only 36 percent of the real price in 1982. The deep worldwide recession of the early 1980s and the decline in other commodity prices also hurt Indonesia's balance of payments, although lower import prices provided

Table 17-1. Effects of External Shocks in Indonesia, 1984–89, as a Percentage of GNP

Effect	*1984*	*1985*	*1986*	*1987*	*1988*	*1989*[a]	*1984–88*
Terms of trade (1981 prices)	2.5	2.0	5.7	15.6	13.3	14.1	8.9
Exchange rate (1981 exchange rate)	−0.2	−0.3	−0.4	0.3	0.9	1.5	0.3
Interest rate (1981 interest rate)	0.6	0.4	0.1	0.0	−0.5	0.0	0.1
Total effect	2.9	2.1	5.4	15.9	13.7	15.6	9.3

a. Estimated.
Source: Ahmed (1989).

partial relief. The adverse effect of the worldwide recession on export volumes was especially severe in 1983.

Another adverse external shock was the depreciation of the U.S. dollar after mid-1985. Since a large proportion of Indonesia's foreign debt is denominated in currencies that have appreciated in relation to the dollar, Indonesia's total debt in dollar terms has surged. These currency fluctuations, together with the loss of export revenue because of falling oil prices, significantly increased Indonesia's debt service payments (interest and principal). Unlike many other developing countries, however, especially in Latin America, Indonesia did not have its debt service burden seriously increased by higher international interest rates, mainly because of the predominantly concessional nature and fixed interest rates of its debt. Another factor in Indonesia's favor was its low borrowing requirements (because of its large oil earnings) during 1978–81 when international borrowing rates surged.

The magnitude of the adverse effects of external shocks on the Indonesian economy is illustrated in table 17-1. On average, Indonesia suffered an income loss equivalent to about 9 percent of its annual gross national product (GNP) due to external disturbances during 1983–88. The loss of income was especially large in 1987 and 1988. As expected, the terms of trade effect was dominant, while the interest rate effect was minimal. The loss of income from international currency fluctuations increased significantly in 1987–88. The burden of external shocks was substantial and presented a major challenge to policymakers. Without a forceful policy response, this large loss of income could easily have destabilized the economy.

Indonesia's Adjustment Program

Indonesia's adjustment program was initiated in 1983 and intensified after the collapse of oil prices in 1986. In broad terms, two types of policy adjustments were made. First, the government adopted more austere macroeconomic policies to restore financial stability. Second, to sustain the development momentum over the medium to longer term, it embarked on a major program to restructure the economy by improving economic efficiency and reducing the country's heavy dependence on oil exports as a source of foreign exchange and budgetary revenue. This structural adjustment program included a range of measures to strengthen domestic resource mobilization, expand nonoil exports, and promote a more competitive and dynamic nonoil economy. A summary of the policy measures initiated through the end of 1988 is presented in table 17-2. These policies can be grouped under four broad categories: exchange rate management, fiscal policy, monetary and financial policies, and trade and other regulatory reforms.

To restore balance of payments stability and sustain growth over the medium term, the government devalued the rupiah by 28 percent in March 1983.[2] At the same time, the flexibility of the exchange rate was increased through a more actively managed float. The rupiah was again devalued by 31 percent in September 1986 in response to the rapid decline in oil prices. Since then, the rupiah has depreciated against a falling U.S. dollar. As a result of two large devaluations, a managed float policy, and the government's ability to restrain inflation, Indonesia's real effective exchange rate depreciated by about 55 percent between December 1981 and December 1988. The downward trend of the real effective exchange rate was generally maintained throughout the adjustment phase. As discussed later, the substantial depreciation of the real exchange rate played a crucial role in the adjustment process by stimulating nonoil exports and restraining imports.

Fiscal Policy

The objectives of both demand restraint and structural change were served by the implementation of strong fiscal measures designed to restrain public expenditure and mobilize public resources. Many large capital-intensive projects were rephased in 1983, with an estimated foreign exchange savings of US$10 billion. In the late 1980s civil service salaries were frozen and real capital spending by the central government was cut by more than one-third. Some actions were also taken to restrain investment in public enterprises. Tight control was kept on the use of nonconcessional import-related credits after 1984, and equity participation in public enterprises funded through the budget was reduced to minimal levels. A sweeping tax reform implemented in 1984–86 boosted nonoil tax revenue and improved the efficiency of the tax system. As a result

Table 17-2. Adjustment Policies Initiated in Indonesia, 1983–88

Policy instrument	*Policy description*
Exchange rate	Rupiah devalued by 28 percent in March 1983.
	Exchange rate made more flexible after March 1983.
	Rupiah devalued by 31 percent in September 1986.
	Exchange rate depreciated against a falling U.S. dollar after September 1986.
Fiscal	Large capital- and import-intensive projects rephased in May 1983.
	Major cutbacks in government real capital spending after 1983.
	Tight control maintained after 1983 on the use of nonconcessional, import-related credits.
	Major tax reform initiated in January 1984.
	Follow-up steps taken to strengthen tax administration.
	Restraints established on civil service employment and salaries.
Monetary and financial	Major financial reform in June 1983 removed interest rate and credit ceilings for state bank operations and introduced new instruments of monetary control.
	New financial measures introduced in October and December 1988 to improve financial sector efficiency and develop capital markets.
	Monetary management for controlling inflation improved.
	Short-term monetary management for curbing exchange rate speculation improved.
Trade and other regulatory	Across-the-board reduction in nominal tariffs implemented in March 1985.
	Measures to provide internationally priced inputs to exporters announced in May 1986.
	Significant reduction in import licensing restrictions initiated in October 1986, January and December 1987, and November 1988.
	Regulatory restrictions for exporters reduced in December 1987 to limit the antiexport bias of trade policy.
	Customs, ports, and shipping reorganized in April 1985 to reduce freight costs and cut procedural time.
	Steps taken in May 1986, October 1986, and January and December 1987 to reduce investment and capacity licensing requirements, relax foreign investment regulations, and reduce the role of the local-content program.
	Substantial deregulation of maritime activities announced in November 1988 to reduce costs and encourage private participation.

of these fiscal measures, total nonoil taxes of the central and local governments as a percentage of nonoil GDP grew from 8.3 percent in 1983 to 11.5 percent in 1989, while the overall public sector deficit declined during that period from 4.9 percent to 3.4 percent of GDP.

Monetary and Financial Policies

Supportive monetary and financial policies were implemented to contain inflationary pressures, prevent capital flight, mobilize financial resources, and improve efficiency in the use of financial resources. A major reform of the financial sector, initiated in June 1983, deregulated state bank interest rates, simplified subsidized lending rates for priority sectors, and replaced credit ceilings with a system of reserve money management (see Balino and Sunderarajan 1986). As a follow-up to this reform, a new set of financial measures was announced in two steps, on October 27 and December 20, 1988. These initiatives were aimed at improving the efficiency of the financial sector by increasing competition, encouraging the development of the capital market, and further improving the effectiveness of monetary management.

Apart from these financial measures, the government's targets for monetary expansion were generally based on maintaining low rates of inflation. The deregulation of domestic interest rates helped restrain capital flight, increase mobilization of private saving by the banking sector (see Chamley and Hussain 1988), and reduce inefficiency in the use of financial resources. The combination of cautious monetary management and austere budgetary management has noticeably reduced the average rate of inflation since the early 1980s.

Trade and Other Regulatory Reforms

The government initiated a series of trade and other regulatory reforms to increase the effectiveness of demand management policies in reducing macroeconomic imbalances and to facilitate economic recovery in the medium term. Trade policy reforms sought to reduce the burden of import licensing and to signal the government's intention to shift to tariffs as the principal instrument of import policy. As a result of these policies, the value of imports subject to controls declined from 43 percent in mid-1986 to 21 percent in December 1988. More important, the proportion of domestic production protected by import licensing restrictions was reduced from 41 percent to 21 percent.

Notable progress was also made in simplifying and reducing other regulatory impediments. Through a series of steps taken between May 1986 and December 1987, the investment approval process was streamlined, licensing requirements were eased, the bias against foreign investment was reduced, and the role of the local-content program was diminished. In May 1989 the government converted the Investment Priority List to a short negative list, thereby simplifying the system and opening up new sectors to domestic and foreign markets. Reforms in the area of customs, ports, and maritime transport implemented in 1985 substantially reduced freight costs and procedural time. Subsequently, the government removed virtually all regulatory constraints on the development of an efficient and responsive maritime transport sector. Along with trade measures, these other regulatory reforms boosted domestic and foreign investment and nonoil exports by improving business confidence and reducing costs.

Economic Performance

The economic effects of Indonesia's adjustment program are discussed below with particular reference to the balance of payments, fiscal deficit, inflation, interest rates, efficiency, growth, and expenditure. The final section looks at the social costs of adjustment.

Balance of Payments

The effect of the adjustment program on the balance of payments is summarized in table 17-3. The current account deficit, following a surge

Table 17-3. Balance of Payments in Indonesia, Selected Years, Fiscal 1982–89
(billions of U.S. dollars at current prices)

Item	*1982*	*1983*	*1986*	*1987*	*1988*	*1989*
Merchandise exports (f.o.b.)	23.0	18.6	18.5	13.7	18.1	19.8
Oil and liquefied natural gas	18.8	14.7	12.3	7.0	8.6	7.7
Nonoil	4.2	3.9	6.2	6.7	9.5	12.1
Merchandise imports (c.i.f.)	−20.0	−20.7	−14.4	−12.7	−14.2	−15.5
Oil and liquefied natural gas	−5.4	−4.8	−3.2	−2.3	−2.4	−2.1
Nonoil	−14.6	−15.8	−11.2	−10.4	−11.8	−13.4
Current account balance	−2.7	−7.3	−2.0	−4.0	−1.6	−1.9
Oil and liquefied natural gas	9.8	7.2	5.9	2.4	3.8	3.0
Nonoil	−12.5	−14.5	−7.9	−6.4	−5.4	−4.9
Public medium- and long-term loans (net)	2.2	4.0	1.4	2.7	2.1	2.7
Other capital (net)	0.6	−0.0	1.5	−1.7	0.7	−1.6
Use of net foreign assets	−0.1	3.3	−0.9	3.0	−1.2	0.8
Current account/GNP (percent)	−3.0	−7.9	−2.4	−5.9	−2.3	−2.5
Noninterest current account balance/GNP (percent)	−1.3	−6.0	0.7	−1.9	2.3	2.1
Medium- and long-term debt service/exports (percent)	10.4	16.8	24.4	37.3	33.9	36.3

a. Estimated.
Sources: Bank Indonesia and World Bank staff estimates.

to 7.9 percent of GNP in 1983, fell to 2.4 percent of GNP in 1986. The collapse of oil prices in 1986 led to another sharp deterioration in the balance of payments, and the current account deficit climbed to 5.9 percent of GNP in 1987. Subsequently, the adjustment measures succeeded in lowering the deficit to less than 3 percent of GNP. Given the large loss of foreign exchange earnings caused by external shocks, the ability to reduce the current account deficit below the preshock level of 1982 is evidence of the success of the government's adjustment program in reducing the external imbalance.

In the initial phase of the adjustment period (1983–85), the balance of payments adjustment was effected largely through a strong reduction in imports. Several factors contributed to this reduction. First, public sector imports of capital goods were reduced sharply by a rephasing of large projects in March 1983 and by reductions in real capital spending in subsequent years. Second, by redefining priorities, the government diverted its expenditures from sectors with a relatively high import-intensiveness (mining and industry) to those that were less import-intensive (agriculture, education, and transport). The government also restrained the import intensity of capital expenditures of state enterprises by imposing strict limits on the use of nonconcessional trade credits. Third, the large depreciation of the real exchange rate raised the price of imports relative to domestic goods, thereby causing private sector demand to shift from imports to domestic substitutes (see Ahmed and Chhibber 1989). Fourth, a strong public investment effort during the oil boom increased import-substitution activities in such important commodities as rice, sugar, processed food, cement, and fertilizer. Fifth, the proliferation of nontariff barriers in the form of import licenses after the early 1980s also led to a compression of imports. (This process was reversed beginning in late 1986 when the government recognized the loss of economic efficiency caused by nontariff barriers. It then initiated a series of measures to deregulate trade and reduced the economy's reliance on import substitution.)

The relatively smaller impact of nonoil exports on balance of payments adjustment during the initial years is partly explained by the small nonoil export base at the start of the adjustment program. For example, the share of nonoil exports in total exports of goods (in real terms) was only 24 percent in 1983. The performance of nonoil exports began to improve immediately after the institution of the competitive exchange rate policy in March 1983.[3] The expansion of nonoil exports was especially encouraging during 1986–88, when they grew by an average of about 20 percent annually in real terms; by fiscal 1989 the share of nonoil exports in total exports (in real terms) had increased to 41 percent.[4] Deregulation measures affecting trade and domestic production also contributed to the expansion of nonoil exports.

Despite Indonesia's good performance in external adjustment and its cautious approach to external borrowing, the debt burden rose sharply in the 1980s. By the end of 1988 the stock of medium- and long-term public and private debt outstanding and disbursed had reached an estimated US$47.5 billion. Reflecting the adverse external environment the country has faced since the early 1980s, many of Indonesia's debt indicators are above the average for all developing countries and in line with those for the seventeen highly indebted countries.[5] Depreciation of the U.S. dollar after 1985 added US$12.6 billion (31 percent) to Indonesia's public debt at the end of 1988 and US$1.9 billion (25 percent) to its debt servicing during 1988.[6] Over the same period, oil prices fell by about one-half, severely reducing Indonesia's export earnings and capacity to service its debt.

Despite the rise in its debt indicators, Indonesia is distinguished from the highly indebted countries in several important respects: (1) it has maintained sound economic policies and a prudent borrowing strategy; (2) as a result, it receives strong financial support from official sources on concessional terms; (3) it has substantial reserves available in the form of foreign exchange and undrawn lines of credit; and (4) it has retained access to new voluntary lending from commercial banks. For these reasons, Indonesia has not faced a foreign exchange crisis or a cash-flow constraint on payment of its external debt obligations. Net transfers of external assistance have risen sharply from US$0.4 billion in 1986 to US$2.0 billion in 1988. At the same time, the government has maintained strict limits on import-related and commercial credits and has reduced exposure to private banks. This voluntary restraint has limited the total net transfer of resources to Indonesia but has improved the structure (maturity and terms) of its external debt. As a result, Indonesia's debt structure is now better than that of most developing countries, with a relatively high share of concessional debt and a relatively low share of variable-interest debt.

Indonesia's recent performance compares favorably with that of the highly indebted countries. Even with recourse to debt reschedulings and moratoriums, net transfers to the most highly indebted countries have turned substantially negative in recent years, reflecting the loss of access to new voluntary lending, especially from commercial banks. As a result, economic growth has been curtailed and per capita consumption has declined in eleven of the seventeen highly indebted countries. Although Indonesia has also made substantial cuts in investment since the early 1980s, the government was able to sustain GDP growth at 3.3 percent a year on average after 1983 through policies to improve efficiency and promote the development of nonoil exports. With prudent external borrowing and better economic performance several of Indonesia's debt indicators have declined, including the ratios of debt outstanding and disbursed to exports, debt outstanding and disbursed to GNP, and debt outstanding and disbursed to resources.[7]

Fiscal Deficit

The effects of the fiscal measures on public resource mobilization and the central government's budget deficit are summarized in table 17-4. Responding to the tax drive, the central government's nonoil taxes grew from 7.4 percent of nonoil GDP in 1983 to 10.8 percent in 1989. Measures to control expenditure were also largely successful. Thus, despite the growing burden of external interest payments, total expenditure declined from 22.7 percent of GDP in 1983 to 20.1 percent of GDP in 1989. As a result of revenue mobilization and expenditure control, the budget deficit narrowed from 4.4 percent to 2.8 percent of GDP over the same period. The restraining influence of the budget is further indicated by the sub-

Table 17-4. Indonesian Central Government Budget, Selected Years, Fiscal 1983–89
(trillions of rupiah at current prices)

Item	*1983*	*1986*	*1987*	*1988*	*1989*[a]
Revenue and grants	11.9	18.8	16.7	21.8	23.5
Oil and liquefied natural gas taxes	7.6	10.7	6.3	10.4	9.5
Nonoil taxes	3.8	6.4	7.9	9.0	11.9
Other	0.5	1.7	2.5	2.4	2.1
Current expenditure	8.2	12.7	13.4	15.5	16.8
External interest	0.7	1.8	2.8	3.8	4.3
Subsidies	1.4	1.1	0.9	1.4	1.0
Other	6.1	9.5	9.7	10.3	11.5
Government savings	3.7	6.1	3.3	6.3	6.7
Capital expenditure	6.6	8.7	7.3	9.2	10.5
Overall balance	−2.9	−2.7	−4.0	−2.9	−3.8
Financed by					
External loans (net)	2.0	1.8	3.7	2.8	4.2
Asset drawdown	0.9	0.9	0.3	0.1	−0.4
Percentage of GDP					
Nonoil taxes (percentage of nonoil GDP)	7.4	8.4	9.8	9.4	10.8
Overall balance	−4.4	−2.8	−3.9	−2.4	−2.8
Total expenditure	22.7	22.6	20.3	20.7	20.1
Net domestic expenditure[b]	11.4	8.5	3.8	4.1	2.2

a. Estimated.
b. Defined as the domestic content of expenditure less nonoil revenues.
Sources: Indonesia Ministry of Finance and World Bank staff estimates.

Table 17-5. Overall Public Sector Balances in Selected Asian Countries, Fiscal 1982–88
(percentage of GDP)

Country	*1982*	*1983*	*1984*	*1985*	*1986*	*1987*	*1988*	*Average, 1982–88*
Bangladesh[a]	−11.7	−11.2	−9.2	−7.5	−7.3	−8.1	−7.8	−9.0
India	−6.5	−7.0	−7.2	−8.6	−8.6	−9.1	n.a.	−7.8
Indonesia	−1.9	−4.9	−2.6	0.6	−3.1	−4.4	−3.2	−2.8
Malaysia	−19.7	−18.0	−15.9	−12.3	−5.3	−9.8	−7.8	−12.7
Pakistan[a]	−5.5	−5.6	−7.4	−6.2	−8.1	−7.7	−8.8	−7.0
Philippines[b]	n.a.	n.a.	−9.0	−8.2	−5.9	−5.4	−3.2	−6.3
Thailand	−7.9	−5.7	−4.5	−6.3	−4.7	−2.6	−2.2	−4.8
Indonesia primary balance[c]	−0.9	−3.7	−0.9	−2.6	−1.2	−1.6	0.1	−0.8

n.a. Not available.
a. Central government deficits.
b. As a percentage of GNP.
c. The overall public sector balance net of interest payments.
Source: World Bank Country Economic Reports.

stantial decline in net domestic expenditure from 11.4 percent of GDP in 1983 to 2.2 percent of GDP in 1989.

The central government's budget deficit, however, understates the true level of the public sector's net claim on resources because it does not include the operation of public enterprises and local governments. Table 17-5 compares overall public sector deficits in Indonesia with those in other Asian countries. This comparison shows that Indonesia has generally maintained cautious fiscal management, despite the loss of oil revenue. Also encouraging is the trend of the primary balance (the public sector deficit net of interest payments), which registered a small surplus during 1988.

Austere budgetary management has been an integral element of the adjustment program and has served to reduce demand pressures on both the balance of payments and prices. By maintaining low deficits and restraining access to bank credit, budgetary management has helped to contain inflation and avoided a crowding-out of private investment. By restraining aggregate demand and lowering the import intensity of expenditures, budgetary management has also assisted in reducing the current account deficit.

Inflation

The effect of the adjustment program on inflation is summarized in table 17-6. All three measures of domestic inflation—consumer price index

Table 17-6. Domestic Inflation Trends in Indonesia, 1973–81 and 1981–88
(average annual percentage rate)

Indicator	*1973–81*	*1981–88*[a]
Domestic inflation		
Consumer price index[b]	15.3	8.4
Wholesale price index (nonoil)	16.6	11.6
Nonoil GDP deflator	15.9	9.3
Selected price indices		
Import goods[c]	13.6	11.4
Export goods[d]	19.0	12.7
Rice[e]	15.7	9.1
Nontraded goods[f]	14.0	8.9

a. Price indices for 1988 were adjusted upward to reflect better the impact of international inflation and rice prices.

b. Because data on the CPI for seventeen cities are available only from 1979, the CPI for Jakarta is used.

c. In domestic currency.

d. In domestic currency, excluding oil.

e. Medium-quality wholesale price.

f. Housing and other services.

Sources: Indonesia Central Bureau of Statistics and World Bank staff estimates.

(CPI), wholesale price index (WPI), and the nonoil GDP deflator—show a significant deceleration of the average rate of inflation. The sharpest reduction is indicated by the CPI, while the WPI shows a more modest decline. Despite large devaluations, cost-push pressures on domestic inflation during 1981–88 were contained by lower levels of world inflation and the government's ability to restrain rice prices. Wage pressures were very limited because of restraints on public sector wages. (Indonesia has a small formal wage employment sector in which the public sector is dominant.) Even in the formal manufacturing sector, available data suggest a slowdown in the growth of wages. In the informal sector, wage adjustments were generally linked to the price of rice, which grew in a stable fashion until 1986, reflecting virtual self-sufficiency in rice and the stabilization of rice prices.[8] On the demand side, austere budgets and the slowdown of domestic income growth assisted in reducing demand pressure on the exchange rate and restraining growth in the prices of nontradables.

The low transmission of inflationary pressures through cost-push and demand-pull forces was supported by an appropriate monetary policy. The government curbed inflation partly by slowing the rate of growth of reserve money but chiefly by inducing people to hold a larger volume of money (M2) by deregulating domestic deposit rates (see table 17-7). The surge in the growth of quasi-money (QM, time and savings deposits),

Table 17-7. Growth of Money and Credit in Indonesia, 1973–81 and 1981–88
(average annual percentage rates)

Item	*1973–81*	*1981–88*
Reserve money	28.0	15.0
Currency and demand deposits (M1)	32.8	12.3
Time and saving deposits (QM)	33.5	39.9
Money supply (M2 = M1 + QM)	33.0	25.1
Domestic credit	21.5	25.7
Private credit	26.6	28.0
Quasi-money/GDP	5.3	13.8
M2/GDP	15.1	24.5

Sources: Bank Indonesia and World Bank staff estimates.

despite much slower growth of nominal income, contributed to a sharp increase in the financial deepening of the economy (reflected in the rise in the QM/GDP and M2/GDP ratios). The increase in demand for money in turn relieved demand pressure in the goods market and brought down inflation.

The financial deepening and the government's austere budgetary stance allowed the expansion of credit to the private sector, thereby avoiding a supply crunch.[9] The ability to bring down inflation even with two major devaluations is a strong indicator of improved overall monetary management. Reserve money growth has been substantially reduced in recent years. Moreover, despite some initial learning costs, short-term monetary management has also improved, as shown by the government's success in curbing speculative pressures on the exchange rate in March–June 1987.

Interest Rates

A major element of the June 1983 financial deregulation package was decontrol of domestic interest rates. The sharp rise in state bank deposit rates in conjunction with lower inflation caused real deposit rates to become strongly positive—increasing from −10.7 percent in 1981 to 9.8 percent in 1985. Similarly, the removal of the ceiling on lending rates led to an increase in the average lending rate. High real lending rates since 1983 have generated some concern about their adverse effect on private investment, however.[10] One factor underlying the high domestic lending rates is the cost of financial intermediation. The current large spread between deposit and lending rates (about 4 percentage points) is a consequence of significant inefficiencies that have persisted in the financial sector despite the 1983 financial reforms. The October–December 1988 financial measures addressed some of these outstanding problems. The reforms are expected to improve efficiency in the financial sector significantly by increasing competition. They are also expected to increase the availability of long-term finance by stimulating the growth of capital markets.

One issue that has evoked intense debate is the role of monetary policy in the determination of domestic interest rates in Indonesia. Because Indonesia does not regulate private international capital flows and the exchange rate is not fully flexible, the domestic interest rate over the long term will be determined by the international interest rate and the expected rate of depreciation of the rupiah.[11]

In the past, three variables affected exchange rate expectations: the swap premium rate,[12] the differential between domestic and international inflation, and the price of oil. Exchange rate expectations appear to have been especially sensitive to oil price movements. From 1983 to 1986 the average difference between the domestic deposit rate and the international interest rate was 6.3 percent, higher than the swap premium (5.1 percent) and inflation differential (CPI) between Indonesia and the United States (4.6 percent). This happened because of uncertainty about the price of oil, which prompted fears of an exchange rate depreciation that would exceed the level implied by the inflation differential or the swap premium.

The September 12, 1986, devaluation and the recovery of oil prices in 1987 tended to dampen these fears in 1987–88, but two offsetting influences were the increases in the inflation differential (5.8 percent) and the swap premium (9.1 percent). These increases widened the difference between domestic and international interest rates even further and fueled additional fears of a depreciation of the exchange rate. The recent move to allow the swap premium to become a market-based value reflecting international interest differentials rather than a policy variable is intended to provide flexibility to the swap rate. In addition, releasing the premium from its role as a policy instrument is intended to persuade people that the swap premium does not reflect the government's view about future exchange rate adjustments.

Since domestic deposit rates will need to be linked to international interest rates to avoid capital flight, Bank Indonesia has rightly maintained that the main way in which monetary policy can affect long-term interest rates is by sustaining low inflation rates and thereby dampening fears of an exchange rate depreciation. In the short term, monetary policy has also been used to protect domestic rates from the destabilizing influences of speculative capital flight.[13] But an expansionary monetary policy designed to achieve low interest rates has generally been avoided because it would be self-defeating over the longer term by leading to high inflation, capital flight, and balance of payments instability.[14]

Economic Efficiency

With the substantial decline in oil revenue and the new limitations on the public sector's capacity to support growth through its expenditure programs, the need to improve economic efficiency and stimulate the private sector became evident. The government recognized that a thorough revamping of the regulatory framework was essential for achieving this goal and, as mentioned previously, began a series of comprehensive and far-reaching deregulatory measures in 1985. Because of the time lag before many of these policy initiatives can affect behavior, it is too early to evaluate their full quantitative impact. Even so, there is some evidence of an improvement in economic efficiency in recent years.

A rough index of productivity is the aggregate return on investment. Large investments financed through the oil boom fueled the growth of the nonoil economy in 1973–81. Given the low initial capital base in these sectors, these investments yielded a fairly high average rate of return (see table 17-8). The return per unit of investment declined sharply in 1982–85 but has picked up noticeably in recent years. A closely related indicator of capital productivity, the incremental capital-output ratio (ICOR), reveals a similar pattern. A more comprehensive measure of the gain in macroeconomic efficiency is the change in total factor productivity (summarized in table 17-8 with the use of value added as a measure of

Table 17-8. Indicators of Aggregate Efficiency in Indonesia, 1973–81 to 1986–88

Indicator	*1973–81*	*1982–85*	*1986–88*
Rate of return on investment (percent a year)[a]	31.4	13.1	21.8
Incremental capital-output ratio	2.8	7.8	5.2
Total factor productivity change (percent a year)[b]			
Value added[c]	8.0	4.0	5.1
Factor inputs			
Labor	3.0	2.8	2.8
Capital[d]	10.7	9.8	5.2
Total factor productivity	0.9	−2.5	1.0

a. Rate of growth of nonoil GDP as a percentage of average investment rate during the period.

b. Total factor productivity change is calculated as the difference between rates of growth of value added and factor inputs (labor and capital); the inputs are weighted by their income shares.

c. Using nonoil GDP.

d. Capital stock was derived by using the perpetual inventory method.

Source: World Bank staff estimates.

Table 17-9. Indonesia's Economic Structure, Fiscal 1982, 1986, and 1989
(percent)

Item	*1982*	*1986*	*1989*
Oil and liquefied natural gas/total exports[a]	80.8	66.6	35.8
Nonoil exports/nonoil imports[a]	28.8	55.4	90.3
Oil and liquefied natural gas revenues/total revenue	70.7	57.5	41.3
Government expenditure/GDP	22.1	22.6	20.1
Private fixed investment/total fixed investment[b]	52.1	47.9	56.9
Manufacturing/nonoil GDP[b]	8.4	8.8	9.5

a. Goods only; in current dollars.
b. Calendar year; in 1983 prices.
Source: World Bank staff estimates.

production). A striking finding is that the main determinant of economic growth in the oil boom period was the rapid buildup of capital stock. Improvement in factor productivity played a marginal role. External shocks reduced factor productivity in 1982–85, but the trend was reversed after 1985. Nevertheless, the low contribution of factor productivity to economic growth illustrates the scope for future gains in efficiency.

The structural reforms that allowed the recent gains in economic efficiency also supported a noticeable improvement in the structure of the economy (table 17-9). Indonesia's dependence on oil was substantially reduced, and the reliance on more promising and sustainable sources of growth increased. Especially encouraging is the strong positive response of nonoil exports and private investment. The process of structural transformation is not yet complete, however. With sustained progress in implementing ongoing reforms and initiating new policy changes in required areas, Indonesia can be expected to reach a higher real growth path on a self-sustained basis.

Economic Growth and Expenditure

The government's balanced adjustment program also helped sustain a rate of economic growth that was better than expected, despite the loss of oil revenue. Although economic growth decelerated significantly over the adjustment period, it remained positive in per capita terms (table 17-10). Given the severity of the external shocks, sustaining a 3 percent annual expansion of the overall economy and 4 percent annual growth

Table 17-10. Overall and Sectoral GDP Performance in Indonesia, 1973–81 to 1988
(annual percentage real growth)

Item	*1973–81*	*1981–88*	*1987*	*1988*
GDP	7.5	3.3	3.9	4.7
Nonoil GDP	8.0	4.3	4.6	5.6
Agriculture	3.4	2.9	1.8	3.8
Manufacturing[a]	14.1	5.2	7.1	9.0
Services	10.0	5.0	5.6	5.6
GDP per capita	5.2	1.3	1.9	2.7

Note: The Central Bureau of Statistics is currently reviewing its data and methodology for estimating GDP. This is expected to result in higher estimates of real growth rates for some sectors, especially in 1988.

a. Excludes liquefied natural gas and oil refineries.

Source: Central Bureau of Statistics.

in the nonoil economy while also substantially reducing financial imbalances is a notable achievement. Although the factors underlying the rapid growth of the 1970s—oil earnings, rice production, and import-substituting manufacturing—weakened during the adjustment phase, nonoil exports, especially manufactured exports, emerged as a new source of growth. Already there are encouraging signs of economic recovery, such as the upward trend in the rate of growth of the nonoil economy since 1987, which reached an estimated 5.6 percent in 1988.

The lower rate of growth of GDP and the deterioration in the terms of trade had an adverse effect on domestic income during 1981–86 (see table 17-11). The shortfall in resources brought about substantial cutbacks in public investment. Private investment fell noticeably until 1985 but has been recovering since then. The growth of private consumption also declined significantly, although it still grew faster than national income. Overall, the main adjustment happened in the public sector. As a result of expenditure restraints, especially the large reduction in budget-financed capital spending, public expenditure (consumption and investment) as a share of GDP fell from 22.4 percent in 1981 to 18 percent in 1988. In the private sector the decline in investment in the first few years of the adjustment period was caused by higher real interest rates and lower aggregate demand (see Ahmed and Chhibber 1989). Since 1986 private investment has been recovering in response to the improved incentives resulting from the regulatory reforms and a more buoyant level of economic activity. Much of this new investment has been directed toward export activities.

Table 17-11. Impact of Adjustment Policies on National Expenditure in Indonesia, 1973–88
(percent)

Item	*Annual growth rate* 1973–81	1981–88	1987	1988	*Share of* GDP[a] 1981	1988
National income	11.4	1.8	4.7	4.8	97.9	88.6
Consumption	8.2	3.3	2.2	4.0	69.5	69.3
Public	10.1	2.2	−3.7	1.5	10.6	9.8
Private	7.8	3.4	3.3	4.4	58.9	59.5
Fixed investment	11.7	−0.5	1.9	7.0	24.7	18.9
Public	11.0	−2.0	−1.7	6.3	11.8	8.2
Private	12.3	0.7	4.9	7.6	12.9	10.7
Per capita national income	9.1	−0.2	2.7	2.8	—	—
Per capita private consumption	5.5	1.4	1.3	2.4	—	—

a. In 1983 prices.
Sources: Indonesia Central Bureau of Statistics and World Bank staff estimates.

The Social Costs of Adjustment

The adjustment process inevitably involved short-term social costs. Despite the recent recovery in economic growth, per capita income was adversely affected by the terms of trade losses. A full assessment of the social costs of adjustment is precluded by the lack of sufficient data on how the adjustment process affected poverty and income inequality. Fragmentary evidence suggests, however, that the urban sector was more adversely affected than the rural sector.

Part of the labor market adjustment took the form of an increased rate of open unemployment in urban areas, especially among young school leavers.[15] Because the flexibility of educated urban job seekers is rather limited, the slowdown in demand resulting from lower economic growth and budgetary constraints on resources reduced the rate of their absorption in employment (especially in the civil service). For the bulk of the urban work force, however, the main burden of adjustment fell on earnings (especially in the informal sector); labor earnings fell in trade, and real wages of construction workers and civil servants stagnated. In manufacturing, real wages continued to grow, although at a slower pace than before the external shocks. The slowdown in demand during 1982–85 hurt manufacturing sector profits, but the recent surge in nonoil manufacturing exports has supported the recovery of profits in export-based manufacturing enterprises, including small-scale enterprises.

The adjustment burden appears to have been generally less severe in rural areas because farm incomes were relatively protected by several factors: the increase in real rice prices; the real exchange rate depreciation, which largely offset lower agricultural export prices; and some profitable diversification away from rice toward nonrice crops, especially fruits and vegetables. Overall agricultural output was pulled down, however, by the slower growth of rice production, which in turn reduced the demand for farm workers. Similarly, a slowdown in real public expenditure reduced the demand for rural construction workers. Because of the flexible nature of rural labor markets, however, the result was not a reduction in employment but rather a stagnation or decline in real agricultural wages (see Papanek 1988; Manning and others 1988).[16] Real wages in rural construction activities apparently also remained flat.

The declining trends in labor earnings are attributable to the major external shocks facing Indonesia and not to the adjustment response itself. Indeed, the government moved to mitigate the social costs of adjustment by reallocating public spending to important social programs. For example, the shares of development expenditure allocated to social services and agriculture were significantly increased from 1983 to 1988. An effort was also made to protect regional transfers, which normally finance small-scale and labor-intensive infrastructure projects at the local level. Given the large magnitude of the income loss, however, there was some scaling back of social programs and some reduction in the quality of service. But without this effort to redefine expenditure priorities in support of lower income groups, the social costs of adjustment would have been much higher. More important, by reducing financial imbalances and promoting restructuring in the economy, the government's reform program prepared the ground for sustaining a higher growth path over the medium term. This is essential for absorption of the rapidly growing labor force at higher levels of productivity and income.

The World Bank's Contribution to the Adjustment Effort

By any standard, the government's efforts to restore macroeconomic stability and to accelerate the process of structural change were remarkably successful. The agenda for policy reform was carefully developed, and the government, by making difficult but correct decisions, has clearly established its credibility since 1983. The World Bank responded to the government's adjustment efforts by focusing policy analysis and advice on the key issues of macroeconomic management and structural reform, while its lending program has expanded significantly to support continued policy reform by the government. At the same time, two adjustment loans and annual economic reports have enabled the World Bank to be a catalyst in mobilizing substantial additional support for the adjustment effort from other external lenders who constitute the Intergovernmental Group on Indonesia.

The World Bank's analysis and policy dialogue have supported the government's efforts to define appropriate policy responses to emerging issues of macroeconomic management. The World Bank prepared major studies of trade and industrial policies in 1981 and 1985 that helped identify the costs of the complex regulatory environment in Indonesia and to show the broad directions for future policy change. With the decline in oil prices, the push for reforms within Indonesia gathered momentum. To support this effort, the World Bank provided analytical inputs on reforms in the trade regime and the regulatory environment.

With the sharp drop in oil prices in 1986 and the rapid increase in the external debt burden, Indonesia needed to rely primarily on concessional aid from official sources, rather than on commercial borrowing, to meet its financing gaps. Indonesia's well-developed agenda for policy reform and the government's well-established credibility for making sound policy decisions enabled the World Bank to support structural adjustment through sectoral loans for housing, urban development, and irrigation and to support macroeconomic reforms through two trade policy adjustment operations.

In general, the World Bank's overall lending program has contributed to important achievements at the sectoral level. Lending for irrigation has supported self-sufficiency in rice production; lending for transmigration and the development of tree crops in the Outer Islands has helped reduce the incidence of rural poverty and increase nonoil export earnings; lending for energy development, transport infrastructure, and industrial finance has helped expand nonagricultural employment and diversify the sources of growth; and lending for human resource development has contributed to a major expansion in the supply of trained staff, the increased availability of health services, and the success of one of the best-managed and -administered population programs in the world.

The World Bank's annual economic reports and two adjustment loans have provided the basis for the support of the Intergovernmental Group on Indonesia, whose members substantially increased their aid flows and made available fast-disbursing, untied balance of payments loans. This assistance provides temporary support to the government while it implements policies to adjust the balance of payments and the budget to external shocks. The response from Intergovernmental Group members has been very encouraging, with disbursements totaling US$3.7 billion over the past three years. This valuable assistance has helped the government push ahead with deregulation and facilitated the recovery of private investment and economic activity. It has also enabled Indonesia to restructure its external debt, by improving the average maturity and terms, while maintaining the confidence of the financial market and investors in the viability of the adjustment program.

Notes

I would like to thank Mark Baird, Amar Bhattacharya, Russell Cheetham, Ajay Chhibber, Javad Khalilzadeh-Shirazi, and Attila Sonmez for helpful comments. Errors are my sole responsibility.

1. The percentage of people falling below the designated poverty line dropped from 57.1 in 1970 to 39.8 in 1980.

2. The magnitude of devaluation is calculated according to the International Monetary Fund (IMF) method, which measures devaluation in terms of the rate of change in the value of foreign currency per unit of the domestic currency (for example, the value of the U.S. dollar per rupiah).

3. Empirical verification of the strong positive response of Indonesia's nonoil exports to depreciation of the real exchange rate is contained in Ahmed and Chhibber (1989) and Kincaid (1983).

4. In current prices, the share of nonoil exports grew from 21 percent in fiscal 1983 to 61 percent in fiscal 1989. This growth reflects the combined effects of higher volumes and prices of nonoil exports and lower oil prices.

5. This group comprises Argentina, Bolivia, Brazil, Chile, Colombia, Costa Rica, Côte d'Ivoire, Ecuador, Jamaica, Mexico, Morocco, Nigeria, Peru, Philippines, Uruguay, Venezuela, and Yugoslavia (see World Bank 1989).

6. Excluding credits for the expansion of liquefied natural gas and liquefied petroleum gas and for paraxyelene projects.

7. The ratios of medium- and long-term debt outstanding and disbursed to exports, and debt outstanding and disbursed to GNP, declined from 236.8 and 71.0 in 1987 to 220.8 and 64.7 in 1988, respectively. The ratio of debt outstanding and disbursed to resources fell from 137.3 in 1987 to 127.1 in 1988. This ratio is obtained as a weighted average of debt outstanding and disbursed to exports and of debt outstanding and disbursed to GNP, and it neutralizes the bias of an exchange rate policy in the measurement of the debt problem (see Cohen 1988).

8. Because the 1987 drought had adversely affected rice output, rice prices surged starting in late 1987, and the upward trend continued until mid-1988. Subsequently, rice prices stabilized in response to improved supply.

9. Indonesia's experience supports the McKinnon-Shaw argument for financial deregulation in developing countries. McKinnon's theory that the rate of inflation can be brought down without reducing real money supply appears to be of strong relevance to Indonesia's experience (see McKinnon 1973; Fry 1988).

10. Ahmed and Chhibber (1989) show that there is a statistically significant negative relationship between the real interest rate and private investment in Indonesia.

11. The domestic rate may adjust to the foreign rate in a lagged fashion, and there may be some transaction costs.

12. The swap facility was set up in 1979 by Bank Indonesia to allow investors borrowing abroad to hedge against the risk of a major devaluation by purchasing a swap rediscountable at a fixed premium. The swap facility provided only a partial arbitrage support, since it was constrained by limited access and a rigidly set premium (until October 1988).

13. This was done very successfully during May–June 1987.

14. A framework linking the interest rate, exchange rate, and inflation in Indonesia is provided in Ahmed and Kapur (1989).

15. Given the structure of Indonesia's labor markets, a slowdown in economic activity is manifested largely in a reduction in labor earnings rather than in employment levels, except in the urban formal sector. Recent data show that more than half of all employment is in agriculture and more than 70 percent in rural areas. Employment outside agriculture is concentrated in services, with manufacturing accounting for only 20 percent of nonagricultural employment. Outside of government service, low and unstable earnings in informal sector activities predominate in urban areas. The considerable flexibility of rural and urban informal labor markets allows a rapid expansion of employment during periods of low economic growth, but at reduced real earnings.

16. There are some exceptions to these trends, especially in areas where a more diversified rural economy and rural-urban linkages have continued to support increases in real agricultural wages (see, for example, Collier and others 1988).

References

Ahmed, Sadiq. 1989. "Indonesia: External Shocks, Policy Response, and Adjustment Performance." Asia Regional Series, Report IDP 39. World Bank, Washington, D.C.

Ahmed, Sadiq, and Ajay Chhibber. 1989. "Reconciling Non-Inflationary Growth and Debt in Indonesia." Asia Region, World Bank, Washington, D.C.

Ahmed, Sadiq, and Basant Kapur. 1989. "A Short-Run Econometric Model of the Indonesian Monetary System." World Bank, Jakarta, Indonesia.

Balino, Thomas, and V. Sunderarajan. 1986. "Financial Reform in Indonesia: Causes, Consequences and Prospects." In Hang-Sheng Cheng, ed., *Financial Policy and Reform in the Pacific Basin.* Lexington, Mass.: Lexington Books.

Chamley, Christophe, and Quaiser Hussain. 1988. "The Effects of Financial Liberalization on Thailand, Indonesia, and the Philippines: A Quantitative Evaluation." PPR Working Paper. Policy, Planning, and Research, World Bank, Washington, D.C.

Cohen, Daniel. 1988. "The Management of the Developing Countries' Debt: Guidelines and Applications to Brazil." *World Bank Economic Review* 2 (1):77–103.

Collier, William, and others. 1988. "Employment Trends in Lowland Javanese Villages." U.S. Agency for International Development, Jakarta, Indonesia.

Fry, Maxwell J. 1988. *Money, Interest, and Banking in Economic Development.* Baltimore, Md.: Johns Hopkins University Press.

Gelb, Alan, and associates. 1988. *Oil Windfalls: Blessing or Curse?* New York: Oxford University Press.

Kincaid, Russell. 1983. "The Impact of the 1978 Exchange Rate Adjustments in Indonesia on the Non-Oil Trade Account." DM/83/60. International Monetary Fund, Washington, D.C.

Manning, Christopher, and others. 1988. "Indonesia: Employment Problems, Prospects, and Policies." World Bank, Jakarta, Indonesia.

McKinnon, Ronald. 1973. *Money and Capital in Economic Development.* Washington, D.C.: Brookings Institution.

Papanek, Gustav. 1988. *Changes in Real Wages: Employment, Poverty, Competitiveness.* DSP 24. Boston, Mass.: Boston Institute for Developing Economies.

World Bank. 1989. *World Debt Tables 1989–90.* Washington, D.C.

Comments

William H. Branson

SADIQ AHMED presents a careful, balanced, and accurate account of Indonesia's adjustment to the fall in oil prices in the mid-1980s and the subsequent liberalization of its trade and industrial policies. In general, I agree with Ahmed's analysis and with the judgment that Indonesia is a successful case in terms of both adjustment and the interaction with the World Bank in the adjustment process. My discussion will focus on Indonesia's macroeconomic adjustment policy as an example for the application of the classic analysis of policy for external and internal balance associated with Salter (1959) and Swan (1963). I will also discuss briefly the desirability of an investment pause during a structural adjustment program, as was observed in Indonesia. Before turning to my analysis, however, I will dispose of the two major points of disagreement I have with the chapter.

The first point concerns the effect of dollar depreciation on debt service, which, Ahmed argues, "significantly increased Indonesia's debt service payments." This effect is included in the exchange rate effect in table 17-1. This interpretation seems to reflect a kind of accounting illusion. If the diversification of Indonesia's debt across currencies reflects the pattern of its export earnings, movements of the dollar against the European Currency Unit or the yen should have no effect on the burden of the debt service. If for historical reasons the debt is not so diversified, the service can be via interest rate swaps. If Indonesia does not diversify its debt service, it is speculating on movements in exchange rates.

The second point concerns the assertion that an external shock is manifested initially in a balance of payments disequilibrium. The recent literature on adjustment shows that this is the case only if the disturbance is perceived to be temporary. But if, for example, the disturbance comes from a variable that is perceived to follow a random walk over time, such as the exchange rate, then each change is permanent. In this case, absorption would adjust immediately to the income effect of the disturbance, and no change would be observed in the balance of payments. This is a standard result from intertemporal maximizing models such as that of McKibbin and Sachs (1988).

Now I turn to a brief examination of Indonesia's macroeconomic policy, which provides a good example for the application of the classic Salter-Swan analysis of policy for internal and external balance in a small open economy with a pegged exchange rate. Indonesia has internationally open capital markets and an exchange rate pegged at any point in time to a currency basket. If we take low inflation as the target of internal balance and stable foreign exchange reserves as the target of external balance, we can apply the Salter-Swan analysis, in which fiscal policy is aimed primarily at internal balance and monetary policy at external balance. With a mild increase in inflation following the 1986 devaluation, and some apparent loss in reserves in 1988, this approach would call for a tightening of both fiscal and monetary policy. This has been the direction of policy in Indonesia since 1987.

In the Salter-Swan analysis, fiscal policy is aimed primarily at internal balance, represented here by a low rate of inflation. Indicators of domestic inflation are shown in table 17-6. The relatively high inflation rates of the early 1980s were reduced to 5 to 7 percent on the general indicators in 1985 and 1986 as the primary budget deficit was reduced. The discrete nominal devaluation in September 1986 raised the prices of traded goods in late 1986 and 1987, but the inflation rate on price indexes for export and import goods slowed in 1988 to about 12 percent.

The single best indicator for internal balance is probably the inflation rate for nontraded goods. With the prices of imported inputs and rice rising, and some shift of demand toward nontraded goods with the devaluation, prices of nontraded goods rose by about 8 percent in 1987. But even with some pressure from the rice price, inflation for nontraded goods was down to about 5 percent in 1988. This shows that the devaluation of 1986 changed the price ratio of traded to nontraded goods and was not passed through as a general increase in prices. In terms of maintenance of internal balance, the tightening of fiscal policy (see table 17-4) was the complement to the devaluation that prevented its spread to the general price level.

The proximate target for monetary policy in the Salter-Swan analysis for Indonesia is external balance, represented by the maintenance of the desired foreign exchange reserve position. This policy objective is required by the combination of open capital markets and a pegged exchange rate. Although the exchange rate is adjusted against a currency basket daily, it is not floating. At any point in time, the authorities are committed to the existing nominal rate against the dollar. In this situation, monetary policy must be tight enough to keep interest rates high enough that the private capital inflow finances the current account deficit less official net borrowing—that is, tight enough to maintain the desired level of reserves. With a stable demand for money that is a function of real income, the price level, expected inflation, and the interest rate, the given values for the first three variables and a proximate target for the interest rate set the demand for money. This, in turn, sets the growth in the domestic component of the monetary base that is consistent with stable foreign exchange reserves. Indonesian monetary policy is a good example of the monetary component of the classic analysis. This is discussed clearly in chapter 17.

The rise in the ratio of quasi-money to GDP since 1984 (implicit in table 17-7) presumably reflects the financial reform that began then and the reduction of inflation. The continued growth in the ratio of quasi-money to GDP since 1986 is also consistent with the public's expectation of continued low inflation despite the devaluation. Thus the movement of the monetary aggregates is consistent with a gradual tightening of policy, combined with a growing public demand for deposits in the banking system. The only modification of this policy stance that might be suggested is the maintenance of a sufficient real international interest differential to maintain the central bank's net foreign asset position.

Finally, I will briefly discuss the investment response to structural adjustment. Adjustment programs in general are attempts to increase the efficiency of the economy, and in general the programs seem to have succeeded. In chapter 11 Riccardo Faini and his associates, using a cross-section regression analysis, find significantly better growth performance in countries with adjustment programs than in those without, and they also find that the amount of World Bank–IMF lending contributes significantly to the result. Indonesia is an example of a country that has improved its growth performance with adjustment, however incomplete.

Faini and his associates also find, however, that the adjusting countries have lower investment/GDP ratios than nonadjusters and that the investment ratio is significantly and negatively related to the amount of lending. In Indonesia private as well as public investment fell during the adjustment period, as suggested by table 17-11. How should we interpret this investment response?

First, consider the extreme case of costless adjustment in a neoclassical growth model. If the adjustment simply rotates the per capita production function up, the golden-rule savings rate will fall as some of the windfall is absorbed by a reduction in investment. The example is greatly strengthened if there are adjustment costs for the current population. The adjustment presumably puts the economy on a higher growth path, which will provide benefits to future generations, but the costs are being borne by the present generation. The costs can be spread equitably into the future if expenditure cuts come out of investment instead of current consumption. This argues for the intertemporal optimality of an investment pause during the adjustment program, if not a permanent reduction in the investment ratio.

This intertemporal efficiency argument may be implicitly recognized by the political attractiveness, if not necessity, of maintaining consumption during the adjustment program. The political justification for the program is that it will provide future benefits. It seems reasonable for the political process to require that the present population be compensated for their efforts in behalf of the future.

The pause in private investment is likely to be motivated by the temporary increase in uncertainty that is caused by the program. In no case is a complete program announced and credibly implemented immediately. Decisions are taken over time and frequently against some political opposition. As a result, some degree of secrecy exists in the political decisionmaking process, which adds to the genuine uncertainty about the best course of the program over time. If this process is understood by private investors, their best course is to wait until the uncertainty is reduced to its normal level. So the investment pause is rational from the private investor's perspective, and is socially rational as well.

An example of this investment response is provided by the Indonesian adjustment in the 1980s, as described by Ahmed. Growth in real private consumption slowed during the stabilization period until 1987, but much less than growth in national income. The growth rate of private real consumption per capita bottomed at 1.3 percent in 1987. Total fixed investment actually fell, while private fixed investment was flat from 1981 to 1986. The private investment slump ended in 1987, and private fixed investment in real terms grew 7.6 percent in 1988, as the shape of the adjustment program became clear. The Indonesian government was clear on the need not to squeeze consumption excessively in the adjustment period, and the policy seems to have succeeded.

References

McKibbin, Warren, and Jeffrey Sachs. 1988. "Coordination of Monetary and Fiscal Policies in the OECD." In J. Frenkel, ed., *International Aspects of Fiscal Policies.* Chicago, Ill.: University of Chicago Press.

Salter, W. 1959. "Internal and External Balance: The Role of Price and Expenditure Effects." *Economic Record* 35 (August):226–38.

Swan, T. W. 1963. "Longer-Run Problems of the Balance of Payments." In H. W. Arndt and W. M. Corden, eds., *The Australian Economy: A Book of Readings.* Melbourne: Cheshire Press. (Reprinted in R. E. Caves and H. G. Johnson, eds., *Readings in International Economics.* Homewood, Ill.: Irwin.)

18 *Korea: Successful Adjustment*

Mansoor Dailami

IN MANY RESPECTS, the process of structural adjustment, which was pursued with varying degrees of intensity by many indebted developing countries in the 1980s, finds its clearest expression in the experience of the Republic of Korea. The economy adjusted to the global shocks of the 1980s with remarkable promptness and success. Economic growth resumed, and the economy is again advancing at a double-digit rate. Inflation was sharply reduced from an average of 13.7 percent in the 1970s and a peak of 29 percent in 1980 to about 7 percent for 1988. The balance of current account underwent a significant turnaround from a deficit of US$5.3 billion (9.4 percent of GNP) in 1980 to a hefty surplus of US$10.0 billion (8.3 percent of GNP) in 1987, and the outstanding level of external debt was reduced by about US$16 billion from its peak of US$48 billion in 1980 (see table 18-1).

These achievements relative to those of other debtor countries place Korea in a unique position that can be compared only with its own "economic miracles" of the 1960s and 1970s. Yet neither the severity of the economic problems faced by Korea at the beginning of the 1980s nor the sagacity of the policy measures undertaken in subsequent years should be underestimated. This chapter describes the crisis of the early 1980s, reviews the policy measures adopted, evaluates the role of the World Bank adjustment lending programs formulated in the context of two structural adjustment loans (SALs) and two industrial finance projects and attempts to draw policy implications for other indebted countries.

Background: Causes and Origins of Crisis

When the global shocks of the early 1980s hit the Korean economy, it was already suffering from several structural and macroeconomic imbalances. These imbalances were reflected most noticeably in high and rising inflation, tight labor market conditions, overvalued exchange rates, deteriorating external competitiveness, high excess capacity in the manufacturing sector (particularly in heavy and chemical industries), low business profitability, high corporate indebtedness, and segmented and overregulated financial markets.

Table 18-1. Macroeconomic and Balance of Payments Developments in Korea, 1970–74 to 1988

Indicator	*1970–74*	*1975–79*	*1980*	*1985*	*1986*	*1987*	*1988*
Real GNP growth (percent)	8.9	9.8	−5.2	5.4	12.3	12.0[a]	12.2[b]
Rate of inflation (CPI, percent)	13.7	16.7	28.7	2.5	2.8	3.0	7.1
Current account balance							
Billions of U.S. dollars	−0.8	−1.5	−5.3	−0.9	4.6	9.9	13.0[a]
Percentage of GNP	−6.6	−3.8	−9.4	−1.0	4.7	8.3[a]	n.a.
External debt (billions of U.S. dollars)	n.a.	n.a.	29.8	48.0	45.1	35.6	32.0[a]

n.a. Not available.

a. Estimate.

b. Based on data for three quarters only.

Sources: Bank of Korea (various years); *Far Eastern Economic Review*, February 9, 1989; and World Bank (1987b).

Domestic Factors

The sources and causes of these imbalances were varied, but there is growing agreement that most could be traced to the rapid growth strategy of the 1960s and 1970s and, most immediately, to the nature of the adjustment to the oil price increase of the mid-1970s. The response to the oil shock was to expand aggregate demand, both internal and external, and thereby to maintain the growth momentum of the 1960s. Between 1973 and 1978 real GDP grew by an average of 10 percent each year, exports by 25 percent, and investment by 21 percent. This strategy avoided interruption in the growth of per capita income, which tripled in real terms between 1960 and 1978.

This vigorous economic growth was accompanied, however, by a substantial shift in industrial structure and resource allocation in the second half of the 1970s. In anticipation of continuing domestic growth and rapid expansion of international trade, the authorities changed course in the second half of the 1970s and promoted large-scale investment in basic chemicals and heavy industries such as steel, ship building, and the manufacture of heavy equipment. The goal of these investments was to restructure the composition of exports and move toward more sophisticated and skill-intensive products. But as demand for these industries' products fell below planned targets, substantial excess capacity emerged.[1] At the same time, this overinvestment in heavy and chemical industries deprived traditional and light industry exports of necessary investment funds, which in turn weakened their external competitiveness.

The industrial restructuring and the associated investment boom exerted unsustainable strains on the country's resources, which were reflected in tight labor market conditions and accelerating inflation. Also contributing to the tightness of labor markets was the departure of a large number of skilled construction workers to the Middle East oil-exporting countries. In response to this development, increases in real wages exceeded gains in productivity by a wide margin, which further aggravated inflationary pressures. And as inflation gained momentum, it threatened external competitiveness and economic growth. Furthermore, with the exchange rate fixed after the devaluation of 1974, the won became progressively overvalued and export growth weakened. In fact, export volume, which had grown at an average annual rate of 27 percent over the previous two decades (1960–78), slowed in 1978 and actually fell by 1 percent in 1979.

The widening structural imbalances in the Korean economy and the ensuing macroeconomic problems originated with the government's basic strategy of deploying finance as a mechanism for channeling resources to priority investment sectors. This strategy, which involved both direct lending to industry through the National Investment Fund and subsidization of the cost of capital via interest rate controls and fiscal incentives, was a hallmark of the Korean approach to industrialization in the 1960s and the 1970s. By exercising control over the funds available to the private business sector, particularly the corporate sector, the government became, in essence, an active partner in the finance process.

Two aspects of this partnership were particularly significant: the system provided funds to the priority sectors at preferential rates and, probably more important, transferred much of the risk of long-term investment to the government. By investing in a project that had the government's blessing, a firm could anticipate a stable and subsidized flow of funds, irrespective of its economic and financial performance. This assurance of funds reduced the cost of financial distress by reducing or even eliminating the risk of bankruptcy.

This interventionist approach to financial allocation seems to have served its objective of increasing industrial investment in the 1960s and 1970s. Over time, however, it led to structural imbalances in the financial markets. First, it made the financial institutions, particularly those in the banking sector, dependent on the government's directives. Second, it led to wide differentials in the cost of capital for various sectors and firms of different sizes. Third, it retarded the development of capital markets for the supply of long-term and risk capital. In a sense, the risk partnership between the government and the private sector functioned as a substitute for organized securities markets.

External Shocks

Because of these widening domestic structural and macroeconomic imbalances, the series of adverse global events of the early 1980s had a particularly profound effect on the Korean economy. The country was so dependent on exports and on imports of essential raw materials and energy products that its external payments position was dealt a major blow by the oil price increases of 1979 and 1980 and the subsequent recession in countries of the Organisation for Economic Co-operation and Development (OECD). Summary indicators of this deterioration in the external environment for 1976–82 (table 18-2) reveal the evolution of three adverse factors: (1) a substantial decline in the terms of trade of about 28 percent from 1979 to 1981; (2) a sharp increase in international interest rates, from an annual average of 6.8 percent for the three-month Eurodollar rate during 1976–78 to 11.6 percent during 1979–82; and (3) a significant slowdown in economic growth among OECD countries, Korea's major trading partners, from an average annual real GDP growth rate of 4.1 percent during 1976–79 to an average of 0.9 percent in 1980–82.

Table 18-2. Summary Indicators of the External Environment Facing Korea, 1976–82

Year	Terms of trade index (1980 = 100)	International interest rate (three-month Eurodollar rate)	Real GDP growth in OECD countries
1976	105.1	5.57	5.0
1977	112.4	6.05	3.9
1978	117.8	8.85	4.0
1979	115.3	2.09	3.3
1980	100.0	14.19	1.3
1981	97.9	16.87	1.6
1982	102.2	13.29	−0.2

Sources: Bank of Korea (various years); IMF (1988); and OECD (various years).

The most immediate and direct impact of these external shocks on the Korean economy was a sharp deterioration in the balance of current account. The current account deficit, which had averaged less than US$0.5 billion during the 1976–78 period, rose sharply to US$4.15 billion (6.9 percent of GNP) in 1979 and to a peak of US$5.3 billion (9.4 percent of GNP) in 1980. Not all of this deterioration can be attributed to external shocks, however. Domestic factors, notably an estimated 23 percent appreciation of the won in real terms during the 1974–79 period also played an important part. A determination of the relative factors at work is not easy, but an analysis of the counterfactual, based on the usual methodology, yields some useful insight by providing a quantitative accounting of the extent of external shocks and the nature of adjustment responses (see table 18-3). The analysis verifies the substantial impact of external shocks on the balance of current account. In 1980 in particular, when various shocks converged to hit the economy with full force, almost all the deterioration in the current account could be attributed to the impact of external shocks.

The analysis also provides some insights into the nature of adjustment responses and their effect on the current account balance. In 1980, for instance, adjustment in the current account took place primarily through a combination of import compression (14 percent decline) and export expansion (11 percent increase in real terms). The nature of adjustment changed fundamentally in 1981, however, when export expansion was large enough to balance the current account and also to permit some increase in imports. Thus, unlike other debtor developing countries which continued to use import compression to achieve external balance, Korea succeeded in weathering the external shocks of the early 1980s through

Table 18-3. External Shocks and Current Account Adjustment in Korea, 1979–82
(percentage of GNP)

Contributing factor	*1979*	*1980*	*1981*	*1982*
Exogenous factors	−1.3	−9.4	−3.2	−2.2
Oil price	−1.9	−4.4	−1.8	+0.3
Foreign interest rates	−0.7	−1.1	−1.1	+0.8
Nonoil terms of trade and other[a]	+1.3	−3.9	−0.3	+1.1
Adjustment efforts	−5.6	+7.3	+4.3	+1.0
Import volume	−9.2	+4.2	−1.3	−1.4
Export volume	+2.4	+3.0	+4.9	+1.8
Other[b]	+1.2	+0.1	+0.7	+0.6
Total change in current account deficit	−6.9	−2.1	+1.1	+3.2

Note: A negative sign indicates an increase in the current account deficit; a positive sign indicates a decrease.

a. Includes the effect of extraordinary rice imports.

b. Mainly the change in net receipts from overseas construction.

Source: World Bank estimates.

strong expansion of exports. The ability to sustain the growth of imports after 1980 facilitated the launching of broader adjustment measures to restructure the industrial sector and liberalize the trade regime.

The Adjustment Program

The government began the process of adjustment in Korea with measures to stabilize the economy by decreasing inflation. It then moved on to policy reforms and structural adjustment.

Stabilization Measures: The Disinflation Process

In the design of stabilization measures in 1979–80 the government gave high priority to restoring price stability and improving external competitiveness by reducing inflation. Inflation was not a new phenomenon for the Korean economy. It had averaged 13.5 percent in the 1960s and 16 percent in the 1970s and has shown a high degree of cyclical sensitivity to external factors, particularly international primary commodity prices (see figure 18-1). What distinguished the inflation of 1977–79 from earlier episodes was its dynamics and the belief that it was mostly homemade. There was growing evidence that the expansionary aggregate demand policies of those years, financed in part by accumulating foreign debt, had exerted excessive pressure on the labor market and pushed real

Figure 18-1. Trends in Inflation and the Import Price Index in Korea: Annual Percentage Rate of Change

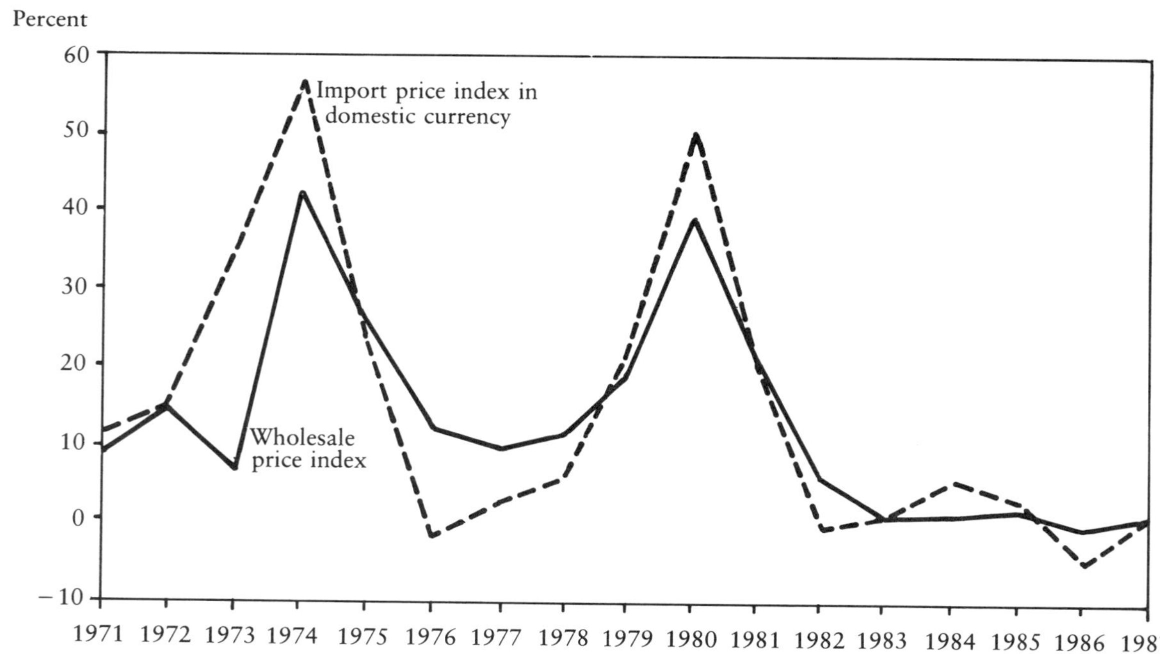

Source: Author's calculations based on data from Bank of Korea (various years).

wages far ahead of gains in productivity. Growth in real wages in the manufacturing sector, for instance, averaged 16.25 percent between 1976 and 1979, compared with a gain in productivity of 12.5 percent over the same period. In addition, the exchange rate had been fixed after the devaluation of 1974, and in this environment of rising inflation it led to considerable overvaluation of the currency, amounting to 23.6 percent between 1973 and 1979 (Corbo and Nam forthcoming).

The inflation of the 1977–79 period prompted an important shift in the management of macroeconomic policy. The goal was no longer simply to promote growth but to promote growth with price stability. The additional requirement of price stability posed a serious challenge to policymakers. Given the overheated state of the economy, some degree of demand contraction seemed to be necessary, which meant curbing the growth of real wages. But such a policy had to be both temporary and perceived as only a brief aberration in the government's traditional approach to macroeconomic management and economic growth, which had been so successful. In the past, Korea's strategy had been accompanied by rising real wages, made possible by rapid increases in labor productivity. To restore such trends in the late 1970s required a resumption in the growth of productivity, which in turn depended on keeping investment high. Encouraging investment, however, conflicted—at least at first glance—with the objective of lowering inflation.

Another aspect of the policy dilemma was how to address the deterioration in trade competitiveness resulting from the rigid exchange rate policy and high inflation at home. Currency devaluation was one option for reversing the downward trend in export volumes, but it would be at the cost of intensifying inflationary pressures, at least in the short run. Trying to improve competitiveness by relying on demand contraction to reduce inflation would also be costly in terms of forgone output and employment.

The policy response adopted by the authorities consisted of a mix of currency devaluation and contractionary demand measures, with a relatively heavy reliance on monetary policy. The won was devalued by 17 percent in January 1980, and monetary policy was tightened. The initial impact of the devaluation was a rapid surge in the rate of inflation, which peaked at 28.7 percent in terms of the consumer price index (CPI) and 38.9 percent in terms of the wholesale price index (WPI) by the end of 1980. At the same time, the tight monetary policy dampened domestic demand so much that in 1980 aggregate private investment declined by 11.5 percent while investment in machinery and equipment registered an even steeper decline of about 25.5 percent (see table 18-4).

Although these measures contributed to the sharp decline in real aggregate output in 1980, they also brought about several improvements; in particular they reversed inflationary trends and restored external com-

Table 18-4. Responses of Macroeconomic Policy Indicators in Korea, 1978–88
(percentage change)

Indicator	*1978*	*1979*	*1980*	*1981*	*1982*	*1983*	*1984*	*1985*	*1986*	*1987*	*1988*
Growth in money supply (M2)	35.0	24.6	26.9	25.0	27.0	15.2	7.7	15.6	18.4	19.1	21.3[a]
Real growth[b]	11.0	3.9	1.3	8.3	19.3	10.9	3.7	11.1	15.3	14.8	n.a.
Growth in credit[c]	47.1	39.2	39.6	26.3	25.1	17.6	14.3	19.0	7.0	12.0	n.a.
Real growth[b]	21.4	16.0	11.5	9.4	17.5	13.2	10.0	14.4	4.2	8.1	n.a.
Real effective exchange rate index (1980 = 100)	104.5	97.1	100.0	96.0	95.1	100.9	103.6	110.1	128.5	n.a.	n.a.
Rate of inflation											
Consumer price index	14.4	18.3	28.7	21.3	7.2	3.4	2.3	2.5	2.8	3.0	7.1
Wholesale price index	11.6	18.8	38.9	20.4	4.7	0.2	0.7	0.9	−1.5	0.5	2.7
Growth in real investment	29.8	15.9	−20.7	−6.3	0.1	17.5	18.6	1.6	10.6	15.1	n.a.
Private	34.0	7.7	−11.5	−4.8	12.4	17.2	10.4	4.3	18.6	n.a.	n.a.
Machinery and equipment	59.9	22.0	−25.5	−2.8	4.3	8.8	15.6	5.2	30.3	16.6	n.a.

n.a. Not available.
a. Preliminary estimate.
b. Deflated by GDP deflator.
c. Total credit to private sector.
Sources: Bank of Korea (various years); Nam (1988).

petitiveness. By 1982 inflation had been lowered to 7.2 percent (in terms of the CPI), and a recovery in output and investment was well under way (see table 18-4). Inflation declined further in the next two years, reaching a low of 2.3 percent in 1984, and remained remarkably stable until 1987 despite vigorous expansion in real aggregate investment and output. Since 1988, however, inflationary pressures have gained momentum and are likely to become a matter of major policy concern again. Nevertheless, the decade of the 1980s was a period of sharp disinflation in Korea, which is comparable, in many respects, to the experience of major industrial countries.

What factors contributed to Korea's achievement of low inflation in the 1980s? Presumably, both internal and external factors played important roles; the evidence, however, is more firmly on the side of external factors, as illustrated by the results of equations 1 through 9 reported in table 18-5. The equations are based on a simple model of the inflationary process in Korea: the rate of inflation in terms of the WPI is explained as a function of lagged inflation, the current and lagged import price index in domestic currency, the rate of growth of the money supply (M2), and the rate of growth of real GNP. The model was estimated by ordinary least squares, using annual data from 1971–87 with several lag specifications. The results are familiar: inflation in Korea was strongly influenced by external inflation and by changes in the exchange rate. Statistically, the estimated coefficient of the import price index (in terms of domestic currency) remains significant and robust throughout all estimated equations, with a short-run elasticity of around 0.5.

Two domestic factors seem of particular importance in Korea's disinflation of the 1980s: (1) the strong performance of business investment, particularly in machinery and equipment, which helped to keep productive capacity in pace with the growth in demand, and (2) the appreciation of the nominal exchange rate. Investment in machinery and equipment averaged 17 percent a year in 1984–88 in real terms, while the exchange rate appreciated in nominal terms by 21 percent during the same period.

From Stabilization to Adjustment

The prompt upturn in aggregate investment and output in 1981, coupled with lower inflation and a flexible exchange rate policy, provided the macroeconomic framework for Korea's broad adjustment efforts encompassing industry, trade, energy, and finance. With hindsight, the roughly two-phased sequencing of these adjustment efforts seems to have been a desirable ordering of reform measures.

The first phase (1981–85) focused on the real side of the economy. The goal of policy was to foster industrial reform, to reduce Korea's high energy consumption and its heavy dependence on petroleum imports, to

Table 18-5. Regression Results for Determinants of Inflation in Korea, 1971–87

Explanatory variable	*Equation* 1	2	3	4	5	6	7	8	9
Constant	−0.07	−0.07	−0.05	−0.07	−0.09	−0.07	0.00	−0.08	−0.09
	(−1.50)	(1.52)	(−0.84)	(−1.04)	(−1.56)	(−1.48)	(0.14)	(−1.46)	(−1.62)
$\hat{P}_{-1}$	0.21	0.40	0.44	0.40	0.33	0.45	0.31	0.23	0.36
	(0.70)	(2.42)	(2.42)	(2.31)	(1.63)	(3.21)	(2.47)	(1.84)	(1.90)
$\hat{P}_{-2}$	0.12	0.09	0.12	0.10	0.07	—	—	—	—
	(0.79)	(0.61)	(0.79)	(0.58)	(0.44)	—	—	—	—
$\hat{PM}$	0.51	0.56	0.57	0.56	0.52	0.54	0.57	0.49	0.50
	(4.64)	(6.28)	(6.12)	(5.33)	(4.91)	(6.66)	(6.62)	(5.35)	(5.39)
$\hat{PM}_{-1}$	0.16	—	—	—	—	—	—	—	—
	(0.72)								
$\hat{Y}_{-1}$	0.74	0.70	0.79	0.72	0.50	0.74	—	—	0.50
	(1.64)	(1.60)	(1.68)	(1.52)	(0.88)	(1.78)	—	—	(0.91)
$\hat{M2}$	—	—	−0.19	—	—	—	—	—	—
			(−0.65)						
$\hat{M2}_{-1}$	—	—	—	−0.05	—	—	—	—	—
				(−0.15)					
$\hat{M2}_{-2}$	—	—	—	—	0.22	—	—	0.46	0.26
	—	—	—	—	(0.59)	—	—	(1.67)	(0.74)
R^2	0.88	0.87	0.88	0.88	0.88	0.87	0.83	0.87	0.88

— Variable not included in the equation.

P = wholesale price index, PM = import price in local currency, Y = real GNP, M2 = money supply, and ˆ = percentage rate of change; *t* statistics are in parentheses.

reduce import barriers, and to promote efficiency in the public sector. These initiatives were supported by two structural adjustment loans from the World Bank (SAL I in December 1981 and SAL II in November 1983) and a one-year standby arrangement with the International Monetary Fund (IMF) in February 1982. In the second phase (1983 to the present), attention turned to the financial sector, where the government has followed a cautious liberalization strategy directed toward deregulation of interest rates, enhanced competition, and a gradual shift from direct intervention in credit allocation and monetary policy to indirect intervention through reserve requirements, open market operations, and market-determined interest rates. These reforms, which were initially supported by two industrial finance project loans from the World Bank (June 1983 and May 1985), have accelerated since the emergence of the current account surplus in 1986.

Policy Reform and Structural Adjustment

Concerns about the sustainability of economic growth and the management of the balance of payments in Korea have traditionally focused on the performance of industry—particularly the manufacturing sector because of its role as the engine of growth and its rapid structural change from light to heavy industry during the 1970s. Thus a key objective of both SALs was to support the government's promotion of industrial efficiency and productivity. To this end, a wide range of medium-term financial, trade, and industrial reforms were initiated to reduce the direct role of the government in the finance process, to provide access to foreign capital and technology, and to expose industry to greater external competition. These reforms were intended to stimulate policy actions that would reduce government direction and control over credit allocation at the enterprise level. Other reforms included relaxation of controls governing interest rate ceilings, liberalization of the import regime by 1986 to the level prevailing in industrial countries, reduction in the spread of tariff rates, and relaxation of foreign investment provisions.

The financial components of policy reform were strengthened and expanded at a later stage under the two industrial finance projects. These reforms included liberalization of commercial banking regulations and supervision, control of corporate indebtedness, and development of an equity market. Collectively, financial reforms were intended to address the main structural weaknesses in the financial sector.

DIRECT AND SUBSIDIZED CREDIT. Although much of the financial reform took place at a later stage of the adjustment process, two measures were initiated under the two SALs: government direction of credit allocation was reduced and interest rates on controlled funds were raised to the level of the minimum rates on commercial bank lending. Directed lending programs through the National Investment Fund and via the rediscounting facilities at the Bank of Korea were the main instruments of direct government intervention in the allocation of credit to industry. Loans arranged through the National Investment Fund were used to finance long-term investment in machinery and equipment and were targeted to high-priority sectors, such as chemicals, power, and heavy industry. For example, of the 4,445 billion won (W) in total loans made over the 1974–84 period, about W2,714 billion, or 61 percent, was earmarked for the heavy and chemical industries (World Bank 1987a).

The other major instrument of government-directed credit allocation was the use of rediscount facilities at the Bank of Korea. Gains from the use of these facilities contributed to commercial bank revenues and provided important incentives to extend credit to priority sectors. Dependence on these facilities also rendered the commercial banks' balance sheets dependent on government finance and hence dampened the commercial banks' initiative and reduced their managerial autonomy.

When viewed from the perspective of the SAL period only, financial sector reform appears to have been slow. When viewed from a longer perspective that includes the two industrial finance projects, however, progress is considerable. Among the important achievements are the following:

- Since 1982, credit allocations through the National Investment Fund have been made on a sectoral basis rather than by targeting specific firms. Banks handling these loans therefore now have greater autonomy in credit evaluation and decisionmaking.
- The volume of loans arranged through the National Investment Fund was reduced from W733 billion in 1983 to W506 billion in 1984.
- Even more important, net contributions to the National Investment Fund were reduced from W444 billion in 1983 to W73 billion in 1984. During 1984 and 1985 the government gradually allowed interest rate ceilings to rise on both lending and deposit rates.
- The government promoted domestic savings by encouraging the introduction of new financial instruments such as negotiable certificates of deposit and cash management accounts.

IMPORT POLICY REFORM. The reform of import policy has been a key aspect of the adjustment program since 1981 with the support of the two SALs. The process accelerated after the 1986 turnaround in Korea's current account position. Major reforms include liberalization of import policy, tariff reduction, and the opening up of financial services, including banking, insurance, and securities.

Government efforts to expose industry to greater external competition have involved a reduction in nontariff barriers and in the rates and dispersion of tariffs. Automatically approved imports as a percentage of total imports (the import liberalization ratio) progressively increased from 69 percent in 1980, to 80 percent 1983, 93.6 percent in 1987, and 94.8 percent in 1988 (Korea Ministry of Trade and Industry 1988). Import liberalization also included phased general reductions in tariff rates and greater uniformity of rates. In compliance with the Tariff Act of 1984, the average (arithmetic) tariff rate was reduced from 31.7 percent in 1982 to 21 percent in 1985 and 18.1 percent in 1988, with a further reduction to 7.5 percent planned by 1993. At the same time, the government continued sliding the tariff schedule downward to narrow the dispersion in the rates. The targets for 1988 were uniform rates of 5 to 10 percent for raw materials, 20 percent for intermediate goods, and 20 to 30 percent for capital goods.

INDUSTRIAL RESTRUCTURING: THE CASE OF THE AUTOMOTIVE INDUSTRY. In the wake of the serious economic difficulties facing the Korean economy in the early 1980s, including low capacity utilization in heavy industry and high oil prices, the World Bank took a pessimistic view of the prospects for expansion of the automobile industry. Several preliminary studies in 1980–82 raised serious questions about the rationale behind this expansion. There were grave doubts about the industry's ability to penetrate foreign markets, particularly in developed countries, because of competitive price structures, sophisticated marketing networks, and the need for advanced product design. For these reasons and in view of the general conditions of excess investment and declining domestic and export demand, the World Bank questioned the wisdom of the government's directed investments in the automobile industry.

Accordingly, under SAL I the government agreed to defer its support for the expansion of automobile plants pending completion of a study reviewing export prospects. Because a relatively higher comparative advantage was thought to exist in the spare auto parts industry, the World Bank recommended that a task force prepare a plan for promoting this industry as a substitute for or complement to the automobile industry.

As events unfolded, however, the outlook for the automotive industry in Korea became far more positive than earlier conditions had led the World Bank to assume.[2] The firm determination of business leaders and a recovery in economic activity in the years following the negotiation of SAL I helped to alleviate the World Bank's concern. Consequently, this issue was not followed up under SAL II eighteen months later. Discussion of the related issue of restructuring the heavy machinery sector was also dropped under SAL II, and attention shifted to other issues, including trade liberalization and energy efficiency.

PROMOTION OF ENERGY EFFICIENCY. A combination of a relatively high energy to output ratio and heavy dependence on petroleum imports in the late 1970s left the Korean economy particularly vulnerable to the vagaries of the world oil market. In 1978 energy consumption relative to GDP was about 60 percent higher in Korea than in other middle-income developing countries. Among the factors accounting for this high energy use was Korea's high stage of industrialization, its concentration on energy-intensive heavy industries, and the relatively heavy use of energy by the residential sector.[3]

The main energy-related objectives of structural adjustment measures under SAL I were to promote overall energy efficiency and to diversify the sources of energy. More specifically, the goals were to lower the elasticity of energy consumption in relation to GDP from the 1.3 average during 1975–80 to 0.9 by the late 1980s and to shift from the use of petroleum toward coal, nuclear energy, and natural gas. To achieve these goals, Korea planned to bring domestic energy prices in line with the world oil price increases of 1979 and 1980, to offer financial and fiscal incentives to promote energy conservation, to cancel or postpone energy-intensive investment projects, to substitute liquefied natural gas for petroleum products, and to strengthen legal and institutional structures to promote energy efficiency. Some of these objectives and proposed measures were initiated under an IMF standby arrangement and then reinforced under SAL I. They were further strengthened and broadened under SAL II to include electric power planning and pricing, refinery pricing and trade deregulation, and formulation of a long-term strategy for the development and deregulation of the coal mining industry.

Judged by several standards, progress in conserving energy and diversifying supply has been remarkable. Even before the SALs the government had demonstrated a bold and strong commitment to the long-term promotion of energy efficiency by raising domestic energy prices in lockstep with increases in world oil prices. Thus between March 1979 and November 1980 electricity rates were raised by 36 percent, coal prices by 14 percent, and petroleum prices by a range from 136 percent (diesel fuel) to as much as 172 percent (gasoline) (see table 18-6). These price adjustments, reinforced by additional policy measures under the two SAL programs, achieved impressive reductions in energy intensity and greater diversity in energy sources. Growth of total energy consumption (measured in tons of oil equivalent) decelerated from an average of 9.8 percent in 1976–80 to about 6.2 percent in 1981–87, and the energy/GDP ratio declined from 1.3 in the late 1970s to 0.7 in the mid-1980s (table 18-7). With regard to the composition of energy the share of petroleum

Table 18-6. Principal Energy Prices in Korea, 1979–81
(U.S. dollars)

Product	March 1979	November 1980	April 1981
Petroleum products (per gallon)			
Gasoline (regular)	0.53	1.44	1.44
		(172)	(0)
Diesel	0.39	0.92	1.07
		(136)	(16)
Bunker	0.36	0.86	0.94
		(139)	(9)
Electricity (per kilowatt hour)	0.066	0.090	0.095
		(36)	(6)
Coal (per ton)	34.09	38.92	41.59
		(14)	(7)

Note: Numbers in parentheses indicate growth rates.
Source: World Bank data.

declined from 61.3 percent in 1980 to 49.1 percent in 1985, while the shares of coal and nuclear power rose to 39.2 percent and 6.4 percent, respectively. These achievements surpassed the targets established under the SAL-supported adjustment programs.

Table 18-7. Changes in the Composition of Energy Consumption in Korea, 1980–87

Composition	1980	1981	1982	1983	1984	1985	1986	1987
Total energy consumption								
Millions of tons of oil equivalent	44.1	46.1	46.0	49.7	53.9	56.0	61.0	67.1
Growth rate (percent)	—	4.5	0.0	8.04	8.4	3.9	8.9	10.0
Energy use by fuel (percentage of total use)								
Coal	29.9	33.1	33.6	33.1	36.8	39.2	37.6	34.2
Petroleum	61.3	58.4	58.0	56.2	52.3	49.1	46.7	47.4
Gas	1.0	1.1	1.6	2.1	2.3	3.8	4.4	3.1
Hydroelectric	1.1	1.5	1.1	1.4	1.1	1.3	1.6	2.0
Nuclear	2.0	1.6	2.0	4.5	5.5	6.4	11.6	14.4
Fuelwood	5.7	5.4	5.3	4.8	4.3	4.0	2.4	2.0
Energy/GDP ratio[a]	0.77	0.75	0.71	0.70	0.70	0.68	0.68	n.a.

n.a. Not available.
a. Energy/GDP ratio = tons of oil equivalent/GDP in billions of U.S. dollars.
Source: Korea Economic Planning Board (various years).

The Bank's Role in the Adjustment Process

The two structural adjustment loans to Korea in 1981 and 1983 were important vehicles of policy dialogue, financial support, and cooperation. Both SALs included conditions for the disbursement of tranches, but all tranches were disbursed on schedule. Given the government's strong commitment to policy reform and its success in macroeconomic management, however, the loan agreements were free of specific conditionality. As a result, the government had a considerable degree of policy flexibility and maneuverability, which proved to be important in the volatile world economic conditions of the early 1980s. For example, the government's unwavering support for the expansion of the automotive industry, despite the World Bank's initial reservations, led to handsome returns as exports of vehicles grew more than fourfold between 1980 and 1985.

The World Bank policy dialogue with the Korean authorities continued in the context of the two industrial finance projects in June 1983 and May 1985. These projects laid the groundwork for later reforms in the financial sector. The reforms were motivated by Korea's awareness of its new role in the international financial system and its understanding that financial sector reforms are as crucial to its transition to the 1990s as export expansion policies and strategies were to the economic growth of the 1960s and 1970s.

It is difficult to evaluate the precise influence of the World Bank's adjustment lending operations and the programs they supported, but there is little doubt that they were important to Korea's successful adjustment experience in the 1980s. Although the two SALs (totaling US$550 million) met 13 percent of Korea's external financing needs during the period of disbursement (1982–83), other aspects of the programs were more important than this resource transfer. Of particular importance were (1) the programs' catalytic role in mobilizing resources in international financial markets by helping Korea maintain its creditworthiness and (2) the policy analysis, discussion, and dialogue which underlay loan operations and agreements. Given their comprehensive and wide-ranging character, the SAL programs provided a broad framework for the design and integration of the various components of policy reforms in industry, trade, energy, and finance. This is an aspect of SAL programs that merits more attention.

Conclusions and Recommendations

According to the major economic indicators, Korea's stabilization and adjustment program can be considered a remarkable success. The Korean economy underwent a fundamental transformation in the 1980s. The most visible and truly impressive aspects of this transformation relate to improvements in internal macroeconomic conditions and external balance, as this chapter has revealed. The extent of this transformation is evident from a comparison of the present state of robust economic growth, contained inflation, and a hefty surplus on current account with the crisis situation in 1980, when the economy was in a deep recession, aggregate output and investment were declining at unprecedented rates of 5 percent and 24 percent, respectively, and inflation was soaring.

Although these macroeconomic successes are impressive, Korea's structural adjustment experience really stands out with respect to its broad and far-reaching policy reforms in trade, industry, energy, and finance. Successive efforts to liberalize imports for industrial production achieved the target import liberalization ratio of 94.8 percent by 1988. The tariff system was simplified, and the average tariff rate was reduced from 31.7 percent in 1982 to 18.1 percent in 1988, with a further reduction to 7.5 percent planned by 1993, a level that corresponds to that in OECD countries. Increased exposure to foreign competition and a reduction in government-directed credit, particularly to specific firms, had an important influence on the industrial sector. The government's perseverance in its plans to expand the automotive industry despite World Bank misgivings reaped large benefits for the industry and the economy. In addition, it made significant advances in reducing the country's growth rate of energy consumption and in diversifying its sources of energy.

In the financial sector, the government has so far followed a cautious strategy of liberalization. The strategy is directed toward deregulating interest rates, enhancing competition, and gradually shifting from direct intervention in credit allocation and the conduct of monetary policy to indirect intervention through reserve requirements, open market operations, and market-determined interest rates.[4] Two important considerations influenced the pace and scope of these reforms: (1) the high degree of corporate indebtedness and (2) the emergence in 1986 of a substantial balance of payments surplus (amounting to US$13.0 billion in 1988). Should this trend in the external payments position continue in the 1990s, it would have significant implications for Korea's relationship with the international financial community, including the World Bank and the IMF. Indeed, Korea's recent acceptance of the obligations of Article VIII of the IMF's Articles of Agreement already marks the beginning of a new era in Korea's international economic position.

Overall, four conclusions emerge from the review presented here. First, success in the design and implementation of structural adjustment efforts affecting the functioning of product and factor markets requires more than the elimination of price distortions and the promotion of competitive forces. The process also requires continuing efforts to strengthen the capability of the economy to respond promptly and favorably to market incentives and signals. Thus changes in both the incentive system and the response capability are integral to the adjustment process. Korea's success in the adjustment process was as much a function of the economy's capability to respond positively and promptly, as reflected by the rapid recovery in private investment in 1981 and its steady growth since then, as it was a function of the government's reforms in the areas of trade, industry, energy, and finance.

Second, Korea's success in adjustment benefited from a favorable external environment. The country's remarkable achievement in controlling and lowering inflation depended significantly on the decline in import prices, including oil prices, which declined from an average of US$40 a barrel in the early 1980s to US$15 in 1988.

Third, the sequencing of policy measures seems to have been important. Korea began with stabilization efforts that laid the foundation for subsequent implementation of industrial restructuring and trade liberalization, which in turn facilitated the liberalization of the financial sector. This seems to have been a desirable ordering of reform measures.

Finally, the 1981–85 period during which the SAL-supported programs were formulated and implemented was characterized by rapid economic growth, low inflation, high savings rates, and vigorous capital formation. Also, the balance of payments adjustment undertaken during this period relied on export expansion and not on import compression.

Notes

1. According to the World Bank's appraisal report for the industrial finance project in 1983, the capacity-utilization rate declined from a high of 88 percent in 1978 to 73 percent in 1980 for the manufacturing sector as a whole and from 75 percent in 1979 to less than 50 percent in 1980 for the machinery subsector.
2. Between 1980 and 1984 production in the automobile industry tripled; production was projected to more than triple by 1990 and reach 1.3 million vehicles. Similarly, automobile exports grew more than fourfold between 1980 and 1985. Of US$1.7 billion total sales revenue in 1986, more than US$500 million was due to exports.
3. Because of a combination of factors, including weather, space-heating techniques, and low coal prices, energy consumption per household in the late 1970s was higher in Korea than in Japan. In 1979, for example, the residential and commercial sectors accounted for about 38 percent of total energy consumption in Korea compared with 19 percent in Japan.
4. For a detailed description of Korea's recent liberalization of the financial sector, see Cho and Cole (forthcoming) and Cho (1988).

References

Bank of Korea. Various years. *Economic Statistics Yearbook*. Seoul.

Cho, Y. J. 1988. "Liberalization of Korea's Financial Market in the 1980s." Paper presented at the East Rock Institute Conference on the Dynamics of U.S.-Korea Trade Relations, Yale University, November 10–12.

Cho, Y. J., and D. C. Cole. Forthcoming. "The Role of the Financial Sector in Korea's Structural Adjustment." In Vittorio Corbo and Sang-Mok Suh, eds., *Structural Adjustment in a Newly Industrialized Country: Lessons from Korea.*

Corbo, Vittorio, and Sang-Woo Nam. Forthcoming. "The Recent Macroeconomic Evolution of the Republic of Korea: An Overview." In Vittorio Corbo and Sang-Mok Suh, eds., *Structural Adjustment in a Newly Industrialized Country: Lessons from Korea.*

IMF. 1988. *International Financial Statistics Yearbook.* Washington, D.C.: International Monetary Fund.

Korea Economic Planning Board. Various years. *Major Statistics of the Korean Economy.* Seoul.

Korea Ministry of Trade and Industry. 1988. *Trade and Industry Bulletin.* Seoul.

Nam, Sang-Woo. 1988. "The Role of Exchange Rate Policy in Four East Asian Countries." Asia Regional Series, Report IDP 15. World Bank, Washington, D.C.

OECD. Various years. *Main Economic Indicators.* Paris: Organisation for Economic Co-operation and Development.

World Bank. 1987a. *Korea: Managing the Industrial Transition.* Vol. 2. Washington, D.C.

———. 1987b. *World Debt Tables.* Washington, D.C.

Comments

Larry E. Westphal

MY REMARKS will concentrate on the structural adjustment aspects of the Korean experience. There appears to be some confusion about what "structural adjustment" means. In my view, there can be little question that the "structure" at issue is the structure of markets, incentives, institutions, and other elements that have an important influence on resource allocation in both static and dynamic terms. Correspondingly, policies aim at structural adjustment insofar as they explicitly seek fundamental changes in existing modes of allocative decisionmaking. Some policy measures, by their nature, entail structural adjustment; privatization, when meaningful, is an example. For some policy measures, the relationship to structural adjustment depends on the context in which they are undertaken. Real devaluation of the exchange rate, for instance, is associated with structural adjustment only insofar as it accompanies a change in development strategy toward greater openness.

The confusion about structural adjustment may result from a failure to recognize the importance of contextual elements in determining whether particular policy measures are or are not related to structural adjustment. There is general agreement, however, that stabilization policies typically do not involve structural adjustment in the sense just outlined. Their objective is clearly understood to be the improvement of economic performance in the short run. Structural adjustment, by contrast, inherently pertains to the longer run. It is concerned with phenomena that are properly seen as being essentially developmental.

Mansoor Dailami's chapter discusses many of the salient ingredients of Korea's overall experience with adjustment in the 1980s but does not always place them in perspective. Thus it does not develop with sufficient clarity the point that Korea's rapid recovery from macroeconomic crisis owed far more to stabilization policies than to concurrent structural adjustment policies. More fundamentally, it does not emphasize that the turnabout owed a great deal to the supply-responsiveness of the private sector—a responsiveness engendered by a much earlier episode of structural adjustment that had put the Korean economy on the path of export-led industrialization. Nor, in this connection, does it adequately reflect the fact that the crisis had its genesis in the evolution of the structure of decisionmaking that followed from the earlier episode of adjustment. It is for these reasons that I wish to focus on the structural adjustment aspects of the Korean experience.

Korea's first episode of structural adjustment came in the early 1960s in response to the exhaustion of opportunities for "easy" import substitution. Two key components of this episode were the institution of a virtually free trade regime for exporters and the establishment of an appropriate exchange rate. For sectors in which Korea could then readily attain international competitiveness, these measures eradicated the antiexport bias of the trade policy and ensured the relative as well as absolute profitability of exporting. In other words, they established the incentives needed for export-led industrialization.

Other components of this adjustment episode included a policy change that led to positive real interest rates and reform of government taxation and expenditure, which greatly enlarged the magnitude of government savings. The reform of interest rate policy was not accomplished by general liberalization of the financial sector, however. Its primary effect was to divert funds from the curb market into regulated financial institutions that served as channels for government-directed credit allocation. In the case of governmental budget reform, however, structural adjustment was accompanied by moves toward a more liberal structure. ("Liberal" here refers to conformance with sound economic management or with free market principles.) Among other things, public enterprises were transformed into profit-maximizing agents.

Import liberalization—in the sense of substantial reductions in import barriers—was not an element of Korea's structural adjustment in the early 1960s. This is not to say, however, that there were no important changes in the rules of the importing game. In fact, there were fundamental changes that virtually abolished unproductive rent-seeking in the use of import licenses. Following those changes, the realization of import quota rents was generally linked to meaningful production, whether for export or for domestic sale. There was some liberalization in the conventional sense of the word, but its effects were modest. The most significant reform in this respect came somewhat later in the 1960s with an administrative change from listing commodities that were approved for import to listing those that were restricted.

The decisionmaking structure that grew out of the reforms of the early 1960s involved significant elements of government intervention that were discretionary and selective as well as coercive in important respects. As already mentioned, much of the credit that flowed from regulated financial institutions was directed by the government toward sectors it considered to have priority. The only major exception was export finance; in this case market forces clearly had the whip hand, but even here there was rationing in the sense that the government stipulated minimum credit allocations in relation to export orders (letters of credit). Inflows of foreign capital were strictly regulated, as were inflows of proprietary foreign technology. In addition, infant industry protection was a central element in the government's efforts to promote new industries. In sum, when all of the government's interventionist policies are taken into account, Korea's effective incentives were more widely dispersed among industries than is the case in countries that adhere to an inward-looking strategy of industrialization.

Just as it would be a mistake to neglect the government's key role in micro decisionmaking, so too would it be a mistake to infer that market-mediated, decentralized decisionmaking played no significant role in Korea's outstanding performance following the first episode of structural adjustment. The structure of decisionmaking was a complex combination of public direction and private enterprise in which the government's use of both carrots and sticks was moderated by frequent, meaningful interaction between public and private decisionmakers.

The critically important nuances of this subtle structure are difficult to capture adequately in a short description. They are nowhere better reflected than in Korea's exceptional export performance during the 1960s and early 1970s, which is not only a testament to the efficacy of "getting the prices right" but also to the potency of export targeting as it was practiced by the Korean government. It would be naive in the extreme to think that government fiat was responsible for Korea's export success, but it would be equally naive to think that the government's close monitoring of exports and responsive fine-tuning of promotional activities was not a major factor.

This structure of decisionmaking served Korea well as long as efficient economic growth was the overriding objective of government intervention and as long as the interventions were pragmatically flexible in the face of changing circumstances. Matters changed radically in the mid-1970s, however, when the government embarked on its campaign to develop heavy industry. The desire to develop capability in armaments production (a sensible desire in the geopolitical context of the time) and the belief that heavy industry is the key to advanced industrial status supplanted the objective of efficient economic growth. But far more important, the government became excessively rigid in its interventions; pragmatic flexibility gave way to ossification as the government lost its ability to see problems as they emerged and to take appropriate corrective action. Thus, whatever one might say about the advisability of the concerted effort to develop heavy industry, there is no denying that there was substantial, even egregious, mismanagement of the effort.

Bad management was most clearly apparent in poor project design and implementation within heavy industry. The long-lasting result was a high degree of excess capacity. The balance between the volume of investment in light and heavy industry was also problematic. Owing to insufficient investment resources, light industry was unable to pursue many profitable opportunities for expanding capacity. Thus the crowding out of export-oriented investment was one cause of the marked deterioration in Korea's export performance over the second half of the 1970s. Adverse real exchange rate movements associated with a fixed nominal rate were another significant cause. In addition, the economy was permitted to become seriously overheated, as manifested by the substantial tightening of the labor market because of the large investment in heavy industry and the simultaneous boom in overseas construction.

The important point here is that the macroeconomic crisis associated with the 1980 fall in real output was fundamentally due to economic mismanagement during the 1970s—mismanagement engendered by sclerosis in the structure of decisionmaking. In fact, serious macroeconomic deterioration was apparent in 1978 and 1979, accompanied by clear evidence of microeconomic mismanagement. The association of macroeconomic deterioration with microeconomic mismanagement was recognized by many contemporary observers, and a vigorous debate ensued about the necessity for radical changes in the structure of decisionmaking. The government embarked on an adjustment program in the first half of 1979. Shortly thereafter the severely adverse shock in the external environment only added to the need for adjustment. Consequently, the adjustment program was greatly strengthened in 1980. The World Bank did not become formally involved until 1981.

The government's stabilization effort is best seen simply as the reintroduction of the sound macroeconomic management it had earlier practiced with great effectiveness. Likewise, the speed and magnitude of the turnaround in macroeconomic performance should be understood in terms of the structure of decisionmaking that had earlier served Korea so well. As Dailami observes, there was very little reform of that structure before the restoration of good macroeconomic performance. But there were major changes in the nature of public intervention. Most important, the objective of efficient economic growth was restored along with flexible pragmatism in the interventions made in its pursuit. As a consequence, the government abandoned the obsessive push to develop heavy industry across a broad front. More generally, it greatly reduced its efforts to promote new industrial activities.

Nonetheless, it is not true that the recovery was associated with a fundamental transformation in the structure of decisionmaking, as Dailami's chapter implies. If allowance is made for differences in circumstances, one sees that the government's role in directing economic activity was no less than it had been earlier. The directions had changed, but not the underlying structure. In short, with the old structure of decisionmaking reestablished, the economy was able to respond vigorously to the improvement in external conditions.

Does the success of the government's stabilization efforts within the preexisting structure of decisionmaking imply that structural adjustment is unnecessary? "No" is the answer of government policymakers, or so it appears from the record of efforts undertaken since 1979. In line with the emerging consensus about policy phasing, the government opted to pursue stabilization before structural adjustment. Seeing its stabilization success, it could have abandoned structural adjustment as unnecessary. The excesses of the second half of the 1970s would then have been considered an aberration rather than indicative of a new, unhealthy tendency. But this is not how policymakers chose to view the matter.

The excesses were seen as symptoms of deficiencies that would, with growing probability, have adverse consequences of increasing severity as the economy became more complex. Policymakers believed that the paramount deficiency was the centralization of decisionmaking with respect to dynamic allocation, which gave the government tremendous influence through directed credit, protection of infant industry, and licensing of foreign capital and technology. Other key deficiencies were either products of past government intervention or concomitants of centralization. An example of the former is the concentration of market power in the *chaebol*, conglomerates which grew extremely large by carrying out many of the government's favored investment projects. An example of the latter deficiency is the many import barriers that remained in the early 1980s. (With respect to these barriers, it is not irrelevant that Korea has been under increasing pressure to open its markets.)

The pace of the second episode of structural adjustment has gradually accelerated since its beginning in the late 1970s. Throughout, the objective has been to achieve a more liberal decisionmaking structure. Liberalization has been pursued with respect to imports, financial intermediation, and inflows of foreign capital and technology. In addition, a great deal of ferment has attended efforts to devise a radically new policy for industrial organization. But, except for a relaxation of restrictions on inflows of foreign capital and technology (which are now freely admitted), liberalization is proceeding at a slow and deliberate pace. A great deal of selective intervention continues as the old structure of decisionmaking is gradually replaced by a more liberal one. Dailami makes this point clearly in regard to the financial sector, but he greatly overstates the pace of liberalization with respect to imports.[1]

The slow pace of liberalization can be justified by the desire to give potentially responsive private enterprise sufficient time to adjust to the new rules of the game. Specific trade liberalization measures have been preannounced in order to foster greater productivity in advance of increased import competition. The slow pace can also be justified by the need to develop adequate processes of decisionmaking within institutions that are expected to assume new decisionmaking roles of considerable consequence. Regulated financial institutions are the obvious case in point.

But, especially with respect to this justification, there is considerable tension between the utility of delay and the imperative of learning by doing. Tremendous interest attaches to knowing how Korean policymakers have managed this tension and how successful they have been. It seems clear that the Korean government will continue for some time its practice of selective intervention coupled with protection of infant industry to generate import substitution. Here again there are significant issues concerning the choice of areas for intervention and the detailed management of intervention. The same is true with respect to the continuation of selective intervention in the restructuring of sick industries. These issues are all related to the management of structural adjustment, which I believe is a more important aspect of the Korean experience than the management of stabilization, which receives great attention in Dailami's presentation.

In addition, Korea's experience has several implications for the time horizons of adjustment. In the first episode of structural adjustment, the export response was strong and virtually instantaneous. Three atypical elements of the reform were largely responsible for this. First, Korea established the equivalent of a virtually free trade regime for exports;

with the exception of the other Gang of Four members, I know of no developing country that has gone this far. Second, the Korean government was committed to export promotion with a seriousness generally unmatched among developing countries. The lesson I draw is that efforts to encourage exports are generally not as extensive as they need to be to elicit a strong response. Third, in the 1980s Korea's macroeconomic response to stabilization was strong and rapid. As already noted, this was due to the underlying strength of the Korean economy, which in turn was the result of its development over the previous two decades. The lesson here is that history matters.

What about the World Bank's role in adjustment? I believe it was useful but minimal. From the beginning of World Bank involvement, the Korean government had the capacity to formulate and implement the requisite policies. It also had the political will. Thus Korean policymakers generally led the World Bank, rather than vice versa. Nonetheless, the World Bank played a useful role in its consultations on policy; World Bank staff served as an effective sounding board for brainstorming and analyzing the full consequences of contemplated actions. Perhaps their most important contribution was to act as a gadfly; they rather consistently emphasized impediments to achieving Korea's targets, pointing out problems that they felt could not be overcome. The problems were typically real enough, but the Korean response was generally to work hard to overcome them, as Dailami notes was the case in the automotive sector. Significantly, the only case I am aware of in which the World Bank foresaw serious problems that were not adequately addressed was the campaign to develop heavy industry in the mid- and late 1970s.

Note

1. See Vittorio Corbo and Sang-Mok Suh, eds., *Structural Adjustment in a Newly Industrialized Country: Lessons from Korea* (forthcoming), especially the chapter by Soo-Gil Young, "Import Liberalization and Industrial Adjustment." Young observes that the import liberalization ratio (which Dailami presents as evidence of actual liberalization) gives at best only part of the story. The ratio does not incorporate several discretionary import licensing schemes that have been used to delay import penetration until competing producers were able to achieve effective competition with imports. Dailami's figures on average tariff rates appear to overstate the rate of tariff reduction by a considerable margin; Young gives averages of 24.8 percent in 1979, 23.7 percent in 1983, and 21.3 percent in 1988.

Comments on Asia

Attila Karaosmanoglu

IN REVIEWS of country experiences with adjustment, considerable attention has focused on the evolution of events rather than on the fundamental aspects of structural adjustment. Much more needs to be known about the cause-result relationships in the processes that are taking place.

Asia provides a rich source of material for analyzing the process of adjustment. The cases of Indonesia and Korea reveal a great deal of the complexities as well as the opportunities connected with adjustment. Other countries in Asia would also make interesting case studies of adjustment programs—studies at least as illuminating as those presented here. The case of the Philippines reveals missed opportunities and wide-ranging prospects. A study of the dynamics of the adjustment process in Thailand would be very instructive. China and India have also undertaken structural reforms in varying degrees and speed, although they have not obtained adjustment loans from the World Bank.

Although Asia as a whole has achieved better results in adjustment and growth than have other regions, its experience nevertheless comprises a range of successes and failures. Generalizations cutting across the varied experiences are therefore necessarily problematic. Two characteristics, however, distinguish the successful cases and the more effective aspects of their adjustment processes.

One characteristic of Asian countries that have achieved higher growth rates and greater efficiency in their economic structures is the continuous nature of the structural adjustment process. Continuity in policy, credibility of reform, and the supply response to policy change are all interlinked. Some of the countries in the economic forefront such as Korea have been engaged in the process for quite some time. Institutional development has been sufficiently advanced to facilitate effective changes in policy. Their track record in carrying out sound policies in turn has lent credibility to their adjustment efforts. Credibility of reform turns out to be a fundamental determinant of the degree of response of economic agents to policy changes.

The second characteristic of the successful cases is their openness and their considerable realism with respect to the world around them. Those countries had, at the starting point, a greater awareness of the importance of foreign trade and a larger volume of trade. They were better prepared to incorporate the changing world conditions into their decisionmaking.

I have often wondered whether the policymakers in the successful Southeast Asian countries are more intelligent and more courageous than those elsewhere or whether something else drives them to make their decisions, to make them in time, and to act on them forcefully. One of my conclusions is that their success is very much related to the openness of their economies. This openness in turn has forced them to become and remain competitive in a rapidly changing world. By reflecting the realities of the world around them in their own economic structures, these economies have avoided losing ground internationally. External competitiveness and macroeconomic stability are mutually interrelated. With considerable openness, the need for macroeconomic adjustments becomes more quickly apparent. This is one of the reasons that adjustment has taken place in that part of the world rather dynamically, continuously, and effectively.

19 Pakistan: Structural Adjustment and Economic Growth

William A. McCleary

PAKISTAN EXPERIENCED a very uneven pattern of development during the 1960s and 1970s. Rapid growth during the 1960s, based mainly on private enterprise and fairly outward-looking policies, was followed by generally poor performance and relative stagnation in the 1970s. Starting in 1969 political disruptions led to the breakaway of Bangladesh and to a new government in Pakistan in 1971 that reversed many of the policies of the 1960s. Most large industries, banks, and insurance companies were nationalized, and massive public investments with long gestation periods were undertaken in industry (most notably steel). To improve the lot of urban workers, consumer price controls and subsidies were instituted, together with low producer prices for crops. Finally, a lack of fiscal and monetary discipline led to high budget deficits, rapid monetary growth, and inflation.

The government that came to power in 1977 sought to reverse this trend by shifting emphasis back to the private sector and restoring fiscal and financial discipline, but the oil price shocks of 1979 and the subsequent slowdown in the world economy made its task more difficult. Between 1979 and 1981 Pakistan's terms of trade fell sharply, and rising interest rates and slackening world trade were additional problems. Pakistan received help in weathering the shocks through large inflows from the International Monetary Fund (IMF) and other external agencies and from migrant worker remittances, which reached US$2.9 billion at their peak in 1983 (compared with US$600 million in 1977). These resources helped smooth Pakistan's adjustment, but they may also have delayed painful policy changes that would otherwise have been necessary.

Improvements in government policy continued, however, and assisted the adjustment to the external shocks. Policies in 1977–81 emphasized reducing the fiscal deficit and government borrowing from the banking system, reinstituting a program of medium-term planning, improving public sector infrastructure and institutions, and strengthening the incentives for private sector participation and efficiency in the key sectors of agriculture, industry, and energy.

Through expenditure restraint and ad hoc tax and price increases, the budget deficit was cut from 8.6 percent of GDP in 1977 to 5.3 percent in 1981, thereby reducing credit expansion and cutting inflation rates. The thrust of medium-term planning was to reestablish real growth in public expenditures for development and to shift resources from activities that could be performed by the private sector to those that strengthened public infrastructure, especially for energy and the social sectors. A shortage of resources, however, suppressed real growth and delayed the shift of resources to priority sectors. Steps were also taken to enlarge the role of the private sector and of price mechanisms. Some agricultural processing and industrial firms were denationalized, tax incentives were introduced for exporters, and a number of joint ventures were entered into with foreign private firms for oil and gas exploration.

Despite such policy improvements and the acceleration in growth during the late 1970s and early 1980s, Pakistan's adjustment to past policy mistakes and to external shocks was incomplete. The economy continued to suffer from structural weaknesses that threatened its potential for rapid growth under conditions of reasonable internal and external balance. Prominent among these weaknesses were the following:

- Relatively low investment and savings rates, which were insufficient to accommodate both the recovery of the private sector and the growing requirements for public economic and social infrastructure
- A fragile external balance, with imports double the size of exports; exports heavily concentrated in rice, cotton, and cotton-based products; and foreign exchange receipts heavily dependent on remittances from migrant workers
- Poor mobilization of resources for the public sector
- Agricultural policies that continued to emphasize low producer prices, public sector distribution and subsidization of agricultural inputs, and investment in major new infrastructure projects (mainly irrigation)
- Heavy protection, continued government regulation of prices and market entry, and inefficient public enterprises in the industrial sector
- Failure to exploit the country's considerable potential in hydropower and hydrocarbons, which led to periodic energy shortages.

The Adjustment Program

From 1981 through 1987 Pakistan pursued a structural adjustment program addressing these problems. Its efforts were supported by an IMF Extended Fund Facility program in 1980–83 and World Bank loans (for structural adjustment in 1982, for energy in 1985, and for export development in 1986). The IMF program and the World Bank's structural adjustment loan (SAL) were drawn up and implemented by the two agencies in close consultation with each other, and although their emphases differed, many conditions overlapped. The IMF program emphasized a continuation and intensification of the government's stabilization efforts, phased implementation of import liberalization, and improved management of the exchange rate. It also included several issues later covered by the SAL (for example, consumer prices for petroleum products, agricultural subsidies, and tariff reform). Because of the IMF's role the early World Bank adjustment operations were able to take the importance of stabilization programs as given and to emphasize issues such as the restoration of medium-term development planning, rationalization of prices in key productive sectors, establishment of a more balanced set of incentives for exports and import substitution, deregulation of industrial prices and investments, and improved institutional performance.

Stabilization Programs

Under the economic stabilization program, fiscal and credit restraints were expected to contain the level of aggregate demand and inflation while exchange rate policies were used to shift resources toward the production of tradables, especially exports. Under the IMF program the government budget deficit was to be held below 5 percent of GDP by curbing expenditure, reducing subsidies, and increasing revenue. Government borrowing from the banking system was to be kept under 2 percent of GDP, thereby helping to hold annual growth in the domestic money supply to 14 to 15 percent, or slightly below the expected nominal growth rate of GDP.

The IMF also monitored the exchange rate. At the urging of the IMF (and the World Bank), the rupee was delinked from the U.S. dollar in January 1982 and subsequently managed flexibly with respect to a basket of currencies of key trading partners. The immediate impact was to reverse the real appreciation of the rupee that had begun in 1979, but the rupee continued to fall in value by more than 40 percent in real terms by 1987 against the basket of currencies.

Until 1983 Pakistan met the fiscal and credit targets of the IMF. In that year, however, an unexpected surge in foreign exchange receipts and government borrowing for budget and commodity operations caused monetary growth to exceed the program limits by a considerable margin. Since the government's budget for the following year already included measures to mobilize resources equivalent to 1.5 percent of GDP, the government was reluctant to undertake the additional measures the IMF was demanding to shrink the size of the budget deficit and reduce the monetary overhang. In November 1983 the IMF credit lapsed, and the final portion was never drawn.

Policy Reforms

The government's adjustment program emphasized a major shift of resources toward the key productive sectors and increased reliance on market-determined prices to provide incentives and encourage efficiency. The major elements in the program were improved resource mobilization and restoration of medium-term planning, trade policy reform, decontrol of input and output pricing, deregulation of private activities, and increased efficiency of public enterprises.

BUDGETARY POLICY AND MEDIUM-TERM PLANNING. The IMF program and various World Bank operations called for improved resource mobilization through improvements in the coverage and elasticity of the tax system and reductions in subsidies. Such policies would have permitted an expansion of government expenditures and a shift toward high-priority sectors, while overall budget deficits remained at acceptable levels. However, the government made relatively little progress in this area either under the IMF program or subsequently. Revenue measures consisted largely of ad hoc changes introduced with each budget (for example, import surcharges and changes in public utility rates or oil and gas prices). No systematic effort was made to introduce new taxes (such as a value added tax or broad-based sales tax) or to expand the coverage of existing taxes. Although some subsidies were eliminated, others were expanded to make up the difference. As a consequence of these failures, budget deficits were a continuing problem through the 1980s.

Increased resource mobilization was also intended to permit directing public expenditures more toward the development of agriculture, water, energy, and social services. Reductions in fertilizer subsidies and in public investments in industry were expected to free additional resources. Development expenditures grew at a real average annual rate of 3 to 4 percent during the 1980s, and substantial progress was made in reorienting expenditures. About 85 percent of expenditure targets under the sixth five-year plan (fiscal 1984–88) were implemented, and public resources were shifted markedly toward power, education, health, agriculture, and rural development. The shift in resources would have been greater but for budgetary constraints and the failure to reduce subsidies (especially for fertilizer) as called for in the plan.[1]

Public investment programs in agriculture and energy received strong support in the adjustment program. In agriculture there was a shift away from activities that could be handled by the private sector (for example, storage and mechanization) and from major new investments to expenditures that would raise the productivity of existing investments. Thus allocations for operations and maintenance in irrigation rose significantly in real terms, extension and research received a growing share of total agricultural expenditures, and irrigation projects emphasized water management, rehabilitation, and drainage in saline areas. In energy the goals were to increase private production and to rationalize investment in and improve financing for public sector programs in oil, gas, and electric power. These efforts substantially increased exploration activity and oil and gas output from private and public sources. The private sector was particularly responsive to the adoption of a new formula for gas producer prices.

TRADE POLICY. Pakistan's trade regime was substantially biased toward import substitution, with pervasive quantitative restrictions and tariffs ranging from zero to 350 percent dominating a duty drawback system and outright subsidies for exports (the "compensatory" rebate). The IMF and World Bank called for substantial trade liberalization, involving a reduction in the coverage of nontariff barriers followed by tariff reform. Coverage by quantitative restrictions dropped from the equivalent of about 66 percent of manufacturing value added to 27 percent, and a negative list of prohibited imports replaced a more restrictive positive list of allowed imports. The tariff reform was not introduced during this period, however, because the study on which it was to be based was not completed until December 1983 and did not contain specific proposals for the government to consider.

Trade policy reform continued after the IMF program and the SAL, through the government's initiative and the World Bank's support under the export development loan. Flexible management of the exchange rate continued as well. Some 136 items were removed from the negative or restricted lists, although about 400 four-digit commodity headings (mostly consumer goods but some important capital goods as well) remained subject to some form of quantitative restriction. The number of tariff rates was reduced from seventeen to ten, while the (unweighted) average tariff rate was reduced from 77 percent to 66 percent. Improvements in the duty drawback and open-bonded manufacturing systems were introduced to move exports toward a free trade basis. These changes, combined with the elimination of export subsidies, have probably improved relative incentives for exports somewhat, but they have left the antiexport bias of the trade regime largely intact.

DEREGULATION. Through regulation, the government had sought to foster efficient development while avoiding the adverse effects of relying on the price mechanism in the absence of foreign competition. The main forms of regulation were investment sanctions, price controls, and cost-plus pricing. During the 1980s several changes were introduced. The size limit for projects requiring government sanction of investment plans was increased substantially; the list of industries requiring government sanctions was shortened (changes in 1987 reduced the list from the equivalent of 40 percent of manufacturing value added to 7 percent); and cost-plus pricing or subsidized pricing was eliminated in key industries such as cement, nitrogenous fertilizer, and vegetable ghee.

By and large, there was considerable progress. The role of government in investment and pricing decisions was significantly reduced, and the economy became more market-oriented. Additional improvements are still needed, however, in particular the removal of investment sanctions based on project size and import content, further shrinkage of the use of price controls and cost-plus arrangements, and increased use of price taxes (rather than location licenses) to ration infrastructure and handle environmental concerns.

PRICING POLICIES. Pricing policies in energy and agriculture shifted their emphasis toward encouraging efficient consumption and production decisions and providing appropriate incentives for domestic producers. Except in the case of certain agricultural inputs (fertilizers and irrigation water), the policy changes were significant. On the consumption side, price increases averaging 24 percent a year during 1981–86 brought natural gas prices to two-thirds of the fuel oil parity level by mid-1985 (three years ahead of schedule). As a result of subsequent declines in world oil prices, gas prices came to exceed fuel oil parity. Domestic oil prices continued to exceed world prices because increases in world prices were fully passed through to domestic consumers but were only partly reversed as oil prices fell. Reversing a long-standing policy of keeping power cheap for social reasons, the government also agreed to adjust power tariffs so that 40 percent of an agreed-on power investment program could be self-financed; subsequent increases in power tariffs have met this objective.

With respect to producer prices for energy, the government responded flexibly in providing appropriate incentives for private sector participation. Through much of the 1980s producer prices for oil discovered under joint ventures were set equal to the official prices for market crude (Arabian light), with an adjustment for quality and a prenegotiated discount. As international oil prices declined, continuation of this practice would have threatened exploration and development. Instead, the government announced a new formula that included sliding-scale discounts, which vary inversely with comparator prices. This revised formula was successful in attracting new companies and maintaining incentives for exploration and development.

Government policy was somewhat slower to change on producer prices for gas. Under the SAL the government initiated a number of joint ventures for gas exploration and development. According to the government's plan, prices, based on a cost-plus formula, would not be agreed on until after discovery. The World Bank had serious doubts about this system because of the considerable uncertainty involved. When after several years no agreements had been reached on this basis, a new formula was introduced under the energy loan. It tied the price to fuel oil parity, less a discount to be negotiated in advance on the basis of such factors as location and geological risk. This formula has been successful in attracting private response.

During the 1980s Pakistan also sought to revise two key agricultural sector policies: support prices and input subsidies. Support prices had been significantly below international prices and constituted a severe tax on agriculture. Under the SAL the government conducted annual price reviews and established appropriate incentives for farmers through price support recommendations based on trends in international prices and in local costs. On the basis of such annual reviews, the prices established for most major crops remained close to world price trends, and the use of support prices to tax agriculture was virtually eliminated. In the case of input subsidies progress was more mixed. Pesticide subsidies were eliminated, but targets for eliminating fertilizer subsidies and increasing the cost recovery of irrigation operations and maintenance were not met.

PERFORMANCE OF PUBLIC ENTERPRISES. Public enterprises are important in the manufacturing sector less for their overall size (15 percent of the sector's value added) than for their dominant role in key subsectors such as steel, cement, fertilizer, and basic chemicals. Government efforts to improve the performance of public enterprises during the 1980s centered on making such firms behave more like those in the private sector and reducing their reliance on budgetary resources. The government implemented a "public enterprise signaling system" for public manufacturing firms, involving information management, and established targets and rewards for performance. Evidence suggests that the system did improve performance and helped to focus government officials' and managers' attention on the need to improve efficiency. It also revealed a number of impediments to improving efficiency, such as insufficient management autonomy, the need for skilled and experienced managers, and excessive government regulation.

In some cases the government has undertaken privatization measures, including disinvestment of shares and denationalization. Progress in this area has been slow, however. A disinvestment committee was established, a few firms were offered for outright sale, and plans were being made to sell shares in a number of important enterprises, such as Pakistan International Airways and Sui Gas Transmission. To date, however, little disinvestment has actually taken place.

Economic Performance

Pakistan is one of the few developing countries whose growth was higher during the 1980s than during 1973–80, to a great extent because of the large scope for reforming the policies that had restrained growth during the 1970s. Improvements in policies affecting stabilization and efficiency had already begun to accelerate growth before the 1979 shock, and policy reforms adopted since then helped to reconfirm the process. Despite substantial progress, however, Pakistan's adjustment is far from complete. Many areas remain in need of considerable improvement, especially public resource mobilization and import liberalization.

Growth, Employment, and Wages

Pakistan grew at an annual rate of 6.5 percent (or 3.3 percent on a per capita basis) during 1980–87 (see table 19-1). This rapid growth was not concentrated in a few sectors but characterized virtually all key sectors. Agricultural expansion of 3.1 percent a year, though somewhat less than government authorities were targeting, was nonetheless respectable. It allowed self-sufficiency in some key commodities (for example, wheat and sugar) and provided surpluses for export in others (for example, rice, cotton, and cotton-based textiles). Although production is still heavily concentrated in these major crops (just over half of value added), some diversification has occurred into minor crops (such as oilseeds) and into livestock and fisheries. Some of the improvement in agricultural performance resulted from favorable weather and private initiative, but government efforts also contributed—for example, better output prices, improvement in the amount and timing of irrigation water, distribution of improved seeds, increased coverage of agricultural credit, and improved balance between the private and public sectors in the distribution of fertilizer and pesticides.

Industrial growth of 9.1 percent a year during 1980–87 was encouraged by improvements in the policy environment for private initiative. The freeing up of prices and investment as well as a reduced role for the public sector were helpful in this regard. The composition of investment shifted heavily toward the private sector: private investment expanded at an annual rate of 23 percent in real terms during fiscal 1984–87, compared with 7 percent for total industrial investment. Overall, 72 percent of industrial investment during that period was contributed by the private sector. Public sector investment grew slowly and was restricted to ongoing projects and some rehabilitation projects. Major contributors to growth in the large-scale industrial sector were cotton yarn, sugar, cement, fertilizer, chemicals, iron and steel, and automobiles. Also important was the rapid expansion of small-scale manufacturing, which

Table 19-1. Economic Indicators for Pakistan

	Share of GDP (current prices)					Growth rates (annual percent in real terms)	
	1980	1985	1986	1987	1988	1973–80	1980–88
Gross domestic product	100.0	100.0	100.0	100.0	100.0	5.4	6.5
Agriculture	26.5	22.8	22.0	23.6	23.5	2.8	4.3
Industry	22.4	24.6	25.3	21.6	21.7	7.0	7.2
Services	40.9	42.8	42.6	44.8	44.0	6.4	7.4
Net indirect taxes	10.2	9.9	10.1	10.0	10.7	—	—
Total expenditure	111.6	112.1	109.5	105.3	107.5	6.3	5.5
Total consumption	93.1	95.3	92.8	86.1	89.4	6.5	5.3
Private consumption	83.1	83.1	80.5	72.6	75.5	6.8	4.4
General government	10.0	12.2	12.2	13.5	13.9	4.0	11.0
Gross domestic investment	18.5	16.8	16.7	19.1	18.1	5.8	6.4
Fixed investment	17.6	15.0	15.1	17.5	16.6	6.7	6.1
Changes in stock	0.9	1.8	1.6	1.6	1.5	—	—
Resource balance	−11.6	−12.1	−9.5	−5.3	−7.5	—	—
Export of goods and nonfactory services	12.5	10.4	12.1	13.8	14.4	4.2	8.9
Import of goods and nonfactory services	24.1	22.5	21.6	19.1	21.9	9.1	3.0
Gross domestic savings	6.9	4.7	7.2	13.9	10.6	−11.6	16.0
Gross national savings	13.6	11.7	13.8	19.6	14.5	4.0	9.5
Overall budgetary deficit	−6.3	−7.4	−8.1	−8.2	−8.6	—	—
Current account deficit (b.o.p.)	−4.8	−5.4	−3.9	−2.2	−4.4	—	—
Debt ratios							
Debt outstanding and disbursed/GDP	42.0	42.9	46.7	50.1	44.5	—	—
Debt outstanding and disbursed/exports	208.9	228.1	228.9	246.0	231.0	—	—
Debt service/exports	18.0	24.2	25.3	26.5	24.7	—	—

— Not applicable.
Source: World Bank data.

also contributed to export growth (for example, garments, towels, hosiery, leather products, and surgical instruments).

In the energy sector, as a result of public and private activities, a record number of wells were drilled for exploration and development. Oil production more than tripled, and Pakistan now supplies about 25 percent of its petroleum requirements (compared with 10 percent in the early 1980s). Expansion in natural gas was more modest, but as investments began to come on-stream growth was expected to average 4.8 percent annually in the sixth plan period. Expansion of electric power, while impressive, is considerably short of projections; even with the acceleration of investment in recent years, capacity will not meet demand before the early 1990s.

With the help of the Middle East oil boom, the domestic labor market was able to absorb, at rising real wages in key sectors, the increases in the labor force. By the early 1980s outmigration to the Middle East was accommodating some 2 million Pakistani workers (the equivalent of about 7 percent of the labor force). Since the labor force was growing by 2.3 percent a year during 1979–85 while employment was growing at 2.2 percent, open unemployment grew slightly from 3.5 percent to 3.7 percent of the labor force. As is typical in developing countries, urban unemployment (5 percent) was higher than rural (3.1 percent), and youth unemployment (7 percent) higher than the national average. A fairly recent phenomenon is the rise of unemployment among the educated urban population, with degree holders experiencing unemployment rates roughly double those of illiterates. Consistent with the strong expansion of the economy and the relatively slow growth of the labor force, real wages have continued to increase. The wages of agricultural laborers grew at 11 percent a year and those of employees in small-scale and large-scale manufacturing grew at 3 to 4 percent a year between 1979 and 1987.

Macroeconomic Balance

DOMESTIC ABSORPTION. Pakistan responded to the crisis of 1979 by reducing the real growth of domestic absorption from an average of 6.3 percent a year in 1973–80 to 5.9 percent in 1980–87, which was below the average real growth of the economy (6.5 percent) in the latter period. The external counterpart to this decrease in absorption showed up in the resource balance, as real growth of exports of goods and nonfactor services accelerated to 9.2 percent a year, while import growth fell sharply to about 2.8 percent a year. Contributing to this performance were a significant fall in the real effective exchange rate, improved policies in the agriculture and energy sectors, and the slow growth of external financing.

The reduced growth in domestic absorption resulted from a fairly sharp shift in the structure of demand. Compared with the 1970s, private consumption grew more slowly while private investment, government consumption, and government investment grew more rapidly. The deceleration of private consumption, though it cannot be explained with certainty, could be the result of rising real rates of return on financial assets such as deposits or government savings schemes, as well as a policy environment that was considerably more hospitable than before to private investment. The acceleration of government expenditures, since it was not accompanied by increased resource mobilization, led to increasingly large budget deficits.

Pakistan's investment rate of 16 to 17 percent of GDP was very low, especially given the economy's relatively high growth rate. It seems implausible that efficiency was as high as an incremental capital-output ratio (ICOR) of 2.6 for 1980–88 would imply. A more plausible explanation is that improved policies made for improved utilization of existing capital and that existing capital was being depleted as the maintenance and the replacement of aging assets were being neglected (as evidenced, for example, in the deteriorating highways and irrigation systems and the neglect of social sector investment). It appears highly likely, therefore, that the ICOR will be much higher in the future.

There was very little improvement in the national savings rate. Improvements in private savings were virtually offset by deterioration in public sector savings. The share of public investment financed from public savings fell to extremely low levels (less than 20 percent in 1985–88 and less than 5 percent in two of those three years). Although the savings performance of public enterprises was far from satisfactory, the deterioration in overall public sector performance emanated from the budget.

BUDGETARY PERFORMANCE. After some improvement during the IMF program, Pakistan's budget situation deteriorated markedly. Overall deficits rose from 5.3 percent of GDP in fiscal 1981 to over 8 percent of GDP in fiscal 1986 and 1987. With the rising deficits came a growing dependence on borrowing, especially from domestic sources. The growth of public domestic indebtedness has been accelerating, and debt-service payments are absorbing a growing share of government expenditures. The budgetary performance of recent years is clearly not sustainable.

The major factors contributing to the budgetary deterioration were the rapid rise of current expenditures and the failure to generate sufficient additional revenue. The growth of development expenditures was relatively slow, and their share in GDP fell. After fiscal 1981 current expenditures rose at an annual rate of 18.8 percent (11.1 percent in real terms), with their share of GDP rising from 15 percent to 19 percent. Defense and interest payments accounted for a large part of that increase. In 1988

Pakistan was spending 25 percent of government expenditures on defense, a significantly larger proportion than the averages in 1985 for low-income (18.6 percent), lower-middle-income (14.2 percent), and industrial countries (16.8 percent). Interest payments as a share of GDP more than doubled in the 1980s. The only bright spot on the current expenditure side was the positive real growth in outlays for the chronically underfunded economic and social sectors.

Over the 1981–88 period revenue remained at 17 to 18 percent of GDP. That this stability was achieved through ad hoc measures introduced yearly indicates a basic inelasticity of the revenue system. Since the early 1980s the IMF and the World Bank have been recommending that the government increase the coverage and elasticity of its revenue-generation system by introducing a broad-based tax on consumption (sales or value added), shifting excise taxes from specific to ad valorem rates and extending the range of goods covered, expanding coverage of the income tax system, and improving cost recovery for public goods and services. Very little was done on these measures, however, before the fiscal 1989 budget.

Both foreign and domestic borrowing for budgetary purposes increased, with domestic borrowing, especially from nonbank sources, growing more rapidly. Domestic interest payments grew at 27 percent a year until they absorbed 14 percent of current expenditure, compared with 8 percent in the early 1980s. The government was able to tap private savings through a number of savings schemes with attractive interest rates and other innovative features. Although tapping private savings enabled the government to postpone tax reform and other resource mobilization measures, the postponement came at a high price in the form of rising interest costs and constraints on more essential government expenditures.

The budgetary performance of the late 1980s was inconsistent with the government's targets for inflation, increased foreign exchange holdings, growth in the private sector, and expansion of essential public economic and social services. Continuation along recent lines would mean that one or more of the government's targets would have to be abandoned. The sustainable long-term deficit appears to be just under 5 percent of GDP, a reduction of 3.0 to 3.5 percentage points from the deficits of recent years.[2]

MONEY, CREDIT, AND PRICES. In Pakistan the objectives of monetary policy are articulated in an annual credit plan, which places ceilings on credit expansion by commercial banks and allocates mandatory minimum credit levels for priority sectors (for example, agriculture, small-scale industry, exports) and indicative levels for other sectors. The government's credit needs and expected changes in net foreign-held assets are also taken into account. After fiscal 1980 the money supply grew at an annual rate of 15 percent and prices at 6.2 percent, roughly in line with the government's targets for real growth and inflation. These increases were a marked improvement over the 1973–78 period when the money supply grew at 22 percent a year and prices at 12 percent.

Generally, the annual plans have called for some modest expansion in net foreign assets, limited public sector reliance on the monetary system, and a growing share for the private sector in the additional credit. Although the private sector has indeed been obtaining a growing share of the additional credit (nearly two-thirds of the increase in recent years, compared with 40 to 50 percent in the late 1970s), credit expansion to both the private and public sectors has often exceeded targets. Thus, although growth of the money supply has generally been in line with government targets, the accommodating factor has been net foreign assets, which have declined in most years since 1980. This is clearly not a sustainable policy. The need to increase official foreign exchange holdings (building up reserve holdings while paying off short-term debt) will raise issues about priorities between the private and public sectors and the possible crowding out of the private sector by public sector credit demands.

The External Sector

BALANCE OF PAYMENTS. During the 1980s Pakistan's balance of payments was affected by several factors over which the government had little control: the instability in international commodity markets (especially rice, cotton, and petroleum products); the sluggish recovery of the world economy; the shrinking markets for migrant workers, especially in the Middle East; and the war in Afghanistan, which affected import levels (to assist refugees) and aid flows. The balance of payments was also affected by factors over which the government did have influence, such as the real devaluation of the rupee after it was delinked from the U.S. dollar, gradual reductions in nontariff barriers and tariff rates, and improvements in sectoral policies (concerning agricultural and energy pricing and investment programs) and policies affecting capital flows (for example, aid disbursements and the creation of new instruments to raise short-term funds from abroad).

The major forces driving Pakistan's balance of payments performance after 1980 were the rapid growth (10 percent a year) in the volume of merchandise exports coupled with a slow growth (4 percent) in merchandise imports; a rise in Pakistan's share in world trade for important export products (such as rice, cotton, cotton textiles and clothing, surgical instruments, and leather goods); the rapid rise in migrant worker remittances following the oil price boom and the subsequent decline; relatively flat (net) long-term capital inflows (mostly official); and increased reliance on short-term capital inflows to slow the decline in (gross) official reserve holdings. As a result of these and other factors, Pakistan's current account deficit declined from US$1.2 billion in fiscal 1980 (4.8 percent of GDP) to US$700 million (or 2.2 percent of GDP) in fiscal 1987.

Despite this improvement, however, Pakistan's external situation at the end of the decade remained fragile. Since delinkage of the rupee from the dollar, Pakistan's real effective exchange rate had depreciated some 40 percent. Although this contributed to improved export performance, there was still no export diversification. Merchandise exports consisted mainly of rice, cotton, and cotton textiles whose share had remained roughly unchanged at 60 percent since 1980. Rice and cotton were subject to substantial year-to-year price fluctuations, and cotton textiles were at the mercy of growing protectionism in the United States and the European Economic Community (EEC). Remittances from migrant workers remained an important source of foreign exchange earnings. Although past declines in remittances were compensated for somewhat by lower oil prices, Pakistan depends on the Middle East as a market for its products and its labor and, on balance, probably benefited from the higher oil prices.

By the end of fiscal 1987 Pakistan's short-term position had deteriorated sharply. Gross official reserves were US$500 million, down from their peak of US$2 billion in 1983 and not much higher than they were in 1980 when trade was substantially smaller. In addition, Pakistan's short-term liabilities stood at US$2.1 billion as a result of increasing reliance on short-term instruments for raising external funds. Although these vehicles have attracted substantial resources, they are highly volatile since they depend on holders' perceptions of exchange rate movements and other economic developments in Pakistan and abroad. This could limit the options for raising additional resources, should this become necessary.

EXTERNAL DEBT AND DEBT SERVICE. Between 1977 and 1982 Pakistan's indebtedness and debt-servicing capacity showed marked improvements because of increased exports, a more than fourfold increase in migrant worker remittances, and relatively conservative financial management. Since then, there has been some deterioration because of falling remittances, increased debt service payments to the IMF and commercial lenders, and a looser fiscal policy stance. Of particular concern, however, is the buildup of all forms of debt since 1982 and the decline in official reserve holdings. With it has come a substantial increase in the debt service/exports ratio from 18 percent in 1980 to 27 percent in 1987.[3] Reserves, which were no higher at the end of 1987 than in 1980, could cover only one-quarter of debt service requirements in 1987 versus two-thirds in 1980. This deterioration suggests that continued progress in

Pakistan's adjustment program will be essential to restoring the viability of its external position and improving its creditworthiness.

Assessment of Conditionality

Adjustment loan conditionality in Pakistan went through two distinct phases. During the first phase the IMF and World Bank programs overlapped; the macroeconomic conditionality of the SAL mirrored that of the IMF. With the IMF and the World Bank in substantial agreement on appropriate stabilization policies, the World Bank concentrated on medium-term planning, the level and structure of the public sector investment program, and sectoral policies—such as appropriate pricing for inputs and outputs, deregulation of prices and investment decisions, and institutional reforms. In the second phase the World Bank's sectoral emphasis remained broadly the same, but it had to take on the monitoring of macroeconomic policy as well because of the absence of the IMF and a failure to reach agreement on a follow-up SAL.

Table 19-2 lists the major conditions that accompanied adjustment loans to Pakistan by degree of compliance. Implementation of some conditions was relatively easy because no readily identifiable major group was harmed by the policy change (for example, medium-term planning, reorientation of public development programs). In some cases positive external shocks eased the policy change; for example, the great drop in international prices made it easy to remove price controls and subsidies on oilseeds and nitrogenous fertilizer since the price drop rendered the policy redundant. Often conditions were implemented after intensive policy dialogue with the World Bank (as in the case of energy pricing) or after a long period of technical assistance and sector work (agricultural pricing, reductions in import bans and restrictions). In cases in which there was little or no progress, it is evident that the political will was lacking (for example, on tariffs, budgetary improvements, irrigation charges) or that the World Bank did not give the government concrete advice in time (the study on effective protection, for example, was late, flawed, and lacking in concrete policy prescriptions).

Sustainability

An interesting and unusual aspect of Pakistan's adjustment program is the lack of policy reversals once reform had begun.[4] Several factors help to explain why reforms were so sustainable. The government's approach to policymaking was very cautious: there were no abrupt changes, and the policy measures adopted were flexible enough to leave the government room for maneuver should the results not be as expected. Moreover, in most instances the government was convinced of the rightness of its

Table 19-2. Implementation of Adjustment Loan Conditionality in Pakistan

Significant progress	*Satisfactory progress*	*Little or no progress*
Exchange rate management	Power tariffs	Budget deficit
Consumer prices of oil and gas	Elimination of cost-plus pricing (for example, of oilseeds, nitrogenous fertilizers, cement)	Tax reform
Producer prices of oil and gas	Elimination of pesticide subsidy	Budget subsidies
Agricultural output prices	Allocation for operation and maintenance of irrigation systems	Tariff reform
Medium-term planning	Reduction in requirements for investment sanctioning	Irrigation cost recovery
	Incentive system for performance in public sector manufacturing	Non-nitrogenous fertilizer subsidies
	Reduction in import bans and restrictions	Disinvestment of public enterprises
	Restructuring of public development budget (overall, and especially for energy, agriculture, irrigation)	
	Revision of duty drawback system for exporters[a]	
	Open-bonded warehousing for exporters[a]	
	Improved credit for exporters[a]	

Note: "Significant" indicates that progress exceeds World Bank–IMF conditions and was not reversed in a succeeding period; "satisfactory" indicates that progress meets World Bank–IMF conditions and was not subsequently reversed.

a. Substantial progress under way, but condition not yet met.

approach in advance (for example, deregulation, agricultural output pricing, gas producer prices) or as a result of the benefits that quickly became apparent (for example, the favorable effects of exchange rate delinkage on exports and migrant worker remittances). In a number of cases (for example, energy, deregulation), the government's confidence was the product of extensive dialogue with the IMF or the World Bank. The stability of Pakistan's growth and the absence of further adverse shocks also certainly aided the reform process.

Tranching

Both the SAL and the energy loan were disbursed in two tranches; the export development loan had only a single tranche, given its small size and the World Bank's expectation that progress in implementation could lead quickly to an industrial sector loan the following year. Release of the second tranche of the SAL was linked to three conditions as well as to satisfactory progress in implementing the remainder of the program: preparation of a three-year public sector investment program, a report on government decisions on agricultural support prices and key input prices, and a report assessing progress in implementing the accelerated program for developing the gas supply. Implementation was judged to be satisfactory, and the second tranche was released on schedule. The tranche release for the energy loan was not as straightforward. The tranche conditions were review of the electricity tariff for fiscal 1987, review of implementation of the core investment program for the energy sector for 1985 and 1986, and agreement on the revised energy investment program for 1987 and 1988. Tranche release was delayed about nine months until it could be determined that power tariffs had been raised sufficiently to finance 40 percent of the power investment program.

World Bank adjustment lending for Pakistan has made sparing use of "up-front" conditionality, which must be met before the loan. The SAL had no up-front conditions because it was introduced at the same time that the IMF program was being successfully implemented. The energy sector loan had two advance conditions related to increases in power tariffs and a new producer pricing formula for natural gas. The export development loan had only one advance condition—appointment of a person of appropriate experience and rank to head the Industrial Incentives Reform Cell—because many of the policy reforms that had been discussed (for example, exchange rate adjustments) were enacted by the government on its own initiative before the loan was presented to the Executive Directors of the World Bank for approval.

Sequencing of Loans

In view of Pakistan's continuing problems with resource mobilization, it would have been logical to follow the first SAL with a second. However, the failure to complete the IMF program, the high visibility of SALs, and the growing political liberalization of Pakistan made negotiation of a follow-up SAL virtually impossible. Instead, the World Bank and the government of Pakistan agreed to a lending program consisting of about 75 percent project loans and 25 percent policy-based sectoral adjustment loans (SECALs) in industry, agriculture, and energy. The policy-based loans depended on agreement on an acceptable program of reform in the relevant sectors *and* on the government's maintaining appropriate overall macroeconomic management. Progress in macroeconomic management was to be monitored in annual reviews by the World Bank and the government. This approach was more acceptable to the government than a SAL because the macroeconomic conditionality would be less intrusive and the sectoral conditionality was broken up into discrete chunks.

As it turned out, however, the procedures for ensuring an appropriate macroeconomic policy environment were not effective. Despite annual consultations, the budgetary situation continued to deteriorate, and the government made little effort to reverse the process. The problem was not that the macroeconomic environment was so unfavorable that sectoral policy changes would have been ineffective; indeed, relatively low inflation rates plus continued effective exchange rate management meant that policy changes involving relative prices and improvements in efficiency would most likely have been effective. Rather, the issues were the deteriorating creditworthiness and the ineffective use of the World Bank's leverage to obtain policy improvements.

With the rapid buildup of debt service requirements on both foreign and domestic debt, Pakistan was quickly approaching the limits of its ability to service such debt. This, in turn, called into question the justification for a larger World Bank lending program in Pakistan. In addition, progress in some sectors was very slow. As a result, the World Bank first slowed its sectoral lending considerably and then suspended it. This outcome highlights the problem of how to ensure appropriate stabilization policies in the absence of an IMF agreement. World Bank consultations are infrequent, and the implied threat of cutting back a lending program seems to lack the urgency and immediacy that accompanies the IMF's quarterly tranche reviews.

Several broad trends in conditionality are discernible in Pakistan's experience in moving from SALs to SECALs. First, the number of conditions attached to any one loan dropped. This is not surprising, although perhaps misleading, since the coverage of sectoral loans is narrower and an array of implicit macroeconomic policy conditions was being monitored concurrently. Second, there was a tendency to focus each loan on about four or five items on which fairly specific—if not necessarily quantifiable—actions were expected. In part, this increasing precision was a product of the World Bank's growing knowledge in a number of areas, progress in the dialogue with the government, and a growing realization that it is better to focus on a few issues that are important and feasible.

Third, the World Bank became more sensitive to the need to adjust the pace of reform to what is politically and institutionally feasible, that is, to make progress in areas where progress is feasible and to leave recalcitrant problems to later follow-up loans. For example, the export development loan capitalized on the government's desire to move forward with export incentives, liberalization of imported inputs, and deregulation, and it left tariff reforms for a later operation. Fourth, significant progress was sometimes made with little specific conditionality. For example, substantial liberalization of government controls on investment and prices was based on a general understanding between the government and the World Bank about deregulation priorities. The precise details, order, and timing were left to the government. Had the World Bank inserted itself into this politically sensitive area with demands for specific actions by specific dates, the process could have been self-defeating.

Conclusions and Lessons

In many respects the Pakistan economy of the late 1980s differed from the economy of 1980. A period of rapid growth and inflows of migrant worker remittances had raised standards of living broadly across the population. Private initiative played a leading role in this expansion, and no longer was public investment in large-scale industry viewed as the engine of growth. The public sector had taken on a supportive role and was beginning to restore the country's neglected economic and social infrastructure while initiating steps to improve the performance of public enterprises. During this time, the economy became substantially more outward-looking, flexible, and market-oriented. More active exchange rate management, combined with better export incentives and reductions in nontariff barriers and, to a lesser extent, tariffs, brought about some improvement in the environment for exports. The government attitude toward regulation became more relaxed: controls on market entry, enforced through investment controls, were significantly reduced, and price controls and cost-plus pricing arrangements were eliminated in some key areas. Agricultural and energy prices were adjusted in line with international prices, improving efficiency and the incentives for increased production.

Although reforms undertaken during the 1980s improved performance and the capacity to respond to economic change, there are some worrisome signs. The continued decline in remittances and the possible leveling off of aid following the end of the Afghanistan War are likely to mean that some painful adjustments can be postponed no longer. Reforms in some areas are still incomplete, while in others progress has been slow or nonexistent. Controls over investment remain intrusive, while in the crucial areas of the budget and the trade regime, major changes are yet to come. Fundamental reform of public sector resource mobilization remains to be undertaken, and budget deficits have been running at unsustainable levels. Many consumer goods remain subject to quantitative restrictions, and the average level of tariffs is still very high, so antiexport bias remains significant.

The dialogue between the government of Pakistan and the World Bank has contributed to the economic improvements in Pakistan. After modest beginnings under the SAL, when the areas amenable to meaningful dialogue were few, the relationship has broadened through improved economic and sector work, experience with successful reforms, and a growing mutual trust. Negotiations now include discussions and actions in areas that could not have been broached in the early years. For example, progress would have been difficult or unthinkable in the early 1980s on such issues as a least-cost investment program for the power sector, an incentive program for exports, reductions in import restrictions for raw materials and intermediate goods, and reforms of producer pricing arrangements in gas and power—areas in which actions have recently been taken or are under way.

Several broad generalizations can be drawn about the adjustment process and the respective roles of the government of Pakistan and the World Bank:

- Progress has been easier and more solid in areas in which the dialogue covered issues that were specific and concrete.
- Reforms in Pakistan have been sustained because of the government's incremental and flexible approach and because continued strong economic performance has obviated the need for reversals.
- When there is broad understanding between the government and the World Bank about the direction and elements of needed change, considerable progress is possible *without* specific conditionality. This finding may be particularly important for application in areas in which reforms are politically sensitive (deregulation is a case in point).
- There are gains to be had from being sensitive to the effects of sequencing and timing. In the long run, for example, it may prove to have been desirable that Pakistan improved export incentives and performance in advance of introducing a strong trade reform program (even granting that progress has been too slow in this area). Similarly, improving private sector performance in oil and gas before attacking this issue in the electric power sector may have improved the prospects for reform in the power sector.
- Trying simultaneously to monitor the macroeconomic situation and hold a government to standards of performance under a program of SECALs without a concurrent IMF program or a SAL has proved to be unsuccessful. In Pakistan the SECALs are supporting useful sectoral reforms, but World Bank attempts to use the size of its lending program and the proportion and number of SECALs to exercise leverage over macroeconomic performance issues have failed to stem an extended decline in budgetary (and credit) performance.

A Postscript for Fiscal 1988 and 1989

In fiscal 1988 Pakistan's economic performance continued to show the effects of large fiscal deficits. Although growth continued at a respectable 7 percent rate, inflationary pressures accelerated and the balance of payments situation deteriorated. At 8.6 percent of GDP, the budget deficit exceeded both original projections and the 1987 deficit by about 0.5 percent. Most inflation indicators jumped into the 5 to 10 percent a year range, some 2 to 3 percentage points higher than in previous years. Although export growth was strong (25 percent in current dollars), imports also surged and remittances continued their decline, which led to a current account deficit of 4.4 percent of GDP (more than double that of the previous year). By year's end, gross official foreign exchange reserves were the equivalent of only three weeks of imports, which was too low to meet any unanticipated short-term fluctuations.

The government has begun an ambitious program of reforms covering the 1989–91 period, partly in the context of an agreement with the IMF and a number of negotiated or potential sectoral loans from the World Bank. Although at this writing the details remain to be worked out, some important initiatives are aimed at reducing the budget deficit to sustainable levels, further liberalizing foreign trade and government regulations, and improving cost recovery in agriculture. Among the most important of these measures are increases in the coverage of the sales tax, a surtax on higher income groups, substantial reductions in the imports subjec to quantitative restrictions, a reduction in the dispersion of tariff ra (through reductions in the maximum tariff rate from 150 to 225 perc to 100 percent and consolidation of rates on inputs into a narrov range), further liberalization of investment controls, and reductions i agricultural subsidies.

Notes

1. Expenditures in all the priority sectors, in real terms and as shares of total development expenditures, were significantly higher in the sixth plan than in the fifth. In most cases, however, the share did not reach the ambitious targets called for in the sixth plan.

2. Deficits on the order of 5 percent of GDP would be consistent with the government's macroeconomic targets and would keep foreign and domestic debt roughly constant as a share of GDP. The calculation is based on the following targets: real GDP growth of 6 percent; domestic debt/GDP of 35 percent; foreign debt/GDP of 35 percent; base money/GDP of 16 percent; inflation of 5 percent; real exchange rate depreciation of 4 percent; domestic real interest rate of 6 percent; and foreign real interest rate of 3 percent.

3. Fiscal years. Debt service includes the service on all forms of debt and repurchases and interest payments on IMF programs. Exports include all goods and nonfactor services, factor services, and current transfers.

4. Although the deterioration in the government's budgetary deficit following the reduction in the deficit under the IMF program could be viewed as a reversal, it can more strongly be argued that no reversal took place because there had been no real reform. The improvement during the IMF period was achieved largely by restraining budgetary expenditures; no important reforms in tax or subsidy policy were introduced that would have made the low budget deficits sustainable over time.

Comments

Mohsin S. Khan

WILLIAM MCCLEARY'S chapter provides a useful account of economic developments in Pakistan during the last twenty-five years or so and, in particular, gives a clear and concise picture of the role of the World Bank in Pakistan during the 1980s.

Pakistan can in certain respects be viewed as a semisuccess story. For example, in 1972–86 real gross national product (GNP) grew at an average annual rate of over 6 percent, and inflation was kept below 12 percent a year on average. In comparison with many other developing countries this is a most creditable performance. The current account deficit was large by developing country standards, however (averaging nearly 5 percent of GNP), and although a large part of it was financed by official aid flows, it did lead to a significant buildup of foreign debt.[1]

McCleary's chapter goes behind these numbers to tell how and why Pakistan was able to achieve this fairly impressive performance, especially in the face of severe external shocks, both economic and political, that hit the country in the 1970s and 1980s. The rendition of history is reasonably accurate, and there is little one could disagree or take issue with.

But the real purpose of McCleary's chapter seems to be to make the case that the World Bank played a significant (and certainly positive) role in the development of the economy during the 1980s through the June 1982 structural adjustment loan (SAL) and subsequent sectoral adjustment loans (SECALS) of 1985 for energy and 1986 for export development. It is with this aspect of McCleary's analysis that I have some difficulties and disagreements.

McCleary contends that circumstances in the 1980s were quite different from those in the 1970s and, by implication, that the 1982 SAL and the 1980–83 arrangement with the International Monetary Fund (IMF) had a lot to do with Pakistan's purportedly better performance in the second period.[2] He believes that a major contributing factor to this performance was the government's promarket and outward-looking approach to development in the 1980s. I would argue, rather, that there was not a great deal of difference in performance between the two decades and that the major economic problems of the 1970s continued into the 1980s—and, for that matter, still remain to be addressed.

As can be seen from the data for the main macroeconomic aggregates table 19C-1), growth rates in the two periods were almost identical.

Table 19C-1. Macroeconomic Indicators for Pakistan, 1972–79 and 1980–86
(percent)

Indicator	*Fiscal 1972–79*	*Fiscal 1980–86*
Growth of real GNP	6.3	6.4
Inflation	14.4	8.0
Current account deficit (percentage of GNP)	6.0	3.4
Debt service ratio	23.9	24.9
External debt (billions of U.S. dollars)	8.6	12.0

Note: Fiscal year starts July 1.
Source: Pakistan Economic Survey, 1985–86 (Islamabad: Government of Pakistan, 1986).

Although inflation was cut by about half, a good part of the increase in the earlier period was a result of the oil price shock in 1973–74. If those two years are dropped from the calculation, the average annual rate of inflation in the 1970s falls to less than 10 percent. A similar adjustment to the current account deficit brings that down from an average of 6 percent of GNP to 4.6 percent of GNP, as compared with 3.4 percent of GNP during 1980–86. Debt servicing was somewhat larger in the second period as the stock of external debt rose sharply. Certainly, it is not obvious from the numbers that the 1970s was characterized "by generally poor performance and relative stagnation" or that the 1980s were so much better on all fronts.

Why was economic performance so similar in the two periods? I would attribute this to the following three factors:

1. *Same policymakers.* For some twenty years the overall direction of economic policy has been in the hands of a few individuals, who generally are not part of the civil service but are supported by it. This small group of technocrats has maintained its central role in economic policymaking despite changes in political regime.
2. *Same political and institutional constraints.* The continuing tensions with neighboring countries have kept defense needs high and absorbed considerable resources. In addition, the power of the agricultural lobby, which has prevented the imposition of an agricultural income tax, was as strong in the 1980s as it was in the 1970s.
3. *Same policies.* The policymakers continued with the same mixture of orthodox policies and direct intervention. The only major change was in the active use of exchange rate policy beginning in 1982. Despite the urging of the World Bank and the IMF, structural reform has proceeded very slowly.

The 1982 SAL was designed to raise savings and investment, strengthen the balance of payments, improve the fiscal situation, raise agricultural production, and reduce protection, among other changes. How successfully were these goals achieved? "Significant" progress was achieved on the exchange rate (the adoption of a managed floating rate in January 1982), pricing policies, and the restoration of medium-term planning. "Little or no" progress was achieved in fiscal reform, tariff reform, and privatization of public enterprises.

Although I do not wish to downplay the positive achievements of the SAL, unfortunately it was unsuccessful in the two areas that seem to me to matter the most—fiscal reform and trade reform. Correcting fiscal imbalances has proved to be an intractable problem for successive governments. From 1972 to the present the fiscal account has been in deficit, and though attempts have been made on several occasions to reduce the deficit, any success has been temporary and limited.

In contrast to the situation in many developing countries, however, the fiscal deficit has not led to spiraling inflation or lowered growth. Rather, the behavior of fiscal deficits is matched by current account deficits (see figure 19C-1). Except for one year (1982) there is almost a one-for-one correspondence between fiscal deficits and current account deficits. These fiscal deficits have been financed in the main by foreign capital, although in more recent years the government has resorted to fairly expensive domestic borrowing.[3]

Since it has been widely recognized that the fiscal situation has put the balance of payments under continual strain and that this position is clearly unsustainable, why has there been no effort to raise sufficient revenue or, failing that, to cut expenditure on a more lasting basis? On the revenue side, it is clear that the tax base of the economy is small. The agricultural sector, which accounts for 25 percent of GDP, has been exempt from direct income taxes. No government has yet been able to impose an agricultural income tax despite the frequent and well-reasoned recommendations of taxation commissions, the IMF, and the World Bank. The problem of revenue is further compounded by the low tax compliance rate—it has been estimated that roughly three-quarters of potential taxpayers do not pay any income tax. The government has relied on ad hoc measures and indirect taxes (particularly trade taxes) to raise revenue.

On the expenditure side, the major share of current expenditure (approximately 35 to 40 percent) has been going to defense. In recent years interest payments on external and domestic debt have risen to about 20 percent of current expenditure. With another 10 percent or so going for subsidies on essential goods, these figures indicate that close to 70 percent of the current budget is virtually untouchable. When the need to continue expenditure for infrastructure and social programs is added in, govern-

Figure 19C-1. Current Account and Fiscal Deficits in Pakistan, 1972–85

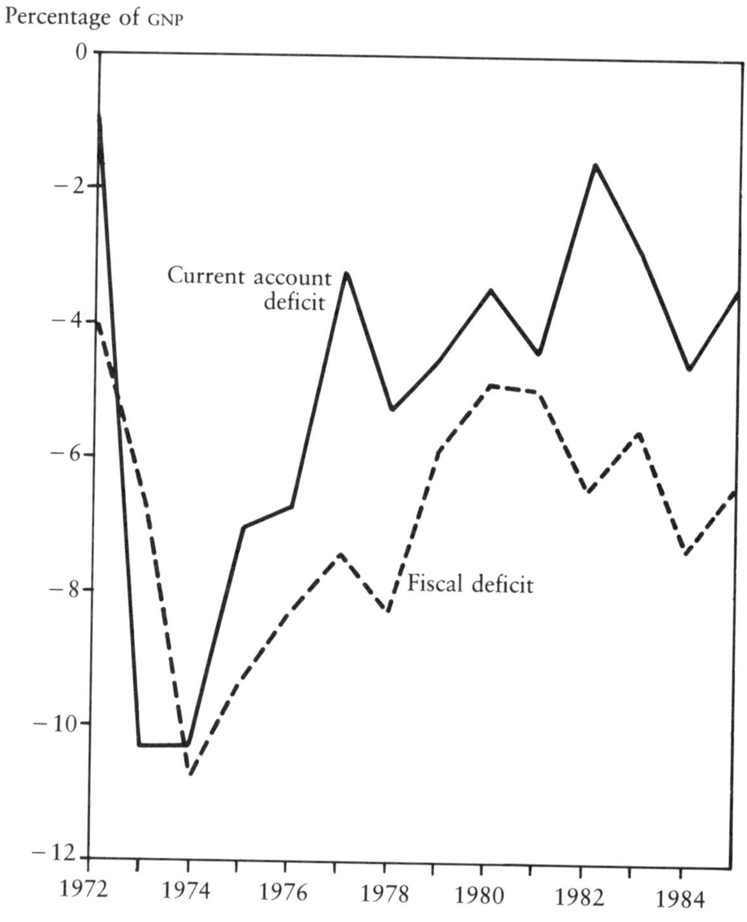

Source: Pakistan Economic Survey, 1985–86 (Islamabad: Government of Pakistan, 1986).

ments find themselves needing to increase expenditure continually while revenue is stagnating.

This budget crunch was a serious problem in the 1970s, and it has, if anything, gotten worse in the 1980s, despite the best intentions of the SAL. The Pakistani government, with the support of the World Bank and the IMF, has now begun to move on revenue generation, but agricultural income taxes are still off the table.

Since fiscal policy has remained expansionary, quantitative controls on trade and payments have been regarded as essential for the balance of payments.[4] Although there have been some attempts at liberalization, the evidence is far too tenuous to argue, as McCleary does, that the economy has become more open and outward-oriented in the 1980s. Broadly speaking, the economy remains regulated, and most foreign trade and capital transactions are still subject to government approval. The changes that have been made have been marginal, and it is doubtful whether those made in the 1980s have been any greater than those of the previous decade. For example, although the government in 1983 moved from the "positive" list of items that could be imported (with all others banned) to a "negative" list of items that were banned (all others could be imported), it is noteworthy that this negative list included 6,000 items. McCleary's reference to the removal of 136 items from the negative list has to be put into that context. The system still has significant barriers to trade and an antiexport bias.

In conclusion, I would not want to say that the SAL and the structural policies pushed by the World Bank did nothing for the economy. Rather, I believe that McCleary has chosen the wrong counterfactual. More informative would have been a comparison of Pakistan's performance under the SAL with the performance of other similarly placed developing countries without SALs. The approach selected here of comparing pre-SAL performance (the 1970s) with performance under the SAL (the 1980s) yields, as I have tried to show here, ambiguous results. The situation in Pakistan was not as bad in the 1970s nor as great in the 1980s as McCleary indicates, but my guess is that relative to the performance of many other developing countries, Pakistan probably did much better than average in the 1980s. If so, one could give some of the credit to the SAL, as well as to the IMF and the government of Pakistan. There would be enough credit to go around.

Notes

1. Between 1971 and 1986 Pakistan received grants and concessional loans of more than US$20 billion. External debt in 1986 was approximately US$12 billion.

2. It is clearly very difficult to disentangle the effects of the SAL from that of the IMF program since many of the policies overlapped.

3. For example, floating and unfunded debt of the government of Pakistan rose from 39.5 billion rupees (17 percent of GDP) to 141.4 billion rupees (26 percent of GDP) between 1975 and 1986.

4. Exchange rate policy, of course, also played a role in the early 1970s after the major devaluation in 1972, and in the 1980s when the rupee peg to the U.S. dollar was eliminated.

20 *Turkey: Structural Transformation and the Threat to Sustainability*

Faezeh Foroutan

DURING THE 1960S AND 1970S Turkey's trade policy was characterized by import substitution with high protection, periodic overvaluation of the exchange rate, and a considerable degree of antiexport bias. Despite this inhospitable setting, however, gross national product (GNP) grew by approximately 6.7 percent a year between 1963 and 1973 (Celâsun and Rodrik 1989). This economic growth was to a great extent stimulated by a rapid increase in worker remittances. The remittances permitted investment to increase almost enough to offset the deterioration occurring in investment efficiency as measured by the incremental capital-output ratio.[1]

As the country's balance of payments position worsened in 1969, the government negotiated a stabilization program with the International Monetary Fund (IMF). The program featured a large devaluation of the Turkish lira and the introduction of several liberalization measures. After the military coup in 1971, the liberalization measures were never implemented, but the lira was devalued considerably in 1970. The devaluation, favorable world economic conditions, and the continuing, buoyant inflow of remittances from Turkish workers abroad helped Turkey expand its exports and GNP from 1971 to 1973. Despite the negative impact of the oil price increase of 1973, the economy grew by more than 7 percent a year between 1973 and 1977, the years corresponding to the ambitious Third Economic Plan. This growth was financed by drawing down reserves and heavy short-term borrowing from abroad. Short-term foreign borrowing, estimated at 7 percent of GDP in 1977, was intensified during 1975–77 through the introduction of a new instrument, the Convertible Turkish Lira Deposit (CTLD).

By 1977, as foreign lenders became aware of the magnitude and unstable structure of Turkey's foreign debt, foreign capital flows ceased. As a result of this foreign debt crisis and the ensuing shortage of foreign exchange, private investment and economic growth collapsed. Because Turkish imports consisted mainly of intermediate and capital goods, the foreign exchange shortage caused a shortage of essential investment goods. Total investment fell from a peak of 25 percent of GNP in 1977 to 18.5 percent of GNP in 1978. The private sector suffered the brunt of the adjustment.

In the absence of foreign borrowing and a lack of infrastructure to permit domestic borrowing, the budget deficit was financed almost exclusively by money creation. As a result, inflation soared to a peak of 141 percent in May 1980 (see table 20-1). Accelerating inflation had a negative impact on both the real exchange rate and the pattern of income distribution. A series of nominal devaluations was undertaken, but the real exchange rate continued to appreciate and Turkey's competitiveness in international markets continued to deteriorate. Income distribution also worsened, with the rural sector and wage earners hit the hardest. Real wages fell by almost the same rate as the rate of the inflation, with a cumulative reduction of 43 percent during 1978–80. The agricultural terms of trade in 1979 were below the level of 1970 (Celâsun and Rodrik 1989).

During the 1977–79 crisis the government made no fundamental changes in its economic philosophy and management. Two standby arrangements with the IMF failed. In the face of this increasing economic deterioration, a new government was formed and its economic reform program was submitted in January 1980. The program represented a radical departure from previous policies and effectively paved the way for support from the IMF and the World Bank and for the resumption of private lending to Turkey.

The 1980 Adjustment Program

Turkey's economic reform program was put together by a group of technocrats headed by the prime minister, Turgut Özal. In the short run the primary goal was to achieve a reasonable degree of price stability, even though this would have to come at the cost of a temporary sacrifice in growth. In the longer run the program aimed at a gradual reduction in the extent of state intervention in production, principally by reforming state economic enterprises; shifting to a more outward-oriented, market-based trade regime; and removing barriers to foreign direct investment.

IMF Programs

In support of the government's 1980 program, a new three-year standby arrangement was reached with the IMF in June 1980 involving 1.25 billion in special drawing rights[2] (approximately US$1.6 billion). Turkey was the first country to have a three-year standby arrangement with the IMF. The key conditions included maintenance of a realistic and flexible exchange rate; improvement of public sector finances, principally via price increases in state-owned enterprises in line with inflation; strict limits on

Table 20-1. *Basic Economic Indicators for Turkey, 1980–88*

Indicator	*1980*	*1981*	*1982*	*1983*	*1984*	*1985*	*1986*	*1987*[a]	*1988*[a]
Macroeconomic balances (percentage of GNP*)*									
Total consumption	84.1	82.0	81.8	83.7	83.3	80.9	77.7	76.1	73.7
Public	12.3	10.7	10.8	10.2	8.8	8.4	8.8	9.1	8.7
Private	71.9	71.3	71.1	73.5	74.5	72.5	68.9	67.0	65.0
Fixed investment	19.5	18.9	18.9	18.8	18.0	20.1	23.6	24.1	24.2
Public	10.9	11.7	11.5	10.6	9.9	11.7	14.0	12.9	11.5
Private	8.5	7.2	7.3	8.2	8.2	8.4	9.6	11.2	12.7
Stock changes	1.9	2.6	1.5	1.1	1.4	0.9	1.4	1.3	0.0
Public	0.5	1.5	0.5	−0.4	0.0	−0.2	0.1	0.4	−0.6
Private	1.4	1.1	1.0	1.5	1.4	1.0	1.3	0.8	0.6
Current account	−5.5	−3.5	−2.2	−3.5	−2.8	−1.9	−2.6	−1.5	2.1
Imports[b]	15.0	16.5	17.9	19.5	23.1	23.5	20.7	20.3	23.6
Exports[b]	7.2	10.9	14.5	15.7	19.5	20.7	18.0	22.3	21.9
GNP (millions of U.S. dollars)	58,327	58,925	53,737	51,237	50,111	53,238	58,082	64,790	n.a.
GNP growth (percent)	−1.1	4.1	4.5	3.3	5.9	5.1	8.1	7.4	3.4
Gross external debt (billions of U.S. dollars)									
Total	16.3	16.9	17.6	18.2	20.8	25.5	32.5	38.3	37.7
Medium to long term	13.8	14.7	15.9	16.0	17.6	20.8	25.6	29.6	30.0
Short term	2.5	2.2	1.8	2.3	3.2	4.8	6.9	8.7	7.7
Debt/GNP	28.0	28.6	32.8	35.6	41.5	47.9	55.9	56.1	53.1
Debt/exports[c]	284.1	198.3	175.0	192.9	180.5	194.5	260.5	227.2	n.a.

Real exchange rate[d]									
Average	100.0	98.4	107.7	107.4	111.3	110.0	131.9	141.8	141.9
End of period	100.0	106.3	110.0	109.4	103.0	114.1	135.4	143.7	n.a.
Nominal exchange rate (Turkish lira to U.S. dollars)									
Average	76.0	111.2	162.6	225.5	366.7	522.0	674.5	857.2	1,422.3
End of period	90.2	133.6	186.8	282.8	444.7	576.9	757.8	1,020.9	1,814.8
Monetary aggregates (percentage of GNP)									
Base money	8.1	8.5	9.7	10.2	9.1	8.7	8.2	7.2[e]	n.a.
M2	14.9	17.4	22.1	23.0	21.7	23.2	23.5	21.4[e]	n.a.
M2X	n.a.	n.a.	n.a.	23.0	22.8	26.0	28.4	28.3[e]	n.a.
Inflation rate									
CPI[f] (year average)	110.9	36.8	23.1	31.4	48.4	44.0	34.6	39.8	75.4
CPI (year end)	89.6	28.3	26.2	37.1	49.7	44.2	30.7	55.1	75.2

n.a. Not available.
a. Estimated.
b. Goods and nonfactor services.
c. Exports of goods, services, and workers' remittances.
d. 1980 export weights.
e. June 1987.
f. Consumer price index.
Source: World Bank data.

Table 20-2. Standby Arrangement between the IMF and Turkey, 1978–85

Period	Millions of special drawing rights		Status
	Committed	Disbursed	
April 1978–April 1980	300	90	Cancelled July 1979
July 1979–July 1980	250	230	Cancelled June 1980
June 1980–June 1983	1,250	1,250	Executed as planned
June 1983–June 1984	225	56	Cancelled April 1984
April 1984–April 1985	225	169	Expired April 1985
Total	2,250	1,795	

Source: Celâsun (1989).

central bank lending to the public sector; and adjustment of interest rates to market levels.

Two more one-year standby arrangements were agreed with the IMF in June 1983 and April 1984 (see table 20-2). The 1983 agreement was canceled early, and the 1984 agreement expired with the funds not yet fully disbursed. Even with the two new standbys, Turkey's net position with the IMF became negative in 1984, which added significantly to the country's debt service burden. Moreover, the IMF's supervisory role ended at the same time as World Bank structural adjustment loans (SALs). Some World Bank audit reports argued that it was premature for the IMF to end its standby arrangements with Turkey in 1985 before stabilization had been achieved. Other people have argued that five years should have been sufficient time for Turkey to reach its stabilization goals; any IMF presence beyond that period would simply have delayed even longer the surfacing of the economic problems that Turkey needed to resolve—and is currently facing.

The OECD Consortium and Debt Restructuring by Commercial Banks

The Organisation for Economic Co-operation and Development (OECD) assisted Turkey in the management of its foreign debt crisis by launching a special rescue operation in 1979 and by arranging for the rescheduling of Turkey's debt.

As part of the four-year rescue operation, the OECD consortium arranged four pledging conferences to increase the volume of bilateral contributions to Turkey above the relatively low levels (US$100 million to US$200 million a year) of the early 1970s. Almost US$4 billion was pledged during the four conferences in the form of program loans, project

Table 20-3. Pledges to Turkey during the OECD Rescue Operation, 1979–82
(millions of U.S. dollars)

Category	*1979*	*1980*	*1981*	*1982*
Program loans	625.1	705.0	649.4	425.0
Project loans	46.2	230.0	124.1	200.0
Export credits	318.0	225.5	190.3	225.0
Total	989.3	1,160.5	973.8	850.0

Source: Wolff (1987).

loans, and export credits (table 20-3). The largest commitments came from the United States and the Federal Republic of Germany. The timing of disbursements and the nature of the loan conditions varied considerably. Conditions ranged from soft terms on long-term program loans to export credits tied to specific purchases at prevailing market rates. After the last pledging conference in 1982, bilateral commitments fell back to their pre-1978 level.

A working group within the OECD consortium arranged for the rescheduling of Turkey's official debt. In all, three rescheduling agreements were signed with Turkey, in 1978, 1979, and 1980. The consolidated debt rescheduled in the three agreements totaled US$5 billion.

Through its pledging conferences and rescheduling operations, the OECD made a significant contribution to Turkey's financing requirements during 1979–82. In all, the rescue operation resulted in a gross capital inflow of at least US$3 billion. If the loan reschedulings are added to this figure, the OECD's contribution exceeded that of all other official agencies. The intervention by the OECD—motivated in part by Turkey's important geopolitical position—makes Turkey's experience atypical among problem debtors. No other country among the highly indebted nations received so much assistance from the international community. This is an important explanatory factor for Turkey's outperforming the other highly indebted nations in economic growth during the 1980s.

The commercial banks also helped Turkey meet its external financing needs by rescheduling accumulated debt and supplying new money. The banks' commitments were conditioned on the conclusion of an agreement with the IMF. Turkey reached agreement with the banks in July 1979, after the OECD rescue operation had begun and a second agreement had been arranged with the IMF.

The rescheduling covered Turkey's short-term liabilities, amounting to US$2.8 billion, mostly in the form of Convertible Turkish Lira Deposits. The agreement provided for the repayment of the debt and the interest arrears in four yearly installments beginning in 1982, and the interest rate was to remain at 1.75 percentage points above the London interbank offer rate. Turkey was not satisfied with this agreement, and in 1982 the banks, under increasing pressure from official lenders, modified the original terms by extending the life of the loan to ten years and the grace period to five years.

After the rescheduling, the commercial banks showed a renewed interest in providing Turkey with fresh funds. In 1983 Turkey received its first new medium-term syndicated loan, and by 1985 commercial banks had provided Turkey with US$1.4 billion in new loans in addition to the US$2.8 billion of rescheduled debt. Although commercial banks clearly made a significant contribution toward easing Turkey's external debt burden, net transfers from commercial banks turned negative in 1981 and remained so until 1986.

The Role of the World Bank

The first adjustment loan to Turkey from the World Bank was in March 1980. The loan agreement was concluded only two months after the Turkish government's announcement of its new economic policy package. By 1988 Turkey had received four more SALS and three sectoral adjustment loans (SECALS) for a total of US$2.5 billion (see table 20-4). These loans supported a comprehensive structural adjustment process that began in January 1980. Although their emphases differed slightly, all the loans addressed basically the same policy objectives—mainly those in the government's 1980 program. The major objectives were:

- Export promotion, through direct incentives and institutional reform, to increase foreign exchange earnings so that Turkey could meet its growing need for imports
- Import liberalization to reduce antiexport bias and the cost of importing the inputs necessary for the production of exports

Table 20-4. World Bank Adjustment Loans to Turkey, 1980–87

Loan	*Year*	*Amount (millions of U.S. dollars)*
SAL I and Supplement	1980	275.0
SAL II	1981	300.0
SAL III	1982	304.5
SAL IV	1983	300.8
SAL V	1984	376.0
SECAL, agriculture	1985	300.0
SECAL, financial sector	1986	300.0
SECAL, energy	1987	325.0
Total		2,481.3

- Rationalization of public investment by reducing it to levels compatible with revenue growth, shifting public investment toward infrastructure while leaving private investment a greater role in manufacturing, and concentrating public investment on fewer projects with higher priority and higher rates of return
- Reform of state enterprises by improving pricing policy, management, and finance so as to enhance their efficiency and productivity and increase their contribution to economic growth
- Development of domestic energy resources by adjusting domestic prices to reflect international prices, by increasing the share of public investment in energy infrastructure, and by rationalizing demand and supply and reducing Turkey's dependence on imported fuel
- Reform of agriculture by modifying the structure of incentives and institutions so as to increase agricultural output and exports
- Financial reform, through fiscal measures affecting financial transactions and through institutional reform, to increase the stability of financial institutions and improve their intermediation capabilities.

Other measures concerned development of a framework for medium-term planning, management of external debt, and reduction in the rate of inflation.

Performance under Structural Adjustment

Turkey has made enormous progress toward many of the policy objectives supported by the SALs and SECALs, with the most spectacular achievements coming in trade. The measures adopted since the beginning of the adjustment program have transformed the country from an inward-oriented, almost closed economy into an outward-looking, open economy. However, other unresolved problems, such as the worsening income distribution and fiscal deficits, could jeopardize the sustainability of the progress made so far if corrective actions are not taken. The following sections examine the extent of Turkey's fulfillment of the policy objectives and conditions of the SALs and SECALs.

Export Promotion

Export promotion was central to the 1980 government program and to all the SALs. It was achieved in three ways: maintenance of a competitive real exchange rate, provision of direct subsidies, and simplification of administrative and bureaucratic procedures (see Milanovic 1986; Foroutan 1987).

The lira was devalued by more than 50 percent in nominal terms in 1980. At the same time, except for a few agricultural inputs, the multiple

Table 20-5. Turkish Export Subsidies, 1980–86
(percentage of total exports)

Subsidy	*1980*	*1981*	*1982*	*1983*	*1984*	*1985*	*1986*
Export tax rebate	0.0	3.6	10.1	11.5	11.1	9.7	7.6
Duty-free imports	5.5	4.4	4.2	5.4	2.9	4.9	6.2
Export credit	16.6	12.5	6.4	6.5	1.1	0.0	0.0
RUSF[a]	0.0	0.0	0.0	0.0	0.0	4.0	2.0
Total	22.1	20.5	20.6	23.4	15.1	18.6	16.0

a. Resource Utilization Support Fund.
Source: Milanovic (1986); Foroutan (1987).

exchange rate system was abolished. After the initial nominal devaluation, the government pursued a policy of slow real devaluation of the Turkish lira that resulted in a cumulative real depreciation of over 33 percent between 1980 and 1986. The government also provided direct incentives to exporters. These measures gave exporters substantial subsidies that to a large extent neutralized the antiexport bias implicit in the import protection system (see table 20-5). A third important support to exporters—although its results are unquantifiable—was the simplification of procedures for obtaining export incentives and the centralization of control over export policy in the State Planning Organization and the Directorate for Exports.

The response of exports to these three measures was spectacular. Merchandise exports rose from US$2.9 billion in 1980 to US$10.3 billion in 1987. Similarly, exports of goods and nonfactor services increased from 7 percent of GDP in 1980 to 21 percent of GDP in 1985.

Optimism about the continuation of such successful export performance must be tempered, however, by four considerations. First, exports started booming during the early 1980s when there was widespread excess productive capacity. This allowed exports to expand without restricting domestic consumption. Today, capacity-utilization rates are much higher (65 to 85 percent, with an average of 72 percent), and further export expansion is possible only through investment in new capacity. As discussed later, industrial investment in the 1980s was rather stagnant, in large part because of very high real rates of interest. Since interest rates are unlikely to fall without a drastic fiscal contraction, the extent of future investment and export expansion remains uncertain.

Second, after 1981 the Iran-Iraq war was important in boosting Turkish exports (see Celâsun and Rodrik 1989). Given the general decline in the purchasing power of the oil-exporting countries and the recent shift of Turkish exports to OECD markets, it seems unlikely that Turkey could increase its exports to these markets at the spectacular rates of growth achieved in the early 1980s.

Third, because export subsidies not only are costly but also violate the rules of the General Agreement on Tariffs and Trade (GATT), it is doubtful whether they can be sustained and consequently whether exports can continue to grow at the same rate as in the early 1980s.[3] Fourth, real wages have been squeezed so hard that it is not clear that the policy of real devaluation can be sustained much longer.

Import Liberalization

The liberalization of imports constituted another focal point of the Turkish government's 1980 policy package and of the SALs. The principal measures were carried out in two steps. First, in mid-1981 the quota list was eliminated. Second, and more far reaching, at the end of 1983 the positive list of imports, which allowed in only the listed commodities, was replaced by a negative list, which allowed the importation of all commodities not explicitly prohibited. By 1988 most other quantitative restrictions in the form of prohibitions and licensing requirements were also abolished.

In addition, a large-scale rationalization of tariffs brought about a reduction in the average rate and the dispersion of rates. The objective of the tariff reform, as agreed with the World Bank, was to lower the average rate of nominal tariff protection to 7 percent by the end of the fifth five-year plan (1989). After 1984, however, import liberalization slowed to some extent because of the growing importance of import levies administered by the extrabudgetary funds. In 1987 levies stood at 6.1 percent of the value of imports, or about 60 percent of the weighted average tariff rate.

Fiscal Stability and Domestic Resource Mobilization

A reduction in the public sector deficit was a principal requirement of the IMF stabilization program and the World Bank's adjustment lending. Little progress was made on this front, however, because of the government's failure to reduce inflation and because of high real interest rates in Turkey.

Inflation can be viewed as a residual tax that allows the government to finance the difference between its total expenditures and all other sources of revenue at its disposal. A similar equilibrating function is played by the real rate of interest. In the absence of perfect capital mobility, because of controls on capital flows or imperfect substitution between domestic and foreign interest-bearing assets, and given the current account target, the interest rate must be high enough to elicit sufficient net savings from the private sector to close the gap between the current account surplus and the public sector deficit. Alternatively, the real rate of interest in Turkey can be viewed as being determined by the real world interest rate and the expected rate of real depreciation of the Turkish lira plus a risk premium. Moreover, on the assumption that the risk premium increases with the stock of government debt, a direct link is again established between the government deficit and the domestic real interest rate.

The public sector deficit, as measured by the public sector borrowing requirement in current prices, improved considerably in 1981 and then remained at about 5 percent of GNP until 1985 (table 20-6). The deficit worsened considerably thereafter as a result of the growing burden of interest payments on domestic and foreign debt and the government's inability to cut expenditures elsewhere. (The high deficit figure in 1984 reflects a shortfall in tax revenue in that year.) Table 20-6 points also to considerable changes in the sources of financing of the deficit. As the government sought greater control over inflation, recourse to central bank financing was curbed and replaced by domestic borrowing. As mentioned, this growing recourse to debt financing substantially worsened the deficit because of high interest payments (these are included in the net transfer figures in table 20-6).

Table 20-6. Public Sector Revenue and Expenditure in Turkey, 1980–87

(percentage of GNP, based on current prices)

Item	*1980*	*1981*	*1982*	*1983*	*1984*	*1985*	*1986*	*1987*[a]
Revenue[b]	19.8	22.2	22.9	22.4	21.8	23.8	28.7	28.0
Current transfers[c]	2.3	2.9	3.2	5.0	5.2	6.1	9.3	11.0
Total disposable income	17.5	19.3	19.7	17.4	16.6	17.7	19.4	16.9
Investment expenditure (including stock changes)	11.5	13.2	12.0	11.5	10.0	11.0	13.6	13.5
Consumption	12.2	10.7	10.8	10.1	9.0	8.5	9.1	9.4
Total expenditure	23.7	23.9	22.8	21.6	19.0	19.5	22.7	22.9
Public sector borrowing requirement (estimate)	9.9	3.7	5.0	5.3	7.9	4.9	6.0	8.2
Net financing								
External borrowing	3.2	2.5	1.0	1.4	2.7	0.5	2.8	4.1
Domestic borrowing	1.1	1.4	1.5	0.9	2.3	2.7	2.9	2.9
Central bank	3.5	2.0	0.3	0.6	0.7	1.3	0.7	1.0
Other	2.2	−2.2	2.2	2.3	2.1	0.4	−0.4	0.2

a. Provisional estimates.

b. Includes factor income from property and the net surplus of social security institutions; excludes wealth tax and capital flows.

c. Includes subsidies and interest payments; excludes capital transfers.

Source: Celâsun (1989).

The increasing burden of interest on the foreign debt reflects mainly the increasing share of nonconcessional loans after 1984. The interest payment on the central government's and the central bank's foreign exchange liabilities increased from approximately 1.6 percent of GNP before 1984 to 3.5 percent in 1987. The interest payment on domestic debt also climbed dramatically. For the central government alone, interest payments rose from less than 1 percent of GNP before 1984 to an estimated 2.5 percent in 1987. The real interest on treasury bills was about 12 percent in 1987. This high real rate of interest is related partly to the generally high real interest rates in Turkey and partly to the way the bills are auctioned. The bills compete with commercial bank loans rather than commercial bank deposits and must therefore offer a comparable interest rate to be attractive to the banks.

Clearly, continued reliance on domestic debt issue is unsustainable at such high rates of interest. These rates are far in excess of the rate of growth of GNP, so the increase in the interest expense of domestic debt exceeds by a wide margin the rate of increase in the debt itself. Thus the government must borrow ever increasing amounts just to finance its interest payments.

What has been the composition of public sector expenditure? How has it affected consumption and investment expenditure in the private sector? These questions are addressed in the following subsection.

Public and Private Investment

In the 1980s the increase in public sector expenditure was due exclusively to investment expenditure. Between 1980 and 1988 government consumption as a share of GNP fell from 12 percent to 9 percent, whereas its investment expenditure increased from 11 percent of GNP in 1980 to 14 percent in 1986 (see table 20-1). Public investment in 1987 accounted for 60 percent of government expenditure, up from 47 percent in 1980. This increase in investment occurred against the advice of the World Bank, which recommended that the overall level of government investment be reduced to match available resources. Although public investment expenditure remained at high levels, the government did shift its composition, in accordance with World Bank guidelines, away from manufacturing and into infrastructure. By 1987 public investment in manufacturing represented only 6.5 percent of total public fixed investment compared with almost 29 percent in 1980.

It has been argued that the shift in public investment in favor of infrastructure may have helped to "crowd in" (as opposed to crowd out) private investment (World Bank 1988b). In a recent study, however, Conway (1989) finds that any crowding-in effect of public investment on private investment relates to private investment in the housing sector;

in other sectors, although public investment may have encouraged private investment initially, this positive impact seems to have reversed itself later with lagged negative effects. Given Conway's additional findings that real currency depreciation, high inflation, and high interest rates have all had a detrimental effect on private investment, it can be concluded that, overall, the developments in the public sector deficit have been a hindrance to private investment in the productive, export-oriented sectors of the economy.

Implementation of Other Objectives

The government's performance in implementing the other major objectives of the SALS, except for the control of inflation, was generally satisfactory, although a number of concerns remain. The failure to lower inflation permanently was strictly related to developments in the public sector deficit. Moreover, reform of the financial sector, by reducing the inflation tax base, contributed to an increase in the average rate of inflation for each level of the deficit.

Reform of the state economic enterprises, particularly price deregulation, considerably improved their operating profits, which became positive in 1984 and accounted for an estimated 1.5 percent of GNP in 1985. Because of heavy investment by the enterprises, however, their overall surplus remained negative even though it improved from −11 percent of GNP in 1980 to −4.5 percent in 1985. Some concern has been expressed that the improvement in the profitability of the state economic enterprises may owe more to their freedom to increase prices than to greater efficiency and reduced costs.

Sectoral Performance

After the completion of the fifth SAL, Turkey received a series of SECALS for agriculture, energy, and finance, the sectors that had earlier received particular attention in the five SALS.

AGRICULTURE. During the 1970s the agricultural sector, much like the industrial sector, grew by following inward-looking policies that stressed food self-sufficiency through subsidized input prices. As part of the structural adjustment program begun in 1980 and supported by the various SALS and an agricultural SECAL, many of these incentive policies were dismantled and more market-oriented policies were introduced. Input subsidies and production price supports were reduced, preferential credit was curtailed, and exports were encouraged through exchange rate devaluation and the relaxation of export-licensing restrictions. Agriculture as a share of public investment increased from 7 percent in 1980 to 10 percent in 1985. As a result of improved criteria for project selection, completion rates for agricultural projects also rose considerably. Commodity support prices were replaced by a system of protective floor prices. In addition, the importation and distribution of fertilizers and seeds were liberalized.

The results of these reforms were generally positive once the initial shock of the subsidy reduction was overcome. The rate of growth of agricultural GDP had fallen to less than 1.5 percent a year during the late 1970s and to 0.9 percent a year in 1980 and 1981. Thereafter, sectoral growth recovered to an average 4 percent a year from 1983 through 1987. Exports of unprocessed agricultural products increased in volume by over 6 percent a year after 1980, but they decreased in value because of adverse world price movements. Exports of processed agro-based products quadrupled after 1980 and now represent about one-third of the combined total for agricultural and agroindustrial exports (about 10 percent in 1980).

ENERGY. The government's energy policy during the 1970s was dominated by supply considerations, with pricing policy, demand management, and energy conservation relegated to a low priority. Until the 1973 oil crisis Turkey had relied almost exclusively on oil imports for its energy needs and had neglected its domestic sources of supply. The situation changed in the second half of the 1970s as the government embarked on a program to curtail energy imports through the substitution of domestic supplies. Considerable resources were invested in the development of indigenous sources of energy, especially lignite and hydropower. By 1984 the share of energy had risen to 40 percent of total government investment and 3 percent of GNP (from 1.5 percent in the early 1970s).

Despite these efforts, the program failed to meet its ambitious targets, mainly because inefficient management of the investment program spread both human and financial resources too thinly across too many projects. The result was frequent and protracted breakdowns in service that were extremely detrimental to industrial users of energy. By the early 1980s problems in the energy sector had reached crisis proportions. They were deep rooted and almost all were linked to inefficiencies in planning, implementation, finance, and operation in the government agencies concerned with energy.

To address these problems the government adopted a new development plan in 1984. It was supported by the World Bank which, after extensive discussions with energy agencies, prepared an energy sector strategy paper. The paper supplemented the government plan by recommending actions to remedy the most pressing problems. The collaboration between the World Bank and the government eventually resulted in the Energy Sector Adjustment Loan of 1987. The government program supported by the loan centered on three areas: institutional reform, including greater private sector participation in the development and supply of energy and greater autonomy for public agencies; economic investment, including measures to minimize the cost of present and future public investment; and improved efficiency, including measures to maximize the operating efficiency of all energy agencies and pricing policies to encourage energy conservation.

FINANCE. The most problematic of the three sectors under examination was the financial sector. The government reform program introduced in January 1980 contained few measures affecting the financial sector other than those for deregulating commercial bank interest rates. The bankruptcy of a major nonbank financial institution in late June 1982 refocused attention on the structural ailments of the financial system. The World Bank supported the new government initiatives by launching a major financial sector study.

The study was the basis for measures adopted under SALS IV and V and helped the government initiate several important financial reforms. The reforms were directed toward reducing the undercapitalization of banks, loosening the interlocking relationships between banks and corporations, increasing the supervisory role of the central bank, and introducing a deposit insurance scheme. The government also took steps to lower the cost of bank intermediation by reducing various taxes on intermediation and established the Capital Market Board and an auctioning system for treasury bills. Financial reform was further advanced by measures introduced during the first Financial Sector Adjustment Loan in 1986. In 1988 a second financial SECAL followed the path laid by the first. According to recent reviews within the World Bank, however, the measures taken have been insufficient to resolve the fundamental instability of the financial sector in Turkey.

The instability of the banking sector and the financial distress of the banks were reviewed extensively in the initiating memorandum for the second financial SECAL (February 1988). The instability was attributed to the large proportion of nonperforming loans in the portfolios of commercial banks and the lack of an appropriate regulatory framework to prevent banks from rolling these loans over indefinitely by capitalizing the interest payments of their problem borrowers. The full extent of the problem is unknown, but current estimates put the stock of bad loans as high as one-third of the banking system's total credits. This means that for some banks, potential losses would exceed the book value of their capital and reserves.

In part, the large number of nonperforming loans was an outcome of the structural reforms undertaken by the government beginning in 1980. These reforms changed the profitability of firms operating under the previous inward-looking policy environment. The problem was aggravated by the extremely high real rates of interest, which in turn were related to the large budget deficits and the policy of continuing real devaluation of the Turkish lira.

In summary, the financial sector requires urgent intervention on several fronts. It needs a stronger regulatory framework, a more effective system of external bank audits, and a restructuring of insolvent banks. In the long run, actions to reduce the very high real rates of interest are vital, since high interest rates have been one of the principal contributing factors to the problem of nonperforming debt.

Income Distribution

Although income distribution was not an explicit objective of the government's 1980 policy reform package, the impact of the reforms on the distribution of income in Turkey was profound. Real wages fell substantially, and the rural sector was adversely affected by the considerable decline in the agricultural terms of trade. Despite the importance of income redistribution to the sustainability of the adjustment policies, the issue was never explicitly addressed in Turkey's SAL program.

Reliable data on employment and income distribution in Turkey are scarce. A World Bank study (1988a) focusing on formal workers in the nonagricultural sector (roughly 23 percent of the domestic civilian labor force) estimated that real wages declined by more than 50 percent between 1977 and 1987. By 1985 real wages in manufacturing had dropped to their 1965 level. Real wages and salaries as a share of nonagricultural factor income were estimated to have fallen from 52 percent in 1977 to 22 percent in 1986.

The decline in real wages changed the factor distribution of income in favor of capital. In the manufacturing industry, for example, it was estimated that the share of interest, rents, and profits increased to 70 percent of manufacturing GDP from approximately 35 percent in the 1960s and 1970s (World Bank 1988a, table 3.10). Although several changes in the fiscal system (changes in income tax brackets and the tax rebate system) since 1984 mitigated to some extent the decline in pretax labor income, wages appear to have absorbed the brunt of the adjustment burden. Moreover, despite the large decline in labor costs, the employment response was not dramatic. The growth in output seems to have been based more on greater utilization of existing capacity and labor than on an expansion of capacity or labor.

Agricultural labor experienced a similar deteriorating trend in income. According to recent estimates (Boratav 1989), the agricultural terms of trade (as measured by the implicit GDP deflator) deteriorated by 53 percent during 1976–86. Such a dramatic relative price change is unique in the postwar history of Turkey.

The dramatic squeeze on real wages together with the partial restoration of civil liberties, including the right to strike, cast doubt on the economic and political feasibility of curbing public sector expenditure through a further reduction in the wage bill or a reduction in certain popular programs, such as the low-cost housing subsidy. Similarly, since real wages have already been squeezed severely, it is hard to believe that the slow but systematic nominal depreciations of the currency will continue to be as easily translated into real devaluations through a further squeezing of labor income.

The redistributional aspects of the adjustment process in Turkey have received insufficient attention in the SAL program. The World Bank's view that the deterioration in labor income in Turkey is a necessary, albeit undesirable, side effect of the adjustment process fails to consider its potentially adverse effect on sustainability.

Conditionality

For each SAL, the government announced the policies it intended to pursue in a Statement of Development Policies. The loan was then granted in support of these enunciated policies, and the time framework was specified. The commitments presented in the Statement of Development Policies can be treated as the true loan conditions even if they were not specifically mentioned as conditions in the loan agreements or as conditions for tranche release. The SALs and SECALs made infrequent and rather imprecise mention of conditions for loan effectiveness or for tranche release. SALs III to V, for example, used such phrases as "satisfactory progress in carrying out" or "adequate progress achieved in."

SAL I was released in three tranches (the other SALs had only two) and had the greatest number of precise conditions for tranche release, that is, conditions requiring implementation of a specific action within a specific time frame. These conditions called for the initiation or completion by specified dates of a review of the feasibility of an export credit and risk facility, a study on the rationalization of the industrial protection system, a study on external debt management, and a review of measures to increase household savings. The results of these studies were expected to guide future action in those areas.

SAL V was the only other SAL that included any precise tranche-release conditions, namely, the completion of the long-awaited fifth five-year plan. Of the SECALs, only the first Financial Sector Adjustment Loan contained any specific conditions; one was that an external audit be required for commercial banks and corporations issuing securities by the beginning of fiscal 1987.

Table 20-7 summarizes the main conditions in each SAL and the extent to which the conditions were fulfilled by the end of each SAL period. Several observations can be made. First, each SAL seems to have so many conditions that it is difficult to pinpoint the main ones. Second, SAL conditions seem to focus mainly on trade liberalization rather than on fundamental macroeconomic balance. The World Bank program apparently focused more closely on measures to increase the efficiency of the economy and left the surveillance of the macroeconomic picture to the IMF stabilization program. Third, the delay in implementing some of the SAL conditions, such as the introduction of a value added tax, was due to the unrealistic time frame specified. This problem was apparently fully understood by the World Bank, since none of the tranche releases was withheld.

In summary, the true SAL conditions were the government commitments specified in its Statement of Development Policy. In this sense, one may speak of a front loading of conditions. With the exception of SAL I, conditions for loan effectiveness or for tranche release were few and flexible; it was left to the negotiators to determine whether satisfactory progress had been made. This flexibility was useful in several respects: it kept the dialogue open with the Turkish authorities; it was politically palatable because it avoided the appearance of being imposed by the World Bank; and it helped the Bank correct its overoptimistic evaluation of the feasibility of carrying out certain reforms within the agreed-on time frame.

World Bank–IMF Relations

Since the first SAL, the World Bank and the IMF have collaborated closely. They have not only exchanged information and participated in joint missions, but also reached agreement on the spheres of involvement. From the beginning, the IMF had primary responsibility for providing advice on macroeconomic issues such as exchange rate, monetary, and fiscal policies. Other policy reforms were of interest to both institutions.

With the expiration of the last IMF standby arrangement with Turkey in 1985, the supervisory role of the IMF ended. Recent argument suggests that the IMF acted prematurely in ending its standby arrangements with Turkey just as the last SAL was also expiring. The World Bank seems to have had difficulty enforcing a sustainable macroeconomic framework through the SECALs alone. The deterioration of the macroeconomic environment in Turkey since 1987 appears to lend indirect support to this argument. It is also possible, however, to argue that if the IMF stabilization program and the World Bank SAL program did not succeed in bringing about a fundamental and lasting change in the macroeconomic picture after five years, then continuation of the programs would not have made much difference. It would only have delayed the surfacing of the economic

Table 20-7. Turkey's Progress in Implementing Structural Adjustment Loan Conditions by the End of Each Loan Period

Significant progress	*Satisfactory progress*	*Little or no progress*
	SAL I *and Supplement (1980, US$245 million)*	
Exchange rate management Export promotion: priority credit to exporters; improvement of institutional arrangements for exporters; financial incentives to exporters; access to duty-free imports Partial liberalization of interest rates	Reduction in budget deficit Autonomy of state enterprises in setting prices Public investment shifted toward infrastructure	Establishment of export credit insurance scheme Reduction in public investment Reduction in subsidized-interest loans to state enterprises External debt management
	SAL II *(1981, US$30 million)*	
Exchange rate management Import liberalization: abolition of quotas; reduction of import guarantee deposits; partial relaxation of quantitative restrictions Further export promotion Reform of the direct tax system Increase in prices of energy to world market levels	Steps toward creation of a stock market Further state enterprise reform: constraints on employment; reduced access to central bank Further rationalization of public investment Incentives for agricultural exports Rationalization of input subsidies for agriculture	Establishment of export credit Introduction of a value added tax Reform of state enterprise management Preparation of a medium-term economic framework External debt management
	SAL III *(1982, US$204.5 million)*	
Continued exchange rate management Continued import liberalization Reduction in bank intermediation tax to reduce cost of loans Continued increase in energy prices to reflect market conditions	Continued rationalization of public investment Continued reform of state enterprises: limit on budgetary transfers; limit on hiring of new personnel Continued reform of the agricultural sector: reorganization of the Ministry of Agriculture; extension of some export incentives to agriculture; phasing out of subsidy on certain inputs	Development of a medium-term economic framework Increased efficiency of state enterprises External debt management

SAL IV (1983, US$300.8 million)		
Reform of the tariff system Further simplification of import procedures Continued export promotion	Continued rationalization of public investment Continued improvement in the financial performance of state enterprises Reduction in public deficit to 0.6 percent of GNP Replacement of agricultural producer price subsidy with floor prices Continued rationalization of energy pricing and investment	Development of medium-term economic framework Control of inflation Reduction in real interest rates on nonpreferential loans Law for regulating the auditing and accounting profession External debt management
SAL V (1984, US$300 million)		
Substantial import liberalization: reduction in average tariffs to 7 percent by the end of five-year plan; elimination of quantitative restrictions Elimination of financial transactions tax Continued autonomy of state enterprises in setting prices Continued policy of flexible exchange rate	Preparation of medium-term economic framework (five-year plan) Review of public investment program Issue of treasury bonds for the public Opening of the stock exchange market Continued reform of the agricultural sector Strengthening of energy conservation programs Increased role of market in setting interest rates	Export credit insurance Diversification of channels for marketing treasury bills Managerial reform of state enterprise Inflation control Balanced budget Privatization of state enterprises

Source: World Bank President's Reports.

problems currently facing Turkey. After all, no country can be supervised forever by multinational agencies.

Conclusions and Lessons

The case of Turkey is often cited as proof that there is life after debt. Turkey has shown that it is indeed possible to reverse the orientation of an economy from an inward-looking, strictly controlled one to an outward-looking, more market-oriented one in a relatively short time when the domestic and international environments are favorable and policymakers are committed to reform and adopt effective policy tools. A closer look at Turkey's experience, however, shows that unless fundamental macroeconomic aggregates are also stabilized on a sustainable path, economic growth may be short-lived and progress may be reversed. In fact, despite the remarkable success achieved during the 1980s, especially in the areas of foreign trade and economic growth, Turkey today is facing some of the same pressing problems that afflicted its economy over ten years ago during the height of its debt crisis. Turkey's public sector deficit is high and growing, inflation is high and accelerating, and the foreign and domestic debt service burden is mounting while investment in key sectors is stagnating.

That these conditions exist does not minimize the remarkable success Turkey has achieved. But current conditions must be examined in order to understand what has gone wrong and what can be done to preserve these achievements. A clear understanding of the policy successes and failures in Turkey is important not only for the case of Turkey, but also for an overall evaluation of the effectiveness of the World Bank's SAL program.

A look at the areas in which success has clearly been achieved, namely high export and economic growth, reveals several lessons and observations. Of primary importance was the ability and willingness of the political authorities to carry out the necessary reforms. It must be stressed that it was the Turkish government rather than any outside economic agent that started the adjustment program in 1980. The international community, including the World Bank and the IMF, simply lent their seal of approval to the program through their financial assistance. The other side of the coin, however, is that the financial assistance of these institutions and the rest of the international community was essential to Turkey's success. The debt reschedulings of the late 1970s and the early 1980s with the OECD consortium and the private commercial banks, as well as the new funds provided by the World Bank, the IMF, and the private lenders in the 1980s, enabled Turkey to spread over time the burden of the necessary adjustment measures. Because sufficient financial resources were available, Turkey was able to avoid the more painful alternative of suppressing economic growth during adjustment, at least until now.

These same two factors—political commitment and external resources—also explain the difficulty Turkey is currently facing in sustaining its growth momentum. Whereas the military regime in 1980–83 was able to implement its adjustment program, including the massive redistribution of income, with relative ease, the newly restored democratic government has had more difficulty traveling along the same path. Similarly, the end of concessional loans in 1984 and the continuation of the policy of real devaluation have meant that the debt burden is growing again and with it the public sector deficit, whose financing has accelerated the inflationary pressures.

An examination of the areas in which the adjustment program has not been so successful also offers valuable lessons. For example, the less successful effort to reform the financial sector raises the issue of the feasibility of sectoral reform in the presence of severe macroeconomic imbalances. It also calls into question some of the World Bank's policy prescriptions related to liberalization of the financial sector or the trade sector before stabilization was clearly achieved. The Turkish experience thus shows that financial deregulation and liberalization of the capital account are inherently destabilizing in an economy that is plagued by inflation, fiscal crisis, and continuous real depreciation (Aricanli and Rodrik 1989).

In sum, despite Turkey's substantial adherence to World Bank policy advice in the 1980s and the remarkable structural transformation of the Turkish economy, the sustainability of progress achieved so far is uncertain. Sustainability is principally threatened by the large and growing public sector budget deficit and its negative impact on inflation, interest rates, private investment, and the stability of financial institutions. Sustainability is also threatened by the sharp deterioration in the purchasing power of wage and salary earners and the rural classes over the past decade. In retrospect, it seems both that the government did not pay sufficient attention to the importance of macroeconomic stability as a prerequisite for sustainable growth and that the SAL program failed to incorporate a mechanism that would guarantee the maintenance of macroeconomic stability. In particular, the SAL program focused more on liberalization than on stabilization and remained largely silent on income redistribution. Although liberalization has borne substantial fruit, decisive additional corrective action is now required on the fiscal front to preserve these hard-won benefits.

Notes

Many thanks to Bela Balassa, Jeffrey Balkind, Jaime de Melo, Francis Geary, Robert Hunt, William McCleary, and Dani Rodrik for their very useful comments on early drafts.

1. The ratio had risen from 1.6 in 1963–67 to 2.4 in 1968–72 (Balassa 1981).

2. IMF funds are denominated in special drawing rights (SDRs), based on a basket of currencies.

3. Considering only the export tax rebate and cash grants, two practices that are most likely to be in violation of the GATT rules, the cost of export promotion can be roughly estimated at US$516 million in 1986, or roughly 5 percent of the central government's revenues. This figure, obtained by multiplying the total value of industrial exports by the average subsidy rate of the two measures,

represents an upper limit because exports of certain manufactures to western markets are not eligible for the cash subsidy.

References

Aricanli, Torsun, and Dani Rodrik, eds. 1989. *The Political Economy of Turkey: Debt, Adjustment, and Sustainability*. London: Macmillan.

Balassa, Bela. 1981. "Policies for Stable Economic Growth in Turkey." In *The Newly Industrializing Countries in the World Economy*. Elmsford, N.Y.: Pergamon Press.

Boratav, K. 1989. "Inter-Class and Intra-Class Relations of Distribution under Structural Adjustment: Turkey During the 1980s." In Aricanli and Rodrik (1989).

Celâsun, M. 1989. "Fiscal Aspects of Adjustment in the 1980s." In Aricanli and Rodrik (1989).

Celâsun, M., and Dani Rodrik. 1989. "Debt, Adjustment, and Growth: Turkey." In Jeffrey Sachs, ed., *Developing Country Debt and Economic Performance: Country Studies*. Chicago, Ill.: University of Chicago Press.

Conway, P. 1989. "A Record on Private Investment in Turkey." In Aricanli and Rodrik (1989).

Foroutan, Faezeh. 1987. "Trade Policy in Turkey in 1986 and 1987: An Evaluation." Trade Policy Division, World Bank, Washington, D.C.

Milanovic, Branko. 1986. *Export Incentives and Turkish Manufactured Exports, 1980–1984*. World Bank Staff Working Paper 768. Washington, D.C.

Wolff, P. 1987. *Stabilization Policy and Structural Adjustment in Turkey, 1980–1985*. Berlin: German Development Institute.

World Bank. 1988a. "Turkey Country Economic Memorandum: Towards Sustainable Growth." Report 7378-TU. Washington, D.C.

———. 1988b. "Turkey: External Debt, Fiscal Policy and Sustainable Growth." Washington, D.C.

Comments

Dani Rodrik

As these words were written (April 1989), Turkey appeared to be headed toward political instability and economic chaos. The government of Turgut Özal, the architect of the economic reform program pursued since

January 1980, had just been badly beaten in local elections. The defeat was due at least in part to Özal's inability to bring down inflation despite applying a rather strong squeeze to the economy during the second half of 1988.

Is Turkey at the end of another one of its infamous ten-year cycles of boom followed by military bust? That would be too hasty a conclusion. After all, Turkey's 1988 current account was in surplus by US$1.5 billion, and exports stood at an all-time high. There was no immediate foreign exchange crisis, although government officials nervously watched foreign creditors and the black-market premium for the dollar.

But after nine years of adjustment, why does the Turkish recovery look so fragile? The answer requires dismantling some of the myths that surround post-1980 Turkish economic policies. Unlike Chile, another frequently cited "success" case, Turkey has followed a path that was quite unorthodox in certain key respects. The chapter by Faezeh Foroutan aptly discusses many of these unconventional approaches: the emphasis on public investment early on, despite World Bank advice to the contrary; the generous use of export subsidies; the substitution of off-budget import levies for the phased-out quantitative restrictions; and, most critically, the lack of any sustained fiscal retrenchment. None of these policies sits well with the idea that Turkey's success derives from liberal, market-oriented policies. Nor does the exchange rate policy look like the product of orthodox prescriptions after nine years of pronounced downward crawl in the real exchange rate—with the expected effect on real wages. In the only area in which Özal has acted as a genuine liberalizer, namely in financial markets, the results have been nothing short of disastrous.[1]

So the first step in understanding the Turkish outcome is to shed preconceived notions about what an outward orientation has meant in terms of day-to-day policy. The Turkish state remains by and large as *dirigiste* as ever. The terms "liberal" and "market-oriented" are quite misleading when used in connection with the Turkish reforms of the 1980s. In view of experience elsewhere, this should come as no surprise: the Republic of Korea's example amply demonstrates the affinity between outward orientation and the visible hand of government. But in contrast to the case in Korea, greater export orientation has not reduced the Turkish economy's proclivity to rent-seeking; it may have actually increased it, thanks to the highly arbitrary and discretionary export subsidy and import levy systems. Özal's great insight was his recognition very early on that the only way Turkey would regain its creditworthiness was by increasing its export base. And that is, above all, what he accomplished.

The second myth to dispel has to do with fiscal adjustment. According to accepted wisdom, fiscal retrenchment is essential to successful adjustment. How does this square with Turkey's conspicuously undistinguished fiscal performance to date? Looking at the borrowing requirements of the public sector, one is struck by the fact that 1981 is the only year with a moderately respectable deficit—and the revenue figures for that year are greatly assisted by the one-time realignment in public enterprise prices and the positive effects on tax collection of the reduction in inflation. The fact is that Turkey has so far not paid the fiscal price of adjustment. In its first few years the Turkish program was underwritten by substantial inflows from multilateral and official sources (this is well described by Foroutan). Since 1983 the export boom has allowed Turkey to turn to private sources of finance: current account deficits have been financed increasingly from private sources[2] and by Turkish workers in Germany. Such inflows did more than provide Turkey with the opportunity "to spread over time the burden of the necessary adjustment measures," as Foroutan puts it; they virtually eliminated the need for fiscal adjustment.

In this light, the success with inflation control and economic growth—at least until very recently—does not look so surprising. The stagflation of the late 1970s was the direct consequence of the shortage of foreign exchange in the aftermath of the mid-1977 debt crisis: the lack of imported inputs had squeezed domestic activity, while the curtailment of foreign borrowing had necessitated recourse to inflationary finance.[3] When the OECD consortium lifted the foreign exchange constraint in 1979—for reasons related to Turkey's strategic location in the Middle East and on the eastern flank of NATO—inflation could be lowered and growth could be restored. Özal's exchange rate policy and generous export subsidies, together with the Iran-Iraq war, ensured that the ensuing spurt in output would be export oriented. This in turn prepared the ground for Turkey's reentry into private capital markets just as official flows were beginning to be phased out.

The present fragility of the Turkish economy can therefore be viewed as the consequence of the long delay in fiscal adjustment. External debt service now exerts a suffocating pressure on fiscal balances; foreign debt stands at 60 percent of GDP, *twice* its level at the start of the adjustment in early 1980. And now there is internal debt to contend with as well. Moreover, the prospects for a serious fiscal effort in the near future are not encouraging. The Özal government is at present weaker politically than it has ever been, while the cumulative deterioration in income distribution leaves it little room to maneuver.

Could the World Bank's lending policies have improved things? Turkey is a critical test case for the Bank's adjustment lending. Not only has Turkey received the largest number of structural adjustment loans of any country to date, but it is also the one important case for which the World Bank can claim some success. As Foroutan's discussion implies, however, the World Bank's main contribution to Turkey lay in the commitment of financial resources rather than in the area of conditionality and policy advice. The conditionality element in the adjustment loans was exceptionally weak, and Turkey was left (in the words of Lance Taylor) on a "long leash." The outline and sequencing of Turkish policies were home-grown, which partly accounts for the heterodox elements in the program. Credit must be given here to Özal's reluctance to undertake a deep cut in public investment early on and to his delay of substantial import policy liberalization until 1984, both of which must have gone against the instincts of World Bank staff. When Özal yielded to foreign pressure, as with his attempted financial liberalization of 1980, the consequences were occasionally disastrous.

The World Bank saw itself primarily as a promoter of economic liberalization, or of what the loan documents called "a development path placing more reliance on market forces." The Turkish economic crisis of the 1970s was attributed to an inward-oriented strategy rather than to a simple mismanagement of macroeconomic policy. But, although the two frequently go hand in hand, it was wrong to think that liberalization on its own could contribute much to the process of macroeconomic stabilization. As a consequence of the emphasis on liberalization, the purely macroeconomic aspects of the program received too little attention and analysis—perhaps, as Foroutan suggests, because the accepted division of labor made them the responsibility of the International Monetary Fund. Whatever the reason, the World bank paid insufficient attention to the fiscal consequences of trade liberalization. (This was later pointed out in a performance audit report.) The World Bank's scheme had the balance between stabilization and liberalization skewed too much toward the latter. This misplaced emphasis on liberalization created other blind spots as well, a key example being the current privatization drive: it is hard to see what the sale of state equity at bargain prices accomplishes other than a worsening of the government's intertemporal budget constraint. It is fortunate that the Turkish government, for the most part, paid little attention to this advice.

Perhaps the most alarming aspect of the Turkish experience is that private investment in tradables has still not revived after nine years of "structural adjustment." One need go no further than the highly unstable macroeconomic and policy environment to understand why. The most important lesson to be learned from the Turkish case is this: one of the chief goals of structural adjustment programs must be to achieve overall stability in the economic environment.[4] Accomplishing that requires putting first things first, in particular, putting macroeconomic stabilization ahead of economic liberalization. Turkish policymakers have wasted too much of their credibility on unsustainable liberalization attempts and in the process have engendered too much instability. The price is now being paid in the form of a dormant private sector.

Notes

1. For an excellent account of efforts to reform the financial market in Turkey, see the chapters by Yilmaz Akyüz and Izak Atiyas in Aricanli and Rodrik (1989).
2. In 1988 Turkey raised US$3.4 billion from private capital markets abroad: US$2.6 billion in bank credits and US$0.8 billion in bond issues (as reported in *Cumhuriyet*, February 7, 1989, p. 10).
3. For an account of this period, see Celâsun and Rodrik (1989).
4. For an extended argument along these lines, see Rodrik (1989).

References

Aricanli, Torsun, and Dani Rodrik, eds. 1989. *The Political Economy of Turkey: Debt, Adjustment, and Sustainability*. London: Macmillan.

Celâsun, M., and Dani Rodrik. 1989. "Debt, Adjustment and Growth: Turkey." In Jeffrey Sachs, ed., *Developing Country Debt and Economic Performance: Country Studies*. Chicago, Ill.: University of Chicago Press.

Rodrik, Dani. 1989. "Liberalization, Sustainability, and the Design of Structural Adjustment Programs." John F. Kennedy School of Government Discussion Paper 177D. Harvard University, Cambridge, Mass.

Comments on Pakistan and Turkey

Hans-Eberhard Köpp

I WOULD LIKE to comment on three themes that have emerged in the preceding chapters: the political economy of adjustment, the time horizon of adjustment, and the role of the World Bank in adjustment.

First, as Shahid Husain, in his concluding remarks on Latin America, has reminded us, the political component is crucial to the adjustment equation. In this respect, the experiences of both Pakistan and Turkey in the 1980s have been extremely instructive, and the political and economic lessons they teach have an important bearing on the consideration of adjustment processes. Along with sociopolitical and economic changes, there has nevertheless been growth throughout—real growth, one hopes, and not just growth conjured up by statisticians.

Second, adjustment turns out to be a drawn-out process that takes longer than was first expected. The presentations here have also confirmed the difficulty of pinning down just when the adjustment process starts and the perhaps even greater difficulty of knowing when it ends. Both Pakistan and Turkey, with all the problems that remain or have reemerged, have shown that adjustment is a gradual process and an almost permanent task. Countries make some progress, they move from here to there, and then they start again. Given the realities of the political environment, the gradual approach is necessary, at least to some extent.

Third, there remains much ambiguity regarding the role of the World Bank, and more generally the external financing agencies, in producing positive results. Despite real difficulties, in both Pakistan and Turkey tremendous progress has been made. Whether that has been due to the World Bank or the International Monetary Fund (IMF) is not really the important issue. Sometimes it is meant as a compliment to say that the government "owns" a program and sometimes it is meant as a criticism—suggesting that the IMF and the World Bank did not play a role. We would all prefer that the government play the guiding role and own the program. If, under those conditions, the World Bank and the IMF appear simply to follow along, in the interest of the countries involved, I would consider that a positive outcome.

Pakistan and Turkey are also good examples of the different ways the World Bank has been involved in adjustment. In Turkey the World Bank provided five structural adjustment loans as well as several sectoral adjustment loans. In Pakistan it undertook just one structural adjustment loan and then entered the sectoral adjustment phase. Since Pakistan's program was built up more from a sectoral base, it is not accidental that the country is again receiving IMF assistance. The long and continuing process of adjustment there led to the need to pull things together under a new IMF program. The question has been raised many times with regard to Turkey whether the World Bank should have stopped with the five structural adjustment loans. Five was indeed an arbitrary number. It needs to be kept in mind that the adjustment process is drawn out, and the effort needs to be continued.

21 *Chile: Economic Crisis and Recovery*

Cristian Moran

DURING THE MID-1970s Chile introduced a series of reforms that radically changed its economic structure and orientation. Price and interest rate controls were eliminated, the economy was opened to international transactions, and the import-substitution policies that had prevailed during the previous three decades were reversed. Free-market-oriented policies were introduced, and both the importance and the size of the public sector were greatly diminished. Simultaneously, the country pursued a set of stabilization policies designed to control inflation (which was running at 1,000 percent in annual terms by the end of 1973) and to correct the external imbalance, which had widened considerably after the first oil shock. Despite certain key improvements (such as fiscal and trade reforms and elimination of price controls), the changes in the economic structure that were introduced during 1975–80 created a highly vulnerable economy.[1]

The Crisis

The fragility of the economy became increasingly evident as the negative external shocks of the early 1980s unfolded and eventually set off an enormous crisis. Decisions in four policy areas in particular helped build a rigid economic structure that was unable to respond to changes in the external environment. These policies and the financial crisis that followed are described in this section.

Domestic Economic Policies

The main policies that set the stage for Chile's economic problems were: (1) the simultaneous adoption of a fixed exchange rate and a wage indexation formula linking nominal wages to past changes in inflation, (2) a privatization process that facilitated the emergence of highly leveraged financial conglomerates, (3) financial liberalization with excessively permissive banking legislation, and (4) the government's delayed response to the events preceding the crisis.

EXCHANGE RATE AND WAGE POLICIES. Despite the adoption of conservative fiscal and monetary policies during 1975–78, inflation proved more stubborn than envisioned. After dropping from about 500 percent in 1973 to 35 percent in 1978, inflation remained at a high level with no sign of abating in the near future. Because the policy of "preannounced exchange rate changes" initiated in 1976 had failed to control inflation, the government decided in mid-1979 to fix the exchange rate in an effort to set a ceiling rate of inflation and to reverse inflationary expectations. In that same year, however, a new labor law was also enacted, which introduced a floor to wage changes by forcing wage adjustments to cover at least the past changes in inflation.

The wage and exchange rate policies introduced excessive rigidity to the economy, however. Lags in the adjustment of domestic inflation to international levels, and a significant increase in capital inflows—prompted by the financial liberalization—resulted in a drastic appreciation of the peso during 1979–81 (table 21-1). At the same time, declining terms of trade and increases in international interest rates during 1980–82 necessitated a real depreciation of the peso in order to limit the increase in the current account deficit. Given Chile's fixed exchange rate policy and the relatively low level of international inflation, achieving a real depreciation of the peso required (under plausible assumptions) a fall in nominal wages.[2] Nominal wages, however, could not fall because of the wage indexation formula. In 1982 a severe balance of payments crisis, following a current account deficit of 14.5 percent of GDP in 1981, forced the government to abandon both the fixed exchange rate and the wage indexation formula.

THE PRIVATIZATION PROCESS. The privatization program of the mid-1970s was carried out in two phases. During the first phase—completed mostly during 1974–75—the firms and agricultural land that had been seized illegally by the government during the previous administration were returned to the private sector. During the second phase—covering 1974–80—the government began to divest firms controlled by the State Development Corporation, CORFO. Most of these firms had required large capital investment and had received state support because the firms had been considered important to the national interest.[3] In 1974 the military government started to transfer these firms to the private sector through a series of public auctions, followed by direct negotiations. This strategy was flawed, however. The firms were generally purchased with only a small down payment (typically between 10 and 20 percent of the sale value), with the rest financed through credit extended by CORFO. The screening procedures, which were intended to ascertain the strength of prospective buyers and any cross-ownership, were not enforced. As a result, this privatization program tended to concentrate assets in indus-

Table 21-1. Basic Macroeconomic Data for Chile, 1978–87

Indicator	*1978*	*1979*	*1980*	*1981*	*1982*	*1983*	*1984*	*1985*	*1986*	*1987*[a]	*Indices (1978–80 = 100)* 1970	1973	1983	1987
National accounts (annual percentage change at 1977 prices)														
GDP	8.2	8.3	7.8	5.5	−14.1	−0.7	6.3	2.4	5.7	5.4	83.9	85.3	97.0	117.6
GNP per capita	6.3	6.0	5.6	2.2	−18.1	−2.3	2.3	2.6	4.8	3.8	98.7	96.6	86.3	98.5
Domestic expenditures	9.7	10.5	9.3	11.6	−24.1	−4.6	8.5	−1.9	5.4	7.3	89.8	93.4	88.4	106.4
Private consumption per capita	5.7	4.7	5.0	8.9	−13.6	−5.0	−0.4	−3.3	3.5	3.5	106.8	114.9	93.6	96.9
Gross fixed investment	17.4	16.8	21.9	16.8	−33.9	−14.9	9.0	14.8	7.1	15.2	107.2	78.7	78.1	120.5
Exports[b]	11.2	14.1	14.3	−9.0	4.7	0.6	6.8	6.9	9.8	6.9	42.8	37.7	109.0	146.0
Imports[b]	17.6	22.7	18.7	15.7	−36.3	−15.1	16.5	−11.0	9.7	16.2	73.0	77.3	74.2	98.1
Prices (annual percentage change)														
Consumer prices	40.1	33.4	35.1	19.7	9.9	27.3	19.9	30.7	19.5	19.9	0.03	0.3	218.9	491.4
Real effective exchange rate	−16.6	1.5	16.1	18.0	−9.6	−18.7	−1.7	−19.3	−15.6	−7.4	245.9	167.2	96.0	59.5
Terms of trade	−1.0	11.3	0.6	−15.7	−4.7	8.9	−4.9	−5.7	4.5	4.8	210.0	212.8	91.2	93.4
Real wages	6.4	8.2	8.6	9.0	0.3	−10.9	0.2	−4.5	2.0	−0.2	121.2	94.1	105.3	102.7
Real minimum wage	18.1	−3.1	0.2	−0.8	−2.0	−19.5	−14.6	−5.1	−3.4	−6.1	103.1	75.6	83.4	60.4
Unemployment (percentage of labor force)														
Open unemployment	14.1	13.6	10.4	11.3	19.6	14.6	14.0	11.9	8.8	7.9	27.6	33.9	114.9	62.2
Emergency programs	3.9	4.0	5.8	4.8	7.4	13.7	8.3	7.4	5.1	2.7	0.0	0.0	300.0	59.1
Total unemployment	18.0	17.6	16.2	16.1	27.0	28.3	22.3	19.3	13.9	10.6	20.3	24.9	163.9	61.4

a. Preliminary estimates.
b. Goods and nonfactor services.
Sources: National accounts data and terms of trade: Central Bank of Chile.
Consumer prices: Instituto Nacional de Estadística (INE), period average.
Real effective exchange rate: 1970–76, World Bank data; 1976–87, IMF (trade weighted, period average). An increase in the index reflects an appreciation of the Chilean peso.
Real (minimum) wages = nominal wages (INE), deflated by the revised consumer price index (Arellano 1988b, table 3, p. 8). Minimum wages were obtained as the average of industrial minimum wages and urban wages and exclude dependent benefits.
Open unemployment rates: INE. Figures for 1978–87 are for the last quarter. The estimate for 1973 is based on the surveys for the Greater Santiago Area conducted by the University of Chile.
Emergency employment programs: Central Bank of Chile. The figures given are those for September of each year.

trial and financial conglomerates with a weak capital base, which made them highly vulnerable to financial collapse.[4]

FINANCIAL LIBERALIZATION. Financial liberalization was also carried out in the second half of the 1970s. Although the liberalization of domestic financial markets was implemented rapidly and was basically complete by 1977, external financial flows remained restricted until mid-1979. These restrictions were gradually lifted during 1979–81, first by eliminating global limits on borrowing, then by restricting monthly inflows, and finally by liberalizing short-term flows.

During the financial liberalization process, prudential regulation and supervision were lax, a problem that was aggravated by the heavy concentration of assets in conglomerates. These conditions permitted continued bank lending to risky projects and to insolvent firms associated with the same groups that owned the banks. As a result, credit was channeled to unprofitable but affiliated firms, and less credit was available for profitable but independent firms (Galvez and Tybout 1985). Furthermore, inadequate supervision under conditions of excess demand for credit encouraged an "adverse selection process"; that is, high-risk borrowers who could temporarily afford the high real interest rates received credit while low-risk low-return borrowers were driven out of the market. In addition, since the government had previously bailed out failing financial institutions, the presumption was that it would do so again. Such implicit deposit insurance provided an incentive for undue risk-taking (Corbo and de Melo 1987).

THE "AUTOMATIC ADJUSTMENT PROCESS." The large real appreciation of the peso during 1979–81 exacerbated the domestic and external imbalances. This problem had serious economic consequences because the government waited several years before initiating the necessary corrective actions. The first sectors to experience significant declines in economic activity were agriculture and industry (and with them, domestic trade and transportation) during the fourth quarter of 1981. At the time, the government insisted that an "automatic adjustment process" would soon reverse the excess demand for tradables and that changes in economic policies were therefore not required. As the decline deepened, however, spreading to construction, finance, and other services and depleting the reserves of the Central Bank, the government was forced to devalue the peso in mid-1982.

With the devaluation, the price of domestic assets in dollar terms fell drastically, and large capital losses occurred. This aggravated the crisis and prompted further speculation against the peso. When commercial bank lending to Latin American countries virtually stopped in the fourth quarter of 1982, after the crisis in Mexico, Chile was in a deep recession.

Real GDP had fallen 14 percent in 1982 and fell another 1 percent in 1983. Unemployment increased to record levels, reaching 28 percent in 1983 (table 21-1)—including those enrolled in the government's two emergency employment programs, the Minimum Employment Program and the Program for Heads of Households.

Despite these signs of economic crisis, the government was still not convinced that major economic policy adjustments were needed. It did intervene in the financial sector, however, and partially reversed the trade policies it had implemented in the 1970s (see below). Not until early 1985, several years after the economy had collapsed, did the government realize that drastic changes in economic policies were needed.

External Shocks

The negative external shocks Chile experienced during the early 1980s triggered the crisis and amplified its economic costs. The deterioration of Chile's terms of trade, in particular, and the increase in international interest rates imposed a heavy burden on the economy. The terms of trade deteriorated by an accumulated 20 percent between 1980 and 1982 (table 21-1), and real interest rates increased from 2.3 percent in 1978–79 to 5.9 percent in 1980–82. The income losses Chile suffered during 1982–83 as a result of these shocks have been estimated at 12.2 percent of GDP.[5]

These figures suggest the magnitude of the external shocks, but they do not explain Chile's economic performance. It is very difficult to separate the strictly exogenous events from the endogenous policy response. Thus, to translate the interest rate effect into a GDP loss (which contributed 60 percent of Chile's total loss), the change in international interest rates during the period analyzed was multiplied by the ratio of debt to GDP. But Chile had a high debt/GDP ratio before the crisis (48 percent, compared with 17 percent for Argentina and 19 percent for Uruguay), which was to a large extent policy induced. Moreover, several studies analyzing the links between recent external shocks and economic performance in developing countries (see, for example, Balassa and McCarthy 1984) have not found a significant correlation between the magnitude of the external shocks and indicators of economic performance. This finding suggests that domestic policy responses, as well as country characteristics such as level of development, are paramount in explaining these links—a conclusion that has been confirmed by more detailed analyses of the case of Chile (Balassa 1985; Corbo and de Melo 1987).

The Financial Crisis and Its Immediate Aftermath

To avoid a complete breakdown of the economy, the Central Bank intervened in the five largest private banks in January 1983, liquidated a few other financial institutions, and provided massive financial support. Bank deposits were publicly guaranteed, upper limits were imposed on passive nominal interest rates, and several emergency credit programs were established. Two of these programs—one providing subsidized credit lines to reschedule peso-denominated private debts and one offering a preferential exchange rate for U.S. dollar-denominated debts—involved significant increases in Central Bank credit to financial intermediaries. Somewhat later, the Central Bank also purchased the nonperforming portfolios of commercial banks.

In early 1984 the economic authorities reached a debt-rescheduling agreement with commercial creditors that provided some new funds in return for a government guarantee of the amounts rescheduled. Chile's new economic team then launched a significant public investment program. GDP increased by 6.3 percent in 1984, and unemployment declined to 22 percent even though the emergency programs were drastically reduced (table 21-1). The recovery was unsustainable over the longer term, however. The trade surplus dropped considerably, and the current account deficit widened from 5.7 percent of GDP in 1983 to 10.7 percent of GDP in 1984. To cope with this imbalance, the government imposed new limits on imports. A 15 percent tariff surtax on selected import items was added in March 1984 on top of a 1983 general increase in tariffs from 10 to 20 percent. Tariffs were finally leveled off at 35 percent at the end of 1984.

The Adjustment Program

By 1985 the severity of Chile's economic problems had become evident to everyone, and the authorities realized that a longer-term strategy was required to address them. The government initiated a three-year adjustment program that emphasized three key areas: export incentives and the balance of payments, domestic resource mobilization, and rehabilitation of the financial and corporate sectors. This program was complemented by an orthodox stabilization package and an explicit attempt to restructure the external debt.

The government's adjustment program was supported by a three-year arrangement with the International Monetary Fund (IMF) approved in August 1985 and totaling 750 million in special drawing rights (SDR)[6] and three consecutive World Bank structural adjustment loans (SALS) totaling US$750 million, approved in October 1985, 1986, and 1987. Both financial packages shared the goals of a more efficient public sector, better budgetary and institutional controls, an open and export-oriented economy, and a revitalized financial sector.

Besides specific fiscal, monetary, and reserve targets, the IMF program stressed the phasing out of the preferential exchange rate system for U.S.

dollar debtors, a lower budget deficit, and a major reduction in Chile's need for new commercial funds. The SALs emphasized the restructuring of the corporate and financial sectors and support for the government's trade, fiscal, and financial reforms.

Macroeconomic Stabilization Policies

After significantly devaluing the peso in September 1984, the government made a commitment to maintain a real exchange rate that would promote new (noncopper) exports. This implied adopting a passive crawling peg system and continuously adjusting the nominal exchange rate according to the difference between domestic and foreign rates of inflation. In practice, devaluations exceeded these differences, and the real effective exchange rate depreciated substantially.

To complement the exchange rate policy, the government adopted an austere fiscal and monetary program. The fiscal policy was designed to reduce the overall nonfinancial public sector deficit by containing fiscal expenditures—particularly wage expenditures. Limits on the Central Bank's creation of credit were also established in order to conform to specific monetary targets set in the context of the IMF program.

Management of External Debt

Two new debt-rescheduling agreements were reached during this period. In 1985 Chile and its foreign creditors agreed to restructure US$5.7 billion of maturities due in 1985–87, and the banks agreed to provide US$1.1 billion of new money for 1985–86. Approval of the first SAL, partial World Bank guarantee of a US$300 million loan with cofinancing, and Chile's participation in the IMF program were instrumental in Chile's obtaining this agreement. In 1987 Chile reached a new agreement with its commercial creditors to postpone payments for US$12.4 billion of maturities falling due in 1988–91, leaving an anticipated financing gap of US$650 million for 1987–88. Two elements negotiated in this last package provided additional relief: repricing (a reduction in the spreads on amounts previously rescheduled in 1983, 1984, and 1985) and retiming (a reduction in the frequency of interest payments). These measures were complemented by agreements with creditor governments to postpone repayments of principal during 1985–88.

Despite the substantial short-term relief provided by these renegotiated agreements, they imposed a heavy burden on the Chilean government. The government agreed to guarantee all rescheduled amounts, including previously unguaranteed foreign debt, thereby eliminating the possibility of major write-offs in case-by-case private negotiations. Through this process, the government effectively "socialized" the huge private losses that could not be serviced, an action whose consequences would become clear during the process of financial rehabilitation.

External debt restructuring was complemented in 1985 by the introduction of two innovative debt-conversion mechanisms. The first, known as a buyback scheme, is open to both foreign and domestic investors and is regulated under chapter 18 of the Central Bank's Rules on International Exchange. Under the buyback scheme, external debt instruments are converted into domestic debt certificates that can be sold in the domestic capital market and used in a variety of domestic transactions. The second mechanism, known as a debt-equity swap, is open only to foreign investors and is regulated under chapter 19. It permits external debt instruments to be converted into equity investment. In both cases, the conversions are made at the official exchange rate. The external debt certificates are bought at a discount in the international secondary market but are recognized at near par value in Chile.[7]

Trade Policy

At the beginning of 1985 the government initiated a series of actions to improve export incentives. It eliminated a stamp tax on export activities and the value added tax on investment for export production and reduced the commercial bank reserves needed for export lending. Import tariffs were lowered from 35 to 30 percent in March 1985, to 20 percent in July 1985, and to 15 percent in January 1988. In addition, the peso was further devalued.

The World Bank's adjustment package emphasized complementary measures to minimize the disruptive effects of fluctuations in international copper prices and to improve incentives for small and medium-size exporters. A pilot copper price stabilization fund was created in early 1986 to smooth out government revenues and avoid short-term pressure on the real exchange rate.[8] Additional incentives to small exporters included temporary fiscal credits in amounts up to 10 percent of the value (f.o.b.) of exports and the allowance of wider margins than those stipulated in the banking law for personal credit for the promotion of new exports. Other measures improved export incentives by offsetting the 20 percent uniform tariff on imported capital goods and intermediate inputs for both direct and indirect exporters, establishing a privately run and unsubsidized export credit insurance program, and expanding institutional and technical assistance to small and medium-size exporters through the state's export development agency, PROCHILE, which also encouraged foreign direct investment in export-oriented activities.

Resource Mobilization

Much of the initial effort to mobilize savings was concentrated in the public sector. Additional savings were needed to cover the transitory imbalance generated by the privatization of the social security system, interest on the public debt, and the losses resulting from the financial crisis. A 1981 reform of the social security system had transformed the publicly supported system into one based on the private investment of individual savings. During the transition, the government continued to pay pensions to those who had already retired and to maintain pension obligations for those who were about to retire, but it no longer received contributions from those who had transferred to the private system. As a result of this reform alone, the overall nonfinancial public sector deficit increased by an estimated 4 percent of GDP in 1982, which accounted for most of the deterioration in public sector savings during that year.[9] In addition, the government had to absorb part of the losses originating from private debts that could not be serviced. Since it had already guaranteed these debts, the government was forced to take direct responsibility for an increasing proportion of Chile's external debt. To cope with these needs, specific targets were adopted to increase public savings to 4.5 percent of GDP in 1986, 4.7 percent in 1987, and 5.5 percent by 1990, compared with a surplus of only 0.4 percent in 1984.

Fiscal reforms initiated in 1984 were intended to encourage private savings and investment. The maximum marginal tax rates were to be decreased gradually from 56 percent to 50 percent, and income tax brackets were enlarged. Retained earnings were exempted from personal income tax and taxed at a flat rate of 10 percent. Other measures gradually phased out the surtax on corporate profits and allowed selected investments to be partially deducted (up to a maximum of 20 percent of the amounts invested) from the personal income tax base. In a later stage, the government announced steps to ease restrictions on institutional investors, including the private pension system, to permit the mobilization of these resources into productive investments.

Rehabilitation of the Financial and Corporate Sectors

Government intervention in Chile's financial sector prevented chaotic bankruptcies, but it led to ownership problems affecting production and investment in the corporate and financial sectors. To address this issue, the government created special commissions to manage the firms in which it had intervened and to define financial programs for their reprivatization. It then pursued the recapitalization of banks and firms through the provision of heavy subsidies and strengthened the supervisory and legal framework of the Superintendency of Banks to prevent future crises.

In 1985 the government initiated a program to recapitalize the banks it had taken over. Their substandard portfolios were purchased by the Central Bank, which paid for them by issuing four-year promissory notes with a 7 percent real interest rate. In return, the banks paid a 5 percent real interest rate for the outstanding portfolios sold to the Central Bank and committed themselves to repurchase these portfolios out of future profits by limiting the distribution of dividends—except in the case of new shareholders, to whom a total of 30 percent of earnings would be distributed as dividends. This mechanism not only avoided a massive expansion of credit and a complete bailout of private shareholders, but also allowed the banks to spread the losses over several years. The Central Bank notes were then capitalized, and the shares were sold to the public.

The corporate sector was recapitalized through Central Bank–financed debt reschedulings, which permitted many firms to stretch their financial servicing costs over a long period. The economic recovery then allowed viable firms to generate sufficient profits to service their debts while improving their overall debt-equity ratios. As soon as these firms regained financial strength and their legal status was settled, the government began to reprivatize them.

To limit the losses arising from the various subsidy schemes, the government announced that no further generalized reprogramming of loans would be made after July 1, 1985. It also announced a gradual phasing out (by early 1987) of the preferential exchange rate for U.S. dollar debtors and reaffirmed its commitment to enforce the repurchase by commercial banks of the substandard portfolios bought by the Central Bank. Despite these policies, the Central Bank incurred heavy losses.

In 1987 a new banking law established greater accountability in banking activities and enhanced the supervisory power of the Superintendency of Banks. The law also provided for the gradual replacement of the state's general deposit guarantee by a limited guarantee system that spread the risk among shareholders, bank creditors, depositors, and the state.

Outcome of Adjustment Policies

Chile's adjustment program permitted a resumption of growth and a continued strengthening of the current account position. It also enabled the country to improve its external debt situation, increase exports, and mobilize resources. These gains, however, have had both financial and social costs.

Macroeconomic Stabilization

GDP growth averaged 5.5 percent a year during 1985–87, led by increases in exports and investment.[10] With strong output growth, unemployment decreased at a significant pace from 22.3 percent in 1984 to 10.6 percent in 1987, its lowest level since 1974. The current account deficit fell from US$2.1 billion in 1984 (10.7 percent of GDP) to US$1.0 billion in 1987

(4.8 percent of GDP) because of significant increases in exports, reductions in international interest rates, and in 1987 improvements in copper prices.

Most of the targets set in the adjustment program were met. Targets for international reserves, for net domestic assets of the Central Bank, and for short-term indebtedness of the public sector at the end of 1987 were even exceeded by wide margins. The public sector deficit also narrowed more rapidly than anticipated, dropping from 4.4 percent of GDP in 1984 to 0.8 percent in 1987 (compared with the target of 1.6 percent). Inflation, however, was marginally above its target in 1987. After increasing to 30.7 percent in 1985, inflation dropped to 19.5 percent in 1986 and then increased slightly to 19.9 percent in 1987 (compared with the target rate of 18.1 percent).

Despite these achievements, concerns about the social impact of the adjustment program remain (see discussion below). Average per capita income has not yet reached its previous level (table 21-1), while consumption per capita in 1987 was still 5 percent below the average level for 1978–80 and 12 percent below the level in 1970.[11] Although unemployment in 1987 was below the average in 1978–80, it was still more than twice the level that prevailed during 1965–73.

External Debt

By following a consistent and austere adjustment program that stressed improvement in the balance of payments, Chile was able to reschedule its external debt successfully. These efforts were complemented by reductions in the spreads on new and rescheduled debt and, more important, by significant declines in international interest rates in both nominal and real terms.

The total level of external debt increased only slightly (from US$19.7 billion in 1984 to US$20.8 billion in 1987, although it declined relative to exports) as the new borrowing was partly compensated for by the external debt-reduction schemes introduced in 1985 (table 21-2). These schemes proved useful in limiting the growth of external debt, but their benefits were limited.

At the end of 1987 Chile had retired US$2.2 billion in external debt through these mechanisms.[12] Slightly more than half this amount (US$1.2 billion) was retired through buybacks under chapter 18, which do not carry remittance rights. The chief benefits under this scheme are that Chile receives not only a reduction in future interest payments (in this case, worth about US$110 million) but also the part of the external discount that is appropriated by the Central Bank (through auctions for the right to participate in these operations). This discount averaged 15 percent during 1985–87 (or about half the discount rate prevailing in international secondary markets), for which Chile received US$190 mil-

Table 21-2. *Chile's External Debt, 1970, 1973, and 1978–87*

Indicator	*1970*	*1973*	*1978*	*1979*	*1980*	*1981*	*1982*	*1983*	*1984*	*1985*	*1986*	*1987*[a]
Total external debt (billions of U.S. dollars)	n.a.	n.a.	7.011	8.663	11.207	15.591	17.159	18.037	19.666	20.404	20.670	20.761
Long-term debt	2.767	3.261	5.923	7.507	9.413	12.553	13.815	14.832	16.963	17.650	17.814	17.356
Public and publicly guaranteed	2.218	2.862	4.353	4.771	4.720	4.415	5.157	6.689	10.601	12.515	14.379	14.729
Private nonguaranteed	0.549	0.399	1.570	2.736	4.693	8.138	8.658	8.143	6.362	5.135	3.435	2.627
Short-term debt	n.a.	n.a.	0.741	0.977	1.671	2.989	3.338	2.599	1.914	1.668	1.574	1.945
IMF net credit	0.002	0.095	0.347	0.179	0.123	0.049	0.006	0.606	0.743	1.085	1.328	1.460
Debt ratios (percent)												
Private nonguaranteed debt/long-term debt	19.8	12.2	26.5	36.5	49.9	64.8	62.7	54.9	37.5	31.1	27.2	15.1
Total external debt/GDP	n.a.	n.a.	45.5	41.8	40.6	47.8	70.5	91.3	102.5	127.6	122.9	110.8
Total external debt/exports	217.2[b]	228.7[b]	235.0	183.5	178.6	277.7	332.9	373.4	408.5	437.0	404.0	343.3
Debt service ratio[c]	24.4[b]	16.1[b]	49.0	42.3	38.8	61.8	62.9	56.5	62.1	49.7	44.4	42.8
Average interest rate[d]	6.8	5.8	10.6	13.0	13.8	15.0	13.2	11.8	12.5	9.5	8.6	n.a.
LIBOR[e]	8.5	9.2	9.1	11.9	14.0	16.7	13.6	9.9	11.3	8.6	6.8	7.2
Real LIBOR[f]	2.8	2.4	1.7	2.9	4.5	6.5	6.7	5.9	6.9	5.1	4.0	3.2

n.a. Not available.
a. Preliminary estimates.
b. Debt ratios for 1970 and 1973 exclude short-term debt and interest payments on short-term debt.
c. Total debt service payments as a percentage of exports of goods and services.
d. Average cost of new commitments on public and publicly guaranteed long-term debt, obtained from the World Bank's Debtor Reporting System.
e. London interbank offer rate (LIBOR) on six-month U.S. dollar deposits.
f. LIBOR deflated by the U.S. GNP deflator.
Source: Central Bank of Chile.

lion (Ffrench-Davis 1987). The remaining portion of the external debt retired during 1985–87 (US$1.0 billion) was processed as debt-equity swaps through chapter 19. The benefits Chile obtained under this scheme may have been even smaller than under the buyback scheme. Under debt-equity swaps, the reduction in interest payments may be neutralized by increases in future profit remittances, and the discounts do not accrue to the Central Bank but are divided between foreign investors—who effectively receive a preferential exchange rate—and commercial banks and other intermediaries.

Three other comments need to be made about the mechanisms for reducing external debt. First, from an accounting point of view, a debt-equity swap has no effect on a country's net liability position with the rest of the world when the debt is redeemed at face value and no new investment requirements are introduced at the time of the swap operation, as is the case in Chile. However, since debt ratios include repayment obligations on loans but exclude interest and dividends on foreign investment, debt ratios are reduced as a consequence of the swap operation. Second, debt-equity swaps can also have significant monetary and fiscal implications because they often increase the domestic money supply and may increase the domestic-currency debt service obligations of the government (when domestic interest rates are higher than the interest rate on the foreign loans). There is little evidence, however, that these negative effects have been important in the case of Chile. Third, although the debt-equity schemes in Chile increased the flow of foreign funds—most of which were used to reprivatize firms (see below)—this increase was partly reversed by a reduction in net foreign direct investment (from an average of US$220 million a year in 1980–84 to US$60 million in 1985–86).

External Trade

Exports benefited greatly from the improved incentives. The volume of merchandise exports increased 7.9 percent a year during 1984–87, compared with 3.7 percent during 1980–84. Agricultural and industrial exports increased even more (by 19 and 15 percent a year during 1984–86, respectively, compared with 8.4 and 4.2 percent a year during 1980–84), helped by a favorable exchange rate and other incentives that effectively redressed the mild antiexport bias prevailing during 1974–81. Although no direct evidence is available, there are indications that investments in export-oriented activities—particularly in fruit, forestry, agroindustry, and mining activities—increased considerably in the late 1980s.

Imports also increased substantially during 1985–87, despite the significant depreciation of the real effective exchange rate. Fueled by the economic recovery, increases in investment, and the decline in tariff rates, the volume of imports rose by 15 percent a year during 1985–87. Because of the relatively low import base (after a significant decline in 1985), however, the trade balance improved from 1.5 percent of GDP in 1984 to 5.8 percent in 1987, despite unchanged terms of trade (table 21-3).

Resource Mobilization

Public sector savings grew significantly, from 0.6 percent of GDP in 1984 to 5.3 percent in 1987, surpassing the 4.7 percent target set in the adjustment program. This performance was due to both increases in revenue and reductions in expenditure. Improvements in the administration of the value added tax, in particular, increased the collection of indirect taxes from an average of 15.0 percent of GDP during 1981–84 to 16.9 percent during 1985–87 (table 21-4). These gains, however, were partly offset by the decline in direct tax collections (from 5.3 percent of GDP in 1981–84 to 3.8 percent in 1985–87) that resulted from the 1984 tax reform—a process that intensified the changes introduced in the previous fiscal reform and increased its regressive distributional consequences.[13] Other changes that complemented the government's savings efforts included an increased surplus in the operation of public enterprises, lower expenditures because of reductions in the emergency employment programs and international interest rates, and continued wage restraint in the public sector.

Private savings also increased from 2.3 percent of GDP in 1984 to 6.8 percent in 1987 but with a significant drop in 1985 (table 21-3). Thus despite significant increases in incentives, private savings averaged only 3.7 percent of GDP in 1985–87 compared with 3.1 percent in 1980–84.

Increased savings (due in part to a cyclical recovery and in part to the adjustment program) and declines in domestic interest rates permitted a recovery of investment. Gross fixed investment increased by 11 percent a year in real terms during 1985–87. As a percentage of GDP, fixed investment increased from 12.4 percent in 1984 to 15.5 percent in 1987, and public investment increased from 6.4 percent to 7.3 percent. The value of these achievements was enhanced because the government restricted investment to the most profitable projects and dropped or scaled down nonessential investments.

Rehabilitation of the Financial and Corporate Sectors

The Central Bank's intervention in failing banks and businesses and the various subsidy schemes it introduced allowed many banks and firms to continue operating. It therefore prevented widespread bankruptcies and their devastating economic consequences, but its losses were enormous.

Table 21-3. Balance of Payments, Savings, and Investment in Chile, 1970, 1973, and 1978–87
(percentage of GDP based on current prices)

Item	*1970*	*1973*	*1978*	*1979*	*1980*	*1981*	*1982*	*1983*	*1984*	*1985*	*1986*	*1987*[a]
Balance of payments												
Trade balance	4.7	−0.3	−2.8	−1.7	−2.8	−8.2	0.3	5.0	1.5	5.3	6.5	5.8
Current account balance	−1.4	−4.2	−7.1	−5.7	−7.1	−14.5	−9.5	−5.7	−10.7	−8.3	−6.5	−4.8
Savings and investment												
External savings[b]	−0.7	1.9	3.3	2.8	4.2	10.3	1.9	−2.7	1.1	−2.8	−3.8	−3.0
Gross domestic savings	17.1	6.1	14.5	15.0	16.8	12.4	9.4	12.5	12.6	16.5	18.4	19.9
Net factor income	−2.2	−1.1	−2.2	−3.0	−3.4	−4.5	−4.5	−7.8	−10.2	−11.9	−11.2	−8.2
Net current transfers	0.3	0.2	0.5	0.4	0.4	0.3	0.5	0.5	0.5	0.4	0.4	0.4
Gross national savings	15.2	5.2	12.8	12.4	13.9	8.2	2.1	4.4	2.9	5.0	7.7	12.1
Private savings	7.9	25.0	4.0	3.4	3.3	2.7	2.9	4.2	2.3	1.2	3.1	6.8
Public savings	7.3	−19.8	8.8	9.0	10.6	5.5	−0.8	0.2	0.6	3.8	4.6	5.3
Gross domestic investment	16.4	7.9	17.8	17.8	21.0	22.7	11.3	9.8	13.6	13.7	14.6	16.9
Gross fixed investment	15.0	12.8	14.7	14.9	16.7	18.6	14.6	12.0	12.4	14.2	14.6	15.5
Change in stocks	1.4	−4.9	3.1	2.9	4.3	4.1	−3.3	−2.2	1.2	−0.5	0.0	1.4

a. Preliminary estimates.
b. Net imports of goods and nonfactor services.
Sources: Central Bank of Chile and World Bank estimates.

Table 21-4. Public Sector Finances in Chile, 1970, 1973, and 1978–87

(percentage of GDP based on current prices)

Item	*1970*	*1973*	*1978*	*1979*	*1980*	*1981*	*1982*	*1983*	*1984*	*1985*	*1986*	*1987*[a]
Nonfinancial public sector												
Current revenue	38.2	21.3	36.7	33.8	35.0	31.8	31.4	30.5	31.2	33.4	32.0	32.6
Direct taxes	7.7	5.7	8.1	7.2	7.3	5.8	5.7	5.0	4.6	3.7	3.7	4.1
Indirect taxes	10.8	10.1	13.7	13.3	13.4	14.8	13.8	14.6	16.6	17.0	17.0	16.8
Other revenue	19.7	5.5	14.9	13.3	14.3	11.2	11.9	10.9	10.0	12.7	11.3	11.7
Current expenditure	30.9	41.1	27.9	24.8	24.4	26.3	32.2	30.3	30.6	29.6	27.4	27.3
Current surplus	7.3	−19.8	8.8	9.0	10.6	5.5	−0.8	0.2	0.6	3.8	4.6	5.3
Capital formation	10.4	8.4	6.7	5.2	5.4	5.0	4.7	4.7	6.4	7.0	7.5	7.3
Overall surplus	−6.7	−30.5	1.5	4.8	5.5	0.8	−3.4	−2.8	−4.4	−2.6	−1.9	−0.8
Central Bank (net income)[b]	n.a.	n.a.	n.a.	n.a.	1.0	1.5	0.5	−6.4	−6.2	−12.6	−9.5	n.a.
Consolidated public sector[c]	n.a.	n.a.	n.a.	n.a.	6.5	2.3	−2.9	−9.2	−10.6	−15.2	−11.4	n.a.

n.a. Not available.

a. Preliminary estimates.

b. These figures were obtained from the Central Bank's statements of income and expenses. Since 1982 they have included the subsidies given to commercial banks (to finance losses originating from the purchase of bad loans) and to individuals and corporations (to finance the restructuring of domestic debts and the preferential exchange rate system). Price adjustments that are due to indexed operations are omitted.

c. Includes Central Bank and nonfinancial public sector.

Sources: Ministry of Finance, Central Bank of Chile, and World Bank estimates.

These losses are estimated to have averaged over 6 percent of GDP during 1983–84 and 11 percent of GDP during 1985–86—for an accumulated total of US$6.0 billion (table 21-4).[14] Moreover, these estimates omit the losses incurred by the State Bank (Banco del Estado), which absorbed the debts of two failing banks valued at US$360 million (Larrain 1988). The losses for 1987 and beyond are expected to be substantially lower than in previous years, however, since most of the subsidy schemes have been phased out, but the extent of the losses will depend to a significant extent on continued economic recovery.

The reprivatization of these banks and firms began shortly after they had been recapitalized. In this new privatization effort—which was mostly completed during 1986—the government deliberately distributed ownership among a large number of proprietors and ensured more careful screening of prospective buyers. Several methods were used to distribute ownership, but the one that attracted the most attention was the system of "popular capitalism." It imposed limits on the maximum stock ownership of individual agents and gave credits to small investors to enable them to participate. But this system also provided tax breaks favoring wealthy individuals and therefore involved heavy subsidies with regressive distributional consequences.

In a later phase, beginning in 1985 and still ongoing, the government continued its attempts to privatize the remaining state enterprises, a process that had been interrupted during the 1982–83 crisis. As of mid-1986, forty state enterprises remained, of which twenty-five were in the hands of CORFO. Three main forms of divestiture have been used: sales in the stock exchange; sales to institutional investors, dominated by private social security corporations; and sales to the workers of the companies being privatized.

The program has raised several issues. First, the government has not developed a phased and carefully planned program but has chosen instead to privatize these firms in a very short time. Second, the government has not clarified the regulatory framework for the privatized companies (some of which are natural monopolies) or the final role that institutional investors will be allowed to play. Both these factors may have depressed the prices offered for the companies. Third, and perhaps most important, the government has not announced how it will use the proceeds from the sales of these firms. If they are used to finance current expenditures rather than investment, particularly in infrastructure and human capital, the net effect on government finances will likely be negative (Larrain 1988).

The Social Costs of Adjustment

Despite significant economic improvements in the late 1980s, there are indications that the social costs of adjustment may have fallen disproportionately on those at the lower end of the income scale. Two factors in particular suggest this outcome. First, the rewards to domestic factors of production benefited capital against labor. Profit rates increased significantly during 1980–87 while real wages remained depressed. Average wages declined by 5 percent in real terms during 1980–87 and by 13 percent during 1982–87 (table 21-1). Second, changes in wage distribution adversely affected low-paying jobs. For example, the minimum wage declined by 44 percent in real terms during 1981–87. Additional indicators suggest that wages for unskilled workers declined much more than did other wages: wages for domestic employees and construction workers declined by 25 and 33 percent, respectively, during 1981–87, compared with declines of 12 and 13 percent, respectively, for wages in the financial and modern sectors of the economy (Arellano 1988a, table 6).

It is likely that the behavior of real wages, along with the economic recovery, encouraged the substantial increase in employment. But real income for low-paying jobs declined substantially. For example, real income for domestic employees and construction workers declined by margins ranging from 3 to 50 percent during 1981–87, while average real income for the economy as a whole (average wages times employment) increased by 3 percent during the same period. Real income for those earning minimum wages also declined markedly.

The apparent deterioration in income distribution is consistent with explicit policy choices adopted by the government. The tax policy, in particular, became more regressive as indirect taxes increased as a proportion of total tax revenue from 58 percent in 1970 to 72 percent in 1980–84 and 82 percent in 1985–87. By comparison, indirect taxes as a proportion of total tax revenue averaged 61 percent for a sample of developing countries with income levels similar to Chile's (Tanzi 1987). This bias was partly reversed in mid-1988 when the government reduced the uniform rate on the value added tax from 20 to 16 percent. Other biases, however, resulted from the financial rehabilitation and reprivatization (which favored U.S. dollar debtors and wealthy individuals) and may also have contributed to the deterioration of income distribution.

The deterioration of real incomes for low-paying jobs has not been accompanied by a deterioration in traditional indicators of mortality and nutrition, however. Improvements in the efficiency of government programs and better targeting of social programs for poor and high-risk groups have resulted in a continued decline in these indicators, although at a slower pace than before (Cornia, Jolly, and Stewart 1987). Nonetheless, a deterioration in health infrastructure and an increase in the incidence of poverty-related health problems followed the significant decline in health expenditures during 1981–86.

Recently, the government increased expenditures in the social sectors, particularly in health. A structural adjustment loan supports a program to maintain the present per capita level of food distribution in maternal and child health programs and to expand preventive care services such as health education, screening, and community education in order to decrease the incidence of chronic illnesses among adults. Other plans call for improvements in health infrastructure, medical equipment, and the administration of the public health system and reinforcement of the private health insurance scheme.

Evaluation of Loan Conditionality

All three SALS were well designed and clearly focused on the main problems facing Chile after the 1982–83 crisis. Appropriately, the emphasis of the loans shifted gradually from the more urgent needs requiring swift and strong stabilization efforts to longer-term, more specific structural reforms. SAL I focused on the balance of payments (export incentives), savings mobilization, and an orderly phasing-out of generalized subsidies such as the preferential exchange rate and interest rate subsidies. SAL II focused on the rehabilitation of the financial and corporate sectors and included measures to strengthen public sector finances and the control of the Superintendency of Banks over financial institutions. SAL III stressed social sector policies, particularly in health, and improvements in the mobilization and allocation of long-term savings. Conditions in SAL III had none of the vagueness that sometimes afflicted SALS I and II (for example, when they merely called for a review of progress in the bank recapitalization program or "satisfactory progress" on particular studies).

All the loans had two tranches, and a significant proportion of the loan conditions (particularly in SALS I and II) had to be met before release of the second tranche. This allowed the World Bank to maintain a close dialogue with the government and to monitor advances in key areas.

The implementation of loan conditions was generally quite successful, although a few areas of concern remain. Policy implementation in export development and public finance, in particular, was very successful. Indeed, the government exceeded the conditions it had agreed to in these areas. The implementation of financial sector reforms was also comprehensive and successful, although some problems remain (particularly concerning the new banking law and the ability of commercial banks to repurchase the portfolios sold to the Central Bank). In one instance the government seems to have backed away from its commitment to end generalized subsidies; in early 1988 it provided a new subsidy to allow banks to reschedule housing loans.

Implications for World Bank Policy

Chile's adjustment program has clearly been successful in meeting its objectives. The success is even more apparent when compared with the experience of other countries that have faced severe debt-servicing problems in recent years. Concerns about the social costs of adjustment remain, however.

There are four main explanations for the success of the adjustment program in Chile: (1) the introduction of a sound macroeconomic program, (2) the elimination of major microeconomic distortions before the establishment of the program, (3) the strength of the government's commitment to policy change, and (4) the provision of adequate external financial assistance.

After the crisis of 1982–83 and a few years of indecision, the government in early 1985 instituted a comprehensive program for macroeconomic reform that eliminated inconsistencies between exchange rate and wage policies and strengthened export development and regulation of the financial sector. Because microeconomic distortions (ad hoc subsidies and price controls) had been eliminated and significant steps toward trade liberalization and fiscal reform had already been taken in the mid-1970s, the economy was able to respond to the new incentives. The government's commitment to policy change and its firm control of the economy were also important to the success of the program. Its long tenure and authoritarian character allowed the military government to pursue strong actions and implement policy changes with relative ease, although the delay before any action was taken after the crisis may have been unnecessarily long. The final significant factor in the success was the external financial assistance from multilateral institutions (the IMF, World Bank, and Inter-American Development Bank) that provided the government with the breathing space it needed to pursue its adjustment program and to reschedule its external debt successfully.

Despite the success of the adjustment program, however, the economy remains vulnerable. Chile's external debt is still substantial, and negative external shocks, such as increases in international interest rates, declining terms of trade, or increases in protectionism among its trading partners, could complicate the management of its external and financial debt. More important, Chile still needs to mobilize sufficient domestic savings to pay its external debt and increase investment (which is still low by international standards), an effort that will be difficult to sustain in the face of strong pressures to increase consumption and expenditure in the social sectors.

Notes

I am grateful to Jaime de Melo, Luis Ernesto Derbez, Richard Newfarmer, Jose Olivares, and other World Bank colleagues for helpful comments on an early draft of this chapter, and to Sheila Fallon for typing the manuscript. All remaining errors and shortcomings are mine.

1. See Corbo (1985), Edwards and Cox-Edwards (1987), and Moran (1989) for a detailed analysis of these policy changes.

2. The real exchange rate (e^r) can be expressed as $e^r = p_t/p_n = ep^*/p_n$, where e is the nominal exchange rate, $p_t(p_n)$ is the price of tradables (nontradables), and p^* is an index of international inflation. But p_n is determined by domestic wages (w) and the user cost of capital. Assuming the latter remains unchanged, changes in the real exchange rate can be expressed as $\hat{e}^r = \hat{e} + \hat{p}^* - \hat{w}$. If $\hat{e} = 0$ (fixed nominal exchange rate) and $\hat{p}^* \approx 0$ (small level of international inflation), then a real depreciation can only be obtained by a fall in nominal wages.

3. CORFO was directly involved in about 50 enterprises in 1970, but by 1973 it had increased its participation to 180 firms.

4. See Marshall and Montt (1987), Larrain (1988), and Moran (1989) for a more detailed discussion of the privatization process in Chile.

5. Compare this figure with losses of 6.7 percent for Argentina during its crisis of 1981–82, for example, or losses of 1.0 percent for Uruguay during 1982–83 (Corbo and de Melo 1987).

6. IMF funds are denominated in SDR, which are based on a basket of currencies.

7. The external discounts fluctuated between 30 and 35 percent from 1985 to mid-1987 but increased to 40 to 45 percent in the second half of 1987 after a significant increase in the supply of these certificates.

8. The fund proved useful and timely and was activated in 1987 as copper prices increased significantly (mostly because of low international stocks and continued demand pressure) to a level above their long-run trend.

9. The cost of this reform increased to 5 percent of GDP in subsequent years and was expected to remain at this level until 1990 and then start decreasing gradually.

10. Preliminary evidence indicates that the economy continued to grow at a significant pace in 1988 as well, so the trend for 1985–87—which is the focus of the chapter—would remain unaffected if 1988 were included (although the levels of particular variables would obviously be affected).

11. The comparison of aggregate consumption levels between 1970 and 1987 may be misleading, however, because of drastic changes in the composition of consumption (Moran 1989).

12. These figures include only the amounts entered under chapters 18 (buybacks) and 19 (debt-equity swaps) of the Central Bank's Rules on International Exchange. They exclude US$0.2 billion entered under Decree Law 600, which regulates foreign direct investment, and other operations (such as partial write-offs or direct buybacks of private unguaranteed foreign debt) that accounted for about US$0.8 billion.

13. Since lower-income families consume a higher proportion of their income than wealthier families, a uniform indirect tax rate (such as the value added tax in Chile) implies that lower-income families spend a higher proportion of their income on taxes than do wealthier families.

14. I am grateful to Edgardo Barandiaran of the World Bank for providing these figures.

References

Arellano, J. P. 1988a. "Crisis y Recuperación en Chile en los Años 80." *Colección Estudios* CIEPLAN 24:63–84.

———. 1988b. "La Situación Social en Chile." Notas Técnicas 94. Santiago: CIEPLAN.

Balassa, Bela. 1985. "Policy Experiments in Chile, 1973–83." In G. M. Walton, ed., *The National Economic Policies of Chile.* Greenwich, Conn.: JAI Press.

Balassa, Bela, and F. Desmond McCarthy. 1984. *Adjustment Policies in Developing Countries, 1979–1983.* World Bank Staff Working Paper 675. Washington, D.C.

Corbo, Vittorio. 1985. "Reforms and Macroeconomic Adjustments in Chile during 1974–83." *World Development* 13:893–916.

Corbo, Vittorio, and Jaime de Melo. 1987. "Lessons from the Southern Cone Policy Reforms." *World Bank Research Observer* 2 (2):111–42.

Cornia, G. A., Richard Jolly, and Frances Stewart. 1987. *Adjustment with a Human Face.* Oxford, U.K.: Clarendon Press for UNICEF.

Edwards, Sebastian, and A. Cox-Edwards. 1987. *Monetarism and Liberalization: the Chilean Experiment.* Cambridge, Mass.: Ballinger.

Ffrench-Davis, R. 1987. "Conversión de Pagares de la Deuda Externa en Chile." *Colección Estudios* CIEPLAN 22:41–62.

Galvez, J., and James Tybout. 1985. "Microeconomic Adjustment in Chile during 1977–81: The Importance of Being a Grupo." *World Development* 13:969–94.

Larrain, F. 1988. "Public Sector Behavior in a Highly Indebted Country: The Contrasting Chilean Experience, 1970–85." Country Policy Department, World Bank, Washington, D.C.

Marshall, J., and F. Montt. 1987. "Privatization in Chile." Country Policy Department, World Bank, Washington, D.C.

Moran, Cristian. 1989. "Economic Stabilization and Structural Transformation: Lessons from the Chilean Experience, 1973–87." *World Development* (April).

Tanzi, Vito. 1987. "Quantitative Characteristics of the Tax System of Developing Countries." In David Newbery and Nicholas Stern, eds., *Theory of Taxation for Developing Countries.* New York: Oxford University Press.

Comments

Sebastian Edwards

THE CHILEAN economic experience since the early 1970s has attracted considerable attention. In the mid- to late 1970s the daring free market reforms implemented by the so-called Chicago boys captured the imagination of the financial media and conservative publicists. When the economy collapsed in 1982—GDP declined by almost 15 percent and unemployment soared to almost 30 percent—many observers wrote off the experiment, claiming that a free-market-oriented regime could not succeed in a small developing nation. When the economy recovered with great vigor in the late 1980s, most experts were surprised. It is not an exaggeration to say that Chile has become a showcase for those interested in understanding and evaluating the economics of structural reform and liberalization.

Cristian Moran's chapter provides an interesting analysis and a substantial amount of information on the evolution of the Chilean economy during the 1980s. Although I disagree with several parts of the analysis, I think this chapter is a timely and useful contribution to the literature on the Chilean experience with structural reform. My comments cover five topics: monetary and fiscal policies, the key role played by exchange rate policy, the time horizon of structural reform, the role of the World Bank in facilitating the process of structural adjustment, and prospects and directions for the future.

One of the most important lessons of the Chilean experience has to do with the influence of macroeconomic stability and macroeconomic management on successful performance. Indeed, macroeconomic management was at the center of both the unleashing of the crisis in 1982 and the recovery in the late 1980s. Moran mentions four main internal causes of the 1982 collapse. Two of them—the simultaneous adoption of a fixed nominal exchange rate and a wage rate indexation rule and the reliance on "automatic adjustment"—are obviously macroeconomic in nature and clearly illustrate how policy mistakes at the level of macroeconomic management can magnify negative external shocks. The other two policy errors identified by Moran refer to the lack of supervision that characterized the privatization and financial liberalization programs. He does not argue, however, that the whole concept of microeconomic reform was a mistake or inappropriate for Chile. In that regard, Moran joins a growing number of scholars who have argued that the Chilean economic problems of the early 1980s were rooted in external shocks, macroeconomic mismanagement, and lack of supervision in implementing some of the key microeconomic reforms.

In the same way that macroeconomic policy helped unleash the 1982 crisis, strong and aggressive macroeconomic management was fundamental to the recovery of the 1980s. After 1985 fiscal policy was based on redirecting public expenditure from current expenditure to public investment. As a result, public investment as a share of GDP increased by more than 7 percentage points between 1985 and 1989. In addition, fiscal policy during this period was directed toward encouraging private savings via a reduction in taxes. What was crucially important, however, was that overall fiscal balance was maintained during this period so that outbursts of inflation and unsustainable pressures on the real exchange rate were avoided.

The monetary policy of the post-1985 period was characterized by active manipulation of the stock of domestic credit, mainly for the purpose of controlling interest rates. Indeed, an overriding concern of the authorities during this period was to avoid repeating the syndrome of high real interest rates of the late 1970s. In this regard, the contrast between the attitude of finance minister Hernan Buchi's team and that of the "Chicago boys" of the 1970s is important. Although Buchi's team had a clearly pragmatic view of the role of active macroeconomic—especially monetary—policy in achieving stability, the 1970s team firmly believed that the only way to tackle macroeconomic problems was to let the economy adjust on its own. A number of observers have argued that the automatic adjustment approach to macroeconomic policy that was followed between 1979 and 1982 was one of the most important mistakes of the time in Chile.

Of the economic policies pursued by Chile in the post-1982 period, there is little doubt that the exchange rate policy based on periodic devaluations was one of the most important. Between 1982 and 1988 the real exchange rate was devalued by approximately 90 percent. This devaluation not only allowed the country to improve its level of competitiveness and thus greatly helped the boom in nontraditional exports, but it also contributed to the maintenance of reasonable interest rate levels and the avoidance of capital flight.

Chile's successful experience with exchange rate management during this period generated a number of important lessons for other countries. Perhaps the most important is the demonstration that by devaluing the nominal exchange rate it is possible to engineer substantial real devaluations without generating very high inflation. In Chile the key to the success of this policy was maintaining fiscal discipline and recognizing that changes in real exchange rate "fundamentals" are important in determining the extent to which the real exchange rate can be altered. ("Fundamentals" are the immediate determinants of the equilibrium real exchange rate, such as international prices, import tariffs, export taxes, real interest rates, capital controls, and so on.) In that regard, the Chilean authorities followed a particularly pragmatic approach in which the pace at which the nominal exchange rate was devalued was determined by several considerations, including the classification of shocks as permanent or transitory, the evolution of terms of trade, and the availability of foreign funds.

It must be emphasized that much of the success observed in Chile during 1987–89 is rooted in the major structural reforms implemented in the mid-1970s. For example, the boom in nontraditional exports occurred as a result of investments that were undertaken almost ten years earlier. Moreover, the flexible and rapid market response to incentives is a direct consequence of the microeconomic reforms of the 1970s. Chile's experience shows that it can take a considerable amount of time—even eight to ten years—for an economy to adapt fully to the new rules of the game and to new incentive structures. The relatively short duration of World Bank adjustment programs may constitute a serious limitation to the achievement of successful structural reform in some cases. Although Moran does not make this point, there is no doubt that in the case of Chile most of the structural reforms were undertaken long before the World Bank got involved through its structural adjustment loans.

Moran's chapter provides information on the most important details of the World Bank's structural adjustment loans to Chile, including their amounts and the changing emphasis of their conditionality, but it does not discuss the nature of the negotiations between the World Bank and the Chilean authorities. This is of relevance to the general question of structural reform for those who would like to draw lessons from what appears to be one of the most—if not *the* most—successful World Bank operation of the 1980s. Were the negotiations difficult? Did the Chilean authorities take a strategic stance? Was it difficult to persuade them to accept some of the more controversial aspects of the loans, or were they willing to accept all conditions? Did the political situation underlying the Chilean military regime simplify acceptance of loan conditions by the authorities? The answers to these and other questions are important, especially at a time when the effectiveness of World Bank (and IMF) conditionality has come under increasing scrutiny.

Moran does discuss, however, some specific details of the adjustment loan programs. I was surprised by his suggestion that the decline in the minimum wage in real terms was a major failure of the Chilean adjustment process. Any attempt to increase the overall efficiency of the economy should try to deal with *all* distorted markets, including the labor market. In that sense, allowing the minimum wage to decline—and thereby reducing the extent of this distortion—cannot be seen as a negative development. Although income distribution certainly represents a (very) weak spot in the Chilean economy, a high minimum wage is not the most efficient way of dealing with the problem. Any formal analysis would clearly indicate that the minimum wage is, at best, an nth best policy; subsidies, social expenditure targeting, and other measures are under almost all circumstances better ways of improving income distribution.

My final point has to do with the outlook for the future. The author argues that despite Chile's recent solid economic performance, the Chilean economy continues to be quite vulnerable. I tend to agree with this view. Three areas of particular weakness in the economy are the levels of investment and savings and the very uneven income distribution. But probably the most urgent issue that the newly elected government will face in the early 1990s concerns the need to maintain fiscal discipline and macroeconomic stability. How will the newly elected democratic government persuade the public that it will actually maintain fiscal discipline and will not resort to the old inflationary ways? The public will surely remember the macro-instability of the 1960s and early 1970s, and consequently there is the danger, even in the absence of any real indiscipline, that public responses to these expectations will generate destabilizing forces.

How then can credibility be obtained? A key step in acquiring much-needed credibility is to make the Central Bank an independent institution. Such an arrangement, by introducing an important "precommitment technology," would greatly reduce the risk of irresponsible fiscal behavior. Legislation to this effect would be greatly beneficial for the country as a whole and should be pursued by all segments of the political spectrum.

22 Mexico: Adjustment and Stabilization

John Nash

MEXICO'S ECONOMIC CRISES of 1982 and 1985 had their origins in the late 1970s. In 1976, in response to severe macroeconomic imbalances and a high debt service ratio, the López Portillo government reached a stabilization agreement with the International Monetary Fund (IMF). Some progress was made in 1976 and 1977 in reducing the fiscal deficit and inflation and improving the balance of payments, but several events in 1977 undermined the momentum of the stabilization program: large oil reserves were discovered, unemployment rose, and for the first time in three decades gross domestic product (GDP) per capita failed to increase. Pressures built up to soften the stabilization measures and to stimulate growth through increased public sector expenditure financed by borrowing against prospective oil revenue.

The public deficit mounted each year until it reached 18 percent of GDP in 1982, with public sector outlays reaching 45 percent of GDP (compared with 21 percent in 1970). An important contributing factor was the expansion of state enterprises. Credit policy, which since 1973 had served to monetize the fiscal deficit (Blanco and Garber 1986), remained expansionary until the government attempted in 1982 to bring the fiscal situation under control through credit restrictions, which were borne largely by the private sector. Despite rising oil export earnings, the merchandise trade balance deteriorated until 1981. Imports rose while nonoil export earnings stagnated.

External conditions, by contrast, had on balance been favorable to Mexico between 1976 and 1982, with improved terms of trade outweighing increased debt service (on the 1977 debt) by a wide margin. The improved terms of trade increased real income by about 4.4 percent of GDP, while increased debt service decreased it by 2.7 percent. Toward the end of the period, however, the terms of trade were no longer improving, the interest rate was increasing, and the debt that the country had to service had increased greatly.

By 1981 foreign lenders had become cautious about providing new money or rolling over short-term debts. The domestic private sector also lost confidence in the authorities' ability to maintain the value of the peso. The nationalization of private commercial banks in September 1982 and the forced conversion of foreign currency accounts into pesos at an artificially low exchange rate further exacerbated the crisis of confidence and led to a massive flight of capital. The government had to resort to large foreign borrowing, mostly short term with rising interest rate spreads. The acute foreign exchange shortage and consequent import restrictions, rather than any improvement in underlying conditions, resulted in a large surplus in the trade balance and a sharp decline in the current account deficit in 1982.

The crisis came to a head in August 1982 when the government of Mexico suspended interest payments on foreign loans. It then negotiated an agreement with the IMF for about US$3.57 billion, with drawings to begin in January 1983 and to continue if certain performance criteria were met. The key element of the program was a drastic reduction in the public sector deficit from 18 percent of GDP in 1982 to 3.5 percent in 1985. The program also called for increases in the trade surplus and foreign exchange reserves. These measures were projected to bring down inflation to 55 percent in 1983, with further reductions in later years. No decline in GDP during 1983 was foreseen, and a fairly robust recovery was expected in the following years.

The Economic Crisis of 1985

The administration of President Miguel de la Madrid, which came into office on December 1, 1982, introduced several measures to increase tax revenue and raised the domestic prices of oil products and public utilities. A commitment was made to reduce budgetary subsidies over time. The 1983 budget also provided for cuts in both current and capital expenditures. The policy of low interest rates was reversed to encourage mobilization of domestic resources and discourage capital flight. The government also entered into negotiations with foreign creditors to refinance the public external debt falling due before 1985 and introduced a scheme to cover the foreign exchange risk on the private sector debt and to facilitate its restructuring.

A sharp reduction in the public sector borrowing requirement in 1983 permitted a large share of credit to shift to the private sector. Reinforced by generous tax allowances for investments and growing confidence, real private sector activity shot up during the last quarter of 1984. However, the underlying incentive structure was distorted by an extensive system of trade and other controls, and it exacerbated the pull of resources from exportable sectors to protected domestic sectors.

The economy remained bottled up behind protectionist walls and vulnerable to modest shortfalls in meeting policy targets (World Bank 1988b). The target for the public sector borrowing requirement for the last quarter of the year was substantially exceeded, and this intensified the competition for domestic savings. Inflation also greatly exceeded the program target, and as inflationary expectations rose, financial disintermediation resumed. The balance of payments position also weakened as the real exchange rate, which had been depreciated by an unprecedented amount in 1982, began to appreciate rapidly. Nonoil exports, which had responded strongly to the real depreciation, slowed and then turned downward, while capital flight accelerated. By mid-1985 the rate of foreign exchange losses had risen to US$500 million monthly. With the approach of congressional elections, monetary and fiscal policy became increasingly expansive, and by July a number of ceilings in the quarterly fiscal and balance of payments program had been surpassed. Drawings of IMF funds were suspended.

Despite the tragic and costly earthquake of September 1985, the government unveiled an austere budget in November 1985. It called for raising the primary fiscal surplus (that is, the surplus net of interest payments) from 3.3 percent of GDP in 1985 to over 9 percent of GDP in 1986. Partly because of a collapse in international oil prices, however, revenue increased less than noninterest expenditure, and the primary surplus fell by 1.6 percent of GDP between 1985 and 1986. Because of the increased cost of debt service, public sector borrowing increased by almost 6 percent of GDP.

In the period leading to the 1985–86 crisis, the net effect of external shocks was again favorable to Mexico, although the movements were in opposite directions from those that occurred before the 1982 crisis. The real interest rate on Mexico's external debt declined by almost half between 1982 and 1985, which reduced the cost of servicing the 1982 debt by about 6.1 percent of GDP, while Mexico's terms of trade declined by about 37.6 percent, the equivalent of a loss of income of about 3.0 percent of GDP. Thus the primary reason for the 1985–86 crisis was the continuation of excessive expenditure—although it must be acknowledged that the 1985 earthquake made all fiscal goals more difficult to attain—in combination with an incentive structure so distorted by trade and other policies that sustainable and efficient growth of the private sector was difficult.

In December 1985 the government of Mexico and the IMF entered into lengthy and at times acrimonious negotiations over the terms of a new standby agreement. Concurrent negotiations with commercial banks and the World Bank produced in July 1986 perhaps the largest and most complex package concluded for a major debtor nation in recent decades. It included US$12 billion in new money, US$2.3 billion in contingent financing (of which only US$0.5 billion was used), and rescheduling of the service falling due on US$70.5 billion of existing external debt (World Bank 1987). Under the IMF standby agreement, Mexico was scheduled to receive up to US$1.7 billion in quarterly disbursements through the first quarter of 1988, contingent upon flexible criteria determined by conditions in the oil market and Mexico's growth performance.

The World Bank played a large role in producing this package of agreements. It agreed to provide new money directly and to cofinance some of the new loans from commercial banks. About half of the new World Bank lending commitments, averaging US$2.0 billion annually during 1986–87, were to be in the form of quick-disbursing policy-based loans. These commitments were triple the amount of World Bank lending to Mexico in the 1981–85 period.

The World Bank also played an important role in triggering the release of up to US$500 million for a Growth Contingency Cofinancing Facility from the commercial banks. If certain conditions (some linked to specific World Bank adjustment loans) were met, and if Mexico's economic recovery did not materialize by March 1987, this facility was to become available for designated investment projects; half the amounts drawn under the facility would be guaranteed by the World Bank. The conditions were met, and these funds became available to Mexico in April 1987.

The Adjustment Program

Before the 1985 crisis the World Bank had made only one policy-based loan to Mexico, a 1983 export-development operation that had mixed success. The loan package negotiated between Mexico and its creditors in 1986 thrust the World Bank into a central role in the policy dialogue, since the release of much of the commercial bank money was linked to various prospective policy-based World Bank loans then under discussion. Between late 1986 and early 1988 the World Bank's Executive Directors approved lending operations totaling more than US$2.2 billion. These loans were based on policy reforms with regard to agriculture, fertilizer, and steel; export development; and changes in the import regime (see table 22-1 for a summary of adjustment measures and their implementation).

Trade Reform

Following the 1982 crisis the government instituted reforms in the trade regime, mostly to promote exports. Controls on temporary imports (used as inputs for exports) were eliminated, exporters were given access to foreign exchange at the controlled rate, and in-bond facilities (for example, customs warehouses) were provided. Administrative procedures for exporters were simplified. Export taxes on certain (largely agricultural) products were eliminated, and the number of products subject to

Table 22-1. Mexico's Implementation of Adjustment Measures

Policy area	*Significant progress*	*Some progress*	*Little or no progress, or regression*
Trade	Reduction of coverage of quantitative import restrictions* Reduction of tariff protection of imports* Reduction of coverage of quantitative export restrictions*	Creation of quasi-free trade status for exporters*	
Macroeconomic	Depreciation of real exchange rate Reduction of sectoral tax incentives	Reduction of noninterest government expenditures	Reduction of total government expenditure Reduction of inflation (signs of dramatic decline in late 1988)
Financial		Reduction of directed credit Decontrol of some types of deposits Reduction of credit subsidies	Denationalization of commercial banks
Public sector	Privatization and liquidation of minor state enterprises	Restructuring and reduction of fiscal losses by state enterprises* Reduction of market power of the National Food Marketing Company (CONASUPO)* Some reduction in public sector employment (after increases until 1984)	Privatization of major public enterprises

Pricing	Reduction of food subsidies	Reduction of coverage of price controls (until the Economic Solidarity Pact) Linkage of agricultural prices to border levels* Reduction of subsidies for public services	
Capital account		Reduction of controls on foreign investment	
Labor market			Reduction in labor market regulations
Administrative		Revision of public sector procurement regulations	
Compensatory measures	Better targeting of food subsidies		

* Related to tranche-release conditions of adjustment loans.
Source: World Bank.

export licenses was reduced. The World Bank supported these measures in the discussions leading to the first export development loan. Although specific loan conditions dealt mainly with export promotion measures, the discussions touched on broader issues, including unification of the exchange rate and maintenance of the rate at a realistic level, reduction of credit subsidies, and replacement of import quotas with tariffs. Most of these measures were eventually adopted by the government.

The major steps in trade policy reform were not taken until 1985. In July the government announced a 20 percent devaluation of the controlled exchange rate, followed soon by the introduction of a managed floating exchange rate and a marked acceleration in the average nominal rate of devaluation. Although a dual exchange rate system was retained, the rates were managed so that they would eventually coalesce into a unified rate. Import liberalization also began in earnest in July 1985 with the rollback of quantitative restrictions on imports, which had formed the basis of an implicit import protection policy for nearly forty years.

In 1986 the government reinforced this move toward greater openness by requesting membership in the association of the General Agreement on Tariffs and Trade (GATT), lowering the maximum tariff from 100 percent to 50 percent, announcing a three-year plan to narrow the range of import tariffs from 0 to 100 percent to 0 to 30 percent, pledging to eliminate all official reference prices on imports (another protective device) by the end of 1987 in concert with the introduction of a GATT-compatible antidumping system, and pledging to further reduce coverage of quantitative restrictions by the equivalent of 5 percent of domestic production by December 31, 1986. Throughout the development of this program, the World Bank and the government of Mexico remained in close touch. Eventually, in 1986, the World Bank approved a US$500 million trade policy loan, with some of these actions as tranche-release conditions.

During 1987 the government met its pledges and accelerated its program of narrowing the tariff range by reducing the maximum tariff to 20 percent. In addition, it further reduced the coverage of quantitative restrictions from 49.8 percent of 1983 national production to 43.1 percent (or to 25 percent of 1986 production figures). This program was supported by a second trade policy loan of US$500 million. These reforms represent tremendous progress, although it is not clear that the antidumping system is consistent with GATT rules, and there is concern that it may be used to provide concealed protection.

Certain administrative reforms governing public sector procurement that were made in January 1988 may also considerably advance import liberalization. Before January 1988 all public entities had to procure domestically all goods available in Mexico at reasonable prices and quality, and public imports valued at more than US$50,000 had to be licensed.

Because the public sector accounted for a large share of total purchases (30 percent) and imports (25 to 33 percent), these procedures created a strong anti-import bias and provided additional protection to industries producing for the public sector. It is still too early to judge whether the new regulations will be effective in redressing this bias, however.

A number of important export-promotion measures were also adopted. Many of these measures were encouraged by the World Bank through two export development loans (1983 and 1987). Domestic letters of credit now permit exporters and their suppliers to obtain export financing and foreign exchange needed for imports. Under an import admission scheme, exporters signing multiyear agreements with the government can import equipment and intermediate inputs with reduced guarantee requirements and receive rebates of duties and indirect taxes. Exporters can now retain all of their foreign exchange earnings for future imports. Credit lines for export financing were consolidated, and export insurance and guarantee schemes simplified. Quantitative export controls were reduced, and the coverage declined from 85 percent of nonoil exports in 1980 to 44 percent in 1985. The government subsequently agreed to remove some of the remaining export controls, which cover mostly agricultural products. For some of these products, especially beef, the government had manipulated the controls to ensure low internal prices and depressed producer prices.

The government's policy of strong exchange rate devaluation, which coincided with a period of declining real wages, increased Mexico's cost advantages over other export-oriented countries. Real manufacturing wages and benefits declined by nearly 25 percent between 1981 and 1987 in local currency (about 40 percent in U.S. dollars), to make Mexico's wage rates among the lowest of the major developing-country exporters.

For several reasons, the reform of trade policy was the most far-reaching and successful of the economic reforms undertaken. First, the de la Madrid administration, with strong support from the World Bank and prompted by declining oil prices, concluded early in its term that Mexico's development required a shift from an inward to an outward orientation. Second, the government's commitment was reinforced by the recognition that import liberalization could be a tool in its fight against inflation. Third, both the World Bank and the government concluded that trade reform was a prerequisite for stabilization and for the success of reforms in other sectors. Fourth, the reforms, though symbolically important and politically difficult, appear not to have been extremely painful. Nontariff barriers and tariffs were not fully binding at the time of the reforms because imports had been severely depressed by general economic conditions. As quantitative restrictions were reduced, official reference prices and tariffs were used to provide continuing, temporary protection before being gradually eliminated or reduced. Depreciation of the exchange rate cushioned the blow to import-substituting industries.

Fiscal Reform

Fiscal reform centered on efforts to reduce the budget deficit and improve the tax structure and incentives. Public sector investment fell from 10 to 5 percent of GDP between 1982 and 1987 while current spending (excluding interest) declined from 26 percent to around 20 percent of GDP. But the effect of inflation on interest rates and, consequently, on the cost of servicing domestic debt left total public spending in 1986 at around 47 percent of GDP, compared with a 1978–81 average of 34 percent. And because spending cuts were concentrated more in investment than in current expenditure (especially the wage bill), the effect on growth was less than hoped. Also on the negative side was the decline in revenue from the sale of already underpriced public sector services such as electricity, transportation, and fertilizer.

Changes in the tax structure and the system of fiscal incentives were also significant. The Tax Reform Act of 1987 is expected to reverse gradually the sharp decline since 1980 in corporate taxes as a share of GDP and should improve collection rates. The use of generous investment depreciation allowances, however, may act to increase subsidies to capital-intensive investment. With respect to fiscal incentives, the reduction in tax subsidies between 1981 and 1987 brought the level of forgone revenue to well under 0.5 percent of GDP. In 1988 all tax subsidies, except those in agriculture, were eliminated. Other tax credits for investment remain in place, targeted by region rather than industry in order to encourage investment outside the three major cities.

Reform of the Domestic Financial Sector

The banking system was nationalized in the last year of the López Portillo administration (1982) and remains under government ownership. The government, however, permitted private brokerage houses to perform some banking functions, which effectively put them in competition with banks for deposits. It was largely these brokers who financed the development of Mexico's first stock market.

Interest rates were kept low before 1983 and became highly negative in real terms in 1982 as inflation surged. This implied large transfers, both from savers to borrowers and from the government budget to borrowers from lending institutions financed by the government. In 1983 most loan rates were raised to positive real levels, although the continuation of large directed credit programs at preferred rates reduced the funds available to nonpreferred borrowers and raised their rates to extremely high levels. Later the government relaxed many of the requirements that banks channel credit to certain sectors, as well as other regulations and implicit taxation of financial intermediation activities.

Although this was a significant step toward limiting bureaucratic control of the financial sector, a substantial amount of regulation remains. Of greater concern, however, is that the public sector continues to absorb 66 percent of available credit. The World Bank, in part because of the political sensitivity of the issue of nationalization, has been reluctant to tackle reforms in this sector in a comprehensive way.

Public Sector Reform

Public sector policy remains a serious obstacle to improving the efficiency of the Mexican economy. From 1970 to 1982 the number of public enterprises increased from fewer than 100 to more than 1,000. Once established, such enterprises are difficult to liquidate or sell, while efforts to make their operations more efficient run up against the political power of the public sector unions.

Despite political opposition, the de la Madrid administration undertook some reforms of the public sector by divesting some firms and restructuring others. Under the current divestiture program, the government proposes to sell 250 firms, liquidate 395, merge 80 with other agencies, and transfer 30 to state governments. This program is one of the most ambitious ever undertaken and will ultimately reduce by 65 percent the number of firms owned by the state. The real impact will be far less, however, since the affected enterprises own only about 10 percent of the sector's assets.

The restructuring effort was modestly successful. In the agricultural and food sectors, the government took steps to improve the operation of the giant National Food Marketing Company, CONASUPO. The federal government assumed over 80 percent of CONASUPO's debt (US$1.8 billion) in return for CONASUPO's pledges to streamline its operations and to promote private sector participation in some markets. CONASUPO's monopoly on imports of maize, sorghum, rice, oilseeds, and barley was eliminated, although it remains the sole legal importer of milk and beans. Many of CONASUPO's retail outlets were moved to low-income neighborhoods to improve targeting of subsidies. In addition, the government took the politically difficult step of closing six high-cost sugar mills and is studying the sale or closure of others. An agricultural loan from the World Bank supported the relocation of the retail CONASUPO stores, closure of sugar mills, and other steps to reduce the role of state agricultural enterprises.

Steps were taken to improve the efficiency of state enterprises in other sectors as well. Plants were closed in the fertilizer and steel sectors. The national railroad is being restructured with support from World Bank lending, shipyards are being restructured to benefit from new technology, and reorganization is being contemplated for the state oil company, the petrochemical industry, and the state truck manufacturing firm. Aeromexico, one of two state-owned airlines, was allowed to go bankrupt and is now being reorganized. To show the seriousness of the reform effort, the government arrested the powerful head of the national oil company (PEMEX), which had operated as a corrupt state-within-the-state and thwarted all previous efforts at reform.

Still, public sector influence in the economy remains far too high. The divestiture program notwithstanding, 650 state enterprises remain, compared with between 39 and 84 in 1970 (depending on the definition used). A cutback of 25,000 public sector staff in 1985 did little to offset the increase in employment in the sector from 3.5 million in 1981 to 4.2 million in 1984. Reducing public enterprises' control over the economy will require building a political consensus. Little real improvement can occur, however, as long as the problem is seen as one of attaining technical efficiency rather than of basing the incentive structure on the decisions of individuals in a market instead of on political pressures.

Pricing Reform

Control of consumer prices in the private sector was relaxed to some extent. In December 1982, 55 percent of national production was under strict controls, but by the end of 1986 coverage was reduced to 37 percent. The changes affected mostly industrial products; about 55 percent of primary agriculture, fishing, livestock, and agroindustry remained under strict control. Under the Economic Solidarity Pact announced in December 1987, the strict control list was extended to all basic commodities. The government's plans after the expiration of the pact (which was extended through July 1989) are not clear but may call for a return to the control system in effect in 1987, followed by a gradual phaseout.

As part of the World Bank's agricultural loan, the government in 1989 agreed for the first time to link the prices of crops under the guarantee price system to border prices. Prices would be maintained within a band around their international levels, adjusted for differences in quality and transport costs. Maize and beans, the most important of the crops under the guarantee price system, were excluded because of their political sensitivity and the technical difficulty of including them in the new scheme. The government also agreed to maintain support prices in 1988 at their real 1987 levels. Because pricing did not conform to these agreements, however, the release of the second tranche of the loan was jeopardized.

After the 1982 crisis the government attempted to reduce the subsidies on goods and services produced by government-owned entities by increasing their real prices. Although it is hard to judge the efficiency effects of these efforts, the budgetary effects were salutary. Raising interest rates on preferential credit lines reduced interest rate subsidies channeled through official development banks from 5.4 percent of GDP in 1982 to

3.1 percent in 1985. The government later announced plans to eliminate all interest rate subsidies except those to low-income agricultural borrowers. Higher real retail prices on controlled basic foods were linked with a phaseout of subsidies to processors, including CONASUPO. These subsidies thus decreased by over 80 percent in real terms between 1983 and 1986. Global food subsidies continue only for sugar and some maize products. Attempts to reduce subsidies for oil derivatives and state-run transportation were complicated by the high and unpredictable inflation of costs, with the result that many of the gains in subsidy reduction were lost. For example, public sector prices were increased by around 80 percent in November 1987, but by March 1988 the increases had been so eroded by inflation that the prices in real terms were only about 20 percent over their November levels.

Capital Account

To mitigate the problems created by its strict rules governing foreign investment, the government clarified the basic legislation regulating foreign investment, simplified the approval process, and expanded the class of businesses in which foreign ownership is permitted. In 1986 the government launched a debt-equity conversion program that enables foreign investors to acquire Mexican public sector external debt in the secondary market at discounts of up to 30 percent. These instruments are redeemed by the government at 75 to 100 percent of face value in domestic currency, which is then used to finance certain equity investments and other investment-related expenses.

As a result, approvals of foreign direct investment increased from around US$0.65 billion annually in 1982–85 to nearly US$2 billion in 1985, US$2.4 billion in 1986, and US$3.9 billion in 1987. However, actual inflows (as opposed to approvals) declined in 1984 and rose only slightly to US$0.5 billion in 1985. Inflows were US$1.5 billion in 1986 and US$3.3 billion in 1987, of which 24 percent in 1986 and 46 percent in 1987 were inflows under the swap program, valued at official conversion rates. Foreign investment is concentrated in the in-bond industrial sector (which is required to export a part of production) because the regulatory framework for other industries is perceived as unfriendly and the macroeconomic situation remains uncertain. After the swap program was suspended in November 1987, foreign investment dropped (World Bank 1988a). Capital flight, which had averaged around US$7 billion annually during 1979–82, was reduced to half that in 1983–85 and was negligible in 1986. Capital flight seems to have resumed in 1988, but it was limited to US$2 billion–US$2.5 billion by the government's reluctance to keep domestic interest rates artificially low.

Labor Market Policy

Because the government has raised the minimum wage much more slowly than the inflation rate, real wages have eroded dramatically—by around 40 percent relative to the U.S. dollar, according to some estimates. There have been no major changes in the cumbersome regulations governing labor relations. These regulations, which make it costly for a firm to reduce its labor force, may impose serious rigidities that could make the economy slow to adjust to the new incentive structure created by trade liberalization. Furthermore, the immobility of labor has contributed to the deep decline of real wages; if the market had been able to reallocate labor from declining to booming sectors, real wages would not have had to fall so steeply in order to maintain employment.[1]

Compensatory Measures

General subsidies on basic foods that were begun on a massive scale in the late 1970s were gradually reduced beginning in 1983 and eliminated altogether in 1987, with the exception of those on sugar and some maize products. World Bank staff estimate that the consequent increases in prices reduced the purchasing power of the poorest 20 percent of the urban population by about US$250 million, or by about 6.5 percent of their income. With the exception of the landless poor, the rural population was not adversely affected by higher food prices since they are subsistence farmers or net producers of these products.

To replace the global subsidies, the government instituted a program of targeted food stamps that could be used to buy tortillas, a staple food of the poor, and expanded two other targeted programs (World Bank 1988c). World Bank staff estimate that expenditures on the targeted programs exceed US$250 million annually, which largely compensates for the price rises. Unfortunately, the price of the tortilla stamps, which were redeemable for a given physical quantity of tortillas, was not linked to the price of tortillas. In a period of high inflation, this caused the subsidy component of the program to grow rapidly and limited the program's ability to serve more of the poor. This issue is being addressed in connection with the agricultural loan.

The Outcome

The stabilization and adjustment program has been successful in producing the surpluses on the current account that Mexico will need to service its debt and return to commercial creditworthiness. The program has been less successful in restructuring the economy and reducing the government's role, although there has been progress.

Macroeconomic Balance

Until 1988 the macroeconomic stabilization program notably failed to control inflation, which increased from 20 to 25 percent in 1978–81 to nearly 160 percent in 1987. The experience of other countries with high rates of inflation shows that prospects are poor for eliminating inflationary expectations once they have become established. Nonetheless, events in the late 1980s suggest that the government may persevere better with its current program than it has with past ones. The underlying causes of the accelerating inflation since 1985 are being addressed, with an increase in the primary fiscal surplus from 5.3 percent of GDP in 1987 to about 7.6 percent in 1988. Monthly inflation was reduced from 16 percent in January 1988 to 0.6 percent in September, as measured by consumer prices, while wholesale prices even declined slightly in September and October. Thereafter, monthly inflation was variable, reaching 2.4 percent in early 1989, but then declining.

The dilemma for the government, which has relied on price controls to break inflationary expectations, is how to remove the controls without rekindling those expectations. Despite the large primary surplus, continued reduction of the fiscal deficit is complicated by high interest rates abroad and a domestic interest rate of around 40 percent in real terms. The high real domestic rate appears to be the result of fears that inflation may reappear. Real money balances have not increased in Mexico as they have in other countries after a dramatic decline in inflation.

The record on other macroeconomic performance indicators is mixed. Real GDP decreased by around 6 percent in 1982–83 and fell again by 3.8 percent in 1986. There was modest growth in 1987 and 1988 (about 1 percent), but the future remains uncertain.

External Balance

The reforms were most successful with respect to external trade, and large trade surpluses were created. In 1987 nonoil merchandise exports, both agricultural and manufacturing, stood at 230 percent of their 1982 level. This increase helped offset the adverse impact of the collapse of oil prices and allowed Mexico to accumulate substantial reserves. Reserve accumulation continued through March 1988, but then higher interest rates, declining oil prices, surging imports, and the effects of an exchange rate frozen as part of the anti-inflation program combined to generate a loss of US$6 billion by year's end. The loss came in spite of a continued expansion of nonoil exports. In early 1989 the government began to devalue the peso through a crawling peg at a 17 percent annual rate. It is not clear, however, that this will be enough to sustain the boom in exports.

It is too early to assess the sustainability and long-run impact of the trade reforms. As the economy recovers and imports increase, pressure to reimpose protection is likely—and may already be occurring. A recent study (World Bank 1988b) concluded that the private sector's initial belief that the reforms would be temporary, as well as the government's sluggishness in reducing other sectoral distortions, has impeded the shift toward export expansion and efficient import substitution. Regulations governing foreign investment and especially the hiring and firing of workers tend to reduce factor mobility. Employers must feel confident about the future before they will expand output by increasing either capital or labor inputs. The government's policy reforms do not yet appear to have reached this level of credibility; consistency over a longer period will be required.

Outlook and Political Sustainability of Adjustment

DEBT SERVICE. One can be guardedly optimistic about Mexico's prospects for servicing its debt. Although gross external public and private debt increased by US$17 billion between 1983 and 1987, official reserves increased by US$13.5 billion, so that net debt increased by only US$3.5 billion. In 1987 the country's medium- and long-term debt was about two and a half times its average level during 1978–81. The interest bill was close to twice the average level during 1978–81 and would have been much higher had it not been for the debt rescheduling and falling interest rates since 1984. On the positive side, the ratio of interest to exports was only slightly higher (25.7 percent, compared with 19.8 percent), and the debt service ratio was lower (40.3 percent, compared with 46.8 percent). These payments will have to be sustained over a longer period of time because of the rescheduling, but this should be possible if international interest rates do not escalate, the oil market does not weaken further, and policy reforms already in place are not reversed.

Not everyone accepts this guardedly optimistic scenario. Some argue that as long as Mexico devotes a large part of its export earnings to debt service instead of capital imports, investment and therefore GDP growth will stagnate and generate irresistible pressure for a suspension of payments. To reduce the debt burden, Mexico has implemented a debt buyback program, but it has met with only limited success, and other proposals have been floated (see Dornbusch and Modigliani 1989). It seems likely, however, that although debt reduction will certainly promote some growth, substantial short-term growth can be expected with or without debt reduction when efficiency-enhancing reforms are made in an economy as distorted as Mexico's.

SUSTAINABILITY. Since 1982 Mexico has had three years of negative GDP growth, and it entered 1988 with a lower standard of living than it had when the stabilization process began. Wages have fallen in real terms by around 40 percent, and open unemployment was around 4.5 percent in 1987, compared with 3.8 percent in 1981. Thus it is not easy to argue that the program can be sustained. The government, however, has convinced the populace of the necessity of persisting with the program. It has also cushioned the blow for a large segment of the urban poor by introducing targeted subsidies as it reduced global subsidies. The Salinas administration appears to realize that Mexico's economic future depends on integrating the economy into world markets and increasing its efficiency. As an indication of this commitment, Salinas has filled key policymaking positions with a first-rate economics team rather than with traditional politicians.

The key question, however, remains unanswered: To what extent can this administration overcome the ideas of economic nationalism and the proper economic role of the state that have been entrenched among the Mexican people ever since the Revolution? Two threats to the program appear to be critical. First, if the economy does not soon show signs that the program is bearing fruit, the pressure for retrenchment from vested interests might become impossible to resist. And if the growth response is further delayed, this pressure could jeopardize the macroeconomic stabilization by making it more difficult to reduce the fiscal deficit. Second, if the government receives a large windfall—for example, from another oil bonanza—political pressure to increase its role in the economy may build.

The outlook for sustained reform could probably be improved by a negotiated reduction in the debt burden or a modest improvement in oil revenue. Even without debt reduction, however, some of the reforms seem to be permanent. Certainly Mexico's trade reforms possess many of the characteristics associated with sustained trade reforms in other countries (Michaely 1988), including a relatively stable political system, a strong start to the reforms, a rapid initial depreciation of the real exchange rate, and an external commitment to the GATT.

The World Bank's Role in the Adjustment Process

Before 1988 the only reforms Mexico introduced as a direct result of World Bank loan requirements were in trade liberalization. However, the discussions on the trade-related loans touched on issues only indirectly related to trade reform and led to agreements or loans in the agricultural, steel, and financial sectors. In other areas, reforms were not the basis for loans, but they were viewed by the World Bank as evidence of the government's willingness to make difficult choices. The World Bank played a supportive rather than a leading role in the adjustment process, but by strengthening the position of reform-minded factions in the government, World Bank support made possible reforms that were more extensive than would otherwise have been the case.

Conditionality in World Bank Adjustment Loans

For several reasons Mexico's four trade-related loans from the World Bank in the 1980s contained few conditions that were legal requirements for putting the loan into effect or for tranche release. First, some conditions, such as maintenance of an appropriate exchange rate, are difficult to quantify and monitor. Second, it was clear that the government intended to meet many of the trade liberalization goals in any case. Third, some goals specified in loan documents, such as reducing the public sector borrowing requirement to less than 4 percent in 1988, would be fulfilled only after the loan was almost fully disbursed. Fourth, some of the goals discussed at the time of the loan negotiations, notably reforms of interest rates and price controls, may have been judged too risky or too tangential to the loans' chief aims to be included as conditions.

Two "hybrid" sectoral adjustment loans, for the steel and fertilizer sectors, contained a quick-disbursing component to finance imports, other investment, and technical assistance. Each has tranche-release conditions related to sectoral restructuring, trade liberalization, and implementation of more efficient pricing policies.

The agricultural loan includes conditions related to targeting food subsidies, streamlining state agricultural enterprises, eliminating some restrictions on agricultural imports and exports, setting some guarantee prices close to border prices, restructuring the Ministry of Agriculture, and conducting studies of input and output pricing policies.

The sequencing and the scope of the trade-related loans were appropriate. They addressed the major trade policy distortions, beginning with barriers to exports. It remains to be seen whether these reforms can succeed in stimulating a supply response while so many distortions remain in other parts of the economy and whether new nontariff barriers will be substituted for the quantitative restrictions that have been removed. In the case of both the fertilizer and agricultural loans, some conditions believed by World Bank staff to be important were dropped during negotiations (for example, reduction of the coverage of food price controls), and other desirable changes were not considered because they were politically sensitive (for example, privatization of fertilizer production).

Since the World Bank has made no structural adjustment loans to Mexico, it has relied on the IMF to monitor macroeconomic performance. Most of the World Bank's sectoral adjustment lending to Mexico has been concurrent with IMF programs. The exception was the first trade policy loan, which was approved in July 1986 after disbursements under the IMF program had been suspended. The trade loan required that Mexico's external financing needs for 1986 be met, and since commercial lending was contingent on Mexico's reaching agreement with the IMF on an adjustment program, this became a de facto condition of effectiveness. Some of the recent sectoral adjustment loans have included a tranche-release condition requiring an appropriate macroeconomic policy framework.

Effectiveness of Implementation

All the conditions included in the four trade-related loans were met, and the reforms have so far been sustained. The government also met many of the goals enumerated in the loans but not identified as requirements for disbursement.

Release of the first tranche of the agricultural loan was delayed because of lack of agreement on the terms of reference of a series of studies and the failure to remove export controls on high-quality cuts of beef. This delay in turn led to a postponement of the release of the second tranche, which is also threatened by the government's failure to adjust producer prices because of its concern about inflation.

The fertilizer loan never went into effect because the agreement negotiated between the Mexican Fertilizer Company and the central government did not call for the plant closures that were required by the loan. Nor were the required increases in fertilizer prices introduced.

Lessons from the Adjustment Experience

The main lessons from Mexico's experience are related to the sequencing of stabilization and adjustment and to the dialogue between the World Bank and the country in the context of policy-based lending. Questions remain, however, about the economy's future response to the changes that have been made.

Sequencing

Some economists have argued that when inflation rates are high (say, greater than 25 percent a year), priority should be given to stabilization, with structural adjustment policies postponed until after inflation rates have fallen (see, for example, Corbo and de Melo 1987; Fischer 1986; and Sachs 1986). In a highly inflationary environment, it is reasoned, relative prices among sectors are so variable that they will give uncertain signals about where investment should occur.

Conversely, Mexico's experience between late 1983 and mid-1985 shows the danger in stabilization without adjustment. Inflation rates were falling and economic activity was rekindling at the beginning of this period, but the recovery occurred in an environment distorted by a protectionist trade structure. Thus resources were attracted to the protected sectors and away from exportable sectors. The consequent balance of payments crisis led to the crash program of trade reform that began in July 1985. Through the end of 1987 that program was carried out during a period of high and rising inflation. Yet in February 1988 the World Bank concluded that the incentive structure had shifted in the expected direction, with both import protection and the bias against exportable sectors having been reduced. Although shifts in investment had been impeded by regulatory and other constraints, the expected shifts in resource allocation were nevertheless apparently beginning (World Bank 1988b).

Inflation, it appears, adds "noise" to relative price movements, but it does not alter the fundamental pattern of shifts in prices following changes in trade policy. To some extent, economic agents know beforehand what sectors will gain or lose from trade reform, and they can check their expectations against average price movements over a fairly short period. Inflation, therefore, should not be considered an insuperable obstacle to adjustment. Other barriers to resource movement, such as regulatory constraints, may be as important. If that is so, then an adjustment program should be wide-ranging and should give special attention to regulatory reforms.

Mexico's second and current attempt at stabilization occurred in a regime of significantly restructured incentives. The boom in nonoil exports, together with external resources from the World Bank, the IMF, and commercial banks, provided reserves that made it possible for the government to use the exchange rate as a nominal anchor in its anti-inflationary program. The fact that the antiexport bias had been greatly reduced while the exchange rate had reached a very competitive level at the end of 1987 meant that the exchange rate could be frozen throughout much of 1988. This led to a real appreciation, without tremendously depressing exports. In Mexico's case, stabilization before adjustment was an unqualified failure, while stabilization after adjustment may tentatively be judged a success.

The Trade Reform Program

The Mexican trade reform program shows how constructive dialogue between the World Bank and a country can be combined with policy-based lending to achieve worthwhile objectives. The government planned its import liberalization program and announced its schedule in advance. When the timing was opportune, the government did not hesitate to accelerate the process since the World Bank had assured Mexico that "overperformance" would be credited toward a second trade loan. The process was carried out in stages, to give time for any necessary adjustment of plans. Tariffs were first substituted for nontariff protection to make the system visible; this in turn made it easier to monitor the reform and eventually to reduce protection. The Mexican experience with import liberalization may provide a model for future World Bank operations in the trade sector.

Liberalization of exports began several years before liberalization of imports, in accordance with the generally accepted argument that imports respond more quickly to liberalization and therefore create a balance of trade deficit unless exports have been liberalized first. As it turned out, imports declined in 1983, 1986, and 1987, apparently because of domestic demand contraction and (in 1983) a shortage of foreign exchange. It is not clear that any balance of payments crisis would have been precipitated had the liberalization sequence been reversed. Export-import sequencing may not be an important determinant of the success of a reform program (see also Michaely 1988).

The trade reform dialogue between Mexico and the World Bank owed its success to two factors. First, the World Bank did not press for reforms that were at odds with the government's own program. Rather, it pressed for more far-reaching reforms than the government might otherwise have considered. The World Bank took into account both the reform-minded and the conservative elements in the government, and by its encouragement and incentives apparently strengthened the former. Second, the dialogue began at a propitious time. In 1982 a new administration was assuming power and policies were still in the formative stage. It was helpful to the World Bank's position that this new administration was in deep need of financial assistance and headed by technocratic elements less steeped in Mexico's traditional politics than previous government leaders. It was also helpful that the government was petitioning for accession to the GATT and was therefore required to fulfill conditions that paralleled those that the World Bank judged necessary for structural adjustment. Mexico was given full credit for reforms it carried out in order to accede to the GATT, even when these were not preexisting loan conditions. The Mexican experience supports Michaely's (1988) conclusion that a multilateral commitment to reform, although it does not guarantee success, at least helps to prevent temporary aberrations in the reform process.

The trade liberalization process largely bypassed agricultural imports; almost all basic food imports are still under direct or indirect government control. The World Bank should continue to press for changes in this area, being careful to reduce protection to agriculture only to the extent that industrial protection is also reduced. (Although this may argue for a rather slow reduction in agricultural tariff rates, it does not argue for sluggishness in eliminating import licensing, government monopolies, and other controls in these markets.) The World Bank should also pay careful attention to any evidence that antidumping, health, safety, and pollution regulations are being used as protection devices.

Complementary Policies

The key question remaining is whether and how quickly the economic structure will respond to these changes in trade policy. Investment has been slow to respond to the new price signals for several reasons (World Bank 1988b). Initially, investors did not find the government's reforms to be credible, and they were also deterred by an unstable real exchange rate. In addition, investible funds were scarce and expensive because the government had tightened monetary policy without substantially reducing its own borrowing requirements.

There has been only a slight reduction in government direction of the economy. The government and the World Bank have only recently begun to address issues of sectoral liberalization. There is a danger—and some evidence of this is surfacing already—that the full gains from trade liberalization will not be realized because of the delays in following through on these other reforms. They should probably constitute the main focus of future World Bank lending to Mexico.

Note

Many thanks to Bela Balassa, Suman Bery, Vittorio Corbo, John Johnson, Don Keesing, Bill McCleary, Jaime de Melo, and Sreenivasa Ramachandran for helpful comments on early drafts of this chapter. Remaining errors, of course, are my responsibility.

1. I owe this point to Vittorio Corbo, chief of the World Bank's Macroeconomic Adjustment and Growth Division.

References

Blanco, H., and P. Garber. 1986. "Recurrent Devaluation and Speculative Attacks on the Mexican Peso." *Journal of Political Economy* (February):148–66.

Corbo, Vittorio, and Jaime de Melo. 1987. "Lessons from the Southern Cone Policy Reforms." *World Bank Research Observer* 2 (2):111–42.

Dornbusch, Rudiger, and F. Modigliani. 1989. "Easing the Mexican Interest Rate." *Wall Street Journal*, January 3.

Fischer, Stanley. 1986. "Issues in Medium-Term Macroeconomic Adjustment." *World Bank Research Observer* 1 (2):163–82.

Michaely, Michael. 1988. "Trade Liberalization Policies: Lessons of Experience." Paper prepared for the conference "For a New Policy Toward Foreign Trade in Brazil." São Paulo, Brazil, April 11–12.

Sachs, Jeffrey. 1986. "Conditionality and the Debt Crisis: Some Thoughts for the World Bank." Development Research Department, World Bank, Washington, D.C.

World Bank. 1987. "Mexico after the Oil Boom: Refashioning a Development Strategy." Latin America and Caribbean Region Report 6659-ME. Washington, D.C.

———. 1988a. "Direct Foreign Investment in Mexico: Past Patterns and Future Strategy." Latin America and Caribbean Region Report. Washington, D.C.

———. 1988b. "Mexico: Trade Policy Reform and Economic Adjustment." Latin America and Caribbean Region Report 7314-ME. Washington, D.C.

———. 1988c. *Targeted Programs for the Poor during Structural Adjustment: A Summary of a Symposium on Poverty and Adjustment, April 1988.* Washington, D.C.

Comments

Vittorio Corbo

JOHN NASH's chapter provides a well-balanced interpretation of Mexico's adjustment program. Since I agree with most of it, my comments will concentrate on certain points that require further elaboration.

Although it is true that the crisis of the early 1980s in Mexico was caused by expansionary fiscal and monetary policies—which, given a fixed exchange rate regime, resulted in appreciation of the real exchange rate, capital flight, and the accumulation of a large foreign debt—one should also recognize that Mexico made major adjustments on the fiscal front after 1982. The primary balance (that is, net of interest payments) improved by nearly 16.0 percent of GDP by 1988. The operational deficit also improved in spite of the high real interest rates on government debt. This fiscal adjustment is all the more remarkable in view of the drastic decline in the terms of trade in 1986 as a result of the drop in the price of oil.

Nash is right to indicate that in the first half of 1985 the elections had a negative impact on fiscal adjustment efforts. After the elections, however, not only were fiscal adjustment efforts intensified, but a major restructuring of trade incentives was initiated.

An aggressive policy of nominal devaluations in 1986–87 resulted in a large surplus in the current account of the balance of payments, as well as an acceleration of inflation. The acceleration of inflation placed the overall adjustment program in jeopardy. To their credit, the Mexican authorities implemented a heterodox stabilization program in late 1987. This program included *further* fiscal adjustment and the use of income policies to deal with the persistent elements of inflation. To date, Mexico's stabilization program, with its large dose of fiscal adjustment, has been quite successful in reducing inflation.

In the area of structural reform, Mexico has also made important progress. After the onset of the debt crisis, Mexico decided to manage the crisis by introducing a host of trade restrictions that further isolated Mexico from the world economy. In the middle of 1985, after much internal discussion, the Mexican government initiated a major restructuring of its trade regime that resulted in a maximum 20 percent tariff rate and eliminated most quantitative restrictions.

Mexico has made major progress in stabilizing and restructuring its very distorted domestic economy. To reap the benefits of its structural reforms, however, Mexico needs to succeed in stabilizing its economy. It also needs to complement its trade policy reforms with a liberalization of the domestic financial system and the rationalization of its highly inefficient system of domestic regulation.

In conclusion, in spite of the heavy burden of debt accumulated mainly to finance capital flight and unproductive public investment, Mexico has made much progress in adjusting its economy. Ultimate success will be achieved when stabilization is more permanent and growth is sustainable. Mexico is well on the way to achieving these objectives.

Comments on Latin America

S. Shahid Husain

IN SUMMING UP the discussion on Latin America, I would like to add my own thoughts on some often neglected, but critical, aspects of the adjustment process: the political economy, including the role of government, and the social dimensions. These sociopolitical considerations bear on the success of economic reforms. They determine how much adjustment is carried out, how long the process takes, and what the results will be.

The two countries discussed here, Chile and Mexico, are relatively large economies that have made substantial progress in adjustment. In the case of Chile adjustment has in recent years been accompanied by rapid growth. No one, however, should ignore the fact that both countries have had a tremendous continuity of government and governmental processes. In the case of Chile continuity came through an authoritarian, dictatorial regime. It is not coincidental that adjustment in Chile is a process that goes back to the mid-1970s and did not begin to bear fruit until well into the middle 1980s. Mexico's government, too, although nominally democratic, has been authoritarian and has had a much greater integration among the civil service, the political process, and labor than do most Latin American countries. So the importance of the continuity of policies is inescapable.

The crisis of economics and economic development in Latin America is fundamentally a crisis of government. The process of adjustment involves, to a great extent, determining how to reduce to reasonable proportions the tremendous amount of rent creation and rent receiving that has proliferated around the government. The question to consider is whether in large, diverse countries such as Brazil and Argentina, with volatile political processes, results similar to those achieved in Mexico and Chile can be expected.

We should not be deluded by the relative smoothness of this process in Chile and Mexico into thinking that it can be duplicated with ease in other countries. The process of adjustment is going to be very discontinuous, in part because of factors related to the cost of adjustment and the society's ability to withstand it. Although Chile and Mexico were able to withstand some of the pain that accompanies adjustment, such as the tremendous decline in real wages in Mexico, a similar decline over an extended period in countries such as Brazil and Argentina is likely to provoke substantial political repercussions. Another issue with regard to the discontinuity of adjustment concerns needed reductions in regulations and in the size of the corporate state. In Chile this process has gone the furthest. How fast can it proceed elsewhere? For example, despite efforts in Argentina to privatize the airlines and the telephone company, the government has not been able to mobilize the political will to implement these changes. Argentinian railways therefore continue to lose a billion dollars a year while carrying only 6 percent of total traffic.

Although we need to talk about the economic issues of adjustment, we should not lose sight of the political and social issues of adjustment. These issues ultimately form the background of economic policies and can limit their effectiveness within a relatively short time. It is precisely in this context that the approach of the latter half of the 1980s has become untenable. We at the World Bank have assumed a total smoothness of the adjustment process, a total synchronization of foreign assistance and domestic adjustment. We have assumed that the frictions in the process of adjustment were going to be very limited and that we could go on increasing the debt of these countries as adjustment proceeded. That approach clearly did not work. It is to be hoped that a meaningful process of reduction of debt service burdens—and I purposely use the term "debt service"—will provide governments with greater maneuverability in the very difficult task of realigning the domestic benefits and costs of the economic policy.

We also need to look more closely at the issue of poverty and the social consequences of adjustment. We learned a good deal in the 1980s about the issues of adjustment, but not enough about the process of adjustment and the issues of transition. This book discusses some of these issues, such as how, in the process of adjustment, governments can and should institute measures and programs that cushion the less-privileged and vulnerable groups. A great deal more work needs to be done in this area if the process of adjustment is going to work in the Latin American countries. This is particularly the case in countries that do not have authoritarian regimes and where people therefore will feel more free to come out onto the streets to protest. If the problem of the less privileged and the poor is not addressed, such protests may contribute to the disruption of the entire adjustment process.

That brings me to the role of the World Bank. Although we have worked hard on adjustment, success has been greatest in cases in which we have essentially supported and complemented the commitments of the government and its own efforts. By and large, in countries where that commitment has not been present, success has been marginal at best, despite major efforts. And that simply means that more of the World Bank's efforts need to go into countries where that fundamental commitment and the proper conditions exist.

We in the World Bank and the international community will have to show a great deal more patience with this process. The factors that led to the present malaise developed over twenty or thirty years as a result of the economic policies in these countries and, in some cases, the policies of international lenders. Consider, for example, the case of Colombia and Honduras, which have massive overinvestment in electric power. This investment was externally financed and has contributed to high debt service obligations. Most of this investment was financed by the World Bank and the Inter-American Development Bank. So responsibility is not one-sided; commercial lenders and to a certain extent official lenders such as the World Bank are also responsible for the economic problems in many of these countries.

Essentially, this means that adjustment will take time. In many cases there will be two steps forward and one step backward, and we will have to look for the second- and third-best solutions.

PART IV

Assessment

23 *Lessons of Experience and the Future of Adjustment Lending*

THIS CHAPTER uses the panel format to bring together a group of distinguished economists and practitioners from the World Bank, the International Monetary Fund, universities, and the governments of adjustment loan recipient countries. They were asked to draw lessons from the decade of experience with adjustment lending that is described in this book. Their views, comments, and criticisms and their forecasts for the future of adjustment lending are presented here.

Joe Abbey

The real issue here is the search for a workable development strategy, and adjustment lending must be viewed as part of that strategy. The question of whether adjustment lending or structural adjustment should be considered a medium- to long-term effort really is a nonissue for many countries because their development effort is necessarily a long-term process. Although this question becomes more pressing at times of crisis, it must not detract developing countries from their major concern, which is to get on with the process of economic development.

What is important, especially for sustainability, is how adjustment programs are formulated and the role of each of the players—governments, the World Bank, and the International Monetary Fund (IMF)—in that process. Governments are confronted by many serious tradeoffs. First are the tradeoffs between the short term and the long term, and quite often governments may be tempted to take the short-run benefits at the expense of long-term gains. Second are the technical tradeoffs and legitimate policy conflicts, such as fiscal prudence versus trade liberalization. A third class of problems facing governments is the result of conflicts in policymaking and advice between the IMF and the World Bank. Those caught in the middle are not amused by such disagreements, particularly when there are legitimate policy conflicts to be resolved.

A look at the totality of difficulties facing a country about to embark on a program of adjustment—institutional rigidities, market weaknesses, administrative and managerial weaknesses—brings certain issues into clearer focus. It is particularly clear that unless the government "owns" the program, in the sense that the political tradeoffs have been taken care of, the program cannot work. When that condition is lacking, the World Bank might believe that a dialogue is taking place, but in fact what is happening is that a country that needs money—very badly, too—is being forced to take a few measures that it does not understand and that the World Bank itself is not really confident about. As this book points out, the countries that have done well are those that had their own programs before IMF or World Bank involvement or those that had the technical capabilities to take these programs and adapt them to their needs. In this regard, there seems to be some argument about whose program the Ghanaian Economic Recovery Program is. Some of us in Ghana, of course, think the program is ours, but frequently it is referred to as the ESAF Program or Ghana SAL I or SAL II.

Nevertheless, the World Bank and the IMF do have a critical role in the adjustment process: to force governments to think through what they plan to do and to understand all the ramifications of their programs. Frequently, the necessary markets or other institutions are not there, or they do not work well or as expected. Failure to take into account institutional characteristics specific to the country can lead to poor advice. Advice must be grounded in thorough and detailed analysis; the blanket recommendation of generally accepted policies can be disastrous in particular circumstances. Financial deregulation, for example, if implemented under unfavorable conditions, can actually lead to increased financial instability. This was the case in Ghana in 1987, when poor advice concerning financial deregulation was imposed on the country. The expectation was that as soon as financial deregulation took place, interest rates on deposits would go up. It was clear to us in Ghana, however, that the absence of nonbank financial intermediaries and of other debt instruments made it unlikely that deregulating interests rates would lead to the expected results. And as events unfolded, the banks in Ghana took advantage of deregulation, widened their margins, and are now paying very low rates of interest to depositors and even turning depositors away. It is not surprising that interest rates are low. The institutional features of Ghana's financial sector were not considered carefully by our international advisers, and now they tell us we must raise interest rates. This is the outcome of inadequate knowledge and poor advice.

Other problems arise because of a narrow focus on aggregates or on only part of the picture, without regard for the reality behind the data. Thus, for example, after the 1987 conference of Ghana's external lenders, there was concern that the country was walking into a death trap because it was facing a 70 percent debt service burden. But everyone failed to consider the net flows. The debt service ratio measures only gross outflow; it says nothing about net inflow or net outflow. Now, however, the other side of the picture is finally being considered. Everybody is talking about the large resources that are being given to the Ghanaian program, and nobody is talking about the debt. Between 1983 and 1988 Ghana received from all sources US$3.6 billion and paid out (to clear arrears in interest and principal) a little over US$2.6 billion. So the net inflow to Ghana was about US$1 billion. This type of thing is missed when people fail to look behind the aggregates.

Another example concerns cuts in social services or social expenditures that accompany adjustment. These aggregates mean nothing unless one takes account of the quality of the expenditures that are being cut and those that remain. Thus, for example, total government expenditure in Chile went down by 5 percent in real terms and yet the quality of life did not deteriorate; in fact, there was an improvement.

When the social costs of adjustment are being analyzed, other intervening factors must be considered as well as the adjustment program. For example, in 1982–83 Ghana had the worst drought in its recorded history, and about a million Ghanaians returned home from abroad. We decided to launch the Economic Recovery Program at the height of the drought because we believed it would be wrong to wait for the drought to abate and then start a program that would require massive increases in imported items. The program would then have been more difficult to manage and would have provoked cynicism. Therefore, we had to move in the middle of the drought. When malnutrition and high infant mortality rates were reported in rural areas in 1983, the blame was put on the program, which had not even started until 1983, instead of on the drought. Of course, if the Ghanaian recovery program was responsible for the malnutrition in 1983–84, it also caused one of the quickest turnabouts in history. As we had predicted, when the rains returned, when the incentives began to work and food production picked up, infant mortality rates improved and dietary problems were eased. But the wrong story had gone out already, and many people believed that Ghana had experienced massive social costs of adjustment.

The only way to go forward is for governments to clearly state their objectives and how they intend to achieve them. Because these things are often not clearly articulated, either by the government or by the international organizations involved, the structural benchmarks are rarely achieved. I believe that the World Bank and IMF can best fulfill their roles not by using their money as leverage, but by forcing the necessary analysis. By compelling governments to spell out how they expect to achieve, if not their ultimate goals, at least their intermediate goals, the World Bank and the IMF can help policymakers avoid the pitfalls experienced by others who blindly tried to follow set paths and came to grief. This imposition of discipline is the more important part of the dialogue process, and many other practices that pass for dialogue are counterproductive. Once we know the groundwork is firm, we can begin to worry about sustainability.

Stanley Fischer

The evaluation of adjustment lending is not only extremely difficult, but also essential. None of the methods of evaluation are entirely satisfactory. First, there are statistical tests that look at countries with and without adjustment lending. Although these tests provide some useful information, they are vulnerable to criticism from those who look at each observation and say "yes, but Korea did this," "yes, but Mali did that"—but that is true of every regression ever done. We work with statistical methods because they provide useful data for evaluation. The second method is case studies, and the information they provide is also useful. Third are econometric models, which are themselves problematic in many ways but do provide information. Fourth is a special group of case studies prepared by the Operations Evaluation Department (OED) in the World Bank. It is surprising how little these are used. That may be because they tend to come in very late and are very long.

In evaluating adjustment, we have to pull the evidence together from wherever we can get it. We are not going to find *definitive* evidence on the success of adjustment lending or, for that matter, on anything in economics. What caused the Great Depression? We do not know with complete certainty. Why did the United States start to grow in 1982? Was it supply-side economics, was it good old-fashioned Keynesian expansion? We do not have a definitive answer. We look at the evidence, make as strong an argument as we can, and then we have to proceed on that basis. As Arjun Sengupta of the IMF emphasizes, the fact that we do not know does not excuse us from making decisions. Our obligation is to evaluate the evidence as best we can, listen to all the arguments, and then make a decision about the actions we want to take, taking into account that our knowledge is imperfect and that we should remain flexible and always on the lookout for new evidence. That is the best that we can hope for.

Of course, there are people who prefer not to look at any evidence. Frank Paish, the British economist and forecaster, said it was very dangerous to look at our past forecasts because that made us lose our nerve. But we have to look back in order to reach decisions that we are willing to stand by on the basis of the best evidence we can find.

The problems of adjustment lending fall into three categories and are related to adjustment in the countries themselves, relations between the World Bank and the countries receiving adjustment loans, and internal World Bank controls that affect adjustment lending.

In looking at problems of adjustment from the country's perspective, it is important to emphasize both short-term macroeconomic adjustment and long-term structural adjustment involving development strategy. An adequate macroeconomic framework is absolutely essential. That is clear from the many cases in which the macroeconomic framework has not been appropriate. I would single out—in addition to the fiscal problem that has already been emphasized—the problem of extremely high inflation rates. No program in which an inflation rate of 600 percent is expected over the next nine months can conceivably be sound, and yet such programs have occasionally been certified as acceptable.

These are long-term and extremely complicated problems. The economic transformations now being attempted in adjustment programs took decades and longer to achieve in the industrial economies. The tendency is to introduce extremely sophisticated financial and governmental structures into countries that probably cannot support them. We should concentrate on fundamentals, however; the countries that require adjustment loans have major distortions and major gaps, and we had better concentrate on correcting them. The refinements—the seventy-ninth condition in an adjustment loan that at best would bring only an epsilon of improvement—are way beyond what is known and what should be imposed on a country that may well lack the capacity to carry it out.

Adjustment is a continuing process. It is still taking place in the industrial economies, and it will take a very long time in the developing economies. Our obligation is to differentiate between what is essential and what is a luxury at a particular stage of development. Joe Abbey emphasized the importance of thinking policies through and looking ahead, and both the World Bank and the IMF can help with this kind of rigorous analysis in their interactions with member countries.

Of the many complications that can arise in adjustment lending, those involving the financial sector, foreign exchange controls, and so on should cause particular concern. An enormous amount of information is needed to deal with these delicate systems; there are matters of trust and matters of prudential regulation. Even many highly developed countries have had great difficulty with their financial systems, and in many developing countries the problems in this sector are clear: massive bankruptcies, interest rates completely out of line, and so forth. These things have to be fixed. When we begin to introduce ultrasophisticated financial instruments, however, I worry whether that is what we ought to be doing.

With respect to the mutual problems between the countries receiving adjustment loans and the World Bank, the crucial issue is "ownership" of the adjustment program. For some countries, ownership is virtually all that is needed. If a country "owns" a program and has the administrative capability necessary to design and implement it, we at the World Bank do not have to do very much. We can discuss the program with the country and see it get under way, but then we should relax. If a country has the commitment but does not have the administrative capacity, we can take a more active role. In those cases, slightly more detailed adjustment lending and greater specification of conditions may be useful.

Ernest Stern in the opening chapter touched on problems related to internal World Bank controls when he said that adjustment lending is addictive both to governments and to the World Bank. One could also say that adjustment lending is seductive—its allure lies in being close to the powerful, in being able to say "I spoke to the president" or "I was assured by the finance minister." Because it is seductive, we need strong procedures, rules within the World Bank delineating the conditions under which adjustment lending will take place, such as assurances that the macroeconomic framework is right. In particular, we need to ensure that the patterns of disbursement will not cause trouble down the road. We do have to control adjustment lending. Some people now believe that World Bank staff cannot even talk to a country unless they give them a great deal of money up front. That is wrong. It is up to the World Bank to perform the economic and sector work and provide the technical advice that will make project lending more attractive to its members and its staff.

Internally, the problem is how to enforce our own controls on adjustment lending. There is pressure to lend from within the World Bank. There is no denying that; indeed there *should* be pressure to lend. We just asked our member governments for US$75 billion because we have a task to do. The pressure to lend comes not from a belief that we should shovel out money regardless of its use, but rather from an implicit contract by World Bank management to deliver loans of a given quality in given amounts. The pressure to lend is the pressure to go out, to find the opportunities, and to set up the good loans.

The World Bank's internal procedures do not encourage simplicity in lending, however. Consider, for instance, the system for reviewing loans internally. Loan documents are distributed for comment, and it is incumbent on everyone to add something, to show that he or she has contributed. Similarly, in the Operations Committee, people pick up on a point here and a point there. By an inevitable process of accretion, the loans become more and more complicated as a result of the World Bank's review process. I do not know how to stop that process, but we have to think about improving it.

One change in internal procedures for which there are strong arguments is from multi-tranche to single-tranche operations. When a country has taken ownership of a program and we are confident, as we are, say, in the case of Indonesia, that the government will deliver what it has promised, then I cannot see the objection to single-tranche lending. These are not one-shot operations; they involve a sequence of operations. Single-tranche lending helps to clarify the ownership issue and it helps to keep loans simple.

The balance of payments link is another important internal issue. We need to maintain that link both for purposes of internal control and to ensure that we do not unnecessarily increase a country's indebtedness. But at the same time we should find a way of undertaking long-term policy lending: providing money in small amounts over longer periods for adjustment, including institutional development, is absolutely crucial to the development effort. We played with that concept in the 1988 report on adjustment lending but could not come up with a satisfactory instrument. We should be using our ingenuity to create some type of loan that disburses less rapidly than adjustment loans but that is nonetheless directed at adjustment. Such a loan would give countries that have undertaken a serious program of institutional and other development the assurance that the World Bank would be there supporting a long-term adjustment process.

With regard to the issue of World Bank–IMF coordination, we have reached a very important new agreement with the IMF. We will no longer try to sort out any macroeconomic disagreements with the IMF in competing negotiations with the debtor countries, but will discuss these disagreements with the IMF. The new agreement recognizes that countries benefit from the different professional opinions offered through the two institutions and requires the institutions to discuss these matters. When there are genuine differences between the World Bank and the IMF concerning macroeconomics from the viewpoint of development, it is extremely important to discuss those issues. We have to work out methods for doing that.

In addition, the agreement gives the World Bank primary responsibility for structural adjustment. From the perspective of development, structural adjustment policies are the crucial ones to deal with. The macroeconomics framework is important, and we have to be sure it is right and that changes do not violate development priorities. But it is the primary responsibility of the World Bank to tackle development issues through the adjustment process. We are going to have to concentrate on this and improve the quality of our analysis. That is the challenge—a crucial one—that we must meet.

Manuel Guitián

A striking feature of the process of adjustment in the 1980s is the extent to which it was dominated by the events of the 1970s. Even more striking is that the factors that complicated the environment in the 1980s included not only the problems but also the solutions from the 1970s. For brevity's sake I will focus on global developments without discussing the role of specific policies pursued by individual countries. I cannot overstress the importance of this caveat because, in many respects, the global trends that I will outline are the joint results of all those policies.

Put briefly, the 1970s were characterized by events such as the sharp changes in terms of trade and corresponding shifts in current account imbalances, by problems such as high inflation and faltering growth, and by solutions such as recycling and large capital flows, particularly from commercial banks to sovereign borrowers. In many respects the 1970s witnessed a revolt against the growing interdependence toward which the international economy had been struggling during the 1950s and 1960s. This revolt was made evident not only by the surge of protectionist pressures but also by the move to flexibility in exchange rates in search of the widely heralded degree of freedom that would give autonomy to national economic policies—a goal that, in the end, proved to be most elusive. But another factor tended to counter these trends: growing capital movements provided cohesion (at least for some time) to the international financial system. The international lending-borrowing process was therefore perceived as part of the solution to the period's difficulties.

The start of the 1980s provided an excellent illustration of the interdependence of economic phenomena, in particular the ease with which the correction of one imbalance can thwart the solution adopted for some other imbalance.

In the industrial world, inflation in the 1970s shifted the pendulum toward policies to bringing it promptly under control. The resolution of the inflation issue was accompanied by the emergence of high real interest rates and a slowdown in economic activity. A by-product of this process was that the decisions made in borrowing countries when real interest rates were negative now became untenable, and the consequences of continuing to follow them soon surfaced: concerns about creditworthiness arose among lenders, and the flow of international loans and capital dried up abruptly.

In effect, the solution of the inflation problem was accompanied by events that brought about the debt service difficulties. In other words, what had been perceived as a solution in the 1970s (recycling) became a problem of the 1980s (debt). Thus a first conclusion is that a most urgent concern must be to ensure that the solutions devised for the difficulties of the 1980s do not become the problems for the 1990s.

Adjustment in the 1980s was aimed at resolving the debt problem, possibly one of the most elusive economic objectives sought in this decade. By now the main stages of the solution are familiar: initially, the pursuit of a debt strategy based on the assurance of external financial support for domestic adjustment efforts; subsequently, reinforcement of the strategy by the addition of the growth imperative—growth to be achieved through structural reforms and continued financial assistance in a variety of forms, including menus of financing modalities; and now, the addition to the financing menus of schemes for reducing debt and debt service, which are supported by international institutions and made available to countries undertaking a strong adjustment effort.

Each stage provided evidence of the difficulties that led to successive adaptations of the strategy. At the outset, improvements in the balance of payments and economic recovery in debtor countries were slower than expected; thus available resources were severely constrained and there was a need for increased domestic efficiency and continued external support to ensure growth. The difficulty in restoring lending and capital flows led, in turn, to menus of financing options and then to internationally supported debt-reduction proposals.

There was scope for dissent at each point, and dissent, of course, surfaced on each occasion. Questions arose concerning the mix and sequencing of adjustment and financing: Was the blend adequate? Which should come first, adjustment or financing? Similar dilemmas surfaced at later stages as perceptions differed (and will continue to differ) about the appropriateness of an adjustment effort, a financing package, a proper rate of growth, or—looking ahead—the proper scope of debt-reduction packages, to name just a few. In the process, however, there is a risk that attention may be diverted from what is possibly the most fundamental question on this front: What are the conditions necessary for the restoration of normality to capital flows? This question brings up another urgent concern for the 1990s: the need to ensure that both the level and the structure of international capital flows freely conform to a market-determined pattern of economic incentives.

The policy issues that will need to be addressed in the years ahead are numerous. For the developing countries, the preceding chapters have examined areas of policy reform and country experiences, and there is little that I can add to these analyses. I will refer to the industrial countries later in the context of the role of international institutions.

But certain general principles and areas are worth stressing with regard to policy issues:

- The complementarity between macroeconomic and structural policies and the importance of consistency among them as well as persistence in their implementation
- The relevance of the varying time horizons in policy formulation and the consequent need to ensure consistency between short- and long-run aims and to take account of the different lags in the effects of policies
- The search for operational criteria for the implementation of structural reforms; for example, their scope (how widespread should they be?),

their pace (how fast should they proceed?), and sequence (which one should go first?).

As in the past, international institutions will continue to have an essential role in the coming decade. They are uniquely placed to provide a genuinely international perspective on issues confronting the world economy. For them to do so appropriately and effectively will require a concern with the system as a whole in order to safeguard common objectives and gauge the responsibility of the parts. A necessary means to these various ends is a commonly agreed code of conduct, which of course exists in the form of the Articles of Agreement of the IMF and of the World Bank (and the General Agreement on Tariffs and Trade as well).

These institutions have a responsibility to demonstrate persistently that the opportunities opened by economic interdependence far outweigh the constraints—a responsibility that calls for a careful balance of international and national considerations. Good economic analysis will help, but also needed is the ability to promptly spot shifts in that balance over time, because such shifts do occur—as happened, for example, in the context of the debt strategy.

Given my affiliation with the IMF, I will focus on the very basic challenge lying ahead for this institution. The challenge calls for yet another delicate balance, one between its jurisdictional or regulatory activities and its financial assistance operations—that is, the balance between surveillance and conditionality. The IMF has to ensure coordination between surveillance and conditionality, so to speak.

Surveillance is needed to ensure a favorable and stable global economic environment. The linkages between the whole and the parts have hardly ever been clearer than in recent years. For example, the world economic setting has been characterized by historically high real interest rates for some time; it seems clear that their return to normal levels will be as important as, if not more important than, some of the schemes under consideration for the resolution of debt problems. To put it more generally, individual countries can be expected to pursue specific domestic policies only if similar behavior is pursued elsewhere. Thus a challenge for the IMF, in addition to the many others that it will have to meet both by itself and cooperatively with the World Bank, will be to bring surveillance back onto center stage along with the more visible conditionality.

The 1990s are likely to be an eventful decade, and we must seek to ensure that its legacy to the next century is one of sustainable solutions rather than recurrent problems.

These are some of the issues that lie ahead:

- Resolving industrial countries' payments imbalances. This will require establishing the respective responsibilities of the deficit and surplus countries, which are by no means symmetrical.

- Restoring balance to the composition of demand (and output) in several dimensions: consumption and investment, public and private, external and internal.
- Determining the role of markets in the process.
- Ensuring continued effectiveness of the debt strategy.
- Returning capital markets to normal.
- Ensuring growth.

The experiences of the 1980s confirm the importance of consistency in policies and persistence in their implementation. Perhaps the main lesson is the limitations of economic policy when it stretches far beyond the setting of a predictable framework for economic decisions.

Gerald Helleiner

Perhaps an appropriate starting point is the observation that we do not have total agreement concerning precisely what "adjustment lending" is. Ernest Stern, in chapter 1, said that structural adjustment "ought to be anchored in balance of payments problems"; others have argued that it is a matter not of macroeconomic variables but of (microeconomic) resource allocation and the institutions and decisionmaking systems that determine it. If we do not agree on the ultimate meaning and purpose of adjustment loans it should not be surprising if we also cannot agree on conclusions about either the key issues or the record.

There can be little doubt that whatever the original balance of payments–related origins of adjustment loans, they quickly acquired all manner of other elements. Everyone who had a view about what was crucial for growth in a particular country rapidly joined the effort to influence local policies through program lending. A veritable Christmas tree of structural policies began to be advocated, some with more obvious balance of payments implications than others. (Obviously, structural reforms frequently *do* have balance of payments implications, and macroeconomic policies motivated by balance of payments difficulties can and often do have structural implications.) Adjustment lending rapidly became a euphemism for good old-fashioned policy-based program lending of the kind long debated in the development literature and aid agencies.

How has adjustment lending actually worked? If there is one conclusion that has dominated the discussion here it is that *everything* takes longer than anticipated. Structural adjustment simply does not happen through short bursts of intensive policy change. The message to those undertaking structural policy reforms seem to be (1) be patient and (2) have faith. They are being told that while there is as yet little firm evidence of the developmental impact of these reforms, the reforms are nonetheless probably the correct ones. This advice to adjusters is strikingly similar to that typically proffered by the International Monetary Fund. But the IMF is probably on stronger ground than the World Bank because the IMF promises less from its recommended policy changes: stabilization rather than development.

What is the evidence that adjustment lending and the principal longer-run reforms it has promoted have contributed to economic growth and development? Granting all the methodological problems—arriving at a suitable counterfactual case, possible sample-selectivity bias, and the like—there is nonetheless evidence of modest improvement in overall economic performance in countries undertaking World Bank–supported adjustment programs. But the evidence is fairly thin. And there are some disconcerting details in the record. Particularly deserving of further exploration is the finding that the intensity of World Bank and IMF lending is negatively and statistically significantly related to the investment rate. This relationship seems to place a very high premium on the increased efficiency that structural reforms are supposed to achieve. Even more provocative is the strong evidence, presented in more than one chapter, that increased imports are strongly associated with improved economic growth and the implication that increased utilization of capacity, rather than any effects of investment, dominates medium-term performance. There is also evidence elsewhere that the *stability* of import volume is a powerful predictor of recent growth performance in developing countries.

A new mood of caution, humility, and uncertainty characterize this book (as well as the 1988 summary report, *Adjustment Lending: An Evaluation of Ten Years of Experience*). It was found in discussions of all the major areas of adjustment policy.

In the sphere of trade, the record indicates greater success in encouraging exports than in liberalizing import policy. Much of the export success was dependent, however, on earlier investments with a long gestation period, as in Chile and Turkey, for example; only in Mexico (and in the return of Ghanaian exports from smuggling) was there rapid switching purely in response to current price incentives. Except for exporters' inputs, import liberalization efforts have been fairly weak and fairly modest in their effects. One is left yearning for more analysis of such issues as the effects of different kinds of import liberalization, differences in its timing, differing degrees of dispersion of trade incentives, and differences in the stability of trade regimes. As is usual in recent discussions of trade policy, there was also some handwringing over the mysterious successes of the heterodox Republic of Korea.

Financial reforms have typically also been weak and, where initially more forceful, have virtually always been subsequently reversed. It seems that financial liberalization has frequently been counterproductive when pushed too fast in the absence of macroeconomic stability, adequate prudential regulatory mechanisms, or at least minimal competition in the financial sector. It is striking that no systematic assessment appears to have been made of the impact of interest rate reforms undertaken in World Bank–IMF programs.

Despite the continuing frequency of advice on the desirability of privatizing public enterprises, the impact of privatization has yet to be systematically studied with the use of the traditional economists' criteria of social efficiency. The summary record suggests that premature efforts to privatize in the absence of market capacities or adequate official preparation have been costly and that privatization deadlines have often proven counterproductive.

Fundamental tax reforms have been few and far between. None has as yet been attributable to adjustment lending.

Chapter 7 on agricultural policy emphasizes the importance of long-term perspectives and of nonprice considerations, particularly in the case of public investment. Price reforms, it argues, do not accelerate growth, whatever improvements in efficiency they may achieve, and they are easily reversed. Price stabilization schemes are likely to remain in place, and rather than waste effort in vainly seeking their elimination, we should work to improve them.

There is some evidence that value added in industry grew a little faster in countries receiving adjustment loans than in others, but the link with conditionality is obscure. The author of the industrial policy study (chapter 8) was reluctant to draw firm conclusions from such scanty data.

The social costs of adjustment and considerations of distributional equity seem to have been universally neglected in World Bank–supported adjustment programs. Where distributional outcomes were relatively benign, they were accidental. Programs to defend the poor may be very difficult to engineer, but the fact is that they have nowhere been seriously tried. Such programs as Ghana's Program of Actions to Mitigate the Social Costs of Adjustment were afterthoughts, added on after the program was launched. The question at issue in the policy discussions was not the desirability (which seems affirmed) so much as the efficacy of targeting measures for the poor within adjustment programs.

In view of current environmental concerns, I note that nowhere in any of the adjustment programs reviewed here was there any specific reference to the environment or to environmental sustainability. There were only glancing references to these issues.

What policy conclusions for the World Bank can one draw from this very mixed and uncertain record of the impact of adjustment reforms and the Bank's own adjustment lending? I would suggest at least the following six.

1. Since structural change and development are long-run processes and supply responses in developing countries are everywhere slow, one should

not expect quick results—even from fast-disbursing loans to governments that are doing everything "right." Trying to move too quickly can be counterproductive. That some policies can be changed faster than others does not mean that they necessarily should be. And overloading an adjustment program can similarly be unhelpful. What is required from outsiders is long-run vision and commitment, steady financial support, and ongoing supportive policy dialogue. The sustainability of change depends upon a stable incentive structure and stable politics as well as stable financing. But stable financing can go a long way.

2. It is perverse to rush to judgment on relative success or failure. It is certainly premature, for instance, to proclaim, as does a recent World Bank document, that in Africa "recovery has begun." Larry Westphal of Swarthmore College has offered elsewhere the dictum—henceforth no doubt to be known as Westphal's Law—that those who know the least about a country are the most prone to seize upon its short-term record of overall performance as an indicator of longer-run success.

3. It is therefore also perverse to impose too many conditions in the short run, conditions for which failure brings cessation of external support. In the face of our uncertainty about the development consequences of so many kinds of policy change, the only possible criterion for disbursing short-term adjustment loan tranches is whether the country did or did not undertake the promised policy changes. We are apparently unable to tell in the short to medium run whether they worked. But is this not a rather tenuous and inappropriate basis for a decision to drop support? By imposing such short-run performance requirements, we risk aborting the flow of external support so necessary for the development process over matters of dubious developmental relevance. Conditions for tranche release must be for a longer-term cycle and should relate to policy outcomes rather than promises.

4. Policy conditionality should not impose unreasonably demanding short-term structural shocks on fragile economies and politics. In view of the considerable uncertainty concerning the effects of specific policy reforms on the economy, political stability, and so on, it may be sensible to prescribe programs of reform that, though less than optimal, are not too disruptive and are both resilient to unforeseen shocks and amenable to change with minimal costs. The skills of the economist are, after all, best employed to reduce the prospect of egregious error, not to attain policy perfection. But once the most grotesque distortions, particularly those related to the real exchange rate and the fiscal deficit, are repaired, further fine-tuning of prices and policies may not be very productive. Straining toward further policy reforms risks disruption of the stable investment flows on which development depends.

5. It is striking that among the case studies presented in this volume, the countries that launched the strongest adjustment programs—Chile,

Korea, Mexico, and Turkey—undertook them out of their own convictions. The World Bank does not seem to have persuaded them of much. Sometimes their own convictions were more orthodox than those of the World Bank! The World Bank and the IMF nevertheless were able to provide assistance with technical specifics and contribute to ongoing policy debates. It would be no small achievement for the World Bank simply to maintain everywhere an open dialogue on development policy, to provide specific technical assistance on matters of detail where requested, and gradually to improve the quality of economic analysis both in the borrowing countries and in the World Bank itself. If these functions were all performed well, the World Bank would have quite enough to be proud of. Its staff should not seek or expect to win all battles. Policy discussions with adjusting countries should truly be dialogues, not a process akin to negotiation in a bazaar.

6. Once gross macroeconomic distortions are overcome, the risk of a program's failing because of underfunding seems at least as great as the risk of failing because of not undertaking recommended policy reforms. The contrast between underfunded Zambia, which, for a while, did all it was asked and still failed, and Ghana, which this year received gross commitments of US$800 million (its population is under 15 million), could hardly be more striking. One cannot help returning to the strong evidence cited earlier regarding the role of imports in growth. What, after all, do we ultimately know about optimal policies for growth? We do know—now better than ever—that more resources help. No effort should be spared to raise them. Since total resources are limited, however, difficult decisions will remain about which countries to support with "adequate" funding.

The debate on adjustment lending has brought development economists back full circle to where they were about twenty-five years ago. Once again they are debating the relative roles of program and project assistance. They now emphasize macroeconomic management rather more than most of them did in those earlier times. In other respects, however, their knowledge has not progressed as much as one might have hoped.

Perhaps the new humility and uncertainty about broad structural reforms will drive more of the World Bank's program lending into less ambitious sectoral loans in the 1990s. And perhaps this move would have the desirable side effect of reducing some of the World Bank's conflict with the IMF. To my mind, such developments would be all to the good.

In any case, let me congratulate the World Bank on its new, more nuanced, more careful, and more objective approaches to the analysis of its policy-based lending activities. I am confident that I speak for the entire development community when I express strong support for this more open intellectual environment.

Pedro S. Malan

After nearly a decade of adjustment lending—about 160 loans to about 60 developing countries—it is time to consider the lessons learned. Elsewhere in this book the World Bank's experience in trade policy is described as "a limited success." The Turkish experience is considered "unfinished business" after five structural adjustment loans, three sectoral adjustment loans, and three standby agreements. The Pakistani case is called a "semisuccess." It is noted that the World Bank underestimated the political difficulties involved in adjustment lending and the protracted nature of the deep-rooted development problems facing too many developing countries in the 1980s. "Mild relative improvements" are seen in countries undertaking adjustment programs with the support of the World Bank and the International Monetary Fund (IMF).

Apparently, the first lesson to be drawn from experience is that the record is a mixed one, which compounds the uncertainties about the future of adjustment lending. There is no point yet in trying to reach a verdict based on the evidence at hand. We need both more studies of individual countries—their successes and failures—and more comparative analysis that cuts across a wide range of experiences.

In evaluating the impacts of adjustment, I would like to organize my remarks around four clusters of observations. The first one is related to the sustainability of adjustment programs. The importance of political commitment to structural reforms by the authorities of the adjusting country has been strongly emphasized by creditor countries and the multilateral institutions they control. This emphasis seems appropriate, but relatively less attention has been given to the importance of public support for policy reform if adjustment efforts are to be sustained. In fact, the political commitment of the authorities and the support of public opinion are not unrelated, and both will be progressively harder to maintain the longer adjustment continues without payoffs in terms of growth and the longer human and social conditions are allowed to deteriorate.

The concern with the social costs of adjustment—or of delayed adjustment—is as legitimate as the concern with protecting the poor during adjustment and reducing poverty over the long term. The argument is often couched in terms of the need to ensure broadly based political support for adjustment. What often derails adjustment programs, however, is not the outcry of the vulnerable poor but the opposition of the vocal special-interest groups that are bound to be affected by reforms in foreign exchange, subsidies, tax benefits, and other areas that affect rent-seeking activities. The benefits of adjustment programs are often perceived to be long term and diffuse, while the losses are shorter term and concentrated. In this context, the vocal have an edge over the vulnerable. Poverty alleviation is a legitimate concern, but to justify it as a means of recruiting the political support of the poor to ensure the sustainability of adjustment is to weaken the argument. This long-term objective should stand on its own.

One last point on sustainability: a consensus seems to be emerging that primary responsibility for the conception of structural adjustment programs must lie with the national authorities that will implement and sustain the program. Although the advice of the World Bank and the IMF may be welcome, the national authorities must be satisfied that the policy actions and reforms represent an appropriate, realistic, and feasible course of action.

The second cluster of issues is related to design. Improving the design of macroeconomic and structural adjustment policies could help to establish credibility for the policies at an early stage. But credibility cannot be established unless the program design takes full account of the country's legacy of real or perceived structural weakness. These are frequently deep-rooted structural problems, such as inadequate infrastructure, poorly developed markets, institutional and managerial weaknesses in the public and private sectors, lack of critical skills, and an undiversified productive base with limited potential for a quick supply response. The macroeconomic and structural adjustment policies will not be effective unless these economic and social realities are addressed in the conditions and performance criteria for the operation. These conditions should be focused, capable of being monitored, few in number, properly sequenced, and concentrated on variables that are under the effective control of the authorities of the country in question.

The concern with social costs and poverty reduction in the design of adjustment programs could well be summarized in a few propositions. One, without growth and development there is no hope of reducing poverty and social costs. Two, the trickle-down process is not enough to make even a dent in the problem of poverty; specific measures directed to the poor are needed, even though identifying the poor may be difficult. And three, poverty-reduction objectives should be integrated in the design of adjustment programs. But there are clearly tradeoffs in trying to put rationality into the quest for equity and humanity into the quest for efficiency. As noted by Arthur Okun, this inescapable conflict may be the reason capitalism and democracy need each other.

A final issue related to design concerns the need for contingency mechanisms in adjustment programs because of the enormous uncertainties they face. Such mechanisms are essential if the programs are to be sustained and perceived to be sustainable over the relevant medium term.

The third cluster of observations is related to the macroeconomics of debt and its implications for the effectiveness of design and for the sustainability of adjustment programs. As recognized explicitly by the managing director of the IMF, "the debt overhang has interfered with the sustained implementation of adjustment policies." Steps to accelerate the reduction of debt and debt-service burdens are essential for the design and implementation of effective and sustainable adjustment programs.

Both the World Bank and the IMF will have to pay increased attention to two factors. First, realistic estimates are needed of sustainable current account deficits or, more precisely, of the feasible balance in trade and nonfactor services over the medium term. Second, adjustment programs must be internally consistent—that is, they require a set of policies that will bring about a financeable fiscal deficit that matches the private savings surplus over investment at levels of investment high enough to sustain output growth. This situation clearly does not exist at the moment for the indebted countries, given the magnitude of the net real resource transfers abroad. For these countries, there can be no sustained implementation of a growth-oriented structural adjustment program unless the design of the program squarely faces the problems posed by the debt overhang.

The fourth cluster of observations concerns the existence of an external environment that is supportive of structural adjustment. Such an environment appears to be a necessary—but not sufficient—condition for sustained domestic reform programs. Four elements are particularly crucial: (1) medium-term external financial support that is adequate (in volume, terms, and conditions) for serious adjustment efforts, (2) growth-oriented adjustment in industrial countries, (3) reduction of protectionist barriers in industrial countries, and (4) no increase in real international interest rates.

Moeen Qureshi

Both within and outside the World Bank there are two groups with opposing views on the issue of adjustment lending—the partisans and the agnostics. My first point to both the apostles and the heretics is that adjustment lending is a child born of sheer necessity. In the early 1980s, following the second oil shock, some of the World Bank's largest borrowers faced very severe balance of payments crises and were forced to cut back drastically on their investment programs. Clearly, they wanted help from the World Bank and the World Bank wanted to help them. But its traditional instruments—especially investment lending—had limited relevance and effectiveness in that situation. These countries could not afford and did not have the counterpart funds to undertake investments, and in any case that was not the highest priority. The highest priorities in most countries were, first, effective demand management and, second, in a more medium-term context, fundamental structural change that would adapt their economies to a changed international economic environment. So, necessity being the mother of invention, adjustment lending was invented by my predecessors in the World Bank. Had that not been the case, the World Bank would have been out of business, and it could not have provided large segments of the developing world with both financial assistance and technical advice.

My second point is that it is important to recognize both the potential and the risks of adjustment lending for the World Bank and the countries that receive such loans. There are countries that received adjustment loans but have nothing to show for them—it has largely been money down the drain. In some of these countries that appear ready to make another effort at adjustment we are prepared to plunge into battle again with unabated faith. Other countries have achieved varying degrees of success in implementing adjustment programs and are clearly better equipped today to use whatever resources they have to support their development process. The key arguments for and against adjustment lending would appear very vividly to anyone taking a sight-seeing tour through the large number of countries in which the World Bank has supported adjustment efforts through both the International Bank for Reconstruction and Development (IBRD) and the International Development Association (IDA).

I will comment briefly on certain operational aspects of adjustment lending. First, how do we formulate and prepare adjustment programs these days? Quite frankly, this is a very imperfect craft, born of an inexact science, and practiced on a patient whose diseases are very hard to diagnose. Therefore I agree with Gerald Helleiner that a measure of modesty and humility is indeed needed. The tendency to overgeneralize should be avoided. Above all, there should be a receptivity to learning the lessons of experience—especially those of failure.

In the adjustment programs that I oversee, the macroeconomic framework is conceptually the easier part but it is rarely done well in our lending operations. Even by my own somewhat out-of-date standards, it is clear that the analytical and conceptual basis for our macroeconomic models needs strengthening. I am looking with expectation to Stanley Fischer and other Policy, Research, and External Affairs staff to provide the intellectual inputs that will refurbish that aspect of our work. The sectoral or structural work in our adjustment loans is much better, although it sometimes lacks thematic cohesion. In the sectoral area, the World Bank's craft has been honed in the forge of experience. The more experienced and skilled practitioners of the art in the World Bank—our technical specialists—are beginning either to retire or to leave, however, because they think adjustment lending is in vogue and their craft is less valued. Nevertheless, they are, and continue to be, the backbone of some of our best work in the adjustment area.

Second, it should be recognized that adjustment lending, in most of its aspects, is a pretty blunt instrument. Macroeconomic policy, for all its conceptual and rather flamboyant architecture, is nonetheless an imprecise operational tool. Therefore one must avoid the tendency, however understandable, to turn this somewhat blunt instrument into a surgeon's scalpel. This is attempted too frequently in our adjustment loans. As Helleiner said, they are festooned with conditions in an attempt to achieve myriad specific policy objectives and targets within the macroeconomic framework.

Third, how much money should we provide to support an adjustment program? The answer is, as little as possible—as little as might be needed to grease the wheels of economic change and catalyze external support for the adjustment programs. Without adequate external support, programs are not likely to succeed. But we cannot and should not take upon ourselves the responsibility for providing the major part of that financing, because that is not a sustainable role for the World Bank and IDA.

Fourth, how long should adjustment lending continue? Conventional wisdom suggests five to seven years. My colleagues who sponsor adjustment lending proposals do not have a precise time period in mind but generally argue for a longer period of adjustment the second time around than the first. Clearly, there is no precise period within which adjustment lending can be said to be completed. It varies a great deal from country to country and depends on a host of factors. In addition, adjustment can, and probably will in most cases, be an interrupted process. In my experience, the period for most countries tends to be not less than five years. But if the process of adjustment is not completed in ten years, we had better ask ourselves whether the will to adjust is really there. Indeed, if the political will is lacking, we might just be throwing good money after bad.

Fifth, the sooner we can make the transition from quick-disbursing assistance to investment lending the better the prospect of moving the country from crisis management to more normal conditions. Planning for the postadjustment period must become an integral part of the financial and economic strategy. In the case of IBRD lending, in particular, this process must be managed carefully so that the World Bank can maintain a role in a country long enough to see the adjustment process through to the end. Otherwise, especially in countries receiving IBRD support, the World Bank is likely to find itself constrained by the limits on its share in total external lending to a given country and by its inability to provide adequate and timely financial support to a country that needs it. In the process of adjustment lending therefore we must not only define the policy changes that are envisaged but also look ahead and plan for World Bank support to the country both during the adjustment period and beyond it.

24 *Summary and Conclusions*

THIS BOOK has assessed the experience of countries with adjustment programs and the effectiveness of adjustment lending from the World Bank in supporting these programs. Introduced by the World Bank in 1980, adjustment lending has provided fast-disbursing, balance of payments financing and support for policy and institutional reforms. During the past decade, the use of adjustment lending has expanded dramatically. This increase has brought mounting criticism of the appropriateness and usefulness of this instrument as a means to provide financing and policy support to countries in distress.

The book has taken an inventory of the decade of experience with adjustment lending in fifty-one countries with loans totaling US$15 billion (from 1980 to 1987). The studies presented here have comprehensively evaluated such aspects of adjustment lending as its design, policy components, conditionality, social implications, macroeconomic interactions, and country performances for a sample of nine countries from all regions of the developing world. In addition, economists and practitioners from both inside and outside the Bank have provided different perspectives on the evolution and success of adjustment lending. Despite the diversity of views and differences of assessments, a number of conclusions as well as open questions can be identified.

Three positive features of adjustment lending emerge from the inventory presented here. First, among countries requiring adjustments, those that have carried out major adjustments have performed better on average in terms of their aggregate economic activity than those that have not. There is a general and positive connection between adjustment lending and this relative improvement, but the connection is not a tight one and performance varies substantially among the loan recipients. A clearer association emerges, however, when the focus is on the sample of early recipients who received several loans rather than on all recipients. There is a significant and positive correlation between relative improvements in macroeconomic performance and the intensity of adjustment lending operations. This result is noteworthy because the recipient countries were subjected to more severe external shocks than were their comparators. It therefore underscores the importance of timely adjustments and sustained efforts in making a difference to performance.

Second, the overall rate of implementation of loan conditionalities seems to have been quite satisfactory. This finding is particularly clear for the conditions in the monitorable components of action programs that were considered especially important by the authors of the country studies. In a sample of about fifty adjustment loans to fifteen countries, 60 percent of the loan conditions were subsequently fulfilled. Yet there is a wide variation in implementation both among policy areas and within a given country. Third, adjustment lending has become a necessary and valuable instrument in the World Bank's kit of tools for supporting the economic development of borrowing members. Furthermore, by virtue of its focus on major economywide and sectoral reforms of policies and institutions, adjustment lending has come to play a pivotal role in the World Bank's dialogue with borrowing countries on the fundamental aspects of macroeconomic and development policy. It has thus placed the World Bank in a central position in the economic adjustment process.

This emphasis should continue—provided the effectiveness of the instrument can be enhanced. Notwithstanding the generally positive review of adjustment lending, the wide variation in its effectiveness raises many questions about when and how to use it and how to improve it. Here again three central issues emerge from the varied analyses in this book: the ownership of the program, the adequacy of macroeconomic stability, and the size of external funding. In each of these areas there is scope for improvement and important lessons to be learned from past mistakes.

Program Ownership

By its very nature, adjustment lending is a high-profile activity. It touches on sensitive policy variables such as the exchange rate, import tariffs, taxes, and agricultural prices. Sustainable policy reforms in these areas are predicated on a commitment by governments and policymakers to the process of change and on the resolution of the tensions inevitably associated with change. Consensus on the merits of the actions to be undertaken is necessary for the success of adjustment operations. This finding underscores the value of country ownership of an adjustment program and implies that the role of the World Bank should be essentially a supportive one, providing assistance in the design, implementation, and supervision of various components of the program.

Judging the commitment of a government to an adjustment path is inherently subjective. There is never uniform and widespread commitment. Typically a core group of policymakers is in favor of a reform program. This group needs and often seeks both financial and intellectual support from outside agencies such as the World Bank. The World Bank, on its part, must often make a commitment of funds and support based on its judgment that this core group will succeed in pushing through a reform package. Mistakes clearly occur, as in Zambia, where the committed group in favor of adjustment was so small that the process had very little hope of succeeding.

These judgments often fail because of the inherent uncertainty about the underlying political processes that lead to or hinder reform. Outside agencies such as the World Bank are not fully cognizant of the underlying sociopolitical forces. One way for lenders to circumvent these problems is to make loans only when the required policy changes have already been executed. Indonesia has repeatedly demonstrated its commitment through prior actions. A second-best alternative is tranching of loans. This involves disbursing a part of the agreed loans only after policy actions have been undertaken on an agreed time schedule. The resort to tranching reflects considerable uncertainty on the part of the lender that agreed actions will be carried out. The record with tranched loans has been mixed, and tranching remains an unsatisfactory and clearly inferior solution to the lack of clear-cut commitment. It is usually very difficult to stop the disbursement of second tranches, and often compromises are made to justify their release. Smaller single-tranched loans seem to be a better alternative, but they naturally involve higher administrative costs.

In a situation fraught with uncertainty the World Bank, as a public international financial organization, must be willing to take greater risks. There are two reasons for this: (1) to counteract what is likely to be the excessive caution of international commercial banks and (2) to maintain the World Bank's long-term relationship with client countries who are also member shareholders of the Bank. The record indicates that the Bank has taken risks in supporting a nascent reform program even when it was not clear that the reforms would work. These actions have often resulted in temporary setbacks or failures, but there have also been notable successes. One case of success is Ghana. In 1982 Ghana's record on reform would have given little hope and much concern to an international lending agency. Yet the World Bank pursued the course with subsequent high payoffs.

Macroeconomic Justification

Taking appropriate risks does not imply being foolhardy. One situation in which reforms are not going to work, however genuine the intentions and commitment, is when there is macroeconomic instability. Macroeconomic stability should be an integral part of the adjustment effort and is critical to its success. This requirement raises many complex questions about the scope, mix, and sequencing of policy measures that must be determined country by country. In particular, the effectiveness of structural adjustment involving changes in relative prices depends critically on a country's ability to restore fiscal balance through more judicious management of aggregate demand.

How much macroeconomic stabilization is necessary in a particular situation also requires judgment. Clearly insufficient macroeconomic stability threatened Turkey's reforms over the past decade, and the World Bank could have been more strict in ensuring greater stability. But both the size and the speed of stabilization matter, and if they are too great they can also threaten reforms. Eliminating in one year a large fiscal deficit of, say, more than 10 percent of GDP can threaten reforms in one of two ways. Either the sharp reduction in the deficit can slide the economy into a sharp recession, or the sharp cuts in income from very rapid and large stabilization can hurt particular income groups (such as the poor or organized urban workers) who may threaten social stability. The size and pace of the required stabilization effort depends on the amount of external funding available to support the reforms.

External Financing

External financing can assist and promote adjustment or it can substitute for it (that is, delay adjustment). There are examples of both. The risk of delayed adjustment is a real one, and it is not easy to judge beforehand which risk is greater. Yet such judgments are made all the time. Once a program is initiated on the assumption that certain external funds will be available, the failure to provide them will kill credibility and can defeat the program.

The adequacy of the funding of adjustment programs, especially in low-income countries with characteristically low supply elasticities, receives considerable attention in the various country studies in this book. Adjustment programs failed in some African countries primarily because they were underfunded. In other countries, particularly the highly indebted ones, the legacy of the debt crisis continues to diminish the domestic availability of the countries' financial resources and to delay the recovery of investment. Low investments in productive assets have in turn handicapped the process of adjustment.

Under these circumstances, taking appropriate measures for debt relief will have a high payoff in terms of macroeconomic stability. At the same time, the use of funds available from debt relief should be monitored so as to improve the position of both creditors and debtors. Debt relief should come with enhanced conditionality to provide the country with the incentive to adjust and, perhaps more critically, to avoid the resumption of unsustainable macroeconomic policies.

With the continuation of debt problems and the likelihood of higher oil prices and higher real interest rates in the early 1990s, the World Bank will be required to assist a new round of structural reforms. Adjustment lending will remain a key instrument for the World Bank in providing financial and policy support to its member countries. The lessons from the experience of the past decade must therefore be taken seriously so that future adjustment operations can be made more effective.

Index